HISTORICAL DICTIONARY

The historical dictionaries present essential information on a broad range of subjects, including American and world history, art, business, cities, countries, cultures, customs, film, global conflicts, international relations, literature, music, philosophy, religion, sports, and theater. Written by experts, all contain highly informative introductory essays of the topic and detailed chronologies that, in some cases, cover vast historical time periods but still manage to heavily feature more recent events.

Brief A–Z entries describe the main people, events, politics, social issues, institutions, and policies that make the topic unique, and entries are cross-referenced for ease of browsing. Extensive bibliographies are divided into several general subject areas, providing excellent access points for students, researchers, and anyone wanting to know more. Additionally, maps, photographs, and appendixes of supplemental information aid high school and college students doing term papers or introductory research projects. In short, the historical dictionaries are the perfect starting point for anyone looking to research in these fields.

HISTORICAL DICTIONARIES OF U.S. POLITICS AND POLITICAL ERAS

Jon Woronoff, Series Editor

Historical Dictionary from the Great War to the Great Depression

Second Edition

Neil A. Wynn

The Scarecrow Press, Inc.
Lanham • Toronto • Plymouth, UK
2014

Published by Scarecrow Press, Inc.
A wholly owned subsidiary of The Rowman & Littlefield Publishing Group, Inc.
4501 Forbes Boulevard, Suite 200, Lanham, Maryland 20706
http://www.scarecrowpress.com

10 Thornbury Road, Plymouth PL6 7PP, United Kingdom

British Library Cataloguing in Publication Information Available

Library of Congress Cataloging-in-Publication Data

Wynn, Neil A.
Historical dictionary from the Great War to the Great Depression / Neil A. Wynn. — Second edition.
pages cm. — (Historical dictionaries of U.S. politics and political eras)
Includes bibliographical references.
ISBN 978-0-8108-8033-7 (cloth : alkaline paper) — ISBN 978-0-8108-8034-4 (ebook)
1. United States—History—1913–1921—Dictionaries. 2. United States—History—1919–1933—Dictionaries. I. Title.
E740.7.W96 2014
973.91003—dc23
2013031843

™
The paper used in this publication meets the minimum requirements of American National Standard for Information Sciences Permanence of Paper for Printed Library Materials, ANSI/NISO Z39.48-1992.

Printed in the United States of America.

Contents

Editor's Foreword

When writing history, there is a temptation to enliven it with such words as *crisis*, *turning point*, or *watershed*, whether or not they are justified. In the period from 1913 to 1933, roughly from the inauguration of Woodrow Wilson to Herbert Hoover's failure to win a second term, these expressions are entirely appropriate in referring to American history. The period opened with a bout of dramatic political change at home, followed by a major international crisis, World War I, which drastically affected the United States. It ended with another major crisis, an economic depression that gradually spread around the world and in its severity and duration justified the description of the Great Depression. There was also considerable social change, change in the situation of women in the workplace and in the election booths, change in the ethnic composition of the country with massive immigration and a flight of blacks to the North, change in the views and status of the working class, and also change in the attitudes of African Americans (although a change in their status lagged behind). In some cases, the change was great enough to be deemed a *turning point.* This is particularly true of America's position in the world, moving from peripheral to central, and shifting from isolationism to active participation in world affairs, although there was a temporary retreat after the war.

This explains why the *Historical Dictionary from the Great War to the Great Depression* is so interesting, and even more so in this expanded second edition. A lot happened in these two decades, perhaps more than usually happens in such a short period. As usual, the broad view is sketched out in the introduction while the details are drawn in the dictionary entries. These entries include the major events, not only political but also economic, social, and cultural, the presidents and other significant persons, organizations and institutions, movements and legal decisions, plus some of the fads and fashions that marked the time. The chronology makes it easier to see how things came together. A handy list of acronyms reminds us of the meanings of this alphabet soup. And the bibliography directs readers who want further information to the relevant literature.

Although most of the volumes in this rapidly expanding—and almost complete—series of Historical Dictionaries of U.S. Politics and Political Eras are written by Americans, some are not. This can have definite advantages when they treat the subject carefully and objectively but from another perspective. The author of this volume is Neil A. Wynn, who grew up and was educated in Great Britain, also studying in the United States, receiving his doctorate from the Open University in England. He presently teaches at the University of Gloucestershire, where he is professor of twentieth-century American history. In addition to lecturing, Dr. Wynn has written extensively on the period, including articles and chapters and three books that he edited or coedited and another three that he authored, among them *From Progressivism to Prosperity: World War I and American Society.* Moreover, he is the author of another volume in the series, the *Historical Dictionary of the Roosevelt-Truman Era.* Having already written the first edition, we are indebted to him for expanding it in a second edition, since the period—as readers will see—is clearly a crucial one.

Jon Woronoff
Series Editor

Preface

The opportunity to produce a new, revised edition of the *Historical Dictionary from Great War to Great Depression* presented a welcome challenge: welcome because there has been much new writing on the era and also because a new edition allowed me to include topics not much touched on in the previous edition, particularly in the social and cultural areas; the challenge was precisely the possible scale of the task—subjects seemed to snowball, and ultimately to include all aspects, details, individuals, and new sources was clearly impossible. The period covered seemed to have increased in relevance to the present day, firstly because issues of social and economic policy and the role of government continue to be matters of public debate, secondly because we will soon be approaching the various anniversaries connected to World War I, and also because the period after the war produced developments that have a particular resonance with recent events. The financial crisis that affected much of the industrial world in the past decade has some remarkable parallels with events that led to the Wall Street Crash of 1929 and the subsequent Great Depression. Comparisons can be made about the economic and political causes of the modern crisis, and also about consequences and responses. It is perhaps remarkable how striking some similarities are and how little the lessons of history appear to have been learned.

There still is a fascination with the period of the 1920s, as the success of the long-running HBO television series *Boardwalk Empire* or the latest film version of F. Scott Fitzgerald's classic novel *The Great Gatsby* testifies. The "Jazz Age" ushered in the consumer society of mass entertainment, the automobile, and communications technologies that are still with us today. The period is both recognizable and yet different in tone and quality. Major issues such as those of race and gender were only just being addressed while those of gay rights were almost totally ignored. Some of these matters are dealt with in this edition of the dictionary. There are now some fifty new entries on, among others, art, crime and policing, education, literature and theater, music and dance, and sports, and extensive additions to the bibliography. Inevitably, there are omissions, despite the good efforts of the series editor Jon Woronoff. That this edition appeared at all was due to his perseverance, and also that of my long-suffering wife, Regina, who wondered whether the task would ever end. Where there are errors, gaps, and omissions, they are solely my responsibility.

In order to facilitate the rapid and efficient location of information and to make this book as useful a reference tool as possible, extensive cross-references have been provided in the dictionary section. Within individual entries, terms that have their own entries are in **boldface type** the first time they appear. Related terms that do not appear in the text are indicated by *see also*. *See* refers to other entries that deal with this topic.

Acronyms and Abbreviations

AAA	Agricultural Adjustment Administration
AAFS	American Ambulance Field Service
ACLU	American Civil Liberties Union
AEF	American Expeditionary Force
AFBF	American Farm Bureau Federation
AFL	American Federation of Labor
APL	American Protective League
APS	American Peace Society
AT&T	American Telephone & Telegraph
AUAM	American Union Against Militarism
BOMC	Book-of-the-Month Club
BSCP	Brotherhood of Sleeping Car Porters
CBS	Columbia Broadcasting System
CIO	Congress of Industrial Organizations
CND	Council of National Defense
COS	Charity Organization Societies
CPI	Committee on Public Information
CPUSA	Communist Party USA
FBI	Federal Bureau of Investigation
FRC	Federal Radio Commission
FTC	Federal Trade Commission
GAO	General Accounting Office
GDP	Gross Domestic Product
GM	General Motors
GNP	Gross National Product
HOLC	Home Owners' Loan Corporation
ILGWU	International Ladies Garment Workers Union
IWW	Industrial Workers of the World

KKK	Ku Klux Klan
MGM	Metro-Goldwyn-Mayer
MPPDA	Motion Picture Producers and Distributors of America
NAACP	National Association for the Advancement of Colored People
NAM	National Association of Manufacturers
NAWSA	National American Woman Suffrage Association
NBC	National Broadcasting Company
NCCC	National Conference of Charities and Corrections
NCL	National Consumers League
NRA	National Recovery Administration
NUL	National Urban League
NWLB	National War Labor Board
NWP	National Woman's Party
PGA	Professional Golfers' Association
POUR	President's Organization on Unemployment Relief
RCA	Radio Corporation of America
RFC	Reconstruction Finance Corporation
RKO	Radio-Keith-Orpheum
SLP	Socialist Labor Party
SPA	Socialist Party of America
UMWA	United Mine Workers of America
UN	United Nations
UNRRA	United Nations Relief and Rehabilitation Administration
USEFC	United States Emergency Fleet Corporation
USHC	United States Housing Corporation
USRA	United States Railroad Administration
USSB	United States Shipping Board
USSR	Union of Soviet Socialist Republics
WCTU	Women's Christian Temperance Union
WFC	War Finance Committee
WIB	War Industries Board

WILPF	Women's International League for Peace and Freedom
WLB	War Labor Board
WPA	Works Progress Administration
WPP	Woman's Peace Party
WTUL	Women's Trade Union League
YMCA	Young Men's Christian Association
YWCA	Young Women's Christian Association

Chronology

1913 9–18 February: The government of Francisco Madero was overthrown by Victoriano Huerta in Mexico. The United States did not recognize the new regime. **25 February:** The Sixteenth Amendment empowering Congress to tax incomes, passed by Congress on 12 July 1909, was ratified. **4 March:** President Woodrow Wilson (Democrat) inaugurated having defeated William Howard Taft (Republican) and Theodore Roosevelt (Progressive) in the election in November 1912. In his inaugural address Wilson promised to address the "fearful physical and spiritual cost" of the country's industrial growth. **30 March:** The Sixteenth Amendment, providing Congress with the power to tax incomes, was ratified. **8 April:** President Wilson broke with tradition and outlined his legislative program in person to a special session of Congress. **31 May:** The Seventeenth Amendment, providing for the direct election of senators, was ratified. **3 October:** The Underwood-Simmons Tariff Act was passed, providing for the first significant lowering of duties since 1861. **November–April 1914:** The Wilson Administration sought to achieve the removal of Huerta from power in Mexico through diplomatic means. **23 December:** Federal Reserve Act passed establishing twelve regional Federal Reserve Banks supervised by the Federal Reserve Board to regulate currency and credit operations in the United States.

1914 27 January: U.S. forces landed in Port-au-Prince, Haiti, to protect American interests until order was restored following the outbreak of revolution on the island. **10 April:** U.S. seamen from USS *Dolphin* were arrested when they landed without permission in Tampico, Mexico. Although the men were soon released and an apology was given, the Wilson Administration demanded that the U.S. flag be given an official salute or suffer the consequences. **21 April:** U.S. Marines occupied Vera Cruz, Mexico, following the Tampico incident and the failure to salute the U.S. flag, and in order to prevent the landing of a shipment of arms. **8 May:** The Smith-Lever Act providing federal funds for agricultural extension colleges and adult education was passed. **28 June:** Archduke Franz Ferdinand was assassinated in Sarajevo, Bosnia, sparking the crisis that led to the outbreak of World War I. **4 August:** Following various declarations of war in Europe, President Wilson announced U.S. neutrality. **29 August:** Fifteen hundred women marched in silence down Fifth Avenue, New York City, in protest against the outbreak of war in Europe. **10 September:** The Federal Trade Commission Act was passed. It abolished the Bureau of Corporation established in 1903 and replaced it with a five-man Federal Trade Commission to supervise business in order to prevent corporations from using unfair means of competition. **15 October:** The Clayton Antitrust Act, strengthening the 1890 Sherman Antitrust Act, was passed. The act prohibited interlocking directorates, forbade corporations from purchasing securities of other companies to eliminate competition, and held company officers personally liable for offenses. It also sought to exclude labor from antitrust legislation by declaring that the "labor of human beings is not a commodity or article of commerce."

1915 A "preparedness" movement developed in the United States in response to the war in Europe and increasing conflict about shipping rights between the United States and belligerent powers; organizations such as the National Security League (formed in December 1914) and the American Defense Society (August 1915), supported by individuals such as Theodore Roosevelt and Senator Henry Cabot Lodge, called for an increase in U.S. military and naval strength. **10 February:** Following a German declaration establishing a war zone around Great Britain, the Wilson Administration announced it would hold Germany strictly accountable for the sinking of U.S. vessels by U-boats. **4 March:** The Seaman's Act, establishing minimum standards for sailors, sponsored by Senator Robert M. La Follette, was passed. **7 May:** The Cunard passenger liner, *Lusitania*, was sunk by German U-boat off Ireland with the loss of 1,200 lives including 128 Americans. The Wilson Administration warned that similar actions could be construed as "deliberately unfriendly." **7 June:** Secretary of State William Jennings Bryan resigned in protest at the strength of Wilson's statement. **28 July:** U.S. forces took control of Haiti following a series of internal revolts. The United States effectively remained in control until 1934. **19 August:** The British liner *Arabic* was sunk by a German U-boat with the loss of two American lives. The German government disavowed the action and temporarily abandoned unrestricted submarine warfare. **4 November:** President Wilson announced his "preparedness" defense program and called for its adoption in the light of growing differences with Germany. The plans included expansion of the Navy and Army.

1916 9 March: Mexican forces led by Pancho Villa attacked Columbus, New Mexico, killing nineteen Americans. **15 March:** A "punitive expedition" of U.S. troops led by General John Pershing entered Mexico in pursuit of Pancho Villa and his forces. The expedition was withdrawn in February 1917. **18 April:** Following the sinking of the unarmed French Channel steamer *Sussex* on 24 March by a German U-boat, President Wilson issued an ultimatum to the German government threatening to sever diplomatic relations. The German government pledged to suspend unrestricted submarine attacks without warning. **15 May:** U.S. forces occupied and took control of Santo Domingo in the Dominican Republic following the overthrow of the government. They remained in control until 1924. **3 June:** The National Defense Act, increasing the strength of the U.S. Army, was passed as part of the "preparedness" campaign. **8–10 June:** The Republican Party convention in Chicago nominated Charles Evans Hughes as presidential candidate. The Progressive Party nominated Roosevelt, who declined and urged his supporters to back Hughes. The Progressive Party disbanded shortly after, but many leading members threw their support behind Woodrow Wilson, who was renominated for the Democratic Party at the convention in St. Louis. The slogan that emerged from the convention was "He kept us out of war." **11 July:** The Federal-Aid Highway Act provided $75 million over five years to match state spending on road building. When the act was renewed in 1921 it introduced the systematic numbering of highways in the United States. **17 July:** The Federal Farm Loan Act was passed, establishing twelve Farm Land Banks supervised by a seven-man Federal Farm Loan Board to provide bank credits for farmers. **22 July:** A Preparedness Day march organized by the Chamber of Commerce in San Francisco was disrupted when a suitcase bomb exploded, killing ten people and wounding forty; despite flimsy evidence, two labor activists—Tom Mooney and Warren K. Billings—were subsequently convicted for the crime. **August:** A Workmen's Compensation Act for federal employees was passed. **4 August:** The Treaty of Denmark confirmed the U.S. purchase of the Virgin Islands. **29 August:** A Council of National Defense was established to direct industrial mobilization as a part of "military preparedness." **1 September:** The Keating-Owen Child Labor Act, prohibiting the shipping across state lines of goods manufactured by companies employing children under fourteen or mines employing children under sixteen, was signed by President Wilson. **3 September:** The Adamson Act passed, introducing the eight-hour day for workers on interstate railways starting from 1 January 1917. The act was passed to avert a general railway strike after railroad presidents had refused to accept the principle voluntarily despite the pleading of President Wilson. **7 September:** The U.S. Shipping Board was created to enlarge the merchant marine. In April 1917 this became the U.S. Emergency Fleet Corporation. **7 November:** President Wilson was reelected. He received over 9 million votes as against 8.5 million for Hughes. Wilson won 277 votes in the Electoral College, a majority of 23. However, the Democratic majority in the Senate was reduced from sixteen to twelve while the balance between the two major parties in the House was held by a handful of Progressives, Independents, and a Socialist.

1917 22 January: In an address to the U.S. Senate, President Wilson called for a "peace without victory" in any postwar settlement. **3 February:** Following the resumption of unrestricted submarine warfare, the United States broke off diplomatic relations with Germany. **5 February:** An Immigration Act introducing a literacy test was passed over President Wilson's veto. **1**

March: Contents of the Zimmerman telegram promising German support for territorial gains by Mexico in the event of a future war with the United States were made public, having been intercepted by the British government on 16 January. **2 March:** The Jones Act established Puerto Rico as a territory and conferred U.S. citizenship on Puerto Ricans. **19 March:** Daylight Savings introduced. The measure was repealed in 1919. **6 April:** Following the resumption of unrestricted submarine warfare, the United States declared war on Germany and joined the Allied countries in World War I. **13 April:** A Committee of Public Information (CPI) chaired by George Creel was established to mobilize public opinion in support of the war. **18 May:** The Selective Service Act introducing wartime conscription was passed. **15 June:** The Espionage Act, providing for fines of up to $10,000 and twenty years in prison for acts of sabotage, was passed. **2 July:** A race riot in which at least twenty-nine African Americans and eight whites died broke out in East St. Louis, Illinois. **28 July:** Several thousand people marched in a silent protest in New York City organized by the National Association for the Advancement of Colored People (NAACP) to protest against race violence. **28 July:** A War Industries Board (WIB) was established to coordinate economic mobilization. Banker Bernard Baruch became head of a strengthened WIB in March 1918. **10 August:** The Lever Food and Fuel Control Act was passed, establishing the U.S. Food Administration and U.S. Fuel Administration. **23 August:** Following several incidents of racial harassment, members of the 3rd battalion of the all–African American 24th Infantry fired indiscriminately on white people in Houston, Texas. Sixteen whites and four blacks were killed in the riot. Thirteen of the black soldiers were subsequently court-martialed and executed in San Antonio in December 1917. **6 October:** Penalties were introduced for anyone trading with the Central Powers under the Trading with the Enemy Act. **21 October:** The first contingents of the American Expeditionary Force entered the line in France. **26 December:** The federal government took control of the railroads under the Rail Administration headed by William Gibbs McAdoo.

1918 January: All industries east of the Mississippi were ordered to close for a week by James A. Garfield, head of the Fuel Administration, in order to break the deadlock in coal supplies. **8 January:** In a speech to Congress President Wilson outlined the "Fourteen Points" on which an armistice with the Central Powers could be signed, including provision for a League of Nations. **March:** The first outbreak in what was to become a worldwide influenza epidemic began at a military camp in Kansas. Eventually more than 650,000 Americans died as a result of the illness. **9 April:** The National War Labor Board (NWLB) was established to mediate in labor disputes affecting war production. **16 May:** Fines of up to $10,000 and prison terms of up to twenty years for anyone uttering, writing, printing, or publishing anything that might hinder the war effort or be deemed critical of the U.S. government or armed forces were introduced under the Sedition Act. **20 May:** The Overman Act, enabling the president to redistribute powers among executive agencies without consulting Congress, was passed to increase government efficiency in wartime. **3 June:** In *Hammer v. Dagenhart* the Supreme Court found by five votes to four that the 1916 Keating-Owen Act was unconstitutional. **July:** 275,000 U.S. troops took part in the battle of the Marne, halting a German offensive. **16 August:** U.S. troops sent to Vladivostock, Siberia, in the Allied intervention in Russian Civil War. **26 September–11 November:** U.S. troops played a leading role in the Meuse-Argonne offensive that ended with the recapture of Sedan and negotiations for an armistice. **5 November:** The Republican Party gained majorities in both the House and Senate in the midterm elections. **8 November:** An armistice was agreed between the Allied and German forces on the western front. **11 November:** The armistice between the Allied Powers and Germany, bringing an end to fighting on the western front, was formally signed at 11 a.m.

1919 The Second Child Labor Act was passed, introducing a tax of 10 percent on products made in businesses employing children under the age of fourteen. The Supreme Court declared the law unconstitutional in 1922. **18 January–28 June:** The Versailles Peace Conference met to agree on the terms of the settlement after World War I. **21 January–10 February:** A strike by shipyard workers in Seattle turned into a general strike, but collapsed in the face of public opposition and police action called by Mayor Ole Hanson. **29 January:** The Eighteenth Amendment introducing prohibition was ratified. **3 March:** In *Schenck v. United States* the U.S. Supreme Court upheld the conviction of Charles T. Schenck on the grounds that the distribution of leaflets urging draft resistance constituted a "clear and present danger" to the country during war. **July:** Two African Americans died during a race riot in Longview, Texas. **27 July:** A race riot began in Chicago. When the riot ended five days later, twenty-three African Americans and fifteen whites were dead. **9 September:** Boston police struck for union recognition. Looting and violence broke out in the city until the State guard was called in to restore order. **22 September–8 January 1920:** A national steel strike took place in an attempt to gain union recognition and win an eight-hour day. The strike was unsuccessful. **26 September:** President Wilson suffered a stroke while on a speaking tour in support of the Versailles Treaty. **30 September:** African American sharecroppers meeting to form a union in Elaine, Arkansas, were involved in a confrontation with a group of white men. After a white deputy sheriff was shot and killed in the clash, violence spread as a white mob attacked the black community. Five whites and "anywhere from 20 to 200" African Americans died in the ensuing violence between 1 and 3 October. **11 October:** The Volstead Act or National Prohibition Act was passed to implement the provisions of the Eighteenth Amendment. **6–23 October:** An Industrial Conference with representatives of employers, labor, and the public met in Washington, D.C., to try to settle the postwar industrial unrest. No agreement was reached. **7 November:** In the first raids authorized by Attorney General A. Mitchell Palmer, six hundred people were arrested as suspected revolutionaries in different cities. **10 November:** In *Abrams v. United States* the U.S. Supreme Court upheld the conviction under the Seditions Act of Julius Abrams for distributing leaflets denouncing American intervention in the Russian Civil War by a majority of seven to two. **11 November:** Wesley Everett, a member of the Industrial Workers of the World (IWW) was castrated and lynched following a confrontation between the IWW and members of the American Legion, aided by the Citizens' Protective League, in Centralia, Washington, in which three members of the Legion were killed.

1920 January—March: A second industrial conference met to consider the problems of industrial relations. It proposed a forty-eight-hour week, minimum wages, and equal pay, but had little impact amid the postwar recession and the "Red Scare." **1 January:** The U.S. census reported that the U.S. population was 117.8 million. For the first time in U.S. history, the urban population exceeded the rural population. **2 January:** The "Palmer Raids" continued. Under the direction of Attorney General A. Mitchell Palmer 2,700 suspected communists were arrested. By the time the raids ended in May, six thousand people had been arrested. **5 January:** Boston Red Sox baseball star Babe Ruth was sold to the New York Yankees for $125,000, the biggest trade deal in baseball up to that time. **15 January:** The League of Nations first met in Paris. **17 January:** The Eighteenth Amendment to the U.S. Constitution went into effect, and Prohibition began with the ban on the making, selling, or the possession and consumption of alcoholic beverages. **24 January:** The U.S. expeditionary forces returned from Europe. **1 March:** The Railroad Transportation Act (Esch-Cummins Act) ended wartime federal control of the railroads, provided federal funds to help rail companies reestablish themselves, and established a Railway Labor Board to mediate in labor disputes. **19 March:** The U.S. Senate refused to join the League of Nations or ratify the Treaty of Versailles. **26 March:** F. Scott Fitzgerald's *This Side of Paradise*, his first novel, was published to wide acclaim. **1 April:** Five elected members of the New York state legislature were expelled for being members of the Socialist Party. **19 May:** Twelve people, mostly men from the detective agency hired by coal operators to stop the organization of mine workers by the United Mine Workers union, were killed at Matewan, West Virginia. **8 June:** The Republican Party convention nominated Warren G. Harding in the convention at Chicago. **28 June:** The Democratic Party convention, divided between pro-League supporters and isolationists, anti-prohibitionists and prohibitionists, nominated James M. Cox on the 44th ballot. **29 July:** First transcontinental airmail service, New York to San Francisco. **1 August:** Jamaican black nationalist leader Marcus Garvey convenes the first International Convention of the Negro Peoples of the World in New York's Madison Square Garden. **26 August:** The Nineteenth Amendment to the U.S. Constitution accepting women's right to vote was ratified. **16 September:** A bomb exploded near the Wall Street offices of J. P. Morgan's company, killing thirty (some accounts say thirty-five). Suspected radicals were arrested and later released, but the perpetrator was never found. **2 November:** Republican Warren G. Harding won the presidential election when he defeated the Democratic candidate James M. Cox by 16.1 million votes to 9.1 million, and 404 Electoral College votes to 127.

1921 4 March: Warren G. Harding was inaugurated as president of the United States. **10 May:** President Harding issued an executive order transferring management of the navy's emergency oil field deposits to the Department of the Interior. One of the oil fields was located at Teapot Dome, Wyoming. **19 May:** The Quota Act limited immigration to no more than 3 percent annually of each nationality, based on the number of that nationality already residing in the United States (as of 1910). **31 May:** The trial of Sacco and Vanzetti, Italian anarchists accused of robbery and murder, began in Dedham, Massachusetts. **31 May:** A race riot in Tulsa, Oklahoma, began. It was estimated that as many as two hundred blacks and fifty whites died in three days of violence. **10 June:** The Budget and Accounting Act was passed, establishing the fiscal year from 1 July to 30 June and creating the General Accounting Office and Bureau of the Budget. **2 July:** First radio broadcast of heavyweight boxing title bout between Georges Carpentier vs. Jack Dempsey from Jersey City, New Jersey. This was also the first time that box office receipts for a boxing match reached $1 million. **14 July:** The case of Sacco and Vanzetti became a cause of national and international protest when they were convicted of murder and sentenced to death. Their conviction appeared to be due more to their immigrant background and political views than the weight of evidence. **9 August:** The Veterans Bureau was established. **25 August:** The peace Treaty between the United States and Germany was signed. **12 November–6 February 1922:** International Disarmament Conference began in Washington, D.C., to address mutual concerns about a developing postwar arms race. U.S. secretary of state Charles Evans Hughes proposed that the major powers stop building large navy ships for ten years. The United States, Britain, France, Japan, and Italy agreed to the terms by the conference's end on 6 February 1922. **23 November:** The Sheppard-Towner Act providing federal funds for maternity and infant health care was passed. It remained in operation until 1929.

1922 1 April: A national coal strike began in protest of wage reductions and industrial and government labor union policies. The strike ended in September with some concessions to the miners. **7 April:** Secretary of the interior Albert B. Fall leased the Navy's Teapot Dome oil field secretly, without competitive bidding, to Harry F. Sinclair and the Mammoth Oil Co. Later, on April 25 and 11 December, Fall leased the Elk Hills Reserve to Edward L. Doheny in similar fashion. It was later found in investigations that Fall had taken bribes for these transactions. **15 May:** The Supreme Court found that the 1919 child labor law was unconstitutional in that a 10 percent tax on goods produced in factories employing children was a selective penalty. **1 July:** Railway shop men went on strike. The strike ended unsuccessfully after several weeks when attorney general Harry Daugherty secured a court injunction severely restricting the strikers' actions. **21 September:** The Fordney-McCumber Tariff Act, raising many duties to the levels of 1909 or earlier, passed to protect new war industries. **21 November:** Rebecca Latimer Felton, appointed in Georgia to fill a deceased senator's unexpired term, became the first female senator in the United States. **4 December:** The Dyer Anti-Lynching Bill, although passed by the House of Representatives, was withdrawn from the Senate after a filibuster by southern states.

1923 1–5 January: A white mob murdered eight African Americans and forced the population of Rosewood, Florida, to flee following an unconfirmed report of an assault on a white woman by a black male. No one was prosecuted for the outrage. **3 March:** The U.S. Senate rejected the proposal for the United States to join the International Court of Justice. **2–3 May:** The first transcontinental airplane flight was made in twenty-six hours, fifty minutes, from New York to San Diego. **2 August:** President Harding died of apoplexy (heart attack) in San Francisco. Vice president Calvin Coolidge took office the next day. **13 August:** U.S. Steel introduced an eight-hour workday at the urging of secretary of commerce Herbert Hoover. On 16 August, the Carnegie Steel Company also accepted the eight-hour workday.

1924 16 January: The first McNary-Haugen bill was introduced in Congress. Intended to raise farm prices artificially by employing a federal farm corporation to store surplus agricultural produce, the measure was defeated in 1924, passed in 1927, and vetoed by President Coolidge in February 1927 and again in May 1928. **3 February:** Former president Wilson died. **28 February:** U.S. troops landed in Honduras to protect American interests. **26 May:** The National Origins Act, limiting immigration to 150,000 a year and further reducing quotas on certain national groups, was passed. The act completely prohibited Japanese immigration, sparking diplomatic protests from Japan. **10 June:** The Republican Party convention in Cleveland nominated Calvin Coolidge and Charles G. Dawes. **24 June:** The Democratic Party nominated John W. Davis as presidential candidate and Charles W. Bryan as vice presidential candidate at the convention in New York. **4 July:** The Conference for Progressive Political Action, an alliance of progressives, farm interests, and the American Federation of Labor, met in Cleveland to form a new Progressive Party with Robert M. La Follette as presidential candidate and Burton K. Wheeler as the vice presidential candidate. **16 August:** The Dawes Plan reducing German reparation payments was adopted by a London conference. The plan's coauthors, U.S. secretary of state Charles G. Dawes and the British foreign secretary, Sir J. Austen Chamberlain, won the Nobel Peace Prize in 1925. **June:** Congress passed the law granting citizenship to American Indians. **10 September:** Nathan Leopold Jr., nineteen, and Richard Loeb, eighteen, who kidnapped and murdered a fourteen-year-old boy on 22 May for sport, were sentenced to life in prison rather than the electric chair following the successful use of the "insanity defense" by Clarence Darrow. **4 November:** Calvin Coolidge was elected president with 15.7 million votes to 8.3 million for the Democrat John W. Davis, and 4.8 million for the Progressive candidate, Robert M. La Follette.

1925 5 January: Nellie Tayloe Ross (Dem.) became the first female state governor when she completed the two years remaining of her dead husband's term in Wyoming. She was defeated in the election of 1926. **18 March:** One of the largest tornadoes on record since 1840 hit the tri-state area of southeastern Missouri, southern Illinois, and southwestern Indiana, destroying several towns in its path. The death toll was in excess of 695. **10 April:** F. Scott Fitzgerald's acclaimed novel of the 1920s, *The Great Gatsby*, was published. **10–25 July:** The "Scopes Monkey Trial" in which John T. Scopes was accused of teaching evolution in a Tennessee school in violation of state law, pitted the leading lawyer, Clarence Darrow (representing Scopes), against the former politician William Jennings Bryan for the prosecution in a great debate that gripped the national media. Scopes was found guilty on July 21 and ordered to pay $100 plus court costs. His fine and the case were dismissed on a technicality on appeal in January 1927 by the Tennessee Supreme Court. **8 August:** An estimated forty thousand Ku Klux Klan members marched through Washington, D.C., as part of the organization's first national congress. **3 September:** The navy dirigible *Shenandoah* crashed in Ohio, killing fourteen airmen. U.S. Air Service general William "Billy" Mitchell, a hero of World War I and early air-power advocate, criticized government administration of its air fleet as incompetent following the airship crash. He was subsequently forced to resign.

1926 The **Railway Labor Act** (Watson-Parker Act) abolished the Railroad Labor Board established in 1920 and replaced it with a National Board of Mediation. **May:** Leading evangelist Aimee Semple McPherson mysteriously disappeared. She reappeared several weeks later, claiming to have been abducted and tortured. Later speculation was that she was actually in hiding with a lover, or pulling a publicity stunt, or both. **2 May:** U.S. troops landed in Nicaragua to restore order following a revolt. **9 May:** U.S. commander Richard E. Byrd and pilot Floyd Bennett became the first people to fly over the North Pole. **26 June:** The McNary-Haugen bill to introduce tariffs on agricultural produce was defeated in the Senate. **6 August:** Gertrude Ederle became the first woman to swim the English Channel, a feat that earned her a New York City ticker tape parade. **23 August:** Rudolph Valentino, star of *The Sheik* and a movie idol, died of a perforated ulcer at age thirty-one. **25 September:** Henry Ford instituted the five-day workweek and eight-hour day to reduce overproduction.

1927 1 March: President Coolidge appointed the first five-man Federal Board of Radio Control to oversee radio broadcasting and issue licenses. **7 March:** The Supreme Court declared the Texas law excluding African Americans from voting in the state's primary election unconstitutional. **16 April:** The worst Mississippi River flooding (until 1937) occurred, eventually covering 4.4 million acres and causing $300 million in damage. **4 May:** U.S. Marines land in Nicaragua to supervise elections. American troops remained until 1932–1933. **20–21 May:** Charles Lindbergh made the first one-person, nonstop transatlantic airplane flight, from New York to Paris, in his *Spirit of St. Louis* monoplane. **20 June–24 August:** An international conference called by President Coolidge met at Geneva to consider further naval limitations. Only Great Britain and Japan took part with the United States and no agreement was reached. **2 August:** President Coolidge unexpectedly announced he "did not choose to run for president in 1928." **23 August:** Sacco and Vanzetti were executed at Charlestown State Prison, Massachusetts. **30 September:** New York Yankees baseball star Babe Ruth hit his sixtieth home run for the season, a mark not again achieved for thirty-four years. **6 October:** The movie *The Jazz Singer* premiered. Although only a partial "talkie" using conversational dialogue as part of a dramatic story, the film was regarded as the first sound picture. It earned more than $3 million, making it one of the biggest hits of the 1920s, and changed the film industry forever. **10 October:** The Supreme Court upheld lower court rulings that Teapot Dome oil leases with Harry Sinclair's Mammoth Oil Co. were fraudulently obtained and should be declared illegal. Earlier, on 28 February, the court ruled oil contracts and leases granted to Edward Doheny by Interior Secretary Albert Fall in 1921 to be illegal and fraudulent. **2 December:** Ford Motor Co. unveiled the Model A to replace the Model T car that had revolutionized motorcar manufacture.

1928 12 January: Ruth Snyder became only the second woman to be electrocuted when she was executed at Sing Sing prison in New York for the murder of her husband. Her lover, Judd Gray, was executed the same day. **15 May:** The Flood Control Act passed to provide a $325 million, ten-year program of flood control on the Mississippi River and tributaries. **June:** The Republican Party convention in Kansas City nominated Herbert Hoover as their candidate to succeed Calvin Coolidge. The Democrats, meeting in Houston, Texas, nominated Al Smith, governor of New York, with Joseph T. Robinson of Arkansas as his running mate. The campaign was to focus on Smith's Catholicism, his opposition to Prohibition, and his urban, immigrant background. **17–18 June:** Amelia Earhart made the first transatlantic flight by a woman, flying with Wilmer Stultz and Louis Gordon. **27 August:** The Kellogg-Briand Pact, outlawing war as an instrument of foreign policy, was signed in Paris. **6 November:** Herbert Hoover was elected president, defeating Al Smith by 21.4 million votes to 15 million, and 444 Electoral College votes to 87. Significantly, while Hoover carried half of the states of the traditionally Democratic former Confederacy, Smith won majorities in the largest cities, most of which had previously voted Republican.

1929 14 February: Seven gangsters were killed in the "St. Valentine's Day Massacre" by members of Al Capone's gang. **3 March:** Herbert Hoover was inaugurated as president of the United States. **20 May:** President Hoover appointed the National Commission on Law Observance and Enforcement (the Wickersham Commission) to examine the impact of Prohibition on crime rates. **June:** The Agricultural Marketing Act or Cooperative Marketing Act passed to assist farmers market produce. **14 September:** The United States joined the International Court. **24 October:** "Black Thursday"—13 million shares were sold in trading on the New York Stock Exchange and began the Wall Street Crash. **29 October:** "Black Tuesday"—a further 16 million shares were sold on the stock exchange as the crash deepened. By 1 December the value of stocks listed on the New York exchange had fallen to $63.5 billion from $89.6 billion on 1 September 1929. **1 November:** Former secretary of the interior Albert Fall became the first cabinet officer convicted of crime while holding office when he was found guilty of accepting bribes in the Teapot Dome scandal. **29 November:** Commander Richard Byrd and pilot Bernt Balchen became the first people to fly over the South Pole.

1930 17 January: The London Naval conference met, with delegates from Britain, France, Italy, Japan, and the United States agreeing to reductions in naval strength. **17 June:** The Hawley-Smoot Tariff was passed, raising import duties to some of the highest levels ever in U.S. history in order to protect American industry in the face of the Depression. The measure proved counterproductive and resulted in retaliatory measures from other powers.

1931 6–9 April: The trial of the "Scottsboro boys," eight black youths accused of rape, took place. Found guilty, they were sentenced to death. Their case became a cause of national and international protest and the convictions were later overturned by the Supreme Court. **1 May:** The Empire State

Building in New York City opened. At the time it was the tallest building in the world. **September:** Following the Wall Street Crash, a bank panic hit the United States and over eight hundred banks closed in September and October.

1932 7 January: The Stimson doctrine, stating opposition to Japanese aggression in Manchuria and refusal to accept any territorial gains from such an act, was set out in a note by secretary of state Henry Stimson. **22 January:** A Reconstruction Finance Corporation was established to provide loans to banks and insurance companies to stabilize the deteriorating banking situation following the Wall Street Crash. It lent $1.5 billion up to 1933, but could not stop the collapse of banking and was widely regarded as a "rich man's dole." **2 February–July:** The United States participated in the Geneva Disarmament Conference, which was to last two years. Despite the involvement of over fifty-seven countries, little agreement was achieved. **1 March:** The baby son of the aviator Charles Lindbergh was kidnapped. Despite payment of a $50,000 ransom, the child was found dead several months later. Bruno Hauptmann was subsequently found guilty of the abduction and murder and executed on 3 April 1936. **3 March:** The Twentieth Amendment ending "lame duck" congresses by introducing the completion of terms of office in January rather than March was ratified. **4 March:** The Senate Committee on Banking and Currency began investigations into the banking practices that led to the Wall Street Crash. **20 May:** Amelia Earhart became the first woman to fly across the Atlantic alone. **29 May–28 July:** The "Bonus Army" of about three thousand World War I veterans marched on Washington, D.C., to lobby for early payment of veterans' bonus. By July some twenty-five thousand people had made camp in the capital. On 28 July armed troops forced the veterans out of the camp, which was then destroyed. **14 June:** President Hoover was renominated at the Republican Party convention in Chicago. **1 July:** Franklin Delano Roosevelt was nominated as the presidential candidate for the Democratic Party. The following day, having flown to Chicago to address the delegates, he promised the American people a "New Deal." **21 July:** President Hoover signed the Emergency Relief and Construction Act into law to provide $300 million in relief loans to the states. **22 July:** The Federal Home Loan Bank Act was passed, establishing Home Loan Banks to provide credit for real estate financing to offset the impact of the Wall Street Crash and Depression. **8 November:** Roosevelt was elected president in a landslide, with 22.8 million votes to Hoover's 15.7 million. Roosevelt became the longest-serving president when he was reelected in 1936, 1940, and 1944.

1933 5 December: The Twenty-first Amendment was ratified, ending Prohibition with the repeal of the Eighteenth Amendment. **15 February:** Giuseppe Zangara attempted to assassinate president-elect Roosevelt during a visit to

Florida. One of the shots hit the mayor of Chicago, Anton Cermak, who was traveling with Roosevelt. Cermak subsequently died, and Zangara was executed on 21 March. **4 March:** Franklin Roosevelt was inaugurated president of the United States. Declaring that the nation had "nothing to fear but fear itself," Roosevelt called for broad powers to combat the impact of the Depression. He was to initiate a program of reform known as the "New Deal," which established the basis of a federal welfare system and shaped American politics through to the 1960s.

Introduction

The period from 1913 to 1933 is not often seen as a coherent entity in the history of the United States. It is more often viewed in terms of two distinct periods with the prewar era of political engagement, idealism, and reform known as "progressivism" separated by World War I from the materialism, conservatism, and disengagement of the "prosperous" 1920s. To many postwar observers and later historians, the entry of the United States into the European conflict in 1917 marked not just a dramatic departure in foreign relations, but also the end of an era of reform. More than this, the war was also often perceived to have brought disruption, conflict, and the suppression of civil liberties at home with little positive benefit.

Such negative views were expressed particularly strongly in the 1930s as war clouds threatened once more. Those in favor of neutrality measures argued that the United States had entered the Great War because of the baleful influence of British propaganda or the vested interests of munitions' manufacturers. Even among those Americans who believed that World War I had been fought for the cause of democracy and freedom, there were many who felt that such aims had been sacrificed in an unjust peace settlement at Versailles. The postwar disillusionment evident in such expressions again seemed to underline the difference between two eras and to separate the 1920s from the prewar years.

The 1920s themselves have often been characterized as a distinct and separate era in United States history, sandwiched between the end of World War I on one side and the onset of the Great Depression on the other. The decade, known variously as the "Jazz Age," "Roaring Twenties," "Prosperity Decade," and "New Era," was depicted by one of its greatest chroniclers, the author F. Scott Fitzgerald, as "an age of miracles, an age of excess," when "a whole race was going hedonistic, deciding on pleasure." The sudden growth in consumerism associated with the automobile industry, new electrical appliances, movies, radio, and sport supported Fitzgerald's view. However, this image overlooked not only some of the harsher realities, but also elements of continuity between this decade and those before and after. There were in fact several common threads running across the decades. Rather than ending them, World War I often accelerated existing political, social, and economic trends. Many of the issues and developments evident before 1914, including some of those on the reformers' agenda, either came to fruition during the war or continued after it, surviving in some instances even into the 1930s.

Whatever the debates, the years from 1913 to 1933 marked a period of enormous change in the history of the United States as the characteristics of modern America—an industrial/urban economy, an increasingly powerful and interventionist national government, a mass national popular culture, and an international role—emerged. The United States had begun to grapple with the consequences of massive industrial growth from the last quarter of the nineteenth century onward, but that development reached its height in the first decade of the twentieth century. Among the most pressing issues was the question of how to deal with the rise of huge corporations and business monopoly, mass immigration and mass urbanization, social inequality and issues of public welfare, and increasing class divisions and social conflict. The political response to this was the movement known as "progressivism," a broad movement of reform beginning at the local and rising to the federal level. There were major differences within this movement over almost every issue, whether it was about the best form capitalism should take, the function of national government, or the tension between demands for social justice as opposed to those for social control. While the call for reform was all-pervasive, these differences were evident in the very fact that progressivism influenced both major parties, Republican and Democratic, produced a third party, the Progressive Party, in 1912, and witnessed the rise of the Socialist Party of America (SPA).

Although diverse, progressivism rejected traditional notions of individualism and limited government enshrined in principles of "laissez faire" so evident in the preceding "Gilded Age." Instead the reformers demanded that government should tackle the economic and social problems facing the nation. They argued too that government itself should be more efficient and more responsive to the public will. Several states adopted referenda, recall, and voter initiatives between 1900 and 1914, and the direct election of senators came into force in 1913. Women were often at the fore of the call for greater social responsibility and a more representative government. Jane Addams, one of the founders of the settlement house movement that played a leading part in urban reform, argued that women's involvement in politics would lead to better "civic housekeeping." The demand for women's suffrage gained increasing support in the years just prior to 1914 and, further spurred on by the impact of World War I, culminated in the passage of the Nineteenth Amendment in 1920.

Other groups were less fortunate. A strong anti-immigrant feeling was evident before, during, and after World War I. The desire to "keep America American" revealed deep-seated ethnic and racial prejudices fueling a nativism that lasted for fifty years or more. While educational reformers argued that greater political participation demanded education for all, some also recognized that education could be used to "Americanize" the new immigrants. This did not apply to African Americans, most of whom still lived in the former Confederate states of the South, where the prewar years saw the final implementation of the system of racial segregation known as "Jim Crow" and an increase in racial violence. The quickening movement of the black population to northern industrial centers in search of greater social and economic opportunities saw the spread of race conflict beyond the confines of the South. However, it also brought with it a growing black consciousness and the rise of new civil rights organizations.

If the domestic concerns of this period were those that were to feature for much of the twentieth century, then so too were the issues in foreign relations. In the 1890s the United States had become an imperial power following the acquisition of the Philippines after the Spanish-American War. However, although increasingly active in the international arena and already becoming the world's leading economic power, the United States was not committed to any alliances and acted largely independently of other nations. Under the presidencies of Theodore Roosevelt and Woodrow Wilson the United States increasingly intervened in the affairs of Central American and Caribbean states in a "policing role." Such intervention brought such deterioration in relations with Mexico that it almost led to war in 1915 and 1917. As far as Europe was concerned, however, most Americans still clung to notions of "isolationism." The outbreak of war in 1914 immediately challenged such assumptions and forced the United States to face the realities of total war in the modern age.

The attempt to insist on both neutrality and the right to trade and travel freely after 1914 failed and America entered the war in 1917. By then her role was justified in terms of high principle, a war to make the "world safe for democracy." The involvement of the United States broke the deadlock on the western front and contributed significantly to the final victory. Sadly, the attempt to establish a liberal world order along the lines indicated by president Woodrow Wilson did not materialize in the Versailles settlement and the treaty, and with it the League of Nations, was rejected by the Senate. Although it appeared that the United States retreated once more to an isolationist position in the 1920s, in reality it was involved through economic concerns and in attempts to lessen the risk of another war. However, for some historians the failure of the United States to join international peacekeeping in the League of Nations, and also to fully accept the responsibilities that went with its now confirmed dominant economic power, contributed to the Great Depression and coming of World War II.

POLITICAL DEVELOPMENTS

The election of the Democratic presidential candidate, Woodrow Wilson, in 1912 and his inauguration on 4 March 1913 marked the culmination of the progressive reform movement. The election had been contested by three major candidates—Wilson, William Howard Taft for the Republican Party, and former Republican president Theodore Roosevelt for the Progressive Party—all of whom could claim to be progressive. In addition Eugene V. Debs stood for the Socialist Party and there was also a candidate for the Prohibition Party. The support of insurgent progressive Republicans like Robert M. La Follette for Roosevelt's candidacy divided the Republican vote and ensured victory for Wilson and the Democrats.

Initially rejecting what he saw as the paternalistic approach of Roosevelt's "New Nationalist" platform, Wilson's "New Freedom" program promised to protect the economic and political liberties that enabled ordinary people to prosper by further empowering the federal government to curb business monopoly, stabilize the financial system, and encourage competition. This was done by introducing sweeping tariff reform, creating the Federal Reserve System, and implementing and extending the antitrust principles of the Sherman Act (1890) through the Clayton Antitrust Act (1914) and the creation of a Federal Trade Commission (1914). Government itself became more responsive to the popular will through the direct election of senators in 1913. Between 1915 and 1916 Wilson also accepted a measure of social policy reform with the passage of the federal workmen's compensation law, the introduction of the eight-hour day for railroad workers, child labor restrictions, and federal farm loans. In doing so, he increased the power and influence of the federal government, and particularly the president, and established a form of liberal capitalism within the existing constitutional framework.

Faced with the possibility of a second Democratic victory in 1916 and critical of Wilson's "cowardice and weakness" in foreign relation, the ever-belligerent Theodore Roosevelt disbanded the Progressive Party. Although not selected as the Republican candidate, Roosevelt threw his support behind the party's choice of Charles Evans Hughes. However, Wilson successfully attracted many of the progressive movement with his record of reform and peace and narrowly secured a historic second election victory.

Wilson's second term in the White House was dominated by foreign affairs following the outbreak of World War I in Europe in 1914. The presence of a large and diverse immigrant population, coupled with a progressive abhorrence of war as a means of settling disputes, guaranteed support for Wilson's policy of neutrality. However, when his attempts to mediate a peaceful settlement failed and the German use of unrestricted submarine warfare threatened both American trade and lives, the president who had been reelected on the slogan "He kept us out of war" was forced to ask Congress for a declaration of war in April 1917. Although the request was granted, divisions still remained within the United States, and the federal government took steps to mobilize the population and silence any opposition. The creation of a propaganda agency, the Committee of Public Information, together with the passage of the Espionage and Sedition Acts, encouraged anti-German feeling and led to the suppression of antiwar groups, most notably with the arrest of leaders of the Socialist Party and Industrial Workers of the World (IWW). These actions contributed to a mood of war hysteria and xenophobia that seriously threatened civil liberties during the war and continued when the war was over.

The need for economic mobilization to wage war led to a plethora of new federal agencies, creating what some contemporaries referred to as "war socialism." The most obvious extension of government authority was in the implementation of selective service through the draft that registered more than 20 million men for service and raised an army of 4 million. A War Industries Board was created to direct economic mobilization, a War Labor Board was established to prevent the disruption of the war effort by labor disputes, food and fuel conservation each became the subject of separate agencies, and transportation came under the direction of the Railroad War Board. However, the federal government relied a great deal on the voluntary cooperation and participation of businessmen and experts in the many war agencies. For example, the Food Administration, headed by Herbert Hoover, unlike its European counterparts relied on persuasion rather than imposing rationing and controls in its efforts to regulate supplies.

Although these many measures were dramatic and certainly confirmed the central role the federal government now played in the lives of American citizens, they were for the duration only. The end of the war brought rapid demobilization both of the American Expeditionary Force in Europe and of the war agencies at home. The election of 1920 in which the Republicans returned to power appeared to indicate a repudiation of government intervention and Wilsonian idealism. The return of former progressive Republicans to their party fold helped to secure Warren Harding's victory and suggested a return to more traditional "conservative" policies. However, politicians like Robert M. La Follette kept aspects of the reform agenda alive throughout the 1920s, and in reality the return to "laissez-faire" was never as complete as it sometimes seemed.

The Republican administrations of Harding, Coolidge, and Hoover shared a number of common features, particularly of cabinet personnel. The most significant cabinet members were Charles Evans Hughes, secretary of state; Henry C. Wallace, secretary of agriculture; Andrew Mellon, secretary of the treasury; and Herbert Hoover himself, who was secretary of commerce under his two presidential predecessors. While Mellon was responsible for many pro-business policies, especially with regard to taxation, Hoover believed that government had a role to encourage and lead businessmen, farmers, and others to cooperate voluntarily in a process of self-regulation to fix standards, stabilize prices, and maintain economic stability. To that end he organized meetings and conferences with the leaders in different sectors of manufacturing and business, supported the formation of trade associations, and had federal agencies compile statistical information.

If Hoover's actions belied those of the traditional conservative and reflected a degree of moral earnestness, this could not be said of some others in the new Republican administration. Warren Harding himself was chosen as the Republican presidential candidate as a compromise choice who would offend least people. He was neither a leading thinker nor speaker, and often seemed more interested in golf and poker games with his cronies than in the business of government. However, he was a popular president and was personally responsible for the early release from prison of some of the antiwar leaders, including the socialist Eugene V. Debs, appointed women to federal bureaus, and spoke out against race violence and in favor of racial equality in politics and economics. His administration, with Hoover particularly active, helped secure the introduction of the eight-hour day in the steel industry, an aim long sought after by labor. However, the Harding government was beset by corruption, most infamously in the Teapot Dome scandal that involved the secretary of the interior, Albert Fall, who received bribes in return for leasing federal oil reserves to private companies. Fall was eventually convicted and jailed for his part in these events, while the attorney general, Harry Daugherty, was forced to resign for his failure to prosecute the case with sufficient rigor.

Harding died in office in 1923 before the scandals became public, but after his death a record of poor appointments and marital infidelity obscured the few successes of his administration and ensured that he was judged harshly by historians. His successor, Calvin Coolidge, elected in his own right in 1924, did not fare much better. Known as "Silent Cal," this taciturn president is often remembered for his apparent inactivity. However, Coolidge allowed his cabinet members to get on with their work, and his administration balanced the budget, reduced government debt, and began construction of a federally funded highway system. Coolidge also presided over a period of considerable economic growth. The election in 1928 of his successor, Herbert Hoover, was in many ways an expression of approval for Coolidge's policies although the fact that the Democratic candidate, mayor Al Smith of New York City, was of Catholic Irish extraction and an opponent of prohibition, was clearly also a factor.

Hoover reflected on his predecessor's success when he suggested in his inaugural address that poverty might soon be a thing of the past. Sadly, events quickly proved him wrong. The Wall Street Crash in October 1929, itself a product of inflated optimism and rash financial practices caused a financial panic that revealed the flaws in "Coolidge prosperity." Hoover's responses, based on his previous experiences as head of the wartime Food Administration, relied on exhortation and appeals to state and local officials and businessmen to act for the public good. The president tried to boost morale, first by using the term "depression" rather than "panic" or "collapse," and by suggesting the crisis would soon be at an end. Although he enacted a series of measures that far exceeded anything previously done, they proved insufficient and were often undercut by other actions. Thus, Hoover initially cut federal taxes and increased spending on public works and created the President's Organization for Unemployment Relief (POUR) to mobilize private funds to aid charities and local relief agencies. More dramatic in terms of direct state intervention was the Reconstruction Finance Corporation (RFC) set up in 1932 to provide loans to businesses and banks in the hope that this would "trickle down" through companies to employees.

All of these measures proved inadequate, and subsequent tax increases and the implementation of tariff barriers against foreign imports only aggravated an already serious situation. As the crisis deepened, Hoover's name soon became synonymous with the depression—the severity, duration, and spread of which led to it being known as the Great Depression.

When World War I veterans who had marched to Washington, D.C., in the "Bonus Army" to call for the early payment of their service bonuses were driven out of the capital by force, Hoover's reputation was in tatters. His defeat in the 1932 presidential election by the Democratic candidate Franklin D. Roosevelt was virtually inevitable. Although Hoover's program included elements that his successor would build on, Roosevelt's victory and his "New Deal" marked a comprehensive return to reform and led to the creation of the modern welfare system in the United States.

ECONOMIC, SOCIAL, AND CULTURAL NEEDS

With the exception of a severe but brief recession after World War I, the period from 1913 to 1933 was one of unprecedented economic growth. The thirty or forty years prior to 1910 had already witnessed the transformation of the United States from an agricultural nation into an industrial giant. The development of key basic industries producing capital goods—railways, iron, coal, and steel, oil, and banking—was combined with the rise of huge business corporations and the expansion of the factory system of production. The late nineteenth century also saw mass immigration and the rise of the city. The years after 1910 brought a greater diversification of the economy and the rise of fully fledged systems of mass production coupled with the growth of a mass-consumer society. Total national income rose from $36.5 billion in 1900 to $60.4 billion in 1920 and $82.8 billion in 1929. From the end of the postwar recession in 1922 to the Wall Street Crash in 1929 the economy grew by 5 percent a year, and the Gross National Product (GNP) rose from $70 billion to $100 billion as manufacturing output increased by 50 percent. The key industries in this phase of economic growth were automobiles, electrical appliances, chemicals, leisure industries or mass-produced entertainment (movies, radio, sport), and advertising itself. At the same time, the nation became more clearly urban in emphasis and gave the appearance of greater homogeneity. However, many of the social tensions and conflicts evident before 1913 were still present during the 1920s, exacerbated to some extent by the increasing rapidity of change.

The basis of the consumer society that emerged in the twentieth century was the system of mass marketing and national markets that had sprung up in the preceding twenty or thirty years. The expansion of agriculture to meet an ever-increasing population, swollen by the huge influx of immigrants who populated the growing cities and worked in the new factories, was coupled with the development of a national railway network and huge national corporations headed by ruthless business entrepreneurs. The exploitation of the United States' rich supply of natural resources inevitably made it one of the world's leading economic powers. By 1929 the United States produced 40 percent of the world's coal, 70 percent of its gasoline, and 50 percent of its steel. The development of new technologies, such as electricity, increased productivity; their application to the home opened up the market for production aimed at the consumer. New companies like General Foods emerged in food processing, and Birdseye led the way in frozen foods. Access to such products was linked to the postwar growth of chain stores such as The Great Atlantic and Pacific Tea Company (A&P) and the Piggly Wiggly.

The nation's economic supremacy was confirmed during World War I as foreign powers such as Great Britain and France sold their investments in the United States and borrowed money to fund their war machines. By the end of the war the United States was no longer a debtor nation but a creditor, owed millions by the European powers. Moreover, the war brought a huge expansion in American industrial production with none of the physical destruction and many fewer military casualties than those experienced by other participants.

The methods of mass production already developing prior to 1914 were accelerated to meet the demands to feed, clothe, and arm Allied and, after 1917, American armed forces. The automobile manufacturer Henry Ford, responsible for developing the moving assembly line production technique before the war, in 1916 employed thirty-two thousand workers; by 1918 this had risen to forty-eight thousand. The workforce at General Motors rose from ten thousand to fifty thousand during the same period. By the 1920s automobile manufacture was second only to steel in value. Henry Ford's Model T Ford, first produced before the war, led the way in developing mass-produced, cheap, standardized vehicles in the 1920s. A total of more than 26 million automobiles were registered by 1929.

Business profits soared during the war, and after a brief recession from 1920 to 1921, this pattern resumed in the 1920s. Farmers were less fortunate. The war gave a considerable impetus to agricultural expansion and farm production rose by over 20 percent despite a fall in the size of the farm labor force. Increased production was achieved by increasing acreage—and increased indebtedness. When the war ended and world trade resumed, farm prices fell and with it farm incomes. Few farmers shared in the prosperity of the 1920s and the problem of agriculture led to repeated calls for assistance. The passage of a succession of McNary-Haugen farm bills to create federal price supports reflected farmers' concerns and the strength of the farm lobby in Congress. They were vetoed by president Calvin Coolidge, who believed that farmers had always been poor and the government could not (and should not) do anything about it.

Like farmers many industrial workers also benefited from the war as the demand for production led to full employment, increased wages, and increasing recognition of labor unions led by the American Federation of Labor (AFL) and Samuel Gompers. The government's War Labor Board acknowledged the right to collective bargaining and incorporated the principle of the eight-hour day and a living wage in many of the cases it adjudicated during the war. While earnings in some cases rose by 50 to 100 percent, membership in labor unions rose from under 3 million in 1914 to over 5 million in 1920. However, those gains were short-lived. The withdrawal of government support with the end of wartime agencies combined with the postwar recession placed labor unions in a weak position. The outbreak of strikes to increase union representation and combat falling wages in 1919 was met with employer resistance and characterized as the work of Bolsheviks in what became known as the "Red Scare." The return of conservative Republican administrations and a less sympathetic attitude toward labor unions, coupled with the prosperity of the 1920s, saw union membership fall back to prewar levels. Nonetheless, in the decade after the war many workers benefited from increased wages and shorter working hours enabling them to spend more on consumer goods and on leisure and entertainment.

While on average real wages rose between 20 and 30 percent during the "prosperity decade" of the 1920s, some areas of the workforce did not share in the boom. Older industries such as steel and coal mining declined and new technology served to displace many workers, if only temporarily. Unemployment, although low, was still a constant feature in many lives, if only for a short period in any year.

The uneven distribution of wealth and income meant that domestic markets had their own limitations. Tariff barriers that limited imports also restricted the ability of foreign nations to purchase goods from the United States. The increasing reliance on credit at home to purchase consumer items was also a major weakness in the economy. These factors taken together with the conservative attitudes toward government intervention contributed significantly to the coming of the Great Depression following the Wall Street Crash in 1929.

The Wall Street Crash ended a boom in the sale of stocks and shares, the "bull market," that had been developing since the end of the postwar recession in 1921 and had quickened in 1927 and 1928. Confidence in the economy had encouraged more and more people to invest, and by 1929 about 4 million owned stock. As stock market prices soared, investments became more than just a reflection of the strength of the economy or consumer spending, both of which were slowing. Instead it became a business itself as speculation and a lack of close banking regulation encouraged dubious or even illegal financial practices. While some unscrupulous entrepreneurs floated multiple investment trusts, many people purchased stock "on margin," putting down a deposit, in some cases as low as 10 percent, on the expectation that values would continue to rise. When, however, prices began to fall, there was a rush to sell in order to cover outstanding debts, and a rapid downward spiral began. As individuals and financial institutions lost their investments, credit shrank. Many small banks that, like the stock exchange, had hardly been regulated, could not meet their obligations. Some five thousand banks failed between 1929 and 1932, wiping out the savings of thousands of Americans in the process. Industry, no longer able to borrow, had to reduce costs and cut wages and labor forces. By 1933 industrial production had fallen to below 50 percent of the 1929 levels and unemployment had risen to 17 million or 25 percent of the labor force. This economic collapse, although it eased somewhat, was to last until well into World War II.

THE SITUATION OF WOMEN AND ETHNIC AND RACIAL MINORITIES

The war boom brought job opportunities to groups previously largely excluded from industrial employment. The economic position of women had already been changing as the number of women in paid employment outside of the home doubled between 1870 and 1910. By then 8 million women workers made up over 20 percent of the labor force. The vast majority worked in domestic service or in industries traditionally associated with women—garment making, textiles, the needle trades. However, there was a rapid increase in female employment as telephonists, typists, and sales assistants in the decade before World War I. These new trends continued as more than a million women entered paid employment during the war. Many women found work in war industries, and others were used for the first time in the uniformed branches of the armed forces. Although many of these jobs were lost after the war, women's employment was clearly more widely accepted and continued in the 1920s. By 1930 10.8 million were in paid employment. The biggest increase took place in clerical occupations—by 1930 2 million women worked as typists, bookkeepers, and clerks. Significantly the number of married women who worked outside the home rose from 1.9 million to 3.1 million.

Women's war work strengthened the demand for political recognition that finally resulted in the passage of the Nineteenth Amendment in 1920. The campaign for the vote, led particularly by the National American Woman Suffrage Association (NAWSA), had been growing from 1900 on and had secured a number of victories at state level. As more states granted the vote during the war, the passage of a federal amendment became inevitable. But with victory won the women's movement divided into separate interest groups and became less conspicuous. However, continued political and economic advances combined to create the notion of the "new woman" in the 1920s. In reality, however, the percentage of women who worked remained constant, as did their proportion in the labor force. New female stereotypes in advertising and the movies that suggested a greater liberation in fact only confirmed gender difference. Similarly, new household appliances made housework lighter, but rather than freeing women this only meant that more women did their own housework rather than employ domestic servants.

The extent to which women's position had advanced was revealed in the 1930s. When the Depression struck the United States, there was a widespread demand for working women to give up their jobs for men and for married women once more to stay in the home. Paradoxically, however, economic necessity often forced more women to seek work if only on a part-time basis in the traditional and poorly paid area of domestic service. It was not until World War II that really significant changes occurred in women's employment.

Like that of women, the situation of African Americans appeared to go through considerable change between 1913 and 1933, but in reality there was a considerable element of continuity. In 1900 the black population of 9 million constituted 12 percent of the United States' population, and 90 percent of them lived in the South, mainly employed in the agricultural pursuits of their slave ancestors. Free in name, the largely propertyless African

Americans were forced into a system of economic dependency in the share-cropping system under which tenant farmers worked the land owned by whites. In the late nineteenth century African Americans had seen their right to vote denied through various legal devices such as the grandfather clause, poll tax, and literacy test. Laws segregating the races on railways and street-cars and in schools and all places of public accommodation were passed throughout the South from the late 1870s on. Where these measures failed violence was used to "keep them in their place." African American leadership was long dominated by the "accommodationist" principal of Tuskegee Institute in Alabama, Booker T. Washington. However, more militant voices were being heard, particularly those of Monroe Trotter and W. E. B. Du Bois. Du Bois joined a small group of white progressives who, shocked by increasing race violence, organized the National Association for the Advancement of Colored People (NAACP) in 1909 to protest on behalf of the African American population.

Initially the NAACP had little impact. Under Woodrow Wilson segregation spread to the federal civil service. Black participation in the military during World War I was only reluctantly accepted and was strictly segregated. Some four hundred thousand African Americans served in the armed forces, but only about forty thousand in combat roles. There was more significant change on the home front where the demand for industrial labor increased and the normal supply of immigrant labor declined. During the war between three hundred thousand and four hundred thousand African Americans moved north in the "Great Migration" to find work in the war industries in centers such as Chicago, Detroit, Philadelphia, and Pittsburgh. This trend continued in the 1920s, and by 1930 almost 1 million African Americans had left the South.

While the move to the North offered African Americans new job opportunities in industry and greater access to education and political influence, it also resulted in race violence as whites reacted to the competition for housing and jobs. Race riots occurred in East St. Louis in 1917 and in Chicago, Washington, D.C., and a number of other towns and cities north and south during the "Red Summer" of 1919. However, African Americans now fought back and a less passive mood was evident in the physical resistance of the "New Negro" and in the cultural expression of the literary and artistic "Harlem Renaissance" that was a feature of the 1920s.

Despite the adoption of African American culture by some white Americans, mainly among the young or literary circles, that gave the 1920s the title "Jazz Age," racial intolerance and race violence continued intermittently throughout the decade. Riots in Tulsa, Oklahoma, 1921, and Rosewood, Florida, 1923, or the case of the Scottsboro boys in 1931, indicated how little the plight of the majority of African Americans who still remained in the South had changed. With the onset of the Depression, black Americans once more found themselves "last hired, first fired," and unemployment rates were twice as high for African Americans as they were for whites. As in the case of women, this situation did not change until World War II.

The persistence of discrimination and prejudice against African Americans, evident in the revival of the Ku Klux Klan in 1915 and its spread into states such as Indiana and Illinois during the 1920s, was indicative of the deep-seated racism in American society. The Klan did not confine its attention just to African Americans, but instead also expressed opposition to Catholics, Jews, and those of nonwhite Anglo-Saxon backgrounds. To a considerable extent this was a continuation of the nativist sentiment evident from the end of the nineteenth century on. Such feelings were heightened during the war with its emphasis on 100 percent Americanism, total loyalty, and the suppression of civil liberties. Anti-German feeling, fanned by war propaganda, easily became antiforeign feeling. In the instability of the immediate postwar period this quickly translated into anti-Bolshevism and led to the "Red Scare" in which hundreds of immigrants were deported. The anti-immigrant sentiment finally culminated in the passage of the Quota Act of 1921 and National Origins Act of 1924, severely restricting immigration along ethnic lines. A hatred of foreigners combined with antiradicalism was also evident in the trial for murder of two Italian anarchists, Sacco and Vanzetti, who were executed in 1927 despite national and international campaigns on their behalf. Anti-Catholicism was also a significant factor in the defeat of the Democratic presidential candidate, Al Smith, in 1928.

CULTURAL CONFLICTS

Anti-Catholicism was evident in American society as far back as the 1840s. Religious fundamentalism stretched back even further. With the anti-immigrant sentiment, both were apparent in the late nineteenth century and could be seen in elements of both Populism and the progressive movement. In the 1920s such beliefs seemed to represent a conservative, rural-based culture in a reaction to the growing challenge of modernism. The battle between the old and the new, the rural and urban was fully illustrated in the Scopes monkey trial in Tennessee in 1925, which pitted the old Populist and fundamentalist William Jennings Bryan against the labor lawyer Clarence Darrow. Although Darrow lost in the sense that his client John Scopes was convicted for teaching Darwinist theories of evolution, the fundamentalist belief in the strict interpretation of the Bible upheld by Bryan was exposed to ridicule and scorn.

Nowhere was the clash of values more evident than in the battle over prohibition. Prohibition too had its origins in the religious movements of the early nineteenth century. It gained support in the moral crusades of the 1880s and 1890s, and was often seen by reformers as a means of tackling poverty, industrial accidents, and the breakup of families. For many of its supporters, saloons were associated with urban immigrant ghettos and political corruption. Nineteen states had already passed prohibition laws prior to 1914. During World War I prohibition was seen as a means of conserving grain; it was also aimed at brewers, many of whom were of German descent. Enacted first as a war measure, prohibition became fully established with the ratification of the Eighteenth Amendment in 1919 and its enforcement from January 1920 on.

Although the consumption of alcohol fell considerably during the 1920s, prohibition was resisted from the outset and the issue divided the Democratic Party between "wets" and "dries" for much of the 1920s. Many reformers like Jane Addams supported the conservative Republicans because of their backing for prohibition. However, it was clear that other Americans did not believe that the law applied to them, and the continued demand for alcoholic beverages led to the rise of an illegal industry with "speakeasies" supplied by "bootleggers" and gangsters led by individuals like Al Capone. The rise of gangsterism and the impossibility of enforcing the law led eventually to the repeal of the amendment in 1933.

Prohibition, religious fundamentalism, racism, anti-immigrant sentiment, and political conservatism reflected the narrow-minded parochialism of the small-town America depicted in the works of novelist Sinclair Lewis, sociologists Robert and Mary Lynd, and social critic H. L. Mencken. These movements also represented a reaction to the rapid social and cultural change that transformed the United States and threatened established values. In 1920 for the first time the census recorded that the urban population exceeded the rural. The city and the factory with their polyglot immigrant inhabitants and industrial workforces were now dominant. While regional, ethnic, and racial differences continued, the growth of national businesses, brand names, chain stores, and mass communication through movies and the radio helped to create a modern and more homogenous national culture. At the heart of this culture were mass consumption, entertainment, and leisure. Movie stars like Charlie Chaplin, Lillian Gish, Douglas Fairbanks Jr., Mary Pickford, and Rudolph Valentino all became national icons. They were also stars who set fashions and created desires. The actresses Clara Bow and Louise Brooks, for example, symbolized the liberated "flapper" both in clothing and in sex appeal. Mass circulation magazines ranging from *True Stories* to the *Saturday Evening Post* advertised cosmetics, soap powders, and electrical appliances. The growth of radio too sold goods through advertising and helped to make national heroes of sportsmen like boxer Jack Dempsey and baseball legend "Babe" Ruth and turned sport into a mass industry. The media also helped to lionize Charles Lindbergh, the lone flyer who crossed the Atlantic in 1927 and demonstrated that the individual could still triumph in the modern age.

It was not just rural traditionalists, however, who resisted or reacted against the social and economic changes of the "new era." On the other side a critical literary and artistic movement, first evident in the prewar Greenwich Village group of writers and artists, developed more fully after World War I in what became known as "modernism." Many were either disillusioned as a consequence of the war itself or alienated by postwar materialism and political complacency. Some like Lewis, Mencken, and Edith Wharton stayed in the United States to produce biting satire or critical observations of their modern society. Others, like Ernest Hemingway, John Dos Passos, F. Scott Fitzgerald, and T. S. Eliot, became temporary or permanent exiles, a "Lost Generation" that adopted the new style and tones of the modernist movement and reinvigorated American arts in the process. Many artists echoed these trends applying modernist approaches to depictions of American industrial and urban landscapes. The identification of such writers and artists with cultural movements elsewhere was exceptional. Most of American popular culture turned its back on Europe, looked steadfastly inward, and reflected a mood often misleadingly described as "isolationist."

FOREIGN AFFAIRS

In foreign affairs, the Republican period was remarkable for the attempts to maintain a world role while at the same time not being enmeshed in international agreements or organizations like the League of Nations. This struggle between internationalism on the one hand and isolationism on the other was already evident at the end of the nineteenth century but increased as a consequence of World War I. For most of the nineteenth century the United States could adhere to the principles enunciated by George Washington and Thomas Jefferson, and further expressed in the Monroe Doctrine—a desire to avoid "entangling alliances" and the maintenance of the independence of the nations of the New World. However, the growth of the United States as an economic power trading in, and affected by, world markets began to challenge those principles. The application of "dollar diplomacy" by the administrations of William McKinley and Theodore Roosevelt saw an increase in United States investments in the Pacific and in the Caribbean. The Spanish-American War in 1898, ostensibly against Spanish imperialism and in defense of the Monroe Doctrine, reflected United States' interests in Cuba and elsewhere. The acquisition of the Philippines and Hawaii following the war marked the United States' entry onto the world stage as an imperial power. The construction of the Panama Canal under American aegis between 1904 and 1914 and the control of the Canal Zone confirmed the United States' authority in Central America and the Caribbean.

When the Democrats gained control of the White House under Woodrow Wilson it was widely assumed that foreign relations would change direction. Many Democrats, like the new secretary of state, William Jennings Bryan, had opposed imperialist ventures overseas and the threatening use of the "big stick" in foreign affairs advocated by Roosevelt. Moves were made toward granting independence to the Philippines, reparations were agreed with Colombia for the loss of Panama (although the treaty was not approved by the Senate until 1921), and thirty conciliation agreements were signed with foreign powers to bring any possible disputes before an international commission. However, the new administration felt obliged to keep United States' troops in Nicaragua to prevent civil war and to protect U.S. financial investments. Troops were also sent to Haiti and Dominica to avert revolutions also perceived as threatening American interests.

Revolution had already occurred in Mexico when Wilson became president. Offers to mediate between the new government of Victoriano Huerta and his opponent, Venustiano Carranza, were rejected by the Mexicans as interference. In 1914 an incident that began with the arrest of American seamen in Tampico became a full diplomatic incident when Admiral Henry Mayo rejected the Mexican apology and demanded a salute to the American flag. Mexico's failure to respond satisfactorily was met with the seizure of Vera Cruz. The threat of war was averted by mediation under the leadership of envoys from Argentina, Brazil, and Chile and by the abdication of Huerta in favor of Carranza in July 1914.

Relations between the United States and Mexico continued to be strained and became more inflamed as a result of the actions of the Mexican military commander, Francisco "Pancho" Villa. Determined to provoke a war, Villa killed sixteen American passengers on a train near Santa Ysabel in January 1916 and then attacked Columbus, New Mexico, killing a further nineteen people on 9 March 1916. A punitive expedition led by General John Pershing pursued Villa deep into Mexico. Clashes with Mexican troops led to casualties on both sides, and the two nations once again came close to war. However, the likelihood of the United States becoming involved in war in Europe forced Wilson to back down. The troops were withdrawn in January 1917 and the Carranza regime was officially recognized in March.

WORLD WAR I

The outbreak of war in Europe in 1914 confirmed to many Americans the validity of the policy of isolation. There was considerable support for President Wilson's call for impartiality in thought and deed. However, the conflict was a total war that involved entire populations and their economies. Supplies were vital, and maritime trade itself was threatened. The Wilson Administration's insistence on the right of United States' citizens to trade with whomever they wished and to travel freely on the high seas soon came into conflict with the reality of modern warfare. The imposition of a tight naval blockade on European ports by the British provoked several protests from the Wilson government but little more. These conflicts could be left to the courts to adjudicate. This was not the case when the German government responded to the blockade by using submarines (the U-boat) to attack merchant and passenger vessels from February 1915 on. The sinking of the passenger ship *Lusitania* with the loss of 128 American lives on 7 May led the Wilson administration to warn that further such attacks would be seen as deliberately unfriendly. William Jennings Bryan considered this response so strong that he resigned as secretary of state. A further protest following the sinking of the *Arabic* in August produced a promise that unrestricted attacks on unarmed passenger vessels would cease. However, in February 1916 the German government announced that armed merchant vessels would be sunk without warning. The Wilson administration refused to warn American citizens against traveling on armed ships and blocked the Gore-McLemore Resolution introduced in Congress to implement such warnings. When a German submarine torpedoed an unarmed ship, the *Sussex*, on 24 March 1916, President Wilson threatened to sever relations with Germany unless the unrestricted submarine campaign ceased. Although the German government acceded, it indicated that it might resume the campaign if the British naval blockade continued.

The growing realization that the war in Europe would not come to a speedy conclusion, combined with the threat it posed to the security of the United States, encouraged a "preparedness campaign" that brought the first steps toward war planning in America. It also led Wilson to initiate proposals to mediate a peace settlement. The first discussions began when Wilson's secretary, Colonel Edward House, went to Europe first in 1915, and again the following year. In January 1917 Wilson went before the Senate and outlined his proposals for a "peace without victory." However, as neither side was willing to give up whatever advantage they held at any given moment, or while a military victory seemed possible, the discussions came to nothing.

On 31 January 1917 the German government announced its intention to resume unrestricted submarine warfare. President Wilson broke off diplomatic relations on 3 February, and on 26 February asked Congress for the power to arm American merchant ships. Opinion in the United States began to mobilize behind such measures, particularly following the publication of the Zimmerman telegram, in which the German foreign secretary proposed an alliance to the Mexican government. Mexico was promised the possibility of regaining New Mexico and Arizona in the event of a victory in a war against the United States. The change of regime in Russia with the overthrow of the Tsar also made the Allied cause seem more attractive as a defense of democracy. However, it was the sinking of several United States ships that forced Wilson to go before Congress on 2 April 1917 to ask for a declaration of war to "make the world safe for democracy." The declaration was approved on 6 April.

About 2 million soldiers from the United States served in France in the American Expeditionary Force (AEF) led by General John J. Pershing between 1917 and 1918. Their arrival could not have been more timely as the submarine campaign threatened Allied supplies, and the withdrawal of the Russians from the war following a second, Bolshevik, revolution in November 1917 freed German troops for the western front. American troops were first thrown into action as part of a unified Allied command in response to the German offensive along the Somme in March 1918. The intervention of additional United States' divisions in the Aisne-Marne offensive in May 1918 led to the victories at Chateau Thierry and Belleau Wood. Over a quarter of a million American soldiers then took part in the Allied counteroffensive along the Marne that opened in July 1918. Another five hundred thousand men of the AEF launched an attack on St. Mihiel on the River Meuse in September, and 1.2 million Americans took part in the Meuse-Argonne offensive that began later that month and concluded with the signing of the armistice that brought the war to an end on 11 November 1918. More than sixty thousand soldiers from the United States died in combat during World War I. Another sixty thousand died of disease, many of them victims of the worldwide influenza pandemic that took 20 million lives across the world in 1918.

VERSAILLES AND AFTER

In January 1918 President Wilson had outlined his war aims in his "Fourteen Points" speech to Congress. His speech stressed self-determination and independence for the people of the former Austro-Hungarian and Ottoman empires, free trade, arms reductions, open treaties openly arrived at, and a world organization to ensure future peace. In December 1918 the president led the American delegation to take part in the peace negotiations in Versailles, near Paris. Only one Republican was included in the group, despite the Republican victories in the congressional elections that gave them control of both houses of Congress. The peace treaty eventually drawn up did not accord with the Fourteen Points. Although independence was granted to Poland, Estonia, Latvia, Lithuania, Czechoslovakia, Hungary, and Yugoslavia, Germany was forced to accept a war guilt clause, lost all of its colonies and some of its lands in Europe, and was required to pay huge reparations. The now-communist Russia was excluded from the peace negotiations, and Allied (including American) troops were sent to Siberia ostensibly to protect war material, but in reality to support the Bolsheviks' opponents. The newly created eastern European countries ringed Russia with a "cordon sanitaire," and the United States denied the Soviet Union recognition until 1933.

Included in the peace settlement was a covenant to establish a League of Nations on which Woodrow Wilson pinned his hopes for future peace. However, Republicans in Congress led by senator Henry Cabot Lodge indicated that they would not accept the league as proposed. Wilson, who refused to accept any amendments, suffered a stroke campaigning in defense of the treaty in September 1919. On 19 November 1919 Democrats, instructed by Wilson to reject any reservations to the treaty, voted with the Republican "Irreconcilables" to reject the Versailles treaty and League of Nations.

FOREIGN RELATIONS DURING THE 1920S

The newly elected Republican president, Warren G. Harding, undoubtedly captured the mood of many of his fellow citizens when he evoked the tradition of isolation in his inaugural address in 1921 and declared, "We do not mean to be entangled." However, certain facts could not be ignored. After World War I the United States was a world power in terms of its naval strength and its merchant marine; it was also the world's greatest financial and economic power. If in appearance the United States may have seemed isolationist, in reality the thrust of its foreign policy in the 1920s was the preservation of peace on its own terms without becoming inextricably involved in the conflicts of other nations.

From 1922 on the United States sent observers to the League of Nations and participated in many of the League's conferences. The Republican administrations also sought to achieve membership for the United States in the Permanent Court of International Justice established under the Covenant of the League of Nations, but separate from it. However, reservations attached to America's proposed membership by isolationists in Congress in 1926 led to the rejection of the United States by the other member countries.

The Republican administrations consistently attempted to ensure peace through arms limitations and played a leading part in the Washington Naval Conference (1921–1922) that resulted in a treaty limiting the size of the navies of the United States, Britain, Japan, France, and Italy. Treaties were also agreed with regard to relations in the Pacific. A further agreement at the London Naval Conference in 1930 restricted the number of smaller ships the respective navies would have. Even more remarkable was the Kellogg-Briand Pact outlawing war as an instrument of policy. Initiated by the French foreign minister Aristide Briand and signed by secretary of state Frank B. Kellogg in 1928, the agreement was eventually joined by sixty-two nations. However, lacking in any power of enforcement, the pact proved meaningless in the face of aggression from nonparticipants.

The issue that most undermined the isolation of the United States during the 1920s was that of war debts and war reparations. During and immediately after the war the United States had lent almost $10 billion to Allied governments. Requests for these debts to be canceled or reduced were rebuffed although tariffs in the United States made it impossible to repay the loans in goods and services. The Allies in turn demanded payment in full of the huge reparations ($33 billion) imposed on Germany. This situation threatened the economic stability of nations already weakened by the war and necessitated further renegotiation. In 1924 a committee headed by Charles G. Dawes and Owen D. Young produced the Dawes Plan, which scaled down the amount owed in reparations and provided for loans from the United States to Germany. A further committee led by Young reduced the reparations payments even further in 1929. Although these efforts eased the immediate financial crisis, they established a dangerous flow of capital that, if broken, could produce an economic collapse. This is precisely what happened following the Wall Street Crash in 1929.

The 1920s also witnessed an improvement in relations with Latin American nations. Charles Evans Hughes, the new secretary of state in 1921, was opposed to Woodrow Wilson's interventionist policies, and initiated the process by which United States' troops were withdrawn from the Dominican Republic in 1924 and from Nicaragua in 1925. Marines returned to Nicaragua in 1927 to assist in the suppression of a revolt and were only gradually withdrawn between 1931 and 1933. Relations with Mexico were more problematic. A slight improvement occurred after Carranza had been replaced by Alvaro Obregon, but when the more radical Plutarcho Calles assumed power in 1924, relations worsened once more. They continued to be difficult until president Calvin Coolidge sent Dwight Morrow as ambassador to Mexico City in 1927. Morrow was able to establish a good working relationship with the Mexican government and set up more friendly links between the two countries. Although the U.S. delegation led by Hughes to the Pan-American Conference in 1932 refused to give an unequivocal promise not to intervene in the affairs of neighboring nations, the Clark Memorandum drawn up in 1928 by the State Department following president-elect Herbert Hoover's visit to Latin America acknowledged that this was the case. Thus the Republican administrations helped to undo some of the policies of their predecessors and lay the groundwork for the "Good Neighbor" policy of the succeeding administration.

A

ABBOTT, EDITH (1876–1957). Edith Abbott studied at the University of Nebraska and completed a PhD in political economics at Chicago in 1905. Abbott then conducted research on **women** in industry for the Carnegie Institution before undertaking a postgraduate program at the London School of Economics. From 1907 to 1908 she taught at Wellesley College and then joined her sister **Grace Abbott** at the **Hull House settlement** in Chicago, where they lived for the next twelve years. Edith Abbott began to assist **Sophonisba Breckinridge** at the Chicago School of Civics and Philanthropy in a program to professionalize **social work**. Her study of *Women in Industry* was published in 1910 and, with Breckinridge, Abbott coauthored *The Delinquent Child and the Home* (1912) and *Truancy and Non-Attendance in the Chicago Schools* (1917).

Abbott became dean of the new School of Social Service Administration at the University of Chicago in 1924. In 1927 she and Breckinridge established the *Social Service Review*, a professional journal for social workers. At the same time Abbott was conducting studies of the employment and behavior of immigrants to the United States, and in 1929 president **Herbert Hoover** appointed her to the Wickersham Commission on Law Observance and Enforcement. Abbott's research, published as the *Report on Crime and Criminal Justice in Relation to the Foreign Born* in 1931, demonstrated that immigrants committed proportionately less crime than the rest of the population.

Abbott's role in social work education was recognized in her election to president of the National Conference of Social Work in 1936. In 1951 she was awarded the National Conference of Social Work's Survey Award for her services.

ABBOTT, GRACE (1878–1939). Like her sister **Edith Abbott**, Grace Abbott began her career as a high school teacher. She studied law at the University of Nebraska before enrolling at the University of Chicago in 1907 and gained a master of philosophy in 1909. Abbott also lived in the **Hull House settlement**, where she became involved in social reform activities. She was active in the Juvenile Protection Association, the Immigrants' Protective League, and the Women's Trade Union League, and in 1915 she chaired a special committee on Penal and Correctional Institutions. In 1917 Abbott published *The Immigrant and the Community*.

In 1917 Abbott joined the **Children's Bureau** in Washington, D.C. She went briefly to Chicago to head the state commission on immigration but returned to Washington, D.C., in 1921 to replace **Julia Lathrop** as head of the Children's Bureau. Abbott led the administration of the **Sheppard-Towner Act**, extending federal aid in maternity and infant child-care services. She was president of the National Conference of Social Work from 1923 to 1924.

Abbot resigned from the Children's Bureau in 1934 to take up a teaching position at the University of Chicago. She also worked on the President's Council on Economic Security, 1934–35, and helped to draft the Social Security Act. Her study of *The Child and the State* was published in 1938.

See also SOCIAL WORK.

ABBOTT, ROBERT SENGSTACKE (1868–1940). Born to former slaves in Georgia, the **newspaper** founder Robert S. Abbott graduated from Hampton Institute, Virginia, in 1896 and then gained a law degree from Kent College of Law, Chicago, in 1896. After failing on several occasions to establish his own legal practice, Abbott set up his own newspaper, the *Chicago Defender*, in 1905. By 1918 it had a circulation of 125,000 and eventually at its height, reached 500,000 in the 1940s. Under his leadership the *Defender* vigorously opposed discrimination and called for destruction of American race prejudice, and the paper had a distribution that went far beyond Chicago making it effectively a black national paper. During **World War I** the *Defender* urged **African Americans** to leave the South and the newspaper was instrumental in encouraging the **Great Migration** to northern centers both through its headlines and via published letters from migrants. In 1919 Abbott sat on the Commission that investigated the **Chicago race riot**. Honored by many institutions and respected as a leading black spokesman, Abbott died in 1940 of Bright's disease.

ABC MEDIATION, 1914. Deteriorating relations between the United States and **Mexico** following the seizure of power by Victoriano Huerta in 1913 threatened to bring the two nations to war. In an attempt to avert conflict the "ABC" powers, Argentina, Brazil, and Chile, offered to mediate. Meetings took place between 18 May and 2 July 1914 but accomplished little. The overthrow of Huerta by Venustiano Carranza in July brought some brief improvement in relations, but war seemed possible again when the United States sent a **punitive expedition** into Mexico in response to the attacks of **Pancho Villa** in 1916.

***ABRAMS V. UNITED STATES* (1919).** In 1919 the **Supreme Court** upheld the conviction of Jacob Abrams under the **Espionage** and **Sedition** legislation by a verdict of seven to two, Justices **Oliver Wendell Holmes** and **Louis Brandeis** dissenting. Abrams, an anarchist who had recently entered the United States, had distributed pamphlets in the tenement area of New York City denouncing American military intervention in Russia.

ADAMSON ACT, 1916. Brought about by a threatened strike of railroad unions, the Adamson Act introduced the eight-hour day, with time and a half for overtime, for workers on interstate railways as of 1 January 1917. The law also established a commission to study the problems of railroad labor.

See also TRADE UNIONS.

ADDAMS, JANE (1860–1935). Social reformer, suffragist, and pacifist, Jane Addams was a leading figure in the prewar **progressive** reform movement. Educated at Rockford Female Seminary, Addams was one of the first generation of college-educated **women**. Unable to continue her medical studies at Philadelphia Medical College, Addams was inspired by a visit to Toynbee Hall, a **settlement house** in London, England. In 1889, with **Ellen Starr** she founded **Hull House** in Chicago, which, as one of the first settlement houses in the United States, became an inspiration for many other reformers. Addams lived there for the rest of her life.

Addams was active in the **women's suffrage** movement, president of the National Conference of Charities and Corrections (later the National Conference of **Social Work**), a founder of the **National Association for the Advancement of Colored People**, the **National Consumers' League**, and in the formation of the **National Progressive Party** in 1912. She was also one of the founders of the **Woman's Peace Party** and became chairperson in 1915. Addams was elected president of the International Congress of Women in The Hague the same year and then president of the Women's International League for Peace and Freedom. She maintained her pacifist stance throughout the war and suffered a decline in popularity as a result. However, her activities in the cause of peace were recognized in 1931, when she became the first American woman to be awarded the Nobel Peace Prize. Addams wrote two accounts of her work, *Twenty Years at Hull House* (1910) and *The Second Twenty Years at Hull House* (1930).

ADKINS V. CHILDREN'S HOSPITAL, **1923.** In 1923 the **Supreme Court** dismissed the defense of minimum wage legislation for **women** brought by **Felix Frankfurter** in the case of *Adkins v. Children's Hospital* when they upheld the concept of "liberty of contract" to strike down a District of Columbia minimum wage law for women.

ADVISORY COMMISSION TO THE COUNCIL OF NATIONAL DEFENSE. The Advisory Commission was a committee of seven experts appointed in 1916 to assist the **Council of National Defense** in mobilizing the nation for war as part of the "Preparedness" program. The members were the chairman, Daniel Willard, president of the Baltimore & Ohio Railroad; **Howard Coffin**, vice president of the Hudson Motor Co.; **Hollis Godfrey**, head of the Drexel Institute; Dr. Franklin Martin, director of the College of Surgeons; **Julius Rosenwald**, president of Sears, Roebuck; **Bernard Baruch**; and **Samuel Gompers**. The use of experts drawn from business and industry on a voluntary basis was a model to be followed during the war, and the Advisory Commission created a plethora of similar subcommittees dealing with all aspects of war production.

AFRICAN AMERICANS. In many respects the period 1913–1933 was one of considerable continuity for the African American population, with racial prejudice, discrimination, poverty, and violence being the constant features. Although only 12 percent of the whole population, the majority of African Americans (90 percent) still lived in rural areas in the former slave states of the South in 1900. In 1930 the proportion was still almost 80 percent despite the "**Great Migration**" to the North that began during **World War I** and continued in the 1920s. The late nineteenth and early twentieth centuries also witnessed the full implementation of the system of racial segregation in the South known as "Jim Crow." The process of excluding African Americans from the political system through poll taxes, grandfather clauses, literacy tests, and open intimidation occurred at the same time. Race violence increased and more than 1,000 black people were lynched between 1900 and 1914. Race riots in which white mobs attacked black communities took place in Atlanta, Georgia, in 1906, and in Springfield, Illinois, in 1908. This violence continued through the war, with thirty-eight lynchings in 1917, sixty-four in 1918, and eighty-three in 1919. There were major riots in **East St. Louis** (1917) and in **Chicago** and other towns and cities during the "**Red Summer**" of 1919. Such outbreaks continued with the riot in **Tulsa**, Oklahoma, in 1921 and in **Rosewood**, Florida, in 1923. Denied a political voice, the African Americans were largely ignored at the federal level by all administrations, whether **Republican** or **Democratic**.

However, there were some significant underlying changes. The "accommodationist" leadership of the black educator Booker T. Washington (who died in 1915), was increasingly challenged by leaders such as **W. E. B. Du Bois**. Du Bois and others demanded full equality, and with a few white **progressives** appalled by the spread of race violence to the North, formed the **National Association for the Advancement of Colored People** (NAACP) in 1910 to campaign against discrimination. The organization grew in the aftermath of World War I, and under the leadership of **James Weldon Johnson** and **Walter White**, led the campaign against lynching and race prejudice generally.

During World War I the issue of race was raised with the implementation of **Selective Service**. Many white southerners opposed the inclusion of African Americans in the military, while blacks demanded the right to fight for their country. African Americans were drafted into the military, but the army and navy were both segregated and blacks were excluded from the marine corps and the army air force. Over 400,000 African Americans served in the army, but only 42,000 in combat roles. On the domestic front the need for industrial labor encouraged the large-scale migration of African Americans to the northern manufacturing centers. While they benefited from new job opportunities, the black workers faced discrimination from **trade unions** and conflicts over housing and transportation.

The disillusionment felt by returning black servicemen and black workers encouraged a mood of militance associated with new leaders such as **Marcus Garvey** and **A. Philip Randolph**. The willingness to fight back was expressed by what **Alain Locke** described as the "**New Negro**" while the sense of black community and pride found a cultural voice in the **Harlem Renaissance** during the 1920s. **African American music** particularly became a major influence on white musical forms and gave its name to the period in the "**jazz age**." The new black northern populations also found a political voice and began to have an influence that came to fruition in the Democratic Party and resulted in some recognition in the **New Deal**. **Eleanor Roosevelt** also conspicuously defended the rights of black Americans, and reactions to the case of the **Scottsboro boys** revealed that many white Americans were now much more sympathetic toward African Americans. Despite this, during the **Great Depression** African Americans were still "last hired, first fired," and there was once more a rise in race violence.

See also ABBOTT, ROBERT SENGSTACKE (1868–1940); ARMSTRONG, LOUIS (1901–1971); BECHET, SIDNEY JOSEPH (1897–1959); FAUSET, JESSIE REDMON (1882–1961); HARLEM; HOUSTON MUTINY, 1917; HUGHES, (JAMES) LANGSTON (1902–1967); JAZZ; JEFFERSON, "BLIND" LEMON (1897–1929); LARSEN, NELLA (1891–1964); LOGAN, RAYFORD WHITTINGHAM (1897–1982); MCKAY, CLAUDE (1890–1948); MILLS, FLORENCE (1896–1927); MIS-

SISSIPPI FLOODS, 1927; MORTON, "JELLY ROLL" (FERDINAND JOSEPH); MOTLEY, ARCHIBALD, JR. (1891–1981); MOTON, ROBERT RUSSA (1867–1940); OWEN, CHANDLER (1889–1967); ROBESON, PAUL LEROY BUSTILL (1898–1976); SCOTT, EMMETT JAY (1873–1957); SISSLE, NOBLE (1889–1975); SMITH, BESSIE (1894–1937); TOOMER, (NATHAN) JEAN (1894–1967); TROTTER, WILLIAM MONROE (1872–1934); WATERS, ETHEL (1896–1977).

AGRICULTURE. *See* FARMING.

AGRICULTURAL CREDITS ACT, 1923. A law passed to provide additional credit facilities to enable farmers to purchase farm equipment and livestock through Federal Intermediate Credit Banks in each of the 12 districts created by the **Federal Farm Loan Act** of 1916. These **banks** could extend loans to farmers for periods of from six months to three years and were administered by the boards of directors of the Federal Land Banks.

AGRICULTURAL MARKETING ACT, 1929. Also known as the Cooperative Marketing Act, the Agricultural Marketing Act passed in June 1929 was intended to assist farmers in marketing their produce. It established a **Federal Farm Board** of eight members appointed by the president, plus the secretary of agriculture. The Board was provided with $500 million to lend to cooperative associations and stabilization corporations that could buy, sell, or store surpluses of the specific commodity with which each corporation dealt. The Board attempted to raise the prices of cotton and wheat by making heavy purchases but was unable to counteract the downward trend in world prices.

AIR COMMERCE ACT, 1926. The gradual development of air transportation in the 1920s led to the passage of the Air Commerce Act to provide for federal safety regulation and control. The Aeronautics Branch of the Department of Commerce was empowered to test and license pilots, guarantee the airworthiness of aircraft, supervise the provision of airports, and investigate air accidents.
    See also AVIATION.

ALEXANDER, WILL WINTON (1884–1956). The southern liberal Will Alexander was educated at Scarritt-Morrisville College, Missouri, and Vanderbilt where he received his BD in 1912. Alexander was ordained as a Methodist minister in 1911 and held a number of pastorates in Tennessee between 1911 and 1917. In 1919 Alexander established the Commission on Interracial Cooperation in Atlanta. The commission, which Alexander directed for 25 years, aimed to improve race relations in the South through programs of education and public information. Details of the activities of the **Ku Klux Klan** collected by the commission were used in press exposés in the 1920s.

Alexander also worked with the Social Science Research Council's Advisory Commission on Race Studies (1927–1928) and on the Commission on Minority Groups in Economic Recovery (1934–1935). Alexander was influential in the **New Deal** and was appointed assistant administrator in the Department of Agriculture's Resettlement Administration in 1935. He was actively involved in the creation of the Farm Security Administration (FSA) in 1937 and was responsible for many of its programs benefiting poor southern farmers. He resigned from FSA in 1940 to accept the chair of the **Rosenwald** Fund where he implemented a number of programs to help **African Americans** in the South follow an education.

See also CIVIL RIGHTS.

ALIEN PROPERTY CUSTODIAN. The office of Alien Property Custodian was established under the terms of the **Trading with the Enemy Act** in 1917. The custodian held enemy property in the United States in order to prevent its use during the war and to sell it once the war was over. Many German patents and other properties were seized and disposed of. Claims were subsequently settled between the United States and Germany and Austria under the Settlement of War Claims Act, 1928.

ALLEN, FREDERICK LEWIS (1890–1954). Allen was a journalist and popular historian whose best-selling portrait of the 1920s *Only Yesterday* (1931) did much to shape views of the decade. After working at the magazines *Atlantic Monthly* and *Century*, Allen became press bureau director for the Boston Writers' Council for Patriotic Service in 1917. In 1918 he became press bureau director of the **Council of National Defense** in Washington, D.C. After the war Allen managed the publicity for Harvard University before becoming articles editor at *Harper's Magazine* in 1925. He later became assistant editor (1931), and then editor in chief (1941). *Only Yesterday* was a retrospective and journalistic view of the "roaring twenties" which tended to emphasize the frivolity of the decade. His subsequent books included *The Lords of Creation* (1935), *Since Yesterday* (1940), *I Remember Distinctly* (1947), *The Great Pierpont Morgan* (1949), and *The Big Change* (1952).

ALLIED POWERS. The term applied to the Allied and Associated powers that fought and defeated the **Central Powers** during the **World War I**. The five leading nations were the United States, Great Britain, France, Italy, and Japan. The other allied and associated states were Belgium, Bolivia, Brazil,

China, Cuba, Czechoslovakia, Ecuador, Greece, Guatemala, the Hejaz, Honduras, Liberia, Nicaragua, Panama, Peru, Poland, Portugal, Romania, Siam, Uruguay, and Yugoslavia.

AMERICAN AMBULANCE FIELD SERVICE (AAFS). With the outbreak of **World War I** in Europe a number of Americans volunteered to serve with the **Allied powers**, particularly the French. One of the most significant groups was the American Ambulance Field Service established by Abram Piatt Andrew in 1915. Many of the more than 2,000 Americans who served in the AAFS in France, Italy, Greece, and Serbia were college graduates, including 325 from Harvard and 187 from Yale. Among these were **Malcolm Cowley**, **e. e. cummings**, **John Dos Passos**, and **Ernest Hemingway**. Some members of the AAFS joined the **American Expeditionary Force** (AEF) after 1917. After the war, the AAFS became the American Field Service and established graduate exchange programs between France and the United States. Eventually the organization evolved into an international youth exchange program.

AMERICAN CIVIL LIBERTIES UNION (ACLU). The American Civil Liberties Union was founded in 1920 by **Roger Baldwin** and other social reformers including **Jane Addams**, **Crystal Eastman**, **Clarence Darrow**, **John Dewey**, **Johannes Muste**, and **Elizabeth Gurley Flynn**. The ACLU developed out of the activities of the **American Union Against Militarism** during **World War I**, and was established to preserve civil liberties guaranteed under the Bill of Rights, namely, freedom of speech, press, and religion. During the 1920s the ACLU supported **Sacco** and **Vanzetti** and **John Scopes**, and was involved in the case of the **Scottsboro boys** in the 1930s.

AMERICAN EXPEDITIONARY FORCE (AEF). The American Expeditionary Force was the name given to the U.S. military contingents commanded by General **John J. Pershing** that joined the **Allied** armies during **World War I**. When war was declared the number of men in the U.S. Army was 200,000, one-third of whom were National Guardsmen called into federal service along the Mexican border. By the end of the war the total force numbered 4.5 million, half of whom actually were overseas. A small number of units were sent in 1917, but the bulk of the U.S. Army arrived in 1918. In total 42 divisions served in France. Following a German spring offensive Pershing placed the entire force at the disposal of the Allied High command, and the American First Army was not created until 24 June 1918. The soldiers in the AEF were often referred to as "**doughboys**."

AMERICAN FARM BUREAU FEDERATION (AFBF). Established in 1919, the American Farm Bureau Federation represented 36 states and developed from the farm extension programs established during **World War I** to disseminate more widely scientific and technical advances in agriculture. The AFBF established lobbies at state and federal level to promote agricultural interests.

See also FARM BLOC; FARMER-LABOR PARTY; FARMING.

AMERICAN FEDERATION OF LABOR (AFL). A federation of **trade unions** formed in 1886 by **Samuel Gompers** and Adolph Strasser. The AFL emerged from the Federation of Trades and Labor Unions formed in 1881, and was an organization of autonomous craft-based unions. Conservative and nonpolitical in outlook, the AFL largely excluded unskilled, immigrant, and black workers. Nonetheless by 1910 it was established as the leading union organization and had a membership of over 2 million. Its support for the administration of **Woodrow Wilson** during the war brought recognition in terms of the inclusion of Gompers in the **Advisory Commission to the Council of National Defense** and in the recognition of unions by the **War Labor Board**. By the end of the war AFL membership had doubled, but in a changing economic climate and without government support, the organization was unable to consolidate upon the wartime advances in the face of employer resistance. Following defeats in the **Steel Strike** of 1919 and other industrial areas, union membership declined once more and by 1924 had fallen to 2.9 million. The AFL maintained its conservative outlook with regard to unskilled and immigrant workers, and this approach continued when **William Green** succeeded Gompers in 1924.

AMERICAN INDIAN CITIZENSHIP ACT, 1924. The **Supreme Court** in 1894 specifically excluded **Native Americans** from the 14th Amendment ruling that "all persons born or naturalized in the United States" are citizens. However, members of the Five Civilized Tribes of Oklahoma were granted citizenship in 1901, and the Burke Act of 1906 granted citizenship to Indians who left their tribes. The Indian Citizenship Act clarified the position when it conferred citizenship on all 350,000 Indians. The act did not, however, end federal control of Indian lands or tribal government.

AMERICAN LEGION. The American Legion was an organization of veterans established by 20 officers from the **American Expeditionary Force** (AEF) in Paris on 15 February 1919 to preserve the memory of war service and promote the welfare of former servicemen. Membership was open to all ex-servicemen on an open footing without any reference to rank. At its height in the interwar years it had 1 million members. Veterans of other wars were subsequently admitted to membership.

AMERICAN PLAN. The "American Plan" was a program launched in 1919 by the National Association of Manufacturers to combat the wartime gains of labor organizations and restore the "open shop." The determination of employers to resist workers' demands contributed to an outbreak of strikes in 1919 and the decline of **trade unions** in the 1920s. More moderate approaches were evident in the programs of "**welfare capitalism**" adopted by some of the larger businesses in the interwar years.

AMERICAN PROTECTIVE LEAGUE (APL). The American Protective League was formed during **World War I** by a Chicago advertising executive, A.M. Briggs, to assist the Justice Department with investigations of disloyal activity, breaking up antiwar meetings, and searching for draft evaders. By 1918 the APL boasted 250,000 operatives in over 600 towns and cities and was involved in 3 million investigations. Although there was some concern about their activities, not all of which were legal, Attorney General **Thomas Gregory** described them as "a most important auxiliary and reserve force of the Bureau of Investigation."

AMERICAN SCENE. The "American Scene" was the name given to the artistic movement of the 1920s and especially the 1930s that saw a concentration on American themes and subjects rather than European modernist images. It included the regionalist painters, **Thomas Hart Benton**, **John Steuart Curry**, and **Grant Wood**, as well as social realists, such as **Edward Hopper**.
　　See also ART; BURCHFIELD, CHARLES EPHRAIM (1893–1967).

AMERICAN UNION AGAINST MILITARISM (AUAM). The American Union Against Militarism was founded in 1916 by **Roger Baldwin**, **Oswald Garrison Villard**, and **Lillian Wald** to lobby against American entry into the **World War I**. In April 1917 the AUAM became the National Civil Liberties Bureau, later the **American Civil Liberties Union**, which campaigned for the protection of civil liberties and the rights of conscientious objectors.

ANDERSON, SHERWOOD (1876–1941). Sherwood Anderson literally rose from rags to riches. Having started work as a laborer without completing high school, he moved from advertising to the mail-order business, and by 1907 was president of his own manufacturing company in Elyria, Ohio. In

1912 he suffered a breakdown, and the following year he left his job and family and established himself among the intellectuals of Chicago. His first novel, *Windy McPherson's Son*, appeared in 1916. Anderson achieved his fame as a writer with the publication in 1919 of a collection of naturalistic stories depicting small-town life entitled *Winesburg, Ohio*. He continued to illustrate the frustrations of modern life in *Poor White* (1920), *Many Marriages* (1923), and *Dark Laughter* (1925). His later writing, much of it autobiographical such as *A Story Teller's Tale* (1924) and *Tar: A Midwestern Childhood* (1926), was less successful, but **H. L. Mencken** nonetheless described him as "America's most distinctive novelist" in 1926. After turning to producing newspapers in 1927, Anderson continued writing through the 1930s and published *Perhaps Women* (1931) and *Beyond Desire* (1932). He died of peritonitis while traveling in the Panama Canal Zone.

See also LITERATURE AND THEATER.

ARABIC. The *Arabic* was a British liner sunk in a German submarine attack with the loss of two American lives on 19 August 1915 while en route to New York. Following American protests the German government pledged to halt attacks on liners without warning and allow for the safety of passengers. The *Arabic* pledge averted American entry into **World War I** until the resumption of unrestricted submarine warfare in 1917.

See also LUSITANIA, SUSSEX.

ARBUCKLE, ROSCOE "FATTY" (1887–1933). Roscoe Arbuckle ("Fatty" because he weighed over 260 pounds) began his career at the turn of the century as a singer of illustrated songs on the vaudeville circuit. Arbuckle appeared with Walter Reed in a smash-hit play, *The Campus*, in Los Angeles in 1910 before touring Hawaii, Japan, China, and the Philippines. On returning to the United States in 1913 he began work at the Keystone Film Company and by 1914 had become the company's biggest star as a slapstick comedian. In 1916 he became Hollywood's highest earner when he joined Paramount Pictures with a contract worth more than $1 million a year. He formed his own production company, the Comique Film Company, and hired **Buster Keaton**. He and Keaton made fifteen films together. In 1921 Arbuckle became the center of scandal when a young actress, Virginia Rappe, suffered convulsions during a party he held in a San Francisco hotel. She died a few days later of acute peritonitis and a ruptured bladder. The police, who believed that Arbuckle had sexually assaulted her and that his weight had caused the injury, charged him with manslaughter.

Arbuckle stood trial amid a public outcry at the Hollywood excesses revealed in the Hearst press. He denied the charges, and evidence was produced to show that Rappe was seriously ill and had previously had several illegal abortions. The trial ended with a hung jury. A second trial in 1922 ended the same way, but in the third trial Arbuckle was acquitted. Shortly after the trial had ended **Will Hays** was appointed to clean up the image of the **movie** industry, and he immediately banned all of Arbuckle's films. The ban was lifted in 1923, but Arbuckle never really recovered. He directed several films and in the late 1920s ran a nightclub in Culver City, California. In 1932 he returned to act under his own name in several movies for Vitaphone, but died amid his comeback.

ARGONNE. A wooded area in eastern France between Toul and Mezieres where the 1st U.S. Army under General **John Pershing** went into action against German positions on 26 September 1918. The fighting continued through October. Although the American advances were initially rapid, they had difficulty establishing their supply systems and it was not until November that the Germans were eventually pushed back to Verdun. By the time the **Armistice** was declared United States and French troops had surrounded the German force near Verdun.
  See also WORLD WAR I, 1914–1918.

ARMED FORCES. Before **World War I** the U.S. military was very limited in its strength and largely confined to patrolling western states and the borders with **Mexico**. However, small numbers of American troops were involved in several interventions in Central American and the Caribbean in order to maintain stability and protect American business and financial interests at various times. These actions included: Cuba (1917–1933), **Dominican Republic** (1916–1924), **Haiti** (1915–1935), Nicaragua (1912–1925, 1926–1933), and Panama (1912, 1918–1920, 1925). A military force also took part in **punitive expedition** against Mexico in 1916–1917. The U.S. Army had a total strength of 98,000 in 1914, 45,000 of whom were overseas. Another 27,000 served in the national guard. The navy consisted of almost 150 ships of different sizes and included 19 modern "dreadnought" battleships; naval manpower numbered 69,000, with 15,000 in the U.S. Marine Corps. There was a rapid expansion in numbers following America's entry into World War I in 1917 and the introduction of **Selective Service**. By 1918 a total of 4.7 million men had been mobilized and over 2 million served in Europe. By 1918 the U.S. Navy had 200,000 seamen, and the marines numbered 72,000.

There was a rapid reduction in military numbers following **demobilization** at the end of the war. The size of the army fell from 1.17 million in 1919 to 343,000 in 1920, and by 1921 the manpower for the army was set at 150,000; total naval strength fell from 121,845 in 1920 to 96,890 by the end of the decade.

New aspects of warfare emerged during the war and were reflected in the creation of the tank corps, but more significantly of an air force. Initially air force operations were carried out under the Aeronautical Division of the Signal Corps of the U.S. Army (1907–1914), but in 1918 a separate U.S. Air Service was created. In 1926 this changed to the U.S. Air Corps and this then became the U.S. Air Forces in 1942. The number of air personnel reached about 195,000 in 1918, but by 1926 this had fallen to under 10,000.

Military service was restricted and segregated for **African Americans** before, during, and after the war. Prior to 1917 service in the army was limited to the two infantry and two cavalry regiments established by Congress after the Civil War. With the introduction of the draft in 1917 the number of African Americans who entered the army rose to almost 400,000 but the majority were assigned to quartermasters, engineers, and other all-black service units. Only 40,000 were given combat roles. Officer training was established for African Americans during the war, but they could only serve with black troops. Roles for African American in the navy were limited to the galleys/kitchens and boiler rooms; African Americans were excluded from the U.S. Marine Corps entirely. After the war service for African Americans was restricted once more, and by the outbreak of World War II their position was almost as it had been in 1917.

More than 35,000 **women** served as auxiliaries in different branches of the armed forces during the war, with over 20,000 in the army nurse corps. Others worked as telephone operators, secretaries, and drivers. After the war numbers again shrank, and service for women was largely confined to the army and navy nursing corps.

See also AMERICAN EXPEDITIONARY FORCE (AEF); ARGONNE; BELLEAU WOOD; CHATEAU-THIERRY; CONSCIENTIOUS OBJECTORS; JOHNSON, HUGH SAMUEL (1882–1942); MACARTHUR, DOUGLAS (1880–1964); MARCH, PEYTON CONWAY (1864–1955); MARNE, BATTLE OF; MEUSE-ARGONNE, BATTLE OF; PERSHING, JOHN JOSEPH (1860–1948); ST. MIHIEL SALIENT; YORK, ALVIN CULLUM (1887–1964).

ARMISTICE. The armistice was an agreement to cease fire between the belligerent powers in **World War I** pending peace negotiations. It was first requested by the German government on 4 October 1918, and was to be based on president **Woodrow Wilson**'s **Fourteen Points**. A temporary cease-fire ordered to allow truce discussions was mistaken by elements of the American press as a final agreement, leading to premature celebrations in the United States on 7 November. The armistice proper was finally agreed after further negotiation on 8 November and signed at 11 a.m. on 11 November. The armistice required German forces to evacuate all territory west of the Rhine, surrender large elements of its war-making capacity, withdraw all its troops from Russia, Rumania, and Turkey, and renounce the treaties of Brest-Litovsk and Bucharest. Armistices had earlier been agreed between the Allies and Bulgaria, Turkey, and Austria-Hungary. The armistice was renewed until the signing of the **Treaty of Versailles**.

ARMORY SHOW, 1913. The Armory Show was the name given to the "International Exhibition of Modern Art" which took place in the armory of the 69th Regiment of the New York National Guard in New York City from 17 February to 15 March 1913. Organized by a group of artists known as the Association of American Painters and Sculptors (1911) and including Walter Kuhn, Arthur B. Davies, and John Sloan, it was the first large exhibition of modern **art** in the United States. Among the work shown to the American public for the first time was that of Kandinsky, Picasso, and Duchamp. Although the subject of much criticism and ridicule, the exhibition of impressionist, post-impressionist, and cubist work had a revolutionary impact on the American art world.

ARMSTRONG, LOUIS (1901–1971). Born in New Orleans, the great **jazz** trumpeter and singer Louis Armstrong was placed in a Colored Waifs' Home for Boys at the age of twelve. He began his career as a professional musician in 1918 playing the cornet in clubs and on Mississippi River paddle steamers. In 1922 Armstrong moved to Chicago to play second cornet in Joe "King" Oliver's Creole Jazz Band. Armstrong made his first recordings between 1923 and 1924 with Oliver, including "Riverside Blues," "Snake Rage," and "Dipper Mouth Blues." He moved to New York City to join **Fletcher Henderson**'s orchestra in 1924. It was this new band that developed the jazz style known as "swing." Armstrong made a number of records playing trumpet with Henderson ("One of these Days," "Copenhagen," and "Everybody Loves My Baby") and also with Clarence Williams's Blue Five, a group featuring **Sydney Bechet** and the singers Ma Rainey and **Bessie Smith**. Armstrong returned to Chicago in 1925 and began to lead his own groups, the Hot Five and the Hot Seven, with whom he made some classic recordings of traditional jazz—"Cornet Chop," "Gut Bucket Blues," "Heebie Jeebies," and others.

Armstrong and his band moved to New York in 1929 and made several records on which he sang, often using his improvised "scat" singing. He achieved great success with "I Can't Give You Anything but Love" and "Ain't Misbehavin'," recorded in 1929. From 1930 through the 1940s Armstrong played with a number of big bands and returned to small combos after World War II. Between 1932 and 1965 he also appeared in almost fifty movies, including *Pennies from Heaven* (1936), *High Society* (1956), and *Hello Dolly* (1969). Armstrong's song "Hello Dolly" had already reached number one on the popular music charts in 1964. Through his long and successful career from the days of the **Harlem Renaissance** through to the post–Civil Rights period of the 1960s, Armstrong—also known as "Satchmo" or "Pops"—was one of the most significant figures in jazz music.

See also AFRICAN AMERICANS; MUSIC AND DANCE.

ART. The visual arts of the 1920s captured something of the dichotomy in the cultural trends of the decade and provided links with both pre–**World War I** trends and those of the 1930s. On the one hand there were a considerable number of artists who, like the "**lost generation**," seemed alienated from America and, following many prewar artists, drew much of their inspiration from and spent most of their time in Europe, particularly Paris. One of the most notable of this group was **Man Ray**, but others who moved to Europe before turning back to the United States and to American themes included **Charles Demuth**, **Marsden Hartley**, **John Marin**, and **Grant Wood**.

Although some of the European influences could be seen in the modernist, impressionistic, or abstract representations of these artists, particularly the poster portraits of Demuth or the cubist work of Max Weber (1881–1961), they also produced more representational work and contributed to the second body of painters who formed the "**American scene**." This group focused particularly on America and its themes, history, and landscapes. While Marin and Hartley concentrated on Maine, **Thomas Hart Benton** depicted Indiana, Missouri, and Kansas; **John Steuart Curry** portrayed landscapes of Wisconsin and historical scenes from Kansas. Other artists like **Charles Burchfield** and **Charles Sheeler** concentrated on cityscapes and representations of industrial and urban scenes and skyscrapers. However, many of these artists include both urban and rural themes in their work; one of the most notable artists associated with the city was **Edward Hopper**, but he was equally famous for his depiction of the coast and sea off Maine and Cape Cod.

A major influence during the decade and beyond was **Alfred Stieglitz**, whose own work in photography both provided links with the prewar era and also marked new departures; his 291 and other galleries also exhibited the work of many of the young, developing artists of the period. He particularly encouraged the work of **Georgia O'Keefe**, whom he married. Like Sheeler, O'Keefe produced photographic work as well as her more famous paintings of flowers and desert scenes. Photography itself was a growing and significant art form in this period as new cameras and film developed rapidly and became more accessible to ordinary people following the introduction of Kodak's Box Brownie in 1900. While realism, as established in the late nineteenth and early twentieth centuries by people like Jacob Riis and Lewis Hine, continued to be very much the focus of photography, people like Stieglitz, **Edward Steichen**, **Paul Strand**, and **Edward Weston** developed the photograph as an art form, using light and shade, or concentrating on objects, landscapes, or buildings in such a way they became almost abstract. Indeed, it was often difficult to distinguish the photographs of people like O'Keefe and Sheeler from their paintings. Many of the photographers of the period were also famous for their portraits, ranging from studio models to famous personalities such as **movie** stars. **Carl Van Vechten**, for example, photographed many of the people involved in the "**Harlem Renaissance**." His work like that of many other photographers appeared in **newspapers and magazines** and paved the way for future fashion photography and photojournalism in the 1930s.

The difficulty of categorizing some of the art of the 1920s lies in the fact that the prewar modernist movement had in many ways become Americanized. The most obvious example of this was in the focus among some artists on the modern city. Demuth, Sheeler, O'Keefe, and **Louis Lozowick** took aspects of the Cubist movement and applied the emphasis on simple, geometric forms to paintings of skyscrapers or industrial plant in what became known as the "precisionist" movement. Buildings themselves became part of the modern machine age, celebrating both new building techniques and also business success. The skyscrapers of New York and Chicago represented the soaring success of American civilization and business and reached their apogee with the art deco Chrysler Building (completed in 1930) and the **Empire State Building** (1931).

The link between architecture and art was best demonstrated in the work of sculptor **John Storrs**, whose abstract works combined the influences of Cubism with those of art deco in his "Studies in Architectural Form." Art deco also influenced **Paul Manship**, whose sculptures of classical subjects appealed nonetheless to the modernists because of their sleek simplicity. Much more abstract was the work of Alexander Calder (1898–1976), who moved from representational wire sculptures in the late 1920s through to his abstract mobiles and installations of the 1930s. The most momentous piece of sculpture was undoubtedly the presidential heads (Washington, Jefferson, Lincoln, and **Theodore Roosevelt**) carved at Mount Rushmore, South Dakota, by the Danish-American artist Gutzon Borglum (1867–1941) between 1927 and 1941, completed after his death by his son.

African American artists of the 1920s reflected different influences from their white counterparts and were very much part of the Harlem Renaissance. The leading black artist, sometimes called the "father of African American art," was **Aaron Douglas**, whose work celebrated African American life, history, and African origins; **Archibald Motley**, on the other hand, concentrated on black urban life and culture, particularly **jazz**, in an often unprecedented fashion.

See also ARMORY SHOW, 1913; BELLOWS, GEORGE WESLEY (1892–1929); HENRI, ROBERT (1865–1929); MODERNISM.

AUTOMOBILE. The rise of the automobile was rapid and dramatic. Charles E. and J. Frank Duryea built the first automobile in the United States in 1892 and sold their first vehicle in 1896. **Henry Ford** produced his first gasoline-powered automobile in 1893 and introduced his Model T Ford in 1908. In 1899 thirty separate automobile companies produced twenty-five hundred vehicles; by 1914 there were more than seventy companies producing two hundred thousand cars a year. The number of registered automobiles reached 469,000 in 1910. **World War I** led to accelerated development as Ford's mass production and assembly line techniques spread. In 1920 there were already over 9 million registered vehicles in the country, but during the 1920s the automobile became the outstanding symbol of the new consumer society. The number of manufacturers declined to forty-four by 1929, with three companies, Ford, **Chrysler**, and General Motors, being responsible for 80 percent of production. Production peaked at 5.3 million vehicles in 1929, by which time there were 26.7 million registered vehicles on the road, one per every 4.5 people. Almost 75 percent of these automobiles were bought on credit.

The impact of this revolution was enormous. Automobile manufacturing employed 750,000 people directly, but 4.5 million more worked in related industries—glass, rubber, oil. While automobile prices fell, purchase was made easier by the development of credit and encouraged by the growth of advertising. The automobile promoted highway building, and federal funding increased with the **Federal Highway Acts** of 1916 and 1921. Gasoline taxes raised $431 million a year in revenue by 1929. The automobile encouraged the start of a motel industry, made the growth of suburbia a possibility, and encouraged a real estate boom. Some people even blamed the automobile for the decline in sexual morality. The slowdown in the economy when Ford switched production to a new model in 1928 was one factor associated with the **Wall Street Crash** and **Great Depression**.

See also CHEVROLET, LOUIS (1878–1841); DURANT, WILLIAM CRAPO (1861–1947).

AVIATION. Following the first air flight of the Wright Brothers in 1903, the first air passengers were carried between limited destinations in California and Florida in 1913 and 1914. Air travel was still slow to develop, and, despite the increased use of aircraft during **World War I**, the aviation industry in the United States remained in its infancy. In 1917 Congress provided $100,000 to fund an air service between New York City and Washington, D.C., operated jointly by the Army and Post Office, and the Post Office Mail Service was established in 1918; by 1924 this had been gradually extended to cover New York to San Francisco. In 1925 the Contract Air Mail Act gave airmail contracts to five independent commercial operators, and in 1926 the **Air Commerce Act** was passed providing for federal regulation of the air industry. Partly as a consequence of this and business consolidations, commercial airline companies such as Trans World Airlines, Northwest Airlines, Western Air Express, and Ford Air Transport Service were formed in 1925 and 1926. Pan American Airways was created in 1927, and in 1929 William Boeing merged Boeing Air Transport with Pratt and Whitney to form United Aircraft and Transport Corporation.

Air travel was given a considerable boost by the publicity that followed **Charles Lindbergh**'s solo crossing of the Atlantic in 1927. In 1925 **Richard E. Byrd** had flown to the North Pole, and in 1929 he flew to the South Pole. Secretary of commerce **Herbert Hoover** campaigned to get towns and cities to build municipal airports, and by 1929 he claimed there were twenty-five thousand miles of government-approved airways. In 1926 six thousand passengers had traveled by air; by 1930 this had risen to four hundred thousand, and aircraft capable of carrying more than one or two passengers were being built.

B

BABBITT, IRVING (1865–1933). Irving Babbitt was a graduate of Harvard who rejoined the university and became a professor in the Department of Romance Languages, where he taught French literature. With **Paul Elmer More**, Babbitt became one of the leaders of the New Humanism, a critique of Romanticism, and a call for restraint and conservatism. Babbitt's published work included *Literature and the American College* (1908), *The New Laokoön* (1910), *Masters of Modern French Criticism* (1912), *Rousseau and Romanticism* (1919), and *Democracy and Leadership* (1924). Although Babbitt influenced a number of writers including **T. S. Eliot**, **H. L. Mencken**, and **Walter Lippmann**, his views tended to find their most receptive audience among conservative intellectuals.

BAILEY V. DREXEL FURNITURE CO. The decision by the **Supreme Court** in 1922, which held that the second **Child Labor** law was unconstitutional because it attempted to regulate child labor by use of a penal tax. The Court states that the tax-raising power of Congress was limited to raising revenue, not correcting social problems, which was the province of the states.

BAKER, NEWTON DIEHL (1871–1937). A graduate of Johns Hopkins University (1892) and Washington and Lee University (1894), Newton Baker first worked as secretary to the postmaster general, William L. Wilson, before moving to Cleveland, Ohio, where he was city solicitor from 1901 to 1909. Baker became mayor of Cleveland in 1911 and served from 1912 to 1916, continuing the reform program of Tom L. Johnson. Although avowedly a pacifist, he became secretary of war in **Woodrow Wilson**'s administration in 1913, a post he held until 1920. Baker's calm handling of the problems with **Mexico**, and the **punitive expedition**, 1916–1917, helped minimize public unease. He was also responsible for the administration of the **Selective Service Act**, which introduced universal military conscription in 1917. Throughout **World War I** Baker loyally supported Wilson's policies. He returned to his law practice in 1921. He continued to support the **League of Nations** and addressed the 1924 Democratic Party convention with some force on the issue. In 1928 he was appointed to the Permanent Court of Arbitration in The Hague. The following year president **Herbert Hoover** appointed Baker to the Law Enforcement Commission and during the 1930s he also served on a number of committees in relation to the armed forces. In 1933 the National Institute of Social Sciences awarded Baker a medal for "services to humanity."

BAKER, RAY STANNARD (1870–1946). A journalist and writer, Baker joined the staff of *McClure's Magazine* in 1897 and the *American Magazine* in 1906. He became famous as one of the "**muckraking**" journalists of the **progressive** era, writing critiques of the railroads and of business and financial malpractice. Baker's famous series of articles on race relations was published as *Following the Color Line* in 1908, and his study of religious life was published as *The Spiritual Unrest* in 1910. Baker contributed to the work of the **Committee on Public Information** during **World War I** and was director of the press bureau for the American Commission to Negotiate Peace at the **Paris Peace Conference** in 1919. He was one of the leading biographers of **Woodrow Wilson** after the war, publishing an eight-volume study between 1927 and 1939, for which he was awarded a Pulitzer Prize in 1940.

BALCH, EMILY GREENE (1867–1961). After graduating from Bryn Mawr in 1889, Emily Balch studied in Paris for a year and published *Public Assistance in France* in 1893. After returning to the United States she became an active reformer and in 1892 helped to found Boston's first **settlement house**, Denison House, and served as its head. In 1895 Balch produced the *Manual for Use in Cases of Juvenile Offenders and Other Minors*. That year she began teaching sociology at Wellesley and she rose to chair of the Department of Economics and Sociology in 1913. Balch produced *Our Slavic Fellow Citizens*, a definitive study of immigrants from the Austro-Hungarian Empire in 1912. She was also active on a variety of local boards, including Boston's City Planning Board, the Massachusetts commission on immigration, and the committee on **immigration** of the **Progressive Party** in 1912. Balch was also one of the founders of the Women's Trade Union League (WTUL) in 1903, and the Boston WTUL in 1904.

Following the outbreak of war in Europe in 1914, Balch joined the peace movement and was one of the founders of the **American Union Against Militarism**. In 1915 she and other members of the **Woman's Peace Party** attended an international peace conference at The Hague that called for a conference of neutral nations, and Balch attended the Stockholm peace conference in 1916. In 1918 she was dismissed from Wellesley because of her pacifism and her reform activities. With **Jane Addams**, Balch attended the founding conference of the Women's International League for Peace and

Freedom in Zurich in 1919, and served as secretary treasurer until 1922. She served again as secretary in 1934, and succeeded Addams as honorary international president in 1937. Balch was one of a group of investigators from the Women's International League to visit **Haiti**, and their report, *Occupied Haiti* (1927), helped to bring about the end of U.S. occupation of the island. In 1946 she was a corecipient of the Nobel Peace Prize.

See also WOMEN.

BALDWIN, ROGER NASH (1884–1981). Described as "America's foremost libertarian," Roger Baldwin graduated with a BA and MA from Harvard in 1905. He became a **social worker** and taught sociology at Washington University, St. Louis, from 1906 to 1909. After becoming involved in reform politics, he moved to New York City in 1911. In 1917 Baldwin and others formed the **American Union Against Militarism** to provide support for pacifists and **conscientious objectors** during **World War I**. He was jailed for nine months in 1918 for refusing to answer the draft. In 1919 Baldwin briefly joined the **Industrial Workers of the World** (IWW) and took to the road. However, in 1920 he was one of the founders of the **American Civil Liberties Union** (ACLU). Baldwin became the ACLU director and served until 1950.

During the 1930s Baldwin visited the Soviet Union and wrote extolling the virtues of the Communist regime. He also supported Popular Front activities to combat the rise of fascism, but following the Nazi-Soviet Pact in 1939 he campaigned to alter the ACLU charter to exclude anyone associated with totalitarian regimes. Baldwin was instrumental in the expulsion of **Elizabeth Gurley Flynn** from the organization. After World War II Baldwin acted as a consultant on civil liberties in Japan and, following his resignation as director, became active in international affairs on similar issues.

BANKING. Historically banking in the United States was a complex political as well as economic issue. Opposition to a strong centralized government led to the demise of the National Bank in 1836. Although national banking was restored with the banking acts of 1863 and 1864, the banking system was complicated and inclined to instability. A three-tier system of national banks chartered by the federal government, state banks chartered by individual states, and local banks, all of which remained independent, and essentially local businesses, existed. Lack of regulation and the impact of local events, such as problems in **farming**, often resulted in bank collapses. Bank panics (the worst in 1907) and the nineteenth-century crisis in farming, had led to demands for regulation that resulted in the creation of the **Federal Reserve** in 1914. While this brought some stability, it did not solve all the problems as only about one-third of all banks registered with the Federal Reserve. In 1921 only about one-third of the 29,018 commercial banks were members of the Reserve. Between 1921 and 1928 five thousand banks were forced to close, mostly in rural areas or small communities. Some of the closures were due to smaller banks being swallowed up in mergers or by the competition from newly created branches of larger banks. The creation of large statewide or even transnational banks such as **Amadeo Giannini**'s Bank of America led to the concentration of control of 46 percent of all banking resources in just 1 percent of the country's banks, but this did not necessarily bring greater security; the majority of banks in 1929 were still small, independent businesses.

With the collapse in investors' confidence following the **Wall Street Crash**, a further 1,345 banks failed in 1930 alone and another 2,294 the following year. Banking failure contributed enormously to the coming of the **Great Depression** as confidence fell, credit shrank, and business loans and mortgages on homes and farms were called in. The collapse of the Bank of the United States in New York City in December 1930 wiped out the savings of over four hundred thousand depositors, affecting almost a third of the city's population. While president **Herbert Hoover** attempted to tackle the problem with the **Reconstruction Finance Corporation** (RFC), **Glass-Steagall**, and **Federal Home Loan Bank Acts** of 1932, many banks remained closed on the eve of **Franklin D. Roosevelt**'s inauguration. It was only with the banking reforms of the **New Deal** that some order and stability returned.

See also INSULL, SAMUEL (1859–1938); MITCHELL, CHARLES EDWIN (1877–1955).

BARA, THEDA (NÉE THEODOSIA BURR GOODMAN) (1885–1955).
The silent **movie** star famous for her roles as a "vamp"—a sexually liberated and dangerous woman—Theda Bara was born in Cincinnati to a Polish father and Swiss/French mother. She attended the University of Cincinnati briefly before moving with her family to New York City in 1905, where she made her Broadway stage debut in *The Devil* in 1908. In 1915, under her changed name, Bara starred as the femme fatale in *A Fool There Was* (1915), based on Rudyard Kipling's poem "The Vampire." She was then given a long-term contract by **William Fox** and for a while was one of the top-earning movie actors of the day. She was to star in some forty films between 1915 and 1926, including *Sin* (1915), *The Vixen* (1916), and most famously *Cleopatra* (1917). Although she appeared in *Romeo and Juliet* in 1916, Bara mainly portrayed exotic, mysterious, and sensual **women**—often in revealing costumes. She made her last film with Fox, *The Lure of Ambition*, in 1919, and her career declined thereafter. She appeared in a handful of mainly unsuccessful roles, the last in *Madam Mystery* in 1926, and then lived in quiet retirement in Beverly Hills until her death from cancer in 1955.

See also FLAPPER.

BARRYMORE, JOHN (1882–1942). Like his brother **Lionel**, John Barrymore was born John Blythe but adopted his parents' stage name. After an education in Great Britain, Barrymore worked for a while as a cartoonist at the New York *Evening Journal* before beginning his acting career in 1901. By 1909 he was established as a leading comic actor and starred in *The Fortune Hunter*, a play that he took on tour for a year after a successful Broadway run in 1909. Barrymore made his first **movie**, *An American Citizen*, in 1914, and he made anther nine films before 1919. He continued to appear on stage in *Justice* (1916), with his brother in *Peter Ibbetson* (1917), and in *Richard III* (1920). He successfully played the lead in a new interpretation of *Hamlet* in 1922 and he also took the play to London in 1925. Barrymore's film career continued with *Beau Brummel* in 1923 and in the first film with a synchronized soundtrack, *Don Juan*, in 1926. He continued to make movies and appear on stage through to the 1940s, even appearing in parodies of his own life as a failing actor (*My Dear Children* [1939–1940], *Playmates* [1941]). Barrymore was one of the most influential actors of his day and he starred in over forty theater plays, sixty films, and one hundred radio shows, including Rudy Vallee's *Sealtest Show* in the 1940s.

See also LITERATURE AND THEATER.

BARRYMORE, LIONEL (1878–1954). Born Lionel Blythe, Barrymore adopted his mother and father's stage name of Barrymore and quickly joined them on the stage in the 1890s. He achieved his first success in 1902 playing a character role in *The Mummy and the Hummingbird* and then in 1903 in a central role in *The Other Girl*. In 1906 Barrymore moved to Paris, France, where he studied art for three years. Returning to the United States, he played in a variety of vaudeville roles, then joined **D. W. Griffith** at the Biograph Studio in New York City and appeared in dozens of **movies** between 1912 and 1914.

Between 1917 and 1920 Barrymore appeared in a number of successful Broadway plays, including with his brother **John** in *Peter Ibbetson* in 1917. He also took part in **Liberty Loan** campaigns during **World War I**. Following a series of Broadway flops in the 1920s, Barrymore turned more and more to films and signed a contract with Metro-Goldwyn-Mayer (MGM) in 1925. He starred with **Greta Garbo** in *The Temptress* (1926) and with **Gloria Swanson** in *Sadie Thompson* (1928). His theater background enabled him to make the transition to sound film, and in 1931 he won an Academy Award for his role in *A Free Soul*. He continued to make movies through the 1930s, several with his brother, and beginning in 1938 made fifteen films in the *Dr. Kildare* series. His last memorable film performance was in *Key Largo* in 1948. In addition to his film and theater work Barrymore also starred in a number of radio series and won recognition for his paintings and for his musical compositions.

See also LITERATURE AND THEATER.

BARTON, BRUCE FAIRCHILD (1886–1967). Bruce Barton graduated from Amherst College in 1907. After a series of jobs in **newspaper and magazine** journalism, he became assistant sales manager for *Collier's* in 1912 and then editor of *Every Week* in 1914, where he developed a skill in writing inspirational articles. He became a regular contributor of such work to the *American Magazine*, *McCall's*, *Collier's*, *Good Housekeeping*, and *Reader's Digest*. Several volumes of his writings were published between 1917 and 1924.

During the war Barton worked as publicity director for the United War Work Agencies. In 1919 he joined Roy S. Durstine and Alex F. Osborne to form an advertising agency, which by 1928 was the fourth largest in the United States. In 1925 Barton published the best-selling *The Man Nobody Knows* in which he portrayed Christ as "the world's greatest salesman." He also wrote a study of the Bible in a similar vein, *The Book Nobody Knows* (1926), and a portrait of St. Paul, *He Upset the World* (1932). In 1937 Barton was elected to fill an unexpired term in Congress as a Republican representative for New York. He won a full term in 1938. He campaigned against the **New Deal** and, together with Joseph Martin and Hamilton Fish, was ridiculed by **Franklin Roosevelt** as one of "Martin, Barton, & Fish." He failed to win election to the Senate in 1940 and returned to his advertising company.

BARUCH, BERNARD MANNES (1870–1965). After graduating from City College in New York, Bernard Baruch became a financier and successful Wall Street investor. Baruch supported **Woodrow Wilson** in 1912 and was appointed to the Advisory Commission to the **Council of National Defense** in 1916. In 1918 he became chairman of the **War Industries Board**, where he directed the industrial war effort. He helped to formulate the economic provisions of the **Versailles Treaty**. Baruch was less in the public eye during the 1920s and 1930s, but as a special adviser to the Roosevelt Administration during World War II he authored a report on postwar conversion. As U.S. representative to the United Nations Atomic Energy Commission, Baruch drew up proposals for the international control of atomic energy in 1946.

See also WORLD WAR I, 1914–1918.

BEARD, CHARLES AUSTIN (1874–1948). Charles Beard was one of America's greatest historians. He studied at DePauw University, Indiana, and gained his PhD from Columbia University in 1904 and then taught history and politics there until 1917, when he resigned in protest against the dismissal of two colleagues opposed to U.S. entry into the war. In 1917 he became director of the Training School for Public Service, a position he held until 1922. A prolific writer, perhaps his most significant work was the *Economic Interpretation of the Constitution* (1913), in which he argued that rather than idealism, many of the Founding Fathers were motivated by economic interests. His *The Rise of American Civilization* (1927), coauthored with his wife, **Mary Beard**, stressed the uniqueness of American history. In the 1930s he became increasingly isolationist in outlook.

See also EDUCATION.

BEARD, MARY RITTER (1876–1958). Mary Beard gained her PhD from DePauw University in 1897, where she met her future husband, **Charles Beard**. Mary Beard was active in reform groups in New York City including the **Women**'s Trade Union League and Woman Suffrage Association and the **Congressional Union**. In addition to collaborating with her husband on a number of publications, Mary Beard made a major contribution to women's history and can be classed as one of the founders of that genre. She wrote *Women's Work in Municipalities* (1915), *A Short History of the American Labor Movement* (1920), *On Understanding Women* (1931), *America through Women's Eyes* (1933), and *Women as Force in History* (1946). Beard also did much to collect material and establish an archive of women's history. With Charles Beard, she wrote *The Rise of American Civilization* (1927), *America in Midpassage* (1939), *The American Spirit* (1942), and *A Basic History of the United States* (1944). One of Mary Beard's last works was *The Making of Charles A. Beard* (1955).

See also EDUCATION.

BECHET, SIDNEY JOSEPH (1897–1959). The great **jazz** saxophonist and clarinetist Sidney Bechet was born in New Orleans, where he learned the clarinet and played in his first bands. Bechet toured various states in America and visited different European countries with bands between 1916 and the early 1920s. He played with **Bessie Smith**, **Duke Ellington**, and other **African American** leading performers in different revues. In 1925 Bechet toured again in France, Belgium, Germany, and Russia, returning to the United States in 1930. Bechet played with **Noble Sissle**'s band on several occasions, and with his own sextet and quartet, recording in different forms as the "New Orleans Feetwarmers." He also recorded with **Louis Armstrong** and **Jelly Roll Morton**. Bechet continued to tour the United States and Europe through to his death of cancer in 1959.

See also MUSIC AND DANCE.

BELLEAU WOOD. The first sizable battle involving troops of the **American Expeditionary Force** (AEF) took place at **Chateau-Thierry** and Belleau Wood in June 1918 and helped stop the German offensive on the **Marne** prior to the **Allied** counteroffensive. The battle became part of the history of the U.S. Marines for their refusal to retreat. More than eighteen hundred American soldiers were killed and almost eight thousand were wounded in the engagement fought over twenty-five days.

BELLOWS, GEORGE WESLEY (1892–1929). The realist painter and printmaker, described shortly after his death as one of America's greatest artists, was born in Columbus, Ohio. He attended Ohio State University between 1901 and 1904 but moved to New York City before graduating in order to study painting at the New York School of **Art** with **Robert Henri**. An associate, though not a member of the group known as "The Eight," Bellows was a major figure in what became known as the Ashcan School of artists who focused on depicting the life of the urban working class in New York's tenements. He also was involved in the famous Armory exhibition of 1913. His portrait of *Little Girl in White* (1913) won the first National Gallery Hallgarten Prize, and he became a member of the National Academy of Design the same year. Among Bellows's many works were *Forty-two Kids* (1907), a portrayal of boys swimming in the East River that offered a counterpoint to Thomas Eakins's idealized depiction of *The Swimming Hole* (1885), the lively street scene in *New York* (1911), and a view of crowded tenement buildings in *The Cliff Dwellers* (1913). As well as cityscapes, Bellows also became known for his many paintings and lithographs of boxing matches such as *Stag at Sharkey's* (1909), *A Knockout* (1921), and *Dempsey and Firpo* (1924) showing **Jack Dempsey** knocked from the ring in the fight against Luis Ángel Firpo, which Dempsey subsequently, if controversially, went on to win.

Bellows taught at the Modern School of Art and Art Students League in New York City and later at Art Institute of Chicago. He was a member of the editorial board and, from 1913, an illustrator for the **Socialist** paper, *The Masses*. Initially he opposed **World War I** and in 1917 produced twenty-five antiwar drawings for the journal. However, he supported American entry into the conflict and he produced a number of paintings of German war atrocities based on various reports, such as *Massacre at Dinant* (1918) and *Return of the Useless* (1918). Among his other lithographs was the depiction of the execution of **Tom Mooney**, *Electrocution* (1917). Bellows provided illustrations for magazines such as *Collier's* and *Harper's Weekly*, and for numerous books, including the works of H. G. Wells. As a painter he also produced a considerable number of portraits of women, including his wife, Emma, in work such as *Emma at the Piano* (1914) and *Emma and Her Children* (1923). Following his sudden death from a ruptured appendix, the Metropolitan Museum of Art held an exhibition in his honor.

BENÉT, STEPHEN VINCENT (1898–1943). Stephen Benét began writing and publishing poetry while still at school. His first book of poetry, *Five Men and Pompey*, was published in 1915. He entered Yale University that year and won a number of literary prizes. He had his *Young Adventure: A Book of Poems* published in 1918. Benét completed his master's at Yale in 1920 and his dissertation, a group of poems, was published that year. Benét's first novel, *The Beginning of Wisdom*, was published in 1921; his second, *Young People's Pride*, in 1922; and the third, *Jean Huguenot*, in 1923. More of his poetry appeared in the *New Republic* and the *Nation*. He achieved commercial and popular success in 1928 with the publication of his narrative poem, *John Brown's Body*, which was widely recited on stage and radio.

Benét then went to Hollywood to write scripts but did not remain long. He was elected to the National Institute of Arts and Letters in 1929 and to the American Academy of Arts and Letters in 1938. His *Ballads and Poems* appeared in 1931 and included the popular "American Names," ending with the line "Bury my heart at Wounded Knee." More poetry and a fourth novel appeared in the 1930s, and during World War II he wrote scripts for the radio series *This Is War* and *Dear Adolf*, in addition to a history of the United States commissioned by the Office of War Information. *Western Star*, published after his death in 1943, won the Pulitzer Prize for poetry in 1944.

See also LITERATURE AND THEATER.

BENTON, THOMAS HART (1889–1975). Born in Neosho, Missouri, Thomas Hart Benton briefly attended military school before going to study at Chicago Art Institute in 1906 and then in Paris from 1908 to 1911. In 1913 Benton moved to New York City where he had his first successful show in 1916 as part of a modernist collection in the Forum exhibition. He served in the navy during **World War I** and afterward abandoned **modernism** in favor of the **American scene** and the rural emphasis associated with Regionalism during the 1930s. During the 1920s he completed eighteen large, mural-size works as part of *The American Historical Epic* and in 1930 Benton produced a series of murals entitled *America Today*. The vibrant colors and depictions of ordinary working people led some critics to compare him to both right- and left-wing **art**. His Indiana murals painted in 1933 to mark a *Century of Progress* and those in *The Social History of the State of Missouri* in the State Capitol in Jefferson, Missouri, celebrated American settlement but also depicted scenes of racism and violence. Nonetheless, Benton made the cover of *Time* magazine in December 1934 and was regarded as one of the country's leading artists.

The richness of color and content in Benton's voluptuous rural scenes, such as *Cradling Wheat* (1938) and *Threshing Wheat* (1939), were in stark contrast to the arid landscapes of the Dustbowl recorded by the photographers of the Farm Security Administration (FSA). His autobiography, *An Artist in America*, appeared in 1937. From 1925 to 1935, Benton taught at the New York Art Students League and then from 1935 to 1941 he taught at the Kansas City Art Institute where one of his students was Jackson Pollock— and during World War II produced several paintings of Nazi atrocities. Although his style went out of fashion in the 1940s and 1950s, in 1961 he completed another mural depicting historical scenes, *Independence and the Opening of the West*, in the Truman library in Independence, Missouri.

See also ART.

BERGER, VICTOR LOUIS (1860–1929). An immigrant from Austria who entered the United States in 1878, Berger joined the Socialist Labor Party in 1889. He was the editor of *Milwaukee Daily Vorwaerts* (1892–1898), *Social Democratic Herald* (1900), and then of the leading U.S. socialist daily newspaper, the *Milwaukee Leader* in 1911. A critic of the conservatism of the **American Federation of Labor** under **Samuel Gompers**, Berger was one of the founders of the Social Democratic Party that then became the **Socialist Party of America** in 1901. He became the first socialist elected to Congress when he entered the House of Representatives in 1911. He served until 1913 and was reelected in 1918. Following his conviction under the **Espionage Act** he was sentenced to twenty years in prison and excluded from the House in 1919. The **Supreme Court** overturned his conviction in 1921, and Berger was elected and seated in the House once more from 1923 to 1929. He succeeded **Eugene Debs** as chair of the Socialist Party's national executive committee in 1927.

BERLIN, IRVING (1888–1989). Born Israel Isidore Baline in Russia, Berlin's family moved to the United States in 1893 and settled in New York's Lower East Side. Berlin grew up in poverty and was forced to work from an early age; he did a variety of casual jobs including being a singing waiter. However, he began writing songs—his first published song in 1907 misprinted his name, which he then changed to Irving Berlin. From 1908 to 1911 he mainly wrote lyrics for other people's **music**, but in 1911 he achieved his first major success with "Alexander's Ragtime Band." He had another hit with "When I Lost You," written following the early death of his first wife in 1912, and marking his move from ragtime to ballads.

Berlin entered the army during **World War I** and staged the revue *Yip Yip Yaphank*. Following the war Berlin wrote for the *Ziegfeld Follies* before establishing his own theater on Broadway, The Music Box. He achieved hits with "What'll I Do" (recorded by **Paul Whiteman)** in 1924, "Always" in 1925, and "Blue Skies" in 1926. "Blue Skies" was performed by **Al Jolson** in the **movie** *The Jazz Singer* (1927). He began to write hit songs again with Rudy Vallee's "How Deep Is the Ocean" in 1932 and then had a string of hits with the Broadway revue *As Thousands Cheer* (1933) including the songs "Easter Parade," "Harlem on My Mind," and "Heat Wave." He also wrote the music for the movie *Top Hat* (1935) and won an Oscar for the song "Cheek to Cheek."

Berlin's film success continued during World War II with *Holiday Inn*—featuring Bing Crosby singing the song that became the most-played Christmas song, "White Christmas"—and the reprise of *Yip Yip Yaphank* retitled *This Is the Army* (1943), based on the revue that had first been staged in 1942. It now included "God Bless America," a song first performed by Kate Smith in 1938, which was so popular during the war it almost became the nation's anthem. His contribution to the nation was recognized by president Harry S. Truman with the award of the Medal of Merit in 1945.

Berlin had a huge success after the war with one of his greatest musicals, *Annie Get Your Gun* (1946), produced by Richard Rodgers and Oscar Hammerstein, including the songs "There's No Business Like Show Business" and "Anything You Can Do." This was made into a successful film in 1950. The movie *Easter Parade* appeared in 1948. However, Berlin's subsequent productions, *Miss Liberty* (1949) and *Mr. President* (1962), were regarded as flops and he largely retired thereafter. He did, however, write "I Like Ike," the campaign song for Dwight D. Eisenhower in 1952. With **George Gershwin**, **Jerome Kern**, and **Cole Porter**, Berlin dominated the popular music of the interwar years. With over fifteen hundred songs, nineteen Broadway shows, and eighteen film scores to his credit, Berlin is rightly remembered as one of America's greatest songwriters.

See also LITERATURE AND THEATER.

BILLINGS, WARREN KNOX. *See* MOONEY, THOMAS JOSEPH (1882–1942).

***BIRTH OF A NATION*, 1915.** Made by director **D. W. Griffith**, *The Birth of a Nation* was a pathbreaking **movie** in terms of technique but also significant for its racial content. The film was the story of the intertwined fortunes of two families, North and South during Civil War and Reconstruction. It depicted the defeated South overrun by ignorant former slaves manipulated by scheming white politicians. It also showed white womanhood threatened by rapacious black men—most of whom were played in the film by white actors in blackface. The **Ku Klux Klan** was presented as the savior of the South. The film was based on Thomas Dixon's play *The Clansman* and reflected many of the views held at the time. President **Woodrow Wilson** said the film was "like writing history with lightning. And my only regret is that it is all terribly true." The showing of the film prompted protest from black groups and the **National Association for the Advancement of Colored People**, but it also led to a revival of the Ku Klux Klan. Technically the film, which lasted almost three hours, included many of the features of modern filmmaking with intercutting of stories, panoramic views of battles, fadeouts, and close-ups, and in that sense it remains a masterpiece.

BLACK BOTTOM. The Black Bottom was one of the several dances, like the **Charleston**, reflecting the more uninhibited styles of the 1920s and developed from a song of the same name. It was made popular in the stage play *Dinah* in 1926.

See also MUSIC AND DANCE.

BLATCH, HARRIOT STANTON (1856–1940). Daughter of an abolitionist and Elizabeth Cady Stanton, a leader of the early **women**'s rights movement, the woman suffrage leader Harriot Stanton Blatch obtained her degree from Vassar in 1878 and then assisted her mother and Susan B. Anthony in writing the *History of Woman Suffrage* (1881). After her marriage Blatch lived in London, England, and became involved in women's reform movements. She returned to the United States in 1902 and set out to revitalize the American suffrage movement by including working women. She established the Equality League of Self-Supporting Women in 1907, and three years later this became the Women's Political Union (WPU). During **World War I** Blatch concentrated on helping the war effort and was head of the **U.S. Food Administration**'s Speakers' Bureau and director of the Woman's Land Army.

Once New York conceded **women's suffrage** in 1917, Blatch combined the WPU with the **Congressional Union** to fight for a federal suffrage amendment. After the vote had been won, Blatch joined the **National Woman's Party** in campaigning for an Equal Rights Amendment. Blatch also joined the **Socialist Party** and made unsuccessful bids to be elected to public office. In addition to her political activities Blatch also campaigned on behalf of the **League of Nations**.

BOK, EDWARD WILLIAM (1863–1930). Born in the Netherlands, Edward Bok immigrated to the United States with his family in 1870. After working as an office boy and reporter Bok became head of advertising for the publisher Charles Scribner in 1887. In 1886 Bok established his own Syndicate Press, supplying material to over 130 newspapers. In 1889 he became editor of the *Ladies' Home Journal*. Under his direction the journal, which increased its circulation from under half a million to over 2 million, supported reform measures including city improvements, **women's suffrage**, sex education, and the Pure Food and Drug Act (1906). The journal was used to support the war effort during **World War I** and to encourage the recruitment of women into the war effort. Bok served as vice president of the Belgian Relief Fund. He resigned the editorship of the *Ladies' Home Journal* in 1919 and established an American Peace Award in 1923 and later the American Foundation to lobby for U.S. entry into the Permanent Court of International Justice. Bok's autobiography, *The Americanization of Edward Bok* (1920), was a best-seller and won the Pulitzer Prize. He published numerous other books, including a second autobiography, *Twice 30* (1925).

See also NEWSPAPERS AND MAGAZINES.

BONUS ARMY. Following the onset of the **Depression**, in the spring of 1932 veterans of **World War I** began to call for the early payment of cash bonuses for military service that were due to be paid in 1945. Starting in Portland, Oregon, some of these groups, calling themselves the "Bonus Expeditionary Force" or "Bonus Army," began to travel to Washington, D.C., to lobby Congress. By the beginning of June some three thousand veterans and their families had established a camp on the Anacostia mud flats just outside the capital. By July almost twenty-five thousand people were assembled there.

The bill to secure the early payment was defeated in the Senate on 17 June and many of the protestors began to leave the city. However, following confrontations with the police in July in which two protestors were shot and killed, it was decided that the veterans posed a threat to public order, and president **Herbert Hoover** authorized the use of military force to remove them from the capital. On 28 July infantry and cavalry, backed by tanks, under the command of General Douglas MacArthur and Major Dwight D. Eisenhower, cleared the streets. Contrary to the president's orders, the troops then went on to destroy the camp in Anacostia. The images of these incidents did much to destroy the last of Hoover's reputation and bring about his political defeat.

BOOTLEGGING. "Bootlegging" was the term used to describe the sale or smuggling of illegal alcohol. Although its origins were in the early history of the West when traders carried a bottle of liquor in their boots, it was widely used during the 1920s and the era of **prohibition**, which followed the passage of the **Eighteenth Amendment** in 1920. Bootleg alcohol was sold in illegal bars or clubs known as "speakeasies."

BORAH, WILLIAM EDGAR (1865–1940). After a limited education in Kansas, Borah passed the bar examinations in law in 1887 and practiced for three years before moving to Idaho. Having stood unsuccessfully for the U.S. House of Representatives as a **Democrat** in 1896, Borah turned to the **Republicans** as a candidate for the Senate in 1902. Unsuccessful again, he was elected in 1906. Borah served six successive terms and was known for his oratory and political independence. In domestic matters he had **progressive** tendencies, supporting antitrust legislation, income tax, popular election of senators, and prohibition. In foreign affairs he was one of the leading opponents of the **Versailles Treaty** and **League of Nations**, but he supported the **Washington Conference** (1921–1922). As chairman of the Foreign Relations Committee from 1924 to 1933, he helped secure ratification of the **Kellogg-Briand** Pact in 1928. He opposed revision of the Neutrality acts passed in the 1930s and also disapproved of many **New Deal** measures.

BOSTON POLICE STRIKE. In September 1919, 75 percent of the Boston police force went on strike when the police commissioner refused to recognize their union. When Governor **Calvin Coolidge** refused to intervene, Mayor Andrew Petes used sections of the militia to break up the strike. Coolidge then ordered the police commissioner to take charge and called out the entire state guard. The strike was broken, but the commissioner refused to allow those who had taken part back into the force. **Samuel Gompers** asked Coolidge to help the policemen regain their jobs—his reply that "there is no right to strike against the public safety by anybody, anywhere, anytime" won him national prominence and led to his inclusion on the Republican ticket in 1920. The strike and disorder associated with it helped to generate the hysteria that led to the "**Red Scare**."
See also TRADE UNIONS.

BOURNE, RANDOLPH SILLIMAN (1886–1918). Randolph Bourne was one of the group of young social and literary critics who emerged in the **progressive** era. He was educated at Columbia University, where he was influenced by **Charles Beard**, **John Dewey**, and **James Harvey Robinson**. Bourne published his first book, *Youth and Life*, in 1913 and in 1914 joined the newly formed progressive journal *New Republic*. In addition to literary criticism he wrote a series of articles and two books, *The Gary Schools* (1916) and *Education and Living* (1917), on progressive **education**. He became increasingly at odds with the other writers for the *New Republic* over

World War I and wrote a series of articles in a new avant-garde journal, *Seven*, rejecting the notion that the war was a moral crusade and criticizing the intellectuals for their naiveté. He died in the **influenza epidemic** in 1918.

See also NEWSPAPERS AND MAGAZINES.

BOW, CLARA GORDON (1905–1965). Known as the "It" girl for her sensuous looks, Clara Bow was the quintessential **movie** "**flapper**." Bow had her first part in a movie in 1921 and signed with Schulberg's Preferred Pictures in 1923. Her reputation as a "jazz baby" was established in *The Plastic Age* and *Kiss Me Again*, both in 1925. Bow moved to Paramount Pictures in 1926 and achieved enormous fame exuding sexual allure in *Mantrap*. In 1927 she appeared in *It*, and she was known as the "It" girl thereafter. Between 1922 and 1930 Bow made fifty-two films, but with the onset of sound movies her career and health faltered. She was fired from Paramount in 1931 and retired. Attempted comebacks in 1932 and 1933 failed, although she did have some success in 1947 on the radio program "Truth or Consequence."

See also WOMEN.

BRANDEIS, LOUIS DEMBITZ (1856–1941). After graduating with the highest honors from Harvard Law School in 1877, Louis Brandeis established a law practice in Boston, where he earned a reputation as the "people's lawyer" and a leading member of the **progressive** movement. Brandeis acted without fees for Boston citizens in their fight to control the price of gas. He also acted for policyholders in an investigation of life insurance companies, and he drafted state legislation to control the companies. On several occasions Brandeis also acted as mediator on behalf of labor in disputes with employers. Brandeis came to national prominence in the 1908 case of *Muller v. Oregon* when he used sociological and economic evidence rather than legal precedent to argue in support of restricting the hours of working **women**.

Brandeis also acted as an informal adviser to both **Robert M. La Follette** and **Woodrow Wilson.** In 1916 Wilson nominated Brandeis to the **Supreme Court**, and after a fierce battle over his nomination, he became the first Jew to serve as Supreme Court justice, a position he held for twenty-three years. Brandeis's opinions tended to be critical of any concentration of power, and he refused to endorse the government's power to restrict freedom of speech. He did, however, uphold the Court's decision in *Schenck v. United States*, but with **Oliver Wendell Holmes** dissented in *Abrams v. United States*, both in 1919. Having written a seminal article on the "Right to Privacy" in 1890, Brandeis argued against the government's use of telephone tapping in *Olmstead v. United States* (1928). He argued for judicial restraint and placed considerable emphasis on the independence of the states, and in *Erie Railroad v. Tompkins* (1938) argued that federal courts had to be bound by the decisions of state supreme courts in state matters.

Outside of the courts, Brandeis was a leader of the American Zionist movement and helped to found the American Jewish Congress, the Palestine Endowment Fund, and the Palestine Cooperative Company.

BRECKINRIDGE, SOPHONISBA PRESTON (1866–1948). Born into a prominent Kentucky family, Sophonisba Breckinridge graduated from Wellesley College in 1888 and after teaching for a while began to study law. In 1894 Breckinridge was the first woman to pass the Kentucky bar examination. However, she then joined the Political Science Department at the University of Chicago, where in 1901 she received the first PhD in political science awarded to an American woman. Breckinridge taught at Chicago until her retirement in 1942 and was a close associate of **Edith Abbott**. She and Abbott founded the *Social Service Review* in 1927 and together the two **women** produced several books on social issues.

In addition to her academic career, Breckinridge served as a Chicago city health inspector, served as a probation officer with the Juvenile Court, and was a member of the executive committee of the Consumers' League, the Women's Trade Union League (WTUL), and the **National Association for the Advancement of Colored People** (NAACP). Breckinridge served on the commission investigating the **Chicago Race Riot** of 1919 and in a later essay blamed prejudice for bringing housing segregation. Breckinridge attended several international conferences on behalf of the U.S. State Department and in 1933 was the official representative at the first Pan-American Conference. In 1934 she was elected president of the American Association of Schools of Social Work.

See also SOCIAL WORK.

BROOKS, LOUISE (1906–1985). Born Mary Louise Brooks in Cherryvale, Kansas, the future **movie** actress began her professional career in 1921 as a dancer with the Denishawn Dancers in New York City. In 1924 she visited London briefly but returned to New York City and joined Florenz Ziegfeld's musical, *Louie the 14th*, and then joined Ziegfeld's *Follies* in 1925. Her first screen appearance was in Paramount Pictures' *Street of Forgotten Men* (1925). In both her private life and in movies, Brooks, like **Clara Bow**, became the personification of the "**flapper**." She was known for her beauty, sensuality, and her slick bobbed hairstyle, which earned her the nickname "the girl in the black helmet." She appeared in a considerable number of silent films, usually in the role of a flapper. They included *The American Venus* (1926), *A Social Celebrity* (1926), *The Show-Off* (1926), *Rolled Stock-*

ings (1927), *A Girl in Every Port* (1928), and *Beggars of Life* (1928). Following a dispute with Paramount, in 1928 Brooks went to Germany, where she starred in G. W. Pabst's *Der Erdgeist* (*The Earth Spirit*) and as the erotic figure of Lulu in *Die Büchse der Pandora* (*Pandora's Box*). After appearing in several more European films, Brooks returned to the United States and had minor roles in several films, the last being *Overland Stage Raiders* (1938). She subsequently established a dance studio in Wichita, Kansas, in the early 1940s and then returned to New York City, where she took part in several radio soap operas but also worked as a salesclerk. In the 1950s Brooks's early films were rediscovered, and she moved to Rochester, New York, where she wrote several journal articles on film and published her autobiography, *Lulu in Hollywood* (1982).

See also WOMEN.

BROOKS, VAN WYCK (1886–1963). The literary critic and cultural historian Van Wyck Brooks entered Harvard University in 1904, published his own poetry in 1905, edited the *Harvard Advocate* (1905), and graduated a year early. Following his graduation he spent two years in England and published *The Wine of the Puritans* on 1908. He returned to the United States in 1909 and taught at Stanford University from 1911 to 1913. After another spell in Britain and France, Brooks returned to America in 1914 and published *John Addington Symonds: A Biographical Study* (1914), *The World of H.G. Wells* (1915), and *America's Coming-of-Age* (1915). In the latter Brooks divided American culture into "highbrow" and "lowbrow," and his criticism of American materialism was to be evident in other writings. From 1916 to 1917 Brooks coedited and published *Seven Arts*, a liberal journal. He gained a national reputation when he published his essays in *Letters and Leadership* in 1918. His studies of *The Ordeal of Mark Twain* (1920) and *The Pilgrimage of Henry James* (1925) were regarded as controversial for their criticism of the two writers. In 1932 Brooks published *The Life of Emerson* and *Sketches in Criticism*. Between 1936 and 1952 he published his five-volume study, *Makers and Finders: A History of the Writer in America*. He continued to write works of criticism and a three-volume autobiography right up until his death.

See also LITERATURE AND THEATER.

BRYAN-CHAMORRO TREATY, 1914. A treaty between the United States and Nicaragua that granted the United States the exclusive right to the option to construct a canal in Nicaragua. The treaty also gave the United States the Great and Little Corn Islands on a ninety-nine-year lease in return for $3 million. Previously rejected by the Senate in 1912, it was accepted in 1914. U.S. troops had been sent to Nicaragua in 1912 and remained until 1924.

See also FOREIGN POLICY.

BRYAN, WILLIAM JENNINGS (1860–1925). Born and educated in Illinois, Bryan moved to Nebraska, where he was elected to Congress in 1890 as a **Democrat**. After two terms he campaigned for the nomination as U.S. senator on a platform of free silver, tariff reform, and income tax. Following his famous "Cross of Gold" speech at the Democratic Party convention in Chicago in 1896, Bryan became the leader of the rural Populist Party as well as the candidate for the Democratic Party. He was defeated by the **Republican** William McKinley. McKinley defeated him again in 1900, when he campaigned on a largely anti-imperialist ticket. He failed to win the Democratic nomination in 1904 but was renominated again in 1908, only to be defeated by **William Howard Taft**. In 1916 he supported the nomination of **Woodrow Wilson** and was rewarded with the appointment as secretary of state. Although a nationalist who expanded U.S. influence in Central America through the **Bryan-Chamorro Treaty**, 1914, he was steadfastly neutral with regard to the European nations involved in war. Fearing that Wilson's demand of "strict accountability" from Germany following the sinking of the *Lusitania* might lead to war, Bryan resigned in 1915.

Although his political influence quickly declined, he remained a voice of rural America and campaigned in support of the **Eighteenth Amendment** that introduced **prohibition**. He was an increasingly vocal supporter of anti-evolution laws and appeared for the prosecution against the teacher **John Scopes** in the famous trial in Dayton, Tennessee. Although Scopes was found guilty of breaking the law by teaching the theories of Charles Darwin, Bryan's defense of the literal interpretation of the Bible left him subject to ridicule and criticism from both scientists and defenders of academic freedom. He died five days after the trial had concluded.

BUDGET AND ACCOUNTING ACT. Passed in 1921, the act created the **General Accounting Office** and **Bureau of the Budget**. The act established the fiscal year running from 1 July to 30 June and required the president to send details of the executive budget to Congress and to recommend new taxes and expenditures.

BULLARD, WILLIAM HANNUM GRUBB (1866–1927). Bullard was a graduate of the U.S. Naval Academy (1907) who became superintendent of the Naval Radio Service in 1912 and director of naval communication from 1919 to 1921. He commanded the battleship *Arkansas* during the war and commanded the Yangtze patrol of the American Asiatic fleet from 1921 until his retirement the following year. He was a founder of the Radio Corporation of America (RCA) and chair of the U.S. Radio Commission.

BULLITT, WILLIAM CHRISTIAN (1891–1967). Bullitt began work as a writer on the Philadelphia *Public Ledger* (1915–17) but joined the State Department in 1917. In 1919 he was sent to Moscow to report on the Bolshevik government and he recommended recognition of the Soviet regime. When this was rejected he became disaffected and spoke against acceptance of the **Versailles Treaty**. He was recalled from relative obscurity and appointed ambassador to the Union of Soviet Socialist Republics (USSR) from 1933 to 1936, and to France from 1936 to 1941. He became a special assistant to the secretary of the navy in 1942, but left to serve as an officer in the Free French Army, 1944 to 1945.
See also FOREIGN POLICY.

BURCHFIELD, CHARLES EPHRAIM (1893–1967). Born in Ohio, Charles Burchfield trained at the Cleveland School of Art and after graduating in 1916 briefly attended the New York Academy of Design. He served in the Army from 1918 to 1919 and then returned to Salem, Ohio. In 1912 he was employed as a wallpaper designer for a company in Buffalo, New York, a job he held until 1928. The focus of much of his painting in the 1920s was on towns and cities, as evident in *Old Tavern at Hammondsville* (1926–1928), *Rainy Night* (1928–1930), and the later *Black Iron* (1935). While most of his work was in water colors, Burchfield did do some work in oil including his *November Evening* (1931–1934). Later he produced works of fantasy such as *The Sphinx and the Milky Way* (1946) and toward the end of his career *Orion in Winter* (1962), but Burchfield is remembered for his often romantic, sometimes fantastic, depiction of nature and the urban landscape as "a recorder of the **American Scene**."
See also ART.

BUREAU OF THE BUDGET. Established in 1921 under the **Budget and Accounting Act**, the Bureau was headed by the director of the budget with the primary function of preparing the annual executive budget. It was also responsible for the supervision of the administrative management of executive agencies, the improvement of federal statistical services, and the promotion of economic and efficient government running.
See also ECONOMY.

BURLESON, ALBERT SIDNEY (1863–1937). After an education at Texas Agricultural and Mechanical College, Baylor University, and the Law Department of the University of Texas, Austin, Albert Burleson practiced law in Austin. From 1885 to 1898 he served as assistant attorney general in Austin and then attorney general for the Twenty-sixth District. In 1898 Burleson was elected as **Democratic** congressman and served until 1913. His support for **Woodrow Wilson** and the backing of **Edward House** led to Burleson's appointment as postmaster general in 1913. Burleson's management of the U.S. Post Office was generally conservative. He introduced the segregation of black and white workers, opposed postal workers' unions, and refused mailing rights to publications he judged to be critical of American involvement in the war. Burleson also attempted to make the Post Office self-sustaining by cutting back on the rural mail service, which he regarded as too expensive. When Congress refused to accept this, he attracted considerable criticism when he altered many carriers' routes and effectively eliminated others. His high-handed management of the U.S. Telegraph and Telephone Administration created during the war also added to his lack of popularity. However, Burleson did establish the airmail service and the parcel post system. In 1920 he returned to Austin and concentrated on his ranching and **banking** interests.

BURNS, WILLIAM JOHN (1861–1932). William Burns began work as a detective in Columbus, Ohio. In 1889 he joined the U.S. Secret Service. He established the William J. Burns Detective Agency with his son in New York City in 1909, and the agency soon became a national body. He was involved in the investigations that led to the conviction of John and James McNamara for the bombing of the *Los Angeles Times* office in 1910, and in the cases of municipal corruption in Atlantic City and Detroit. In the trial of **Leo Frank** in 1914, Burns presented strong evidence of Frank's innocence. In 1921 Attorney General **Harry S. Daugherty** appointed him as chief of the **Federal Bureau of Investigation**, a position he held until 1924. He then returned to his private practice. During the trial of one of his clients, the oil producer **Harry F. Sinclair**, in 1927–1928, Burns was convicted of "shadowing" the jury and sentenced to jail for contempt. He was, however, released because no deliberate act was proven on his part.
    See also CRIME AND POLICING.

BURROUGHS, EDGAR RICE (1875–1950). Burroughs was the author who created the fictional character of Tarzan. He served in the army attached to the Seventh Cavalry in the 1890s, had a stint as a cattleman, worked for his father, and then held a variety of different jobs including gold mining, janitor, door-to-door salesman, and seller of pencil sharpeners. He published his first short story, a science fiction tale, in *All-Story*, a pulp fiction magazine in 1912. Burroughs's first Tarzan story was published later that year, and *Tarzan and the Apes* appeared in book form in 1914. It was a national best seller and was followed by a total of twenty-five more Tarzan novels. The first **movie** version of *Tarzan and the Apes* appeared in 1918 and was one of the first half-dozen films to gross more than $1 million. Tarzan films continued to be made right through into the 1990s. The Tarzan stories were turned into radio shows in the late 1920s and were also syndicated in comic strip form in daily and Sunday newspapers beginning in 1931. A Tarzan television series began in 1966. In addition Burroughs wrote over twenty space novels, several Westerns and historical romances, and a number of social satires. During World War II he served as a war correspondent.

See also LITERATURE AND THEATER.

BUTLER, NICHOLAS MURRAY (1862–1947). Nicholas Butler graduated from Columbia University in 1882 and went on to gain his MA in 1883 and PhD in 1884. After a year in Europe, Butler returned to Columbia as a teacher in 1885. His essays on educational methodology were published as *The Meaning of Education* in 1915. In 1887 Butler became president of the Industrial **Education** society of New York and established the teachers college the same year. The college was affiliated with Columbia in 1890, and Butler became professor of philosophy and education. He established the journal *Educational Review* in 1891 and edited it until 1919.

Butler was involved in New York politics in matters relating to public education and was president of the National Education Association, 1894–1895. In 1902 Butler became president of Columbia. Under his leadership for forty-six years, the university grew in size and renown. He insisted the university be run along business lines but insisted too that donors would not affect the university's independence. Butler was active in **Republican** politics and was an adviser to successive presidents, and was offered a number of political posts but declined them all. In 1925 he became president of the Carnegie Endowment for Peace and held the position until 1945. He was a sponsor of the **Kellogg-Briand Treaty** in 1929 and was awarded the Nobel Peace Prize in 1931 with **Jane Addams**.

BUTLER, PIERCE (1866–1939). Pierce Butler was admitted to the Minnesota bar in 1888. He was briefly assistant county attorney and was elected county attorney in 1892 and 1894. In 1908 he was chosen as president of the Minnesota State Bar Association. A **Democrat**, Butler narrowly lost election to the state senate in 1906 but continued to advise state governors. As a member of the Board of Regents of the University of Minnesota during **World War I**, Butler supported the dismissal of professors who expressed pacifist or radical opinions. In 1922 president **Warren Harding** nominated him to the U.S. **Supreme Court**, and he served until 1939. He was generally conservative and opposed any expansion of the power of the federal government and voted against the majority of **New Deal** measures. Butler was also conservative on issues of civil liberties and **civil rights** and he opposed the rejection of the conviction of the **Scottsboro boys** in 1932.

BYRD, RICHARD EVELYN (1888–1957). Richard Byrd gained his commission from the U.S. Naval Academy, Annapolis, in 1912. He learned to fly during **World War I** and pioneered nighttime and sea flight navigation. In 1918 he became commander of the U.S. air forces in Canada. In 1915 Byrd took part in an expedition to Greenland, directing the aviation unit. In 1926 he and pilot Floyd Bennett became the first people to fly over the North Pole, although Byrd's diary caused some later writers to question whether they had in fact reached the Pole. Both men were awarded the Medal of Honor. Byrd led the first American expedition to the Antarctic since 1840 between 1928 and 1930. Together with pilot Bernt Balchen, Byrd became the first person to fly over the South Pole in 1929. He was appointed rear admiral in 1930 and took part in two further expeditions to the Antarctic, in 1933–1935 and 1939–1941. The latter was an official U.S. expedition. After World War II Byrd was involved in two further expeditions in 1946 and 1955. He wrote two books about his experiences, *Skyward* (1928) and *Little America* (1930).

See also AVIATION.

C

CALLOWAY, "CAB" (CABELL) (1907–1994). The **African American** entertainer Cab Calloway began his professional career in vaudeville in Baltimore from 1924 on. He also played basketball in the black professional basketball league for the Baltimore Athenians. In 1927 Calloway joined the *Plantation Days Revue* and traveled to Chicago, where he sang in the Dreamland Café with **Louis Armstrong**'s band. After a brief and unsuccessful tour to New York in 1929 Calloway obtained a part in Connie's *Hot Chocolates*, a successful Broadway revue that also went to Boston and Philadelphia. He returned to New York in 1930 and made his first recordings with his orchestra, including "St. Louis Blues," "Some of These Days," and "St. James Infirmary." In 1931 Calloway and his band moved to the Cotton Club in Harlem, the black area of New York City, where they alternated with **Duke Ellington**'s orchestra. Calloway performed there regularly until 1936, when the Cotton Club moved from Harlem. Calloway performed at the new location until 1940.

Radio broadcasts from the Cotton Club made Calloway a national star, renowned for his singing and "jive" talk. Having already achieved recording success, in 1931 Calloway had an enormous hit with his first of several versions of "Minnie the Moocher." Calloway's scat singing made him the "King of Hi-de-ho" and provided the inspiration for **George Gershwin**'s character Sportin' Life in *Porgy and Bess* (1935). A number of Calloway's performances figured in cartoons starring Betty Boop in the 1930s, and he made several short films, *Cab Calloway's Jitterbug Party* (1935), *Hi De Ho* (1937), and *Manhattan Merry-go-round* (1937). In addition Calloway also published a *Hepsters Dictionary* in 1938, and the sixth edition, *The New Cab Calloway's Hepsters Dictionary: Language of Jive* (1944), sold over 1 million copies. In 1941 Calloway's band played in the **movie** *Roadshow*, and in 1943 Calloway costarred with Lena Horne in *Stormy Weather*. He continued to perform on stage and in film through to the 1980s. In addition to roles in *The Blues Brothers* (1980) and *The Cotton Club* (1984), Calloway also made regular appearances on the children's television show *Sesame Street*. In 1989 he appeared with Janet Jackson in her music video "Alright." Calloway's career as a performer and bandleader places him among the great showmen of the twentieth century.

See also HARLEM RENAISSANCE, c. 1920–c. 1933; JAZZ; MUSIC AND DANCE.

CANNON, JOSEPH GURNEY (1836–1926). After qualifying as a lawyer in North Carolina, Cannon moved to Illinois to practice law. He was elected to the House of Representatives (1873–1891, 1893–1913, and 1915–1923). He became leader of the "Old Guard" (conservative) **Republicans**, and as speaker he used his power to appoint legislative committees in a dictatorial manner until the speaker's powers were restricted in 1910 by **progressive** Republicans and **Democrats**. Cannon continued to serve in the House until his retirement at the age of eighty-seven in 1923. Cannon's forty-six-year-long tenure in Congress was the longest of any member before World War II.

CANTOR, EDDIE (1892–1964). The singer and actor Eddie Cantor was born Israel Iskowitz in New York City. He later changed his name when he began performing as a comedian and singer in music hall in 1907. Cantor played in a number of musicals and revues in London, New York, and Los Angeles between 1911 and 1916. He made a successful appearance in the *Ziegfeld Follies* in 1917, 1918, and 1919. He also led the strike that established the Actor's Equity Association and later he was to become president of the Screen Actors' Guild, the American Federation of Radio Artists, and the American Guild of Variety Artists. Cantor continued to appear in musical reviews in the early 1920s, and he achieved a major success in one of the decade's longest-running Broadway musicals, *Kid Boots*. He appeared in a silent film version of this in 1926 and in *Special Delivery* in 1927.

Cantor returned as the central performer in the *Ziegfeld Follies* in 1927, followed by *Whoopee*, which opened in 1928. Despite losing his personal fortune in the **Wall Street Crash**, Cantor achieved greater success in the 1930s and was a leading star in film and **radio**. From 1931 to 1934 he starred in the radio *Chase and Sanborn Hour*, and with other sponsors through to 1940. He made several **movies** with **Samuel Goldwyn** including *Palmy Days* (1931), *The Kid from Spain* (1932), and *Roman Scandals* (1933). During World War II Cantor performed for wounded GIs in hospitals and also continued making movies—*Thank Your Lucky Stars* (1943), *Show Business* (1944), and *If You Knew Susie* (1948). He recorded the soundtrack to the *Eddie Cantor Story* in 1953, and appeared on television programs including *The Eddie Cantor Comedy Theater*. He retired due to ill health in 1957. One of the first stars to succeed in stage, film, and radio, Cantor was also active in social causes, among them the March of Dimes established to fight polio. In 1964 president Lyndon Johnson awarded Cantor the Medal of Freedom in recognition of his achievements.

See also MUSIC AND DANCE.

CAPONE, AL (ALPHONSE) (1899–1947). Al Capone, the man who achieved fame as a gangster during the 1920s, was born in Brooklyn, where he grew up among the street gangs. In 1917 he was scarred in a knife fight and earned the nickname "Scarface." Capone moved to Chicago around 1920 to work with John Torrio, who had taken over leadership of organized crime in the city. With the onset of **Prohibition** the sale and distribution of **bootleg liquor** provided new opportunities for criminal activity. In 1924 Capone organized gunmen to determine the election in Cicero, just west of Chicago. In 1925 Capone took over the Torrio operation and rose to fame through a number of acts of violence. An assistant state attorney was assassinated in 1926, bombings occurred to influence the election of Mayor **William Thompson**'s candidates in 1928, and in 1929 Capone's rivals were eliminated in the St. Valentine's Day massacre. In 1927 Capone was forced to move out of Chicago by police pressure, and he established a base in Florida. He was arrested in 1929 and jailed for a year for carrying a concealed weapon. Released in 1930, Capone was indicted for income tax fraud in 1931. Found guilty, he was sentenced to eleven years in prison. Diagnosed with fatal syphilis of the brain, Capone was released from Alcatraz in 1939 and retired to his home.

See also CRIME AND POLICING.

CAPPER, ARTHUR (1865–1951). Arthur Capper was the first native-born Kansan to serve his state as governor and U.S. senator. Capper began his career as a journalist and newspaper owner. A **Republican**, Capper narrowly failed to win the gubernatorial election in 1912 but won it in 1914 and was reelected in 1916. In 1918 Capper was elected to the U.S. Senate, where he served until 1949. He voted for the **League of Nations** with reservations but tended to be isolationist until World War II. Capper was a leader of the **Farm Bloc** and supported measures to aid farm cooperatives. During the Depression Capper supported many of the **New Deal** reforms.

CARAWAY, HATTIE OPHELIA WYATT (1878–1950). Hattie Caraway graduated from Dickson Normal College in Tennessee in 1896. She married Thaddeus Caraway in 1902, and they settled in Arkansas, where she raised three children. Thaddeus Caraway served first in the U.S. House of Representatives from 1912 and then in the U.S. Senate from 1921. When he died in 1931, Hattie Caraway was appointed to fill his vacant seat. She then became the first woman ever elected to the Senate when, supported by the Arkansas **Democratic** Party, she won a special election. In 1932 Hattie Caraway defeated six challengers in the Democratic primary and was reelected in her own right in 1932. Caraway won election again in 1938 and went on to become the first **woman** to preside over the Senate, first to conduct a Senate committee hearing, first to chair a committee, and first senior senator. She cosponsored the Equal Rights Amendment in 1943. She was defeated in the Democratic primary in 1944 by J. William Fulbright, who went on to win her seat. Caraway subsequently served on the Employees' Compensation Commission and Employees' Compensation Appeals Board.

CARDOZO, BENJAMIN NATHAN (1870–1938). After graduating from Columbia Law School in 1889 and practicing law in New York City, Cardozo served as a justice of the Supreme Court of New York from 1913 to 1914, when he moved to the New York court of appeals. In 1932 President **Hoover** appointed him to the **Supreme Court** to succeed **Oliver Wendell Holmes**. Cardozo demonstrated a liberal inclination in generally supporting **New Deal** legislation and arguing strongly in favor of sociological jurisprudence. Cardozo was also active in a number of Jewish organizations.

CATHER, WILLA SILBERT (1876–1947). The novelist Willa Cather was born in Virginia but brought up in Nebraska. After graduating from the University of Nebraska (1895) she became a staff writer for the Pittsburgh *Daily Leader* (1898–1901) and then associate editor of *McClure's Magazine* (1906–1912). She began publishing poetry and short stories, and her first novel, *Alexander's Bridge*, appeared in 1912. She became established with *O Pioneers!* (1913) and then the classic *My Antonia* (1918), both of which focused on the role of immigrants, particularly **women**, in the West. Her novel about **World War I**, *One of Ours* (1922), was awarded the Pulitzer Prize, and she continued to produce novels through the 1920s, including *A Lost Lady* (1923) and *Death Comes for the Archbishop* (1927). Several more novels and collections of Cather's stories appeared in the 1930s. She is widely regarded as one of the leading American writers of the twentieth century.
See also LITERATURE AND THEATER.

CATT, CARRIE CLINTON CHAPMAN (1859–1947). Educated at Iowa State Agricultural College, the **women's suffrage** leader, formerly a schoolteacher and principal, Carrie Catt became an organizer and campaigner for the Iowa Woman Suffrage Association in 1890 and for the **National American Woman Suffrage Association** (NAWSA) from 1892. She was president of NAWSA from 1900 to 1904 and again from 1915 till her death, leading the campaign that resulted in women gaining the vote with the **Nineteenth Amendment** in 1920. Catt also founded the International Woman Suffrage Alliance (IWSA) in 1902 and was also president of the organization from 1904 to 1923. Following the passage of the amendment Catt participated in forming the **League of Women Voters**. She was a supporter of the **League of Nations** and was head of the National Committee on the Cause and Cure of War from 1925 to 1932. Catt continued to support the committee until it ended in 1941.

CENTRAL POWERS. Originally a term used to describe Germany, Austria-Hungary, and Italy following the Triple Alliance of 1882, the name was given to the group of nations that opposed the **Allied Powers** during **World War I**, comprising Germany, Austria-Hungary, Turkey, and Bulgaria. The alliance disintegrated as each nation sought an armistice in 1918.
See also FOREIGN POLICY.

CENTRALIA "MASSACRE," 1919. Following a background of conflict and previous attacks on their union building, on 11 November 1919 members of the **Industrial Workers of the World (IWW)** fired on veterans taking part in the **American Legion** parade celebrating the anniversary of **Armistice** Day in Centralia, Washington, killing four of the Legionnaires. Several members of the IWW were arrested and held in jail. Later that same night a mob broke into the jail and seized one of the union members, Wesley Everest, and lynched him from a nearby bridge. He had been shot several times, and it was rumored he had been castrated. In the subsequent trial seven members of the IWW were convicted of second-degree murder and sentenced to fifteen to twenty-five years in prison. All but one had been released by 1932. No one was convicted for the murder of Everest.
See also RED SCARE, 1919.

CERMAK, ANTON JOSEPH (1873–1933). Born in Austria-Hungary (now the Czech Republic), Anton Cermak came to the United States with his family in 1874. After working in the coal mines Cermak began a hauling business in Chicago. He joined the **Democratic Party** and rose from precinct captain to win a seat in the Illinois state legislature in 1902. In 1909 he became a Chicago City alderman and then bailiff of the municipal court before returning to the city council once more in 1919. In 1922 Cermak was elected to the Cook County Board of Commissioners, and he was soon the leader of the Chicago Democratic machine. In 1931 Cermak defeated the **Republican** incumbent, **Bill Thompson**, to become mayor. In February 1933 he traveled to Miami to meet president-elect **Franklin D. Roosevelt**.

On 15 February Cermak was seriously wounded when **Giuseppe Zangara** fired several shots intended for Roosevelt. Cermak died on 8 March, and Zangara was executed thirteen days later.

CHAMBERLAIN, GEORGE EARLE (1854–1928). Admitted to the bar in Oregon (1878), Chamberlain served in the state legislature as a **Democrat**, 1880–1882, and was attorney general of Oregon, 1891–1894, and governor of Oregon, 1902–1909. He was U.S. senator from 1909 to 1921, where he chaired the Public Lands Committee. As chair of the Military Affairs Committee from 1913 to 1921, Chamberlain was responsible for such legislation as selective service, food controls, and war finances. He was appointed to the U.S. Shipping Board in 1920.

CHANEY, LON (1883–1930). Born Leonidas, Lon Chaney dropped out of school and began work in the theater in 1895. He joined a vaudeville group and moved to California, where he began his film career in slapstick comedies in 1913. In 1915 Chaney joined the Universal film company and made numerous **movies** with them before moving to Paramount in 1919. Chaney made a name for himself by using contortion and makeup in films such as *The Miracle Man* (1919), in which he played a frog; *The Hunchback of Notre Dame* (1923) as Quasimodo; the phantom in *The Phantom of the Opera* (1925); and the lead role in *Mr. Wu* (1927). Altogether Chaney made over 150 films and earned the name "The Man of a Thousand Faces." His son was also successful as an actor under the name Lon Chaney Jr.

CHAPLIN, CHARLES (SPENCER) (1889–1977). One of the greatest performers in silent **movies**, Charlie Chaplin was born in London, England, where he performed in music halls and plays in his early teens. In 1913 while on tour in America Chaplin signed a contract with **Mack Sennett** at the Keystone film studios. He first appeared in a motion picture in 1914 and he made thirty-five films with Keystone and then fourteen with Essanay before moving to the Mutual Film Corporation in 1916. He quickly established his film persona in movies such as *The Tramp* (1915), *The Vagabond* (1917), and *The Immigrant* (1917). As the little tramp with his distinctive walk, little mustache, bowler hat, and large shoes, Chaplin effectively combined slapstick with pathos. By 1917 he was a huge star and had signed a $1 million contract with the First National Exhibitors' Circuit to make eight films. In 1919 Chaplin joined with **Mary Pickford**, **Douglas Fairbanks**, and **D. W. Griffith** to establish United Artists to produce their own films.

Chaplin scored critical and box office successes with *The Kid* (1921) and *The Gold Rush* (1925). His first sound film was *City Lights* (1931), which had a musical score but no dialogue. Chaplin turned to social comment in the

1930s, firstly again without dialogue in *Modern Times* (1936), and in his first real dialogue film, *The Great Dictator* (1940), in which Chaplin parodied Hitler. During the 1940s Chaplin's reputation was damaged by revelations concerning his personal life and charges of immorality. His marriage to the eighteen-year-old Oona O'Neill in 1943 further tarnished his name. Chaplin's support for the Soviet Union during and immediately after World War II also led to criticism from conservative groups. His next two films, *Monsieur Verdoux* (1947) and *Limelight* (1952), did badly. In 1952 Chaplin, still a resident alien, applied for a reentry permit to the United States prior to a visit to Europe. Shortly after he had set sail his permit was revoked, and it was announced that he would not be readmitted before he answered questions about his political views and moral behavior. Chaplin then took up permanent residence in Switzerland. Subsequently he made only two more films. He visited the United States again in 1972 and was granted a special Oscar for his contribution to film. Queen Elizabeth II knighted him in 1975.

CHARLESTON. The Charleston became a popular dance of the 1920s following its inclusion in the *Ziegfeld Follies* in 1923. It was associated with the new spirit of the "Jazz Age" and the liberated **women** known as "**flappers**."
   See also MUSIC AND DANCE.

CHATEAU-THIERRY. Chateau-Thierry was a French town about forty miles east of Paris where troops of the **American Expeditionary Force** (AEF) first played a significant part in **World War I** in June 1918. In helping to push back the German offensive on the Marne here and the nearby **Belleau Wood**, the American forces gave the **Allies** an enormous military and psychological boost.

CHEVROLET, LOUIS (1878–1841). The racing driver and **automobile** designer Louis Chevrolet was born in Switzerland. His family moved to France in 1884, and Chevrolet began work there as a mechanic. In 1900 he was sent to Canada to work, and shortly after he moved to New York to work for another French car dealership. Chevrolet began racing cars in 1905 and by 1907 was regarded as one of the best drivers in the world. He joined the Buick Motor Car Company under **William Durant** that year. Durant later asked Chevrolet to design a mass-produced car with his six-cylinder engine, and the Chevrolet Motor Company was established in Detroit in 1910. Differences over the decision to switch production from high-performance cars to cheaper, mass-produced vehicles led Chevrolet to sell his interests in the company in 1915. He and his brother, Arthur, established their own Frontenac Motor Company in 1916 and continued their career in motor racing. While the Chevrolets continued their success on the racing track, their business ventures were less successful. In 1928 Glenn Martin helped them to establish the Chevrolet Aircraft Corporation, but the company was a failure. By 1933 Louis Chevrolet had liquidated all of his investments, and he was forced to find work as a mechanic in the Chevrolet Division of General Motors in Detroit until ill health forced his retirement in 1938.

CHICAGO RACE RIOT, 1919. On 27 July 1919 a black youth swimming at the Chicago lakeside drowned after being stoned for crossing into a white area. When police failed to arrest the perpetrator scuffles broke out between black and white onlookers. The violence spread and developed into a full riot lasting five days in which white crowds stopped streetcars and pulled off black passengers and beat them. Other black workers were pursued and beaten or stoned to death. A total of twenty-three **African Americans** and fifteen whites died, and more than three hundred were injured in the violence in the worst riot of the "**Red Summer**." The Chicago riot had been preceded by friction over housing and jobs following the influx of thousands of African Americans who had moved north in the "**Great Migration**" to find work in war industries. Between 1917 and 1919 more than twenty-four bombings of black homes occurred, and there was a history of considerable conflict in the workplace, particularly between unionized white labor and nonunion black workers. An unstable political situation also added to the wartime tensions.

CHICAGO WHITE SOX. *See* WORLD SERIES, 1919. *See also* SPORTS.

CHILD LABOR. The employment of children in industrial, mining, and **agricultural** occupations was widespread in late-nineteenth- to early-twentieth-century America. In 1900 it was estimated that 1.7 million children, 20 percent of all those under the age of sixteen, were in employment. By 1930 the figure was less than 5 percent, although attempts to get a federal child labor law on the statute books had twice failed to meet the **Supreme Court**'s objections. This was finally accomplished with the Fair Labor Standards Act in 1938.
   See also ECONOMY.

CHILD LABOR LAWS. One of the major concerns of prewar **progressives** was to limit the employment of children. Although almost all states had introduced some legislation to control **child labor** by 1914, there were many variations and loopholes. The first federal child labor law, the Keating-Owen Act, was passed in 1916. It prohibited the shipping across state lines of products made in factories which employed children under fourteen years of age, or mines which employed children under sixteen, or any producer which employed children at night or for more than eight hours. The law was declared unconstitutional by the **Supreme Court** in *Hammer v. Dagenhart* on the grounds that regulation of interstate commerce could not be applied to conditions of labor. A **second child labor law** passed in 1919, imposing a 10 percent tax on the products of factories or mines employing children, but this too was declared unconstitutional in 1922 in *Bailey v. Drexel Furniture Co.* A child labor amendment was introduced following this decision and passed both houses of Congress in 1924 but failed to win ratification in the states. Child labor was not effectively prohibited until **New Deal** legislation in the 1930s.

CHILDREN'S BUREAU. Established in 1912 as an agency of the **Department of Labor**, the Children's Bureau was to investigate and report on problems of child welfare. Its first head was **Julia Lathrop**.

CHRYSLER, WALTER PERRY (1875–1940). The influential **automobile** manufacturer Walter Chrysler began work as a mechanical engineer in the railroad industry in the 1890s. He constantly moved to new positions—from general foreman with the Colorado & Southern Railroad in 1902, master mechanic with Fort Worth & Denver City Railroad in 1903, supervisor with Chicago Great Western Railroad in 1905, and works manager of the American Locomotive Company, Allegheny in 1910. In 1912 Chrysler took over the management of the Buick Motor Company in Flint, Michigan, as part of General Motors. Chrysler introduced a considerable number of innovations and created new production processes at the plant, making it one of the most efficient of its day. Chrysler stayed with the company when **William C. Durant** regained control in 1916 but resigned in 1919 after disagreements about construction projects.

In 1920 Chrysler became executive vice president of the Willys-Overland truck manufacturer, a position he held until the company was liquidated in 1921. In 1923 Chrysler became president of the reorganized Maxwell Motor Company, and in 1924 Maxwell produced the successful Chrysler Six automobile. The Maxwell Company was renamed "Chrysler" in 1925. By 1928, when Chrysler incorporated the Dodge Motor Company and developed the Plymouth motor car, it was the third largest motor manufacturer in the United States. The company also built the seventy-seven-story Chrysler Building in New York City in 1930. Despite the **Depression** the Chrysler Company became the second largest car company ahead of **Ford** in the mid-1930s when Walter Chrysler handed over the presidency to K. T. Keller.

See also TRANSPORTATION.

CIVIL RIGHTS. *See* AFRICAN AMERICANS.

CLARK MEMORANDUM. A statement of **foreign policy** prepared in December 1928 following president-elect **Herbert Hoover**'s visit to Latin America, released by undersecretary of state J. Reuben Clark in 1930. The memorandum declared the 1904 Roosevelt Corollary to the Monroe Doctrine invalid and that the United States did not have the right to intervene in the affairs of Latin American countries. This statement was written into the Declaration of the Montevideo Conference in 1933 and formally ratified by the Senate in 1934.

CLARKE, JOHN HESSIN (1857–1945). John Clarke graduated from Ohio Western Reserve College in 1877 and qualified in law in 1878. He practiced law and became part owner of a Democratic newspaper, the Youngstown *Vindicator*, but eventually became partner in a leading Cleveland law firm. Clarke failed to win election to the U.S. Senate in 1904 and failed to gain the **Democratic Party**'s nomination for the seat in 1916. **Woodrow Wilson** nominated him for a federal judgeship that year, and shortly after he replaced **Charles Evans Hughes** on the **Supreme Court**. Clarke concentrated his work on patent and antitrust law and took a liberal position in enforcing the Sherman Antitrust Act. He supported **child labor laws** in dissenting decisions in *Hammer v. Dagenhart* (1918) and *Bailey v. Drexel Furniture Co.* (1922). However, he wrote the majority opinion that upheld the convictions of the six Russians in *Abrams v. United States* (1919). He resigned from the court in 1922 and became a leading advocate of U.S. entry to the **League of Nations** and **Permanent Court of International Justice**.

CLAYTON ANTITRUST ACT, 1914. Legislation introduced by Henry De Lamar Clayton, the **Democratic** chair of the House Judiciary Committee in 1914. The act was a supplement to the 1890 Sherman Antitrust Act, and it was an attempt to exempt organized labor from the restrictions of the Sherman Act on the grounds that it was not an item of commerce. Regarded as "Labor's Magna Carta," many mistakenly believed the Clayton Act would allow peaceful strikes and boycotts without the threat of injunctions. The law also forbade interlocking directorates in the same industry and ruled that corporation officers could be held personally liable for violations of the antitrust laws.

See also TRADE UNIONS.

COBB, TYRUS RAYMOND (1886–1961). The baseball player and manager Ty Cobb grew up in Georgia. He left home in 1904 to become a professional baseball player. In 1905 he was the South Atlantic League's outstanding player, and the Detroit Tigers of the American League signed him that year. In 1907 Cobb became the league's outstanding performer, leading in batting average, base hits, runs batted in, and stolen bases. The Tigers won three consecutive pennants with Cobb (known as the "Georgia Peach"), and he was probably the best-known player at the time. From 1919 on, however, the big-hitting **Babe Ruth** challenged Cobb's domination.

From 1922 until 1926 Cobb also managed the Detroit team. He resigned following accusations that in 1919 he and others had been involved in fixing games. The baseball commissioner Kenesaw Mountain Landis subsequently exonerated Cobb, and he signed as a player with the Philadelphia Athletics. Cobb played successfully for two seasons before he retired, having made his fortune in the game and through shrewd investments. He was the first man elected to the National Baseball Hall of Fame when it opened in Coopers-town, New York, in 1939.

See also SPORTS.

COFFIN, CHARLES ALBERT (1844–1926). Charles Coffin began a shoe manufacturing company in Lynn, Massachusetts, in the 1870s and as part of a syndicate purchased the American Electric Company of Connecticut in 1883. In 1892 the company consolidated with Edison General of New York and took the name of General Electric with Coffin as president. From 1913 to 1922 Coffin was chair of the board of directors, and he contributed to the expansion that made General Electric Company into one of the major companies in the country. During **World War I** Coffin established the War Relief Clearing House in 1915, later taken over by the Red Cross. His war work was recognized by a number of foreign awards including the French Legion of Honor.

COLUMBUS, NEW MEXICO. In 1916 the Mexican bandit **Francisco "Pancho" Villa** attacked Columbus. Nineteen Americans were killed, and the town was set on fire. As a consequence the U.S. Army pursued Villa in a **punitive expedition** into **Mexico** that almost brought the two countries to war.

See also FOREIGN POLICY.

COMMERCE, DEPARTMENT OF. *See* DEPARTMENT OF COMMERCE.

COMMITTEE OF FORTY-EIGHT. In 1919 **Amos Pinchot** established a committee across the forty-eight states to unite **Progressives** and to ensure their election to Congress. However, the committee failed to agree upon candidates or establish the hoped for unity with representatives of labor at the two conventions held in 1919 and 1920. It was succeeded in 1922 by the **Conference for Progressive Political Action.**

COMMITTEE ON PUBLIC INFORMATION (CPI). The Committee on Public Information was established on 13 April 1917 to mobilize public opinion in support of the American war effort and to carry out a program of propaganda abroad to win over neutrals and undermine the morale of the enemy during **World War I**. The committee, which became one of the most important of wartime agencies, consisted of the secretaries of war, navy, and state departments but was dominated by its civilian chairman, **George Creel**. Initially the CPI's main function was to act as a conduit for news stories for the press and to provide information through an *Official Bulletin*. However, in the face of criticism from the press and Congress, and as censorship was increasingly handled by the postmaster general's office or Censorship Board, the CPI concentrated more on selling the war.

Drawing on the participation of well-known writers, journalists, academics, artists, actors, and other celebrities, the CPI bombarded the country with over 100 million pieces of literature in the form of pamphlets, leaflets, and posters. It made films and enlisted movie stars such as **Douglas Fairbanks Jr.**, **Charlie Chaplin**, and **Mary Pickford** to help to "sell" the war and outline America's war aims. Over seventy-five thousand volunteer "Four Minute Men" were used to address theater and movie audiences on themes indicated by the CPI. At the time the CPI was often criticized for acting as an agency of **Woodrow Wilson**'s administration and for limiting free expression. After the war it became increasingly associated with the mood of war hysteria and "100 percent Americanism" that had swept the nation in a wave of intolerance.

COMMUNICATIONS ACT, 1927. *See* FEDERAL RADIO COMMISSION (FRC).

COMMUNIST PARTY USA (CPUSA). Communism was established in America in 1919 with the creation of the Communist and Communist Labor Parties which had been formed by elements of the **Socialist Party** and others, following the 1917 Bolshevik revolution and the launching of the Third International or Comintern in March 1919. The two groups merged in 1921 and shortly after assumed the title of Workers' Party of America. In 1928 it was renamed again as the Communist Party. The party always remained a minority party with a large foreign-language and immigrant membership. Its greatest electoral support came during the Depression when it secured 102,991 votes in the 1932 presidential election. It did not field presidential candidates after 1940 but resumed again in 1968. Its support continued to be insignificant.

See also FLYNN, ELIZABETH GURLEY (1890–1964); FOSTER, WILLIAM Z. (1881–1961); POLITICAL PARTIES; SCOTTSBORO BOYS; SOCIALIST LABOR PARTY (SLP).

CONFERENCE FOR PROGRESSIVE POLITICAL ACTION, 1922. Following World War I, **Robert M. La Follette** organized a loose alliance of **progressive** groups, including the **Nonpartisan League**, the **Farmer-Labor party**, and a number of labor organizations including the sixteen railroad brotherhoods to try to ensure the election of progressives to Congress and promote liberal legislation. At a national convention in Cleveland, 4–6 July 1924, the group nominated La Follette as presidential candidate with **Burton K. Wheeler** as his running mate under the banner of the **Progressive Party**. The party polled nearly 5 million votes, 17 percent of the votes cast. The party carried only the state of Wisconsin. The Progressive Party faded away thereafter, and many supporters voted for **Herbert Hoover** in 1928.

See also COMMITTEE OF FORTY-EIGHT.

CONGRESSIONAL UNION. A militant **women's suffrage** organization formed in 1913 by **Alice Paul** and **Lucy Burns**, and forerunner of the **National Woman's Party**.

CONSCIENTIOUS OBJECTORS. When **Selective Service** was introduced in the United States in 1917 the act provided for the right to conscientious objection for those members of "well-recognized religious sects or organizations whose creed forbids participation." In December 1917 secretary of war **Newton Baker** extended this to include those who objected on grounds of "moral scruple." However, those exempted from armed service were expected to accept noncombatant duties and to join other servicemen at military camps, subject to military discipline and the "persuasion" of the other men in the camps. Out of 20 million men who were registered for military service 65,000 claimed conscientious objector status and 20,813 were inducted. Of these, 16,000 gave up their claims at the camps, 1,300 accepted noncombatant roles, 1,200 were furloughed out to farms, and 99 assisted with Quaker relief. Only 1,390 "absolutists" refused to accept any form of war-related service and faced courts-martial. By the time the war had ended five hundred had been tried. Of these, 17 were sentenced to death, 142 to life imprisonment, and the rest to terms from 10 to 99 years. All death sentences were commuted, and most of those jailed were released shortly after the **Armistice**. Some, however, experienced very harsh treatment in prison and several died during their incarceration.

See also AMERICAN UNION AGAINST MILITARISM (AUAM); ARMED FORCES; BALDWIN, ROGER NASH (1884–1981); EASTMAN, CRYSTAL (1881–1928); PEACE MOVEMENTS.

COOLIDGE, CALVIN (1872–1933). Thirtieth president of the United States. Born in Plymouth, Vermont, Coolidge was an Amherst graduate, a qualified lawyer who served in town politics in Northampton, Massachusetts, where he became mayor, 1910–1911. A member of the Massachusetts senate, 1912–1915, and lieutenant governor of Massachusetts, 1916–1918, Coolidge became governor of Massachusetts, 1919–1920. As governor Coolidge supported the **Nineteenth Amendment** and regulation of child and female labor. He gained national prominence when he spoke out against striking **Boston** police, saying, "There is no right to strike against public safety by anybody, anywhere, anytime." In 1920 he was selected as **Warren Harding**'s running mate, and on Harding's death in 1923 Coolidge became president. He was elected in his own right in 1924, when he defeated Democrat **John W. Davis** by 15,718,211 votes to 8,385,283 and 382 Electoral College votes to 136. The third candidate, the Progressive **Robert M. La Follette**, received 4,831,289 votes and 13 Electoral College votes. The **Republican Party** slogan, "Keep Cool with Coolidge," was an implicit reference to the apparent prosperity that contributed to his victory

Coolidge was a sharp contrast to Harding in that he was rather stiff, shy, sober, abstemious, cautious, and famously laconic. He quickly demanded attorney general **Harry Daugherty**'s resignation for his failure to comply with Senate investigators looking into the Harding scandals. Coolidge also appointed special counselors to investigate the **Teapot Dome** scandal. Coolidge was often dismissed by contemporary writers and historians as "Silent Cal," a "do-nothing" president who slept most in the White House. Contrary to that image, recent historians have painted a more sympathetic view of Coolidge. The president entertained more visitors than his predecessor in the White House and established regular press conferences, although his remarks had to be attributed to a "White House spokesman," and he received the questions in advance. Coolidge kept on several members of Harding's cabinet, most notably **Herbert Hoover, Charles Hughes,** and **Andrew Mellon,** and he left his cabinet officers alone to do their jobs.

Coolidge continued many of the policies of his predecessor, particularly with regard to business, which he described as "the chief business of America." His administration cut taxes, including surtax and estates tax, in 1926 and 1928 and failed to pursue **Federal Trade Commission** investigations of illegal corporate activity. Coolidge acted to block two important measures passed by Congress, namely plans to take over **Muscle Shoals** in a government-operated project which he stopped by pocket veto in 1928, and two **McNary-Haugen** bills that he vetoed in 1927 and 1928. He also blocked the payment of a bonus to veterans. However, Coolidge also achieved a balanced budget every year and used the surplus to reduce the national debt by one third. The president also supported the promotion and regulation of aviation, the establishment of the **Federal Radio Commission** in 1927, and a federal building program in 1926 that included the National Archives and Federal Triangle. Coolidge believed that America should be "kept American" and supported the passage of the **Immigration Act** of 1924.

In **foreign policy** Coolidge continued the cautious policies of limited involvement established by his predecessor. He refused to cancel Allied war debts but did accept the renegotiations of German war **reparations** in the **Dawes** and **Young plans**. Coolidge recommended American membership of the **Permanent Court of International Justice** (or World Court) to the Senate but failed to push the measure when the **League of Nations** asked for clarification of Senate reservations. The Coolidge Administration supported attempts at naval reduction and called the **Geneva Naval conference** in 1927. Coolidge also supported the **Kellogg-Briand** pact in 1928. Relations with Latin America improved following negotiations with Nicaragua and **Mexico** and participation in the fifth and sixth Pan-American conferences in 1923 and 1928 which paved the way for the **Clark Memorandum**.

While vacationing in the Black Hills of Dakota in August 1927 unexpectedly and without further elaboration Coolidge issued the statement "I do not choose to run for President in nineteen twenty-eight" and so left the way open for the nomination of Herbert Hoover as the Republican candidate. His enigmatic statement encouraged some historians to believe that Coolidge had foreseen the coming **Crash** and **Depression**. Although there is some evidence to support this, it seems more likely that he wished to retire after almost ten years in Washington, D.C. After he left office he took a position as director of the New York Life Insurance Company, wrote for various journals and in a syndicated daily newspaper column, and published *The Autobiography of Calvin Coolidge* (1929). The only public office he held was as a member of the National Transportation Committee set up to advise on the nation's transportation systems.

See also COOLIDGE, GRACE ANNA GOODHUE (1879–1957).

COOLIDGE, GRACE ANNA GOODHUE (1879–1957). Born Grace Goodhue in Burlington, Vermont, the future wife of president **Calvin Coolidge** graduated from the University of Vermont in 1902 and took up a teaching position at Clark Institute for the Deaf. She married Coolidge in 1905, and they had two sons, John and Calvin Jr. Mrs. Coolidge was an attractive and vivacious individual, much respected as a hostess at the White House. After the death of Calvin Jr. of blood poisoning in 1924, she devoted herself to renovating the White House. Mrs. Coolidge also supported projects related to the deaf and became a trustee of the Clark Institute and was an active member of the college sorority Pi Beta Phi.

See also WOMEN.

COPLAND, AARON (1900–1990). The son of Russian Jewish immigrants, Copland was to become one of America's greatest modern composers. His work combined the influences of Igor Stravinsky with that of jazz and American folk melodies. He wrote for radio, theater, and movies, and his first major piece was S*ymphony for Organ and Orchestra*, composed in 1924. During the 1920s Copland was very much part of the avant-garde and contributed articles to the new journal *Modern Music.* He established the American Festivals of contemporary Music at Saratoga Springs in 1932. His *El Salon Mexico* (1936) was influenced by visits to South and Central America. He is best known for his later ballets *Billy the Kid* (1938), *Rodeo* (1942), and *Appalachian Spring* (1944), and for the patriotic pieces written in 1942, *A Lincoln Portrait* and *Fanfare for the Common Man.* In 1949 Copland won an Oscar for his music for the movie *The Heiress*.

See also MUSIC AND DANCE.

COSTIGAN, EDWARD PRENTISS (1874–1939). After studying law and graduating from Harvard Law School in 1899, Edward Costigan established a law practice in Denver. Costigan was a progressive Republican committed to municipal reform and was founder and attorney to Denver's Honest Election League (1903–1906) and the Law Enforcement League (1906–1908). He was also president of the Civil Service Reform Association and chairman of the Dry Denver Campaign Committee. Costigan was a founding member of the Citizen's Party that carried Denver in 1912.

Costigan was one of the leaders of the Colorado Progressive Republican League that opposed **William Howard Taft** in 1912. Costigan first backed **Robert M. La Follette** and then **Theodore Roosevelt** in the presidential campaign. Costigan himself stood unsuccessfully for governor of Colorado on the **Progressive** ticket in 1912 and 1914. The Colorado mining strike of 1914 divided the state's Progressive Party. Costigan served as legal counsel to the miners. In 1916 he endorsed **Woodrow Wilson**'s election on the basis of his reform program and in 1917 was appointed to the Tariff Commission. He was increasingly critical of the Republican appointments to the commission and in 1928 resigned.

Costigan supported La Follette in 1924 and **Alfred E. Smith** in 1928. He became a **Democrat** in 1930 and was elected to the U.S. Senate from Colorado. He supported the **New Deal** program and measures to open the sugar trade and antilynching bills. He retired from politics due to ill health in 1936.

COUNCIL OF NATIONAL DEFENSE (CND). The Council of National Defense was established under the Army Appropriations Act of 1916 as part of the program of "Preparedness." Consisting of the secretaries of war, navy, interior, agriculture, commerce, and labor, the CND was authorized to "supervise and direct investigations and make recommendations" relating to the railroads, the mobilization of military and naval resources, and domestic industrial production in order to effect "the immediate concentration and utilization of the resources of the Nation." It was assisted by an **Advisory Commission of the Council of National Defense** and a network of subcommittees.

See also ARMED FORCES.

COWLEY, MALCOLM (1898–1989). A literary critic, journalist, poet, novelist, and historian of the 1920s literary scene, Malcolm Cowley was born in western Pennsylvania. He attended school in Pittsburgh before going to Harvard University in 1915. In 1917 he left to join the **American Ambulance Field Service (AAFS)** in France during World War I but returned to join the U.S. Army. He graduated from Harvard in 1920. For a time he worked as a book reviewer, copywriter, and poet but in 1921 he and his wife joined the American expatriate community in Paris where he met **Ernest Hemingway** and **Ezra Pound** among many others. In 1923 Cowley moved back to **Greenwich Village** and edited an avant-garde magazine, *Broom*, and published poetry—including the prize-winning "The Urn" in 1926. In 1929, encouraged by **Hart Crane**, he published his best-known poems under the title *Blue Juniata*.

From 1929 to 1940 Cowley was the literary editor for the *New Republic*, and in 1934 he published *Exiles Return*, a major study of the expatriate American writers of the **"Lost Generation"**—although this only became a success in its second revised edition in 1951. During the Depression Cowley had joined other left-wing writers in establishing the League of American Writers. Although he left that body because of the influence of the **Communist Party USA**, when during World War II Cowley was appointed deputy director to the Office of Facts and Figures he was attacked by conservatives in Congress for his communist sympathies. He resigned in 1942 and became an adviser to the Viking Press. In that role Cowley edited various collections of major writers including those of Hemingway and **William Faulkner**. Later still he edited work by **F. Scott Fitzgerald** and **Sherwood Anderson**. His own other writing included *Black Cargoes* (1962), a study of the Atlantic slave trade; a study of *Fitzgerald and the Jazz Age* (1962); and *A Second Flowering: Works and Days of the Lost Generation* (1973). Cowley's autobiography, *And I Worked* (1980), won a U.S. National Book Award.

See also LITERATURE AND THEATER.

COX, JAMES MIDDLETON (1870–1957). Formerly a newspaper owner, Cox served in the House of Representatives as **Democratic Party** congressman from Ohio from 1909 to 1913. He was governor of Ohio from 1913 to 1915 and again from 1917 to 1921. In 1920 he was chosen as the Democratic presidential candidate on the forty-fourth ballot with **Franklin Delano Roosevelt** as his running mate. Cox, a committed supporter of **Woodrow Wilson** and the League of Nations, was defeated by the Republican **Warren G. Harding**. Cox received just over 9 million votes, 34 percent of the vote, and 127 electoral college votes to Harding's 16 million votes and 404 electoral college votes.

After the election Cox completed his term as governor of Ohio and then returned to the newspaper business. He acquired several more newspapers in the 1920s and established Dayton's first radio station. In 1933 Roosevelt sent Cox as vice chairman of the U.S. delegation to the world economic conference in London. Cox's autobiography, *Journey through My Life*, was published in 1946.

CRANE, (HAROLD) HART (1889–1932). The poet Hart Crane was born in Garrettsville, Ohio, to a wealthy family. However, his parents' bitter divorce affected him and he dropped his first name in favor of his mother's maiden name. Crane's first poetry was published in 1916 shortly before he moved to New York City, ostensibly to study at Columbia University. Instead he became part of the **Greenwich Village** literary and artistic avantgarde, supporting himself as a copywriter and occasional work in his father's factory in Cleveland. He worked briefly in a munitions plant in Cleveland during **World War I** before resuming his literary career. He published several short poems between 1917 and 1923, when his longer "For the Marriage of Faustus and Helen" appeared. Intended as a riposte to the pessimism of **T. S. Eliot**'s *The Waste Land*, Crane extended this work in a collection entitled *White Buildings* (1926), incorporating both the influence of Walt Whitman and the **jazz** rhythms in a celebration of the modern. After a brief stay in Paris between 1928 and 1929, a second collection using the motif of the Brooklyn Bridge and titled simply *The Bridge* appeared in 1930 published by **Harry Crosby**'s Black Sun Press and received with some acclaim by the critics.

In 1931 Crane was awarded a Guggenheim Fellowship and went to Mexico where he joined an artistic colony near Mexico City and had an affair with the wife of **Malcolm Cowley**. A conflicted individual, Crane had several affairs both homo- and heterosexual, and he was also given to bouts of heavy drinking. Traveling back to the United States in 1932 he jumped off the ship into the sea and drowned in what has been assumed to be a suicide. His significance as a poet was disputed, and for some time his work was ignored, but it underwent something of a revival in the 1970s and 1980s.

See also LITERATURE AND THEATER.

CREEL, GEORGE (1876–1953). George Creel was a newspaperman and publicist who rose to national prominence as chairman of the **Committee on Public Information** (CPI) during **World War I**. He was editor of the Kansas City *Independent* (1899–1909), the Denver *Post* (1909–1910), and the *Rocky Mountain News* (1911–1913). A committed reformer, Creel served as police commissioner in Denver from 1912–1913. He wrote several **muckraking** articles for *Harper's Weekly* and other journals and was responsible for the **Democratic Party**'s publicity in 1916 and became a personal friend of president **Woodrow Wilson**. He was often accused of producing propaganda on behalf of the president while chair of the CPI and he made enemies with his acerbic comments about Congress and critics of the war effort. He accompanied the president to the Paris Peace Conference in 1919 and visited various European countries on the president's behalf. In 1920 he began work as a feature writer at *Collier's*. In 1933 he chaired the Regional Labor Board for California, Utah, and Nevada and directed the West Coast office of the National Recovery Administration. Unsuccessful in his attempt to win the Democratic nomination for governor of California in 1934 he returned to *Collier's*. After the World War II he supported senator Joseph McCarthy's anti-Communist campaign.

See also NEWSPAPERS AND MAGAZINES.

CRIME AND POLICING. The rise of the large industrial city in the late nineteenth century brought a growing concern about crime, policing, and political corruption. The cities were often seen as places of lawlessness and street crime that was attributed to the huge influx of new immigrants. Ethnic gangs were already a feature of city life and became more prevalent after the introduction of **Prohibition** in 1920. Policing was still largely a local and state matter, and during the period of **progressivism** many cities and several states established civil service police forces and police commissioners to separate policing and politics and create more professional police forces. Federal involvement became increasingly common with the passage of legislation such as the Mann Act in 1911 prohibiting the transportation of women across state lines for sexual purposes, or the **Dyer Act** (National Motor Vehicle Theft Act) of 1919 that made it a federal offense to drive a stolen car across state lines. **World War I** witnessed an enormous increase in federal law enforcement with the passage of the **Selective Service**, and **Espionage** and **Sedition** acts. The **Red Scare** after the war and the growth of crime syndicates also encouraged greater expansion of federal police power and led to the growth of the Bureau of Investigation within the Justice Department. This became the **Federal Bureau of Investigation** (FBI) in 1921. The federal prison service also grew from its first creation by Congress in 1891. By 1925 there were three federal prisons (Leavenworth, Atlanta, McNeil Island); a further two were added by 1930, one of them in Alderson, West Virginia, for **women**. The number of federal prisoners was approximately two thousand in 1915 and twenty-six thousand in 1930 (half of them military prisoners). A Federal Bureau of Prisons was created within the Department of Justice in 1930.

President **Herbert Hoover** suggested during his inaugural in 1928 that crime was increasing. However, although the 1920s has a reputation for lawlessness, the evidence is not entirely clear. If prison population size can be taken as one measure of criminal activity, then there seemed to be some increase during the 1920s, although figures are unreliable. In 1926, when statistics were first recorded by the Bureau of Census, the number of prisoners in state and federal institutions was ninety-six thousand compared to about fifty-seven thousand in 1900. By way of comparison, the number at the end of the twentieth century was more than 1.25 million. Some historians point to a fall in crime and disorderly behavior in the early twentieth century as industrial society placed greater emphasis on discipline, punctuality, and regimentation; others have argued that bank robbery, murder, and other serious crimes were few in number during the 1920s, which is why cases such as those of **Sacco and Vanzetti** or **Leopold** and **Loeb** captured the public's attention.

Changes in the law created new crimes: laws to deal with the rise of the **automobile** and the creation of traffic offenses ranging from speeding to drunk driving were one of the most obvious examples. Of course, the police also became increasingly motorized. During the Progressive era (c. 1900–c. 1917) attempts were made to eradicate certain crimes with the introduction of tighter **immigration** controls and laws against prostitution, gambling, and drinking. Regulation was introduced to dance halls, and during World War I 110 red light districts were closed down to protect men in uniform from vice and safeguard their social welfare. The saloon was a particular focus of progressive concern as it was often linked to political machines and party bosses. By 1900 the Anti-Saloon League had become the most powerful voice calling for Prohibition, and the war provided additional arguments to regulate the manufacture and sale of liquor. With the passage of the **Eighteenth Amendment** and **Volstead Act** in 1920 a new market for illegal goods was created, which led in turn to the rise of organized crime as new ethnic gangs seized the opportunities for economic success otherwise denied to them. Smuggling alcohol into the country, or **bootlegging**, became big business. Interlocking interests of gambling, vice, bootlegging, and politics arose in almost every major city across the country, and rival gangs competed for control of the markets. In Chicago rivalry between **Al Capone** and other gangs culminated in the **St. Valentine's Day Massacre** in 1929; like Capone, New York gangsters **Arnold Rothstein,** Jack "Legs" Diamond, and **Dutch Schultz** became nationally known figures. The gangs were so powerful that in 1929 they could hold a national convention in Atlantic City, New Jersey.

In the year immediately after the introduction of Prohibition crime rates rose by 24 percent in thirty major cities, and during the "beer wars" between 1924 and 1930 there were some seven hundred murders in Chicago alone; the national homicide rate rose from 6.2 per 100,000 of population in 1914 to 9.7 in 1933. In 1921 there were almost thirty thousand federal prosecutions for Prohibition-related crimes and by 1932 this had risen to almost sixty-six thousand cases. The demand for alcohol and the small number of federal officers employed to enforce the law meant that the government was largely ineffective despite the exploits of officers like **Eliot Ness**. The report of the Commission on Law Observance and Enforcement chaired by **George Wickersham** in 1931 pointed to the widespread police and political corruption combined with a lack of public will as the cause of Prohibition's failure. It was not until 1933 that Prohibition was repealed and a new attorney general, **Homer S. Cummings**, declared war on organized crime. At the same time the head of the FBI, **J. Edgar Hoover**, announced gangsters to be "public enemy number one," but by then the "mob" had become well established.

Another major form of crime, although not one the FBI tackled until much later in the century, was race crime. Race violence was a constant feature of American life, particularly in the South where it was primarily directed against **African Americans**. Lynching was the most public form of race violence with over one thousand lynchings occurring between 1900 and 1914. They continued during World War I, which also witnessed an outbreak of race riots in northern cities beginning with East St. Louis in 1917, and Chicago and other centers during the "**Red Summer**" of 1919. The attacks on African Americans in the cities were partly a response to the **Great Migration**, and the growth of black ghettos, but racial feelings were also heightened by the rise of the second **Ku Klux Klan** (KKK). The KKK was also associated with several attacks on Jews and Catholics during the 1920s: a Klan member murdered a Catholic priest in Birmingham, Alabama, in 1921, and in Naperville, Illinois, a Catholic church was burned in 1922; a Catholic priest was also tarred and feathered in Slaton, Texas, that year. Although the KKK was not directly involved, anti-Semitism was clearly involved in the murder of **Leo Frank** in 1915.

Vigilantism was not just confined to the KKK, nor to attacks on racial or religious groups. Individuals who were thought to be pro-German or not sufficiently patriotic were tarred and feathered during the war, and one, a German coal miner named Robert Prager, was lynched by a mob in Collinsville, Illinois, in 1918. During and immediately after World War I violence was directed against radical labor organizations; in 1919, Wesley Everest, a member of the **Industrial Workers of the World** (IWW), was lynched by a mob in **Centralia**, Washington, during the Red Scare. Such acts of violence decreased after 1919 but did not disappear altogether.

See also DYER ANTI-LYNCHING BILL.

CROLY, HERBERT DAVID (1869–1930). Although he failed to complete his academic studies at Harvard University, Herbert Croly was to gain enormous influence as a political philosopher and editor during the **progressive** period. He began writing in his father's journals, *Real Estate Record and Builders' Guide* and the *Architectural Record*, in 1889 and later coauthored books on architectural style and urban planning. In 1909 his influential work of political philosophy, *The Promise of American Life*, was published. Calling for an abandonment of laissez-faire principles and simple individualism, Croly advocated federal regulation and reform to tackle the problems of industrialism. **Theodore Roosevelt** incorporated aspects of Croly's philosophy, including the phrase "new nationalism," into his **Progressive Party** campaign in 1912.

In 1914 Croly became editor of a new journal, *New Republic*, which quickly became the mouthpiece of the reform movement. Increasingly the journal supported preparedness and **Woodrow Wilson**'s administration. However, Croly and other writers viewed the **Versailles peace** settlement as a great betrayal of wartime idealism and turned against Wilson. The *New Republic* continued to espouse progressive ideals during the 1920s and supported **Robert M. La Follette** in the 1924 presidential campaign. In 1928 it backed **Democrat Al Smith**. Frustrated by the conservative politics of the decade, Croly began to show more interest in literary, religious, and philosophical issues. He suffered a massive stroke in 1928 that left him incapacitated until his death.

See also NEWSPAPERS AND MAGAZINES.

CROSBY, CARESSE (NÉE MARY "POLLY" JACOB) (1892–1970). Born into a wealthy family in New York City and educated in exclusive private schools, Caresse Crosby was to become one of the symbolic figures of the 1920s. Prior to her first marriage, to Richard Peabody in 1915, Polly Jacob aspired to be an inventor and is credited with designing the first backless brassiere, which was patented in 1914. Her marriage to Peabody ended in 1921 because of her affair with **Harry Crosby**, whom she married the following year. She changed her name to Caresse, and she and Harry settled in Paris, where they wrote and published poetry and other **literature** and became part of the American expatriate community. She and Harry enjoyed a wild lifestyle of drink, drugs, and affairs.

Caresse Crosby's first collection of poetry, *Crosses of Gold*, was published privately by the couple in 1924; her second, *Graven Images*, was published by Houghton Mifflin in 1928. Together the Crosbys set up their own publishing company originally called Éditions Narcisse, later renamed as the Black Sun Press. She continued the press after her husband's suicide in 1929 and published work by, among others, **William Faulkner**, **Ernest Hemingway**, and **Dorothy Parker**. Having returned to the United States, Caresse continued to publish avant-garde writers in the Black Sun *Portfolio: An Intercontinental Quarterly*, which appeared between 1945 and 1947; she also supported and wrote pornography for the author Henry Miller. Dividing her time between homes in Rome, Washington, D.C., and New York City, Crosby continued to be a part of the literary and artistic bohemian world until her death from heart disease.

CROSBY, HARRY STURGIS (1898–1929). Often seen as the epitome of the "**Lost Generation**" and the very personification of the "**Jazz Age**," Harry Crosby was born into a wealthy, long-established Boston family and educated at prep school before he volunteered to serve in the **American Ambulance Field Service** in France during **World War I**. He later continued in the same role in the U.S. Army. He was awarded the Croix de Guerre by the French government after the war in recognition of his service. On his return home Crosby enrolled as a student at Harvard University and graduated with a BA in 1921. He was sent to work in a branch of the Morgan bank in Paris by his family shortly afterward because of his developing love affair with the married New York socialite Mary Jacob Peabody, but the couple married shortly after her divorce and they established a home in Paris in 1922, where they became a part of the American expatriate literary and artistic circle. The Crosbys became notorious for their hedonistic lifestyle of wild parties, drink, drugs, and many sexual liaisons.

Harry published a collection of his favorite poetry in *Anthology* in 1924 and then established his own publishing house with his wife, now renamed Caresse, in 1927. First called Éditions Narcisse, the press was renamed Black Sun Press a year later and became known for publishing beautifully produced, limited editions of work by writers including Edgar Allan Poe as well as new authors including James Joyce, D. H. Lawrence, Archibald MacLeish, **Hart Crane**, and **Ernest Hemingway**.

The Crosbys continued to publish their own rather unexceptional poetry and writing and to enjoy an extravagant social life. However, Harry Crosby became increasingly fixated with a young American woman, Josephine Rotch Bigelow, and in December 1929 the two were found dead in a hotel in New York City, victims of what appeared to be a suicide pact. Editions of the Crosbys' poems and the publications of the Black Sun Press are now rare collectors' items.

See also LITERATURE AND THEATER.

CROWDER, ENOCH HERBERT (1859–1932). An army officer and graduate of West Point, Crowder served as judge advocate of the expeditionary forces and the Department of the Pacific in the Spanish-American War (1898) and associate justice of the Philippines supreme court, 1899–1901. In 1911 he was appointed judge advocate general of the U.S. Army and became provost marshal general to administer the **Selective Service Act** in 1917. From 1923 to 1927 he was the first U.S. ambassador to Cuba.

CUMMINGS, EDWARD ESTLIN (1894–1962). Later known as e. e. cummings, the poet and artist Edward Cummings was educated at Cambridge Latin School and Harvard University where he graduated in 1916. His first book of poems appeared with those of **John Dos Passos** in *Eight Harvard Poets* in 1917. That same year Cummings volunteered for the ambulance corps in France. After five months he and a colleague were detained in a French prison camp for expressing antiwar views. Sent back to the United States, Cummings was drafted and served in the Army in Massachusetts in 1918. After the war Cummings moved to New York where his cubist paintings and avant-garde poetry won him recognition in literary circles. His novel based on his experience of prison appeared as *The Enormous Room* in 1922. Cummings's presentation of poems in a visual form on the page, and his usage of language and absence of capitalization and punctuation appeared in print in various journals before publication as *Tulips and Chimneys* (1923), *XLI Poems* (1925), and *Is 5* (1926).

Cummings visited Europe on several occasions during the 1920s and was influenced by the Dada movement and Surrealism. Some of this was evident in his play *Him* (1927). A visit to the Soviet Union in 1931 led him to record his experiences (and disappointment) in literary form in *Eimi* in 1933. In 1935 Cummings authored *Tom*, a satirical ballet based on *Uncle Tom's Cabin*. Cummings continued to publish through the 1950s and received recognition as one of leaders of the group of postwar literary writers known as the "**Lost Generation**."
See also LITERATURE AND THEATER.

CUMMINGS, HOMER STILLÉ (1870–1956). Homer Cummings graduated from Yale Law School in 1893 and began to practice law in Stamford, Connecticut. In 1900 he was elected mayor of Stamford where he carried out a moderate program of reform during his three terms. In 1914 Cummings became state's attorney in Fairfield County, a post he held until 1924. Throughout this time Cummings was active in the national **Democratic Party** organization, and he was national chairman from 1914 to 1920. Cummings supported **Franklin D. Roosevelt** in 1932 and as a reward he was initially offered the post of governor-general of the Philippines. However, when **Thomas Walsh**, the attorney general designate, died en route to the inaugural, Roosevelt offered the post to Cummings. Cummings held the position until 1939 and was responsible for extending the federal role in fighting **crime**. He also drafted the so-called "court-packing" measure, the 1936 Judicial Reorganization Act, which would have enabled Roosevelt to appoint new justices to the **Supreme Court**. The measure became the center of political controversy and was never enacted. Cummings retired in 1939 and practiced law in Washington, D.C.

CUMMINS, ALBERT BAIRD (1850–1926). Admitted to the bar in Illinois in 1875, Cummins practiced law in Des Moines, Iowa, where he won recognition as attorney for the Farmers' Protective Association against the "barbed wire trusts." Cummins was active in state **Republican Party** politics as a leader of the progressive faction of the party. He failed to win election to the U.S. Senate in 1894 and again in 1900, but was elected governor of Iowa in 1901 and served three terms until 1908. Cummins was selected to fill a vacant Senate seat in 1908, and he held the position until his death. He sided with **Robert M. La Follette** in the insurgent reform movement of the Republican Party in 1912 and joined the National Progressive Republican League. Cummins supported **Theodore Roosevelt** rather than La Follette but remained within the Republican Party.

Although he supported much of **Woodrow Wilson**'s **New Freedom** program, Cummins opposed intervention in **World War I** and was one of the "little group of willful men" who filibustered against the arming of merchant ships in 1917. Cummins was an "**irreconcilable**" in his opposition to the **League of Nations**. As chair of the Committee on Interstate Commerce he helped to prepare the Esch-Cummins Railroad **Transportation Act** (1920) that returned the railroads to private ownership. Increasingly conservative in the 1920s, Cummins lost the 1926 primary to a supporter of La Follette.

CURLEY, JAMES MICHAEL (1874–1958). Curley dominated Boston politics for much of the first half of the twentieth century as mayor. Born of Irish **immigrant** stock, he grew up in an Irish tenement neighborhood in Boston where he built a powerful political machine. A conviction for fraud after taking a federal civil service examination for one of his constituents in 1901 only seemed to further his career. A member of the **Democratic Party**, he served as a Boston city alderman from 1903, and in the U.S. House of Representatives from 1910; he was first elected mayor of Boston in 1914, lost in 1918, reelected in 1922, lost in 1926, and won again in 1930. In contrast to the mood in national politics, Curly favored active, interventionist government and his period as mayor saw millions spent on the City Hospital, schools, parks, and other public facilities as well as a program of public works to counter the effects of the **Great Depression**. He was subsequently governor of Massachusetts (1935–1937), U.S. congressman (1942–1946), and mayor of Boston again (1947–1950).

See also POLITICAL PARTIES.

CURRY, JOHN STEUART (1897–1946). Born in Kansas, John Steuart Curry studied **art** at Kansas City **Art** Institute in 1916; the Art Institute of Chicago, 1916–1918; and Geneva College, Pennsylvania, 1918–1919. He worked as an art teacher and illustrator for magazines and novels in New York City and spent a year in Paris in 1926. He established his studio in Westport, Connecticut, in 1928, but much of his work focused on Kansas and its landscapes. One of the Regionalists—the group of artists who concentrated on rural scenes—much of Curry's work depicted American landscapes and themes in American history such as his *Baptism in Kansas* (1928), *Tornado Over Kansas* (1929), and *Wisconsin Landscape* (1937–1938). In 1934 Curry completed several murals in public buildings for the Federal Art Project. In 1936 he became artist in residence at the University of Wisconsin, Madison. In 1937 his murals in the Kansas statehouse, showing an angry figure of John Brown, and also including members of the **Ku Klux Klan**, were regarded as controversial, and he did not complete the four panels originally projected. In his last years Curry concentrated mainly on book illustrations and lithographs.

CURTIS, CHARLES (1860–1936). Thirty-first vice president, 1929–1933. Admitted to the Kansas bar in 1881, Curtis practiced law in Topeka, Kansas. He was elected county attorney in 1884 and was elected as a **Republican** to the House of Representatives in 1892. A mixed-blood Kaw Indian, Curtis sponsored the Curtis Act, which abolished tribal courts and the Five Civilized Tribes in Oklahoma in 1898. He also fought for the rights of Indian women and mixed-blood children, but served as an attorney for energy companies taking natural resources from Indian reservations. In 1907 he became a senator and served until 1913 and again from 1915–1929. He was cosponsor of the **Dyer Anti-Lynching Bill**. In 1924 Curtis was chosen majority leader in the Senate. In 1928 he was chosen as the vice presidential candidate to appease the farm interests. His contributions as vice president were limited and he retired from politics to return to his law practice in 1932.

See also NATIVE AMERICANS.

D

DANIELS, JOSEPHUS (1862–1941). Daniels began his career as a reform journalist and publisher in his home state of North Carolina, where he owned and edited several **newspapers** including the *Raleigh State Chronicle* and the *North Carolinian*. In 1893 he became chief clerk in the Department of the Interior in the administration of Grover Cleveland, but returned to Raleigh in 1895 as owner/editor of the Raleigh *News and Observer*. He supported causes such as **child labor** laws, **trades unionism**, better hospital provision, and regulation of the railroads. Having previously supported **William Jennings Bryan**, Daniels backed **Woodrow Wilson** in 1912 and was rewarded with the appointment of secretary of the navy in 1913. He instituted a number of reforms to open access to the navy and promotions and in 1914 banned alcohol on all naval vessels. During **World War I** Daniels was seen as responsible for the "Bridge of Ships'" that safely transported the U.S. Army to Europe. After the war he returned to his role at the *News and Observer* but returned to political life when **Franklin D. Roosevelt** appointed him ambassador to Mexico in 1933. In this post until 1942 he was an upholder of Roosevelt's "Good Neighbor" policy. Daniels spent the rest of his life at his newspaper and completing his five-volume autobiography.

DARROW, CLARENCE SEWARD (1857–1938). Leading labor and criminal lawyer Clarence Darrow was educated at Allegheny College and the University of Michigan Law School. He became a member of the Ohio bar in 1878. In 1887 Darrow moved to Chicago and in 1890 became general attorney to the Chicago and North Western Railway. However, he became famous for his defense of **Eugene V. Debs** in the railroad conspiracy case (1894) and of **William D. Haywood** in 1907. Increasingly associated with labor and with the disadvantaged, Darrow defended several of those people charged under the wartime **Espionage** and **Sedition acts**. In 1924 Darrow saved **Leopold** and **Loeb** from the death penalty by using expert witnesses to argue that they were not responsible for their actions. Perhaps Darrow's most famous case was his defense of **John Scopes** in the **Scopes Monkey Trial** in

1925. In 1926 he also defended Ossian Sweet, a black man who had used violence to defend himself against a mob who attacked his home in Detroit. Darrow also worked on the case of the **Scottsboro boys** in 1932.

DAUGHERTY, HARRY MICAJAH (1860–1941). Harry Daugherty practiced law in Washington Court House, Ohio, before he entered city and then state politics. After serving as prosecuting attorney for Fayette County, he was elected as a **Republican** to the Ohio House of Representatives where he served from 1891–1895. His electoral career was effectively ended after he had been accused of accepting $3,500 to vote for a senatorial candidate. However, he continued to be active in Ohio politics and was chair of **William Howard Taft**'s election campaign in 1912. He played a part in securing the Republican presidential nomination for **Warren Harding** and managed Harding's campaign in 1920 and in return was appointed attorney general.

As attorney general Daugherty appointed several Republican Party cronies to the Justice Department and was chief among the "Ohio gang" of poker players and whiskey drinkers who socialized with President Harding. Daugherty's role in the series of scandals that came to light in 1923 forever tarnished the Harding administration's legacy. As the scandal began to emerge, Daugherty's assistant, Jess Smith, committed suicide in 1923. It transpired that he had acted as go-between in arranging payments from the office of the **Alien Property Custodian** to claimants in return for a payment of **Liberty Bonds**. The bonds were then sold and monies were paid into a bank run by the attorney general's brother, Mal S. Daugherty. Ledgers relating to bank accounts held jointly by Smith and Harry Daugherty were destroyed. Daugherty also refused to hand over Justice Department files to the committees investigating **Teapot Dome**; when the attorney general failed to prosecute the guilty parties, **Calvin Coolidge** forced him to resign in 1924. Daugherty was twice indicted for fraud by a grand jury on corruption charges but was acquitted due to lack of evidence. He returned to Ohio to practice law.

DAVIDSON, DONALD (1893–1968). The southern poet, historian, and literary critic Donald Davidson studied at Vanderbilt University, Nashville. He served in the army during World War I and returned to complete his MA in 1922. He later became professor of English at Vanderbilt. Davidson was part of the Nashville literary group the Fugitives, which included **John Crowe Ransom**, **Allen Tate**, and Robert Penn Warren. Davidson's own writing included *An Outland Piper* (1926), *The Tall Men* (1927), and *Lee in the Mountains* (1927). Like the other Fugitives, Davidson was a defender of the

South and contributed to the collection of essays presenting their case, *I'll Take My Stand* (1930). Davidson also wrote *The Attack on the Leviathan: Regionalism and Nationalism in the United States* (1938).

See also LITERATURE AND THEATER.

DAVIS, DWIGHT FILLEY (1879–1945). Dwight Davis graduated from Harvard in 1900. While he was at the university Davis was twice runner-up in the national men's tennis singles championship and three times winner of the doubles championship with Holcombe Ward. In 1900 he donated a trophy for the International Lawn Tennis Challenge Trophy, which became known as the Davis Cup. Davis captained the victorious U.S. team in 1900 and played on the 1902 team that also won. Davis graduated in law from Washington University in 1903 but devoted himself to a life of public service, locally and nationally. During **World War I** Davis became involved in military training and then enlisted in the Missouri National Guard. He served in France and won the Distinguished Service Cross for heroism during the **St. Mihiel** and **Meuse Argonne** offensives.

In 1920 Davis failed to gain the **Republican** nomination for the U.S. Senate but was appointed to the **War Finance Corporation** by **Warren Harding**. In 1923 he was appointed as assistant secretary of war, and in 1925 **Calvin Coolidge** chose him to succeed John Weeks as secretary of war. Davis served until 1929 and was responsible for developing plans for a comprehensive industrial mobilization. He opposed General William Mitchell's advocacy of air power but backed the recommendations of the President's Aircraft Board for developing military air power but not a separate air force. Davis also encouraged the development of a tank force.

In 1929 **Herbert Hoover** appointed Davis governor general of the Philippines where he did much to further internal improvements. He resigned in 1932. Although a critic of the **New Deal**, **Franklin D. Roosevelt** appointed Davis as director general of the Army Specialist Corps in 1942. When the Corps, which provided commissions for highly skilled individuals that did not meet the army's physical standards, was incorporated in the Army Service Forces, Davis remained in an advisory role until the end of the war.

See also ARMED FORCES.

DAVIS, JAMES JOHN (1873–1947). Born in Wales, Davis immigrated to the United States in 1891 and was employed as a puddler in the Pennsylvania steel mills. Davis was active in the Amalgamated Association of Iron, Steel, and Tin Plate Makers. He served as secretary of labor, 1921–1929, and subsequently was elected to the Senate. As secretary of labor Davis established the Border Patrol to limit the influx of illegal immigrants. Although he served under **Warren Harding**, **Calvin Coolidge**, and **Herbert Hoover**,

Davis was perhaps best known for his leading role in the Loyal Order of the Moose, a fraternal order. In the Senate he cosponsored the Davis-Bacon Act, which set wage levels at local rates on federal construction projects in order to stop cutthroat wage slashing in bids.

See also IMMIGRATION.

DAVIS, JOHN WILLIAM (1873–1955). John W. Davis was a lawyer who served as a **Democrat** in the House of Representatives for Virginia from 1911 to 1913 and was responsible for drafting parts of the **Clayton Antitrust Act**. As U.S solicitor general from 1913 to 1918, he argued a number of important constitutional cases. These included successfully defending the federal government's right to regulate interstate oil pipelines and to regulate railroad wages under the **Adamson Act**, a ruling against Oklahoma's "grandfather clause" denying **African Americans** the vote, and against Alabama's use of leased convict labor. In 1918 he was appointed ambassador to Great Britain, a post he held until 1921. He then became head of a Wall Street law firm.

In 1924 Davis became the Democratic presidential candidate in 1924 on the 103rd ballot when the convention was deadlocked between supporters of **Alfred E. Smith** and **William Gibbs McAdoo**. He lost support through his criticism of the **Ku Klux Klan** and his advocacy for American participation in the **League of Nations**. In the election he was easily defeated by **Calvin Coolidge**, winning only 8.3 million popular votes and 136 Electoral College votes to Coolidge's 15.7 million and 382 votes respectively. Davis supported **Al Smith** in 1928 and initially backed **Franklin D. Roosevelt** in 1932. However, as a believer in states' rights and the strict interpretation of the Constitution Davis was critical of much of the **New Deal** and was one of the organizers of the conservative Liberty League. He was later a critic of Harry S. Truman's Fair Deal. His greatest legal victory came in 1952 in the ruling in *Youngstown Sheet & Tube Co.* against Truman's seizure of the steel industry. Davis also argued in favor of the "separate but equal" doctrine in the *Brown v. Topeka Board of Education* school segregation case in 1954, but he acted as counsel for J. Robert Oppenheimer, the atomic scientist accused of being a security risk, the same year.

DAVIS, NORMAN HEZEKIAH (1878–1944). Norman Davis was a financier and diplomat who organized the Trust Company of Cuba (1905–1917) and became U.S. Treasury representative to Great Britain and France in 1918 and served as chair of the finance section of the Supreme Economic Council. **Woodrow Wilson** appointed him assistant secretary of the treasury, 1919–1920, and he was undersecretary of state, 1920–1921. He served as a delegate to the International Economic Council in Geneva, 1927, and to the **Geneva Disarmament Conference** in 1932. He headed the U.S. delegation to the International Sugar Conference in 1937.

DAWES, CHARLES GATES (1865–1951). Thirtieth vice president, 1925–1929, Dawes was a financier who was U.S. comptroller of the currency, 1897–1901. In 1902 he organized the Central Union Trust Company of Chicago and served as president and later chairman of the board. During the war he was chief of supply procurement of the **American Expeditionary Force**. From 1921 to 1922 he was the first director of the **Bureau of the Budget**. As chairman of the Allied Reparations Commission (1923–1924), he was instrumental in drawing up the **Dawes Plan**. He was elected vice president on the **Republican** ticket in 1924. In 1925 he won the Nobel Peace Prize (with Austen Chamberlain of Great Britain), and from 1929 to 1932 he was U.S. ambassador to Britain. He was appointed chairman of the **Reconstruction Finance Corporation** (RFC) in 1932. His own bank in Chicago received a loan from the RFC, but only after he had left office.
See also BANKING.

DAWES PLAN 1924. The Dawes plan was drawn up by various European representatives under the direction of **Charles G. Dawes** to solve the problem of the collection of reparations for war losses from Germany. The plan stabilized the German currency with a loan raised by mortgaging German railways and other industries and set reparations at one billion gold marks rising to 2.5 billion by 1928. The plan was replaced by the **Young Plan** in 1929.

DAYLIGHT SAVINGS. Daylight savings, achieved by advancing clocks forward by one hour on the first Sunday of April, was introduced as part of the Standard Time Act of 19 March 1918 that established the continental time zones introduced by the railways in 1883 as part of federal law. Daylight savings was repealed in 1919 and reintroduced in 1942. It was repealed with the end of World War II and reintroduced again in 1966.

DEBS, EUGENE VICTOR (1855–1926). Debs was a **trade union** activist who began his career as a railroad fireman and served as an official of the Brotherhood of Railway Firemen. He was elected city clerk of Terre Haute as a **Democrat** in 1879 and in 1884 was elected to the Indiana General Assembly. Debs founded the first industrial union in the United States, the American Railway Union (1893), and was jailed for contempt of court as leader of the Pullman strike in 1894. He helped organize the Social Democrat Party in 1897 and was a founding member of the **Socialist Party of America**

and ran as the party's presidential candidate in 1900, 1904, 1908, 1912, and 1920. In June 1918 in Canton, Ohio, Debs spoke out publicly against **World War I** and compared the American businessmen with the Kaiser's Junkers in Germany. As a result he was convicted under the **Espionage Act**. He was sentenced to ten years in prison. He campaigned for the presidency from prison and won almost 1 million votes. President **Warren Harding** commuted his sentence, and he was released on Christmas Day 1921 and returned home to Terre Haute.

DEFOREST, LEE (1873–1961). Lee was a pioneer inventor who patented hundreds of inventions in the areas of wireless telegraphy, motion picture sound, radio, telephone, and television. He added a third electrode to the electron tube, designed and installed the U.S. Navy's first high-power radio stations, broadcast the first radio news in 1916, and developed sound-on-film motion pictures shown in New York City in 1923.

DELL, FLOYD JAMES (1887–1969). The novelist and critic Floyd Dell moved from Davenport, Iowa, to Chicago in 1908 and in 1909 became an associate editor with the *Chicago Evening Post*'s "Friday Literary Review." Dell became editor in 1911, and he encouraged a number of writers such as **Theodore Dreiser** and **Upton Sinclair**. In 1913 Dell moved to **Greenwich Village**, New York, where he became an associate editor on the radical magazine *The Masses*. In 1918 Dell and **Max Eastman** were tried twice for attempting to obstruct the draft. After two hung juries the charges were dropped.

Dell's first novel, *Moon-Calf*, was published to critical acclaim in 1920. His second novel, *The Briary Bush*, appeared in 1921. His third novel, *Janet March* (1923), was withdrawn by the publishers because of its treatment of sex and abortion. Dell's other writing did not have the success of his earlier work. In 1935 he assumed an editorial role in the Works Progress Administration (WPA) and continued to write for the government until 1947. He continued to write after his retirement but published little.

See also LITERATURE AND THEATER.

DE MILLE, CECIL BLOUNT (1881–1959). The pioneer motion picture director-producer Cecil B. De Mille trained as an actor at the American Academy of Dramatic Arts in New York and worked in the theater from 1900 to 1912. In 1913 he entered into partnership with Jesse Lasky and Samuel Goldfish (**Samuel Goldwyn**) to produce **movies** in the Jesse L. Lasky Feature Play Company. Their first film, *The Squaw Man*, was successfully released in 1914. The energetic, dictatorial De Mille quickly made a reputation as a successful producer, particularly of films dealing with moral issues of sex, sin, and high society, often starring **Gloria Swanson** in sensual roles. However, in 1923 De Mille scored a huge success with the epic *The Ten Commandments*. In 1925 he established his own studio and had another success with the life of Jesus, *King of Kings* (1927). However, later films were less successful, and De Mille was forced to join Metro-Goldwyn-Mayer (MGM) in 1928. In 1931 he joined Paramount. He achieved success once more with historical and biblical epics—*The Sign of the Cross* (1932), *Cleopatra* (1934), *Samson and Delilah* (1949). *The Greatest Show on Earth* (1952) won De Mille an Oscar for best film, and his last film, a remake of *The Ten Commandments* (1956), was a huge commercial success. De Mille was planning a new film when he died in Hollywood. His legacy was seventy films, many of which set pathbreaking precedents and broke box-office records.

DEMOBILIZATION. When **World War I** ended on 11 November 1918 little preparation had been made to return the U.S. **armed forces** home. Plans to return soldiers gradually on the basis of their skills and occupations were quickly abandoned in favor of a unit-by-unit demobilization that was carried out at the rate of fifteen thousand a day. The returning forces were carried in converted cargo vessels and U.S. warships. The U.S. Navy also discharged four hundred thousand men in a year, and the U.S. Marine Corps discharged fifty thousand. By August 1919 only a force of forty thousand Americans remained in occupied Germany, and the U.S. military presence continued until 1923. During the 1920s the U.S. armed forces were reduced to little more than a token force.

DEMOCRATIC PARTY. Excluded from the White House and the minority party in Congress since 1892, the Democratic Party benefited from divisions in the **Republican Party** to gradually gain control first of Congress, and then of the White House with the election of **Woodrow Wilson** in 1912. The Democrats held a majority in both the Senate and the House of Representatives during the 63rd (1913–1915) and 64th Congress, and maintained a majority in the Senate during the 65th Congress (1917–1919). After 1919 the Democrats were divided on the issues of **Prohibition**, the **League of Nations**, and on race. The divisions often reflected the differences between rural and urban areas, and the South and North. They were not able to unite again until the election of 1932, when, in the face of the **Depression**, they united behind **Franklin D. Roosevelt** and recaptured control of both the House and the Senate.

See also POLITICAL PARTIES.

DEMPSEY, JACK (1895–1983). The future world heavyweight boxing champion Jack Dempsey was born William Harrison Dempsey and grew up in a poor family in the West. He traveled as a hobo from 1911 to 1916 and built a reputation as a boxer. In 1919 Dempsey defeated the reigning heavyweight champion, Jess Willard, in three rounds. The following year Dempsey, who had not seen military service during **World War I**, faced trial accused of draft evasion. He was acquitted as sole supporter of his wife and mother, but his reputation was damaged. In 1921 Dempsey successfully defended his title in a match with the Frenchman Georges Carpentier in front of a crowd of eighty thousand.

Dempsey's popularity was enhanced by his appearances in movies—in a serial, *Daredevil Jack* in 1920, and in the series *Fight and Win* in 1924. His tough fighting style earned him the title of "Manassa Mauler." In 1926, after a long absence from the ring, Dempsey unsuccessfully defended his title against **Gene Tunney**. In the rematch in 1927 Dempsey knocked Tunney down but failed to retreat to a neutral ring, and Tunney benefited from the "long count" to go on to win. Dempsey did not fight again. Having lost much of his wealth following the **Wall Street Crash** in 1929, Dempsey earned a living in boxing exhibitions and wrestling. During World War II he served in the coast guard and directed the physical fitness program. He was inducted into the International Boxing Hall of Fame in 1990.

See also SPORTS.

DEMUTH, CHARLES HENRY BUCKIUS (1883–1935). One of the leading American modernist artists, Charles Demuth was born in Lancaster, Pennsylvania, the son of a wealthy tobacco merchant. He was a graduate of the Franklin & Marshall Academy in Lancaster and subsequently studied at the Drexel Institute and Pennsylvania Academy of Fine Arts in Philadelphia. In 1912 he traveled to Paris where he joined the avant-garde community; among his close friends was **Marsden Hartley**. Returning to the United States, Demuth established his studio in Lancaster but was a frequent visitor to New York City where he had his first one-man exhibition in 1914. He was also a regular visitor to the **Greenwich Village** community, and some of his work from this period included *Dancing Sailors* (1918) and *Turkish Bath* (1918), both of which hinted at homosexual themes.

From 1919 on Demuth began a series of paintings of buildings in Lancaster that marked him as a leader in the Precisionist school; this included one of his most famous works, *My Egypt* (1927), depicting grain elevators. Demuth was very much part of the wider artist community, and in 1925 he started working with **Alfred Stieglitz** and was a member of the American Place Gallery in New York. He also produced several poster portraits, abstract representations of individuals such as **John Marin** and **Gertrude Stein**; his most famous portrait was *I Saw the Figure Five in Gold* (1928), an homage to the poet **William Carlos Williams.** Often suffering from ill health, Demuth died from diabetes at the age of fifty-one. With **John Marin**, he was one of America's foremost watercolorists.

See also ART.

DENBY, EDWIN L. (1870–1929). Denby, son of the U.S. minister to China, where he was educated, qualified as a lawyer in 1896 and practiced in Detroit until 1898. He enlisted in the navy during the Spanish-American War in 1898, then returned to his practice. He served as a **Republican** congressman from Michigan in the U.S. House of Representatives from 1905 to 1911. Following his political defeat Denby founded the Hupp Motor Company and was involved in the Federal Motor Truck Company and the Detroit Motor Bus Company. He was president of the Detroit Board of Commerce from 1916 to 1917. In 1917 he reenlisted in the U.S. Marines and rose to the rank of major. At the end of the war he became chief probation officer in the Detroit recorder's court and chief probation officer in Wayne County.

In 1921 Denby was **Warren Harding**'s surprise choice as secretary of the navy. His career ended when he became implicated in the **Teapot Dome** scandal. It was Denby who transferred the naval oil reserves to the Department of the Interior because, he believed, he had been instructed to do so by the president and because the Department of Interior would be better able to handle the oil reserves. In the light of the investigation into the affair Denby resigned in 1924. In 1927 the **Supreme Court** found that Denby had taken "no active part" in the negotiations, and the head of the Senate investigating committee, senator **Thomas Walsh**, also acquitted Denby of any wrongdoing. Denby successfully returned to his law practice in Detroit and his work in the **automobile** manufacturing and **banking** businesses.

DEPARTMENT OF COMMERCE. The Department of Commerce was established under the administration of **William Howard Taft** in 1913 with the reorganization of the Department of Commerce and Labor (established 1903). The function of the Department was to promote domestic and foreign commerce; collect, analyze, and disseminate information relating to commerce; carry out the census; and establish weights and measures.

DEPARTMENT OF LABOR. Established as an executive department under the administration of **William Howard Taft** in 1913 following the division of the Department of Commerce and Labor (originally set up in 1903), and the creation of a separate **Department of Commerce**. The function of the Department of Labor was to "foster, promote and develop the welfare of wage earners," which it did primarily through the investigation of, and publication of information relating to, labor conditions and problems. It contained divisions dealing with children, women, wages and hours, and labor statistics.

DEPRESSION. *See* GREAT DEPRESSION.

DE PRIEST, OSCAR STANTON (1871–1951). Born in Alabama, the son of a former slave, Oscar De Priest migrated first to Salina, Kansas, and then to Chicago where he established a successful real estate business. He entered local politics and with a power base of **African American** votes he became Cook County commissioner in 1904 and 1906. In 1915 he was elected to the city council where he introduced a civil rights ordinance and campaigned against job discrimination. In 1917 he was accused of taking a bribe from a gambling house but was successfully defended by **Clarence Darrow**.

De Priest was elected a ward committeeman in 1924 and 1928, and in return for his support for Mayor **William Hale Thompson** he was appointed assistant Illinois commerce commissioner in 1927. In 1928 he won the **Republican** nomination for Congress and was elected despite facing an indictment for gambling connections and vote fraud. The case against him was eventually dropped, and De Priest was the first African American congressman for twenty-eight years, and the first from a northern state. He was reelected in 1930 and 1932. He campaigned against lynching, fought to defend the **Scottsboro boys**, and in 1933 obtained the inclusion of an amendment prohibiting discrimination in the bill creating the Civilian Conservation Corps. In 1934 he was defeated by the first black **Democrat** elected to Congress, Arthur W. Miller, and returned to local politics and his real estate business.

DEWEY, JOHN (1859–1952). Perhaps America's greatest philosopher, John Dewey was educated at the University of Vermont and Johns Hopkins University. Dewey taught at the universities of Minnesota, 1885–1889; Michigan, 1889–1894; Chicago, 1894–1904; and Columbia, 1904–1939. He wrote on **education**, psychology, and philosophy and became president of the American Psychological Association, 1899–1900; president of the American Philosophical Association, 1905–1906; and vice president of the American Association for the Advancement of Science in 1909. Involved in the **settlement houses** at Hull House and Henry Street, his work showed the influence of William James's notions of pragmatism. Dewey referred to the "instrumentalism" of ideas, meaning that ideas were instruments that could be used in social reform to tackle the problems that were created by society, not nature. He viewed education as a means to improving society and he established an experimental school at the University of Chicago. Over the years Dewey developed and modified his theories and shifted emphasis from biology and psychology to anthropology and history as determinants of human nature. Increasingly, too, Dewey argued that the value of ideas was measured by their outcome, and this could only be ascertained by continuous testing. His work ranged over ethics, logic, education and pedagogy, art, and religion.

Dewey supported American participation in **World War I** as a means of securing a lasting peace, but he defended the right to dissent and principles of academic freedom. He was one of the founders of the **American Civil Liberties Union**. After the war Dewey visited Japan, Mexico, and later the Union of Soviet Socialist Republics (USSR). He called upon the United States to recognize the communist regime. In 1937 he chaired an unofficial commission to examine the charges brought against the Russian revolutionary Leon Trotsky in the Moscow show trials of 1936. After several meetings with Trotsky, the commission found him not guilty.

During the 1930s Dewey was an advocate of American neutrality but he abandoned this position following the German invasion of Poland in 1939. He was one of the organizers of the Committee for Cultural Freedom that criticized the "repression of intellectual freedom" in Germany, Italy, Spain, and the Soviet Union. After World War II Dewey spoke out against the activities of the House Un-American Activities Committee and the exclusion by some universities of staff accused of communist sympathies. Dewey's many publications included: *Psychology* (1887), *The Study of Ethics* (1894), *School and Society* (1899), *How We Think* (1910), *Democracy and Education* (1916), *Human Nature and Conduct* (1922), *Experience and Nature* (1925), *The Quest for Certainty* (1929), *Art as Experience* (1934), *Liberalism and Social Action* (1935), *Logic: The Theory of Inquiry* (1938).

See also FOREIGN POLICY.

DEWSON, MOLLY (MARY WILLIAMS) (1874–1962). Molly Dewson graduated from Wellesley College in 1897 and joined the Women's Educational and Industrial Union in Boston. In 1900 Dewson became the superintendent of the parole department of the Massachusetts State Industrial School for Girls in Lancaster. She resigned in 1912 to take part in the campaign to establish a minimum wage for **women** workers in Massachusetts, the first in the United States.

In 1917 Dewson and her partner, Mary G. Porter, volunteered for service in France with the American Red Cross, and then settled in New York City in 1919. From 1919 to 1924 Dewson was the research secretary of the National Consumers' League, and she became president of the New York Consumers' League until 1931. An active campaigner on behalf of the **Democratic Party**, Dewson ran the Women's Division of the Democratic National Committee from 1933 to 1937, and she worked closely with both **Eleanor** and

Franklin D. Roosevelt. She was a member of the Committee on Economic Security in 1934 that helped to draw up the Social Security legislation, and in 1937 Dewson became a member of the Social Security Board. She retired from government service in 1938 and spent the rest of her life with Porter.

DOHENY, EDWARD LAURENCE (1856–1935). Edward Doheny began his business career in 1892, when he opened the Los Angeles oil fields. He went on to develop the Tampico oil field in Mexico and organized the Mexican Petroleum Company of California. In 1922 he secured a contract from the U.S. government to build a naval fuel station at Pearl Harbor, Hawaii, and also obtained drilling rights in the naval oil reserves at Elk Hills, California. However, a Senate investigation into the **Teapot Dome** scandal revealed that Doheny had given secretary of the interior **Albert Fall** $100,000 in cash. Doheny claimed this was a loan, but he and Fall were indicted in 1925 for bribery and conspiracy. In 1926 both were acquitted of conspiracy, and in 1930 the judge instructed the jury that they could acquit Doheny of giving a bribe but convict Fall of receiving it. Nonetheless, the government canceled Doheny's oil leases, and he was required to repay profits made from them.

DOMINICAN REPUBLIC. In 1916 U.S. troops were sent to the Dominican Republic, in the West Indies, when internal unrest threatened American business interests on the island. The troops remained until 1924.

See also FOREIGN POLICY.

DORR, RHETA CHILDE (1866–1948). Rheta Dorr began her career as a journalist reporting on the Klondike gold rush for the New York *Sun* from her vantage point in Seattle. She left her husband in 1898 and moved to New York where she became a full-time reporter for the *Evening Post*. Having reported on **women** in work, she became an activist campaigning for **women's suffrage**, minimum wage laws, and better working conditions for women. In 1906 Dorr left her job, visited Europe, and subsequently worked in department stores and garment industries. Her accounts of these experiences were published in *Harper's Weekly*, *Everybody's Magazine*, and *Hampton's Magazine*, and formed the basis of her book *What Eight Million Women Want* in 1910. After spending time with Emmeline Pankhurst in England, Dorr founded and edited the *Suffragist* for the Congressional Union of Woman in 1914. Dorr reported on the Russian Revolution in 1917 and was a war correspondent for the New York *Evening Mail* for three months. After the war she spent time in Europe and served as a foreign correspondent for the New York *Herald Tribune* from 1920 to 1923. In 1928 she published a *Biography of Susan B. Anthony*, one of the leading American suffragists.

See also NEWSPAPERS AND MAGAZINES.

DOS PASSOS, JOHN RODERIGO (1896–1970). John Dos Passos's first poems were published with those of **e. e. cummings** in *Eight Harvard Poets* in 1917. After graduating from Harvard University that year Dos Passos served through **World War I** as an ambulance man in Italy. He won recognition for his books, *One Man's Initiation* (1919) and *Three Soldiers* (1921), based on his war experiences. In 1925 *Manhattan Transfer*, his first book written in the style mixing fact and fiction ("faction") that was to become his trademark, appeared.

In addition to poetry and travel writing, Dos Passos wrote three plays during the 1920s—*The Garbage Man* (1926), *Airways, Inc.* (1928), and *Fortune Heights* (1933). His *United States* trilogy, consisting of *The 42nd Parallel* (1930), *Nineteen Nineteen* (1931), and *The Big Money* (1936), continued in the realist vein and offered a radical critique of American capitalism through the eyes of various fictional and real characters and a commentary by the narrator acting as the "Camera Eye." Dos Passos defended **Sacco** and **Vanzetti** in 1927 in *Facing the Chair: Story of the Americanization of Two Foreign-Born Workmen*. Dos Passos also reported on strikes and covered the trials of the **Scottsboro boys**. During the 1930s he spent time in and reported on events in Spain. His political concerns were reflected in his *District of Columbia* trilogy—*Adventures of a Young Man* (1939), *Number One* (1943), and *Year of Decision* (1943). He also wrote books on Thomas Jefferson and Tom Paine. During World War II Dos Passos was a war correspondent for *Life* magazine in the Pacific. After the war he wrote a number of historical works focusing on the founding years of the American republic and continued to write books on travel. He is mainly remembered with e. e. cummings, **Ernest Hemingway**, and **William Faulkner** for his writings in the interwar years and for his use of new styles.

See also LITERATURE AND THEATER.

"DOUGHBOYS". The nickname given to the men who served in the **American Expeditionary Force (AEF)**. The origins of the term are unclear: possibly coined during campaigns in the West or the Philippines when infantry men appeared covered in dust resembling the color of adobe buildings or dough. Others suggested it was because the buttons on the infantryman's blouse was shaped like a dough dumpling; alternatively it was claimed it was because, compared to their French counterparts, they were loaded with "dough," meaning money.

DOUGLAS, AARON (1899–1979). Born in Topeka, Kansas, the leading **African American** artist of the **Harlem Renaissance** Aaron Douglas began studying **art** at the University of Nebraska in Lincoln. His studies were broken by **World War I** when he worked in factories in Detroit and then

Minneapolis. He returned to Lincoln after the war and gained a Bachelor of Fine Arts from University of Nebraska in 1922 and then a Bachelor of Arts from the University of Kansas in 1923. He taught art at Lincoln High School in Kansas City between 1923 and 1925. In 1925 he moved to **Harlem** in New York City and took classes with the German artist Winold Reiss. Douglas soon established himself as an artist, providing illustrations for the **National Association for the Advancement of Colored People**'s (NAACP) magazine *Crisis* and the **National Urban League**'s (NUL) journal *Opportunity*. His work was also included in **Alain Locke**'s collection *The New Negro*, and that of various leading black writers including **Langston Hughes** and **James Weldon Johnson**. From 1930 on Douglas worked on several large murals of *Symbolic Negro History* for Fisk University and *Aspects of Negro Life* for the Schomburg Collection of the New York Library. After a year in Paris in 1931 Douglas became the first president of the Harlem Artists Guild. In 1939 he moved to Nashville, Tennessee, to establish the art department at Fisk. He obtained in his MA there in 1944, and he continued to teach until his death.

DREIER, MARY ELIZABETH (1875–1963). Like her sister, **Margaret Dreier Robins**, Mary Dreier attended the New York School of Philanthropy and was involved in Asacog House, a **settlement house** in Brooklyn. Both sisters joined the Women's Trade Union League (WTUL), and Mary Dreier succeeded Margaret as president in 1906 and served until 1914. As a wealthy middle-class woman her arrest in support of strikers in the Triangle Waist Company in 1909 brought considerable publicity to the **women**'s cause. In 1911 Dreier was the only woman appointed to the New York State Factory Investigating Commission established following the Triangle Waist Company fire in which 146 women had died. Dreier served until 1915, when she joined the New York City Board of Education.

Dreier resigned from the WTUL in 1915 and became chair of the New York City Woman Suffrage Party's industrial section and concentrated on the **women's suffrage** campaign. During **World War I** she headed the New York State Women in Industry Committee. After the war Dreier campaigned for protective legislation for women and in 1924 was elected to the WTUL's executive. In 1935 Dreier was appointed vice president of the WTUL and served until the organization ended in 1950.

See also SOCIAL WORK.

DREISER, THEODORE (1871–1945). The son of German immigrants, Theodore Dreiser became one of the leading figures in the prewar literary naturalism movement, which depicted characters as victims of their internal drives or social environment. He wrote as a journalist for several years for the Chicago *Globe*, St. Louis *Globe-Democrat* and *Republic*, and the Pittsburgh *Dispatch*. He edited *Smith's Magazine* (1905–1906), *Broadway Magazine* (1906–1907), and *American Spectator* (1907–1934). In 1900 he published *Sister Carrie*, showing a **woman** driven by her desire for material success above all moral values. *Jennie Gerhardt* (1911) focused on an immigrant girl disowned by her family when she becomes pregnant out of wedlock. In *The Financier* (1912) and *The Titan* (1914) he focused on the rise to power and influence of an amoral businessman, based on the life of businessman Charles Yerkes. The final volume in the trilogy, *The Stoic*, was published in 1947.

In 1919 Dreiser moved to Hollywood where he worked on film scripts. His great postwar novel, *An American Tragedy* (1925), was widely regarded as his masterpiece. In it, the main protagonist was a young man, who, driven by sexual desire and greed, murdered his pregnant mistress to marry a wealthy woman but was discovered, convicted, and executed. Like a number of his works, this attracted the attention of some censors for its supposedly immoral content, but the book was a commercial success. In 1927 Dreiser visited the Soviet Union and he subsequently wrote positively of communism during the **Depression**. He became a political activist in the thirties as a member of the League of American Writers and chair of the National Committee for the Defense of Political Prisoners. His *Tragic America* (1932) was a critique of large corporations, **banks**, and railroads. In 1938 he attended an international peace conference and campaigned in America on behalf of the Spanish Republican forces. He argued against U.S. involvement in the war in Europe in 1941. In 1945 he very publicly joined the Communist Party. In addition to his novels Dreiser published several collections of poetry, short stories, travel books, and works of journalism, but he is remembered as perhaps America's greatest writer of naturalist fiction.

See also LITERATURE AND THEATER; NEWSPAPERS AND MAGAZINES.

DUBINSKY, DAVID (1892–1982). Born in Poland, Dubinsky was imprisoned in Siberia for his early **trade union** activities. He immigrated to the United States in 1911, found work as a cutter in the garment industry, and joined the International Ladies Garment Workers Union (ILGWU) and the **Socialist Party**. He became secretary-treasurer of the union in 1929 and president in 1932. He held the position until 1966. In 1934 he became vice president of the **American Federation of Labor** (AFL) but left to help form the Congress of Industrial Organizations (CIO) in 1936. He was one of the leading **trade union** supporters of **Franklin D. Roosevelt** and the **New Deal** and in 1936 he left the Socialist Party to help found the American Labor Party (ALP). He left the CIO in 1938, and the ILGWU was independent until 1945, when it rejoined the AFL. Dubinsky left the ALP in 1944 and was one of the founders of the Liberal Party. He was also active in Americans for

Democratic Action formed in 1947 to oppose communism. After the war Dubinsky was involved in combating racketeering in the unions and was a member of the AFL-CIO Committee on Ethical Practices.

DU BOIS, WILLIAM EDWARD BURGHARDT (1868–1963). W. E. B. Du Bois was an **African American** scholar—historian, sociologist, poet— and **civil rights** leader. From Great Barrington, Massachusetts, he was educated at Fisk, Harvard, and Berlin, and gained his PhD from Harvard in 1895. Professor of economics and history at Atlanta University, his influential collection of essays *The Souls of Black Folk* (1903) included an attack on the "accommodationist" leadership of Booker T. Washington. In 1905 Du Bois was one of the African Americans who called together black leaders in the Niagara Movement to challenge segregation. In 1909 a number of white liberals joined with African Americans to form the **National Association for the Advancement of Colored People** (NAACP), and Du Bois was appointed editor of the journal *The Crisis*. Under his editorship *The Crisis* became a major outlet for the expression of black culture and opinion. Du Bois's own writings on subjects such as lynching, support for the American war effort, and postwar race relations were of major influence.

After **World War I**, Du Bois was active in the Pan African movement and attended congresses in Paris (1919), London, Brussels, and Paris (all in 1921), and London and Lisbon (1923). Du Bois increasingly questioned the gradualist approach of the NAACP and he resigned in 1934 and concentrated on teaching and writing as professor at Atlanta. In 1935 Du Bois published *Black Reconstruction in America*, a work that still stands as a major study of the post–Civil War period. After World War II he was an advocate of world peace and nuclear disarmament and as such was seen as a communist sympathizer. Du Bois prepared *An Appeal to the World*, a petition to the United Nations protesting the plight of African Americans tabled by the Union of Soviet Socialist Republics (USSR) in 1947. His membership of the Peace Information Center led to his indictment under anticommunist legislation. He was acquitted, but denied a passport until 1958. Du Bois left the United States to live in Ghana in 1961 and renounced his U.S. citizenship a year later.

DURANT, WILLIAM CRAPO (1861–1947). The **automobile** manufacturer and financier William Durant began his working career as a patent medicine and cigar salesman in the 1880s. In 1886 he and J. D. Dort bought a company making horse-drawn carriages which they moved to Flint, Michigan. By 1900 the Durant-Dort Company was the largest of its type in the United States. In 1904 Durant moved into automobile manufacturing when he took over the struggling Buick Motor Company, and in 1908 he established the General Motors Corporation (GM) and added Oldsmobile and Cadillac in addition to another twenty companies to the new organization.

Durant lost managerial control of General Motors in 1910. The following year he financed the production of a touring car by **Louis Chevrolet** and in 1913 created the Chevrolet Motor Company. By 1915 Chevrolet was the country's second largest automobile manufacturer. Using Chevrolet shares, Durant regained control of GM in 1916. Another financial crisis in 1920 forced Durant to give up the presidency of the company once more. In 1921 he established Durant Motors, and in two years the new company had captured a fifth of the automobile market. The shaky foundations of the company were exposed by the **Wall Street Crash** in 1929, and Durant was forced to declare bankruptcy in 1936. He opened a supermarket in New Jersey in 1936 and a chain of bowling alleys in Flint in 1940, but he was never able to regain the heights he had formerly held.

See also FORD, HENRY (1863–1947).

DYER ACT, 1919. The National Motor Vehicle Theft Act, named after its primary sponsor, Leonidas C. Dyer, a **Republican** representative from Missouri, made it a federal offense to drive a stolen motor vehicle or **automobile** across state lines, or to deal in stolen vehicles that had crossed state lines.

See also CRIME AND POLICING.

DYER ANTI-LYNCHING BILL. A bill to outlaw illegal lynching by penalizing mob violence introduced in Congress by **Republican** Representative Leonidas C. Dyer of Missouri and Congressman **Charles Curtis**, Republican representative for Kansas in 1919. It passed in the House of Representatives but was rejected by the Senate in 1921 and again in 1923.

See also CRIME AND POLICING.

EARHART, AMELIA (1898–1937). Amelia Earhart learned to fly in 1921 and became an exhibition flyer. She became the first **woman** to fly across the Atlantic when she flew in a plane piloted by two men from Newfoundland to Wales on 17 June 1928. She was feted in London and New York. Earhart toured the United States promoting **aviation** and the new airmail service with **Charles Lindbergh**, and speaking on behalf of equal rights for women. In 1932 she flew single-handed from Newfoundland to Londonderry, Ireland, and was awarded the U.S. Distinguished Flying Cross for her achievements. In 1935 Earhart flew across the Pacific from Honolulu to California. In 1937 she went missing over the Pacific with navigator Fred Noonan while trying to fly around the world from east to west.

EASTMAN, CRYSTAL (1881–1928). A law graduate, Eastman investigated labor conditions as part of the Russell Sage Foundation's Pittsburgh Survey and published a report on *Work, Accidents, and the Law* in 1910. She was the first **woman** to serve on New York State's Commission on Employers' Liability and Causes of Industrial Accidents, and was responsible for drafting the state's workmen's compensation law, the first in the country. Between 1913 and 1914 she was an investigating attorney for the U.S. Commission on Industrial Relations. A committed suffragist, she was one of the founders of the militant **Congressional Union**. In 1915 she founded the **Woman's Peace Party** and led the New York branch. She became an executive director of the **American Union Against Militarism** which attempted to keep the United States out of the war and then became an advocate for **conscientious objectors** in the National Civil Liberties Bureau in April 1917. When the war ended she organized the First Feminist Congress in 1919 and with her brother, **Max Eastman**, became copublisher of the radical journal *The Liberator*. As labor lawyer, social worker, suffragist, pacifist, and defender of civil liberties, Crystal Eastman was an example of the new women's activism during and after the **progressive** era.

EASTMAN, MAX FORRESTER (1883–1969). The radical editor Max Eastman was educated at Williams College and Columbia University. Influenced by his sister, **Crystal Eastman**, he joined the literary circles in **Greenwich Village** in 1910 and in 1912 became editor of *The Masses*. Eastman revitalized the left-wing journal and attracted some of the leading writers of the day to contribute. During **World War I** Eastman and six others associated with *The Masses* were indicted for sedition and conspiracy to obstruct military enlistment, but they were acquitted when two juries failed to reach a verdict. *The Masses* collapsed in 1917 after being denied its mailing privileges under wartime legislation. In 1918 Eastman established *The Liberator*, which survived until 1924. In 1922 Eastman traveled to the Soviet Union and after two years, to Europe. He returned to the United States in 1927 and for a while was Leon Trotsky's literary agent. Eastman increasingly wrote critical studies of Joseph Stalin's Soviet policies and renounced socialism in *Marxism: Is it Science?* in 1940. In 1941 he became an editor with the *Reader's Digest*, and in the 1950s he even supported senator Joseph McCarthy's anti-Communist crusade. Eastman's memoirs *Enjoyment of Living* (1948) and *Love and Revolution* 1964), plus his many essays, provide a detailed insight into the "lyrical left."

See also NEWSPAPERS AND MAGAZINES.

EAST ST. LOUIS RACE RIOT, 1917. On 2 July a race riot broke out in East St. Louis, Illinois, in which thirty-nine **African Americans** and eight whites died. Unofficial estimates put the figure for black deaths much higher. East St. Louis had seen an increase in black population of about five thousand due to the increased job opportunities in defense industries. The city was also a terminus through which many African Americans passed on their way to other towns and cities. This influx created conflict over housing and employment.

In response to the riot and the general increase in racial violence, the **National Association for the Advancement of Colored People** (NAACP) organized a silent protest march on 28 July in which several thousand African Americans marched down Fifth Avenue, New York. Further race violence erupted in the "**Red Summer**" of 1919.

See also GREAT MIGRATION.

ECONOMY. After an initial downturn in the economy in 1915 due mainly to a fall in exports, **World War I** brought a boom as **farming** and manufacturing sought to meet the increased demand for food and war materials for both the **Allied** nations and, after 1917, for the United States. Gross national product (GNP) almost doubled in the war years, and the war speeded up processes of mass production that were to continue in the following decade.

By the end of the war, the United States had the most powerful economy in the world, and it had changed from being a debtor nation to a creditor nation as a consequence of war loans and sales to the Allied powers. Much of this expansion was overseen and directed by new federal war agencies, particularly the **War Industries Board**, the **War Finance Corporation**, the **U.S. Food Administration**, and the **War Labor Board**. However, these agencies disappeared with the end of the war, and rapid, unplanned demobilization brought a period of sharp readjustment and dislocation as industry switched from wartime to peacetime production and returning soldiers flooded the labor market. As GNP dropped by 17 percent, unemployment rose dramatically to nearly 12 percent; this was coupled with an outbreak of industrial conflict that continued despite **industrial conferences** called by **Woodrow Wilson**'s administration. The situation improved as an upturn in the economy began with an increasing demand for consumer goods.

The years after the postwar recession were marked by dramatic growth as manufacturing output increased by an average of 5 percent a year. GNP rose from about $70 billion in 1922 to almost $100 billion in 1929. New technology, the development of chemical and plastic industries, the rise of the **automobile**, and the rapid introduction of electric power to industry and for domestic use all had an enormous impact on productivity and brought a wave of new consumer goods. In 1920 less than 50 percent of American homes had electric power; by 1930 over 70 percent had electricity. The widespread use of radios, vacuum cleaners, fans, and other domestic appliances powered by electricity was a major feature of the decade. The purchase of such products was encouraged by the growth of advertising, which became an industry in its own right. However, much of the spending on consumer goods was based on credit, and even this decade of apparent growth witnessed recessions in 1924 and 1927, and following the **Wall Street Crash** in 1929 the economy plunged rapidly into the **Great Depression**.

Other features of the economy contributed to the coming of the Depression after 1929. The 1920s witnessed a considerable consolidation of American businesses due to mergers. The automobile industry was increasingly concentrated in just a few companies, but so too was meat-packing, food production, soap products, and other areas including **banking**. Chain stores such as The Great Atlantic & Pacific Tea Company (A&P) grew in number. By 1929 the two hundred largest corporations controlled almost half of the country's corporate wealth. While some industries boomed, others did not—coalmining struggled through the decade, as did **farming**. Income distribution was also uneven, and although average incomes rose by 11 percent corporate profit rose by 62 percent. While there were estimated to be fifteen thousand millionaires in 1929, more than 12 million people, 42 percent of the population, lived on less than $1,500 per annum, and even workers in growth industries like automobile experienced occasional periods of unemployment.

While such factors limited domestic purchasing power, the introduction or raising of **tariffs** during the decade made exports more difficult. At the same time, the linking of the American economy with that of European nations through war loans, and loans to Germany after the war, ensured that financial failure quickly became international in its impact.

See also DAWES PLAN 1924; DEPARTMENT OF COMMERCE; EMERGENCY RELIEF AND CONSTRUCTION ACT, 1932; EXCESS PROFITS TAX; FORDNEY-MCCUMBER ACT, 1922; HOOVER, HERBERT CLARK (1874–1964); LEVER FOOD AND FUEL ACT, 1917; MCNARY-HAUGEN BILL; PRESIDENT'S EMERGENCY COMMITTEE FOR EMPLOYMENT, 1930–1931; PRESIDENT'S ORGANIZATION ON UNEMPLOYMENT RELIEF (POUR), 1931–1932; PRESIDENT'S UNEMPLOYMENT CONFERENCE, 1921; RECONSTRUCTION FINANCE CORPORATION (RFC); TRADE UNIONS; YOUNG PLAN, 1929.

EDERLE, GERTRUDE (1906–2003). Gertrude Ederle began swimming as a child and was already a world-record holder by the age of twelve. By the time she was seventeen she held eighteen swimming world records. In 1924 at the Paris Olympics Ederle won one gold and two bronze medals. After failing to swim the English Channel in 1925 she turned professional in order to finance a second attempt. In 1926 Ederle broke the record for the channel swim and became the first woman to complete the challenge when she swam the distance in fourteen hours thirty-one minutes. This time was soon beaten by men, but remained the record time for **women** until 1964. Ederle swam in exhibitions for a time after her success but increasingly suffered from hearing loss due to the aggravation to an existing problem by the saltwater. In 1933 she fell and damaged her spine and was in casts for four years. During World War II Ederle worked in aircraft factories. After the war she became a swimming instructor for deaf children. She was inducted to the Swimming Hall of Fame in 1965.

EDUCATION. The period from **Progressivism** before World War I through to the end of the 1920s witnessed continuous growth in the field of education. Free elementary education for almost all children was achieved by the end of the nineteenth century, and most states outside of the South also required attendance at high school up to the age of sixteen or eighteen. Education was seen by many reformers as an important means toward Americanization, and **Settlement Houses** often provided basic programs in literacy for their occupants. **World War I** had also served to underline the importance of education to the nation as concern was expressed about the poor educational background of many of those registered for the draft, 25 percent of whom were found to be illiterate or failing in the newly introduced intelligence tests.

Wartime training programs were established within the **Army**. A Vocational Rehabilitation Division was established at the end of the war to help train disabled servicemen for civilian work and this program was later transferred to the Veterans Administration. The influence of **John Dewey**'s ideas on education, spread through the Progressive Education Association founded in 1919 and challenging the commonly held notion that schooling was simply about literacy and classical learning, could be seen in a number of developments including the spread of vocational educational programs in schools. These developments were assisted by matching federal funds provided under the **Smith-Lever Act** (1914) providing for agricultural education and the **Smith-Hughes Act** (1917) that provided for commercial, industrial, and domestic science training programs.

Between 1919 and 1928 the number of Americans in all levels of education rose by over 6 million: the number in elementary and secondary school rose from 17.8 million in 1910 to 21.58 million in 1920 and 25.678 million in 1930; the percentage of those between fourteen and seventeen years of age in school rose from 32 percent in 1920 to 51 percent in 1930 (from 83,417 to 99,168). The quality of education varied according to region and race. Many schools in 1920 were still one-room, single-teacher institutions, the majority of them in rural areas and particularly in the South. Motorized transportation facilitated rural school consolidation and led to a considerable drop in the number of one-teacher schools. Schools remained segregated in the South, and **African Americans** did not benefit from improvements in education; spending on schools, books, equipment, and teachers' salaries for African Americans remained consistently much lower than for whites.

The number of colleges and universities increased from 977 in 1900 to 1,041 in 1920 and to 1,409 by 1930; the number of college students rose by almost 300 percent between 1900 and 1930, from 132,489 to 388,755, and the university population rose by 500,000 during the 1920s and had reached 1.1 million by 1930. By 1926 over 12 percent of Americans between eighteen and twenty-one were in some form of higher education. While colleges provided mainly training in business-related courses, law, medicine, engineering and education, universities were becoming centers of research; the number of doctorates awarded rose from 615 to 2,299 in the decade. The number of students enrolled in colleges and universities in America was four or five times the number in European countries.

The development of new subjects particular in the social sciences was evident in a number of universities, the progressive belief in a rational and efficient approach to politics and society was also evident in the role of social scientists such as **William F. Ogburn** and **Charles E. Merriam** on presidential committees and advisory bodies. The precedents for **Franklin D. Roosevelt**'s later "Brain Trust" were already established to some extent by his predecessors, particularly **Herbert Hoover**.

See also BEARD, CHARLES AUSTIN (1874–1948); BEARD, MARY RITTER (1876–1958); BRECKINRIDGE, SOPHONISBA PRESTON (1866–1948); BUTLER, NICHOLAS MURRAY (1862–1947); HOUSTON, DAVID FRANKLIN (1866–1940); JOHNSON, JAMES WELDON (1871–1938); JORDAN, DAVID STARR (1851–1931); KALLEN, HORACE MEYER (1882–1974); KELLER, HELEN (1880–1968); LAWRENCE, ERNEST ORLANDO (1901–1958); LOCKE, ALAIN (1886–1954); LOGAN, RAYFORD WHITTINGHAM (1897–1982); MILLIKAN, ROBERT ANDREWS (1868–1953); MOTON, ROBERT RUSSA (1867–1940); MUMFORD, LEWIS (1895–1990); ROBINSON, JAMES HARVEY (1863–1936); ROSS, EDWARD ALSWORTH (1866–1951); SCHURMAN, JACOB GOULD (1854–1942); STARR, ELLEN GATES (1859–1940); VAN RENSSELAER, MARTHA (1864–1932).

EIGHTEENTH AMENDMENT. The Eighteenth Amendment to the Constitution prohibiting the manufacture, sale, or transportation of alcohol was adopted by both houses of Congress in December 1917 and ratified by the necessary two-thirds of the states in January 1919. It was put into force by the **National Prohibition Act** in October 1919. (See appendix 2.)

ELAINE, ARKANSAS. Elaine was the location of one of the race riots that swept America during the "**Red Summer**" of 1919. On 30 September 1919, **African American** sharecroppers meeting to form a union were involved in a confrontation with a group of white men. After a white deputy sheriff was shot and killed in the clash, violence spread as a white mob attacked the black community. Five whites and "anywhere from 20 to 200" African Americans died in the ensuing violence between 1 and 3 October. Hundreds of African Americans were arrested, and twelve were subsequently sentenced to death for murder in a number of very short trials. The **National Association for the Advancement of Colored People** (NAACP) financed their appeals, and all the defendants were eventually released following the **Supreme Court** ruling in *Moore v. Dempsey* in 1923, which found that the trials were conducted against a mood of public passion that led to the accused being denied their constitutional rights.

ELIOT, T. S. (THOMAS STEARNS) (1888–1965). The poet T. S. Eliot was born in St. Louis, Missouri, but he settled in England in 1915 and became a British subject in 1927. Eliot was educated at Smith Academy, Harvard, the Sorbonne in Paris, and Oxford University. In England Eliot was introduced to the literary circles by **Ezra Pound**. Eliot's first collection of poems, *Prufrock and other Observations*, was published in 1917, and the second collection, *Poems*, in 1919. Eliot's poem "The Waste Land" was published in 1922 and became one of the major works of the **"Lost Generation"** of postwar disillusioned writers and the modernist school. The poem first appeared in the *Criterion*, which Eliot edited for seventeen years. When the journal was taken over by the publishers Faber and Faber, Eliot became a director with the company and helped to publish the work of major English writers such as W. H. Auden and Stephen Spender. Eliot also became one of the leading literary critics on the interwar period.

Eliot's later work such as "Journey of the Magi" (1927), "Ash Wednesday" (1930), and the essays for *Lancelot Andrewes* (1928) reflected his conversion to the Anglican Church in 1927. The subject of Christianity was also evident in his plays, the history of the Church in *The Rock* (1934), *Murder in the Cathedral* (1935), and *The Family Reunion* (1939). Eliot's last work of nondramatic poetry, regarded by many critics as his greatest work, was published as *Four Quartets* in 1943. After World War II he continued to write chiefly for the theater, and *The Cocktail Party* (1949) was one of his most successful plays.

See also LITERATURE AND THEATER.

ELLINGTON, "DUKE" (EDWARD KENNEDY) (1899–1974). The **African American jazz** musician and composer was born Edward Kennedy Ellington but acquired the nickname "Duke" as a schoolboy in Washington, D.C. Ellington did not have professional musical training but learned how to play from other black musicians. He formed his first group in 1917 and in 1923 he and several band members moved to Harlem, New York, where they found work in clubs. In 1924 Ellington became the bandleader and developed an improvisational style of composition. In 1926 the Ellington band recorded "East St. Louis Toodle-Oo," followed in 1927 by "Birmingham Breakdown" and "Black and Tan Fantasy." It was in 1927 that the band became the resident band at Harlem's famous Cotton Club. Over the coming years Ellington and his band composed and recorded what were to become jazz classics: "Creole Love Call" (1927), "Mood Indigo," "Sophisticated Lady" (1932), "Solitude" (1934), and many more. With successful recording and live broadcasts from the Cotton Club from 1931 on, Ellington became a major figure in popular music.

Ellington continued to produce great jazz hits through band and record label changes. In 1940 the band recorded "Take the 'A' Train," "Cotton Tail," and "Ko-Ko." After a brief lull in their success the Ellington band had a revival of fortunes following a performance at the Newport Jazz Festival in 1956. Before he died Ellington had been awarded honorary degrees, membership in the American Institute of Arts and Letters, the French Legion of Honor, and the Presidential Medal of Freedom.

See also MUSIC AND DANCE.

ELLSWORTH, LINCOLN (1880–1951). Lincoln Ellsworth was an explorer who led a geological expedition to the Andes in 1924, went with Amundsen from Spitsbergen to Alaska by seaplane in 1925, and made a trans-Arctic submarine expedition in 1931. In 1935 he flew 2,300 miles across the Antarctic claiming the new land for the United States. He was the author, with Amundsen, of *First Crossing of the Polar Sea* (1927), and sole author of *Beyond Horizons* (1938).

EMERGENCY QUOTA ACT. *See* QUOTA ACT, 1921.

EMERGENCY RELIEF AND CONSTRUCTION ACT, 1932. Signed by president **Herbert Hoover** on 21 July 1932 in response to the deepening **Depression**, the Emergency Relief and Construction Act provided $300 million for the **Reconstruction Finance Corporation** to make relief loans available to states. It also authorized funds for federal, state, and local public works. These relief programs were to be far exceeded during the **New Deal**.

EMPIRE STATE BUILDING. When it opened on 1 May 1931 the Empire State Building on Fifth Avenue, between 33rd and 34th Streets in New York City, was, at an original height of 1,250 feet, for a time the tallest building in the world. Ironically, much of the new office space provided was not initially used because of the onset of the **Great Depression**.

ENTERTAINMENT, ARTS, AND LEISURE. *See* ART; LITERATURE AND THEATER; MOVIES; MUSIC AND DANCE; RADIO; SPORTS.

ESCH, JOHN JACOB (1861–1941). John Esch graduated from the University of Wisconsin in 1882. He took a law degree in 1887, was admitted to the bar, and began to practice law in La Crosse, Wisconsin. Active in the state guard, from 1894 to 1896 Esch served as judge advocate general with the rank of colonel. He was a delegate to the **Republican Party** convention in 1894 and 1896, and in 1898 was elected to the U.S. House of Representatives. He served for twenty-two years. Esch's major contribution was on the Committee on Interstate and Foreign Commerce where he supported measures to increase the power of the Interstate Commerce Commission. Esch opposed U.S. involvement in **World War I** and voted against the declaration of war in 1917.

As chair of the House Commerce Committee after the war, Esch was cosponsor of the **Esch-Cummins Act**. Criticism from senator **Robert La Follette**, who argued that the act would increase rail costs and consumer prices, led to Esch's defeat in the Republican primary in 1920. President **Warren Harding** appointed Esch to the Interstate Commerce Commission in 1921, and he served as chairman in 1927. Southern politicians voted against confirming his renomination in 1928, and Esch then established a law practice in Washington, D.C. He also served as president of the American Peace Society from 1930 to 1938.

ESCH-CUMMINS ACT. *See* RAILROAD TRANSPORTATION ACT, 1920.

ESPIONAGE ACT, 1917. Passed in June 1917 shortly after the American entry into **World War I**, the Espionage Act established a $10,000 fine and up to twenty years' imprisonment for acts of sabotage, promoting the success of the enemy, or obstructing military recruitment and operations in wartime. Anyone using the mail in violation of the statute was liable to a $5,000 fine and up to five years' imprisonment. By May 1918 forty-five newspapers or journals had had their mailing rights suspended under the legislation. The act was further amended in 1918 under the **Sedition Act** to give even greater powers of suppression to the government.

EVANS, HIRAM WESLEY (1881–1966). Evans was a dentist from Texas who rose through the ranks of the **Ku Klux Klan** to become imperial wizard from 1922 to 1939. The Klan expanded and became a significant force in several northern states under his leadership in the mid-1920s. Evans wrote several books, including *The Menace of Modern Immigration* (1923), *The Klan Tomorrow* (1924), and *The Rising Storm* (1929).

EXCESS PROFITS TAX. First levied by Congress in 1916 to deal with high war profits during **World War I** and raise money for the war effort, the excess profits tax was a graduated tax on business profits in excess of a fixed percentage of capital investment or of average profits. In its first year it yielded approximately $2 billion. The law was repealed in 1921 but reintroduced in 1933.

See also ECONOMY.

FAIRBANKS, DOUGLAS (1883–1939). Born Douglas Elton Ulman, Fairbanks changed his name in 1900. In 1902 he made his acting debut in New York and he became a leading Broadway star and was one of New York's best-paid leading men by 1914. In 1915 he joined Triangle Film Productions, and he had appeared in twenty-three **movies** by 1918. By 1916 he was writing his own scripts and producing his own films. By 1919 Fairbanks was America's leading movie star, and he had also authored three books: *Laugh and Live* (1917), *Assuming Responsibilities* (1918), and *Making Life Worth While* (1918). That year he joined with director **D. W. Griffith** and two other stars, **Charlie Chaplin** and **Mary Pickford**, to form the United Artists Film Corporation. In 1920 Fairbanks married Pickford, and they became an internationally known "couple."

Starting with *The Mark of Zorro* in 1920 Fairbanks turned to the swashbuckling costume dramas with which he was forever associated. The enormously successful *Robin Hood* (1922) followed the *Three Musketeers* (1921). *The Thief of Baghdad* (1924), *Don Q. Son of Zorro* (1925), and *The Black Pirate* (1926) crowned Fairbanks's success. Several other silent movies followed, but Fairbanks's style seemed increasingly dated as the talkies took over and later as the **Depression** undercut the optimism and exuberance central to his movies. In 1935 he and Pickford were divorced, and by 1938 **Samuel Goldwyn** had acquired major control of United Artists, which was renamed Samuel Goldwyn Studios. In 1939 Fairbanks won a posthumous Academy Award for his contribution to the development of motion pictures.

FALL, ALBERT BACON (1861–1944). Albert Fall grew up in Tennessee where he later began teaching and studying law. He moved to Kansas and then Texas in 1881 before prospecting in New Mexico where he settled in 1887. Initially a **Democrat**, Grover Cleveland appointed him judge on the territorial bench in 1893, and he served until 1895. He subsequently established a law practice in El Paso, Texas, and became involved in a variety of business activities in Mexico and New Mexico. Fall served in New Mexico's legislature from 1891 to 1895, 1897, and 1903 to 1905. He changed political allegiance in 1904, when he supported the **Republican** platform and was Republican senator for New Mexico from 1912 until **Warren Harding** appointed him secretary of the interior in 1921. He resigned in 1923, and in 1924 a Senate investigation revealed he had accepted large bribes from his friends in the oil business, **Edward Doheny** and **Harry Sinclair**, in return for leasing naval oil reserves in **Teapot Dome**, Wyoming, and California. Fall was convicted of bribery in 1929 and served nine months of a one-year prison sentence, the first cabinet officer to be convicted of a felony committed while in office.

FARM BLOC. The Farm Bloc was a congressional coalition of western **Republicans** and southern **Democrats** led by **Arthur Capper** that fought for legislation to improve the plight of farmers during the 1920s. The twenty-five senators and approximately one hundred representatives supported the **Agricultural Credit** and **Agricultural Marketing Acts**, and the **McNary-Haugen** bills. The Bloc also managed to obtain the passage of legislation in 1922 exempting farmers' cooperatives from antitrust legislation.
See also FARMING.

FARMER-LABOR PARTY. A third party formed in 1919 by members of the **Committee of Forty-eight** in an attempt to unite farmers and the labor movement under a reform program. The party first nominated **Robert M. La Follette** as its presidential candidate, but when he rejected the nomination the party turned instead to Parley P. Christensen of Utah. In the 1920 election he received 260,000 votes. In 1924 the Farmer-Labor Party supported La Follette's **Progressive Party**.
See also FARM BLOC; FARMING.

FARMING. For much of its history the United States was a predominantly agrarian economy. The industrial revolution in the early nineteenth century stimulated the expansion of agriculture, and the move westward after the Civil War (1861–1865) led to growth in machine technology with the use of threshers, reapers, and combined harvesters. The new large-scale farming, linked to eastern cities by the **railroads**, provided the food for growing industrial, urban populations. But by the 1890s manufacturing output began to exceed agricultural production, and as the farmers were displaced socially and politically, they also experienced increasing economic problems due to overproduction and worldwide competition that resulted in falling prices. Angry farmers blamed their indebtedness on the high interest charged by **banks**, the rates levied by the railroads, and **tariffs** that protected industry but raised consumers' costs. In the 1880s and 1890s this anger saw the rise of a farmers' movement and the creation of the Populist Party in 1892. A depression in 1893 only worsened their situation, and in 1896 the Populist Party supported the **Democratic Party**'s candidate, **William Jennings Bryan**. Bryan's defeat signaled the demise of Populism and the domination of the political system by the **Republicans** until 1912.

Many of the Populists' demands for railroad and bank regulation were incorporated in the agenda of the **Progressives**, and rising prices saw some improvement in the farmers' situation. **World War I** brought a boom in agriculture, as world trade was limited. The demand for grain and food to feed both the U.S. and **Allied** armies brought an expansion in farm acreage and output. Mechanization and the use of tractors contributed further to farm efficiency. After the war, however, world competition resumed and the artificially high commodity prices fell. American farmers once again struggled to pay off the debts they had incurred, and 453,000 farmers lost their property in the immediate postwar crash. The farm population, over 32 million in 1910, was 31.9 million in 1920, and had fallen to 30.5 million by 1930. As a proportion of the total population this represented a drop from over 30 percent to just under 25 percent.

Despite falling numbers, this vital sector in the **economy** failed to share fully or evenly in the prosperity of the 1920s. In 1919 gross farm income accounted for 16 percent of the national income; by 1929 it was 8 percent, and average per capita farm income was 25 percent of the national average as the value of farm products fell by half. Some farmers did prosper during the 1920s, but many smaller farmers and tenant farmers struggled to make a living. Falling farm property values and the fall in price of farm produce led to increased indebtedness. Farmers in the midwest organized in the **Non-Partisan League** echoed Populist demands for federal action to control prices on their behalf but had limited success. The **American Farm Bureau Federation** (AFBF) established a lobby in Washington, D.C., and a **Farm Bloc** of western Republicans and southern Democrats struggled to achieve the passage of legislation to protect farmers but with little effect.

The **Great Depression** only worsened the situation of farmers as agricultural prices collapsed after 1929. By 1932 average farm income had dropped by two-thirds. With many farmers unable to meet mortgage repayments almost a million farms were repossessed between 1930 and 1934. The drought and dust storms of the 1930s only added to the misery. Desperate farmers declared "farm holidays" in which they withheld their produce from the market or dumped it in the roads. Farm sales following evictions were often blocked, and farmers demonstrated in their neighboring towns. President **Herbert Hoover** responded by signing the **Agricultural Marketing Act** and attempted to stabilize prices through **Federal Farm Boards**. However, this had little immediate effect, and it was not until the coming of the **New Deal** that farming began to experience a recovery.

See also CAPPER, ARTHUR (1865–1951); FEDERAL FARM LOAN ACT, 1916; FORDNEY-MCCUMBER ACT, 1922; MCNARY-HAUGEN BILL; TOWNLEY, CHARLES ARTHUR (1880–1959); WALLACE, HENRY CANTWELL (1866–1924).

FAULKNER, WILLIAM HARRISON (1897–1962). William Faulkner was one of the greatest southern writers of the twentieth century. Born William Cuthbert Falkner in Mississippi, he had a desultory education, worked in the family bank, and spent some time at the University of Mississippi. Rejected by the U.S. Army Faulkner joined the British Royal Air Force in Canada in 1918. After the war he studied at the University of Mississippi from 1919–1921 and published various poems and reviews. Faulkner earned a living as postmaster at the University until 1924. His first book, *The Marble Faun*, was published that year to be followed by many others including *Soldier's Pay* (1926), *Sartoris* (1929), *The Sound and the Fury* (1929), *As I Lay Dying* (1930), *Sanctuary* (1931), *Light in August* (1932), *Absalom, Absalom!* (1936), *Intruder in the Dust* (1948), *Requiem for a Nun* (1951), and *The Reivers* (1962). In many of these novels Faulkner traced the decline of the Old South through the stories of fictional families in "Jefferson," a composite Mississippi town in the mythical county of Yoknapatawpha. He was the winner of the Nobel Prize in Literature in 1950.
See also LITERATURE AND THEATER.

FAUSET, JESSIE REDMON (1882–1961). Jessie Fauset was the first **African American** woman admitted to Cornell University. She graduated in 1905 and completed an MA at the University of Pennsylvania. After a period of study in France, Fauset taught in high schools in Baltimore, Washington, D.C., and New York City. From 1919 until 1926 she was literary editor of the **National Association for the Advancement of Colored People** (NAACP) journal, the *Crisis*. Fauset was a part of the **Harlem Renaissance**, and her books, *There Is Confusion* (1924), *Plum Bun* (1928), *The Chinaberry Tree* (1931), and *Comedy: American Style* (1933), deal with black middle-class society and issues of "passing," miscegenation, lynching, and race pride.
See also LITERATURE AND THEATER.

FEDERAL BUREAU OF INVESTIGATION (FBI). The FBI began when attorney general Charles J. Bonaparte created a corps of special agents within the Department of Justice in 1908 to investigate **crime** at a federal level. In 1909 it was named the Bureau of Investigation. Following America's entry into **World War I**, the Bureau became responsible for investigating violations of the **Selective Service Act**, **Espionage Act**, and **Sabotage Acts**.

Headed by A. Bruce Bielaski the Bureau grew in size and influence. This growth continued during the **Red Scare** of 1919 and under the new leadership of William J. Flynn who assumed the title of director that year. The Justice Department widened its brief with the creation of a General Intelligence Division headed by **J. Edgar Hoover**. The Federal Bureau was created in 1924 to investigate violations of federal law with Hoover as its head.

FEDERAL FARM BOARD. The Federal Farm Board was a nine-man agency, eight appointed by the president, plus the secretary of agriculture, created by the **Agricultural Marketing Act** in 1929. Provided with a fund of $500 million, the Board was empowered to establish stabilization corporations to make purchases in agricultural commodities in order to support price levels. Two such corporations, for grain and cotton, were established but achieved very little. Having used all of its appropriation to little effect, it was abolished in 1933.
   See also FARMING.

FEDERAL FARM LOAN ACT, 1916. Passed on 17 July 1916, the Farm Loan Act established twelve Federal Land **Banks** along similar lines to the Federal Reserve Banks (*see* Federal Reserve Act) in order to provide more accessible credit to farmers through farm loan associations. The Federal Land Banks were under the control of a Federal Farm Labor Board consisting of the secretary of the treasury and six members appointed by the president. The Land Banks were funded initially with a minimum capital of $750,000. Mortgages of up to 50 percent of land value and 20 percent of improvements were issued to run from five to forty years.

FEDERAL FOOD ADMINISTRATION. *See* U.S. FOOD ADMINISTRATION.

FEDERAL HIGHWAY ACTS, 1916, 1921, 1925. The first Federal Highway Act provided matching federal funds to states and local authorities for highway building. The planned program was overtaken by the outbreak of World War I, necessitating further legislation in 1921. Under the second Highway Act in 1921, additional federal funds were provided for highway building, increasing spending from $19.5 million in 1920 to $88 million in 1923. The act of 1925 continued federal funding and provided for the replacement of the previous named highways such as the Lincoln Highway (1913), each of which had different colored systems of road signs, with the numbered U.S. Highway System such as Route 66 with even numbered routes running east to west and odd numbers running south to north.
   See also TRANSPORTATION.

FEDERAL HOME LOAN BANK ACT, 1932. Passed in July 1932, following the **Wall Street Crash**, the Federal Home Loan Bank Act established a series of discount **banks** for home mortgages, similar to the service provided by the **Federal Reserve System**. The failure of banks to cooperate limited the act's success.

FEDERAL RADIO COMMISSION (FRC). The Federal Radio Commission (FRC) was a five-man regulatory body established under the Communications Act of 1927 that took over the regulation of radio from the Department of Commerce. The commission had authority to grant licenses to broadcasting stations and approve their locations. It could also prescribe wavelengths and hours of operation but did not control program content other than to forbid the use of "obscene, indecent or profane language." A Federal Communications Commission established in 1934 replaced the FRC.

FEDERAL RAILROAD ADMINISTRATION. *See* U.S. RAILROAD ADMINISTRATION (USRA). *See also* TRANSPORTATION.

FEDERAL RESERVE ACT, 1913. Passed on 23 December 1913, the Federal Reserve Act, or Glass-Owen Act, was the first major **banking** and currency reform since the Civil War. It was intended to stabilize banking, limit the power of the bank trusts, and make access to credit easier. However, rather than create one central institution, the act established a Federal Reserve that consisted of twelve regional bodies, each one acting as a central bank run by local bankers. These banks were depositories for all national banks and for state banks and trust companies that wished to join. Each member bank subscribed 6 percent of its capital to the Federal Reserve and deposited a portion of its reserve there. The Reserve Banks were able to rediscount member banks' loans, that is, take over loans in return for Federal Reserve Notes that could then be used to make further loans. A Federal Reserve Board consisting of seven members appointed by the president was established to supervise the system and to review the rediscount rates as necessary.
See also ECONOMY.

FEDERAL TRADE COMMISSION ACT, 1914. The Federal Trade Commission Act established a Federal Trade Commission (FTC) consisting of five members appointed by the president to prevent unfair methods of competition. The Commission replaced the Bureau of Corporations established in 1903, and had new powers to define unfair trade practices and to issue cease and desist orders. In practice the commission proved sympathetic to business, offering advice on how to avoid antitrust prosecutions.

FEDERAL WATER POWER ACT, 1920. The Federal Water Power Act established a five-man Federal Power Commission to license the use of navigable rivers for power and set rates for power used in interstate commerce. The licenses enabled the construction of hydroelectric power stations.

FELTON, REBECCA LATIMER (1835–1930). Rebecca Felton, a campaigner for prison reform, temperance, and **women's suffrage**, was an influence on Georgia politics through her regular contributions to the *Atlanta Journal* and her book, *My Memoirs of Georgia Politics* (1911). She became the first **woman** to become senator when she was symbolically appointed by the governor of Georgia in October 1922 to fill a temporary vacancy caused by the death of the incumbent. Her tenure lasted an hour until the regularly elected male was sworn in.

FERGUSON, MIRIAM AMANDA WALLACE ("MA") (1875–1961). When Miriam Ferguson's husband, the **Democratic** twice-governor of Texas, James Ferguson, was impeached and convicted of misusing state funds in 1917, she entered the gubernatorial campaign in 1924 to clear his name. Campaigning with her husband, she appealed to "the mothers, sisters, and wives of Texas to help clear her family's name" and earned the nickname "Ma." She defeated the **Ku Klux Klan** candidate Felix Robertson to become the second **woman** governor (the first was **Nellie Tayloe Ross**). As governor she secured passage of a law prohibiting the wearing of masks in public (aimed at the Klan), and an amnesty for her husband, who she appointed a commissioner to the State Highways Commission. Ferguson granted a total of 3,595 pardons while governor, leading to suggestions that pardons were being sold by her husband. She failed to gain the nominations in 1926 and 1930 but was reelected in 1932. Ferguson supported the **New Deal** and approved a "bread bond" to raise money for the poor. Her attempts to raise taxes on the oil industry and on corporate business were unsuccessful. She later supported pensions for those over sixty-five and federal and state aid for farmers but failed to regain the Democratic nomination in 1940.

FIELDS, W. C. (WILLIAM CLAUDE) (1880–1946). The vaudeville, film and **radio** comedian W. C. Fields was born William Claude Dukenfield. His early theatrical career began as a juggler, and in the 1890s through to 1915 he toured America and Europe. In 1915 Fields joined the *Ziegfeld Follies* on Broadway and appeared in a successful Broadway musical, *Poppy* from 1923 to 1924. The film version of *Poppy*, *Sally of the Sawdust* appeared in 1925, and Fields also appeared in numerous other silent **movies** in the 1920s developing his comic persona as the con man or harassed husband, both with a strong dislike of children. In the 1930s he moved to Hollywood where he wrote scripts and starred in several films including *It's a Gift* (1934), *David Copperfield* (1935), and *The Bank Dick* (1940). Other successful films included *You Can't Cheat an Honest Man* (1939), *Never Give a Sucker an Even Break* (1941), and *My Little Chickadee* (1940), which also starred Mae West. Fields also had a successful radio career on *The Chase & Sanborn Hour* starting in 1937.

See also MOVIES.

FITZGERALD, F. (FRANCIS) SCOTT (1896–1940). F. Scott Fitzgerald was the writer who perhaps more than any other captured the spirit of the 1920s in America. He even gave the period its name, "The Jazz Age." Born in St. Paul, Minnesota, Fitzgerald went to Princeton in 1913. In 1917 he left to take up a commission in the infantry, but the war ended before Fitzgerald could see action. While serving in Alabama he met his future wife, **Zelda Sayre Fitzgerald**. She agreed to marry him following the publication of his first book, *This Side of Paradise*, in 1920. The book, which seemed to capture the new postwar morality of the young, was a great success. His second book, *The Beautiful and the Damned* (1922), was less successful, but the Fitzgeralds were able to support their extravagant lifestyle, much of it spent in Europe, with earnings from short stories published in magazines and in collections such as *Flappers and Philosophers* (1920) and *Tales of the Jazz Age* (1922).

Fitzgerald's reputation was assured with the publication of *The Great Gatsby* (1925). The book, which caught many of the elements of moral and material corruption of the decade, stood as a lasting commentary on the American Dream itself. Despite this success Fitzgerald's life was not easy. Financial worries, tensions in his marriage, and Zelda's nervous breakdown delayed the publication of his next book, *Tender Is the Night*, until 1934. In 1937 Fitzgerald began work as a scriptwriter for Metro-Goldwyn-Mayer, and his last book, *The Last Tycoon*, was based on his observations inside the studios. Incomplete when he died, the novel was published in 1993.

See also LITERATURE AND THEATER; "LOST GENERATION".

FITZGERALD, ZELDA SAYRE (1900–1948). The wife of **F. Scott Fitzgerald** and one of the celebrities of the 1920s, Zelda Fitzgerald was a writer and artist in her own right. As the daughter of an associate justice of the Alabama Supreme Court, Zelda was a notoriously rebellious teenager known for her unconventional behavior and dress as well as her striking good looks when she met her future husband in 1918. She was to be the model for many of his female characters. In both her lifestyle and some of the articles she wrote for **magazines** Zelda Fitzgerald portrayed the **flapper**. Sadly she suffered several nervous breakdowns requiring institutional care. In 1948 she died in a fire in Highland Hospital in Asheville, North Carolina.

See also JAZZ; LITERATURE AND THEATER.

FIVE POWER TREATY. *See* WASHINGTON NAVAL TREATY.

FLAPPER. Used prior to **World War I** to mean a headstrong **woman**, the term "flapper" was used much more widely in the 1920s to describe the "new woman," liberated politically with the vote, economically by new work opportunities, and socially with new fashions. With her bobbed hair, straight dresses that stopped just below the knee, the flapper smoked and drank in public and discussed sexual matters in a manner inconceivable to older generations of women. However, the extent of this "revolution in manners and morals" was probably exaggerated by images in the **movies**, magazines, and advertising. A film called *The Flapper* appeared in 1920, and several actresses including **Theda Bara** and **Louise Brooks** were identified with the term. The writer **F. Scott Fitzgerald** was often thought to have invented the flapper of the 1920s, and his first collection of short stories was entitled *Flappers and Philosophers* (1920); his wife, **Zelda Fitzgerald**, was in many ways the personification of the flapper. The term used for the male equivalent of flapper was "sheikh," probably from the films of **Rudolph Valentino**.

FLYNN, ELIZABETH GURLEY (1890–1964). Socialist labor organizer Elizabeth Gurley Flynn became a full-time organizer for the **Industrial Workers of the World** in 1907 and was involved in so many strikes that she became known as the "Rebel Girl." After the war she helped to found the **American Civil Liberties Union** and was a leading campaigner in defense of **Sacco** and **Vanzetti**. She also spoke on behalf of **women**'s rights and birth control. In 1936 Flynn joined the **Communist Party USA**. In 1952 she was convicted of advocating the overthrow of the U.S. government and jailed for two years. She became national chairperson of the Communist Party in 1961. Flynn died during a visit to the Soviet Union where she was given a state funeral before being flown back to the United States for burial.

FORD, HENRY (1863–1947). Henry Ford's name became synonymous with the 1920s with the development and sale of his mass-produced **Model T Ford**. Ford began work as a mechanic in Detroit in 1879. In 1891 he found employment with the Edison Illuminating Company and was chief engineer from 1887 to 1889. Ford built his first car in 1896 and in 1899 established the

Detroit Automobile Company. For a time Ford concentrated on building racing cars, and his company became the Cadillac Motor Car Company in 1902.

Ford returned to **automobile** manufacture when he established the Ford Motor Company in 1903. He first began production of the Model T Ford in 1909 using the concept of mass-produced standardized parts and developed it further at his new Highland Park factory in 1910. In 1913 Ford developed the moving assembly line method of production enabling an enormous increase in production and a reduction in price that made motorcar ownership a possibility for masses of ordinary people. In 1914 he introduced a profit-sharing scheme and a five-dollar eight-hour day for his workers and later introduced the five-day week. However, he also attempted to control workers through a personnel department that implemented mandatory English lessons for immigrant workers, and a no-smoking, no-drinking, and nonunion policy. Ford also established a museum at Dearborn dedicated to preserving the rural past, complete with one-room schoolhouse and McGuffey readers.

Ford was a pacifist, and he personally funded an attempt to bring peace when he purchased a "peace ship," *Oscar II*, in 1915 that went with delegates to Oslo where a conference of neutral powers was held. Once America entered the war the Ford Company turned to producing engines, tractors, and vehicles for the government. Ford opened the world's largest single manufacturing plant at River Rouge, Detroit, in 1916. Such was Ford's public stature that in 1916 he won the **Republican** presidential primary in Michigan without campaigning. In 1918 Ford was persuaded to run for election to the Senate by **Woodrow Wilson**, but a Republican opponent defeated him. There were attempts to persuade him to stand for the presidency in 1920 and 1923, but Ford supported **Warren Harding** and **Calvin Coolidge**. During the early 1920s Ford's magazine, the *Dearborn Independent*, published a series of anti-Semitic articles, and in 1938 the German Nazi government honored Ford.

After **World War I** Ford expanded his operation to develop luxury cars (the Lincoln) and airplanes. In 1927 he ceased production of the now out-of-date Model T and began producing the Model A. This did not match up to other cars, particularly the **Chevrolet**. In 1932 Ford introduced the new V-8 engine, but the Ford Company did not recover its early domination of the market. By 1936 Ford ran third behind **General Motors** and **Chrysler** in terms of its market share. The Ford Company held out against the **trade union** drives of the 1930s despite some bitter struggles on the part of workers. Union recognition was only granted in 1941.

During World War II the Ford Company converted entirely to war production and built a huge aircraft production plant at Willow Run outside Detroit. Ford himself was increasingly unwell, and in 1945 he was forced to yield control to his grandson, Henry Ford II. Despite this, Ford's name remained synonymous with modern car production.

FORDNEY, JOSEPH WARREN (1853–1932). Joseph Fordney began work from an early age in the lumber industry in Michigan. He became a prominent businessman and entered politics in 1895 as a **Republican** alderman in Saginaw, Michigan. In 1898 he was elected to the U.S. House of Representatives, where he became an advocate of timber and sugar tariffs. In 1920 he became chair of the Ways and Means Committee and in 1922 achieved his protectionist objectives with the **Fordney-McCumber Act**. Fordney retired the following year to concentrate on his business interests.

FORDNEY-MCCUMBER ACT, 1922. The Fordney-McCumber Act raised **tariffs** to levels higher than any previously in American history in an attempt to bolster the postwar economy, protect new war industries, and aid **farmers**. Duties on chinaware, pig iron, textiles, sugar, and rails were restored to the high levels of 1907, and increases ranging from 60 to 400 percent were established on dyes, chemicals, silk and rayon textiles, and hardware. Tariffs on a variety of agricultural produce were raised. While the tariffs encouraged the growth of monopoly in the United States, they also made it difficult for European powers to earn sufficient dollars to repay war debts. Other nations responded by increasing their tariffs, thus limiting U.S. exports and constricting the market. These factors helped to create the weaknesses that produced the Depression.

See also ECONOMY; FORDNEY, JOSEPH WARREN (1853–1932).

FOREIGN POLICY. For much of its history the United States was content to look inward and concentrate on westward expansion and settlement rather than concern itself with affairs beyond its borders. Traditionally the main feature of the country's foreign policy was **isolationism**. However, as the nation grew and as it became increasingly a world economic power, it began to look outward. The Spanish-American War (1898) resulted in the acquisition of an empire—the Philippines, Hawaii, and Puerto Rico—and concern for trade saw a widening interest in Asia and the growth of the U.S. Navy. The building of the Panama Canal (1904–1914) was funded by the United States and carried out under the supervision of **George W. Goethals**. Increasingly too, the notion of separate spheres with the United States dominant in the new world found a more aggressive expression in **Theodore Roosevelt**'s "Roosevelt Corollary" (1904) justifying an interventionist policing and protectorate policy in Central and Latin America. This was also linked to the "dollar diplomacy" that witnessed a growth of the U.S. economic interests in this area. This new role lay behind the interventions in Panama (1903), Cuba (1906, 1912, 1917), the **Dominican Republic** (1905, 1916), **Haiti** (1915), and Nicaragua (1912, 1927). It also affected relations with **Mexico** and almost brought the two countries to war during **Woodrow Wilson**'s presidency. Relations with Latin America began to improve under the presidencies of **Warren Harding**, **Calvin Coolidge**, and particularly **Herbert Hoover** who began the "Good Neighbor" policy that was to continue under **Franklin D. Roosevelt**. The Roosevelt Corollary was repudiated under the **Clark Memorandum** in 1928.

Wilson's moralistic and idealist approach to foreign affairs, evident in his relations with Mexico, was also apparent during **World War I**. The outbreak of war in Europe demonstrated how difficult it was for a world power with a large immigrant population and growing trading links to remain unaffected by the conflict. Great Britain actively tried to persuade the United State to enter the war on the side of **Allied Powers** by use of propaganda and did exert some influence when it made the **Zimmerman telegram** public. However, relations between Britain and the United States were strained early on due to the imposition of a naval blockade by the British from 1914 onward, and relations became increasingly strained by 1916. However, it was Germany's use of unrestricted submarine warfare that ultimately led to the declaration of war.

The U.S. entry into the war in 1917, justified as a war to "make the world safe for democracy," seemed to mark an end to the policy of isolationism. Wilson's **Fourteen Points** and his commitment to the **League of Nations** appeared to confirm this. However, the rejection of the **Versailles Treaty** and the League by the Senate in 1919 demonstrated the strength of traditional views, particularly in the **Republican Party**. The defeat of the **Democratic Party** in the presidential election of 1920 and the Republican domination through the 1920s suggested a return to isolationism, but in reality the war had underlined America's position as a leading world power.

Following the Bolshevik Revolution of 1917, the United States had refused to recognize the new Russian government and had sent troops as part of a multinational force ostensibly to protect property and supplies but in reality supporting the White Russian forces. Over ten thousand U.S. troops were sent to Vladivostok and Archangel in 1918 but were withdrawn in 1920. The new Soviet Union was not recognized until 1933, although trading relations improved throughout the 1920s.

During the 1920s the Republican administrations were involved in disarmament plans at the **Washington** and **London Naval Conferences**, and in initiating attempts to outlaw war in the **Kellogg-Briand Pact**. Moreover, the country was vitally involved in the world's economy. In 1920 the United

States produced one-sixth of all world exports and received one-eighth of all imports. Before the war the United States was a debtor nation, owing $4 billion in foreign investments; after the war it was a creditor nation, owed $12.5 billion in war debts by nations like France and Great Britain. In addition American financiers lent money to Germany throughout the 1920s enabling the payment of reparations. The Allied Powers of Great Britain and France wished to renegotiate the payment of war debts as they could meet their payments, and reduced payments were agreed in 1923. The United States also took a lead in renegotiating reparations through the **Dawes** and **Young Plans**. Thus the raising of **tariffs** and the withdrawal of credit to foreign powers following the **Wall Street Crash** contributed to the **Great Depression** becoming worldwide phenomena. The British government suspended payment of war loans in 1932 after the Germans had ceased to pay reparations the previous year.

Although isolationist tendencies reappeared as world conflict spread during the 1930s, Franklin D. Roosevelt took a much more interventionist position than his predecessors, and entry into World War II in 1941 revolutionized the U.S. foreign policy.

See also BRYAN, WILLIAM JENNINGS (1860–1925); HUGHES, CHARLES EVANS (1862–1948); ISOLATIONISM; STIMSON, HENRY LEWIS (1867–1950).

FOSDICK, RAYMOND BLAINE. A graduate of Princeton University (1905) and New York Law School (1908), Raymond Fosdick became assistant corporation counsel for the city of New York and established a reputation as a reformer during investigations of motion picture theaters, prostitution, and loan sharking. In 1912 Fosdick became comptroller and auditor of the national **Democratic Party**. In 1916 he was appointed assistant to the secretary of war **Newton D. Baker** and during **World War I** was chair of the Commission on Training Camp Activities. In that role Fosdick encouraged the development of educational and other programs for U.S. servicemen.

In 1919 **Woodrow Wilson** appointed Fosdick first undersecretary to the **League of Nations**, but he resigned when the Senate refused to ratify the League of Nations Covenant. He continued to support the League through the League of Nations Association that he founded. Fosdick established a legal practice in New York City and was involved on the boards of a variety of organizations associated with **Rockefeller** family philanthropies. In 1936 he became president of the Rockefeller Foundation and Rockefeller Education Board. Fosdick continued to advocate U.S. involvement in international affairs and supported the world court and the United Nations.

FOSTER, WILLIAM Z. (1881–1961). Having traveled the country as an itinerant worker, Foster joined the **Socialist Party** in 1901 but later left to join the **Industrial Workers of the World** (IWW). Foster gradually moved away from the IWW in favor of converting existing **trade unions** to syndicalism. In 1912 he established the Syndicalist League of North America, which became the Independent Trade Union League in 1914. As an organizer for the Chicago Federation of Labor during World War I, Foster helped to mobilize the meatpacking workers. The **American Federation of Labor** then appointed Foster to lead the drive to unionize the steel industry in 1919. The resultant strike ended in defeat, partially because Foster's past affiliations were used to brand the strikers as revolutionaries. Foster converted to communism in the early 1920s and was the **Communist Party USA** candidate in the 1924, 1928, and 1932 presidential elections. In 1932 he won over one hundred thousand votes.

Foster resumed the leadership of the American Communist Party following the ideological differences between the established executive and Moscow in 1945. In 1948 Foster was one of eleven Communist leaders indicted by the government under the 1940 Smith Act. He was not jailed because of his ill health, but his codefendants were. Foster died in Moscow in 1961 and received a state funeral there before his ashes were flown back to the United States.

FOUR MINUTE MEN. The Four Minute Men were volunteers mobilized by the **Committee of Public Information** during **World War I** to address audiences at theaters, movie halls, and public places on issues relating to the war. Some seventy-five thousand people took part in this propaganda exercise, and there were also Junior Four Minute Men who spoke on patriotic themes in school competitions.

FOUR-POWER TREATY, 1921. One of the several agreements made during the **Washington Naval Conference** in 1921, the Four-Power Treaty was between the United States, France, Great Britain, and Japan. The signatories agreed to recognize each other's possessions in the Pacific and approved joint action in the event of any aggression in the Pacific by a non-signatory power.

See also FOREIGN POLICY.

FOURTEEN POINTS. In a speech to Congress in January 1918 president **Woodrow Wilson** laid out the basis for an armistice with the **Central Powers**. This program, a list of fourteen points, included such principles as freedom of the seas, open covenants openly arrived at, removal of trade barriers, equal adjustment of colonial claims, and the establishment of a **League of Nations** to prevent further wars.

See also FOREIGN POLICY.

FOX, WILLIAM (1879–1952). The **movie** executive and producer William Fox was born Wilhelm Fuchs in Tulchva, Hungary. His family immigrated to the United States in 1880 and took the name "Fox." Fox built up a clothing company which he sold in 1903 and bought a nickleodeon theater. Fox gradually built this into a network of theaters, and he moved into the area of film production. In 1911 Fox successfully challenged the Edison Motion Picture Patents Company's (MPPC) monopolistic control of film equipment and opened the way for independent film producers and distributors. By 1927 Fox owned more than one thousand movie theaters, and he invested money in developing sound pictures and also Fox Movietone News. In 1929 he bought a controlling interest in Loews Corporation, the parent company of Metro-Goldwyn-Mayer (MGM), but was forced to sell the stock back when the Justice Department launched an antitrust suit against him. His financial dealings forced him to sell Fox Films in 1930, and the company merged with **Darryl F. Zanuck**'s Twentieth Century Pictures to become Twentieth Century-Fox in 1935. Accused of financial malpractice, Fox was first of all forced into bankruptcy in 1936 and in 1942 was jailed for bribing a judge in his bankruptcy hearings.

FRANK, LEO (1884–1915). Leo Frank graduated in mechanical engineering from Columbia University in 1906. He moved to Atlanta, Georgia, and became superintendent of the National Pencil Factory. A Jew, Frank became president of the Atlanta B'nai B'rith in 1912. On 27 April 1913 a night watchman at the National Pencil Factory found the body of thirteen-year-old Mary Phagan, who had been brutally murdered. Two days later Frank was arrested and charged with the murder. The Atlanta press created a mood of hysteria by focusing on Frank's religion and printing lurid and false tales about his personal and religious life. In this climate Frank was convicted in August and sentenced to death despite clear doubts about his guilt. A national outcry developed, and the case was covered in a number of northern journals, including *Collier's* and *Everybody's*. After reviewing the case the governor of Georgia, John M. Slaton, commuted the death sentence. There was considerable public anger in Georgia orchestrated particularly by the political leader Tom Watson, and on 15 August 1915 a mob broke into the jail, abducted Frank, and hanged him outside the town of Marietta. No one was ever charged for the murder. Tom Watson was elected to the U.S. Senate in 1920.

Mary Phagan's killing was said to have encouraged the revival of the **Ku Klux Klan**, and Leo Frank's murder was clearly indicative of the racial and religious tensions evident in this period.

See also CRIME AND POLICING.

FRANKFURTER, FELIX (1882–1965). Born in Austria, Felix Frankfurter's family immigrated to America in 1894. Frankfurter gained a law degree at the College of New York and went on to Harvard University where he graduated in 1906. Frankfurter practiced briefly in New York and then became an assistant to **Henry Stimson**, a U.S. attorney in New York. Frankfurter became a professor in the Harvard Law School in 1914, a position he held until 1939. Influenced by **Louis Brandeis**, Frankfurter was a close associate of the editors of the *New Republic* and a part of the **progressive** movement. During **World War I** he became assistant secretary of labor and served as secretary for the **President's Mediation Commission** that investigated the labor unrest in the West in 1917. In the light of protests from **trade unions** and others, in 1916 President **Wilson** asked Frankfurter to investigate the convictions of **Tom Mooney** and **Warren Billings**, the labor leaders sentenced to death for a bombing in San Francisco in which ten people had died. Frankfurter reported that there were several grounds for a retrial, and as a consequence the death sentences were commuted. In 1918 Frankfurter was appointed to chair the War Labor Policies Board to unify labor standards used by federal agencies.

After the war Frankfurter called for recognition of the Bolshevik regime in Russia, defended immigrant members of left-wing groups against deportation, and called for a retrial in the case of **Sacco** and **Vanzetti**. Frankfurter and his protégés were influential in drawing up various pieces of **New Deal** legislation, and in 1938 **Franklin D. Roosevelt** nominated him to the **Supreme Court** where he served until 1962. Frankfurter was not consistently "liberal" as a justice, and is most remembered for his dissents in *West Virginia State Board of Education v. Barnette* in 1943 and *Baker v. Carr* in 1962. In the first he rejected the argument that the First Amendment barred mandatory flag salutes; in the second, he rejected any judicial remedy for malapportioned legislatures. Frankfurter was, however, conspicuous in his support of **African Americans**, and he wholeheartedly supported the decision against segregated schools in *Brown v. Board of Education* in 1954. He did not, though, support picketing by African Americans to secure employment in supermarkets (*Hughes v. Superior Court of California*, 1950), nor did he approve of sit-ins or other militant tactics.

FROST, ROBERT LEE (1875–1963). Perhaps the greatest American poet of the twentieth century, Robert Frost did not complete his university education but for a while divided his time between farming, teaching, and writing poetry. In 1912 he sold his farm and moved to England and in 1913 published his first collection of verse, *A Boy's Will*. His second collection, *North of Boston*, was published in 1914. Having achieved some critical success, Frost and his family returned to the United States in 1915. *Mountain Interval* was published in 1916, and Frost was appointed to a teaching post at Amherst. He left his post in 1920, established a summer study program at Middlebury College, and was "poet in residence" at Ann Arbor. In 1923 *Selected Poems* and *New Hampshire* appeared; *New Hampshire* won the first of four Pulitzer Prizes that Frost was awarded. For the rest of his career Frost divided his time among teaching appointments at different colleges.

Frost produced several more volumes of poetry. His *Collected Poems* (1930), *A Further Range* (1936), and *The Witness Tree* (1942) were awarded Pulitzers, and *In the Clearing* (1962) was well received. In 1961 Frost read one of his poems, "The Gift Outright," at president John F. Kennedy's inaugural and was awarded the Congressional Medal. Frost is remembered above all for his variations on blank verse, and the use of rural images and references to New England in a language easily accessible to the ordinary person.

See also LITERATURE AND THEATER.

G

GARBO, GRETA (1905–1990). The **movie** star Greta Garbo was born Greta Lovisa Gustafsson in Stockholm, Sweden. Her work as an advertising model in a department store led to a career in film beginning with *Peter the Tramp* (1920). From 1922 to 1924 Garbo studied at the Royal Swedish Dramatic Theater, and she acquired her stage name and reputation as an actress in *The Story of Gosta Berling* (1924). Following her success in Sweden, she moved to Hollywood in 1925, where her beauty and her husky voice perfectly enabled her to play roles of sexual passion. Garbo made a total of twenty-four films in Hollywood. Her films, in which she often played the part of the tragic heroine, included *Flesh and the Devil* (1927), *Love* (1927), *Anna Christie* (1930), *Mata Hari* (1932), *Grand Hotel* (1932), *Anna Karenina* (1935), *Camille* (1936), and *Ninotchka* (1939). Garbo received four Academy Award nominations for best actress. She retired at age thirty-six in 1941 and moved to New York City to live a secluded life. Famous for the "Garbo mystique" that she deliberately fostered, she was given a special Oscar in 1954 for unforgettable performances.

GARFIELD, HARRY AUGUSTUS (1863–1942). The son of president James A. Garfield, Harry Garfield studied law at Columbia University and practiced in Cleveland from 1888 to 1903. He taught law at Western Reserve University and then politics at Princeton University from 1903 to 1908 before becoming president of Williams College from 1908 to 1934. During **World War I** Garfield headed the **U.S. Fuel Administration** and was responsible for bringing some stability to the coal industry. However, faced with competing demands for fuel from industry and the railroads, he ordered a temporary closure of all industry east of the Mississippi. This led to such criticism of **Woodrow Wilson**'s administration that it then asserted greater centralized control of the war economy. After the war Garfield resumed his position at Williams College. He was elected president of the American Political Science Association in 1923.

GARNER, JOHN NANCE (1868–1967). The 32nd vice president of the United States, John Nance Garner was born in a log cabin in Texas. After limited schooling he attended Vanderbilt University briefly, studied law, and qualified for the bar on 1890. Garner practiced law in Uvalde, where he became county judge, 1893–1896. He was elected as a **Democrat** to the state house of representatives in 1898 and to the U.S. House of Representatives in 1903. Garner served until 1933. He was not conspicuous in legislation—it was eight years before he made his first speech—but he gained power by virtue of seniority. Garner eventually became speaker of the House from 1931 to 1933, when he was elected vice president to **Franklin D. Roosevelt**. His experience gave him a crucial role as liaison with Congress, and the Texas connection gave him influence with a number of key figures and he was reelected in 1936. He has been described as the "most powerful vice president in history." Initially a supporter of the **New Deal**, Garner was increasingly unhappy with the social welfare and pro-labor aspects of Roosevelt's program. He became openly hostile when Roosevelt attempted to alter the composition of the **Supreme Court** in 1937 and stood against FDR for the nomination in 1940. When he was unsuccessful, Garner retired to his ranch in Uvalde and took no further part in politics.

GARVEY, MARCUS MOZIAH (1887–1940). Marcus Garvey was the Jamaican-born leader of the **Universal Negro Improvement Association** (UNIA), the black nationalist organization he first established in Jamaica in 1914 and then brought to the United States in 1916. Garvey's brand of nationalism, with its call to people of African origin to unite under "One Aim, One God, One Destiny," had a particular appeal to disillusioned **African Americans** after **World War I**. He encouraged black economic self-determination and established a Negro Factories Corporation and a Black Cross as well as a Black Star Shipping Line to assist the movement back to Africa. The UNIA paper, the *Negro World*, was published in several languages and reached an international audience. Garvey claimed over 2 million supporters, but actual members were probably more in the thousands, but with chapters in thirty cities. He outraged many black Americans by meeting the leader of the **Ku Klux Klan** in Georgia and suggesting that their policies of racial separation had much in common. As a consequence of financial irregularities in the running of the Black Star Line, he was convicted of mail fraud in 1922 and went to jail in 1925. His sentence was commuted after two years, and he was deported to Jamaica. The UNIA failed to recover from this turn of events, and Garvey died in relative obscurity in London, where he had moved in 1935.

GARY, ELBERT HENRY (1846–1927). Elbert Gary served briefly in the Civil War (1861–1865), qualified in law, and eventually established his own law firm. Gary served as a county judge (1882–1890) and was president of the Chicago Bar Association (1893–1894). In 1898 he became president of the Federal Steel Company and moved to New York City. In 1901 the banker J. P. Morgan gave Gary the responsibility of organizing the U.S. Steel Corporation. Gary became a dominant figure in the corporation for the next twenty-five years. The steel town of Gary, Indiana, was named after him when it was created in 1913. Gary was also known for his advocacy of the open shop, and his refusal to negotiate with **trade unions** provoked the **steel strike of 1919**.

GEHRIG, LOU (HEINRICH LUDWIG) (1903–1941). Born Heinrich Ludwig Gehrig, Lou Gehrig was outstanding at football and baseball at school. He went to Columbia University in 1921 but was not able to take part in **sport** until the 1922–1923 season because of earlier professional appearances. His performances in baseball led to his signing for the New York Yankees in 1923. He opened the season with the Yankees in 1925 and played every season until 1940. Gehrig hit forty-one or more home runs, set the major league record for grand slams (twenty-three), and in 1932 was the first American League player to hit four home runs in a single game. His career batting average of .340 ranked him close to **Babe Ruth**, and he earned the Most Valuable Player award in 1927, 1934, and 1936. Gehrig removed himself from the Yankees' lineup in 1939 and shortly after was diagnosed with a rare, crippling, and incurable neuromuscular disease. Gehrig was elected to the Baseball Hall of Fame in 1939. Mayor **Fiorello La Guardia** appointed him to New York's city parole commission, and he continued working in that role until his death.
    See also SPORTS.

GENERAL ACCOUNTING OFFICE (GAO). The General Accounting Office was established in the Budget and Accounting Act of 1929 to supervise accounting procedures in the executive departments and agencies of the federal government and to audit federal expenditures.

GENERAL MOTORS CORPORATION. General Motors (GM), now one of the largest **automobile** manufacturers in the world, was founded in Michigan in 1908 by **William C. Durant** when he brought together the Buick, Oakland, and Oldsmobile companies.

GENEVA DISARMAMENT CONFERENCE, 1932. A conference of fifty-seven nations convened by the **League of Nations** to discuss worldwide disarmament. Although not a member of the League, the United States sent a delegation. Among the many proposals was that of president **Herbert Hoover**, who called for an immediate one-third reduction in existing national armaments and the outlawing of chemical warfare, bomber planes, heavy artillery, and tanks. On 27 May 1933, the U.S. delegation announced that the American government would be prepared to consult with other nations in the face of a threat to peace. The conference proved powerless and collapsed following the withdrawal of Germany in October 1933.

See also FOREIGN POLICY.

GENEVA NAVAL CONFERENCE, 1927. The Geneva conference, which took place in Switzerland from 20 June to 24 August 1927, was called by president **Calvin Coolidge** to consider further naval limitations following on from the earlier **Washington Naval Conference**. France and Italy did not accept the invitation, but representatives of Great Britain and Japan took part in discussions with the Americans. The U.S. proposals to extend the previously agreed ratios to cover other vessels were rejected by the British, and the conference ended without agreement.

See also FOREIGN POLICY.

GERARD, JAMES WATSON (1867–1952). Gerard was a lawyer and diplomat who had qualified in law at Columbia University and practiced law in New York City from 1892 to 1908, when he became an associate justice of the New York Supreme Court. In 1913 he was appointed ambassador to Germany by **Woodrow Wilson** and served until 1917. Gerard was central in representing the U.S. government's responses to the use of submarines by the Germans. Although he did express some sympathy for the German position, Gerard made it known publicly that unless some peace settlement was reached in 1916, then unrestricted submarine warfare would resume. When this occurred in 1917, the U.S. government broke off diplomatic relations, and Gerard was recalled. Gerard published two accounts of his experiences, *My Four Years in Germany* (1917) and *Face to Face with Kaiserism* (1918). During the war he addressed numerous **Liberty Bond** rallies.

In 1920 Gerard declared himself a candidate for the **Democratic** presidential nomination. He failed to win that or the vice presidential nomination but became chairman of the campaign finance committee. He continued in this or a similar capacity for the next thirty years. When World War II broke out, Gerard advocated U.S. intervention and spoke out in favor of Lend-Lease in

1941. In 1950 president Harry S. Truman appointed Gerard to the Advisory Board on International Development. The following year Gerard published his memoirs, *My First Eighty-Three Years in America.*

See also FOREIGN POLICY; WORLD WAR I, 1914–1918.

GERSHWIN, GEORGE (1898–1937). George Gershwin, born Jacob Gershvin, became one of America's most famous composers of orchestral works, popular songs, **jazz**, and musical comedies. He worked as a pianist for a **music** publisher from 1914 to 1917, when he became a theater pianist. In 1919 he achieved his first hit with "Swanee," later recorded by **Al Jolson**. From 1920 on Gershwin composed musical reviews, Broadway plays, and orchestral pieces. His best-known works were *Rhapsody in Blue* (1923), *Piano Concerto in F* (1925), *An American in Paris* (1928), and the opera *Porgy and Bess* (1935), all notable for their combination of jazz and orchestral music.

Together with his brother, **Ira Gershwin**, George Gershwin composed many hit songs for musicals. Among the best-known songs in these were "Fascinating Rhythm," "Someone to Watch Over Me," "'S Wonderful," "Embraceable You," and "I Got Rhythm." In 1936 the Gershwins went to Hollywood, where they wrote the music for *Shall We Dance?* in 1937. Starring Fred Astaire and Ginger Rogers, the movie included such hits as "Let's Call the Whole Thing Off" and "They Can't Take That Away from Me." The Gershwins provided the music for two more **movies**, *A Damsel in Distress* (1937) and *The Goldwyn Follies* (1937), before George's death. Gershwin's music was incorporated into a number of films after his death—*Rhapsody in Blue* (1945), *An American in Paris* (1951), and *Manhattan* (1979).

GERSHWIN, IRA (1896–1983). Born Israel Gershvin, Ira was the brother of **George Gershwin**. Ira provided the lyrics for many of George's compositions including the songs for the musicals *Lady Be Good* (1924), *Tiptoes* (1925), *Oh, Kay!* (1926), *Funny Face* (1927), *Strike Up the Band* (1927), and the Pulitzer Prize–winning *Of Thee I Sing* (1931). From 1936 Ira provided the lyrics for George's **music** in a number of Hollywood **movies**. Following George's death Ira wrote the lyrics for *Lady in the Dark* (1940), *Cover Girl* (1944), *Firebrand of Florence* (1945), *Park Avenue* (1946), *The Barkleys of Broadway* (1949), *A Star Is Born* (1954), and *The Country Girl* (1954). He was involved in the making of *An American in Paris* (1951), which incorporated some of his and George's earlier work and which won an Academy Award.

GIANNINI, AMADEO PETER (1870–1949). Born in San Jose of Italian immigrant parents, Amadeo Giannini first began work at the age of fourteen in his parents' fruit and vegetable wholesale business in San Francisco. However, in 1901 he joined his father-in-law's **bank**, Columbus Savings and Loan, but, frustrated by their conservative lending policies, he left in 1904 and established his own Bank of Italy in San Francisco. Giannini was prepared to lend money not just to the wealthy but also to middle- and working-class borrowers based on his estimates of their character and ability to repay. Following the 1906 earthquake and fire in San Francisco, Giannini was able to relocate his business and continue operating while other banks remained closed because their vaults were either too hot to open or inaccessible due to damage. Giannini also showed confidence in the city by making loans to enable people to rebuild their homes and businesses.

Building on his success, Giannini began to move beyond the traditional local bank and opened a number of branches; in 1918 he established California's first statewide bank. In 1921 he opened the Liberty Bank in San Francisco and in 1924 joined with Orra E. Monnette's Bank of America Los Angeles to create the Bank of America, which was to become one of the first transnational banks and one of the largest financial institutions in America. In 1928 further additions and expansion beyond California led to the consolidation of Giannini's holdings, including the Bank of America, in the Transamerica Corporation.

Giannini's success enabled him to finance the building of the Golden Gate Bridge, completed in 1937, and also to support Walt Disney in the making of the first animated **movie**, *Snow White and the Seven Dwarfs*, when it went over budget the same year. During World War II Giannini helped to bankroll Henry Kaiser's shipbuilding business and after the war he also helped to arrange financing to enable the Italian car manufacturer Fiat to rebuild. *Time* magazine, which featured him on its cover on 28 April 1928, described Giannini as one the "builders and titans" of the twentieth century.

See also ECONOMY.

GIFFORD, WALTER SHERMAN (1885–1966). Walter Gifford graduated from Harvard University in 1905. He had already begun work for the Western Electric Telegraph Company and in 1905 he became the company's assistant secretary and treasurer in New York City. In 1908 Gifford joined the parent company, American Telephone & Telegraph (AT&T), as a statistician and after a brief break to manage a copper mine, in 1911 he became the company's chief statistician. In 1916 Gifford was appointed supervising director of the Committee on Industrial Preparedness of the Naval Consulting Board and later director of the **Council of National Defense**. After the war Gifford was involved in the **Paris Peace Conference** as a member of the Inter-Allied Munitions Committee.

Gifford returned to AT&T as its comptroller in 1918. He became vice president of finance in 1920, was elected to the board of directors in 1922, and became executive vice president in 1923. Gifford sold AT&T's seventeen radio stations to the National Broadcasting Corporation (NBC) in order to avoid prosecution of the company under the antitrust laws. In 1925 he sold foreign telephone operations to International Telephone & Telegraph Company (IT&T). During the 1930s AT&T automated its operations and also marketed telephones to middle-class families. Under Gifford's leadership AT&T had become the largest corporation in America by the 1930s. During World War II Gifford was a member of the War Resources Board and chair of the Industry Advisory Committee of the Board of War Communications. In 1948 he gave up his leading role at AT&T and in 1949 became honorary chairman of the board. In 1950 president Harry S. Truman appointed Gifford as ambassador to Great Britain. He retired in 1953.

See also ECONOMY.

GILLETT, FREDERICK HUNTINGTON (1851–1935). The future congressman and senator for Massachusetts, Frederick Gillett graduated from Amherst in 1874 and Harvard Law School in 1877. He began a law practice in Springfield the same year and became assistant attorney general for Massachusetts in 1879. Gillett served in the state house of representatives from 1890 to 1891 and then was elected as a **Republican** to the U.S. House of Representatives in 1893, serving until 1925. Gillett made a name for himself as an able orator, and he spoke in defense of **African American** voting rights in the South and in favor of civil service reform. During **World War I** Gillett was a member of the Appropriations Subcommittee responsible for reviewing the details of military spending bills. He became speaker of the House in 1919 and held the position until 1924, when he was elected to the Senate. Gillett had opposed the **League of Nations** but supported the **Permanent Court of International Justice**. He endorsed **Prohibition** and the **Volstead Act**. Gillett retired from public office in 1931.

GILMAN, CHARLOTTE PERKINS (1860–1935). The great-niece of Harriet Beecher Stowe, writer, economist, and **women**'s rights theorist Charlotte Perkins Gilman grew up in a poor family in Connecticut. She had little formal schooling but studied art for a brief period at Rhode Island School of Design and began work designing greetings cards, teaching art, and offering private tuition. Following her marriage and the birth of her daughter in 1885, Gilman suffered from acute depression and was advised by a well-known neurologist, Dr. Silas Weir Mitchell, to give up all work, never touch a pen or brush, and devote herself to family life. Gilman rejected this remedy, moved to California, and in 1894 divorced her husband with whom she left her daughter. Gilman supported herself thereafter through her prolific writing and lecturing.

Gilman wrote some two hundred short stories, ten novels, plus various works of theory. Between 1909 and 1916 she produced her own journal, *Forerunner*. In much of her writing she argued that women's oppression began in the home. Gilman urged women to find their own identity and stressed particularly the need for economic independence. Her famous short story, "Yellow Wallpaper" (1892), was based on her own experience of illness and response to the medical diagnosis. Her international reputation was established with the publication of *Women and Economics: A Study of the Economic Relation between Men and Women* (1898). Gilman's other work included *Concerning Children* (1903), *The Man-Made World* (1911), *His Religion and Hers* (1923), and the novels *What Diantha Did* (1910), *The Crux* (1911), and *Herland: A Feminist Utopian Novel*, published in serial form in 1915. That year Gilman cofounded the Woman's Peace Party with **Jane Addams**. In 1935 Gilman, suffering from inoperable cancer, took her own life.

GISH, DOROTHY (1898–1968). The younger sister of **Lillian Gish**, Dorothy Gish appeared on the stage in touring melodramas in 1902. In 1912, with Lillian, she began work in film under the direction of **D. W. Griffith**. She made over twenty **movies** in the next few years and in 1917 rose to stardom in Griffith's *Hearts of the World*. Gish made a name as the "female **Chaplin**" playing comic roles, and in 1918 she was signed by Paramount. After playing comic roles in several films, she scored another success in serious parts in *Orphans of the Storm* (1922) and *Nell Gwyn* (1926). The latter was an English-made film. After several more movies with British director Herbert Wilcox, Gish returned to Broadway in 1928 and spent the next thirty years in the theater. She appeared to some acclaim in *The Inspector General*, *Getting Married*, and *The Pillars of Society* in 1931. She retired from the stage finally in 1956. Gish also made appearances on television in the 1950s and made her final film appearance in *The Cardinal* (1964).

GISH, LILLIAN (1893–1993). Along with **Clara Bow** and **Mary Pickford**, Lillian Gish was one of the great stars of early silent **movies**. However, her career on both stage and screen continued successfully well beyond the silent era. Her stage career began in 1902, but in 1912 she and her sister, **Dorothy**, met the film director **D. W. Griffith**, who cast them in *An Unseen Enemy* (1912). Gish worked with Griffith for ten years and starred in his classic film ***Birth of a Nation*** (1915) and *Intolerance* (1916). In these and other movies she developed the role of the pure, virgin heroine. During

World War I she starred in several of Griffith's propaganda films including *Hearts of the World* (1918). In the early 1920s Gish and Griffith parted company, and she worked first with Inspiration Films and then Metro-Goldwyn-Mayer. After making several more movies including *La Boheme* (1926), *The Scarlet Letter* (1926), and *The Wind* (1928), she returned to the stage and won critical acclaim in *Uncle Vanya, Hamlet, The Star Maker,* and other productions.

In the mid-1940s Gish returned to Hollywood in supporting roles in several films including *Duel in the Sun* (1947)—for which she was nominated for an Academy Award—and *Night of the Hunter* (1955). Gish also worked in television and starred in several dramas and television films including *Arsenic and Old Lace* (1969) and *Hobson's Choice* (1983). In 1971 Gish was awarded an honorary Oscar and in 1984 the American Film Institute's Lifetime Achievement Award. Her last film role was in *Whales of August* (1987).

GLASGOW, ELLEN ANDERSON GHOLSON (1873–1945). Ellen Glasgow was born and bred into a wealthy family in Virginia. Educated at home, she began writing as a teenager. Her novels presented a fictional social history of Virginia since 1850 that rejected the romantic stereotypes of southern life and showed instead the class conflicts of the region. Her first novel, *The Descendant,* was published anonymously in 1897. Her later works included *The Voice of the People* (1900) and *The Deliverance* (1904). In *Virginia* (1913), *Life and Gabriella* (1916), and *Barren Ground* (1925) Glasgow concentrated on **women** and their responses to the patriarchal code of the South. Female characters were also central in her comedies, *The Romantic Comedians* (1926), *They Stooped to Folly* (1929), and *The Sheltered Life* (1932). Several of Glasgow's novels were on the best-seller list in the 1920s, and in 1942 she was awarded the Pulitzer Prize for *In This Our Life* (1941). Her autobiography, *The Woman Within,* was published posthumously in 1954.

See also LITERATURE AND THEATER.

GLASS, CARTER (1858–1946). After holding various types of employment, Carter Glass began work as a reporter in Virginia in 1880 and eventually became a **newspaper** editor and owner. He served in the state senate from 1899 to 1903 as a **Democrat** and then represented Virginia in the House of Representatives from 1902 to 1919 and in the Senate from 1920 until his death. An advocate of **banking** reform he sponsored the **Federal Reserve Act** in 1913 and was secretary of the treasury between 1918 and 1920. Glass was a member of the Democratic National Committee from 1916 to 1928 and, unusually for a southerner, he supported **Al Smith** in 1928. In 1932, with Representative Henry Steagall, he cosponsored the act that kept the United States on the Gold Standard; in 1933 he cosponsored the **Glass-**

Steagall Banking Act, which established the Federal Deposit Insurance Corporation. Increasingly, however, as an advocate of states' rights Glass opposed the **New Deal**. He did support **Roosevelt**'s foreign policy and opposed isolationism.

GLASS-OWEN ACT. *See* FEDERAL RESERVE ACT, 1913.

GLASS-STEAGALL BANKING ACT, 1932. A measure passed to stop gold withdrawals and stabilize **banking** during the **Depression** by providing government securities to guarantee Federal Reserve notes.
   See also GLASS, CARTER (1858–1946).

GOETHALS, GEORGE WASHINGTON (1858–1928). A graduate of West Point Military Academy, Goethals served in the Army Corps of Engineers. He worked on a number of navigational improvements of U.S. rivers and in 1907 was appointed chief engineer on the Panama construction project by **Theodore Roosevelt**. The canal was opened ahead of schedule in 1914. He was appointed governor of the Panama Canal Zone in 1914. He was briefly general manager of the **U.S. Shipping Board's Emergency Fleet Corporation** in 1917 but resigned in opposition to the expansion of the merchant fleet with wooden vessels. In 1918 Goethals became head of the War Department's Division of Purchase and supplies. He retired in 1919 and established his own firm of consulting engineers.

GOLDMAN, EMMA (1869–1940). Born in Lithuania, Goldman immigrated to the United States in 1885. Together with the Polish-born Alexander Berkman she became a leader in the American Anarchist movement and editor from 1906 to 1917 of *Mother Earth*. A campaigner for sexual equality, birth control, and the right of free speech, Goldman also denounced **World War I** as an imperialist conflict. Together with Berkman she was tried and convicted for violation of the draft laws. Sentenced to two years in prison in 1918, she was deported to the Union of Soviet Socialist Republics (USSR) on her release after twenty months as a part of the **Palmer Raids** in 1919. She was expelled from the Soviet Union in 1921 and lived in Great Britain and Canada. Goldman visited Spain in the 1930s and campaigned on behalf of anarchists involved in the Spanish Civil War. Her autobiography, *Living My Life*, was published in 1931.
   See also WOMEN.

GOLDWYN, SAMUEL (1882–1974). The pioneer Hollywood film producer Samuel Goldwyn was born Schmuel Gelbfisz in Warsaw, Poland. He fled Poland in 1894 and made his way first to England and then in 1898 to the

United States, where he took the name Samuel Goldfish. Goldwyn found work as a glove cutter in New York and then became a traveling salesman. In 1912 Goldwyn established a film company with his brother-in-law, Jesse L. Lasky. In 1916 the company merged with Adolph Zukor's Famous Players to become the Famous Players-Lasky company, which later became Paramount Pictures. Goldwyn left the company in 1915 and established Goldwyn Pictures Corporation—and changed his name. The company in turn became Metro-Goldwyn-Mayer in 1924, but Goldwyn again left to establish his own Samuel Goldwyn Presents and in 1925 joined United Artists. In 1941 he signed with RKO, where he remained until the end of his career. From 1923 to 1959 Goldwyn produced eighty motion pictures, many of high quality. Among his **movies** were *Bulldog Drummond* (1929), *Dodsworth* (1936), *Wuthering Heights* (1939), *The Best Years of Our Lives* (1946), *Guys and Dolls* (1955), and *Porgy and Bess* (1959). In his long career Goldwyn helped establish the studio system in Hollywood and discovered many movie stars.

GOMPERS, SAMUEL (1850–1924). The American labor leader was born of Dutch-Jewish parents in London. Gompers's family immigrated to New York, where he worked as a cigar maker. A leading member of the Cigarmakers International Union, he became a founder, and the first president of the Federation of Organized Trades and Labor Unions of the United States and Canada in 1881, which became the **American Federation of Labor** (AFL) in 1886. He was elected first president of the AFL, a position he held until his death apart from 1894–1895. Under his leadership the AFL adopted a conservative position, representing skilled craft workers, rejecting state intervention in the workplace or welfare, and was essentially apolitical. However, in the face of **Republican** antipathy Gompers actively supported **Woodrow Wilson** in the 1912 election. He strongly backed Wilson's war policies, became a member of the **Advisory Committee to the Council of National Defense**, and discouraged strikes or other "disloyal" activity. He was part of the U.S. delegation to the **Versailles Peace Conference** at the end of the war and served as chair of the Commission on International Labor Legislation in 1919. Gompers's significance declined with that of the labor movement after the war and the return of a Republican administration. By the time of his death, when he was succeeded by **William Green**, the AFL was little stronger than it had been before the war.

See also TRADE UNIONS.

GORE, THOMAS PRYOR (1870–1949). Although blind from childhood, Thomas Gore qualified as a lawyer in Tennessee and established a practice in Texas. In 1901 he moved to the Oklahoma territory, where he was elected as a **Democrat** to the territorial council in 1902. He became one of the state's first two senators in 1907 and was the first totally blind person to become a U.S. senator. He supported **Woodrow Wilson**'s program but opposed entry into **World War I**. In 1916 he drew up a resolution warning Americans against traveling on the ships of belligerent powers. During the war he spoke against the introduction of selective service and government controls. He also opposed the **League of Nations**. He failed to regain the Democratic nomination in 1920 and practiced law until he returned to the Senate until 1930. He failed to be reelected in 1936 due to his opposition to the **New Deal**. Gore remained in Washington, D.C., to practice law and added Indian affairs to his areas of expertise.

See also FOREIGN POLICY.

GRANGE, "RED" (HAROLD EDWARD) (1903–1991). The famous 1920s football player, coach, and broadcaster Red Grange was born Harold Edward Grange but was nicknamed "Red" because of his hair color. Grange was a gifted athlete from school age on, and when he went to the University of Illinois in 1922 he immediately became a successful football player. In 1924 Grange became a national hero when he amassed 480 yards in the game against the University of Michigan team. Three weeks later he scored three touchdowns and amassed another 450 yards in the game against the University of Chicago. He continued to perform at that level the following season and then announced that he was turning professional. In 1925 Grange made his first appearance for the Chicago Bears, and his performances were to give a considerable boost to the fledgling National Football League (NFL). The following year Grange played for the new American Football League team the New York Yankees, later readmitted to the NFL. Grange was injured in 1927, returned to the Chicago Bears in 1929, and played until 1934.

After leaving football Grange worked for a soft drink company and then became an insurance broker in 1942. In 1942 he became the first athlete to become a sportscaster when he began part-time radio broadcasting. He was to cover more than 480 games before he retired in 1969. Grange was named to the Football Hall of Fame in 1951 and the Professional Football Hall of Fame in 1963.

See also SPORTS.

GRANT, MADISON (1865–1937). Although qualified in law, Madison Grant's chief interests were in natural history and ethnology. He was one of the founders of the New York Zoological Society in 1895 and served first as its secretary until 1924 and as president from 1925 until his death. He was, however, better known for his writing on theories of racial superiority and his support of **immigration** control. His writings included *The Passing of the Great Race* (1916), *The Conquest of a Continent* (1933), and, with C. S.

Davison, *The Founders of the Republic on Immigration, Naturalization, and Aliens* (1928) and *The Alien in our Midst* (1930). From 1922 until 1937 Grant was vice president of the Immigration Restriction League, and he helped to frame the **Quota Act of 1924**, which further restricted immigration to the United States.

   See also STODDARD, (THEODORE) LOTHROP (1883–1950).

GREAT DEPRESSION. The "Great Depression" was the worldwide economic crisis that followed the **Wall Street Crash** and the Depression that began in the United States in 1929. The calling in or cessation of foreign loans and the imposition of high tariffs led to a shrinking in international trade. As prices fell and trade shrank, the number of unemployed workers worldwide was estimated to be more than 30 million by 1933, with two-thirds of those in Germany, Great Britain, and the United States.

   The Wall Street Crash was not the cause of the collapse, merely the trigger that revealed the underlying weaknesses of international markets and the U.S. **economy** in particular. The apparent prosperity of the "**Roaring Twenties**" masked a number of flaws including the maldistribution of incomes, overproduction and the buildup of inventories, the problems of **farming**, the instability of **banks**, and imbalances in the international economy. The breakdown of financial institutions in the United States led to the failure of more than five thousand banks between 1929 and 1932, and as money and credit dried up businesses also reduced output or failed completely. Workers found their wages or hours of work cut, and many were laid off altogether. By 1933 industrial production had fallen to less than 50 percent of its 1929 levels. The **automobile** industry that had played such a part in the prosperity of the 1920s was operating on 20 percent of its capacity.

   Unemployment had reached an estimated 17 million, or 25 percent of the labor force. Farmers, already suffering in the 1920s, saw their situation deteriorate further as commodity prices fell by 55 percent between 1929 and 1932. Almost a quarter of farmers lost their property through foreclosures, and others were driven out by drought and dust storms in the early 1930s, joining the thousands of migrants, the "Okies" and "Arkies," heading west. Urban workers too took to the road as 250,000 families lost their homes in addition to their jobs. Many men abandoned their families, and the number of female-headed households increased. Although many **women** were now forced to seek work, gender-based discrimination increased as priority was often given to men. Similarly, **African Americans** found themselves "last hired, first fired," and black unemployment rates were twice as high as those of whites. Prejudice against Hispanic Americans forced half a million to return to Mexico in the 1930s.

Many Americans began to protest as their economic plight worsened. Farmers destroyed produce or poured milk into the road; foreclosures were prevented by mob action; unemployed workers marched in protest sometimes organized by **Socialists** or **Communists**. In 1932 veterans of **World War I** marched on Washington, D.C., as part of a **Bonus Army** calling for payment of war bonuses. Their forcible removal from the capital was the last nail in the political coffin of president **Herbert Hoover**, whose name had become synonymous with the Depression. Hoover's inability to abandon a commitment to limited federal action and his reliance on "voluntarism" led to his political defeat by **Franklin D. Roosevelt** in the election of 1932. Roosevelt promised the nation a "**New Deal**," and the 1930s were to witness a whole series of programs aimed at bringing "relief, recovery, and reform." The result of this political change was the transformation of American politics and the beginning of a welfare state. However, although the situation was considerably alleviated by the New Deal, it was the expansion of industry that came with World War II that finally ended the Depression. That conflict was itself in part a result of the economic and political problems caused by the Great Depression in Europe and elsewhere.

GREAT MIGRATION. During **World War I African Americans** found new employment opportunities as war industries boomed and **immigration**, the traditional source of factory labor, declined. As a consequence labor agents from northern industries set out to recruit black workers from the South. The black press, particularly the *Chicago Defender* and the *Crisis* (the journal of the **National Association for the Advancement of Colored People** [NAACP]), also called on the black population to escape discrimination and segregation for a better life in the North. As a result approximately four hundred thousand African Americans migrated to northern industrial centers between 1915 and 1920. Over sixty-five thousand African Americans moved to Chicago alone. New York City and Philadelphia also attracted huge numbers. The new workers crowded into already congested ghettos such as Harlem in New York, leading to problems of overcrowding. Competition for housing and jobs created tensions that led to riots in **East St. Louis** in 1917, and **Chicago**, **Washington, D.C.**, and other towns in the "**Red Summer**" of 1919. However, out of the violence and the new urban centers grew a mood of defiance articulated by "**New Negro**" and a celebration of blackness in the **Harlem Renaissance**.

GREAT WAR. *See* WORLD WAR I, 1914–1918.

GREEN, WILLIAM (1870–1952). The labor leader William Green was an Ohio coal miner who rose through the ranks of the United Mine Workers of America (UMWA) to become president of the Ohio district in 1906. In 1910 he was elected to the Ohio state senate as a **Democrat** and served two terms. As the Democratic Party floor leader he helped secure the passage of Ohio's Workmen's Compensation Act, a law restricting **women**'s working hours, and the introduction of income tax. In 1911 he returned to the UMWA as union statistician and in 1913 was elected UMWA secretary-treasurer, a post he held until 1924. In 1913 **Samuel Gompers** appointed him vice president of the **American Federation of Labor** (AFL). He succeeded Gompers in 1924 and continued his predecessor's conservative policies. He opposed strikes and although he personally believed in industrial rather than craft unionism, he did not actively campaign for it. Green resisted those in the AFL Committee of Industrial Organizations and he continued his opposition after the formation of the Congress of Industrial Organizations (CIO) in 1938. The AFL's conservative policy remained largely unchanged, and the two labor organizations stayed divided until after his death.

See also TRADE UNIONS.

GREENWICH VILLAGE. Greenwich Village is a residential area of Manhattan, New York City, centered on Washington Square Park. In the decade or so before World War I it became the focus for a literary and artistic community.

See also ART; LITERATURE AND THEATER.

GREGORY, THOMAS WATT (1861–1933). Thomas Gregory qualified in law from the University of Texas in 1885 and established a law practice in Austin until 1913. Gregory was a leading Texas **Democrat** and became Austin's assistant city attorney from 1891 to 1894. He supported **Woodrow Wilson**'s nomination in 1912, and in 1913 was appointed special assistant to the attorney general. In 1914 Gregory became attorney general and after America had entered **World War I** was responsible for enforcing the **Espionage** and **Sedition** acts. Gregory also encouraged citizens to report disloyal acts, and he enlisted the aid of voluntary vigilante organizations like the **American Protective League**. Gregory resigned in 1919 and took part in the **Paris Peace Conference** as an adviser. From October 1919 to January 1920 Gregory was involved in President Wilson's Second Industrial Conference convened to improve postwar labor relations. He then returned to a law practice in Washington, D.C. He supported the election of **Franklin D. Roosevelt** in 1932.

GREY, (PEARL) ZANE (1872–1939). The famous writer of Western fiction, Zane Grey, was born in Ohio and christened Pearl Zane Gray but later changed his name. Grey trained in dentistry but published his first novel, *Betty Zane*, in 1903. In 1907 he visited the West and produced his first Western, *The Last of the Plainsmen*, in 1908. His first popular success was achieved with *Riders of the Purple Sage* in 1912. *The Lone Star Ranger* (1915) reached the best-seller list, and Grey was one of the most widely read authors of his day. Many of his stories first appeared in serial form, but altogether he wrote more than eighty western adventure stories that formed the basis for almost one hundred movies. Grey was also a keen fisherman and wrote many books on the subject including *Tales of Swordfish and Tuna* (1927) and *Tales of Tahitian Waters* (1931). Grey died deep-sea fishing in California.

    See also LITERATURE AND THEATER.

GRIFFITH, DAVID WARK (1875–1948). D. W. Griffith was one of the great pioneers of motion pictures. After working in theater he became first an actor and then a director with the American Mutoscope and Biograph Company in 1908. He developed a group of new **movie** stars including **Mary Pickford** and **Lillian Gish**, but also with cameraman Billy Bitzer established new techniques with location filming, long shots, and close-ups. He left Biograph in 1913 after making almost five hundred films to become an independent producer and established his reputation with the first four-reel film, *Judith of Bethulia* (1914), *The Birth of a Nation* (1915), and *Intolerance* (1916). His *Hearts of the World* (1918) was an enormously successful propaganda epic about the war.

    In 1920 Griffith joined with **Charlie Chaplin**, **Douglas Fairbanks**, and Pickford to form their own production company, the United Artists Corporation. He directed *Broken Blossoms* (1919), *Way Down East* (1920), *The Orphans of the Storm* (1922), *America* (1924), *Battle of the Sexes* (1928), and *The Lady of the Pavements* (1929). Griffith also made two talkies—*Abraham Lincoln* (1930) and *The Struggle* (1931). However, his later films in the 1920s did not match his earlier successes, and he sold his interest in United Artists in 1933.

H

HAGEN, WALTER CHARLES (1892–1969). Born the son of a blacksmith in Rochester, New York, Walter Hagen began work as a golf caddy before taking up the **sport** as a professional. With **Bobby Jones**, Hagen became one of the greatest golfers of the 1920s and is still ranked among the top ten golfers. A flamboyant player both in style and appearance, who challenged amateurism and raised the profile of professional players, in all Hagen won eleven major titles: the U.S. Open twice (1914, 1919), the British Open four times (1922, 1924, 1928, and 1929), and the Professional Golfers' Association (PGA) Championship five times between 1921 and 1927. Hagen played in the Ryder Cup five times between 1927 and 1935, and he captained the U.S. side on six occasions. He retired in 1940. Hagen was one of the sportsmen who earned a large income during the 1920s—he was said to be the first sporting millionaire—much of it from exhibition games and from his work with the Wilson sports equipment manufacturer.

HAITI. After **Philander Knox** had persuaded U.S. financiers to invest in the national bank of the Caribbean republic of Haiti in 1910, there was considerable concern for those interests when a revolution broke out the following year. After further disturbances U.S. Marines were sent to the island in 1915, and American officials were placed in control of customs, policing, and other aspects of government. The marines were not withdrawn until 1934.

See also FOREIGN POLICY.

HAMMER V. DAGENHART. In 1918 the U.S. **Supreme Court** ruled 5-4 in *Hammer v. Dagenhart* that the **Child Labor law** of 1916 was unconstitutional on the grounds that the regulation of interstate commerce could not extend to the conditions of labor.

HAND, (BILLINGS) LEARNED (1872–1961). Educated at Albany Academy and Harvard, Learned Hand graduated from Harvard Law School in 1896. From 1897 to 1902 he practiced law in Albany, then moved to New York City. President **William Howard Taft** named Hand a district judge in

New York in 1909. Hand was a supporter of civic reform and an acquaintance of **Theodore Roosevelt**, **Herbert Croly**, and **Walter Lippmann**. He supported Roosevelt's **Progressive Party** campaign in 1912 and was involved in the founding of the *New Republic* in 1914. In 1924 Hand was named to the Court of Appeals for the Second Circuit, covering New York, Connecticut, and Vermont. He became chief judge of that court in 1939 and served until he retired in 1951.

In the course of his fifty-two years on the federal bench, Hand wrote more than two thousand opinions and established a reputation as one of the leading jurists of his day. During **World War I** Hand's rulings did much to protect the publication of antiwar sentiments during a period of hysteria. Regarded as "the best judge never to become a **Supreme Court** justice," Hand was the author of *Spirit of Liberty* (1952) and *The Bill of Rights* (1958).

HANSON, OLE (1874–1940). Ole Hanson was born to Norwegian parents in Wisconsin, where he grew up and studied law. Hanson went to Chicago, where he was briefly a mining broker before he set off on travels of the South and Midwest before settling in Seattle in 1902. Hanson was fairly successful in the real estate business and in 1908 was elected to the Washington State legislature. In 1918 he was elected mayor of Seattle on a nonpartisan ticket, and he rose to national prominence during the **Seattle General Strike** in 1919. Hanson characterized the strike as the work of anarchists and Bolsheviks, and in a reference to the Russian Revolution of 1917, warned that Seattle could become the "Petrograd of America." He strengthened the police force and threatened to use violence against the strikers if necessary, but the strike collapsed of its own accord. Hanson then crisscrossed the country speaking about the Bolshevik threat and adding to the mood that fueled the "**Red Scare**." He indicated that he would be a candidate for the **Republican** presidential nomination but to little effect. Having resigned as mayor, Hanson gave up politics and moved to California, where he again established a successful real estate business.

HAPGOOD, NORMAN (1868–1937). The journalist and political reformer Norman Hapgood graduated from Harvard University in 1890 and from Harvard Law School in 1893. After a year in a law firm he became a **newspaper** reporter and worked at the *Chicago Evening Post*, the *Milwaukee Sentinel*, *New York Evening Post*, and *New-York Commercial Advertiser*. Hapgood also published a number of historical biographies—*Abraham Lincoln* (1899) and *George Washington* (1901)—and *The Stage in America, 1897–1900* (1901). In 1902 he became editor of *Collier's Weekly* and contributed to **progressive** campaigns in favor of pure food and drug legislation and conservation. Hapgood continued to produce books with a study of *Theodore*

Roosevelt (1905) and *Industry and Progress* (1911). In 1912 he resigned from *Collier's* because of its support for **Theodore Roosevelt** rather than **Woodrow Wilson**.

In 1913 Hapgood became editor of *Harper's Weekly*, which was strongly pro-Wilson. He left the journal in 1913. In 1916 he was appointed U.S. minister to Denmark, but he resigned in the face of Senate opposition to his appointment. From 1923 to 1925 Hapgood took over *Hearst's International Magazine* and used it to criticize conservative groups including the **Ku Klux Klan**. Hapgood supported **Robert M. La Follette** in 1924 and governor **Al Smith** throughout the 1920s. When Smith lost the **Democratic** presidential nomination to **Franklin Roosevelt** in 1932, Hapgood became a supporter of elements of the **New Deal**. He also spoke out against the dangers of Fascism and Nazism in Europe. From 1936 until his death Hapgood edited the *Christian Register*.

HARDING, FLORENCE MABEL KLING DEWOLFE (1860–1924). The future wife of president **Warren Harding** was born Florence Kling in Marion, Ohio. She studied music at the Cincinnati Conservatory but in 1879 eloped with Henry DeWolfe by whom she had a son. She divorced DeWolfe in 1886 and married Harding in 1891. Florence Harding assisted her husband with the production of his newspaper, the *Marion Star*, and supported his political ambitions. Referred to by her husband as "the duchess," Mrs. Harding was a hardworking first lady. She was involved in veterans' causes, began public tours of the White House, entertained a large number of visitors to the White House, and reinstated the Easter egg roll on the White House lawns. She also read her husband's speeches and apparently made suggestions as to their content. Mrs. Harding supported **women's suffrage** and accepted an honorary membership in the **National Woman's Party**. Following President Harding's death in 1923, some observers suggested that Mrs. Harding had poisoned her husband either because she discovered he had a mistress or because of the scandals surrounding his administration. Most historians discount such claims.

See also WOMEN.

HARDING, WARREN GAMALIEL (1865–1923). Twenty-ninth president of the United States. Harding was a **Republican** politician often depicted as a political nonentity by historians. Born in Blooming Grove, Ohio, he was a successful small-town newspaper owner-editor who had served as Ohio state senator, 1900–1904; lieutenant governor of Ohio, 1904–1906; and U.S. senator, 1915–1921. Harding was a supporter of **William Howard Taft** in 1912 and became chairman of the Republican National Convention in 1916. As a senator he supported **women's suffrage** and national **Prohibition**

but was one of those who opposed the **League of Nations** and **Versailles settlement**. When the 1920 Republican convention in Chicago became dead-locked between **Leonard Wood** and **Frank O. Lowden**, the affable and convivial Harding was recognized as the most available candidate—not just, as legend has it, by a group of senators meeting in the famous "smoke-filled room" in the Blackstone Hotel but also by many delegates as their "second choice" candidate. He was nominated on the 10th ballot. Described as "the best of the second-raters," whose only qualification was his looks, Harding was in fact quite a popular president. In an election with a low turnout, he defeated the **Democratic** candidate **James M. Cox** by 16,143,407 votes to 9,130,328 and by 404 Electoral College votes to 127. His success was seen as a repudiation of the idealism of **Woodrow Wilson** and a reflection of the mood of postwar reaction, which Harding captured in a speech promising "a return to normalcy."

In his first address to Congress, Harding called for a reduction in the size of government, the lowering of taxes, a reduction of **railroad** rates, the promotion of agricultural interests, a national budget system, and a depart-ment of public welfare. However, the president did little to push these meas-ures through, and his most significant accomplishment was the creation of the **Bureau of the Budget** with **Charles G. Dawes** as director. Harding vetoed the soldiers' bonus bill and supported the passage of the **Fordney-McCumber Tariff Act** of 1922. He did speak out against discrimination against black Americans and he reversed Wilson's policies of excluding **African Americans** from federal appointments. Harding also approved the **Sheppard Towner Act** in 1921 and called for the creation of a federal department of public welfare. Significantly Harding also personally ap-proved the pardon of **Eugene Debs**. Little was done to counter the postwar recession, and rising unemployment and mounting farm distress in the first year of the Harding Administration were reflected in the setbacks for the Republicans in the 1922 congressional elections. President Harding also al-lowed attorney general **Harry S. Daugherty** to use injunctions in suppress-ing the national miners' strike in 1922. However, he supported **Herbert Hoover** in bringing pressure on the steel industry to accept the eight-hour day for workers.

In general Harding allowed his cabinet officers to get on with their own business, and the key cabinet officers were secretary of commerce Hoover, secretary of the treasury **Andrew Mellon**, secretary of agriculture **Henry C. Wallace**, and secretary of state **Charles Evans Hughes**. It was the latter who was responsible for improving relations with Latin American countries, sending observers to the League of Nations, and calling the **Washington Conference** to limit armaments.

Although the Harding Administration clearly included several distinguished individuals, it would be remembered most of all for scandal and corruption. Harding himself has been judged a failure, who although personally honest, appointed more venal friends and cronies to government office. While the president seemed more concerned with his golf game and poker evenings, his former campaign manager Harry S. Daugherty, now attorney general, turned a blind eye to failures within the Justice Department and was probably personally involved in other major scandals. The director of the newly created Veterans' Bureau, **Charles R. Forbes**, sold off government surplus and accepted bribes. Secretary of the interior **Albert Fall** was eventually convicted and jailed for taking bribes from oilmen **Harry Sinclair** and **Edward Doheny** in return for leases of naval oil reserves in California and at **Teapot Dome**, Wyoming.

As some of these developments began to surface and in response to his declining popularity, in June 1923 Harding began a "Voyage of Understanding," a national tour that started in Alaska. En route from there to California, he collapsed and died suddenly as a result of a thrombosis. How much he knew of the scandals that quickly emerged following his death is not clear, but his own reputation was damaged by the later claims by Nan Britton that she had an affair with the president and that he had fathered her daughter. A former security man confirmed these claims in his own memoirs and also suggested that Harding might have been poisoned. Historians have largely discounted such stories, although it does now appear that Harding had an extramarital relationship with another woman, Cary Phillips.

HARLEM. The area a few blocks north of 125th Street, bounded by Seventh and Lenox Avenues in New York City, became the center of the city's **African American** population from the early 1900s on when a black realtor, Philip Payton, began to rent property. As white families moved out and property prices fell, more African Americans moved in. In 1914 the black population was estimated to be fifty thousand. This number increased dramatically following the **Great Migration** of African Americans from the South during **World War I**. By 1930 Harlem was almost entirely a black community numbering more than two hundred thousand, and it had become the cultural capital for African Americans.

See also HARLEM RENAISSANCE, c. 1920–c. 1933; JAZZ.

HARLEM RENAISSANCE, c. 1920–c. 1933. The Harlem Renaissance was the sudden growth in African American cultural expression following World War I that centered on the black community in New York City. The African American urban population in the North had grown during the Great Migration and was to provide a base for new movements and ideas such as

Marcus Garvey's Universal Negro Improvement Association. The remarkable literary and artistic development in many ways reflected the mood of the "New Negro" in its demonstration of black consciousness and celebration of the African heritage. African American writers like Claude McKay, Jean Toomer, Countee Cullen, Zora Neale Hurston, Nella Larsen, and Langston Hughes were encouraged by editors such as Charles S. Johnson of the National Urban League's *Opportunity*, W. E. B. Du Bois and Jessie Fauset of the National Association for the Advancement of Colored People's (NAACP) *Crisis*, and by white critics such as Carl Van Vechten. Some of their work was also published in *The New Negro* (1925), edited by Alain Locke. Black artists such as Aaron Douglas, Richmond Barthe, and Nancy Prophet produced African-inspired sculptures and paintings while Archibald J. Motley, and later Jacob Lawrence, depicted scenes of black life in the United States. It could be said that black music came of age during the 1920s with the development and acceptance in white culture of jazz. Bandleaders and musicians like Duke Ellington, Fletcher Henderson, and Louis Armstrong became major performers and recording stars during the period. To some extent the Renaissance ended with the onset of the Depression but also with the sense of increasing pessimism that followed the Harlem race riot of 1935.

See also ART; LITERATURE AND THEATER; MUSIC AND DANCE.

HARVEY, GEORGE BRINTON MCCLELLAN (1864–1928). George Harvey was a journalist who became the owner and editor of the *North American Review* (1899–1926), the president with a controlling interest in the publisher Harper & Brothers (1900–1915), and editor of *Harper's Weekly* (1918–1921) and *Harvey's Weekly* (1918–1921). He supported Woodrow Wilson for governor of New Jersey and for the presidency but opposed the League of Nations. It was in Harvey's room in the Blackstone Hotel, Chicago, later famously known as the "smoke-filled room," that the deadlock over the Republican nomination was broken in favor of Warren Harding. Harvey's support for Harding in 1920 was rewarded with his appointment as ambassador to Great Britain, 1921–1923. In 1924 he described the choice in the election as "Coolidge or chaos."

See also NEWSPAPERS AND MAGAZINES.

HAUGEN, GILBERT NELSON (1859–1933). Gilbert Haugen studied at Decorah Institute and Janesville Business College, Iowa, before establishing his own farm and farm service businesses in Kensett in 1877. He was elected a justice of the peace in 1880 and country treasurer in 1887. In 1893 Haugen, a **Republican**, was elected to the lower house of the Iowa General Assembly but failed to regain the nomination in 1897. In 1898 he was elected to the U.S. House of Representatives. He was to serve for seventeen terms, a total of thirty-four years, before losing his seat in 1932.

Haugen increasingly moved into the progressive Republican camp and he later supported much of **Woodrow Wilson**'s domestic program. However, he opposed U.S. entry into **World War I** and tried to protect farmers' interests during the war. After the war Haugen was instrumental in the repeal of the **Daylight Savings Act** in 1919. His main concern, however, was farm prices, and he was cosponsor of the several **McNary-Haugen** bills introduced and passed by Congress in 1927 and 1928 but vetoed by **Calvin Coolidge**.

HAWLEY-SMOOT TARIFF ACT, 1930. Approved by president **Herbert Hoover** despite the appeals of over a thousand leading economists to reject it, the Hawley-Smoot Tariff Act raised the tariffs of the **Fordney-McCumber Act** and set import duties at some of the highest levels in American history. Proposed by representative Willis Hawley of Oregon and senator **Reed Smoot** of Utah, the tariff was intended to help particularly agriculture in the face of falling prices. However, it was extended to cover many aspects of manufacturing industry. Its effects were disastrous as foreign nations introduced their own retaliatory duties leading to a further fall in American and world trade and only increasing the impact of the **Great Depression**.

See also ECONOMY.

HAYS, WILLIAM HARRISON (1879–1954). Will Hays qualified in law in Indiana and established a practice in Sullivan, where he became the city attorney. He became chair of the Republican National Committee in 1918 and was credited with helping to reunite the **Republican Party** in 1920. President **Warren Harding** appointed Hays postmaster general and during his year in that position he established the Post Office Welfare Department, extended rural free mail deliveries, restored second-class mailing for **newspapers**, and reduced the Post Office expenses. Following a number of scandals in Hollywood (including the case of **"Fatty" Arbuckle**), Hays was appointed as head of the newly created Motion Picture Producers and Distributors of America (MPPDA). Under his leadership the MPPDA established a code of practice to censor movies and to control material of a violent, sexual, or otherwise immoral nature. Hays claimed that "good taste is good business," but his taste often reflected that of small-town rural America. In 1945 Hays resigned his post but continued in the role as adviser to the Motion Picture Association of America. The censorship code survived until the 1960s.

See also MOVIES.

HAYWOOD, WILLIAM DUDLEY (1869–1928). Known as "Big Bill," Haywood was a miner from the age of fifteen and rose to become a militant leader of the Western Miners' Federation and one of the organizers of the **Industrial Workers of the World** (IWW) in 1905. In 1907 he was tried for conspiring to murder the governor of Idaho in 1905. Haywood was defended by **Clarence Darrow** and found not guilty. He stood unsuccessfully as a **Socialist** candidate in the election for governor of Colorado in 1906 but was removed from the party's executive committee for his militant language in 1913. Haywood returned to the IWW and led the Lawrence and Paterson textile workers' strikes in 1912 and 1913. He supported uncompromising militant mass action and opposed U.S. entry into the war in 1917. Arrested in 1917, he was convicted of sedition in 1919 and sentenced to twenty years in prison, but in 1921 he jumped bail and fled to the Soviet Union, where he spent the rest of his life.

See also TRADE UNIONS.

HEARST, WILLIAM RANDOLPH (1863–1951). After studying at Harvard University (1882–1885), William Hearst began a career as a journalist and gradually built up a **newspaper** empire, acquiring ownership of the San Francisco *Examiner*, Chicago *American*, New York *Journal-American*, and *Daily Mirror*. Hearst also owned several magazines including *International-Cosmopolitan*, *Harper's Bazaar*, and *Good Housekeeping*, and he created nationwide news syndicates. His papers became known for their sensationalism that earned the description "yellow journalism." They were also known for their nationalism—he was reported to have said to the artist Frederic Remington, who was in Cuba in 1898, "You furnish the pictures and I'll furnish the war."

Hearst entered politics as a **Democrat**, becoming a member of the U.S. House of Representatives from 1903 to 1907. He failed in his bid to become mayor of New York City in 1905 and 1909, and also in his attempt to become governor of New York in 1906. In 1908 he created his own Independence League in another attempt to win the gubernatorial race but failed again.

During **World War I** Hearst's press adopted a passionately anti-British line that was abandoned once America entered the conflict. Hearst strongly opposed the **League of Nations** and U.S. participation in the **Permanent Court of International Justice**. He continued to be an influential voice during the 1920s, supporting **Calvin Coolidge** and **Andrew Mellon**. However, in 1932 the Hearst press backed the Democrat **John Nance Garner** for the presidency but was persuaded to switch support to **Franklin D. Roosevelt**. Hearst gradually turned against the **New Deal** because of its regulation of business. The Hearst empire was badly hit by the Depression, and he was forced to surrender control in 1937. Nonetheless the company emerged from the crisis as the biggest publishing organization in the United States. Hearst's great wealth was evident in the huge art collection he amassed at his home in San Simeon, California, and Hearst provided the model for the fictional character in Orson Welles' **movie** *Citizen Kane* (1941).

See also FOREIGN POLICY.

HELD, JOHN (1889–1958). The cartoonist and illustrator John Held began publishing his work at the age of fourteen in the Salt Lake City *Tribune*. In 1910 he moved to New York City and found work designing posters and as a display designer. In 1917 he spent a year as the artist attached to the Carnegie Institute's archeological expedition to Central America. When he returned in 1918 he began selling illustrations, covers, and cartoons to *Judge*, *Puck*, *Vanity Fair*, and *Life* magazines. His ironic cartoons of young people, particularly the college students and the **flappers**, seemed to capture the mood of the 1920s and were enormously successful. In 1924 Held began producing a comic strip called *Oh! Margy!*, which later became *Merely Margy* and then *Rah Rah Rosalie*. Held suffered an economic and nervous collapse in the 1930s, and the popularity of his work also declined. In the 1940s Held worked for the signal corps as an illustrator.

See also NEWSPAPERS AND MAGAZINES.

HEMINGWAY, ERNEST MILLER (1899–1961). If **F. Scott Fitzgerald** captured the mood of 1920s America, Ernest Hemingway was probably the most significant voice of the "**lost generation**" of alienated Americans after **World War I**. In 1917 he began work as a reporter for the Kansas City *Star*, but in 1918 he went to Italy as a volunteer ambulance driver for the American Red Cross. He was wounded and hospitalized shortly after his arrival. In 1920 he found work with the Toronto *Star* and he continued to submit articles first from Chicago and then after 1922, from Paris, France.

Hemingway published a number of short stories while he was in Paris, where he became one of a group of expatriate writers and artists. His first collection of stories, *In Our Time* (1925), was followed by *The Sun Also Rises* (1926), *Men Without Women* (1927), and *A Farewell to Arms* (1929). It was in the latter that he wrote famously that after the war "all gods were dead."

Hemingway returned to America in 1928 and settled in Key West, where he wrote a study of bullfighting, *Death in the Afternoon* (1932), followed by *Winner Take Nothing* (1933) and *Green Hills of Africa* (1935). He also published short stories and magazine articles. In 1937 Hemingway went to Spain to report on the civil war. His book *To Have and Have Not* was published the same year.

In 1939 Hemingway went to Havana, where he wrote his novel of the Spanish Civil War, *For Whom the Bell Tolls*, published in 1940. Hemingway was to write little of substance after this point, but he went to Europe as a war reporter for *Collier's* in 1944. In 1952 *The Old Man and the Sea* was published to considerable acclaim, and Hemingway was awarded the Pulitzer Prize for Fiction in 1953. In 1954 he was awarded the Nobel Prize in Literature. Despite these successes Hemingway suffered increasingly from depression, and in 1961 he committed suicide.

See also LITERATURE AND THEATER.

HENDERSON, (JAMES) FLETCHER (1898–1952). Fletcher Henderson studied the piano from the age of six and although he later obtained a degree in science from Atlanta University in 1920, he began playing the piano professionally in New York City. From 1920 to 1924 he worked in W. C. Handy's **music** company and a phonograph company. Henderson formed his own big band in 1924 and toured widely. Henderson's band, believed to be the first organized by a jazzman, was the first **African American** band broadcast regularly on the radio and one of the most commercially successful. Many influential musicians, including **Louis Armstrong** and saxophonist Coleman Hawkins, played with Henderson who some commentators believe was the "King of Swing." In 1939 Henderson joined the Benny Goodman orchestra. He left Goodman between 1943 and 1947 and formed several smaller groups himself before rejoining Goodman in 1947. Ill health forced him into retirement in 1950.

See also HARLEM RENAISSANCE, c. 1920–c. 1933; JAZZ.

HENRI, ROBERT (1865–1929). The influential artist and teacher was born Robert Henry Cozad in Cincinnati, Ohio, but his family moved to Nebraska, where they established a town called Cozad. Henri changed his name after his father was involved in a fatal shooting and the family were forced to move again, this time to Denver, and then in 1883 to New York City and then Atlantic City, New Jersey. In 1886 Henri began his **art** studies at the Pennsylvania Academy of Fine Arts in Philadelphia and in 1888 at the Académie Julian and École des Beaux Arts in France, returning to Philadelphia in 1891. He began teaching in the Philadelphia School of Design for Women in 1892 and had his first solo exhibition at the Pennsylvania Academy in 1897.

In 1902 Henri took up a teaching position in the New York School of Art, where his students included **George Bellows**, **Edward Hopper**, and **Joseph Stella**. In 1908 he organized an exhibition called "The Eight," initiating what later became known as the Ashcan School because of the realistic portrayals of everyday life in the city. Henri also helped to organize the famous **Armory Show**, an exhibition of international modern art, in 1913. Henri had his own art school from 1909 to 1910 and he then taught at the Modern School (1911–1918). From 1915 to 1927 he taught at the Art Students League of New York, but he also spent time in Sante Fe, New Mexico, where he had a considerable influence. His book *The Art Spirit* (1923), a collection of thoughts and ideas, was widely read in the art world. In 1929 the Arts Council of New York listed Henri as one of the top three living artists, and a memorial exhibition of his work was held by the Metropolitan Museum of Art in his honor in 1931. Among his best-known works were *Snow in New York* (1902), *Salome* (1909), *The Laundress* (1916), and his many portraits including several, such as *Irish Lass* (1913) and *The Little Irishman* (1913), from his visits to Ireland.

HEYWARD, (EDWIN) DUBOSE (1885–1940). DuBose Heyward grew up in Charleston, South Carolina, where he became a businessman before turning to writing. His first collection of poetry, *Carolina Chansons*, was published in 1922. His greatest success, however, was with the novel of black life, *Porgy* (1925), which Heyward and his wife, Dorothy, successfully converted to a play of the same name in 1927. Heyward then wrote the libretto for **George Gershwin**'s folk-opera masterpiece, *Porgy and Bess* (1935). Another novel, *Mamba's Daughters*, also based on the black community of Charleston, appeared in 1929 and was dramatized by the Heywards in 1939. DuBose Heyward wrote several novels and children's stories, was the co-founder of the Poetry Society of South Carolina, and was a contributor to the renaissance of southern literature and culture in the interwar years.
    See also LITERATURE AND THEATER.

HILLMAN, SIDNEY (1887–1946). Sidney Hillman was born in Lithuania. He came to the United States in 1907 and found work in the clothing industry. In 1915 he became president of the newly created Amalgamated Clothing Workers Union. During the 1920s Hillman espoused a New Unionism that stressed cooperation with employers and workers' educational, social, and welfare programs. Hillman supported **Franklin D. Roosevelt**'s **New Deal** during the **Depression** and worked with other unionists to secure Roosevelt's reelection in 1936. In 1935 he was one of the founders of the Congress of Industrial Organizations (CIO) and became one of its vice presidents. In 1936 he helped to found the American Labor Party, a left-wing group in New York. During World War II Hillman headed the labor section of the Office of Production Management and then was vice chairman of the War Production Board. He established the political action committee in the CIO to support Roosevelt.
    See also TRADE UNIONS.

HILLQUIT, MORRIS (1869–1933). Morris Hillquit was born in Riga, Russia (now Latvia), and immigrated to the United States in 1886. He worked for the *Arbeiter Zeitung*, the first American-Yiddish newspaper. Hillquit joined the Socialist Labor Party in 1886 and then later the Social Democratic party and became a leading policy maker in the emergence of the **Socialist Party of America** (SPA). As America faced entry into **World War I**, Hillquit drew up the peace platform adopted by the party in 1917. He stood unsuccessfully as a socialist candidate in the elections for the mayor of New York City in 1917, and also stood unsuccessfully five times as a candidate for the House of Representatives. After the war Hillquit was involved in the various factional debates involving socialists and communists that led to the SPA joining the Union of Socialist Parties rather than the Communist International in 1920. In 1922 Hillquit and **Victor Berger** were active in supporting the **Conference for Progressive Political Action** and the call for an independent labor party. When this failed, Hillquit supported **Robert M. La Follette** and the **Progressive Party** in 1924. Hillquit last ran for office himself when he stood again as a candidate for the mayor of New York. Although unsuccessful, he did win 250,000 votes. In addition to his organizational activities, Hillquit wrote several works on socialism and was the author of the *History of Socialism in the United States* (1903).

HINES, WALKER DOWNER (1879–1934). Hines was a successful lawyer who worked as an attorney for **railroad** companies. During World War I he became assistant director to the **U.S. Railroad Administration** and then succeeded his chief, **William Gibbs McAdoo**, as director-general of the **railroads** from 1919 to 1920. He returned to his law practice in New York City after the war but was also a director of a railroad company. Hines wrote *The War History of the American Railroads* (1929), and in 1925 he wrote a report on Danube Navigation for the **League of Nations**. In 1926 Hines became president of the Cotton-Textile Institute formed to promote the development of the cotton industry. He was vice president of the New York City Bar Association from 1932 until his death.

HOLMES, OLIVER WENDELL (1841–1935). After graduating from Harvard University in 1861, Oliver Wendell Holmes served in the Union Army during the Civil War and was wounded three times. He graduated from Harvard Law School in 1866 and practiced in Boston. Following the publication of *The Common Law* (1881), in which he declared, "The life of the law has not been logic, but experience," Holmes became a professor of law at Harvard Law School in 1882 and associate justice to the Massachusetts supreme court the same year. He served as the chief justice in the Massachusetts court from 1899 to 1902, when he was appointed associate justice to the

U.S. **Supreme Court**. Holmes served on the court until 1932 and was famous for his liberal dissent from majority decisions against social welfare and labor legislation, most famously in *Lochner v. New York* (1905). For Holmes the law had to reflect social realities, rather than simply legal principle. However, in *Schenck v. United States*, he authored the decision that upheld the wartime **Espionage Act** on the grounds that in wartime there was "a clear and present danger" that justified restricting free speech that was not absolute. In *Abrams v. United States* he dissented from the decision upholding the conviction for the distribution of pamphlets denouncing U.S. involvement in Russia on the grounds that it presented no clear threat to the prosecution of the war.

HOME LOAN BANK ACT, 1932. The Home Loan Bank Act was passed to establish credit facilities for urban real estate financing. It created a system similar to the **Federal Reserve** System with twelve Federal Home Loan Banks that could offer credit to member banks and savings and loan associations to assist banks in financing real estate development. The act was supplemented by the **Home Owners' Loan Act, 1933**.

HOME OWNERS' LOAN ACT, 1933. Passed as a supplement to the **Home Loan Bank Act, 1932**, the Home Owners' Loan Act established a Home Owners' Loan Corporation (HOLC) with $200 million capital to refinance first mortgages on homes valued up to $20,000 at lower interest rates. Over a three-year period the HOLC helped to save the homes of hundreds of thousands of people. When it ceased its operations in 1936, it had refinanced more than 1 million mortgages.

HOOVER, HERBERT CLARK (1874–1964). Thirty-first president of the United States. Born in West Branch, Iowa, Herbert Hoover was orphaned at the age of nine. He grew up with relatives and went on to qualify in geology at Stanford University, California, in 1895. Hoover became a millionaire working as a mining engineer in various western states and in Australia and China between 1895 and 1913. In 1914 he became chair of the American Relief Commission in London and from 1915 to 1919 chair of the Commission for Relief in Belgium. In 1917 Hoover rose to national prominence when **Woodrow Wilson** appointed him to head the **U.S. Food Administration**. He launched a massive national effort to maximize production and minimize private consumption through a program of propaganda that encouraged voluntary controls. Such was his public appeal that both political parties considered him as a potential presidential candidate in 1920, but he declined to run. **Warren Harding** appointed Hoover as secretary of commerce in 1921, and he was reappointed by **Calvin Coolidge** in 1924.

As secretary of commerce and, as one commentator said, "under-secretary of every thing else," Hoover modernized the Department of Commerce and made it one of the most important federal agencies of its day. He used his position to encourage efficiency and the reduction of waste in industry. He fostered trade associations, mergers, and standardization of production through private agreements. Although historians have regarded both the Harding and Coolidge administrations as conservative, Hoover was in many ways "progressive" in that he hoped to bring about economic and social improvement through programs of education and "voluntarism." He chaired the **unemployment conference** in 1921 to encourage business and local voluntary initiatives to counter the postwar recession. In 1921 he helped to persuade U.S. Steel to accept the eight-hour day. Hoover also backed the postwar "Own Your Own Homes" campaign and the Better Homes of America organization. Hoover also supported children's concerns and was president of the American Child Health Association from 1923 to 1935. He is generally credited with drawing up the Children's Bill of Rights in 1923 that was later incorporated in the nineteen-point Children's Charter drawn up at the White House Conference on Child Health and Protection in 1930.

In 1927 Hoover led the mobilization of relief following the **Mississippi flood**. Again relying on voluntary and charitable relief, he raised $17 million to provide assistance for the thousands affected and further enhanced his reputation. When Coolidge declined to stand for reelection in 1928 Hoover won the **Republican Party**'s nomination and defeated **Democrat Al Smith** by a massive margin of 58 percent to 41 percent of the vote, carrying forty states to Smith's eight. While awaiting his inauguration, Hoover embarked on a six-week "goodwill" tour of Latin America and laid some of the foundations for **Franklin D. Roosevelt**'s "Good Neighbor policy."

On taking office, Hoover's activity contrasted with his predecessor's inertia. He supported labor legislation that resulted in the Norris–La Guardia Anti-Injunction Act (1932); set limits on oil drilling and withdrew all federally held oil lands from further leasing; and ordered all large government rebates on income, estate, and gift taxes to be made public. The new president took action against corrupt patronage practices, supported land conservation, and made some attempt to win the support of black voters with his "southern strategy." However, Hoover's administration fell victim to the **Wall Street Crash** of 1929 and was quickly overwhelmed by the **Great Depression** that followed.

Hoover attempted to address some of the economic problems facing America early in his administration. In an effort to deal with the problems of **agriculture** he called a special session of Congress that passed his **Agricultural Marketing Act** in 1929. A second special session was called to revise the 1922 tariff in order to help farmers. After fourteen months of deliberation the result was the **Hawley-Smoot Tariff**, which in the end proved counterproductive.

Following the Wall Street Crash, Hoover held a series of conferences at the White House with industrialists, representatives of agriculture, and union leaders to try and ensure the maintenance of production, employment, and wage levels by voluntary action. The president called upon state and city officials to increase public works expenditure, and in 1930 he secured federal appropriations of $150 million for river and harbor improvement, new public buildings, and the building of the Boulder Dam. In all the federal government would spend an unprecedented $700 million on public works, but Hoover was insistent that there would be no direct federal relief. Publicly Hoover tried to restore confidence with comments such as the forecast in March 1930 that "the worst effects on unemployment will have passed in the next 60 days." In May he observed, "We have now passed the worst," and later remarked, "At least no one has starved." All of these would come back to haunt him when the Depression continued to deepen.

In 1931 Hoover recognized that the Depression was a worldwide problem and attempted to ease the international economic crisis by declaring a moratorium on the payment of reparations and Allied debts. At home, the earlier President's Emergency Committee for Unemployment in 1931 became the **President's Organization for Unemployment Relief** (POUR) headed by **Walter Gifford**. The aim of this committee was to provide direction and coordination of state and local activity, but this proved increasingly ineffectual given the lack of resources at that level. More effective were the **Home Loan Banks** and the passage of **Glass-Steagall Banking Act** to stabilize credit and banking passed with Hoover's support in 1932. Equally significant was his approval of the Emergency and Relief Construction Act in 1932, which appropriated $2 billion for public works and $300 million for direct loans to states for relief purposes. However, he also called for increased taxation in order to balance the budget, and the 1932 Revenue Act, which raised taxes by one-third, further restricted consumption.

In 1932 Hoover established the **Reconstruction Finance Corporation** to lend money to banks, industries, and **railroads** to get the **economy** going again, but this had a limited effect and was seen by many Americans as a "rich man's dole." As discontent increased across the country Hoover's name became synonymous with the Depression. Tramps lived in "Hoovervilles," and the newspapers they covered themselves in for warmth were "Hoover blankets." When the **Bonus Army** was driven out of Washington, D.C., in 1932 Hoover's popularity fell even further. Despite this, an unenthusiastic Republican Party renominated him for the presidency. The outcome of the election in 1932 confirmed the voters' disapproval. Franklin D. Roosevelt gained 22.8 million votes to Hoover's 15.7 million, and Hoover won only 59 Electoral College votes from six states.

After his defeat Hoover dropped from the public's view. He was critical of the **New Deal** and later of America's Cold War policies. He opposed the formation of the North Atlantic Treaty Organization (NATO) in 1949 and the Korean War, 1950–1953. In 1949 he was appointed chair of the Commission on Organization of the Executive Branch of Government, and many of his recommendations were implemented by Harry S. Truman's administration.

See also FOREIGN POLICY; HOOVER, LOU HENRY (1874–1944).

HOOVER, JOHN EDGAR (1895–1972). J. Edgar Hoover was a lawyer and criminologist who joined the staff of the Alien Enemy Bureau in the Justice Department in 1917 and was active in the campaign against radicals during and after the war. As head of a newly created Radical Division, Hoover's encouragement of **A. Mitchell Palmer** did much to bring about the **Red Scare** of 1919. Hoover planned and directed the **Palmer Raids** of November 1919 and January 1920. In 1921 Hoover became assistant director of the Bureau of Investigation, which later became the **Federal Bureau of Investigation** (FBI).

As director of the FBI from 1924 until his death, Hoover was to achieve enormous power. During the 1930s he became a national figure in leading the attack on organized **crime** and against infamous criminals such as John Dillinger. Hoover was also involved in the investigation and trial of American Nazis after 1938 and of German saboteurs in 1942. He took a key role in the postwar anticommunist campaigns and provided evidence for the prosecution of leaders of the American Communist Party in 1948 and was also involved in the spy investigations that led to the trial and execution of Julius and Ethel Rosenberg in 1953. In the late 1950s Hoover developed a Counter Intelligence Program (COINTELPRO) that was used successively against communist groups, the **Ku Klux Klan**, and in the 1960s, against black organizations. Hoover personally led investigations to undermine the position of the civil rights leader Dr. Martin Luther King Jr. and even threatened him with blackmail. Later Senate investigations produced a report highly critical of Hoover and many of the FBI's domestic activities, but such was his power that no president was able to remove him from office.

HOOVER, LOU HENRY (1874–1944). The future wife of president **Herbert Hoover** was born Lou Henry in Waterloo, Iowa. She moved to Whittier, California, in 1887 and became fascinated by the outdoors. She studied geology at Stanford University, where she met Herbert Hoover. They married in 1899, and Lou traveled with her husband to China, where they were caught in the Boxer Rebellion. Lou Hoover accompanied her husband with their two children to Australia, Burma, Japan, and Siberia. In 1914 she and her husband were in London when **World War I** broke out, and they assisted stranded American tourists. Lou Hoover became president of the American Women's War Relief Fund while Herbert directed the commission for Relief in Belgium. The Hoovers returned to the United States in 1917, and Lou spoke at **U.S. Food Administration** and other events.

Mrs. Hoover was not a prominent first lady and was more private than her predecessor, **Grace Coolidge**. While she encouraged emerging artists through cultural gatherings in the White House, there is no evidence that she had any influence on her husband's speeches or policies. Mrs. Hoover also initiated a history of the White House. However, she did become the center of controversy when she invited the wife of the black congressman, **Oscar De Priest** to a White House tea for congressional wives, an action she and her husband both stood by. After the crash, Mrs. Hoover often privately provided relief to needy families, and she arranged for food and bedding to be sent to the Bonus Marchers' camp. In 1930 a school the Hoovers had built for the children of the area was opened in the Blue Ridge Mountains.

In 1917 Lou Hoover began a lifelong involvement with the Girl Scouts when she became a troop leader and a national Girl Scout commissioner the same year. Mrs. Hoover became vice president of the Girl Scouts in 1921 and president in 1922 until 1925. Her work for the organization became one of her main activities until her death, and she was president again from 1935 to 1937. Mrs. Hoover also served as president of the **women**'s section of the Amateur Athletics Association from 1923 to 1941.

HOPKINS, HARRY LLOYD (1890–1946). The famous **New Deal** administrator Harry Hopkins was educated at Grinnell College, Iowa. In 1912 he moved to New York City, where he became a social worker. He became executive secretary of New York's Board of Child Welfare and during **World War I** was involved in civilian relief for the families of servicemen for the Red Cross. In 1923 Hopkins became president of the American Association of Social Workers and in 1924 the director of the New York Tuberculosis Association. In 1931 Hopkins was appointed by Governor **Franklin D. Roosevelt** to direct New York's Temporary Emergency Relief Administration and then in 1933 to head the Federal Emergency Relief Administration, which spent $1 billion in two years providing jobs for the unemployed.

When initial relief measures proved too slow, Roosevelt put Hopkins in charge of the Civil Works Administration (CWA), which employed 4 million people in six months working on public building projects. From 1935 to 1940 Hopkins directed the Works Progress Administration (WPA), which put over 8 million workers on the federal payroll and spent $10.5 billion dollars. He became secretary of commerce in 1938 and considered running for the presidential nomination in 1940. However, ill health forced him to abandon such ambitions, and he supported Roosevelt before resigning from the administration.

During World War II Hopkins became a diplomat. He was first of all sent as a special envoy to Great Britain in 1941 and then to the Soviet Union. He organized Lend-Lease to the Allies before America entered the war and after 1941 headed the Munitions Assignments Board to allocate war material to different allied powers. Hopkins continued to work in the war administration despite his own poor health and the death of a son in combat. He was an influential figure at the Teheran Conference in 1943 and at Yalta in 1945, and played a part in ensuring Soviet participation in the United Nations conference in San Francisco in 1945. That year Hopkins resigned from government and was awarded the Distinguished Service Medal.

See also FOREIGN POLICY; NEW DEAL.

HOUSE, EDWARD MANDELL (1858–1938). Edward House was drawn into politics in Texas, where he ran his family's properties. His work in mobilizing support for the **Democratic** governor James Hogg in 1892 was rewarded with the title of "colonel." In 1911 House met and formed a friendship with **Woodrow Wilson**, and he became his adviser and confidante. Following the election of 1912 House advised Wilson on cabinet appointments and other issues. During **World War I** in Europe House was involved in negotiations in 1916 with Sir Edward Grey, the British foreign secretary, that resulted in an agreement for the Wilson Administration to call a peace conference when the **Allies** indicated. The agreement was not invoked, but it indicated the administration's move toward the Allied cause. House was involved in preparing the constitution of the proposed **League of Nations** in 1918 and with negotiating the armistice with Germany. House continued to support the League and American participation through the 1920s. He also continued to work within the Democratic Party and supported the nomination of **Franklin D. Roosevelt** in 1932.

HOUSTON, DAVID FRANKLIN (1866–1940). After graduating from Carolina College and Harvard University, David Houston became president of Texas A&M from 1902 to 1905 and then of the University of Texas, 1905–1908. In 1908 he was chancellor of Washington University in St. Louis. In 1913 **Woodrow Wilson** appointed Houston secretary of **agriculture**, and he held that post until 1919, when he became secretary of the U.S. Treasury, a position he held until 1921. In 1926 he wrote *Eight Years with Wilson's Cabinet*.

HOUSTON MUTINY, 1917. After a series of incidents of racial harassment and provocation, **African American** troops of the 3rd Battalion of the 24th Infantry stationed at Camp Logan, near Houston, Texas, seized weapons and marched into the city, where they fired on white townspeople. Sixteen whites and four blacks were killed in the violence. Following a court-martial in which sixty-three African American soldiers were tried, thirteen were executed in San Antonio on 22 December without review or opportunity to appeal.

HOWE, FREDERIC CLEMSON (1867–1940). Frederic Howe was typical of many **progressive** reformers. He obtained a PhD from Johns Hopkins University in 1892 with a dissertation on "The History of the Internal Revenue System" and later qualified in law and moved to Cleveland, Ohio, where he specialized in tax issues. Howe worked in the **settlement houses** in Cleveland and was secretary to the reform organization, the Municipal Association. In 1901 Howe was elected to the city council and served two years. In 1906 he was elected to the Ohio State Senate and then became a member of the Cleveland Board of Tax Assessors until 1910. He moved to New York City in 1910 and became director of the People's Institute, an educational organization for the poor.

In 1911 Howe became secretary of the National Progressive Republican League supporting **Robert M. La Follette** and wrote a study entitled *Wisconsin, an Experiment in Democracy* (1912). When La Follette failed to win the nomination, Howe switched support to **Woodrow Wilson** who appointed Howe commissioner of **immigration** for the Port of New York. Howe's humane approach to immigrants led him to resign during the 1919 **Red Scare** rather than deport alien radicals. He campaigned in support of the **Plumb Plan** to continue government control of the **railroads**, and in 1922 was involved in the **Conference for Progressive Political Action**. Howe supported La Follette once more in the election of 1924. In 1932 he supported **Franklin D. Roosevelt** and was appointed consumers' counsel on the Agricultural Adjustment Board in 1933. In 1937 Howe became adviser to the Philippine government on farm tenancy and cooperatives, and the following year was a consultant on agricultural commodities for the National Economic Committee investigating monopolies.

HOWE, LOUIS MCHENRY (1871–1936). Louis Howe began his career as a salesman and reporter working for his father before moving to the New York *Herald* in 1906. He then became involved in politics working first as a personal assistant to Mayor Thomas Osborne and then for **Franklin D.**

Roosevelt, managing his reelection to the New York senate in 1912. Howe continued as Roosevelt's assistant, speechwriter, and publicist through to the election of 1932 after which he became the president's secretary.

HUDSON, MANLEY OTTMER (1886–1960). Manley Hudson graduated from Harvard Law School in 1910. He was a member of the American commission at the **Paris Peace Conference** in 1919. In 1923 Hudson became professor of international law at Harvard and wrote several books on international law and international affairs. In 1936 he became a judge on the **Permanent Court of International Justice**.

HUGHES, CHARLES EVANS (1862–1948). Associate justice of the U.S. Supreme Court 1910–1916, secretary of state 1921–1925, eleventh chief justice of the U.S. Supreme Court, 1930–1941. A graduate of Columbia Law School, Hughes practiced law in New York City and served as counsel for the New York state legislature's committee investigating gas companies in 1906. He achieved national prominence when, as counsel for a similar committee investigating insurance companies (1905–1906), he exposed corrupt practices. As **Republican** governor of New York state from 1907 to 1910, Hughes established the public service commission, and introduced insurance law reforms and several pieces of labor legislation. He then served as associate justice to the U.S. **Supreme Court** until 1916, when he stood as the Republican presidential candidate. He lost the election to **Democrat Woodrow Wilson** by one of the narrowest margins.

Hughes was appointed secretary of state by presidents **Warren Harding** and **Calvin Coolidge** from 1921 to 1925. In 1926 he became a member of the Hague Tribunal and also a judge on the **Permanent Court of Internal Justice** (1928–1930). He was appointed chief justice to the U.S. Supreme Court by **Herbert Hoover** in 1930 and served until 1941. As chief justice, Hughes generally held a moderately conservative position. Although he wrote the opinion in *Schechter Poultry Corp. v. United States* that found the National Recovery Administration (NRA) unconstitutional in 1935, he generally voted in favor of upholding **New Deal** legislation. He vigorously opposed **Franklin D. Roosevelt**'s attempts to reorganize the Court in 1937.

HUGHES, (JAMES) LANGSTON (1902–1967). One of the major figures of the **Harlem Renaissance**, the **African American** poet Langston Hughes published his first significant poem, "The Negro Speaks of Rivers," in *Crisis* magazine in 1921, a year after he left high school. He spent a year at Columbia University in New York City before becoming a seaman, visiting West Africa and spending time in France and Italy. Two books of verse drawing on the black folk idiom, *The Weary Blues* and *Fine Clothes to the Jew*, appeared in 1926 and 1927 respectively. Hughes enrolled at Lincoln University in 1926 and graduated in 1929. Supported by a wealthy white patron, Charlotte Osgood Mason, from 1927 until 1931, Hughes produced his first novel, *Not Without Laughter*, in 1930.

After traveling to Haiti, the USSR, and Mexico Hughes wrote *Mulatto*, a play that enjoyed a long run on Broadway following its opening in 1935. Hughes's autobiography *The Big Sea* appeared in 1940 and another volume of poems, *Shakespeare in Harlem*, in 1942. Later collections such as *Fields of Wonder* (1947), *One-Way Ticket* (1949), and *Montage of a Dream Deferred* (1951) combined the blues idiom with **jazz** rhythms. Hughes also published regularly in journals and the press, and wrote a regular newspaper column featuring a humorous character called Jesse B. Semple, or Simple. These stories were published in the 1950s. Criticized for his earlier left-wing sympathies, Hughes toured Africa and other countries for the State Department. His second volume of autobiography, *I Wonder as I Wander*, was published in 1956. He continued to publish poetry, essays, and works of history through to his death. Such was his reputation that he was known as the "Shakespeare of Harlem." He was admitted to the National Institute of Arts and Letters in 1961.

See also LITERATURE AND THEATER.

HULL, CORDELL (1871–1955). A graduate of Cumberland University, Hull practiced law in Tennessee, where he became a judge on the 5th judicial circuit, 1903–1907. In 1907 he was elected to the U.S. House of Representatives and served until 1921. He was reelected in 1923 and served until 1931. Hull drew up the federal **income tax** law in 1913 and the federal estate and inheritance laws in 1916. In 1931 Hull was elected to the Senate, but in 1933 became **Franklin D. Roosevelt**'s secretary of state, a position he held until 1944. He worked particularly in improving relations with Latin American nations and in fostering the "Good Neighbor Policy." In 1945 he was awarded the Nobel Peace Prize.

See also FOREIGN POLICY.

HULL HOUSE. Founded in Chicago in 1889 by **Jane Addams** and **Ellen Starr**, Hull House was one of the first **settlement houses** in the United States Hull House was modeled on the example of Toynbee Hall in London's East End and acted as a welfare agency for the **immigrant** population. Funded entirely by voluntary contributions from individuals and social agencies, Hull House became one of the largest settlement houses in the United States and an example that was copied across the country in the **progressive era**.

See also SOCIAL WORK.

HURLEY, EDWARD NASH (1864–1933). Edward Hurley rose from being a railway worker to become a Chicago machine tool and appliance manufacturer and a prominent supporter of scientific management and industrial rationalization before the war. In 1896 Hurley established the Standard Pneumatic Tool Company. Having become a millionaire, he retired from the company. In 1908 he established the Hurley Machine Company, producing electrical home labor-saving devices, and was president of the First National Bank of Wheaton.

Hurley was a supporter of **Woodrow Wilson** who appointed him vice chairman of the **Federal Trade Commission** (FTC) and in 1917 chair of the **U.S. Shipping Board**, where he energetically supported the expansion of the U.S. merchant marine. Hurley also took part in the peace negotiations in Paris as a shipping adviser and was awarded the Distinguished Service Medal for his work. Following his retirement from public service in 1919 Hurley served as director of a number of companies and put the case for a large merchant marine in *The New Merchant Marine* (1920). He also wrote an account of his war experience in *The Bridge to France* (1927). In 1924 president **Calvin Coolidge** appointed Hurley to the World War Funding Commission. He was also a member of president **Herbert Hoover**'s Advisory Shipping Commission.

HURLEY, PATRICK JAY (1883–1963). After an education at the Indian University, Muskogee, and National University law school, Patrick Hurley practiced law in Tulsa, Oklahoma, before becoming a lieutenant colonel in **World War I**. He was appointed secretary of war by president **Herbert Hoover** in 1929. It was Hurley who, in 1932, issued the orders for the expulsion of the **Bonus Army** from Washington, D.C. During World War II Hurley served as minister to New Zealand and then as **Franklin D. Roosevelt**'s personal representative in the Near and Middle East and went on missions to Afghanistan and China. He became U.S. ambassador to China in 1944 but resigned in protest over the administration's China policy in 1945. In 1946 Hurley was awarded the Medal of Merit for his services to China. Hurley ran unsuccessfully for election to the U.S. Senate from New Mexico in 1946, 1948, and 1952.

See also FOREIGN POLICY.

HURSTON, ZORA NEALE (1891–1960). Born in Alabama, the **African American** novelist, folklorist, and anthropologist Zora Neale Hurston grew up in Florida in a community she was to later turn into a subject of study. Hurston studied at Howard University from 1919 to 1923 and then at Barnard College in New York City, where she studied with Franz Boas. She later began but did not complete a PhD at Columbia. Joining the growing literary movement of the **Harlem Renaissance**, Hurston published a number of short stories in magazines such as *Opportunity* and several pieces on southern folklore based on her fieldwork in Florida and other parts of the South. Her first novel, *Jonah's Gourd Vine*, was published in 1934. Her second book, *Mules and Men* (1935), was based on her field trips. Hurston's most acclaimed novel, *Their Eyes Were Watching God*, appeared in 1937 and focuses particularly on the plight of black **women**. *Moses, Man of the Mountains* (1939) was a version of the book of Exodus written in black vernacular. Although Hurston continued to publish in newspapers and journals through the 1950s, her career declined from the 1940s on, and she died in relative obscurity. The author Alice Walker, who did much to inspire a revival in interest in Hurston's work in the 1970s, subsequently found and marked her grave.

See also LITERATURE AND THEATER.

I

ICKES, HAROLD LECLAIR (1874–1952). A graduate of the University of Chicago, Ickes began work as a newspaper reporter, then gained his degree in law from the University of Chicago in 1904. Ickes practiced law in that city and was active in **Republican Party** politics. During **World War I** Ickes served in Europe with the Young Men's Christian Association (YMCA). Despite the political climate, he continued to be active in Republican Party politics and as a **reformer**, he supported **Hiram Johnson**'s presidential nomination in 1924. With the onset of the **Great Depression** Ickes worked for **Franklin D. Roosevelt** and was appointed secretary of the interior in 1933, a post he held until 1946, becoming in the process one of the greatest public administrators of all time. Under his leadership the Department of Interior expanded conservation policies and established several new national parks. Ickes was appointed head of the Public Works Administration (PWA) in 1933, but his cautious approach led to the creation of the Civil Works Administration (CWA) under **Harry Hopkins**. During World War II Ickes was petroleum and solid fuels administrator. After the war he retired from politics and spent most of his time writing his memoirs and columns for various newspapers.

See also NEW DEAL.

IMMIGRATION. The movement of people from one country or land to another was central to American history. The United States was "a nation of immigrants." Until about 1890 most immigrants came from northern and western Europe—England, Scotland, Ireland, France, the Netherlands, Germany, and Scandinavia. These "old immigrants" were predominantly (the Irish being the largest and most notable exception) white Anglo-Saxon Protestants. This changed in the late nineteenth century, and the "new immigrants" were increasingly from central, southern, and eastern Europe, and were Catholics, Jews, or Russian and Greek Orthodox in religion. The scale of immigration also reached new heights with 8.7 million new arrivals entering the United States between 1900 and 1910, and another 5.7 million between 1910 and 1920. The majority of the last group in fact came before **World War I**. A million immigrants entered the country in 1913 alone.

The majority of the "new immigrants" found work in the growing industries of the North and Northeast and settled in the growing urban centers such as New York, Chicago, and Pittsburgh. Many Americans associated immigrants with urban squalor, industrial unrest, and a threat to traditional values. A powerful nativist movement calling for immigration controls developed as a consequence and eventually achieved success with the passage of the **Quota Acts** of 1921 and 1924.

INDUSTRIAL CONFERENCES. In 1919 president **Woodrow Wilson** called an Industrial Conference in order to reach "a meeting of minds" and find a settlement to the postwar strikes and lockouts. The conference of sixty-one representatives of labor, management, and the public, chaired by secretary of the interior **Franklin Lane**, met from 6 to 23 October. The conference ended having achieved nothing. A second conference, chaired by **Herbert Hoover**, met from January to March 1920. The conference produced a report with various recommendations such as the forty-eight-hour week, minimum wages, and equal pay, but it had no power or authority to implement these proposals.

INDUSTRIAL WORKERS OF THE WORLD (IWW). Often known as the "Wobblies," or IWW, the Industrial Workers of the World was a radical industrial union formed in Chicago in 1905 by **William "Big Bill" Haywood** and Daniel Deleon. The object of the IWW was to organize all workers into "One Big Union" in order to achieve a revolutionary overthrow of capitalism. It concentrated on organizing the unskilled workers on an industry-wide basis using direct action methods of strike and sabotage. It was particularly successful in organizing migrant workers and miners in the West and **immigrant** groups such as the textile workers in the East. Faced with suppression under the syndicalist laws in various western states, the IWW launched Free Speech campaigns in western states and led the Lawrence, Massachusetts, textile strike in 1912 and the silk workers' strike in Paterson, New Jersey, in 1913. The IWW espoused direct action tactics, which included "striking on the job" (sabotage). An unofficial policy of opposition to involvement in **World War I**, plus its continued involvement in strikes, particularly in western lumber and mining industries, led to suppression under the **Espionage** laws. Following raids on its offices in 1918, 173 IWW leaders were convicted. Seriously weakened, the organization went into decline in the postwar years.

See also TRADE UNIONS.

INFLUENZA EPIDEMIC, 1918. In March 1918 U.S. troops at a military camp in Kansas became ill with influenza, sometimes known as Spanish influenza, or the three-day fever. Within days several of the soldiers were dead, and the virus spread across the United States and to Europe. A second wave of the illness hit in August, and a final wave in the winter. Eventually over 650,000 Americans and between 20 and 40 million people worldwide died in the epidemic. When the illness reached its height in the United States, 195,000 died in October alone. Unusually, twenty- to forty-year-olds seemed particularly vulnerable to the virus, and the deaths had a considerable impact on long-term birth rates.

INSULL, SAMUEL (1859–1938). Born in London, England, Samuel Insull epitomized the rags-to-riches story of business success that dominated the 1920s. He began work as an office boy in the London office of Thomas Edison's telephone company in 1878. In 1881 he came to the United States to work as Edison's private secretary and financial manager, and he became an American citizen in 1896.

Insull was involved in the consolidation of several Edison companies to create Edison General Electric in 1889; this merged with another company, the Thomas-Houston Electric Company, to form the General Electric Company (forerunner of the present-day General Electric) in 1892. When Insull failed to be made president of the new body, he took over the Chicago Edison Company. Insull acquired one of the several Chicago power stations and, using variable charges for off-peak usage and offering cheap wiring to individual homes, he created one of the largest power plants in the world at the Harrison Street Station. By the end of the decade Insull's companies provided power for 4 million consumers in thirty-two states. His success enabled him to take over several other power companies and invest in local transit, which was consolidated in the Chicago Rapid Transit company in 1924. In 1921 Insull was joint partner with Westinghouse in the creation of Chicago's first **radio** station, KYW; this amalgamated with other Chicago radio stations and was sold to NBC in 1931. Insull also contributed to the building of an opera house for the Chicago Civic Opera.

By the beginning of the 1930s Insull was chairman of the board of sixty-five different companies and president of eleven, with interests in operations ranging from land irrigation to dairy cattle. Much of his empire was based on the sale of low-priced bonds and stock and on a complicated system of holding companies that established monopoly power and controlled prices of utility companies across several states. Many of the shares of these utility companies were held by Insull Utility Investments, established in 1928. The interlocking pyramid organization of Insull's companies hid debts incurred by borrowing. Having initially withstood the effects of the **Wall Street Crash**, Insull believed that the depression would be short-lived and continued to borrow to finance expansion. While the value of utility stocks rose this was not a problem, but when they collapsed in March 1932 with a drop in value of $175 million, six hundred thousand ordinary investors lost their savings, and Insull owed $16 million. Forced to resign his many company positions, Insull fled the country. In October 1932 he was indicted in the Cook County courts on charges of embezzlement, larceny, and mail fraud, and in 1934 he was extradited from Turkey to stand trial. Although he was acquitted of all charges in three trials, Insull returned to Europe and died of a heart attack in the Paris subway in 1938. While at the time Insull was seen as the personification of the business malpractice that led to the Crash and **Great Depression**, some historians suggest that he was a scapegoat and ultimately a victim of aggressive banking or inadequate **banking** regulation.

IRRECONCILABLES. A group of sixteen western and midwestern senators led by **William Borah** of Idaho and **Robert M. La Follette** of Wisconsin. They were unalterably opposed to the **Versailles Peace Treaty** because of the harsh terms imposed on Germany and because of the potentially permanent U.S. participation in world affairs through the **League of Nations**. Their opposition and **Woodrow Wilson**'s unwillingness to compromise led to the Senate's failure to ratify the peace settlement and join the League.

ISOLATIONISM. The traditional **foreign policy** of the United States of noninvolvement and independence was established with George Washington's famous recommendation in his Farewell Address (1796) to avoid "permanent alliances." This was further confirmed in the Monroe Doctrine in 1823, which also established the principle of "separate spheres" of interest between the old world and the new. These positions were seriously challenged following the outbreak of **World War I**, and the U.S. entry into the war marked a major departure in foreign policy. However, isolationist sentiment reasserted itself after the war and led to the rejection of the **Versailles Treaty** and American involvement in the **League of Nations**. However, the United States remained active in foreign affairs and took a lead in disarmament conferences and the attempt to prevent future outbreaks of war through the **Kellogg-Briand Pact**. While attempts were made to maintain an isolated position from the growing conflict in Europe in the 1930s, ultimately these failed, and the U.S. participation in World War II marked the end of isolationism as accepted policy.

See also LONDON NAVAL CONFERENCE, 1930; WASHINGTON NAVAL CONFERENCE, 1921–1922; WASHINGTON NAVAL TREATY.

IVES, CHARLES EDWARD (1874–1954). One of America's greatest composers, Charles Ives studied at Yale University and then entered the insurance business. His business was very successful, and he retired a wealthy man in 1930. Ives sold insurance by day and composed at night. Strongly influenced by his bandleader father and by church and folk **music**, Ives wrote complicated pieces combining hymns, gospel, folk, and other influences in a variety of pieces ranging from music for piano or organ to string quartets and full symphonies. He published his *Concord Sonata* and a collection of 114 other pieces in 1922. Ives wrote little after that and it was only in the later 1930s that he gained recognition for his Piano Sonata no. 2. In 1947 his Symphony no. 3 was awarded the Pulitzer Prize.

J

JADWIN, EDGAR (1865–1931). Edgar Jadwin graduated from West Point in 1890 and received a commission in the Army Corps of Engineers. He worked on various river and harbor improvements and commanded a battalion in Cuba from 1898 to 1899. After holding a number of different appointments in the United States Jadwin worked as an assistant to General **George Goethals** on the construction of the Panama Canal, from 1907 to 1911, when he returned to the United States to work in Tennessee and Pittsburgh. During **World War I** Jadwin served in France, organizing and directing the construction of railways, roads, docks, and barracks. In 1919 he went first to Poland as part of the American Mission and then to the Ukraine as an observer. Resuming his rank as a colonel Jadwin then returned to the United States and worked on different projects. In 1926 he was promoted to chief of engineers with the rank of major general. Following the **Mississippi flood** in 1927 Jadwin ordered a complete investigation of flood control methods, and his proposals formed the basis of all subsequent flood control work on the lower Mississippi. After his retirement in 1929 Jadwin served as a delegate to the World Engineering Congress and later became chairman of the Interoceanic Canal Board that examined the possibilities of increasing the capacity of the Panama Canal.

JARDINE, WILLIAM MARION (1879–1955). After working in forestry and farming in Idaho, William Jardine studied at Utah Agricultural College and graduated with a degree in agronomy in 1904. In 1907 Jardine joined the Department of Agriculture in Washington, D.C. Three years later he joined the Kansas State Agricultural College and became dean of agriculture in 1913. During **World War I** he organized the planning of agricultural production in Kansas. In 1918 Jardine became president of the Agricultural College, but in 1925 **Calvin Coolidge** appointed him as secretary of **agriculture**. Jardine placed considerable emphasis on the marketing rather than production side of farming. He was an outspoken opponent of the **McNary-Haugen** bill and suggested instead that farmers use cooperatives to increase efficiency. In 1929 **Herbert Hoover** appointed Jardine as minister to Egypt.

He returned to the United States in 1933 and became state treasurer of Kansas for a year. In 1934 Jardine became president of the Municipal University of Wichita (now Wichita State University). He retired in 1949.

JAZZ. "Jazz" was the name given to the form of popular **music** that emerged from the **African American** community and became widely popular in the 1920s. The music had its origins in slave songs, chants, and hollers that developed into blues songs. Jazz was the instrumental form, which relied on simple rhythms and improvisation around a recurring melody line. The term was first reported being used among the black community of New Orleans in the 1870s to refer to fast, syncopated music, and jazz music was said to have originated in New Orleans at the end of the nineteenth century. It found expression in marching songs and in ragtime. As a result of the **Great Migration** of African Americans from the South during **World War I**, jazz moved into northern cities such as Chicago with bands like that of Joe "King" Oliver and the all-white Original Dixieland Jazz Band. Oliver made some of the first significant jazz recordings in the 1920s and introduced **Louis Armstrong** to a wider audience. As jazz spread it began to appeal to a white audience, and the most popular jazz music was the modified form of jazz combined with traditional band and symphony orchestra music performed by white musicians such as **Paul Whiteman**. The new, uninhibited aspects of jazz seemed to capture the sense of liberation that followed the war, particularly among the young; it also seemed to capture the sounds of the machine age. The writer **F. Scott Fitzgerald** used the term to describe the 1920s in his *Tales of the Jazz Age* (1922), and the phrase has stuck ever since.

See also CALLOWAY, "CAB" (CABELL) (1907–1994); ELLINGTON, "DUKE" (EDWARD KENNEDY) (1899–1974); HARLEM; HARLEM RENAISSANCE, c. 1920–c. 1933; HENDERSON, (JAMES) FLETCHER (1898–1952).

THE JAZZ SINGER, 1927. Starring **Al Jolson**, the *Jazz Singer* is normally credited as being the first sound motion picture.

See also JAZZ; MOVIES.

JEFFERSON, "BLIND" LEMON (1897–1929). The **African American** blues singer and guitarist Lemon Jefferson was born in Texas but traveled the South as an itinerant musician through the 1920s before being recorded by Paramount Records in its "Race Artists" series. In 1927 Jefferson's records were released at a rate of about one a month, and his forty-three records sold more than 1 million copies. His influence on other blues and **jazz** musicians was considerable, and his "Match Box Blues" was recorded by Larry Hensely (1934), Carl Perkins (1955), and the Beatles (1964) among others.

See also MUSIC AND DANCE.

JOHNSON, CHARLES SPURGEON (1893–1956). The black sociologist Charles Johnson graduated from Virginia Union University and in 1917 moved to Chicago, where he obtained his PhD. Johnson served briefly in France during **World War I**. On his return to the United States he was a researcher for the **National Urban League** (NUL) and the principal author of the study of the **Chicago race riot** of 1919, commissioned by the Chicago Commission on Race Relations, *The Negro in Chicago* (1922). Two years later Johnson moved to New York City, where he edited the NUL's publication *Opportunity: A Journal of Negro Life* from 1922 to 1928. Under Johnson's guidance *Opportunity* became a forum for the writers and artists of the **Harlem Renaissance**.

In 1926 Johnson became professor of sociology at Fisk University. He was the first **African American** appointed to the board of trustees of the **Julius Rosenwald** fund in 1934, and in 1937 became vice president of the American Sociological Society. In 1942 Johnson established the Institute of Race Relations at Fisk. Johnson was the author of seventeen books including *The Negro in American Civilization* (1930), *The Collapse of Cotton Tenancy* (1935), *Growing Up in the Black Belt* (1941), and *Patterns of Negro Segregation* (1943).

JOHNSON, HIRAM WARREN (1866–1945). Hiram Johnson qualified in law in 1888 and practiced in Sacramento and San Francisco. He made a name in cases against political corruption in San Francisco and was elected **Republican** governor of California in 1910 and initiated a program of reform. The various measures included **railroad** and public utility regulation; initiative, referendum, and recall; workmen's compensation and child labor laws; the eight-hour day for women workers; and state commissions on industrial welfare, industrial accidents, **immigration**, and housing. In 1912 he was **Theodore Roosevelt**'s running mate for the unsuccessful **Progressive Party**, and returned as governor of California in 1914. He was elected U.S. senator for the state in 1916 as a Republican and Progressive. Johnson supported the declaration of war on Germany in 1917 but opposed some of **Woodrow Wilson**'s war measures such as the **Sedition Act**. In 1919 Johnson, as a strict isolationist, took a prominent part as one of the "**irreconcilables**" in opposing the **League of Nations** in any form. In 1920 he became a leading contender for the Republican presidential nomination but lost to

Warren Harding. He declined the vice presidential nomination, failed to gain the Republican presidential nomination in 1924, and continued to serve as U.S. senator until his death.

Johnson's biggest achievement as senator was to see through approval of the Boulder (later renamed Hoover) Dam in 1928. In 1932 he declared his support for **Franklin D. Roosevelt** and actively campaigned on his behalf. He subsequently declined the offer to become secretary of the interior but continued to support most **New Deal** measures until 1937. In 1934 Johnson won both the Republican and **Democratic** nominations for reelection. He maintained his opposition to American foreign involvement and during the 1930s supported the neutrality acts. Johnson was reelected again in 1940 but then supported Republican Wendell Willkie's presidential campaign. In 1941 Johnson led the unsuccessful opposition to Roosevelt's Lend-Lease measures. Ill health limited his further participation in the Senate, but in 1945 Johnson voted against the United Nations Charter. Johnson's long political career in various ways charted the path followed by many progressives.

JOHNSON, HUGH SAMUEL (1882–1942). Hugh Johnson grew up in Oklahoma, graduated from West Point in 1903, and served with the First Cavalry in the Philippines and on national park duties. He wrote popular stories about military life for magazines such as *Collier's*, *Century*, and *Scribners*. Johnson qualified in law in 1916 and served briefly as judge advocate with General **John Pershing** in the **punitive expedition** in **Mexico**. During **World War I** Johnson was involved in the development of the **Selective Service** system and became army representative to the **War Industries Board**. He rose to the rank of brigadier general.

Following his resignation from the army in 1919 Johnson became an executive with the Moline Plow Company. He also became an investigator for **Bernard Baruch** in 1927, and in 1933 became part of **Franklin D. Roosevelt**'s team of advisers known as the "Brain Trust." In this role Johnson helped to write the National Industrial Recovery Act and was then appointed as administrator of the National Recovery Administration (NRA). Johnson's rather volatile leadership of the NRA attracted considerable criticism, and he was replaced in 1934. He then served briefly as head of the Works Progress Administration (WPA) in New York City but became increasingly critical of the **New Deal**. In 1940 he supported the Republican presidential candidate, Wendell Willkie, and also helped found the America First Committee to preserve U.S. neutrality.

JOHNSON, JAMES WELDON (1871–1938). James Weldon Johnson graduated from Atlanta University in 1894, taught briefly, and was admitted to the Florida bar in 1897. He practiced law in Florida from 1897 to 1901. In

1900, with his brother Rosamond, Johnson wrote, "Lift Every Voice and Sing," a song commemorating Lincoln's birth. The song was to become known as the "Negro National Anthem." With Bob Cole, the Johnsons were to write a number of other successful songs.

In 1906 Johnson was appointed U.S. consul to Venezuela, and in 1909 to Nicaragua, where he served until 1912. In 1917 Johnson became field secretary for the **National Association for the Advancement of Colored People** (NAACP) and in 1920 became the organization's first **African American** secretary. He was awarded the Spingarn medal for services to black Americans in 1925. It was Johnson who coined the phrase "**Red Summer**" to describe the wave of violence directed against African Americans after World War I, and he actively led the campaign to secure the passage of anti-lynching bills in the 1920s. Johnson actively encouraged the new wave of black writers that emerged during the **Harlem Renaissance**. From 1930 Johnson was the professor of creative literature at Fisk University. He was the author of *The Autobiography of an Ex-Colored Man* (1912), *Fifty Years and Other Poems* (1917), *God's Trombones* (1927), and editor of *The Book of Negro Poetry* (1922). He also published collections of Negro spirituals. Johnson died in an automobile accident in 1938.

See also LITERATURE AND THEATER.

JOHNSON-REED ACT. *See* QUOTA ACT, 1924.

JOLSON, AL (1886–1950). Born Asa Yoelson in Lithuania, Jolson's family immigrated to the United States about 1894 or 1895. Jolson left home with his brother and began a career as a song and dance man on the stage. He was particularly known for his blackface minstrel performances and achieved his first Broadway success in 1911 with *La Belle Paree*. Jolson became nationally known as a musical comedy performer in a series of successful stage performances, including *The Honeymoon Express* (1913), *Dancing Around* (1914), *Robinson Crusoe Jr.* (1916), and *Sinbad* (1918). It was in the latter that Jolson introduced **George Gershwin**'s songs "Swanee" and "My Mammy." He is best known for his appearance in the first sound motion picture, *The Jazz Singer*, 1927, in which he sang "Swanee," "My Mammy," and "April Showers." Jolson made a number of **movies** with Warner Brothers including *Mammy's Boy* and *Singing Fool*, both in 1928. Jolson's last Broadway show was *Hold on to Your Hats* in 1941, but his career declined after the 1930s although he entertained the troops during the World War II and provided the voice to the *Jolson Story* made in 1946.

See also MUSIC AND DANCE.

JONES ACT, 1916. An act passed in 1916 that provide civil government for the Philippines and conferred Philippine citizenship upon all inhabitants of the islands on 11 April 1899. It granted the vote to all literate adult males and established an elected legislature consisting of a Senate and House of Representatives.

JONES ACT. *See* ORGANIC ACT OF PUERTO RICO, 1917.

JONES ACT. *See* MERCHANT MARINE ACT, 1920.

JONES, JESSE HOLMAN (1874–1956). Jesse Jones was a successful Texas businessman who contributed to the development of Houston as a center of commerce and banking. In 1917 he was appointed director general of military relief for the Red Cross. Jones was a **Democratic Party** activist, and he accompanied **Woodrow Wilson** to the **Versailles Peace Conference** in 1918. In 1924 he acted as finance chairman for the Democratic presidential campaign. In 1932 **Herbert Hoover** appointed Jones to the **Reconstruction Finance Corporation** (RFC). **Franklin D. Roosevelt** made him chairman of the RFC in 1933, a position he held until 1939, when he became federal loan administrator. In 1940 he became secretary of commerce but he resigned all his political offices in 1945 following a disagreement with vice president Harry S. Truman.

JONES, ROBERT TYRE "BOBBY" (1902–1971). One of the leading sportsmen of the 1920s and regarded as the most successful amateur golfer ever to play at national or international level, Bobby Jones was born in Atlanta, Georgia. He attended Georgia Institute of Technology and gained a degree in mechanical engineering in 1922; he then took a degree in literature from Harvard in 1924, and finally qualified in law at Emory Law School and worked as a lawyer in Atlanta. Jones only played golf for three months in any year and did not achieve success until he had overcome his fiery temper. He first played in the U.S. Amateur championship in 1916 and the U.S. Open in 1920. He won his first major tournament in 1923, then went on to win the U.S. Amateur five times (1924, 1925, 1927, 1928, and 1930), the U.S. Open four times (1923, 1926, 1929, and 1930), the British Open three times (1926, 1927, and 1930; he was the first amateur to win), and the British Amateur in 1930. In five Walker Cup tournaments between the U.S. and British amateur teams, he won nine of ten matches. In 1930 Jones won the "Grand Slam"—the U.S. Amateur, British Amateur, British Open, and U.S. Open in the same year. He subsequently retired from competitive golf. He helped to create the Augusta National Golf Course and was one of the founders of the U.S. Masters tournament there from its inception in 1934. Jones served as an officer in the U.S. Army Air Force during World War II and was an interrogator of prisoners of war in Europe. He suffered increasingly from ill health and died of *syringomyelia*, a disease of the spine. Jones's record as a golfer was not matched until the 1970s and he is still ranked as one of the greatest golfers of all time.

See also HAGEN, WALTER CHARLES (1892–1969); SPORTS.

JONES, WESLEY LIVSEY (1863–1932). After qualifying and practicing law in Illinois, Wesley Jones moved to Washington State, where he entered **Republican** politics. He was elected to the House of Representatives in 1898 and to the Senate in 1909. He served until 1932. A "conservative progressive," Jones supported **William Howard Taft**, and backed secretary of the interior Richard Ballinger in the dispute over conservation policy with chief forester **Gifford Pinchot**. Jones did agree with reform measures such as the **Adamson Act**, **Clayton Antitrust Act**, and a **child labor** law. Although in favor of a **League of Nations**, he voted for the **Lodge amendments** in 1918. In 1920 Jones sponsored the **Merchant Marine Act** and a further amendment in 1928 authorizing the sale of vessels not already disposed of. Throughout the 1920s Jones supported measures to protect the lumber industry and the enforcement of **Prohibition**. From 1929 until 1932 Jones chaired the Senate Appropriations Committee. His backing for **Herbert Hoover** cost him reelection in 1932, and he died shortly after his defeat.

JORDAN, DAVID STARR (1851–1931). David Starr Jordan was a graduate of Cornell University and of Indiana Medical School. After holding a number of teaching positions he was appointed professor of natural history at Indiana University in 1879 and became president of that institution in 1885. Jordan's skill as an administrator contributed considerably to the growth of Indiana University, and in 1891 he was invited to become president of the newly created Stanford University. He was president of Stanford until 1913 and then chancellor until 1916. Jordan became well known for dismissing the sociologist **Edward Ross** in 1900 because of his political views, an incident that did much to define academic freedom in the United States. Despite this, under Jordan's guidance Stanford became one of the country's leading educational institutions.

As well as being an administrator, Jordan published numerous books and articles but became increasingly well known as an advocate for world peace, and in 1909 became head of the World Peace Foundation. He campaigned against America's entry into **World War I** but supported the war effort after 1917. Jordan was awarded the Raphael Herman Prize for his writings on "International Justice and Friendship."

See also EDUCATION.

K

KAISER, HENRY JOHN (1882–1967). Henry Kaiser began his career as a photographer in Lake Placid, New York, but moved to Spokane, Washington, in 1906, where he worked first as a salesman and then in highway construction. In 1914 he established his own construction company in Vancouver. As his company expanded on the West Coast, Kaiser moved his base to Oakland, California, in 1921. In 1931 he joined a consortium which won the bid to build the Hoover Dam and later for the Bonneville and Grand Coulee dams.

In 1940 Kaiser won a contract to build cargo ships for Great Britain, and following America's entry into World War II, established new yards to produce "Liberty ships" for the United States. His company became famous for producing one third of the nation's wartime cargo vessels. In 1945 Kaiser established the Kaiser-Frazer **automobile** manufacturing company that was successful for a time in the immediate postwar period. However, faced with competition from Ford, General Motors, and Chrysler, the company ceased production in 1955. The Kaiser Steel and Aluminum companies, however, continued to be successful. Equally successful was the Kaiser health and hospital program that had begun in 1938—with 1.5 million members by 1967, it was the country's largest health insurance program. Kaiser retired to Hawaii in 1954 and devoted his time to developing the island of Oahu and sponsoring television programs.

KALLEN, HORACE MEYER (1882–1974). Horace Kallen was born in Germany. His family immigrated to the United States in 1888, and Kallen grew up in Boston. He graduated from Harvard University in 1903 and completed his PhD there in 1908 having specialized in philosophy. He remained at Harvard as a lecturer but in 1911 joined the University of Wisconsin as a lecturer in psychology and philosophy. Kallen was forced to resign in 1918 because he spoke in defense of pacifists during **World War I**. In 1919 he helped to establish the New School for Social Research in New York City and he remained associated with it even in retirement. Kallen's considerable output of writing covered a broad area. His first book was *William James and*

Henri Bergson: *A Study in Contrasting Theories of Life* (1914), while his second was *The Book of Job as a Greek Tragedy* (1918). However, perhaps his most significant contribution was in propounding the philosophy of cultural pluralism in preference to ideas of a "melting pot" in his *Culture and Democracy in the United States* (1924). Kallen also wrote extensively about Judaism and was a leader of the American Jewish Congress (1922) and a member of the executive of the World Jewish Congress. Among his other works were *Individualism: An American Way of Life* (1933), *The Decline and Rise of the Consumer* (1936), *Art and Freedom* (1942), and *Americanism and Its Makers* (1945).

See also EDUCATION.

KEATING-OWEN ACT. *See* CHILD LABOR LAWS.

KEATON, BUSTER (1895–1966). Born Joseph Francis Keaton, Buster Keaton was born into a theater family and began work in vaudeville at age three. In 1917 he joined the Comique Film Company with **Roscoe "Fatty" Arbuckle**. Keaton established his trademark "stone face" in a number of silent comedies and later in a series of full-length features built in acrobatic comedy with melodramatic narratives. He achieved considerable success with *The Navigator* (1924) and *Battling Butler* (1926), but his epic *The General* (1927) was a commercial failure. In 1928 Keaton moved to Metro-Goldwyn-Mayer (MGM) and made two more silent **movies** and then appeared in a number of sound films starting with *The Hollywood Revue of 1929*. Keaton was fired from MGM in 1933 and starred in a number of lesser-known productions for Educational Films and Columbia Pictures. He returned to MGM in 1937 as a gagman and technical adviser and played minor roles in films such as *Hollywood Cavalcade* (1939). In the late 1940s and early 1950s he appeared in European circuses and variety shows and also made appearances on popular television shows. It was during these later years that Keaton was increasingly recognized as one of the greats of the silent movie era.

KELLER, HELEN (1880–1968). Helen Keller was struck deaf and blind as a baby but learned to communicate through Braille and sign language. She was able to gain a full education and attended Radcliffe College and graduated with honors in English and German in 1904. Keller achieved considerable fame through her writing including *The Story of My Life* (1902) and *The World I Live In* (1908). Prior to World War I Keller worked on behalf of the American Foundation for the Blind, joined the **Socialist Party**, supported **women's suffrage**, and defended the **Industrial Workers of the World**. During the 1920s Keller appeared in a **movie** of her life and toured the vaudeville circuit to raise money for the blind. Keller's writing continued to attract public acclaim with *My Religion* (1927), *Midstream—My Later Life* (1929), and *Helen Keller's Journal* (1938). Her life, which demonstrated the triumph of potential over disability, was celebrated in two films, *The Miracle Worker* (1962), and a documentary, *The Unconquered* (1953). In 1964 Keller was awarded the Presidential Medal of Freedom.

See also EDUCATION; WOMEN.

KELLEY, FLORENCE (1859–1932). Kelley was one of the many **women** who played a leading part in the **progressive** movement. Following her degree from Cornell University, she studied in Zurich, where she translated Engels's *The Condition of the Working-Class in England* (1887) and became a socialist. In 1891 she worked with **Jane Addams** at **Hull House** and then became the first chief factory inspector in Illinois in 1893, and secretary of the **National Consumers' League** in 1899. She assisted **Louis Brandeis** in the preparation of the brief in the **Supreme Court** case *Muller v. Oregon* establishing the legality of restricting the working hours of women. She was also a suffragist, a founder of the **National Association for the Advancement of Colored People** (NAACP), and a member of peace organizations. She campaigned in support of the establishment of a federal **Children's Bureau**, created in 1912, and later to secure the passage of the **Sheppard-Towner Act** in 1921.

KELLOGG, CHARLES BILLINGS (1856–1937). Charles Kellogg practiced law in St. Paul, Minnesota, and gained a reputation as special counsel in antitrust prosecutions and in investigations of the **railroads**. He served as senator from 1917 to 1923 and was one of the few **Republicans** to support the **League of Nations**. He was ambassador to Great Britain from 1924 to 1925 before succeeding **Charles E. Hughes** as secretary of state. In 1928 he negotiated the **Kellogg-Briand Pact** with Aristide Briand, foreign minister for France. He was awarded the Nobel Peace Prize in 1929 and served as a judge of the **Permanent Court of International Justice**, 1930–1935.

KELLOGG, PAUL (1879–1958). After graduating from the New York School of Social Work in 1902, Kellogg began work as a writer for *The Survey* (formerly *Charities Magazine*), a journal focused on social issues and conditions that became the leading journal of **social work** in the United States. In 1912 he became editor. He conducted a detailed study of social conditions in Pittsburgh that was published as the *Pittsburgh Survey* between 1910 and 1914 and became a model of research to aid social reform. Like many **progressives**, Kellogg opposed U.S. entry into the World War I and was one of those who persuaded **Henry Ford** to organize the **Peace Conference in Stockholm** in 1916. He was also one of the founders of the **American Civil Liberties Union**.

KELLOGG-BRIAND PACT. Also known as the Pact of Paris and the Pact of Peace, the Kellogg-Briand Pact began as a bilateral agreement between **Charles Kellogg** and the French foreign minister, Aristide Briand, in 1928 to renounce war as an instrument of national policy. Thirteen other countries signed that year, and ultimately sixty-two countries were to ratify it. However, its effectiveness was limited due to the lack of any powers of enforcement.

See also FOREIGN POLICY.

KELLOR, FRANCES ALICE (1873–1952). A graduate of Cornell Law School (1897) and the University of Chicago (1901), Frances Kellor became a leading social reformer and specialist in arbitration. In 1904 she published *Out of Work*, a study of employment agencies in New York, and helped to draft the state legislation to control employment agencies. In 1906 Kellor founded the National League for the Protection of Colored Women to help southern **African American** migrant **women**. In 1910 Kellor was appointed head of the New York State Bureau of Industries and Immigration. In 1912 Kellor supported **Theodore Roosevelt** and the **National Progressive Party**. She continued after the election defeat to work to implement reform at state level.

In 1915 Kellor organized "National Americanization Day" and was an active campaigner for Americanization during **World War I**. She continued these activities through the Inter-Racial Council formed in 1918. During the 1920s Kellor focused more on the resolution of industrial disputes and in 1926 was one of the founders of the American Arbitration Association.

KENNEDY, JOSEPH PATRICK (1888–1969). The father of the future president, John F. Kennedy, Joseph Kennedy was educated at the Boston Latin School and Harvard University. He began work in 1912 as a state bank examiner and by 1914 had become president of a bank founded by his father. In 1914 he married Rose Fitzgerald, daughter of one of the first Irish Catholic Americans to be mayor of Boston. In 1917 Kennedy became assistant general manager of the Bethlehem Steel shipyards at Quincy and after the war he became manager of an investment banking company. From 1926 until 1930 Kennedy was part of a syndicate that bought a chain of movie theaters in the Northeast and was also involved in the merger that created RKO pictures. By the 1930s he was a multimillionaire.

Kennedy made significant financial contributions to the election campaign of **Franklin D. Roosevelt** and held a number of positions under the **New Deal**. From 1934 to 1935 he was chair of the Securities Exchange Commission and in 1937 was chair of the U.S. Maritime Commission. Kennedy was appointed ambassador to Great Britain in 1938 but increasingly seemed to support appeasement, and he returned home in 1940. In the 1950s Kennedy was a supporter of senator Joseph McCarthy and other conservatives. He transferred his political ambitions to his sons, and when Joseph Sr. was killed during World War II, the focus passed to John. While his great wealth helped secure the election of John F. Kennedy as president in 1960, his previous support for right-wingers was something of a handicap. Nonetheless, Joseph Kennedy will be remembered for creating a political dynasty.

KERN, JEROME DAVID (1885–1945). Born to a family of German Jewish immigrants in New York City, Jerome Kern moved to Newark, New Jersey, where he attended Newark High School. He wrote his first musicals while at school and studied **music** from 1902 to 1903 at New York College of Music. He worked as a pianist and song plugger for a musical publisher and as a pianist on Broadway. He visited London in 1906 and some of his songs were used in theaters there. Kern's first complete score was for *The Red Petticoat* (1912), but his earliest major success was the song "They Didn't Believe Me" (lyrics by Herbert Reynolds), written for the New York version of *The Girl from Utah*. He wrote sixteen Broadway scores between 1915 and 1920, some of which were also successful in London. Kern was a prolific composer and produced one show almost every year throughout the 1920s. In 1925 he teamed up with Oscar Hammerstein II to write the music for *Show Boat*, often regarded as the most influential Broadway musical ever. It included songs such as "Ol' Man River," "Can't Help Lovin' Dat Man," and "Why Do I Love You?," all of which became musical standards. He and Hammerstein also wrote the songs for *Sweet Adeline* (1929), among many others, but he also collaborated with other lyricists such as Otto Horbach on songs such as "Smoke Gets in Your Eyes" (from *Roberta* [1933]). Kern also began to write for Hollywood from 1929 onward and won two Academy Awards—for "The Way You Look Tonight" (lyrics by Dorothy Fields) in *Swing Time* (1936), and "The Last Time I Saw Paris" (lyrics by Hammerstein) in *Lady Be Good* (1940). In total Kern wrote over one thousand songs and more than one hundred complete scores. Among his classic compositions were "The Folks Who Live on the Hill" and "All the Things You Are." With **Irving Berlin, Cole Porter**, and **George Gershwin**, Kern was probably one of the most influential musical composers of the interwar period.

See also LITERATURE AND THEATER.

KITCHIN, CLAUDE (1869–1923). Claude Kitchin graduated from Wake Forest College in 1888, studied law, and was admitted to the bar. In 1900 he was elected to the U.S. House of Representatives as a **Democrat** from North Carolina and was to serve for twelve terms. Kitchin was an effective speaker and by 1915 was majority leader in the House. A supporter of **Woodrow Wilson**, particularly on the **tariff** issue, Kitchin nonetheless opposed the "preparedness" campaign and entry into **World War I** in 1917. However, he actively supported the administration's war measures and helped secure passage of the finance bills. He was incapacitated by a cerebral hemorrhage in 1920.

KNOX, PHILANDER CHASE (1853–1921). Knox was a qualified lawyer who served as assistant U.S. district attorney for western Pennsylvania from 1876 to 1877. A corporation lawyer, Knox was involved in the formation of the Carnegie Steel Company in 1900. In 1901 president William McKinley appointed Knox attorney general, and he continued in that position under **Theodore Roosevelt**. Knox initiated the famous suit against the Northern Securities company that marked the beginning of Roosevelt's "trust-busting." He also drafted the legislation establishing the Department of Commerce and Labor in 1903. In 1904 the governor of Pennsylvania appointed Lane to the U.S. Senate to complete the term of a deceased senator. He was elected in his own right as a **Republican** in 1905.

In 1908 **William Howard Taft** appointed Knox as secretary of state. Knox promoted the policy of "dollar diplomacy" encouraging U.S. corporations to invest in Latin America and Asia. He declined an appointment to the **Supreme Court** in 1911 and resumed his law practice in 1913. In 1916 he was again elected as a senator for Pennsylvania. Knox was one of the leading opponents of the **Versailles Treaty** in 1919, and he drafted the "round robin" against the league signed by thirty-seven Republicans. It was Knox who proposed the resolutions rescinding the declarations of war against Austria and Germany in lieu of a peace treaty that **Woodrow Wilson** vetoed. The resolution was passed after Wilson left office in 1921.

KREUGER, IVAR (1880–1932). After a successful career as a civil engineer and cofounder of the construction company Kreuger and Toll, the Swedish-born civil engineer and financier took over his family-owned matchmaking factories and formed the Swedish Match company in 1917. In return for loans to national governments he was able to set up monopolies in several European and Central and South American countries to create a worldwide company. He established the International Match Corporation in New York in 1923 and earned the name of "the match king." Using shares in his existing companies, Kreuger invested in banks, mining companies, **railroads**, timber and paper firms, film distributors, and real estate in several European cities. He had a major interest in the Swedish film company AB Svensk Filmindustri, established in 1919, and a controlling share of L.M. Ericsson & Co., Sweden's leading telephone company. He also controlled a large proportion of the world market in iron ore and cellulose. Drawing on his influence as an international businessman, Kreuger used share and bond issues in New York to raise loans for foreign governments such as Ecuador, Bolivia, Peru, Poland, Greece, Hungary, Yugoslavia, Romania, and even France and Germany. By 1929 Kreuger was said to be the third-richest man in the world. Just days before the **Wall Street Crash**, he made a loan to Germany of $125 million raised largely from U.S. investors.

However, much of Kreuger's empire was based on pyramid selling and fraud with dividends paid out of capital, not profit, and money moved from one part of his vast network to another, much of it done secretly. His success was based on confidence, but when the Swedish national bank refused to make further loans to him without full access to his accounts, it became apparent that much of his business was built on shaky foundations, and confidence collapsed. Faced with exposure, Kreuger shot himself in a Paris apartment on 12 March 1932; his death triggered the collapse of his company and brought about the so-called "Kreuger crash" that wiped out the savings of thousands of investors, many of them in the United States. In 1933 and 1934 Congress passed the Securities Act and Securities and Exchange Act, requiring full disclosure of information by sellers and dealers in securities partly as a consequence of the revelations of the financial malpractice of Kreuger and others, such as **Samuel Insull**.

See also BANKING.

KU KLUX KLAN (KKK). Originally formed in the aftermath of the Civil War, the Ku Klux Klan was revived in 1915 at Stone Mountain, Georgia, by **William J. Simmons**, apparently inspired by **D. W. Griffith**'s movie *The Birth of a Nation*. The Klan represented the white Anglo-Saxon Protestant and older rural values. During the 1920s it was antiblack, anti-immigrant, anti-Catholic, and anti-Jewish. In 1920 Simmons enlisted the assistance of Edward Young Clark and Elizabeth Tyler and their Southern Publicity Association to help build up Klan membership. Although strongest in southern states, the Klan spread beyond the South and gained political influence in Colorado, Indiana, Illinois, Ohio, and Pennsylvania. Reports in the press, particularly coverage in the *New York World* in 1921 of 152 acts of violence, only seemed to encourage the growth.

Under the leadership of **Hiram Wesley Evans** from 1922, the Klan grew in number and influence and by 1924 was estimated to have over 4 million members. In 1925 forty thousand Klansmen took part in a march in Washington, D.C. The Klan's influence was evident particularly in the **Democratic**

Party and affected the nominations in 1924. However, scandals and reactions against violence led to its decline. In March 1925 David C. Stephenson, Grand Dragon of the Indiana Klan, was convicted of the murder and rape of his secretary and sentenced to life imprisonment. A lawsuit against a breakaway group of Klansmen in 1927 also exposed much of the Klan's activities. In 1939 Evans sold his interest in the Klan, and in 1944 the official organization was dissolved. Various unofficial versions of the organization appeared in the 1950s and 1960s.

L

LABOR, DEPARTMENT OF. *See* DEPARTMENT OF LABOR.

LADD, EDWIN FREMONT (1859–1925). A graduate of the University of Maine, Ladd worked as an agricultural chemist at the New York Agricultural Experiment Station from 1884 until 1890. That year he was appointed as agricultural chemist at the North Dakota Agricultural College in Fargo. He also became editor of the *North Dakota Farmer and Sanitary Home* newspaper. In addition to his teaching duties, Ladd was responsible for enforcing state pure food legislation and inspecting paint products. In 1909 the state courts and the U.S. Department of Agriculture upheld Ladd's argument that bleached flour was unfit for human consumption. His studies were instrumental in securing the passage of a federal Grain Standards Act in 1916. In 1920 the **Nonpartisan League** nominated Ladd for the U.S. Senate, and he defeated the incumbent **Republican** and **Democratic** opposition. He was part of the **Farm Bloc** in Congress and supported measures to bring economic cooperation. He also called for diplomatic recognition of the USSR.

LA FOLLETTE, ROBERT MARION (1855–1925). A Republican/Progressive politician, La Follette was elected to the House of Representatives as a **Republican** from Wisconsin in 1885 and served until 1891. He became governor of Wisconsin in 1901 and quickly turned the state into what **Theodore Roosevelt** described as "the laboratory of democracy." He was responsible for the introduction of regulation of the **railroad** rates, civil service reform, the use of specialist advisers in government, public health and pure food laws, conservation legislation, workmen's compensation laws, and the nation's first state income tax. The "Wisconsin Idea" also included the democratization of the political process through the use of referenda, initiatives, and the direct primary.

La Follette was elected senator in 1905 and served until his death. He sponsored the Seaman's Act of 1915, which introduced regulation of working conditions and wages on river, lake, and seagoing vessels. In 1911 La Follette was one of the founders of the National Progressive Republican

League critical of **William Howard Taft**'s administration, and La Follette contested the Republican presidential nomination in 1912. When Taft was renominated, La Follette joined Theodore Roosevelt in the **Progressive Party**. He opposed American entry into **World War I** and subsequently the **League of Nations**. He led the call for investigation into the **Teapot Dome** scandal. In 1924 he won almost 5 million votes and thirteen Electoral College votes as the Progressive Party candidate in the election.

LA GUARDIA, FIORELLO HENRY (1882–1947). Fiorello La Guardia was born in New York City and raised in Arizona. His family went to Trieste in 1898, and La Guardia worked for the U.S. consular service; from 1904 to 1906 he was acting consular agent at Fiume (now Croatia). He returned to the United States in 1907, graduated from New York University Law School in 1910, and practiced law in New York City. He served as a major in the U.S. Air Force during **World War I**. La Guardia served in the U.S. House of Representatives from 1917 to 1921 and from 1923 to 1933 as a **Republican**. He was president of the New York City Board of Aldermen, 1920–1921. While in Congress La Guardia was cosponsor of the **Norris–La Guardia Act**. He lost his seat in Congress in the **Democratic** landslide of 1932, but in 1933 he was elected mayor of New York on a Fusion ticket, supported by Republicans and reform groups.

The diminutive mayor, known as "the Little Flower," established a reputation for honesty and for reforming the city government. La Guardia's administration witnessed slum clearance and public housing development, the building of hospitals and child-care facilities, and the construction of roads and bridges (including the Triborough Bridge and the airport that bears his name). He held the office until 1945 and was president of the U.S. Conference of Mayors from 1936 until 1945. During World War II La Guardia was appointed head of the U.S. Office of Civilian Defense until 1942. In 1946 he became director of the United Nations Relief and Rehabilitation Administration (UNRRA).

LAMONT, THOMAS WILLIAM (1870–1948). Following his graduation from Harvard University in 1892, Thomas Lamont started work as a reporter on the New York *Tribune*. After two years he moved into marketing and established his own company in 1898. He joined the Bankers Trust in 1903, became vice president of the First National Bank in 1909, and became a partner in J. P. Morgan and Co. in 1911. He became chairman of the board in 1943.

In 1917 Lamont joined the **Liberty Loan** committee to aid the Treasury in selling war bonds. He was also appointed as an unofficial adviser to the **Allies** and served as a Treasury representative at the **Versailles Peace Con-**

ference in 1918. In 1924 Lamont was involved in drafting the **Dawes Plan** and in 1929 the **Young Plan** to deal with German reparations. Lamont also headed a commission to deal with the problem of Mexico's debts, and he took part in a consortium established to lend money to China and Japan. Lamont's other role was to liaise with the press and government bodies on behalf of J. P. Morgan and Co.

A generous benefactor, Lamont donated funds to assist in the rebuilding of Canterbury Cathedral, England, after World War II, and he left a sizable bequest to the Metropolitan Museum of Art.

LANDES, BERTHA KNIGHT (1868–1943). After graduating from Indiana University, Bertha Knight Landes moved to Seattle in 1895. She became a leading member of the **Women**'s University Club, the League of Women Voters, and president of the Seattle Federation of Women's Clubs. She was elected to the Seattle City Council in 1922 and became president of the council. In 1926 Landes challenged the incumbent mayor, Dr. Edwin Brown, and defeated him on an anticorruption platform to become the first female mayor of a major city in the United States. As part of her campaign to clean up the city, she dismissed the chief of police. Despite some success Landes was defeated in 1928 and concentrated on social work activities and writing articles advocating greater participation of women in politics.

LANDIS, KENESAW MOUNTAIN (1866–1944). Qualified as a lawyer, Landis briefly worked as a personal assistant to Walter Gresham, secretary of state in the 1890s. He served as U.S. district judge in the Northern District of Illinois from 1905 to 1922. In the course of his term he imposed a fine of $29 million on the Standard Oil Company, attempted to bring a murder indictment against Kaiser Wilhelm II following the sinking of the *Lusitania*, and presided over the trial of 113 members of the **Industrial Workers of the World** in 1918. He imposed heavy fines and prison sentences on those convicted, including **"Big Bill" Haywood**. Landis was equally severe during the subsequent trial under the **Espionage Act** of the Socialist leader **Victor Berger**, on whom he imposed a twenty-year sentence but wished he could have been shot. His intemperate remarks led to the overturn of the conviction. In 1920, following the scandal of the **Chicago White Sox** in 1919, he was appointed commissioner for the American and National Leagues of Professional Baseball Clubs. He claimed to have "cleaned up" the national **sport** by taking a tough moral stand.

See also WORLD WAR I, 1914–1918.

LANE, FRANKLIN KNIGHT (1864–1921). Franklin Lane was born in Canada. His family migrated to San Francisco in 1871. Lane went to the University of California at Berkeley and Hastings Law School and passed the California bar examinations in 1888. However, he made his career initially as a journalist working for the *San Francisco Chronicle*, *Arthur McEwen's Letter*, and the *Tacoma Daily News*, which he owned. He became a partner in his brother's law firm in San Francisco in 1895. In 1897 Lane joined the committee responsible for drawing up San Francisco's new charter, and he subsequently held the office of city attorney for three terms beginning in 1898. In 1902 Lane was unsuccessful in the Californian gubernatorial election. Although a **Democrat**, he supported **Theodore Roosevelt**, who appointed him to the Interstate Commerce Commission in 1906. **William Howard Taft** reappointed him for a second term in 1911.

In 1913 **Woodrow Wilson** appointed Lane as secretary of the interior. He supported several measures to further the development of natural resources on federal lands: the Reclamation Extension Act, the Alaskan **Railroad** Act, the Alaskan Coal Leasing Act, the Federal Water Power Act, and the General Leasing Act. In addition Lane endorsed the National Park Service Act (1916), which established the National Park system.

Lane supported Wilson's wartime policies and served on the **Council of National Defense**. He supported Americanization programs through the Department's Bureau of Education and proposed a land reclamation scheme to provide farms for returning veterans as part of postwar reconstruction. In 1919 he chaired the **Industrial Conference** established to try to end the postwar labor conflicts. In 1920 he resigned from the cabinet and became vice president of a petroleum company.

LANGDON, HARRY PHILMORE (1884–1944). Harry Langdon joined a traveling medicine-show company at the age of twelve and toured as a vaudeville comedian in the years before **World War I**. From 1923 on he worked with the film producer **Mack Sennett** and he made over two dozen silent **movies** between 1924 and 1926. He later joined director Frank Capra and made *Tramp, Tramp, Tramp* (1926), *The Strong Man* (1926), and *Long Pants* (1927). With **Charlie Chaplin**, Langdon was one of the most popular comedians of the silent film era. Langdon did not make the transition to sound film very well, and his last significant role was in *Hallelujah, I'm a Bum* (1933). He made some films in the 1930s with Laurel and Hardy and appeared on stage during World War II.

LANSING, ROBERT (1864–1928). Lansing was admitted to the New York bar in 1889 and worked in his father's law firm. He became a specialist in international law. He was the founder and editor of the *American Journal of*

International Law and acted in various capacities in the Bering Sea arbitration (1892), the Alaskan Boundary Tribunal (1903), and U.S. and British Claims Arbitration. In 1914 Lansing was appointed as counselor in the State Department and the following year he succeeded **William Jennings Bryan** as secretary of state. Lansing supported the dispatch of U.S. troops to **Haiti** and the **Dominican Republic** in 1915–1916, and he had a considerable influence in shaping the policies of **Woodrow Wilson**'s administration toward Germany after the outbreak of **World War I** in 1914. In 1917 Lansing negotiated the **Lansing-Ishii Agreement** with Japan, and at the end the war he was one of the five U.S. delegates to attend the **Versailles Peace Conference** in 1919. However, he disagreed with Wilson about aspects of the peace treaty and the proposals for a **League of Nations**. When Lansing began to chair the cabinet meetings after the president's stroke in October 1919, Wilson called for his resignation. From 1920 until 1925 he practiced law in Washington, D.C., and acted as counsel to several foreign governments.

LANSING-ISHII AGREEMENT. Negotiated in November 1917, the agreement between the United States and Japan pledged to uphold the "Open Door" policy and respect the territorial integrity of China. Further negotiations during the **Washington Naval conference** abrogated this agreement.
See also LANSING, ROBERT (1864–1928).

LARSEN, NELLA (1891–1964). The **African American** writer Nella Larsen was born of a Danish mother and African American father. Her mother subsequently married Peter Larson, from whom Nella took her surname. Larsen studied science at Fisk University from 1907 to 1910, when she moved to Copenhagen. She returned to New York City in 1912 and trained as a nurse. From 1915 she worked as a nurse. **Jessie Fauset** published Larsen's first stories in 1926, and Larsen became part of the **Harlem Renaissance**. Her first novel, *Quicksand*, was published to some acclaim in 1928; her second and last, *Passing*, appeared in 1929. In 1930 Larsen became the first black **woman** to receive a Guggenheim Fellowship, but that year she was accused of plagiarism in one of her short stories. Although she proved her innocence, she was not published again in her lifetime. Following a sensational divorce in 1933, Larsen faded into obscurity and lived the rest of her life as a nurse.
See also LITERATURE AND THEATER.

LATHROP, JULIA CLIFFORD (1858–1932). The **social worker** Julia Lathrop was educated at Rockford Seminary and Vassar. In 1890 she went to Chicago, where she worked at **Hull House** until 1912. Lathrop was a member of the Illinois State Board of Charities (1893–1901, 1905–1909). In 1899

Lathrop was one of the campaigners who helped bring about the creation of the first juvenile court in America. She also helped to establish the Chicago School of Civics and Philanthropy. In 1912 president **William Howard Taft** appointed her head of the Children's Bureau in the U.S. **Department of Labor**. She held the position until 1921. Lathrop was president of the Illinois League of Women Voters from 1922 to 1924, and from 1925 to 1932 she was a member of the advisory committee on child welfare to the **League of Nations**.

See also WOMEN.

LAWRENCE, ERNEST ORLANDO (1901–1958). The physicist Ernest Lawrence was educated at St. Olaf College, Northfield, Minnesota, the University of South Dakota, and the University of Minnesota. He completed his studies at Yale University, where he gained a PhD in 1925. Lawrence remained at Yale as a National Research council fellow and assistant professor until 1928, and he established a reputation as a brilliant experimentalist in the field of photo-electricity. Lawrence conducted a considerable amount of research in the area of television, and he was to obtain a number of patents in the field in his later years.

In 1928 Lawrence accepted a position at the University of California, Berkeley. In 1931 he developed the cyclotron, or particle accelerator, which accelerated protons to initiate nuclear reactions. In 1936 Lawrence became director of the university's Radiation Laboratory. He was awarded the 1939 Nobel Prize in Physics for the invention of the cyclotron. During World War II he was involved in research connected with the development of radar and in the Manhattan Project to develop the atomic bomb. Lawrence's work won him numerous awards and medals.

See also EDUCATION.

LEAGUE OF NATIONS. The first major world organization established to prevent further outbreaks of war following **World War I**. The League was initially proposed in **Woodrow Wilson**'s **Fourteen Points** speech in 1918, and its constitution, the Covenant, was formally included in the **Treaty of Versailles** in 1919. Although many Americans supported the idea of a League and were prepared to agree to the Versailles settlement in some form, it faced unshakable opposition from fourteen Republican senators, known as the "**Irreconcilables**," led by **Henry Cabot Lodge**. More moderate politicians in both parties sought compromise, but Wilson's refusal to allow any concession led to failure to ratify the peace treaty in the Senate in 1920.

Established in Geneva, the League was to be fatally weakened by the absence of the United States. Germany was only a member from 1926 to 1933, and the Soviet Union from 1933. Japan withdrew from the League in

1933, and Italy did the same in 1937. Although it achieved some success in research and refugee work, and in settling disputes between smaller nations, the League had no force to back up its decisions and relied on sanctions to enforce its will. It was unable to prevent the aggression by Japan in Manchuria and China from 1931 on, by Italy in Abyssinia, 1935–1936, or by Russia against Finland in 1939. The League proved powerless to prevent the sequence of events that eventually led to World War II in 1939 despite holding various disarmament conferences. In 1946 the League of Nations was formally dissolved. It was succeeded by the United Nations Organization.

See also FOREIGN POLICY.

LEAGUE OF WOMEN VOTERS. After the passage of the **Nineteenth Amendment**, the **National American Woman Suffrage Association** became the League of Women Voters in 1920 to educate **women** as citizens and to mobilize them on women's issues.

LEGGE, ALEXANDER (1866–1933). After working for a time as a cowboy in Wyoming in the 1880s, Alexander Legge found work with the McCormick Harvesting Machine Company in Omaha. In 1902 he was made manager of domestic sales in the company that had since become the International Harvester Company. By 1918 he had become senior vice president of the entire company. In 1917 he joined **Bernard Baruch** in the raw materials division of the **War Industries Board**, and he later became manager of the Allied Purchasing Commission. In 1918 Legge joined the foreign mission of the War Industries Board and was involved in formulating economic provisions in the **Versailles Peace Treaty**.

After the war Legge returned to International Harvester and was made president in 1922. He advised **Herbert Hoover** on the reorganization of the Department of Commerce, and he took part in president **Warren Harding**'s **Unemployment Conference**. When Hoover became president he asked Legge to become secretary of commerce, but Legge declined the offer. He became chair of the Federal Farm Board in 1929 and in 1932 served as a member of the National Transportation Committee. In 1933 Legge established the Farm Foundation to encourage cooperation among farmers. He had earlier established the Katherine Legge Memorial to care for working women.

LEHMAN, HERBERT HENRY (1878–1963). Herbert Lehman, New York's longest-serving governor, began work in a textile company in 1899. By 1906 he had risen to become vice president and treasurer of the company. In 1908 he joined his father's investment **banking** company, Lehman Brothers. Lehman worked for a number of charitable organizations, particularly the Joint Distribution Committee formed during **World War I** to aid Jews in Eastern Europe. During the war he served in the General Staff Corps in Washington, D.C., as a captain and was responsible for purchase and traffic.

After the war Lehman entered **Democratic** politics as a friend and associate of **Alfred E. Smith** and had various roles in Smith's election campaigns in 1924 and 1928. Lehman became **Franklin D. Roosevelt**'s lieutenant governor in 1928, a position he held until 1932. In 1932 he was elected governor in his own right, and reelected again in 1934 and 1936. In 1938 he was elected to the first four-year term in the same capacity. Under his direction New York established a "little **New Deal**" of relief and recovery programs to alleviate the impact of the **Depression**, including unemployment insurance, minimum wages, and public housing. He resigned as governor in 1942 to become head of the Office of Foreign Relief and Rehabilitation Operations in the State Department. In 1943 this became the United Nations Relief and Rehabilitation Administration (UNRRA), and Lehman was chosen as director general. He held the position until his resignation in 1946.

Unsuccessful in his bid for a seat in the U.S. Senate in 1946, Lehman was elected in 1950, and he fought for liberal causes and opposed senator Joseph McCarthy. He retired from the Senate in 1956.

LEMKE, WILLIAM FREDERICK (1878–1950). William Lemke studied at the University of North Dakota, Georgetown University, and Yale University. After gaining his law degree, he set up practice in Fargo. Associated with farmers and farmers' movements, Lemke became attorney for the **Nonpartisan League** in 1916. The league captured control of the state's **Republican Party**, and Lemke became party chairman. In 1920 he was elected state attorney general. However, his reputation was seriously damaged that year when he and others were accused of allowing state funds to be invested in an insolvent private institution. Although the charges were quashed, Lemke was defeated in a recall election in 1921. He retired to his law practice for the remainder of the decade.

In 1932 Lemke was elected to the U.S. House of Representatives, where he sponsored legislation to ease bankruptcy proceedings against farmers and a proposal for the federal government to assist farmers in paying off their mortgages. When **Franklin D. Roosevelt**'s administration opposed this last measure, Lemke turned against the **New Deal** and joined Father Charles Coughlin, Dr. Francis Townsend, and Gerald K. Smith in the National Union. He was nominated the Union's presidential candidate in 1936 but secured less than 2 percent of the national vote. He failed to win election to the Senate in 1940 but remained in Congress for the rest of his life.

LENROOT, IRVINE LUTHER (1869–1949). Irvine Lenroot studied law and was admitted to the bar in Superior, Wisconsin, in 1897. A **Republican** and supporter of **Robert M. La Follette**, he was elected to the state assembly in 1900 and served as the speaker in 1903 and 1905. Unsuccessful in an attempt to gain the gubernatorial nomination in 1906, Lenroot was elected to the U.S. House of Representatives in 1908, where he became one of the leaders of the progressive Republicans. In 1917 his support for La Follette ended when Lenroot supported war against Germany. In 1918 Lenroot defeated La Follette's candidate for the nomination for the vacant Senate seat and then won the general election. He was reelected in 1920.

Lenroot played a prominent role in the Senate's deliberations over the **Treaty of Versailles** and **League of Nations**. He was in favor of mild reservations to the treaty, and he wrote several of the "**Lodge amendments**" adopted by the Senate but rejected by **Woodrow Wilson**. Lenroot continued in his role as a moderate progressive during the administrations of **Warren Harding** and **Calvin Coolidge** and chaired the Committee on Public Lands. However, some critics felt he was slow to respond to the **Teapot Dome** scandal, and he failed to be renominated in the senatorial primary election in 1926.

In 1929 Coolidge nominated Lenroot to a judgeship of the U.S. Court of Customs Appeals, and president **Herbert Hoover** resubmitted his nomination when Congress returned from adjournment. He served on the court, renamed Court of Patent and Customs Appeals, until 1944.

LEOPOLD, NATHAN FREUDENTHAL (1904–1971). *See* LEOPOLD AND LOEB CASE.

LEOPOLD AND LOEB CASE. In 1924 two well-to-do Chicago students, nineteen-year-old Nathan Leopold, the son of a millionaire box manufacturer, and eighteen-year-old Richard Loeb, son of a retired Sears, Roebuck vice president, were charged with the abduction and murder of Robert Franks, aged fourteen. The trial became a sensation because of the relationship between the two murderers and their motive for the **crime**. The trial involved detailed psychiatric debate and raised the issue of the death penalty to national prominence. Loeb deliberately set out to commit the perfect crime; Leopold, his lover, was apparently influenced by Friedrich Nietzsche's notion of a "superman" beyond moral codes, a role in which he saw Loeb. After murdering Franks, the boys disfigured his body with acid and hid it in a drain. They then created the impression that Franks had been kidnapped. The two were only linked to the murder when a pair of spectacles was discovered near the body that were traced back to Leopold, and both boys eventually confessed under questioning.

Clarence Darrow was hired for the defense, and he changed the "not guilty" pleas to "guilty" in order not to face a jury and to avoid the death sentence. Both sides used psychiatric evidence, and even Sigmund Freud was consulted. Ultimately Darrow's impassioned argument, in a twelve-hour summation, that the boys were victims of their own psyche and that the death penalty would be as cruel as the murder, won the day. Judge John Caverly sentenced both boys to life imprisonment and ninety-nine years.

Loeb died in 1936 following a razor attack in Joliet prison. Leopold studied languages, mathematics, and physics, organized the prison library, and took part in experiments to combat malaria in prison. He was released in 1958 and moved to Puerto Rico, where he graduated with an MA, taught mathematics, worked in hospitals, and produced a study of *The Birds of Puerto Rico*. He died in 1971.

LEVER FOOD AND FUEL ACT, 1917. The Food and Fuel Act empowered president **Woodrow Wilson** to establish and maintain government control "of foods, feeds, and fuel" in order to "prevent scarcity, monopolization, hoarding, injurious speculation, manipulation." Under this measure the president established the **U.S. Food Administration** and the **U.S. Fuel Administration** to maintain adequate supplies and prevent shortages or profiteering during **World War I**.

See also ECONOMY.

LEWIS, JOHN LLEWELLYN (1880–1969). John L. Lewis began work in the coal mines in Iowa in the 1890s. In 1907 he moved to Illinois and he was elected president of the United Mine Workers of America (UMWA) local in 1910. In 1911 Lewis was appointed as field representative for the **American Federation of Labor** (AFL) and in 1917 became vice president of the UMWA. He was elected president in 1920, and Lewis held the position until his retirement in 1960.

UMWA membership declined during the 1920s as the coal industry shrank in the face of foreign competition and the increased use of oil. The deterioration in membership increased with the onset of the **Depression** in the 1930s. Lewis, however, capitalized on the change of political climate with the advent of the **New Deal** and began to mobilize the union membership. Lewis argued for the AFL to take a more militant approach and to focus on organizing workers on an industry-wide basis rather than crafts. As differences within the AFL exploded into physical conflict in 1935, Lewis joined with **Sidney Hillman** and **David Dubinsky** to establish a Committee for Industrial Organization (CIO). The CIO became the leading force in increasing union membership during the 1930s, and Lewis played an active role in these developments. In 1938 the CIO became an autonomous labor organization, the Congress of Industrial Organizations.

Lewis became increasingly critical of the administration of **Franklin D. Roosevelt** and in 1940 openly supported the **Republican** candidate, Wendell Willkie. In 1940 he also stepped down as president of the CIO. Lewis's growing opposition to Roosevelt's war administration caused differences with the CIO leadership, and in 1942 Lewis took the UMWA out of the organization. His conflict with Roosevelt heightened when Lewis led the miners in a series of strikes in 1943. He continued his confrontational methods after the war, and strikes in the face of a federal injunction in 1946 resulted in massive fines for the union. In the 1950s Lewis collaborated more with mine owners in return for pension and health-care programs for the coal miners. After his retirement Lewis was director of the union retirement and welfare funds, and some of his decisions with regard to investments were detrimental to the funds' viability.

See also TRADE UNIONS.

LEWIS, SINCLAIR (1885–1951). Sinclair Lewis was born Harry Sinclair Lewis in Sauk Centre, Minnesota. After graduating from Yale University he worked as a newspaper reporter in Iowa and California, and then in publishing in New York City. Between 1912 and 1920 he wrote several novels and short stories for the *Saturday Evening Post*. However, it was with his critique of small-town life in *Main Street* (1920) that Lewis achieved a national reputation. The novel sold almost three hundred thousand copies in its first year. He followed this with a portrait of a small-town businessman, *Babbitt* (1922), which, like *Main Street* was judged by some reviewers and readers to be too critical of American life and values. Lewis's next book, *Arrowsmith* (1925), dealt with the failures of the medical profession and was awarded the Pulitzer Prize. Lewis rejected the award on the grounds that the terms of the honor, requiring the presentation of the "wholesome atmosphere of American life," inhibited authors from writing freely. In *Elmer Gantry* (1927), Lewis turned his attack on the hypocrisy of religious fundamentalists, while *Dodsworth* (1929) offered a more sympathetic portrait of the businessman/inventor.

Not all critics, many of whom argued that he showed America in too negative a light, welcomed Lewis's award of the Nobel Prize in **Literature** in 1930. In his acceptance speech Lewis in turn criticized the American literary establishment. Although he published a number of novels in the 1930s, Lewis did not reach the heights of his previous work. Only his satirical study of American fascism, *It Can't Happen Here* (1935), was particularly successful both as a novel and then as a play. *Kingsblood Royal* (1947), which dealt with the issue of race and racial identity, also achieved some critical acclaim if only for its treatment of a vital social issue, but most of Lewis's other postwar writing was judged to have little merit.

LIBERTY LOANS. Liberty Loans were the series of five bonds issued during **World War I** by the Treasury between May 1917 and April 1919 to raise money to help finance the war effort (the last was known as the Victory bond). With interest rates of between 3.5 and 4.5 percent and purchase symbolic of patriotism, the bonds were oversubscribed and raised over $21 billion dollars. Finance was also raised through the increased taxation brought about by the **Revenue Acts** of 1916 and 1917.

LINDBERGH, CHARLES AUGUSTUS (1902–1974). Charles Lindbergh became a national hero after making the first single-handed nonstop transatlantic flight from New York to Paris in his airplane called the *Spirit of St. Louis* on 20 May 1927. He previously had flown in the Army Air Service and as an airmail pilot between Chicago and St. Louis. As a result of his flight he was awarded the Congressional Medal of Honor, and *Time* magazine made him its first "Man of the Year." He subsequently worked to promote aviation and was employed by various airline companies. Lindbergh was in the headlines again in 1932, when his twenty-month-old son was abducted and found dead two months later.

The Lindberghs left the United States in 1935 to live first in England and then France. While in Europe Lindbergh inspected air forces in Germany, Poland, and Czechoslovakia and became convinced that Germany had a superior air force and that any war could destroy western civilization. He returned to the United States in 1939 and became a leading noninterventionist and a member of the America First Committee. He was much criticized for comments that appeared anti-Semitic and pro-Nazi.

With American entry into World War II in 1941 Lindbergh tested aircraft as a civilian. Nonetheless he flew combat missions in the Pacific in 1944. After the war Lindbergh continued to work for the U.S. Air Force and Defense Department, and in 1954 president Dwight D. Eisenhower promoted him to brigadier general. His autobiography, *The Spirit of St. Louis* (1953), was awarded a Pulitzer Prize in 1954.

See also AVIATION.

LINDSAY, (NICHOLAS) VACHEL (1879–1931). Vachel Lindsay attended Chicago Art Institute from 1901 to 1903 and the New York School of Art from 1903 to 1904. He was unsuccessful in getting his poetry published so took to the road, selling his verse on the streets and giving lectures and spoken performances. Lindsay's poem "General William Booth Enters into

Heaven" was published in *Poetry* in 1913 and won considerable recognition. **Charles Ives** set it to music in 1914. Collections of his poetry were published in 1913 and 1914. Lindsay toured extensively, gave recitals before **Woodrow Wilson**'s cabinet, and met with reformers, industrialists, and filmmakers. In 1920 he visited England and was acclaimed as "easily the most important living American poet." His career declined following the poor reception given to his prose work, *The Golden Book of Springfield* (1920), and he suffered increasingly from financial hardship and ill health. He committed suicide in 1931.

See also LITERATURE AND THEATER.

LIPPMANN, WALTER (1889–1974). Walter Lippmann made a name as a brilliant student at Harvard. He left university in 1910 to become a journalist on the socialist *Boston Common*. Part of the radical **Greenwich Village** set, Lippmann produced a call for reform in his *Preface to Politics* in 1912. In 1914 he published *Drift and Mastery*, which captured much of the **progressive** ethos in advocating for a government run scientifically by a public-minded elite. The same year Lippmann joined the staff of the *New Republic*. He supported U.S. entry into **World War I** and joined a team of planners to draw up plans for the postwar world. He was one of the group of American advisers at the **Versailles Peace Conference** but was disillusioned by the terms of the peace treaty, and became a critic of it and the **League of Nations**. His wartime experience also made him skeptical of the democratic process, and his *Liberty and the News* (1920) and *Public Opinion* (1922) suggested that government was best left to experts.

In 1922 Lippmann joined the New York *World*, where he established a reputation as one of the leading journalists of his day. His book, *A Preface to Morals* (1929), also found a wide readership. Lippmann became a contributor to the conservative *New York Herald-Tribune* in 1931, and his columns were widely syndicated, nationally and internationally. In the late 1930s he advocated U.S. support for Great Britain against Nazi Germany and during the war wrote a best-seller entitled *United States Foreign Policy: Shield of the Republic* (1943), advocating a continuation of the Grand Alliance with Great Britain and the USSR. When the alliance broke up after the war Lippmann wrote a critical study of containment, *The Cold War* (1947), and was probably the originator of the phrase used to describe postwar relations with the Soviet Union.

Lippmann was awarded the Presidential Medal of Freedom in 1964 and worked on the CBS television network for a number of years. However, he became increasingly critical of Lyndon Johnson's policies in Vietnam and he retired from journalism in 1967.

See also NEWSPAPERS AND MAGAZINES.

LITERACY TEST. Literacy testing was proposed by **Henry Cabot Lodge** in 1891 as an addition to **immigration** legislation in order to restrict the number of immigrants. Bills introducing such a measure were vetoed by presidents Grover Cleveland (in 1897), **William Howard Taft** (in 1913), and **Woodrow Wilson** (in 1915 and 1917). The law was passed over Wilson's veto in 1917.

LITERATURE AND THEATER. The 1920s saw the continued success of already-established writers such as the naturalist author **Theodore Dreiser** and others including **Willa Cather, Upton Sinclair,** and **Edith Wharton**. The era also saw the first Pulitzer Prize awarded for poetry—to **Edwin Robinson**—and the emergence of one of America's greatest poets, **Robert Frost**. However, the decade was marked by the appearance of a new group of writers often collectively referred to as the "**Lost Generation,**" several of whom like the novelists **Ernest Hemingway, John Dos Passos**, and poet **e. e. cummings** returned to the U.S. mentally, and sometimes physically, scarred by their service in **World War I**. These and others such as **T. S. Eliot** and **F. Scott Fitzgerald** rejected the idealism and optimism of the prewar **Progressives** and, often using new stylistic approaches, expressed a mood of disillusionment and cynicism often described as **modernism**. Some, like poet **Ezra Pound**, sought temporary or permanent exile in Europe, fleeing what they perceived as the empty materialism of modern America. Others, such as **Sinclair Lewis**, remained at home to write critical novels of small-town America and Main Street society often echoing the acerbic writing of **H. L. Mencken**. The small town was also the focus of much of **Sherwood Anderson**'s fiction.

Despite the criticism of American society as a cultural wasteland during the decade, the 1920s witnessed a revival in southern writing in the early novels of **William Faulkner**, the work of **Ellen Glasgow** and **Evelyn Scott**, and the poetry of **Donald Davidson, John Crowe Ransom**, and **Allen Tate**. **African American** writers and poets also found voice in the **Harlem Renaissance** that produced the work of **Nella Larsen, Langston Hughes, James Weldon Johnson, Claude McKay**, and many others often encouraged by **W. E. B. Du Bois** in his role as editor of the **National Association for the Advancement of Colored People**'s (NAACP) journal *The Crisis*.

Women writers too made a significant contribution to the literature of the 1920s, often reflecting their new "liberation." One of the leading authors of this type was **Edna St. Vincent Millay**, whose poetry won her the Pulitzer Prize in 1923.

Theater also saw new writers emerge, particularly from the Provincetown Theater Group (1915) and later Theater Guild (1919). Most notable was **Eugene O'Neill**, whose plays reflected some of the influences of Sigmund Freud in their exploration of alienation and sexual tension. Expressionism exploring the world of feelings, and Realism looking at man in the new industrial and urban environment, were also among the main features of this period as evidenced in the plays of **Elmer Rice**. With these new developments theater boomed, and there were an average of more than two hundred stage productions a year throughout the decade as well as a rise in the number of independent or "little theaters" and repertory theaters.

Many of the critically acclaimed writers of literature were ignored by the wider readership. The mail-order Book-of-the-Month Club (BOMC), established in 1926, and its rival, the Literary Guild, created the following year, overlooked Fitzgerald, Hemingway, and Eugene O'Neill in favor of works with a mass appeal. The BOMC had a membership of 110,000 by 1929. Among the wider reading public popular literature included the Westerns of **Zane Grey**, the moralistic novels of **Harold Bell**, and those of **Gene Stratton-Porter**. A new form of American literature also emerged in the **crime** and detective stories in pulp fiction such as *Black Mask*, a magazine launched in 1920 by Mencken and **George Nathan**. Among the writers of crime fiction in the 1920s was Dashiell Hammett, whose novels featuring Sam Spade, the eponymous private eye, appeared in the 1930s and were made famous in the **movies** starring Humphrey Bogart and others.

See also BENÉT, STEPHEN VINCENT (1898–1943); COWLEY, MAL-COLM (1898–1989); CROSBY, HARRY STURGIS (1898–1929); DELL, FLOYD JAMES (1887–1969); FAUSET, JESSIE REDMON (1882–1961); HURSTON, ZORA NEALE (1891–1960); LINDSAY, (NICHOLAS) VACHEL (1879–1931); LOCKE, ALAIN (1886–1954); MASTERS, EDGAR LEE (1869–1950); PARKER, DOROTHY (1893–1967); ROBINSON, EDWIN ARLINGTON (1869–1935); SANDBURG, CARL (1878–1967); STEIN, GERTRUDE (1874–1951); TARKINGTON, BOOTH (1869–1946); VAN VECHTEN, CARL (1880–1964); WILDER, THORNTON NIVEN (1897–1975); WILSON, EDMUND (1895–1972); WOLFE, THOMAS (1900–1938); YEZIERSKA, ANZIA (1880–1970).

LLOYD, HAROLD CLAYTON (1893–1971). The comedian Harold Lloyd began work in the theater as a child and then in 1913 worked with the Edison Film Company in San Diego. Later that year he moved to Los Angeles and worked with Hal Roach at Universal Pictures. In 1917 he conceived his film character, Harold. Wearing his trademark horn-rimmed glasses and straw hat Lloyd went on to make many **movies** involving remarkable stunts which he performed himself. In his best-known movie, *Safety Last* (1923), Lloyd was filmed hanging onto the clock face of a tall building. His later films included *Girl Shy* (1924), *The Freshman* (1925), *For Heaven's Sake* (1926), *The Kid Brother* (1927), and *Speedy* (1928). With the coming of sound, Lloyd's films were less successful, but with **Charlie Chaplin** and **Buster Keaton** he was one of the greatest silent film comics.

LOCKE, ALAIN (1886–1954). An **African American** writer and critic, Alain Locke was a brilliant student and graduated from Harvard University magna cum laude in 1907. The first African American Rhodes Scholar, he studied in Berlin and Paris before assuming a position at Howard University in Washington, D.C. He completed his PhD at Harvard in 1918 and became chair of the philosophy department at Howard, a position he held until 1953. In 1925 Locke edited a selection of articles from *Survey Graphic* showing the talent of new African American writers, and published them as *The New Negro*. Locke actively encouraged and supported writers who were emerging as part of the **Harlem Renaissance**, and with T. Montgomery Gregory he edited *Plays of Negro Life* in 1927. Locke was a regular reviewer and critic of black art and culture and a leader in the field of education.

See also LITERATURE AND THEATER.

LODGE, HENRY CABOT (1850–1924). A leading conservative **Republican** politician and historian, Lodge was one of the first people to earn a PhD in history in the United States. He taught at Harvard University and published several historical biographies before turning to politics. He served as a member of the House of Representatives for Massachusetts from 1887 to 1893 and as senator from 1893 to 1924. Although essentially conservative on domestic matters, Lodge supported most of the policies of **Theodore Roosevelt**, particularly in foreign affairs. He remained loyal to **William Howard Taft** in 1912 despite his friendship with Roosevelt. He was one of **Woodrow Wilson**'s greatest critics, and as chair of the Senate Foreign Affair Committee he successfully led the opposition to the Covenant of the **League of Nations**. His reservations were expressed in the **Lodge amendments**. Lodge was a delegate to the **Washington Naval Conference** and successfully guided the agreement through the Senate in 1922.

See also FOREIGN POLICY.

LODGE AMENDMENTS. On 6 November 1919 senator **Henry Cabot Lodge** tabled fifteen proposed amendments to the **Versailles Peace Treaty** and **League of Nations** covenant specifically aimed at limiting American participation in the League. These amendments or reservations included allowing the United States to determine its own financial and military obligations to the League and exempting the Monroe Doctrine from external interference. When president **Woodrow Wilson** refused to accept any amendments, the opposition was such as to prevent ratification of the treaty.

See also FOREIGN POLICY.

LOEB, RICHARD ALLEN (1905–1936). *See* LEOPOLD AND LOEB CASE.

LOGAN, RAYFORD WHITTINGHAM (1897–1982). The **African American** historian Rayford Logan graduated from Williams College in 1917 and joined the Army, where he rose to lieutenant. Disillusioned by the discrimination he experienced in the Army, Logan remained in France for five years after **World War I** ended. He returned to the United States in 1924 and taught at Lincoln University while completing his PhD from Harvard (1936). He also taught at Atlanta University from 1933 to 1938 before moving to Howard University, where he worked for the remainder of his career. Logan's *The Diplomatic Relations of the United States with Haiti* was published in 1941.

Logan campaigned for full black inclusion in the war effort in World War II and was a leader of **A. Philip Randolph**'s March on Washington Movement in 1941. In 1944 he edited *What the Negro Wants*, spelling out African American opposition to segregation. After World War II Logan was chief adviser on international affairs for the **National Association for the Advancement of Colored People** (NAACP). He was the author of *The Negro in American Life and Thought, 1877–1901* (1953).

LOMBARD, CAROLE (1908–1942). Born Jane Alice Peters, Carole Lombard had her first role in motion pictures in 1920. Fox studios employed her when she was sixteen. Despite facial scarring from an automobile accident, Lombard was able to sign a contract with the **Mack Sennett** company in 1927 and appeared in a number of comic roles before she left in 1928. In 1930 Lombard joined Paramount Pictures and made several minor **movies** before making a name for her acting in *Twentieth Century* (1934), *Hands Across the Table* (1935), *My Man Godfrey* (1936), *True Confession* (1937), and *Nothing Sacred* (1937). Her "screwball" comic roles reflected the mood of the 1930s. During World War II Lombard campaigned across the country to help sell war bonds. She died when her flight back from one of these appearances crashed near Las Vegas.

LONDON NAVAL CONFERENCE, 1930. A follow-up to the **Washington Naval Conference**, the conference of the United States, Great Britain, France, Italy, and Japan convened in London to agree on limits on smaller naval vessels not covered in the previous agreement. The French and Italians withdrew when other delegates refused to increase their ratios. Agreements were reached between United States, Great Britain, and Japan on a ratio of cruisers and destroyers of 10:10:7 and equal tonnage in submarines.

See also FOREIGN POLICY.

LONG, HUEY PIERCE (1893–1935). Known as the "Kingfish," Long was a largely self-taught lawyer who entered Louisiana politics as a member of the **Railroad** Commission (1918–1921), which then became the Public Service Commission (1921–1928). After failing to win election in 1924, he was elected governor of Louisiana for the **Democratic Party** in 1928 and built a reputation as a populist reformer. He raised taxes to pay for schoolbooks and embarked on a program of bridge and road building, and improving the University of Louisiana at Baton Rouge. He ran the state largely as a one-party state, using patronage and intimidation to maintain control.

Long was elected to the U.S. Senate in 1930 but continued as governor until one of his supporters could replace him in 1932. Initially sympathetic, Long became increasingly critical of **Franklin D. Roosevelt**'s **New Deal**. In 1934 he outlined his "Share Our Wealth" program, which promised every family a guaranteed cash income, old age pensions, and reduced working hours financed by placing a ceiling on incomes and property ownership. In 1935 he announced his candidacy for the Democratic presidential nomination, and it appeared likely that he could attract as much as 10 percent of the vote. Franklin Roosevelt, who described him as one of the "two most dangerous men in America," regarded him as a serious threat, and the revenue bill he submitted to Congress was in part a response to Long's challenge. However, Long died on 10 September 1935 after being gunned down on the steps of the State Capitol in Baton Rouge by the son-in-law of a political opponent.

LONGVIEW, TEXAS. In July 1919 tension between the black and white populations of the rural community of Longview, Texas, erupted in violence. Following the murder of two black men, one hundred national guardsmen were drafted into the town to restore order. Texas Rangers arrested seventeen white men and twenty-one **African Americans**, but none were tried. The Longview riot was one of twenty-five in the "**Red Summer**" following **World War I**.

LONGWORTH, NICHOLAS (1869–1931). Born into one of Cincinnati's oldest and wealthiest families, Nicholas Longworth was educated at Harvard and Cincinnati Law School, from where he graduated in 1894. A **Republican**, he was elected to the Cincinnati Board of Education in 1898, the Ohio House of Representatives in 1899, and Ohio Senate in 1901. In 1902 Longworth was elected to the U.S. House of Representatives. In 1912 he was defeated due to the split in the Republican Party, but he was reelected in 1914 and served until his death. In 1923 he became Republican majority floor leader and worked with **Calvin Coolidge**'s administration to ensure tax reductions, a veterans' bonus, and the settlement of the European war debt. Longworth's ability as a conciliator helped to bring about the passage of 594 bills between 1923 and 1925 and was recognized in his appointment as speaker of the House in 1925. As speaker Longworth exercised considerable authority and introduced a number of reforms in the business of the House including making the *Congressional Record* more reliable and ending some of the discriminatory practices against **women**.

LOOS, (CORINNE) ANITA (1893–1981). The author Anita Loos began her career as a child actress before writing screenplays, the first of which was produced in 1912. In 1915 she moved to Hollywood and began writing for **D. W. Griffith**. Loos wrote and cowrote over two hundred film scripts during her years in Hollywood. However, her greatest success was with the novel *Gentlemen Prefer Blondes*, first serialized in *Harper's Bazaar* in 1925. Loos produced a successful dramatized version of the book, and it eventually became a **movie** starring Marilyn Monroe in 1953. A sequel, *But Gentlemen Marry Brunettes*, was published in 1928. In 1931 Loos began work at MGM and wrote the screenplay for several successful sound films beginning with *Red-Headed Woman* (1932). She also continued to write for the theater and produced the script for *Gigi* in 1951. Her autobiography was published in two volumes, *A Girl Like I* (1966) and *Kiss Hollywood Good-by* (1974).

"LOST GENERATION". The title of the "Lost Generation" was used by **Gertrude Stein** to describe all those young people who had served in **World War I**. She had first heard the term applied by her French garage owner, but it was taken up by **Ernest Hemingway** in his novel *The Sun Also Rises* (1926). While the Lost Generation was used simply to refer to the war dead in some European countries, in the United States it described the group of writers such as Hemingway, **F. Scott Fitzgerald**, **John Dos Passos**, and others who rejected prewar values and attitudes and expressed a sense of alienation and disillusionment from modern America. Many became part of the expatriate literary and artistic community in postwar Paris.

See also ANDERSON, SHERWOOD (1876–1941); CRANE, (HAROLD) HART (1889–1932); CROSBY, HARRY STURGIS (1898–1929); LITERATURE AND THEATER.

LOWDEN, FRANK ORREN (1861–1943). After studying at rural schools, Frank Lowden became a teacher in Minnesota at the age of fourteen. In 1885 he graduated from the University of Iowa and went on to study law at the Union College of Law, Chicago. He graduated in 1887 and practiced law in Chicago, where he entered politics as a **Republican**. He was first appointed to Congress in 1906 and elected to the post in 1908. He retired from Congress in 1910 but remained active in state politics. In 1916 Lowden was elected governor of Illinois and continued his reputation as a moderate reformer. In 1920 he was a contender for the Republican presidential nomination but returned to private life after **Warren Harding**'s victory. In the 1920s he was active in a number of farming organizations and campaigned for the **McNary-Haugen** bill. In 1929 Lowden became head of the Country Life Commission. In the 1930s he was an isolationist and active in the America First Committee.

LOZOWICK, LOUIS (1892–1973). The artist (painter and printmaker) Louis Lozowick was born in the Ukraine (then part of Russia) and studied in the Kiev Art Institute until 1906, when he immigrated to the United States. He attended the National Academy of Design in New York City and Ohio State University, where he graduated with a degree in **art** in 1918. After a year in the army, Lozowick spent the period between 1920 and 1924 in Paris, Berlin, and Moscow. He wrote extensively on Soviet art and when he returned to the United States he joined the editorial board of the left-wing journal *New Masses* and eventually became its art editor. He was also one of the founders of the **John Reed** Club in 1929.

Lozowick became one of several artists in the Precisionist school who focused on urban scenes, and he was best known for his lithographs of New York City and images of Brooklyn Bridge. He also painted the skyscrapers of Pittsburgh (1920), Chicago (1923), Cleveland (1926), and Seattle (1927). His essay on "The Americanization of Art" (1927) was a celebration of the new machine-age aesthetic. He supplemented his income with commercial work and taught art history and lithography classes, lectured, and wrote about art at the John Reed Club School of Art and the American Artists School. During the **Great Depression** he worked with the Public Works of Art Project, New York City, for a brief time in 1934. Between 1935 and 1940, he was employed by the Graphic Arts Division of the Works Progress Administration and produced a mural for the New York General Post Office in 1936. In 1935, Lozowick was one of the organizers of the first American Artists' Congress and became the group's executive secretary. His work won several awards and is now part of several permanent collections.

LUCE, HENRY ROBINSON (1898–1967). The son of a missionary, Henry Luce was born in China. He was a student at Yale and became a commissioned officer in the U.S. Army in 1918. He returned to college in 1919 and graduated in 1920. After a brief period of study at Oxford, England, Luce returned to the United States, where, with Briton Hadden, he established *Time* magazine in 1923. In 1930 Luce founded *Fortune*, a journal aimed at businessmen. Time Inc. expanded and in 1935 began a documentary newsreel series, "The March of Time." In 1936 Luce began production of *Life*, a magazine of photojournalism. *Time* and *Life* became enormously influential journals and had a huge circulation until they were undermined by the advent of television.

In an editorial entitled "The American Century" in *Life* in 1941 Luce argued that America should abandon **isolationism** and take a lead in rebuilding a peaceful world after an Allied victory. Luce supported the presidential campaign of the **Republican** Wendell Willkie in 1940. After the war Luce was an advocate of resistance to perceived Soviet expansion. In 1949 Luce blamed Harry S. Truman's administration for the "loss" of China to the communists and supported the election of Dwight D. Eisenhower in 1952. Later Luce supported the war in Vietnam. Luce retired in 1964.

See also FOREIGN POLICY; NEWSPAPERS AND MAGAZINES.

LUHAN, MABEL DODGE (1879–1962). A leading patron of the **arts** during the interwar years, Mabel Dodge Luhan (born Mabel Ganson) established a salon on Fifth Avenue, New York, where intellectuals such as **Max Eastman**, **Emma Goldman**, **Walter Lippmann**, and **John Reed** were entertained. Luhan herself contributed articles on pacifism to the radical journal *The Masses* during **World War I**. After the war she married a Native American, Tony Luhan, and established an artist colony in Taos, New Mexico. Among her guests there were the English author D. H. Lawrence and the American artist **Georgia O'Keefe**. Mabel Luhan wrote several volumes of autobiography, including *Intimate Memories* (1933), *European Experiences* (1936), and *Edge of Taos Desert* (1937).

See also WOMEN.

LUSITANIA. The British passenger liner, torpedoed and sunk by a German submarine off the coast of Ireland, 7 May 1915 en route from New York to Liverpool. One of the largest and fastest ships of its day, the *Lusitania* sank within twenty minutes of being hit by two torpedoes. Of 651 crew and 1,255 passengers, 1,198, including 124 Americans, died. The sinking of the ship caused great outrage in the United States despite the fact that passengers boarding in New York had been warned they were at danger. It also transpired that the vessel was carrying armaments. President **Woodrow Wilson** described the sinking as an illegal and inhuman act and warned the German government that any further such action would be regarded as "deliberately unfriendly." Secretary of state **William Jennings Bryan** felt this response was too strong and resigned.

See also FOREIGN POLICY; WORLD WAR I, 1914–1918.

LUSK LAWS. The Lusk laws expressing the antiradical sentiment that followed World War I were produced by New York state senator Clayton R. Lusk and were intended particularly to prevent unpatriotic or subversive activities in schools by issuing licenses to teachers.

LYND, HELEN MERRELL (1896–1982). The sociologist and social philosopher Helen Lynd obtained a BA from Wellesley College in 1919. After two years teaching in school she began postgraduate studies and earned an MA (1922) and PhD (1944) from Columbia University. She was best known for her work with her husband, **Robert S. Lynd**, and their famous study of Muncie, Indiana, *Middletown: A Study in Contemporary American Culture* (1929) and *Middletown in Transition: A Study of Cultural Conflicts* (1937). Helen Lynd taught at Sarah Lawrence College from 1928 to 1965. Her own work covered a number of fields, and she published *England in the Eighteen Eighties* (1945), *Field Work in College Education* (1945), and *Shame and the Search for Identity* (1958). During the 1950s she was attacked for alleged communist sympathies, an accusation she denied when called before the Senate Internal Security Committee in 1953. She later wrote a defense of civil liberties included in a collection of reviews, *Toward Discovery*, published in 1965.

See also EDUCATION; WOMEN.

LYND, ROBERT STAUGHTON (1892–1970). The famous sociologist and coauthor with **Helen Lynd** of one of the key studies of American society during the 1920s, Robert Lynd graduated from Princeton University in 1914. He then worked for four years as an assistant magazine editor before serving briefly in the field artillery during **World War I**. After the war Lynd became a Unitarian and earned his DD from the Union Theological Seminary in 1923. In the early 1920s he served as a missionary preacher and wrote articles based on his experiences in the oil fields. In 1923 Lynd and his wife, Helen, began a study of small-town life sponsored by the Committee on Social and Religious Surveys. Their work, based on Muncie, Indiana, resulted in the book *Middletown: A Study in Contemporary American Culture* (1929). *Middletown* became a classic study that contrasted white urban values in the age of mass consumption with the sense of community and harmony the Lynds' believed had existed in the 1890s. Lynd's research earned him a PhD from Columbia University, where he became professor of sociology in 1931. A further study of Muncie, *Middletown in Transition: A Study of Cultural Conflicts*, appeared in 1937, and Lynd's final book, *Knowledge for What?*, appeared in 1939. The Lynds' *Middletown* ranked with the writing of

Sinclair Lewis and **H. L. Mencken**, and like them offered a critical view of the narrow-minded conformity and materialism that was evident in parts of the United States in the 1920s.

See also EDUCATION.

M

MACARTHUR, DOUGLAS (1880–1964). Douglas MacArthur graduated first in his class from West Point in 1903. He was a member of the General Staff in France during **World War I** and commanded the 42nd (Rainbow) Division. After the war MacArthur became superintendent at West Point from 1919 to 1922. He became a major general in 1928 and commander of the Philippines Department in 1928. From 1930 to 1935 MacArthur was general and chief of staff of the U.S. Army. In 1932 he led the troops who forcibly ejected the **Bonus Army** from Washington, D.C. He was director of organization of national defense for the Philippines from 1935 to 1937, when he retired. Recalled to active service in 1941 as a lieutenant general, MacArthur was placed in command of the U.S. Forces in the Far East. He was forced to flee the Philippines following the Japanese invasion in 1941 but announced, "I shall return."

MacArthur was made supreme commander of Allied Forces in the Southwest Pacific in 1942. As he had promised, MacArthur led the forces that retook the Philippines in 1944. He received the Japanese surrender in Tokyo in September 1945, and became supreme commander for the Allied Powers in Japan until 1951. In 1950 MacArthur became commander of the United Nations forces that responded to the attack of North Korea upon the South. He was dismissed in 1951 because of his public differences with president Harry S. Truman but returned to the United States as a public hero. He clearly had presidential ambitions, but after playing a key role at the **Republican Party** convention in 1952, he failed to get the nomination and faded from the political scene.

See also ARMED FORCES.

MAN RAY (1890–1976). Born Emmanuel Radnitsky to Russian Jewish immigrant parents in Philadelphia, the artist, photographer, and "maker of objects" became Man Ray when his family changed their name to Ray in 1911. He studied at New York University, the National Academy of Design, and the Art Students League and held his first one-man show in 1915 in New York City. A close friend of the French artist Marcel Duchamp, Man Ray became the leading American exponent of Dada and published the single issue of *New York Dada* in 1920. Despairing that Dada could not succeed in the United States, he moved to Paris in 1921, where he became a leading member of the surrealist art movement. Man Ray produced paintings, films, physical objects, and a new form of photograph he called "rayographs." Several of his photographs were published in the fashion magazines *Harper's Bazaar*, *Vanity Fair*, and *Vogue*. He returned to New York in 1940 and then moved to California before returning to Paris in 1951. His autobiography, *Self Portrait*, was published in 1963. Although not really recognized in the United States in his lifetime, Man Ray's influence was acknowledged later: a retrospective exhibition was mounted by the National Museum of American Art in 1988, and it was shown in several major cities in the following two years.

See also ART; MODERNISM.

MANSHIP, PAUL HOWARD (1885–1966). Born in St. Paul, Minnesota, the sculptor Paul Manship studied at St. Paul School of **Art**, Pennsylvania Academy of Fine Arts, and New York's Art Students League. In 1909 he won the American Prix de Rome, which enabled him to study and work there until 1912. He was influenced by Greek and Roman sculpture but refined it in a more simplistic and modern form. He held his first exhibition in New York in 1917 and subsequently received many commissions. His over seven hundred works included busts and statues of **John D. Rockefeller** (1918) and J. Pierpoint Morgan (1920), but he is best remembered for his classical or mythological figures such as *Dancer with Gazelles* (1917) and various studies of *Indian Hunter with His Dog* (1926). Although his style became less popular as the modern abstract styles grew in popularity, Manship produced the huge gilded *Prometheus Fountain* for the Rockefeller Center Plaza and the Paul J. Rainey memorial Gate to the Bronx Zoo in 1934, and the *Time and the Fates Sundial* and accompanying *Moods of Time* for the 1939–1940 New York World's Fair. Among his other works were the monuments at the American cemeteries for **World War I** at Thiacourt in France (1926) and for World War II at Anzio, in Italy. Manship received many awards and honors, and in 1945 he was awarded the gold medal for sculpture by the National Institute of Arts and Letters; he was elected the president of the American Academy of Arts and Letters in 1948.

MARCH, PEYTON CONWAY (1864–1955). Peyton C. March trained at the United States Military Academy at West Point from 1884 to 1888 and became a specialist in artillery. During the Spanish-American War in 1898 he organized an artillery battery financed by John Jacob Astor and took it to the **Philippines**, where he fought in the battle of Manila. From 1899 to 1901 March saw action against the Philippine guerrillas in Luzon. He received five citations for gallantry.

After his return to the United States, March held a number of administrative positions before joining the General Staff in 1903. From 1911 to 1916 he served as an adjutant general with the War Department. With the U.S. entry into **World War I** March was promoted to major general and went to France with the **American Expeditionary Force** (AEF) in command of artillery. In March 1918 he was recalled to the United States as a general to take over as chief of staff. March's efficient leadership and centralized direction speeded up the flow of troops to France, and he was also responsible for organizing their return from 1918 to 1919. After the war he drew up plans for a peacetime army of five hundred thousand, but Congress rejected the proposal. March resigned in 1921 and spent several years traveling. In 1953 president Dwight D. Eisenhower awarded him the Thanks of Congress for his efforts during World War I.

See also ARMED FORCES.

MARIN, JOHN CHERI (1870–1953). John Marin studied mechanical engineering and then became an architectural draftsman in the 1890s. From 1899 to 1905 he studied fine **art** in Philadelphia and New York and then spent six years in Europe, mainly in Paris. Marin produced a number of watercolors and etching during his travels and exhibited in Paris and in **Alfred Stieglitz**'s 291 gallery in the United States. Marin returned to the United States in 1912, and he demonstrated the modernist influences in his many paintings of New York City. Some of his work was shown at the **Armory Show** in 1913. During the 1920s, when he became the country's leading watercolorist, Marin produced many paintings of Maine's ocean scenes. Some of his best-known work includes *Sun, Isles, and Sea* (1921), *Deer Island, Maine* (1922), *Lower Manhattan* (1922), *Rocks and Seas* (1932). He also painted cityscapes with studies of the Woolworth building and Brooklyn Bridge. The first large-scale public showing of his work, outside of Steiglitz's galleries, was a retrospective in the Museum of Modern Art in 1936. Marin continued to paint through the 1940s, and in 1948 a survey of artists and art critics in *Look* magazine voted him the number one painter in the United States.

MARNE, BATTLE OF. The second battle of the Marne took place in response to the German offensive across the river Marne in July 1918. (The first battle took place in September 1914, when the German armies were halted in their advance into France.) The attack was met with a successful **Allied** counteroffensive that involved 275,000 U.S. troops.

See also WORLD WAR I, 1914–1918.

MARSHALL, THOMAS RILEY (1854–1925). Twenty-eighth vice president of the United States, Thomas Marshall attended Wabash College, studied law, and was admitted to the bar in 1875 and established a law practice in Columbia City, Indiana. In 1908 he was elected **Democratic** governor of the state. Marshall sponsored a considerable amount of reform legislation, most notably proposals for a new state constitution. While he was unsuccessful in this and a number of other measures, he did succeed in seeing through a **child labor** law. Marshall was nominated as the Democratic vice presidential candidate in 1912 and served two terms under **Woodrow Wilson**. Marshall's role was largely to serve as a representative of the administration at social and official functions. He is best known for the remark made in the Senate in 1917—"What this country needs is a really good five cent cigar." Marshall was the first vice president to chair cabinet meetings while Wilson was absent at the **Versailles Peace Conference**. After leaving office Marshall resumed his law practice and wrote his memoirs. He was a member of the Federal Coal Commission from 1922 to 1923.

MASTERS, EDGAR LEE (1869–1950). Qualified as a lawyer, Edgar Masters practiced law in Chicago but also began writing a series of poems about experiences in Illinois in 1914. These were published as the *Spoon River Anthology* in 1915. The poems took the form of dramatic graveside monologues from a representative group of individuals from a small Midwestern town. Although Masters continued writing poetry, novels, and biographies for almost thirty years, it was this collection that made his reputation. His biographies included *Lincoln* (1931), *Vachel Lindsay* (1935), *Whitman* (1937), and *Mark Twain* (1938).

See also LITERATURE AND THEATER.

MAYER, LOUIS BURT (1885–1957). The legendary Hollywood **movie** producer Louis B. Mayer was born Lazar Meir (or Eliezer Mayer) in either Dumier in the Ukraine or Minsk, Russia. His family immigrated to St. John, New Brunswick, in 1887. After working in his father's scrap metal business, in 1904 Mayer moved to Boston and bought the first of a chain of movie theaters near the city in 1907. Building on his success, Mayer established his own distribution company in 1914, and in 1917 he established Louis B. Mayer Pictures. His first film was *Virtuous Wives*. Mayer moved to Los Angeles in 1918 and in 1924 formed Metro Goldwyn Mayer (MGM) with Marcus Loew and **Samuel Goldwyn**. Mayer was to be production chief from 1924 until 1951 and with **Irving Thalberg** as producer established MGM as the leading film studio by the mid-1930s.

Mayer regarded the company as a film factory with the movie stars as "assembly-line workers." The studio produced massive hits ranging from *Ben Hur* (1926) to *Grand Hotel* (1932) and produced major stars such as **Greta Garbo**, **Lon Chaney**, Joan Crawford, Clark Gable, and **John** and **Lionel Barrymore**. In 1927 Mayer helped to establish the Academy of Motion Picture Arts and Sciences. His career effectively ended in 1951, when he resigned from MGM after a difference over production styles.

MCADOO, WILLIAM GIBBS (1863–1941). William McAdoo studied law in Tennessee and for a while was president of the Knoxville Street Railway Company. In 1892 he moved to New York City to sell **railroad** bonds and secured the funding for the Hudson River tunnels. In 1902 McAdoo became president of the Hudson & Manhattan **Railroad**, the company that developed the rapid-transit tunnels between New York City and New Jersey. He was vice chairman of the Democratic National Committee in 1912 and served as **Woodrow Wilson**'s secretary of the treasury from 1913 to 1918. During **World War I** McAdoo chaired the **Federal Reserve Board** and **War Finance Corporation**, and was director general of the railways when the government took over the temporary running of the system. Married to the president's daughter, McAdoo was seen by many as the **Democratic Party**'s "heir apparent" in 1920. However, he did not campaign openly nor did he receive Wilson's endorsement. McAdoo's support for **Prohibition** might also have contributed to his failure to win the nomination. He established a home in California from where he unsuccessfully fought for the Democratic presidential nomination against **Al Smith** in 1924. Faced with deadlock between the two, the convention turned instead to **John W. Davis**. McAdoo was elected U.S. senator for California in 1932 and served until 1938, when he was defeated.

MCCORMICK, MEDELL (1877–1925). After graduating from Yale University in 1900 McCormick began work as a police reporter on the *Chicago Tribune*, which was owned by his grandfather. By 1907 McCormick was vice president, secretary, and treasurer of the Tribune Company. In 1908 he went to Europe to be treated for depression by Carl Jung. In 1909 he left the *Tribune* and turned to politics. He joined the **Progressive Party** in 1911 and was the vice chairman of the Progressive National Committee from 1912 to 1914. In 1912 McCormick was one of the Progressives elected to the Illinois House of Representatives. He was reelected in 1914. In 1914 McCormick also went to Mexico as a reporter for *Harper's*.

In 1915 McCormick resigned from the Progressive Party and in 1916 became chairman of the Illinois State Republican Convention. Now a **Republican**, McCormick was elected state representative at large for Illinois, and as such he became a critic of **Woodrow Wilson**'s administration. In 1918 he was elected to the U.S. Senate, where he became prominent among the group of "**Irreconcilables**" opposed to the **Versailles Treaty** and U.S. participation in the **League of Nations**. In domestic politics McCormick supported budget reform, proposed the **child labor** amendment, called for the replacement of the Department of the Interior with departments of public works and public welfare, and endorsed civil government in the U.S. protectorates of **Haiti** and Santo Domingo. In 1924 he committed suicide after his defeat in the Republican primary.

MCCOY, FRANK ROSS (1874–1954). Frank McCoy graduated from West Point in 1897 and served in Cuba, the Philippines, Mexico in 1915, and the **American Expeditionary Force**, 1917–1919. He was assistant to the governor of the Philippines, 1921 to 1925, and director of the Red Cross in Japan in 1923. In 1928 president **Calvin Coolidge** appointed McCoy to oversee the elections in **Nicaragua**, and the following year he chaired the mediation commission between Bolivia and Paraguay. In 1932 McCoy was a member of the **League of Nations**' commission investigating the Japanese invasion of Manchuria.

MCKAY, CLAUDE (1890–1948). Born Festus Claudius McKay in Jamaica, McKay had already published two volumes of poetry when he immigrated to the United States in 1912. He initially enrolled at Tuskegee Institute in Alabama but moved to Kansas State College before finally settling in New York City in 1914, where he became editor of a Socialist journal, *The Liberator*. McKay became one of the best-known voices of the "**New Negro**" with the publication of his poem of defiance, "If We Must Die," in 1919. McKay lived in London between 1919 and 1921, then returned to the United States. His poetry collection *Harlem Shadows* was published the following year, and his novel *Home to Harlem* appeared in 1928. For much of the 1920s McKay traveled in Europe and Africa. He returned to the United States in 1934 and was employed on the Federal Writers Project. He published his autobiography, *A Long Way from Home*, in 1937 and a nonfiction work, *Harlem: Negro Metropolis*, in 1940, the year he became a U.S. citizen.

  See also AFRICAN AMERICANS; HARLEM RENAISSANCE, c. 1920–c. 1933.

MCLEMORE, ATKINS JEFFERSON (JEFF) (1857–1929). Jeff McLemore worked for a time as a cowboy, miner, and newspaper reporter in Texas, Colorado, and New Mexico before starting a full-time career in journalism in Texas in 1883. In 1892 he was elected as a **Democrat** to the Texas House of Representatives. He served two terms and then moved to Austin, where he became a member of the board of city aldermen. In 1914 McLemore was elected the Democratic congressman at large for Texas. McLemore was an outspoken critic of the **prohibition** movement. He was also increasingly critical of the **Woodrow Wilson** administration's position with regard to neutrality after 1914, and with senator **Thomas Gore** of Oklahoma was responsible for the **Gore-McLemore Resolution** in 1916 warning U.S. citizens against traveling on armed belligerent vessels. McLemore was reelected in 1916, but having voted against the declaration of war in 1917, he was defeated in 1918. He published a newspaper in Texas after 1919 and failed to gain election to the Senate in 1928.

MCNARY, CHARLES LINZA (1874–1944). Charles McNary was admitted to the bar in Oregon in 1898 and was appointed dean of the law school at Willamette University in 1908. In 1913 he became an associate justice to the Oregon Supreme Court. In 1917, McNary, a progressive **Republican**, was appointed to fill the vacant Senate seat for Oregon. He supported **Woodrow Wilson**'s war policies and was elected to a full Senate term in 1918. During the 1920s he sponsored a number of bills to protect the nation's forests and to assist the country's farmers. He was cosponsor of the **McNary-Haugen Bill**. Although associated with western progressives, McNary backed **Calvin Coolidge** rather than **La Follette** in 1924. In 1932 he became Republican Senate minority leader. He supported much of the **New Deal** until **Franklin D. Roosevelt**'s attempt to alter the composition of the **Supreme Court** in 1937. He was inclined toward **isolationism** until the attack on Pearl Harbor in 1941. In 1940 McNary ran as Wendell Willkie's running mate and after the election declined Roosevelt's offer of a cabinet position.

MCNARY-HAUGEN BILL. Between 1924 and 1928 five bills were introduced in Congress known as McNary-Haugen bills, after their proposers, congressman **Gilbert Haugen** and senator **Charles McNary**. The intention of these measures was to alleviate the economic situation of farmers by establishing an export corporation to purchase agricultural surpluses and sell them in overseas markets in order to maintain domestic prices. The last two bills passed Congress but were vetoed by president **Calvin Coolidge**.
    See also AGRICULTURE.

MCPHERSON, AIMEE SEMPLE (1890–1944). Born in Canada and christened Aimee Elizabeth Kennedy, Aimee Semple McPherson was an evangelist who founded the International Church of the Foursquare Gospel. She had undergone a Pentecostal evangelical conversion in 1907 and married a preacher, Robert Semple, with whom she went as a missionary to Asia in 1910. When her husband died she returned to the United States and married

Harold McPherson. She conducted a revival campaign in the eastern states from her "gospel automobile" from 1916 to 1918 and started a monthly paper, the *Bridal Call*.

In 1918 McPherson moved to Los Angeles, from where she conducted widespread revival meetings. She established a permanent base for her "Foursquare Gospel" movement with the opening of a temple in 1923. Her radio station, the first full-time religious station, began broadcasting from the temple in 1924, and the International Church of the Foursquare Gospel was officially incorporated in 1927. A consummate publicist, McPherson became a national figure and the leading female evangelist. In 1926 she mysteriously disappeared while swimming and was assumed drowned. A month later she reappeared and claimed to have been kidnapped. Her accounts to a grand jury led to a charge of perjury in 1927, but the case was dropped. Nonetheless McPherson had achieved national celebrity status. She continued her evangelical activities in the United States and overseas through the 1930s, and the church continued to grow until her death in 1944.

See also WOMEN.

MCREYNOLDS, JAMES CLARK (1862–1946). James McReynolds graduated from Vanderbilt University in 1882 and the University of Virginia Law School in 1884. He established a law practice in Nashville, where he became a leading member of the legal, political, and social establishment. In 1903 McReynolds was hired by the Justice Department and was the chief prosecutor of the American Tobacco Trust. He resigned in 1911 but in 1913 was appointed attorney general by **Woodrow Wilson**. He was again responsible for filing several major antitrust suits. In 1914 Wilson nominated McReynolds to serve on the **Supreme Court**. McReynolds did not play a particularly significant role on the court until the 1930s when he became a persistent critic of **Franklin D. Roosevelt** and opponent of the extension of federal power under the **New Deal**. Critics regarded McReynolds as one of the worst and most conservative justices to serve on the court. In 1941 he retired in despair following Roosevelt's third election victory.

MELLON, ANDREW WILLIAM (1855–1937). Andrew Mellon was born in Pittsburgh, Pennsylvania. He graduated from the Western University of Pennsylvania in 1873 and in 1880 joined his father's **banking** business, which he soon took over with his brother Richard; in 1889 Mellon established the Union Trust Company of Pittsburgh. In addition to holding interests in various industries, Mellon helped establish the Aluminum Company of America (now ALCOA) and became a multimillionaire and one of the wealthiest men of the 1920s. During **World War I** Mellon was a very active fund-raiser for bodies such as the Red Cross. In 1921 he became secretary of the treasury, a post he held until 1932 under presidents **Warren Harding**, **Calvin Coolidge**, and **Herbert Hoover**. He was associated with the conservative fiscal policy that produced the reduction of income and corporation taxes and surtaxes. He still managed to reduce the national debt from $24 billion in 1920 to $16 billion in 1930. Some of the tax cuts were made secretly to his own companies, and in 1932, faced with the possibility of impeachment, Mellon resigned. He was appointed as ambassador to Great Britain and served from 1932 to 1933. Many of his critics believed that his policies had contributed to the **Wall Street** Crash. Mellon was also a philanthropist and founded the Mellon Institute of Industrial Research in Pittsburgh in 1913 and in 1937 donated his own art collection to the nation and funded the building of the National Gallery of Art in Washington, D.C.

MENCKEN, HENRY LOUIS (1880–1956). After graduating from Baltimore Polytechnic, H. L. Mencken worked for two years in his father's cigar factory. In 1898 he became a reporter on the Baltimore *Herald* and by 1905 he had risen to become editor. In 1906 he became the editor of the Sunday edition of the Baltimore *Sun*. Mencken also published a volume of poetry, *Ventures into Verse* (1903), and two scholarly works, *George Bernard Shaw: His Plays* (1905) and *The Philosophy of Friedrich Nietzsche* (1908). In 1908 Mencken became literary editor of a monthly publication the *Smart Set* and he was later to become coeditor of the magazine with **George Jean Nathan**. He and Nathan founded the *American Mercury* in 1923, and Mencken remained as editor until 1933.

Mencken became one of the distinctive voices of the 1920s through his columns and reviews. He was often a scathing critic of American values and morality, and was particularly savage about the American South and small towns, which he claimed were occupied by the "booboisie." Mencken was equally critical of politicians and clergymen. His accounts of the **Scopes Monkey Trial** were widely reprinted, and he described **William Jennings Bryan** in his obituary as a "peasant come home to the dung-heap."

In addition to his social comment, Mencken was famous for his studies of *The American Language* (first printed in 1919), six volumes of *Prejudices* (1919–1927), *Notes on Democracy* (1926), and a later series of autobiographical works. He continued to work on these and new editions of *The American Language* through World War II. He suffered a severe stroke in 1948 that left him incapacitated. His autobiography, *My Life as Author and Editor*, was not published until after his death.

See also LITERATURE AND THEATER; NEWSPAPERS AND MAGAZINES.

MERCHANT MARINE ACT, 1920. An act passed in order to liquidate the government-owned merchant fleet built during **World War I** and run by the **U.S. Shipping Board**, and yet maintain a large merchant fleet. The act provided for the disposal of ships to private companies, and those companies were also given heavy mail subsidies. Preferential tariffs were to be applied to goods carried on American-owned ships. Many of the ships were sold at a fraction of their cost, and further subsidies were granted in a second Merchant Marine Act in 1928. However, the U.S. merchant fleet continued to be inferior to foreign competition, and many companies collapsed in the **Depression**.

MERRIAM, CHARLES EDWARD (1874–1953). The political scientist Charles Merriam took his first degree in Lenox College, Hopkinton, taught for a year, studied law at the State University of Iowa for a year, and then went to Columbia University, where he completed his MA in 1897 and his PhD in 1900. Merriam took a teaching position at the University of Chicago in 1900 and by 1911 had risen to full professor. He was active in Chicago's reform politics and was elected as **Republican** alderman to the city council in 1909 and served until 1917. Having sat on three city council commissions, Merriam ran for mayor in 1911 as a progressive Republican but was narrowly defeated. With **Harold Ickes**, Merriam established the Illinois Progressive Party and backed first **Robert M. La Follette** and then **Theodore Roosevelt**.

Merriam worked as an examiner for the Chicago aviation board and later the **Committee of Public information** during **World War I**. In 1918 he acted as American high commissioner of information in Rome. In the 1920s Merriam built up the Political Science Department at Chicago into one of the leading schools of its type. In 1923 he was one of the founders of the Social Science Research Council and in 1925 he was elected president of the American Political Science Association. From 1929 to 1933 Merriam served on president **Herbert Hoover**'s Research Committee on Social Trends, which issued its report in 1933. In 1933 **Franklin D. Roosevelt** appointed Merriam to the National Planning Board, and he remained one of the team of planners throughout the **New Deal**. Merriam's many publications included *American Political Ideas* (1920), *The American Political System* (1922), and *New Aspects of Politics* (1925).

See also EDUCATION.

MEUSE-ARGONNE, BATTLE OF. The assault on a twenty-five-mile front along the river Meuse in France from 26 September to 11 November 1918 was the last general push by the **Allied** forces during **World War I**. It was led by the U.S. forces under the command of general **John Pershing** and ended with the capture of Sedan and the negotiation of the general **armistice**. The U.S. forces captured 48,800 prisoners and 1,424 guns and suffered 117,000 dead and wounded during the offensive.

MEXICAN PUNITIVE EXPEDITION. *See* PUNITIVE EXPEDITION, 1916–1917.

MEXICO. U.S. relations with Mexico deteriorated following the overthrow and execution of Francisco Madero by Victoriano Huerta in February 1913. **Woodrow Wilson** refused to recognize the new Mexican government and offered support to the opposition to Huerta led by Venustiano Carranza. Relations further deteriorated following the **Tampico** incident and later the seizure of **Vera Cruz** by U.S. marines in April 1914. Relations improved slightly when Carranza replaced Huerta, but the raid on **Columbus**, New Mexico, by **Pancho Villa** in 1916 led to a **punitive expedition** by U.S. troops into Mexico. Ongoing negotiations were further threatened by the release of the **Zimmerman telegram** by the British government in 1917, but further conflict did not follow.

Relations between the two nations improved a little under the postwar **Republican** administrations. Secretary of state **Charles Hughes** attempted to arrive at a resolution of outstanding differences with Carranza's successor. When legislation by the Mexican Congress in 1925 threatened the considerable American property holdings in Mexico, president **Calvin Coolidge**'s ambassador to Mexico, **Dwight Morrow**, was able to reach some agreement on these issues. A goodwill visit by **Herbert Hoover** prior to his inaugural also helped to continue the improving relations and paved the way for **Franklin D. Roosevelt**'s "Good Neighbor" policies.

See also FOREIGN POLICY.

MILLAY, EDNA ST. VINCENT (1892–1950). Already publishing poetry in high school, Edna St. Vincent Millay graduated from Vassar College in 1917, and her collection of poetry *Renascence and Other Poems* was published the same year. She joined the **Greenwich Village** literary set in New York City, wrote several pieces in *Vanity Fair*, and published her second volume, *A Few Figs from Thistles*, in 1920. The latter, which included "My Candle Burns at Both Ends," did much to establish her reputation as a liberated "new" **woman**. *The Harper-Weaver and Other Poems* was published in 1923, and Millay wrote the libretto for **Deems Taylor**'s opera, *The King's Henchman* (1927). Millay became the first female poet to be awarded the Pulitzer Prize in 1923. She was elected to the National Institute of Arts and Letters in 1929 and the American Academy of Arts and Letters in 1940. Her later work included *The Buck in Snow* (1928), *Fatal Interview* (1931), *Wine from These Grapes* (1934), *Conversation at Midnight* (1937), and *Huntsman, What Quarry?* (1939).

In addition to writing poetry that captured aspects of the mood of the 1920s, Millay was one of many intellectuals who defended **Sacco and Vanzetti**. She was arrested and jailed during a protest following their execution in 1927.

See also LITERATURE AND THEATER.

MILLIKAN, ROBERT ANDREWS (1868–1953). Robert Millikan earned a master's degree in physics at Oberlin College in 1893 and then undertook postgraduate research at Columbia University. Millikan took up a teaching position at Chicago University in 1896 and wrote several introductory physics textbooks, including the widely published *A First Course in Physics*. He also taught courses on X-rays, radioactivity, and quantum and electron physics, and carried out major research in those areas. During **World War I** Millikan chaired the General Antisubmarine Committee for the National Research Council. In 1921 he took up an appointment at the new California Institute of Technology, where he established a world-class physics department. He was awarded the Nobel Prize in 1923 for his work in electron physics. Millikan's work included articles in popular magazines and a book on *Evolution in Science and Religion* (1927). His subsequent work focused on cosmic rays, and he published *Cosmic Rays* in 1939. He retired in 1945.

See also EDUCATION.

MILLS, FLORENCE (1896–1927). The **African American** singer and dancer was born Florence Winfrey in Washington, D.C., to parents who had been slaves, Florence began performing at the age of six as part of the "Mills Sisters" with her sisters after the family had moved to New York City. Mills continued as a solo artist when her sisters left, and she performed in a variety of vaudeville and cabaret shows before achieving her breakthrough in *Shuffle Along*, the first black Broadway musical and a major part of the **Harlem Renaissance**. She subsequently appeared in *Plantation Revue* (1922), which was also put on in London, England. In 1924 she was a huge success in another Broadway revue, *Dixie to Broadway*, in which she introduced her famous signature song, "I'm a Little Blackbird Looking for a Bluebird." The song became the centerpiece of the 1925 revue *Blackbirds*, which was a success in New York, Paris, and London, and brought Mills international stardom. Sadly she was taken ill and died following surgery. Over 75,000 mourners viewed her body in **Harlem**, and 150,000 watched the funeral procession.

See also LITERATURE AND THEATER; MUSIC AND DANCE.

MILLS, OGDEN LIVINGSTON (1884–1937). Ogden Mills, a graduate of Harvard University, was admitted to the New York bar in 1908 and practiced law in the city. He became active in **Republican Party** affairs in 1911 and was treasurer of the Republican County Committee of New York until 1926. He stood unsuccessfully for Congress in 1912 but was elected to the state senate in 1914 and served until 1917, when he enlisted in the U.S. Army. He served as a captain in France and was elected to the House of Representatives from New York in 1921 and served until 1927. He was an unsuccessful candidate in the New York gubernatorial election in 1926 but was appointed undersecretary of the treasury by **Calvin Coolidge** in 1927. President **Herbert Hoover** appointed him secretary of the treasury in 1932 following the resignation of **Andrew Mellon** to become ambassador to Great Britain. Mills supported a conservative fiscal policy, a balanced budget, and the gold standard. After leaving the Treasury Department in 1933 he was highly critical of the **New Deal** and published his views in *What of Tomorrow* (1935) and *The Seventeen Million* (1937). He continued to be active in business as a director for several large corporations, including the Lackawanna Steel Company and Shredded Wheat Company.

MISSISSIPPI FLOODS, 1927. Following abnormally high rainfall from September 1926, exceptionally heavy rains in April 1927 brought some of the worst flooding of the Mississippi River in history. From Cairo, Illinois, to New Orleans, Louisiana, the Mississippi and its tributaries flooded, covering some twenty-six thousand square miles. At some points the Mississippi was sixty miles across. An estimated 246 people died in the floods, but hundreds more are thought to have died of exposure or illness subsequently as more than six hundred thousand were forced to leave their homes. Almost half of those affected were **African Americans**. Secretary of commerce **Herbert Hoover** directed Red Cross relief operations, which established 154 camps for the homeless. Hoover's popularity increased as a result, ensuring his nomination as president **Calvin Coolidge**'s successor in 1928. The Flood Control Act of 1928 increased the role of the U.S. Army Corps of Engineers in improving flood defenses as outlined by **Edgar Jadwin**.

MITCHELL, CHARLES EDWIN (1877–1955). The man said by some politicians and commentators to have been personally more responsible than any other individual for the **Wall Street Crash**, Charles Mitchell was born in Chelsea, Massachusetts. He graduated from Amherst College in 1899 and went to work in Western Electric in Chicago until 1906, when he became the assistant to the president of the Trust Company of America in New York City. In 1911 he established his own investment house, C. E. Mitchell & Co., and in 1916 he became vice president of National City Company, an affiliate of the National City **Bank** (now Citibank). In 1921 Mitchell was president of National City Bank, and in 1929 he became chair of the company. He turned the company into a private investment bank and established branches across the country and abroad—by 1930 National City Company had over one hundred branches in twenty-three countries and was the biggest bank in the world.

Known as "Sunshine Charley" because of his unending optimism, when the Federal Reserve called for a curb on lending in March 1929, Mitchell offered to lend $25 million to traders in securities. However, when in 1932 the Senate launched an investigation in banking practices, it became clear that Mitchell had been involved in illegal stock dealing, speculation in his own bank's securities, and tax evasion. He was forced to resign his position and in 1933 was charged with tax evasion. Although cleared of the charges, he subsequently paid back $1.4 million in tax and interest. The 1933 Glass-Steagall, or Banking Act, separating commercial and investment banking, was passed in part as a response to Mitchell's practices. Despite this he continued to work in banking as chair of Blythe & Co. and was able to restore both his fortune and reputation to some extent.

MITCHELL, WESLEY CLAIR (1874–1948). After obtaining his PhD at the University of Chicago in 1899, Wesley Mitchell taught at the University of California, Columbia University, and the New School for Social Research. During **World War I** he served as head of the Price Section of the **War Industries Board**. Mitchell founded the National Bureau of Economic Research in 1920 to undertake quantitative studies of the U.S. business cycle. Mitchell published a number of key texts, including two works entitled *Business Cycles* (1913, 1927). In 1921 he took part in the **President's Unemployment Conference**. Mitchell succeeded **Charles Merriam** as chair of the Social Science Research Council in 1927, led the group that produced the president's *Report on Recent Economic Changes* (1929), and chaired president **Herbert Hoover**'s **Research Committee on Social Trends**, which reported in 1933. That year Mitchell was appointed to the National Planning Board created to serve the Public Works Administration. He resigned in 1935.

See also EDUCATION.

MITCHELL, WILLIAM LENDRUM (1879–1936). The **World War I** air ace "Billy" Mitchell served as a private in the infantry in the Spanish-American War of 1898. He received a commission in the signal corps and served in Cuba, the Philippines, and Alaska. In 1915 he was assigned to the **aviation** section of the signal corps. During World War I Mitchell commanded air forces in a number of important engagements, and he was awarded the Distinguished Service Cross and Distinguished Service Medal in addition to the *Croix de Guerre* for his services. After the war Mitchell became assistant chief of the Army Air Service and an advocate for the development of U.S. air power and unified air force. His outspoken criticism of military policy and accusations of incompetence on the part of the War and Navy Departments after the loss of the dirigible *Shenandoah* in 1925 led to his court-martial. Demoted and suspended in rank, Mitchell resigned in 1926. He was posthumously awarded the Congressional Medal of Honor in 1946 for his contribution to the development of an American air force.

MODEL T FORD. Known as the "tin lizzie," **Henry Ford**'s mass-produced **automobile** was intended to make car ownership a possibility for the masses by producing a simple but serviceable vehicle (the buyer could have any color as long as it was black) using standard interchangeable parts. First manufactured in 1908, by 1927 the company had produced over 15 million Model T Fords, and the price had fallen from just under $1,000 to just under $300. The new Model A Ford was introduced in 1927.

MODERNISM. "Modernism" is a term used to describe the changes that affected **art** as well as **literature and theater**, and intellectual approaches to life in the period from about 1900 through to the 1920s. It marked the end of old established traditions and beliefs of certainty which were replaced instead with doubt, questioning, and innovation. Writing and art became more personal, more intuitive, influenced by the work of Sigmund Freud or the theories of Albert Einstein or radical politics. For many people, **World War I** and the emergence of a "**lost generation**" marked the birth of modernism and the destruction of the old order, but new technology and forms of industrial mass production, consumerism, and the rise of the city also contributed to new forms of expression and style.

MOONEY, THOMAS JOSEPH (1882–1942). Tom Mooney was a radical labor activist involved in various socialist and labor organizations in California. In 1913 he and Warren Billings (1893–1972) were involved in a protracted and bitter electrical workers' strike in San Francisco. Billings was found carrying dynamite, and he and Mooney were charged with illegal possession of explosives. After three trials Mooney was eventually acquitted in 1914 and he resumed his labor activities. However, when a bomb went off during the Preparedness Day Parade in San Francisco on 22 July 1916, killing ten people, Billings and Mooney were both rearrested. Billings was tried and sentenced to life imprisonment. Mooney's wife, Rena, and two other men were acquitted. Mooney, tried separately, was found guilty and sentenced to death despite the lack of real substantial evidence against him. A supposed eyewitness was later found to have perjured himself in his statement.

Mooney's sentence caused an outcry of protest from labor leaders and reformers both nationally and internationally, and in 1918 president **Woodrow Wilson** intervened to ask governor William D. Stephens of California to delay execution. A review of the case led to the commutation of Mooney's sentence to life imprisonment. Legal efforts continued to secure a retrial for both Mooney and Billings over the next twenty years, but it was not until 1939 that Mooney was granted a pardon and released. Billings had his sentence commuted and was also released; he was finally pardoned in 1961.

MORGENTHAU, HENRY (1856–1946). Henry Morgenthau immigrated to the United States from Germany in 1866 with his family. He graduated from Columbia Law School and established a law practice in New York City after he graduated in 1877. Morgenthau later established his own real estate businesses, but in 1913 he turned to public service. In 1907 he had helped to found the Free Synagogue, which was committed to community service. In 1911 he established Bronx House, a **settlement house** and music school. Morgenthau was a generous supporter of **Woodrow Wilson** and served as chairman of the Democratic National Committee's finance committee in 1912. In 1913 Wilson appointed him as ambassador to Turkey, and after the **Allied** nations broke off relations with Turkey in 1914, he also represented their citizens. He was decorated by Great Britain and France for this service, and offered a cabinet post by the Turkish government. Morgenthau resigned in 1916. In 1917 he was sent to negotiate a separate peace with Turkey, but the mission was aborted.

After the war Morgenthau campaigned on behalf of U.S. membership in the **League of Nations**, took part in the establishment of the International Red Cross (1919), advised on Turkish issues at the **Versailles Peace Conference**, and was vice president of the Armenian Relief Committee. He was appointed as ambassador to **Mexico** in 1920, but the appointment was not confirmed due to the unrest in Mexico. In 1923 Morgenthau successfully chaired the League of Nations' Greek Refugee Settlement Commission. In 1933 he was a technical delegate to the World Monetary and Economic Conference in London.

See also FOREIGN POLICY.

MORROW, DWIGHT WHITNEY (1873–1931). A graduate of Amherst College in 1895 and Columbia Law School in 1899, Dwight Morrow practiced law in New York City. In 1914 he accepted a partnership with J. P. Morgan and worked with the company until 1927. During **World War I,**

Morrow played a major part in the Allied Maritime Transport Council allocating shipping resources. In 1921 he advised on the reorganization of Cuba's finances. In 1927 **Calvin Coolidge** appointed Morrow as ambassador to **Mexico**, and he worked to improve relations between the two countries for three years. Morrow was a delegate to the **London Naval Conference** in 1930. Later that year he was elected to the U.S. Senate for New Jersey and became a close adviser to president **Herbert Hoover**. He was to lead the U.S. delegation to the World Disarmament Conference in 1931, when he died suddenly.

MORTON, "JELLY ROLL" (FERDINAND JOSEPH). Born Ferdinand Lamothe, Morton acquired a new name when his mother remarried. A Creole, he grew up with the **African American jazz** musicians in New Orleans, where he learned to play the piano and began to compose his own tunes including "New Orleans Blues" (1902?) and "Jelly Roll Blues" (1905). From 1907 to 1917 Morton traveled around the United States before settling in Los Angeles until 1922. He then moved on to Chicago, where he made his first recordings with the New Orleans Rhythm Kings in 1923. Morton also made a considerable number of solo recordings in the 1920s.

In 1928 Morton moved to New York City, but increasingly his New Orleans and ragtime style were becoming outdated as swing and boogie woogie played by people like **Duke Ellington** and **Fletcher Henderson** began to dominate. Nonetheless recordings made in the 1940s with the musicologist Alan Lomax for the Library of Congress demonstrated the breadth of his talent as a pianist and composer and his knowledge of the history of jazz.

See also ARMSTRONG, LOUIS (1901–1971); BECHET, SIDNEY JOSEPH (1897–1959); MUSIC AND DANCE.

MOSKOWITZ, BELLE LINDNER ISRAELS (1877–1933). After attending the Teachers' College at Columbia University for a year, Belle Moskowitz began work as a resident **social worker** at the Educational Alliance, a Jewish **settlement house** on New York's Lower East Side, in 1900. After her marriage in 1903 Moskowitz worked part-time for the journal *Survey* and on various projects for the United Hebrew Charities and the New York State Conference on Charities and Corrections. In 1908 she was responsible for the implementation of licensing of commercial dance halls. From 1913 until 1916 Moskowitz worked with the Dress and Waist Manufacturers' Association in its grievance and arbitration service. She then established a firm of industrial consultants.

In 1918 Moskowitz supported **Alfred Smith**'s gubernatorial election campaign. Following his victory Moskowitz was appointed executive secretary to New York State's Reconstruction Commission, which proposed many ideas that Smith later enacted. Moskowitz became a close adviser to Smith, and she helped secure his election again in 1922. She became publicity director for the New York State Democratic Committee and acted as a speechwriter and public relations consultant for the governor. She helped to mobilize support for Smith's successful bid to win the **Democratic** nomination in 1928, and she was the only woman on the executive committee of the Democratic National Committee. Moskowitz continued as Smith's press agent after his defeat. She died in 1932 following a car accident.

MOTION PICTURES. *See* MOVIES.

MOTLEY, ARCHIBALD, JR. (1891–1981). Born in New Orleans, the **African American** artist Archibald Motley grew up in Chicago, where he went to high school and later attended the **Art** Institute. He graduated in 1918. Motley's work was reminiscent of that of **Thomas Hart Benton** and **Grant Wood** in his use of rich colors and rounded images. His painting *Old Snuff Taker* won the Harmon Foundation Gold Medal Award in 1928, and Motley was awarded a Guggenheim scholarship in 1929. He spent some time studying in Paris and was influenced by the art of the European Renaissance. He painted several scenes from Chicago's social scene and nightlife including *Cocktails* (1926), *Stomp* (1927), *Jockey Club* (1929), *Blues* (1929), *Saturday Night* (1935), and *Nightlife* (1943). He returned to the United States in 1931 and worked for the Works Progress Administration in the 1930s producing a number of murals on aspects of African American history in public buildings in Illinois.

MOTON, ROBERT RUSSA (1867–1940). The **African American educator** received his training at Hampton Institute, Virginia, and he remained there in a number of roles after his graduation in 1890. In 1915 he succeeded the black leader Booker T. Washington as head of Tuskegee Institute in Alabama. During **World War I** Moton was successful in leading the call for a black-officer-training program and the use of black troops in combat roles. He also helped to secure the appointment of **Emmett Scott** as special adviser to the secretary of war. In 1918 Moton was sent by president **Woodrow Wilson** to report on the conditions of African American servicemen, and did much to challenge accusations of black military failure. However, in general Moton continued Booker T. Washington's accommodationist policies and while in Europe he urged the black soldiers not to challenge the racial status quo on their return home. He continued to develop Tuskegee in the 1920s and was awarded the Harmon Foundation Award for his contribution to improved race relations in 1930 and the Spingarn Medal in 1932. In addition

to contributions to **Alain Locke**'s *New Negro* (1925), Moton authored *Racial Good Will* (1916), *What the Negro Thinks* (1929), and his autobiography, *Finding a Way Out* (1920).
See also EDUCATION.

MOTT, JOHN RALEIGH (1865–1955). John Mott attended Iowa University from 1881 until 1885, when he went to Cornell University, where he obtained a PhD in 1888. While at Cornell Mott attended a Christian student conference and pledged to work in foreign missions. From 1888 until 1928 he worked with the Young Men's Christian Association (YMCA) in a variety of roles. He was general secretary of the YMCA's foreign department from 1901 to 1915, general secretary of the International Committee of the YMCA, 1915–1928, and president of the YMCA's World Committee, 1926–1937. In addition Mott held positions in the Student Volunteer Movement and the World Student Christian Federation, which he helped to create in 1895. Mott personally toured many countries encouraging student Christian organizations. President **Woodrow Wilson** asked Mott to become U.S. ambassador to China while Mott was there in 1913, but he declined the offer. He did, however, take part in the High Commission sent to **Mexico** in 1916 to defuse tension following the **punitive expedition** in pursuit of **Pancho Villa**. In 1917 Mott went to Moscow with the U.S. mission following the revolution, and he also attended the **Versailles Peace Conference**.

During **World War I** Mott became general secretary of the YMCA War Work Council established to provide social service programs for the military. After the war he was involved in the Interchurch World Movement and the later Institute of Social and Religious Research. During the 1920s he devoted more of his time to the International Missionary Council, which he chaired until 1941, encouraging ecumenical movements around the world. He was involved in the foundation of the World Council of Churches after World War II and was appointed its honorary president. In 1946 Mott shared the Nobel Peace Prize with **Emily Greene Balch**.

MOVIES. Moving film images emerged at the end of the nineteenth century from revolving discs with images in kinemascopes or kinematographs, hence the use of term "cinema" in some countries. W. K. L. Dickson's development of moving film for Thomas Edison in 1894 and then the use of film projectors led to the silent film shorts shown in five-cent theaters called "nickelodeons." The first film with a story was *The Great Train Robbery* (1903), and by 1907 there were over five thousand theaters and the term "movie" was well established. Most of the early films were made in New York City or New Jersey, but gradually producers such as **D. W. Griffith** and **Cecil B. De Mille** moved to California. There the climate, access to space, and cheap labor led to the growth of Hollywood, outside of Los Angeles, as the center of the film industry. Griffith also led the way in making movies beyond the one-reel shorts and developing the cinematic devices of panning shots, close ups, and film editing in narrating complicated plots. These were best exemplified in his three-hour epic, *The Birth of a Nation* (1915).

It was in Hollywood that the studio system developed in the 1920s following the breakup between 1912 and 1918 of the Edison Motion Picture Patents Company's (MPPC) monopolistic control of cameras and projectors. **Adolph Zukor** began the process of vertical integration that gave studios control of the film "product" from its making to distribution through cinema chains all owned by his Paramount company. Other companies such as Warner Brothers, **Samuel Goldwyn** and **Louis B. Mayer**'s Metro-Goldwyn-Mayer (MGM), **William Fox**'s Fox Film (later Twentieth Century-Fox), and Radio-Keith-Orpheum (RKO) quickly joined Paramount to dominate the growing industry. Smaller companies including Carl Laemmle's Universal Pictures, Jack and Harry Cohn's Columbia Pictures, and United Artist, formed in 1919 by the movie stars and director **Charlie Chaplin**, **Douglas Fairbanks**, **Mary Pickford**, and D. W. Griffith, also added to the industry. There were also a handful of independent producers like **David O. Selznick**.

By 1926 nickelodeons were being replaced by huge "picture palaces," the motion picture industry was grossing $1.5 billion a year, and cinema attendance averaged 60 million a week. Actors like Chaplin, Fairbanks, Pickford, **Clara Bow**, **Rudolph Valentino**, **Lillian Gish**, **Gloria Swanson**, and **Greta Garbo** became huge stars whose life on and off the screen became the subject of personal interest. Sound—music and special effects—was first used in 1926. The first feature-length film using talking sound (the "talkie") was Warner Brothers' *The Jazz Singer* (1927), starring **Al Jolson**. By 1930 an average of 80 million people a week were going to the movies. Movie audiences did fall in the early years of the **Great Depression**, but after 1933 attendance rose once more and the movie industry enjoyed its greatest years during the 1930s and 1940s.

See also ARBUCKLE, ROSCOE "FATTY" (1887–1933); CHANEY, LON (1883–1930); FIELDS, W. C. (WILLIAM CLAUDE) (1880–1946); HAYS, WILLIAM HARRISON (1879–1954); KEATON, BUSTER (1895–1966); LLOYD, HAROLD CLAYTON (1893–1971); LOMBARD, CAROLE (1908–1942); NEGRI, POLA (1899–1987); SENNETT, MACK (1880–1960); VIDOR, KING WALLIS (1894–1982).

MUMFORD, LEWIS (1895–1990). Lewis Mumford studied at City College, Columbia University, and the New School for Social Research, but did not graduate. Despite this lack of a degree, Mumford was to become an intellectual polymath, philosopher, architectural critic, urban historian and planner, and expert in American studies. He became visiting professor at

Dartmouth, Stanford, Berkeley, the University of Pennsylvania, Wesleyan, and Massachusetts Institute of Technology. He was to receive honorary degrees from Edinburgh and Rome, and was awarded the Presidential Medal of Freedom (1964), the National Medal for Literature (1972), and the National Medal of Arts (1986).

Mumford served in the U.S. Navy from 1918 to 1919 and joined the staff of *The Dial* in 1919. His first book, *The Story of Utopias* (1922), was an examination of ideal societies from Plato to the nineteenth century. His *Technics and Civilization* (1934) was a history of technology, and *The Culture of Cities* (1938) and *The City in History* (1961) used history to argue for smaller, planned, and balanced urban development. Mumford was one of the founders of the Regional Planning Association of America in 1923, and he advised on a number of urban developments. He was the author of a number of works on architecture, starting with *Sticks and Stones* in 1924. Mumford also wrote on American culture in *The Golden Day* (1926) and *Herman Melville* (1929).

Mumford also spoke out on political issues—he opposed appeasement in the 1930s and supported American intervention in World War II. He campaigned against atomic weapons and was one of the first to speak out against the war in Vietnam in the 1960s.

See also EDUCATION; LITERATURE AND THEATER.

MUSIC AND DANCE. Often known as the "**Jazz Age**" (a title given to the decade by writer **F. Scott Fitzgerald**) the 1920s did see the increased influence of **African American** musical forms across all musical genres. In its rejection of tradition and liberation from established forms, **jazz** reflected American modernity—it was the music of the "**flapper**" and the young, the rebel and the intellectual, often captured in the images of cartoonist **John Held**. Black in origin, jazz was first popularized through prewar Ragtime, and by the white Original Dixieland Jazz Band from 1917 on, and then later by band leaders like **Duke Ellington, Fletcher Henderson**, and **Paul Whiteman**, and performers such as **Louis Armstrong, Sidney Bechet**, and **Jelly Roll Morton**.

In its most popular form, jazz became Swing, but the term was also used loosely to describe all forms of syncopated music. It also influenced classical music, particularly in the work of **George Gershwin** and later **Aaron Copland**. Popular music was however, segregated, and many African American musicians had their worked recorded on "race records," labels of major record companies targeted specifically at black audiences. Among these performers were female singers like Mamie Smith, Gertrude "Ma" Rainey, and **Bessie Smith**.

Dance was also influenced by African American music and culture, often from all-black Broadway musicals such as *Shuffle Along* (1921). Best known of all dances of the era was the **Charleston**, but others included the **black bottom**, cakewalk, and the shimmy. **Movies** also did much to popularize new dance forms such as the tango. Traditional dances such as the waltz and foxtrot still continued to be very popular. Modern dance also became more expressive under the influence of Isadora Duncan and Martha Graham, but ballet remained in its infancy during the decade despite the creation of Adolph Bolm's Ballet in 1918 and the Pavely-Oukrainsky Ballet in 1921, both in Chicago.

Not all music in the decade was jazz—probably the most popular songs and records came from vaudeville and from Broadway musicals, where the sentimental ballads of **Irving Berlin**, **Jerome Kern**, and **Cole Porter** had a huge impact and often proved to have an enduring appeal. By the end of the decade **movies** were also providing a vehicle for the musicals and for dance entertainment.

See also CALLOWAY, "CAB" (CABELL) (1907–1994); CANTOR, EDDIE (1892–1964); GERSHWIN, IRA (1896–1983); IVES, CHARLES EDWARD (1874–1954); JOLSON, AL (1886–1950); MILLS, FLORENCE (1896–1927); ROBESON, PAUL LEROY BUSTILL (1898–1976); SISSLE, NOBLE (1889–1975); WATERS, ETHEL (1896–1977).

MUSTE, ABRAHAM JOHANNES (1885–1967). Clergyman, labor activist, pacifist, and exponent of nonviolent protest, Muste was born in Holland and moved to the United States with his family in 1891. Ordained to the ministry of the Dutch Reformed Church in 1918, Muste became a minster in the Society of Friends (Quakers) and later worked for the **American Civil Liberties Union**. He played a leading role in the strike of textile workers in Lawrence, Massachusetts, in 1919 and was general secretary of the Amalgamated Textile Workers of America in 1920 and 1921. He was educational director at Brookwood College, New York, from 1921 to 1933. Muste was the founder of the radical Conference for Progressive Labor Action in 1929. This organization later became the American Workers' Party and then later merged with the Trotskyite Communist League of America. He was executive director of the Fellowship of Reconciliation, an organization of reformist and pacifist clergymen, from 1940 to 1953, and author of *Non-violence in an Aggressive World* (1940). In his later years Muste was an adviser to Martin Luther King Jr. and an active campaigner against the war in Vietnam.

N

NATHAN, GEORGE JEAN (1882–1958). George Nathan began his career as writer and critic while attending Cornell University (1900–1904), where he edited the student **newspaper** and literary magazine. In 1905 he became a reporter with the *New York Herald* and then a writer for magazines such as *Harper's Weekly, Puck, Judge, Vanity Fair,* and *Esquire.* In 1908 he began writing for the *Smart Set* and in 1914 became coeditor with **H. L. Mencken.** Together the two men turned the magazine into one of the leading publications of the early 1920s, renowned for its famous contributors, such as **F. Scott Fitzgerald,** and for its lively independent style. In 1923 Nathan and Mencken left the *Smart Set* to set up the *American Mercury,* but Nathan resigned in 1924 although he continued as drama critic. In the 1930s Nathan, together with **Eugene O'Neill, Ernest Boyd,** and **Theodore Dreiser,** launched the *American Spectator,* a more literary journal than the *Mercury.* Nathan gave this up in 1935 and resumed work for the *Mercury* during the 1940s. He also published an annual *Theater Book of the Year* until 1951. Nathan also wrote works of literary and social criticism, and in total published some forty volumes.

See also NEWSPAPERS AND MAGAZINES.

NATIONAL AMERICAN WOMAN SUFFRAGE ASSOCIATION (NAWSA). Formed in 1890 with a merger of the National Woman Suffrage Association and the American Woman Suffrage Association, NAWSA was the leading organization demanding votes for **women.** Led by **Carrie Chapman Catt** from 1900 NAWSA campaigned not on the grounds of their equality with men, but on the claim that they were morally superior and would introduce higher standards to government. Fighting both at local and national level, their campaign eventually secured the passage of the **Nineteenth Amendment** in 1920.

See also WOMEN'S SUFFRAGE MOVEMENT.

NATIONAL ASSOCIATION FOR THE ADVANCEMENT OF COLORED PEOPLE (NAACP). Formed in 1910 as an outgrowth of the 1909 National Negro Congress called by **Oswald Garrison Villard, Mary White Ovington**, and William Walling following the race riot in Springfield, Illinois, the NAACP became the leading civil rights organization in the United States until the 1950s. With its monthly journal, *The Crisis*, edited by **W. E. B. Du Bois**, the NAACP quickly grew in size and by 1919 had a membership of ninety thousand. Although many of the leading officers were white, the organization was increasingly influenced by its **African American** national secretary, **James Weldon Johnson**, and field secretary **Walter White**. The NAACP organized a silent protest following the **East St. Louis** riot in 1917, led the campaign against lynching in the 1920s, took part in the defense of the **Scottsboro boys**, and in the 1930s initiated the legal challenges to segregation that culminated in the *Brown v. Board of Education* decision in 1954.

NATIONAL CONSUMERS LEAGUE (NCL). A consumer protection and social advocacy organization formed in 1899 to campaign for the protection and welfare of consumers and workers. Its aim was to ensure that goods were of reasonable quality and price and produced in "fair, safe, and healthy working conditions." It was one of a number of **progressive** organizations that campaigned for minimum wages, limited working hours, and the protection of **women** workers. The NCL was led by **Florence Kelley** until her death in 1932, and its members included **Grace** and **Edith Abbott**, **Jane Addams**, **Emily Balch**, and **Eleanor Roosevelt**, among many others.

NATIONAL DEFENSE ACT, 1916. The National Defense Act was passed as part of the preparedness campaign prior to U.S. entry into **World War I**. It authorized an increase in the size of the regular army, provided for the federalization of the National Guard, and created civilian training camps and military schools at universities. The act also empowered the secretary of war to make a census of industrial capacity with regard to potential war orders.

NATIONAL ORIGINS ACT, 1924. *See* QUOTA ACT, 1924.

NATIONAL PROHIBITION ACT, 1919. Known as the **Volstead Act**, the National Prohibition Act was passed in October 1919 to implement the provisions of the **Eighteenth Amendment**. The act defined intoxicating liquor as anything that contained 0.5 percent alcohol by volume, but allowed the sale of alcohol for medicinal, sacramental, or industrial purposes. The act was more easily passed than enforced, and the rise of criminal activity associated with the illegal sale of alcohol, and increased public opposition to the legislation, led to its repeal.

See also PROHIBITION.

NATIONAL URBAN LEAGUE (NUL). The National Urban League was formed in New York City in 1911 in response to the increasing migration of **African Americans** from the South. The Urban League helped to find housing and work, and carried out research into race discrimination. In 1923 the League began to publish a journal, *Opportunity*, to publicize its research and to offer opportunities for black writers.

NATIONAL WAR LABOR BOARD (NWLB). The National War Labor Board was established on 9 April 1918 to "settle by mediation and conciliation" any labor disputes threatening war production during **World War I**. It followed the recommendations of the War Labor Conference Board established in response to the wave of strikes in 1917. The Board recognized the right to collective bargaining and established minimum wage levels and the eight-hour day as the norm in settling disputes. The Board adjudicated in some 1,245 cases.
See also ECONOMY; TRADE UNIONS.

NATIONAL WOMAN'S PARTY (NWP). **Alice Paul** and others frustrated by the slow progress of the **National American Woman Suffrage Association**'s state-by-state campaign to enfranchise **women** formed the National Woman's Party as the successor to the **Congressional Union** in 1916. The NWP instead focused on the federal government and opposed whatever party was in power. In 1917 the NWP began picketing the White House, and several women were jailed. When they went on a hunger strike, they were force-fed. After the passage of the **Nineteenth Amendment** the NWP began a campaign in favor of an **Equal Rights Amendment**. It continued to campaign into the 1960s.

NATIVE AMERICANS. From the late nineteenth century to the late twentieth century Native Americans constituted the poorest and most overlooked minority in the United States. Native Americans numbered 250,000 in 1900, and the majority of them were located on reservations in the West and Southwest. While the massacre at Wounded Knee in 1890 may have been the last chapter in the subjugation of the Indian tribes, it did not mark the end of their suffering. The Dawes Severalty Act of 1887 encouraged the breakup of Indian lands and allowed the disposal of land not allotted to families. By 1930 almost half of their territory, over 86 million acres, had gone to white Americans. A proposal by senator Holm Bursum of New Mexico to dispossess the Pueblo Indians of lands led to the first Pueblo council meeting since the seventeenth century in 1922. White reformers and the American Indian Defense Association led by John Collier also protested, and the Bursum bill was dropped.

During **World War I** seventeen thousand Native Americans registered for military service, and eight thousand were inducted. Unlike **African Americans**, they were not segregated as many reformers hoped that the war would facilitate their assimilation into white society. Partially as a result of this service and also to remove inconsistencies and confusion, full citizenship was granted to Native Americans in the **American Indian Citizenship Act** in 1924. In the mid-1920s secretary of the interior **Herbert Work** established a commission under Lewis Meriam to conduct a survey of conditions on the reservations. The report, *The Problem of Indian Administration* (1928), declared categorically that "an overwhelming majority of Indians are poor, even extremely poor." The commission called for changes in federal policy and more spending on health, education, and welfare provision. Further surveys were conducted under the administration of **Herbert Hoover**, and some changes took place in education. However, little else had changed, and the **Great Depression**, coupled with the effects of drought in the 1930s, exacerbated the already poor conditions. It was not until the **New Deal** and the appointment of Collier as Indian commissioner that the problems of Native Americans first began to be tackled seriously.

NEARING, SCOTT (1883–1983). A socialist and pacifist, Scott Nearing was the author of *The Solution of the Child Labor Problem* (1911) and *Women and Social Progress* (1912) whose outspoken critiques of industrial employers led to his dismissal from the University of Pennsylvania in 1915. He was subsequently offered a position at the University of Toledo in Ohio but was dismissed in 1917 for his opposition to U.S. entry into the war. Nearing joined the **Socialist Party** and was employed at the radical Rand School of Social Science in New York City. He was charged under the **Espionage Act** following the publication of his antiwar pamphlet, *The Great Madness* (1917), and stood trial in February 1919. Although the American Socialist Party was fined for publishing the pamphlet, Nearing was acquitted. He was an active campaigner for black civil rights and author of *Black America* (1929) and *Freeborn* (1932).

NEGRI, POLA (1899–1987). Born Barbara Apolonia Chalupiec in Poland, Pola Negri trained in ballet and appeared in a number of early Polish and then German films. In 1923 she began a contract with Paramount films in the United States, and she made a series of **movies** as the femme fatale—*Bella Donna*, *The Cheat*, *The Spanish Dancer*, and *Hotel Imperial*. Her career was enhanced by publicity attached to her private life, particularly her affair with

Rudolph Valentino. Her entry into sound pictures in 1932 with *A Woman Commands* was a failure, and she returned to Germany. She returned to the United States in 1941 but did not make any more films of significance.

See also WOMEN.

NESS, ELIOT (1903–1957). Eliot Ness found fame as the special agent leading a team of so-called "Untouchables" in the war against organized **crime** during the **prohibition** era. Ness, a graduate from the University of Chicago in 1925, found work first investigating insurance applicants for the Retail Credit Company and then in the Prohibition Bureau of the U.S. Treasury Department. In 1928 Ness was transferred to the Justice Department as a special agent, where with a team of agents, he targeted the **bootlegging** businesses of the mob in Chicago. Ness's team was disbanded following the conviction of **Al Capone** in 1931 and the repeal of prohibition two years later.

In 1934 Ness moved to the Alcohol Tax Unit in Cleveland, Ohio, and a year later became director of public safety in Cleveland responsible for attacking corruption in the police force. He resigned the post in 1942 and found employment with the Federal Social Protection program in Washington, D.C. In 1944 he became the chairman of a safe and lock company in Cleveland and then treasurer and vice president of an import/export company. He was defeated in his attempt to become mayor of Cleveland in 1947. In 1957 he wrote *The Untouchables*, but he did not live to see it published or the successful television series that sprang from it in 1959. An equally successful film version was made in 1987.

NEW DEAL. Addressing the **Democratic Party** convention in Chicago in June 1932 the newly nominated presidential candidate **Franklin D. Roosevelt** pledged "a new deal for the American people." The term "New Deal" was then applied to his program of relief, recovery, and reform to tackle the problems of the **Depression**. The New Deal was to become one of the greatest periods of political change in U.S. history.

NEW FREEDOM. The New Freedom was the title given to **Woodrow Wilson**'s political program in 1912. It reflected the influence of the progressive lawyer **Louis D. Brandeis** and proposed that federal power be used positively to correct monopoly abuses of competition and restore a more open economic order with social justice and opportunity for all. Rather than the "regulated monopoly" proposed in **Theodore Roosevelt**'s "**New Nationalism**," Wilson wanted "regulated competition." This would be achieved through the use of antitrust legislation and the reduction of protectionist tariffs. Wilson felt he had achieved these aims with the introduction of the **Underwood-Simmons Tariff Act**, the **Federal Reserve Act**, the **Clayton Antitrust Act**, and the creation of the **Federal Trade Commission**.

See also DEMOCRATIC PARTY; POLITICAL PARTIES.

"NEW NEGRO". Following the outbreaks of violence directed against **African Americans** in the **Red Summer** of 1919, a new mood of anger and assertiveness emerged among the black population evident in its willingness to fight back against white oppression. This was apparent both in the armed resistance to white violence in the riots in Washington, D.C., and Chicago, in rising black membership of the National Association for the Advancement of Colored People (NAACP), and in the statements of leaders such as **W. E. B. Du Bois**. This new mood found voice too in the work of writers such as **Claude McKay** and in the **Harlem Renaissance.**

See also DOUGLAS, AARON (1899–1979); LOCKE, ALAIN (1886–1954).

NEWSPAPERS AND MAGAZINES. Despite the rise of **radio**, the **movies**, and newsreel, printed newspapers and magazines reached new levels of popularity in this period. In 1920 there were over 2,000 English-language daily papers in 1,295 towns and cities, with a total circulation of 27.8 million. By 1930 circulation had reached 40 million. Although circulation increased, the number of newspapers fell—from 2,325 dailies in 1920 to 1,903 in 1933. The fall in number of weekly papers was even more marked, from 12,876 to 4,218 over the same period. While the **political party** affiliation of newspapers had declined since 1870, control of the press had become more concentrated in the hands of chains. By 1927 chains owned more than 230 newspapers: in 1929 the Scripps-Howard chain owned twenty-five daily newspapers; **William Randolph Hearst**'s company owned twenty dailies and eleven Sundays in thirteen cities. The 1920s saw the growth of the "**jazz**" or tabloid press with an emphasis on sensationalism. In 1919 Joseph Medill Patterson began the *Illustrated Daily News*, which became the *New York Daily News* in 1924 and had the largest single circulation of 750,000 as a consequence of its lurid tales, **crime** and sex stories, and use of photojournalism, such as the photograph of the execution of **Ruth Snyder**. Hearst established a rival tabloid in 1924, the *New York Daily Mirror*, and Bernarr MacFadden produced the even more salacious *New York Evening Graphic* later that year. The *New York Times*, in contrast, continued to build on its reputation as the national newspaper of record established after being taken over in 1896 by Adolph Simon Ochs and its emphasis on "All the News That's Fit to Print."

African American newspapers also reached a growing urban population during these years. During the 1920s the *Chicago Defender*, established in 1905 by **Robert S. Abbott**, became the leading black newspaper. Reaching an audience even in the South, the *Defender* played a part in encouraging the **Great Migration**. The New York *Amsterdam News* (1909) and *Pittsburgh Courier* (1910) were also important black newspapers.

Magazines for white middle-class readers were a major feature of the 1920s. The *Saturday Evening Post*, a long-established magazine, taken over by Cyrus Curtis in 1897, became one of the most popular magazines of the 1920s and 1930s with a circulation of over 1 million, famous for its covers by artists like J. C. Leyendecker and Norman Rockwell, and for its varied articles. Various magazines like *Collier's* continued to have a mass circulation, while progressively minded readers still supported *The Nation* and *New Republic*. New magazines with short articles providing coverage of current affairs or issues relevant to the day appeared in the form of the *Reader's Digest* established by De Witt Wallace in 1922, and *Time* created by **Henry Luce** and Briton Hadden in 1923.

Women were the target audience of *Ladies' Home Journal*, a magazine created in 1883 and already before **World War I** one of the most widely read for its mixture of recipes, household hints, short stories, and fashion—and advertising; *Good Housekeeping*, founded in 1885 and taken over by the Hearst Corporation in 1911, emphasized food and food production, and the phrase "the *Good Housekeeping* seal of approval" became established as a recommendation for kitchen products and appliances. Advertising also supported *Better Homes and Gardens* (1924), the very title of which suggested a comfortable and well-off readership. Condé Nast's *Dress and Vanity Fair* (1913), which became simply *Vanity Fair* in 1914, was more focused on fashion, but also included fairly wide-ranging articles of a literary nature, as did *The New Yorker* (1925) and **H. L. Mencken** and **George Nathan**'s *American Mercury* (1923). *Vanity Fair* closed in 1936, a victim of the **Great Depression**, but the others continued in one form or the other.

The 1920s also saw the rise of popular story magazines with an emphasis on sex and romance such as *True Story* (1919) *True Confessions* (1922), or crime fiction (often known as "pulp fiction") in *Argosy*, *Blue Book*, and *Short Stories*, all established before World War I and others like Mencken and Nathan's *Back Mask* launched in 1920. The **movies** also gave rise to a new genre of publication, the fan magazine covering the lives of stars and new motion pictures such as MacFadden's *Motion Picture Magazine* (1911–1977) and *Photoplay* (1911–1941).

See also EASTMAN, MAX FORRESTER (1883–1969); HAPGOOD, NORMAN (1868–1937); HELD, JOHN (1889–1958); SULLIVAN, MARK (1874–1952); TARBELL, IDA MINERVA (1857–1944); TROTTER,

WILLIAM MONROE (1872–1934); VAN DOREN, CARL (CLINTON) (1885–1950); VILLARD, OSWALD GARRISON (1872–1949); WHITE, WILLIAM ALLEN (1868–1944); WILSON, EDMUND (1895–1972).

NINETEENTH AMENDMENT. The Nineteenth Amendment to the Constitution, first introduced in 1878, ratified on 18 August 1920, recognized **women**'s right to vote. It had been passed by Congress in 1919 and achieved the two-thirds majority needed for ratification when it was approved by Tennessee. It came into effect with the elections in 1920. (See appendix 2.)

NONPARTISAN LEAGUE. The Nonpartisan League was established by the former Socialist **Charles A. Townley** in North Dakota in 1915, and it quickly spread into neighboring states. The League represented mainly farmers and others disgruntled by monopoly control in the wheat trade. It echoed many of the demands of the Populist movement in calling for public ownership of marketing facilities, grain elevators, flour mills, railroads, and banks. The program was adopted by the North Dakota legislature in 1919, and the movement had some electoral success in other Midwestern states. However, its membership declined following the war although elements of it were evident in the "Farm Bloc" and in the **Progressive Party** of 1924.

NORBECK, PETER (1870–1936). Peter Norbeck established an artesian well drilling company in South Dakota in the 1890s and was elected to the state senate, where he served from 1909 to 1915. He was one of the leaders of the **Progressive Republicans** who supported first **Robert M. La Follette** and then **Theodore Roosevelt** in 1912. Norbeck was elected lieutenant governor in 1914 and became governor of South Dakota in 1916 and 1918. As governor Norbeck led a program of reform that included rural credits for farmers, highway building schemes, workmen's compensation, and reform in state government. In 1920 Norbeck was elected to the U.S. Senate, where he served until his death. In Congress he supported farm relief programs such as the **McNary-Haugen** bills and the later Agricultural Adjustment Act (1933). Norbeck supported most **New Deal** measures.

NORRIS, GEORGE WILLIAM (1861–1944). George Norris qualified in law in Indiana in 1883. He moved to Nebraska in 1885 and established a law practice. A **Republican**, Norris won election as a county prosecuting attorney in 1892, judge in 1895, and congressman in the U.S. House of Representatives in 1902. He held that position until 1912, when he was elected to the U.S. Senate, a seat he held almost until his death. An independently minded progressive, Norris opposed U.S. intervention in the affairs of Latin American nations, and he supported neutrality in the war in Europe. Norris was one of the six senators (**Robert M. La Follette, James K. Vardaman, William Stone**, Asle J. Gronna [Republican, North Dakota], and Harry Lane [Democrat, Oregon] being the others) who voted against the declaration of war in 1917. He voted against the **Versailles Peace Treaty** and entry into the **League of Nations** in 1919.

Throughout the 1920s Norris increasingly sided with Republican insurgents in favor of policies to aid the farmers, and he supported the **McNary-Haugen** bills. He was particularly conspicuous in calling for public ownership and development of the **Muscle Shoals** facilities in Alabama. Norris was cosponsor of the **Norris-LaGuardia Anti-Injunction Act of 1932** that extended some protection to organized labor in the event of strikes. He also sponsored the **Twentieth Amendment** to the Constitution, ending the "lame duck" congresses that had sat from December to March following elections.

Although a Republican, Norris supported **Franklin D. Roosevelt** and the **New Deal** during the 1930s and led the fight in favor of the Tennessee Valley Authority (TVA) in 1933. He also increasingly supported Roosevelt in foreign affairs, moving away from his earlier **isolationist** stance. In 1936 Norris was reelected as an Independent Progressive but was defeated in 1942 and retired from public life.

NORRIS–LA GUARDIA ANTI-INJUNCTION ACT, 1932. Cosponsored by **George Norris** and **Fiorello La Guardia**, this act declared "Yellow Dog Contracts" that prohibited a worker from joining a union unenforceable in federal courts. It also prevented federal courts from issuing injunctions against striking workers, those encouraging others to strike, or those picketing, speaking, or writing in support of strikes. Similar measures were passed at state level in the following years.

See also TRADE UNIONS.

OGBURN, WILLIAM FIELDING (1886–1959). William Ogburn got a PhD in sociology from Columbia University in 1912 and then taught in Portland, Oregon, and at the University of Washington. He returned to Columbia in 1919 and taught there until 1927. He established his reputation with the publication of S*ocial Change with Respect to Cultural and Original Nature* (1922), in which he outlined his theory of "cultural lag," arguing that changes in material culture occur before changes in cultural life occur in response. He also later argued that because scientific discoveries were made by more than one person, inventions were inevitable. Ogburn's use of statistical analysis was also evident in his work on "How Women Vote" published in *Political Science Quarterly* [34] in 1919.

Ogburn was managing editor of the *Journal of the American Statistical Association* from 1920 to 1926 and became president of the American Sociological Society in 1929. In 1931 he was president of the American Statistical Association, and from 1937 to 1939 chair of the **Social Science Research Council**. In 1927 he became professor of sociology at the University of Chicago and in 1933 was appointed Sewell L. Avery Distinguished Service Professor. He remained at Chicago until his retirement in 1951. In 1929 Ogburn was one of several social scientists increasingly employed by the federal government when he was appointed director of president **Herbert Hoover**'s **Research Committee on Recent Social Trends**, which reported in 1933. From 1933 to 1935 he was director of the Consumer's Advisory Board of the National Recovery Administration, and from 1935 to 1943 a research consultant to the Science Committee of the National Resource Committee. Ogburn's *Sociology* (1940), written with Meyer Nimkoff, became a standard text for many years.

See also EDUCATION.

O'HARE, KATE RICHARDS (1876–1948). Born Carrie Kathleen Richards, Kate O'Hare worked as a machinist and was one of the first **women** to join the International Association of Machinists. After working in social welfare in Kansas City in the late 1890s, O'Hare became a Socialist, married

Patrick O'Hare, and trained as a party organizer. She wrote for the *Appeal to Reason* and in 1910 assumed leadership of the Kansas **Socialist Party**. O'Hare became a major figure on the socialist speaking circuit and held several leading positions in the party. She was a candidate for the party's vice presidential nomination in 1916 and she was the first ever woman to run for the U.S. Senate, albeit unsuccessfully. She consistently spoke out against U.S. involvement in **World War I** and was jailed under the **Espionage Act** following an antiwar speech in 1917. Woodrow Wilson commuted her sentence in 1920. O'Hare then campaigned for prison reform and an amnesty for all political prisoners. In the 1930s O'Hare supported **Upton Sinclair**'s End Poverty in California campaign, and then worked as assistant to the state director of the California Department of Penology.

O'KEEFE, GEORGIA (1887–1986). Georgia O'Keefe studied **art** in the Art Institute of Chicago and Art Students League in New York. In 1909 she began work as an illustrator in Chicago, briefly taught in Amarillo, Texas, and at the University of Virginia, and in 1915 at Columbia College in South Carolina. O'Keefe returned to New York in 1916, where her work was shown by **Alfred Stieglitz** in his 291 gallery. Stieglitz showed her work again in 1918, 1923, and 1924. Having married that year, Stieglitz was to show O'Keefe's work regularly thereafter and to include her and her work in his own photographs. O'Keefe's painting included Texan landscapes, close-ups of flowers and seashells, and studies of bones, skulls, and antlers in the New Mexico desert and incorporated rich vivid colors in powerful images. By the 1930s her work was widely viewed, and her reputation as one of America's leading artists was established. In 1946 the New York Museum of Modern Art showed her work in its first one-**woman** exhibition. O'Keefe continued painting through to the 1960s until her eyesight failed.

O'NEILL, EUGENE (1888–1953). Born Eugene Gladstone O'Neill, the future great dramatist had an erratic school education and spent two semesters at Princeton University, 1906–1907. From 1909 to 1912 O'Neill wandered various parts of the world—Honduras, Argentina—and worked his passage to England on a number of occasions. He was confined to a sanatorium due to ill health in 1912 but began writing one-act plays shortly thereafter. In 1914 O'Neill went to Harvard University, where he spent a year studying playwriting. After spending some time in **Greenwich Village**, O'Neill moved to Provincetown, Massachusetts, where, with a group of writers and artists, he formed "The Provincetown Players," who put on plays in New York City. Several of O'Neill's one-act plays were staged, and some were published in *Seven Arts* and *The Smart Set*. His first professional success came with *Beyond the Horizon*, awarded the Pulitzer Prize in 1920.

O'Neill produced a number of plays in 1919 and 1920, most significantly *The Emperor Jones* (1920). He received his second Pulitzer for *Anna Christie* (1921), and in 1923 he was awarded a gold medal by the National Institute of Arts and Letters. That same year *All God's Chillun Got Wings*, dealing with miscegenation, appeared, followed the next year by *Desire Under the Elms*, which dealt with incest.

O'Neill won his third Pulitzer for *Strange Interlude*, which appeared in 1928 and ran for over four hundred performances in New York City before it toured the United States and then Europe. Further success came with *Mourning Becomes Electra* in 1929. In 1936 O'Neill was awarded the Nobel Prize in Literature. In 1939 he completed one of his greatest works, *The Iceman Cometh*, and this was followed by *Long Day's Journey into Night* (1939–1941), which won a posthumous Pulitzer, and *A Moon for the Misbegotten* (1943). O'Neill was regarded as one of the greatest twentieth-century playwrights. He defied convention in terms of content, subject, and style.

See also LITERATURE AND THEATER.

OPEN SHOP MOVEMENT. *See* AMERICAN PLAN.

ORGANIC ACT OF PUERTO RICO, 1917. Also known as the Jones Act, the Organic Act of Puerto Rico was an amendment to the original legislation, the Foraker Act (1900), which had established a government of Puerto Rico following its acquisition from Spain in 1898. The legislation passed in 1917 conferred U.S. citizenship on Puerto Ricans and established an elected upper house. The power to veto legislation and appoint the governor and senior officials still remained with the U.S. president. Greater autonomy was granted in a further act of 1947, and Puerto Rico adopted its own constitution in 1952.

OVERMAN ACT, 1918. A measure introduced by senator Lee Overman of South Carolina in 1918. The Overman Act extended president **Woodrow Wilson**'s wartime powers to enable him to redistribute personnel, functions, and powers of federal agencies as necessary and without congressional approval.

See also WORLD WAR I, 1914–1918.

OVINGTON, MARY WHITE (1865–1951). After attending Packer Collegiate Institute and Radcliffe College, in 1893 Mary White Ovington opened a **settlement house** in New York City known as the Greenpoint Settlement of the Pratt Institute Neighborhood Association. Following her resignation due to illness in 1903, Ovington began to study the problems of **African Americans**. She became involved with the Niagara Movement, a protest organization formed by black leaders including **W. E. B. Du Bois**, and with the Lincoln settlement for African Americans. Her study, *Half Man: The Status of the Negro in New York*, was published in 1911. Ovington was instrumental in calling the meeting that led to the National Conference on the Negro following the race riot in Springfield, Illinois, in 1908. The outcome of the conference was the formation of the **National Association for the Advancement of Colored People** (NAACP) in 1910. Ovington held a number of positions in the NAACP and was chair of the board from 1919 until 1932, when she became treasurer. She retired from the NAACP in 1947.

See also WOMEN.

OWEN, CHANDLER (1889–1967). A graduate of Virginia Union University in Richmond, Chandler Owen moved to New York City, where he received one of the **National Urban League**'s first social work fellowships to study at Columbia University and the New York School of Philanthropy. Together with **A. Philip Randolph**, whom he met in 1915, Owen joined the **Socialist Party**. The two young **African Americans** established and edited *The Messenger*, a left-wing monthly journal, from 1917 to 1928. They were critical of American entry into **World War I**, which they opposed as a class war and a "white man's war." Owen and Randolph were charged under the **Sedition Act** with impeding the war effort, but a judge who could not accept that the antiwar publications were their own work dismissed the charges. Owen was inducted into the army in 1918 and served until the war ended.

During the **Red Scare** *The Messenger* was classed by the Justice Department as "the most dangerous Negro magazine," but the two editors escaped further prosecution. For a while Owen still supported the Socialist Party, and he ran for election to the New York state assembly in 1920 but failed. He and Randolph were extremely critical of **Marcus Garvey**, and in 1923 Owen was one of a number of African Americans who wrote to the attorney general urging speedy prosecution of the West Indian. In 1923 Owen moved to Chicago and edited the *Chicago Bee* and later became a regular columnist for the *Chicago Daily News*. He later joined the **Republican Party** and ran unsuccessfully for election to the House of Representatives in 1928. After 1941 both Owen and Randolph were supporters of U.S. involvement in World War II and Owen wrote a widely circulated government pamphlet, *Negroes and the War*, in 1942. He also wrote speeches for the Republican presidential candidates Wendell Willkie and Thomas Dewey and later campaigned on behalf of Dwight D. Eisenhower. Owen's influence was, however, largely limited to the 1920s and 1930s.

OWEN, RUTH BRYAN (1885–1954). Ruth Owen, daughter of **William Jennings Bryan**, was educated at the University of Nebraska. Owen married a British man, and after spending several years in Jamaica, West Indies, she moved to London, England, in 1912. Owen worked with the American Women's War Relief Fund during **World War I** and served as a nurse in the Voluntary Aid Detachment during the Egypt-Palestine campaign, 1915–1918. After the war, Owen settled in Miami, where she was a Lyceum and Chautauqua lecturer, vice president of the University of Miami board of regents, and a member of the faculty, 1926–1928.

Owen was the first **woman** elected to Congress from Florida when she became the **Democratic Party** representative in 1928. Her election was challenged on the grounds that she had not been a citizen for the required period (having taken her husband's citizenship on marriage). Owen won her case— her husband had died and she had "renaturalized"—and she was reelected in 1930. She failed to regain the nomination in 1932 but became the first American woman diplomat when **Franklin D. Roosevelt** appointed her minister to Denmark in 1933. Owen held the position until 1936, when she resigned, having married a Dane. Owen was a member of the Advisory Board of the Federal Reformatory for Women, 1938–1954, and in 1945 acted as a special assistant at the San Francisco Conference. She continued to lecture and to write on various subjects.

P

PACIFICISM. *See* PEACE MOVEMENTS

PACT OF PARIS. *See* KELLOGG-BRIAND PACT.

PALMER, A. (ALEXANDER) MITCHELL (1872–1936). The **Democratic Party** politician and attorney general A. Mitchell Palmer was educated at Swarthmore College and worked as an attorney in Pennsylvania. He served in the House of Representatives from 1909 to 1915. As a member of the Democratic Party National Committee he helped secure the nomination for **Woodrow Wilson** in 1912. Palmer was defeated in his bid to become a U.S. senator in 1914 by the conservative Republican Boies Penrose. In 1916 Wilson appointed him **Alien Property Custodian** responsible for enemy-owned property in the United States during **World War I**. He became attorney general in 1918. Palmer used wartime powers to obtain injunctions against striking miners and railroad workers in 1919.

In response to pressures from Congress, the wave of postwar strikes, and several bomb attacks in 1919, including one on his own home, which encouraged the belief that an attempted revolution was imminent (a fear known as the as **Red Scare**), he instigated the **Palmer Raids** of January 1920. It was believed that Palmer hoped to win the Democratic presidential nomination by capitalizing on antiradical feelings, but his biographer points out that Palmer, who had a Quaker and reform background, had been criticized for delay in dealing with the imagined revolutionary threat. The criticism provoked by his actions, particularly against labor, ensured his defeat in the campaign for the presidential nomination, and he returned to his private law practice. Palmer's last significant political act was to draft the Democratic platform in 1932. He was working on the platform for 1936 when he died.

PALMER RAIDS, 1919–1920. Following a wave of industrial strikes and a postal bombing campaign in April and June 1919, attorney general **A. Mitchell Palmer** determined to crack down on radical activities. Using the powers provided in the 1918 Immigration Act, on 7 November 1919 the

Justice Department arrested some six hundred people in raids in eleven different cities across the country. A further three thousand people were detained in a second series of raids in January 1920. Over eight hundred were deported as undesirable aliens, among them the longtime residents in the United States anarchists **Emma Goldman** and **Alexander Berkman**, but the vast majority of the arrests were dismissed by the acting secretary of labor, Louis B. Post. When the Bolshevik rising predicted by Palmer (advised by **J. Edgar Hoover**) for 1 May failed to occur, there was increasing criticism of Palmer's actions and the threat to civil liberties involved.

See also RED SCARE, 1919; WALL STREET BOMBING, 1920.

PARIS PEACE CONFERENCE. *See* VERSAILLES PEACE CONFERENCE.

PARKER, DOROTHY (1893–1967). Dorothy Parker had her first poem published in *Vanity Fair* in 1915, and she was hired as a caption writer, first for *Vogue* then for *Vanity Fair*. In 1918 she succeeded P. G. Wodehouse as the drama critic at *Vanity Fair*. Parker also published some of her more acerbic and satirical pieces in *Ainslee's* and *Life*, and she wrote fiction and essays for the *Saturday Evening Post* and *Ladies' Home Journal*. Parker was soon well known for her wit, puns, and epigrams. Parker's first book of poems, *Enough Rope*, was published in 1926, and her second, *Sunset Gun*, in 1928. As well as a humorist and a poet, Parker expressed social concerns about racial and gender discrimination. In 1927 she was arrested in Boston for protesting against the execution of **Sacco and Vanzetti**.

In 1927 Parker joined the staff of the *New Yorker* as a book reviewer and later as drama critic. Two volumes of her short stories, *Laments for the Living* and *After Such Pleasures*, were published in 1930 and 1933, and her third volume of poetry, *Death and Taxes*, appeared in 1931. During the 1930s Parker turned to writing Hollywood screenplays. She also helped to organize the Anti-Nazi League and she reported on the Spanish Civil War. As a consequence of her activities in the 1930s the House Un-American Affairs Committee questioned Parker in 1952. During the 1950s she wrote very little. She was inducted into the American Academy of Arts and Letters in 1959 and taught briefly at California State College, Los Angeles, in the 1960s. She lived most of her last years in solitude in New York City, where she died.

See also LITERATURE AND THEATER; NEWSPAPERS AND MAGAZINES; WOMEN.

PAUL, ALICE (1885–1977). A Quaker, Alice Paul was educated at Swarthmore College and the University of Pennsylvania, where she gained her PhD in 1912. She later gained a law degree from Washington College and a PhD in law from American University in 1928. Paul studied at Woodbridge Quaker College in England and the London School of Economics from 1907 to 1910. Paul was active in the British suffragette movement, and after returning to the United States in 1910 she organized demonstrations for the **National American Woman Suffrage Association**.

In 1916 Paul and **Lucy Burns** established the more militant **National Woman's Party**. She mobilized pickets outside the White House in 1917, demanding that "America be made safe for democracy" and was jailed. When she went on hunger strike, Paul was force-fed. Once the vote had been gained Paul led the campaign for equal rights in support of the **Equal Rights Amendment** first introduced in 1923. In the 1930s Paul traveled to Europe, where she established a World Woman's Party. She continued to campaign for the Equal Rights Amendment and in the 1960s was involved in protests against the war in Vietnam.

See also WOMEN'S SUFFRAGE MOVEMENT.

PEACE MOVEMENTS. Peace movements had a long history in the United States stretching back to the late eighteenth to early nineteenth centuries and Quaker and other religious groups. The "largest and oldest" group still in existence in 1900 was the American Peace Society (APS), formed in 1828. The peace movement experienced a surge of interest following the Spanish-American War (1898) and in response to international imperialism. **Progressivism** too, with its emphasis on rational solutions to man-made problems, encouraged action to outlaw war as a means of settling disputes. Many Americans attended the first Hague Peace Conference in 1899, and between 1901 and 1914 some forty-five new peace organizations came into existence in the United States. Chief among these were **Jane Addams**'s International Welfare Organization (1904), **Elihu Root**'s American Society of International Law (1906), and the World Peace Foundation and Carnegie Endowment for Peace, both formed in 1910.

The American peace activists continued their campaigns after the outbreak of **World War I** in 1914 and called for a negotiated peace. A Woman's Peace Parade in New York City in August 1914 led to the formation of the **Woman's Peace Party** (WPP) in 1915 involving **Carrie Chapman Catt** and **Rosika Schwimmer**. The WPP lost some support following its backing of **Henry Ford**'s failed "Peace Ship" mission in 1915, and it lost more supporters after the United States entered the war in 1917. **Women**'s involvement in the international peace movement found fruition in the Women's International League for Peace and Freedom (WILPF) formed in The Hague in April 1915 with Jane Addams as its first president.

After 1917 the American peace movement was thrown into disarray as most organizations patriotically supported the war. Opposition to the war came chiefly from the **Socialist Party** and radical peace activists who formed the **American Union Against Militarism**. The terms of the **Treaty of Versailles** also divided American peace activists as some felt the terms were too harsh, and others were prepared to accept it in order to ensure participation in the **League of Nations**. The postwar reactions to the horrors of World War I did, however, lead to support for disarmament and backing for the **Washington** and **London Naval Conferences** and the **Kellogg-Briand Pact**. New organizations like the Women's Committee for World Disarmament and National Council for Prevention of War joined the older groups in the 1920s.

PEEK, GEORGE NELSON (1873–1943). George Peek studied briefly at Northwestern University, Illinois, in 1891. He then worked first as an office assistant and subsequently found employment with Deere and Webber, a branch of the John Deere Plow Company. In 1901 Peek became general manager of the Deere Company in Omaha, and in 1914 vice president in charge of sales in Deere's main offices in Moline, Illinois. During **World War I** he was an industrial representative on the **War Industries Board** and in 1918 became commissioner of finished products. In 1919 secretary of commerce William C. Redfield appointed Peek to chair the Industrial Board of the **Department of Commerce**, but Peek resigned after a few months due to conflict with the railroad director, **Walker D. Hines**, over price issues.

From 1919 to 1923 Peek was president and general manager of the Moline Plow Company. He resigned over differences with the company's vice president, **Hugh S. Johnson**. As president of the American Council of Agriculture Peek supported government farm-support initiatives as proposed in the **McNary-Haugen** bills between 1924 and 1928. He was an active supporter of **Franklin D. Roosevelt** in 1932 and was appointed to head the Agricultural Adjustment Administration (AAA) in 1933. However, Peek did not accept that there was a farm surplus and opposed the program to reduce production at the heart of the AAA and Roosevelt was forced to ask for his resignation after a few months. He was appointed instead as adviser on foreign trade and president of the Export-Import Bank, but again differences over policy led to his resignation in 1935. Peek increasingly became a critic of **New Deal** farm policies and of Roosevelt's interventionist policies. Peek was a member of the national committee of the America First Committee established in 1940 to keep the United States out of the European war.

See also ECONOMY; FARMING.

PERKINS, FRANCES (1882–1965). Born Fannie Coralie Perkins, Frances Perkins was a graduate of Mount Holyoke College and Columbia University. She became executive secretary of the New York Consumer's League from 1910 to 1912 and worked as an authority on industrial safety with the New York Committee of Safety (1912–1917). Perkins served on the Industrial Commission of New York State in 1921 and was appointed chair of the New York State Industrial Board in 1926. She held the position until 1929, when she became New York secretary of labor under Governor **Franklin D. Roosevelt**. Following his election to the presidency, Roosevelt made Perkins the first woman cabinet officer when he appointed her secretary of labor in 1933. Perkins was a member of the U.S. Civil Service Commission in 1946. She held a number of teaching positions after World War II, and in the late 1950s held a visiting professorship at Cornell.

See also WOMEN.

PERMANENT COURT OF INTERNATIONAL JUSTICE. Often referred to as the World Court, the Permanent Court of International Justice was established under Article XIV of the covenant of the **League of Nations**. It was intended that the court would act as arbiter in international disputes and offer advice on disputes to the Council of the League. Although the United States did not become a member, **Charles Evans Hughes** and **Frank B. Kellogg** were among four Americans who served as judges.

PERSHING, JOHN JOSEPH (1860–1948). Pershing was a career soldier who graduated from West Point in 1886 and served in the Indian wars and Spanish-American War (1898). In 1916 he led the **punitive expedition** into **Mexico** in pursuit of Francisco "Pancho" Villa following the attack on **Columbus**, New Mexico. Although unsuccessful, Pershing carried out his orders to the letter and without upsetting the Mexican government. As a result he became commander in chief of the **American Expeditionary Force (AEF)** in 1917. He successfully maintained the unity of the American army rather than have it divided among other **Allied** forces, and he supported the strategy of concentrating on the western front over other theaters in the war. In 1921 Pershing was appointed chief of staff of the U.S. Army, a position he held until he retired in 1924.

PICKFORD, MARY (1892–1979). Mary Pickford, who was to become one of the great stars of the silent **movies**, was born Gladys Louise Smith in Toronto, Canada. When her father died in 1897 the family turned to the stage to make a living. After some success on Broadway, Pickford turned to movies in 1909 when she found work at the Biograph studio with director **D. W. Griffith**, with whom she made over twenty films. After a brief return to

Broadway, Pickford joined **Adolph Zukor**, head of the Famous Players company, which eventually became Paramount studios. In the five years at Famous Players Pickford achieved enormous financial success, having negotiated a share of net profits from her movies. Her many roles, in films such as *A Poor Little Rich Girl* (1917) and *Rebecca of Sunnybrook Farm* (1917), generally depicted a very young, almost childlike figure with the distinctive girlish curls by which she became known.

In 1917 Pickford met **Douglas Fairbanks** and together with **Charlie Chaplin** and D. W. Griffith, they established the United Artists Company. She and Fairbanks married in 1920. During their honeymoon in Europe crowds of ecstatic fans mobbed them. Her first films with United Artists, *Pollyanna* (1920) and *Little Lord Fauntleroy* (1920) (in which she played both the boy of the title and his mother), were major successes. Attempts to play more adult roles were less successful, and she returned to her normal type in the box-office smash *Little Annie Rooney* in 1925. However, it was becoming increasingly difficult for Pickford to play the young parts. In 1928 she was given an Academy Award for best actress in her first talkie, *Coquette*. In 1929 she costarred for the first and only time with Fairbanks in *The Taming of the Shrew*. She effectively retired from acting in 1933, and she and Fairbanks were divorced in 1935. In 1934 Pickford's book *Why Not Try God?* was a best seller and she wrote a novel, *The Demi-Widow*, in 1935 and her autobiography, *Sunshine and Shadow*, in 1955. She became more and more a recluse in later years and sent a taped message of thanks to the Motion Picture Academy in 1976 in response to the award of an honorary Oscar.

See also WOMEN.

PINCHOT, AMOS RICHARDS ENO (1873–1944). Not as well-known as his famous older brother, **Gifford Pinchot**, Amos Pinchot studied at Yale University and dropped out of Columbia Law School to serve in the Spanish-American War, 1898. He subsequently qualified in law, served briefly as deputy district attorney in New York City (1900–1901), and became active in politics following Gifford Pinchot's dismissal in 1910. Amos Pinchot became committed to exposing what he saw as the threat to government of organized wealth, and he wrote several articles on the subject. Together with Gifford he established the National Progressive Republican League in 1911 to secure the election of progressive candidates and supported the creation of the **Progressive Party**.

Pinchot opposed America's entry into **World War I** and supported conscientious objectors. In 1920 he headed the **Committee of Forty-Eight** in an attempt to resurrect the defunct Progressive Party. His *History of the Progressive Party* was published posthumously in 1958. Pinchot was opposed to **Franklin D. Roosevelt**'s **New Deal** and was an early member of the **isolationist** America First Committee.

PINCHOT, GIFFORD (1865–1946). The first head of the forestry division in the Department of Agriculture in 1898 and then the U.S. Forest Service in 1905, Pinchot graduated from Yale University in 1889 and studied conservation in France and Germany. In 1896 he was appointed to the National Forest Commission and became head of the Division of Forestry in the Department of Agriculture in 1898. Pinchot became a leader in the conservation movement in the administration of **Theodore Roosevelt**. Pinchot favored controlled commercial use of the national forest reserves rather their preservation simply as wilderness areas. His conflict with president **William Howard Taft**'s secretary of the interior, **Richard A. Ballinger**, over conservation practices in Alaska led to Pinchot's dismissal in 1910 and resulted in division in the **Republican Party**. Pinchot and his brother, **Amos**, were involved in founding the National Progressive Republican League in 1911 and aiding the return of Roosevelt to the political arena. After campaigning on Roosevelt's behalf Pinchot established and taught at the forestry school at Yale and was then elected governor of Pennsylvania in 1923 until 1927 and again from 1931 to 1935. He modernized the Pennsylvania administration and increased regulation of state utilities. He also introduced a "mini-**New Deal**" in the state during the **Depression**.

PLUMB PLAN. Proposed in 1919 by Glenn E. Plumb, counsel for **railroad** unions, the plan called for a degree of federal-public ownership of the railroads to replace the wartime Railroad Administration. The government would purchase the railroads at approved values, and a corporation representing government, employees, and operators would run the system. Congress did not accept the measure, but the railroads experienced greater government regulation after 1920.

POLITICAL PARTIES. The **Republican** and **Democratic** parties continued to be the main political groups throughout this period. The Democrats under **Woodrow Wilson** had captured the White House in 1912, when **Theodore Roosevelt** effectively divided the Republican vote by standing as a candidate for the **Progressive Party**. Wilson was reelected in 1916, but following **World War I** the Republicans regained control of the White House with the election of **Warren Harding** in 1920. The period of Republican control continued with the presidencies of **Calvin Coolidge** (1923–1929), who succeeded Harding after his death in 1923, and **Herbert Hoover** (1929–1933). The Republican Party also had majorities in both Senate and House of Representatives from 1919 on, a position that was only reversed after the onset of the **Great Depression** and the return of the Democrats to the White House with the election of **Franklin D. Roosevelt** in 1932.

The Progressive Party fielded a presidential candidate again in 1924 with **Robert M. La Follette** but won only 16.6 percent of the popular vote and thirteen Electoral College votes. Other minority parties fielded candidates in the presidential elections: the **Socialist Party** in 1912, 1916, 1920, and 1928—in 1924 it endorsed La Follette's candidacy; the **Socialist Labor Party** in every election between 1916 and 1932; the Prohibition Party also fielded candidates in every election even after the passage of the **Eighteenth Amendment** in 1920. The **Farmer-Labor Party** contested the 1920 election but merged with the Progressives in 1924. The **Communist Party USA** had candidates in presidential elections from 1928 onward.

POMERENE, ATLEE (1863–1937). Atlee Pomerene qualified in law and was admitted to the bar in Cincinnati in 1886. He served on the city board of education and in 1896 was elected county prosecuting attorney. As a **Democrat** he was a supporter of the reformer Tom L. Johnson. In 1910 Pomerene was elected as Ohio's lieutenant governor, but the state legislature immediately chose him as U.S. senator. Pomerene was reelected in 1916 and won a reputation as an independent-minded progressive. He opposed both the **Eighteenth** and **Nineteenth Amendments** and failed to retain his seat in the 1922 election. In 1924 president **Calvin Coolidge** named Pomerene as one of the two special counsels to prosecute those involved in the **Teapot Dome** scandals. He successfully secured the cancellation of the leases and the conviction of **Albert Fall** for taking bribes. In 1927 he was appointed as special assistant to the attorney general to assist in further related prosecutions. Pomerene failed to gain reelection to the Senate in 1926 and failed to gain the Democratic nomination for the presidency in 1928. President **Herbert Hoover** named Pomerene to chair the **Reconstruction Finance Corporation** in 1932, but his nomination was never confirmed. Pomerene was an outspoken critic of the **New Deal**, particularly its banking and farm policies.

POPULATION. The U.S. population continued to grow during the interwar years but at a marginally slower rate due to declining **immigration** figures. The total population in 1910 was 92.2 million; in 1920 it was 106.4 million; and in 1930 122.7 million. Immigration in the decade 1901–1910 had been 8.795 million (8 million from Europe); for 1911–1920 it was 5.73 million, and for 1921–1930, 4.1 million. Men outnumbered **women** in the population by 2.1 million in 1920, but this had fallen by 500,000 in 1930. The **African American** population numbered 9.8 million in 1910 and 11.8 million by 1930. This represented approximately 10 percent of the population. In 1920 for the first time more than 50 percent of the population was classed as urban. The largest cities were New York City, Chicago, and by 1930, Detroit, respectively.

PORTER, COLE (1891–1964). The prolific songwriter Cole Porter was educated at Worcester Academy, Yale, and Harvard's law and **music** schools. Having already written several musical comedies and hundreds of songs at Yale, in 1916 he and T. Lawrason Riggs wrote a musical comedy, *See America First*, produced on Broadway in 1916. Porter went to France in 1917. A number of his songs were included in English musical shows from 1918 to 1922. Porter's music was included in *Within the Quota* performed in Paris and New York in 1923, the *Greenwich Village Follies* in 1924, *Paris* in 1928, *La Revue des Ambassadeurs* (Paris, 1928), and *Wake Up and Dream* (London, 1929). Porter rose to even greater prominence in the 1930s with songs for shows and **movies**, the most famous being "Night and Day" from *The Gay Divorcee* (1932), "I Get a Kick Out of You" from *Anything Goes* (1934), "Begin the Beguine" from *Jubilee* (1935), "I've Got You Under My Skin" from the movie *Born to Dance* (1936), and "In the Still of the Night" in the film *Rosalie* (1937). He continued to write through the 1940s and 1950s, most notably for *Kiss Me, Kate* (1948), *Can-Can* (1953), and the film *High Society* (1956) for which Porter's song "True Love" won an Academy Award. However, Porter's sophisticated, languid, and often-sensual music seemed to belong more appropriately in the interwar period.

See also MUSIC.

POUND, EZRA (WESTON) LOOMIS (1885–1972). Ezra Pound studied at the University of Pennsylvania and Hamilton College in Clinton, New York, and graduated with an MA from Pennsylvania in 1906. After being dismissed from a teaching position in 1907 for "bohemian" behavior, Pound traveled in Europe before settling in London, where he became part of the literary avant-garde from 1908 until 1920. He remained an expatriate for the rest of his life. Pound's first volume of poetry, *A Lume Spento*, was published in 1908. This was followed by *Personae* (1909), *Canzoni* (1911), and *Ripostes* (1912). During this period Pound established the Imagist movement and later joined the Vorticists with whom he published two volumes of *BLAST: A Review of the Great English Vortex* between 1914 and 1915. After **World War I** Pound published *Hugh Selwyn Mauberley* (1920) and worked with **T. S. Eliot** on Eliot's manuscript of the *Waste Land*. In 1921 Pound joined the expatriate set including **Gertrude Stein** and **Ernest Hemingway** in Paris, but in 1924 moved to Rapallo, Italy, where he remained until the end of World War II.

During the interwar period Pound produced his *Cantos* series of poems, published from 1925 to 1940. He increasingly identified with Italy and Mussolini and between 1941 and 1943 made several broadcasts for Radio Rome attacking U.S. policies. Accused of treason, Pound was arrested in 1945, and after an imprisonment in Pisa was transferred to Washington, D.C., where he was found unfit to stand trial. From 1945 until 1958 Pound was held in an insane asylum. His work the *Pisan Cantos* appeared in 1948 and was awarded the Bollingen poetry prize in 1949. Pound was awarded the Pulitzer Prize in Poetry in 1950. Those who felt that Pound had been a traitor during the war criticized both awards. Pound published several other works before his death, but none reached the levels of his earlier poetry.

See also LITERATURE AND THEATER.

PRESIDENT'S EMERGENCY COMMITTEE FOR EMPLOYMENT, 1930–1931. Established by president **Herbert Hoover** in 1930 the Committee for Employment consisted of the secretaries of agriculture, commerce, interior, labor, and the treasury and was intended to encourage local and state relief activity in response to the **Great Depression**. Provided with only a limited budget, the committee could do very little, and it was replaced by the **President's Organization on Unemployment Relief** (POUR).

PRESIDENT'S ORGANIZATION ON UNEMPLOYMENT RELIEF (POUR), 1931–1932. **Herbert Hoover** established the President's Organization on Unemployment Relief in 1931 to encourage, coordinate, and gather information about local and state provision of relief for the increasing number of people left unemployed. Chaired by **Walter Gifford**, the organization relied on traditional voluntary and charitable relief agencies to tackle the problems of the **Great Depression**, and it soon proved ineffectual.

PRESIDENT'S RESEARCH COMMITTEE ON RECENT SOCIAL TRENDS. Established by President **Hoover** in 1929, the Committee on Recent Social Trends was instructed to carry out a survey of the nation's social development to provide a basis for future government policy. The committee of leading social scientists and other academics was chaired jointly by **Charles Merriam** and **Wesley Mitchell**, and funded by the Laura Spelman Rockefeller Memorial. Its detailed report, published as *Recent Social Trends in the United States* in 1933, provided a useful source of information for future historians but was little use at the time as the country was hit by the **Great Depression**.

See also EDUCATION.

PRESIDENT'S UNEMPLOYMENT CONFERENCE, 1921. Suggested and chaired by secretary of commerce **Herbert Hoover**, president **Warren Harding** called a conference of social scientists and trade officials in response to the recession following World War I. The committee called for local voluntary relief programs and for detailed study of economic trends. Such a study was undertaken under the leadership of **Wesley Clair Mitchell**

between 1927 and 1929 and resulted in a two-volume study, *Recent Economic Changes in the United States* (1929). Much of the report was made redundant by the impact of the **Depression**.

PROGRESSIVISM. The "Progressive era" was the period from about 1890 to World **War I** in which Americans from different backgrounds and **political parties** responded to the problems produced by the rapid industrialization and urbanization of the United States. Progressivism was a diverse movement that almost defies definition. On the one hand, reformers wanted to regulate industry to allow for fairer competition, protect workers and consumers, and on the other, they wished to democratize the political processes and make government more accountable. They also attempted to tackle urban problems such as poor housing, sanitation, and public transport, and many reformers worked in the **settlement houses**. Some reformers were more concerned with moral issues such as **prohibition** or prostitution, while others emphasized "Americanization" and issues related to **immigration**.

The origins of the Progressive movement lay in the earlier agrarian Populist movement and abolitionism. It also reflected a religious revival with the rise of the "Social Gospel" and development of the Young Men's Christian Association (YMCA) (1851) and the Salvation Army (1880). The increase in the number of college-educated professional workers influenced by the new social sciences and also by "human interest" stories written in the new journals such as *Harper's* and *McClure's* by journalists (described by **Theodore Roosevelt** as "Muckrakers") was also an important factor. Significant too was the rise in the number of college-educated **women**, many of whom found an outlet for their skills in the settlement houses. Increased employment of women brought calls for regulation and reform, and many women contributed to the growing call for **women's suffrage**. A wave of social unrest with violent strikes in the 1890s, and the rise of new movements like the **Socialist Party of America** and **Industrial Workers of the World**, motivated many among the middle classes to demand reform.

As the Progressive movement spread from the city to state to national level, it influenced both major parties and spawned new ones, such as the **Progressive Party** and Prohibition Party. In 1912 the presidential election was contested by **Woodrow Wilson** (Democrat), **William Howard Taft** (Republican), Roosevelt (Progressive), and **Eugene V. Debs** (Socialist Party), all of whom could claim to be progressive.

Among the Progressive movement's many accomplishments were: reform in city and state government, improvements in housing and the provision of public utilities, regulation of industry to improve safety and to protect workers, regulation of monopolies to make for fairer competition, **tariff** regulation, protection for consumers, and a more democratic political system with the use of referenda, initiatives, recall, the direct election of senators (**Seventeenth Amendment**), and votes for women (**Nineteenth Amendment**). Some progressives also supported prohibition and immigration control.

PROGRESSIVE PARTY, 1912. The Progressive Party, or "Bull Moose" Party, sprang from **Republicans** disaffected with **William Howard Taft**'s presidency. Originally supporting **Robert M. La Follette**, the dissidents threw their backing behind **Theodore Roosevelt** and his "New Nationalism" in February 1912. When the Republican Party managers ensured that Taft was renominated despite overwhelming victories for Roosevelt in the primaries, Roosevelt and his followers broke away to establish the Progressive Party in August 1912 with Roosevelt as presidential candidate and **Hiram Johnson** as his running mate. The party platform included political reform, **women's suffrage**, further antitrust legislation, **tariff** reform, prohibition of **child labor** and regulation of female labor, and legislation to protect workers. In the election Roosevelt was ahead of Taft with over 4 million votes, but the split in the Republican Party gave victory to the Democrats and **Woodrow Wilson**.
    See also POLITICAL PARTIES.

PROGRESSIVE PARTY, 1924. Republicans disillusioned with the return to conservatism in the postwar era joined forces with elements of the "**Farm Bloc**," members of the **American Federation of Labor**, and Socialists to endorse the third-party candidacy of **Robert M. La Follette**. The party platform called for further legislation against monopolies, greater farm relief, and the public ownership of utilities and the **railroads**. La Follette won almost 5 million votes and carried his own state of Wisconsin but trailed in third behind **Calvin Coolidge** and **John W. Davis**.
    See also POLITICAL PARTIES.

PROHIBITION. The Prohibition movement had its origins in the temperance movement, which began in colonial America and grew with the religious and reform movements of the 1830s. The Prohibition Party originated in 1869 and in 1892 the party gained over 270,000 votes in the presidential election. **Women**'s groups were particularly associated with the movement and in 1874 the Women's Christian Temperance Union (WCTU) was founded in Cleveland, Ohio. Led by Frances Willard from 1879–1898, the WCTU was a powerful force. It was aided by the Anti-Saloon League created in 1893, and together the organizations mobilized a campaign to achieve the legal prohibition of alcohol. By 1914 fourteen states had passed Prohibition legislation.

During **World War I** the need to conserve grain and anti-German feelings directed against brewers strengthened the call for national prohibition. In December 1917 Congress passed the **Eighteenth Amendment**. It was ratified on 16 January 1919. The legal ban on the manufacture, sale, or transportation of alcohol in the United States came into force following the passage of the amendment and **National Prohibition Act** (known as the Volstead Act) from midnight on 16 January 1920 until its repeal in 1933. Prohibition gave the 1920s a colorful reputation for violence and lawlessness associated with the rise of criminal organizations producing and distributing "**bootleg**" alcohol to "speakeasies" (illegal saloons) as it appeared that broad sections of the public were prepared to break the law. However, annual per capita consumption of alcohol fell from 2.6 gallons before the war to 0.97 gallons in 1934. Opposition was mobilized by the Association Against the Prohibition Amendment, which secured the passage of the **Twenty-first Amendment** in December 1933. After repeal liquor control once more became a matter of state rather than federal government.

See also CRIME AND POLICING; POLITICAL PARTIES; PROGRESSIVISM.

PUERTO RICO. *See* ORGANIC ACT OF PUERTO RICO, 1917.

PUNITIVE EXPEDITION, 1916–1917. Following the murder of sixteen American citizens taken from a train near Chihuahua City, **Mexico**, and of nineteen more in an attack on **Columbus**, New Mexico, by **Pancho Villa**, a force of fifteen thousand American troops led by Brigadier General **John Pershing** crossed into Mexico on 15 March 1916 in pursuit of Villa and his men. Initially the Mexican government agreed to this punitive raid, but as U.S. troops penetrated several hundred miles into Mexico, there were armed clashes with Mexican troops with casualties sustained on both sides. As relations deteriorated war between the United States and Mexico seemed a real possibility. Protracted negotiations took place from September to January 1917, and finally **Woodrow Wilson**'s administration recalled the expedition in February although Villa had not been captured.

See FOREIGN POLICY.

QUOTA ACT, 1921. Also known as the Emergency Quota Act, this legislation, signed on 19 May 1921, was one of the first of president **Warren Harding**'s administration. The act limited the number of **immigrants** from any nationality to 3 percent of the number of that nationality resident in the United States as determined by the census of 1910. The measure, which was renewed in 1922 for a further two years, was intended to favor immigrants from northern and western Europe over those of southern and eastern Europe. When it failed to achieve this objective, it was replaced by the **Quota Act of 1924.**

QUOTA ACT, 1924. Also known as the Johnson-Reed Act or Immigration Act, the Quota Act of 1924 replaced the Emergency Quota Act. It reduced the proportion of **immigrants** of any national group to 2 percent of that nationality resident in the United States in 1890, and was intended to reduce the number of "new" immigrants arriving from southern and eastern European countries. While it exempted countries in the western hemisphere, it abrogated previous agreements with Japan and prohibited all further immigration from that country. Under the legislation a new quota based on the proportion of people from any nationality group to the American population as a whole residing in the United States in 1920 was to come into effect in 1927 with a maximum total immigration of 150,000.

R

RADIO. Before **World War I** radio, only developed in the 1890s by Guglielmo Marconi, was still in its infancy and used as a means of communication between individuals. New developments, particularly during **World War I**, enabled the transmission of sound and a shift in emphasis to broadcasting to a wide audience. The Radio Corporation of America (RCA) was chartered in 1919, and the first announced broadcast was made when the Westinghouse Company's KDKA station in Pittsburgh broadcast the presidential election returns on 2 November 1920. The new medium spread rapidly—by 1922 3 million homes had radios and by the mid-1920s there were 530 local stations with an estimated audience of 50 million. The RCA network was joined by the National Broadcasting Company (NBC) in 1926 and the Columbia Broadcasting System (CBS) in 1927. Federal regulation was initiated with the **Federal Radio Commission** in 1927. The spread of commercial radio encouraged the consumer boom through advertising and with the **movies** helped to further "nationalize" American culture.

See also NEWSPAPERS AND MAGAZINES.

RAILROAD LABOR ACT, 1926. Following the bitter **railroad strike of 1922**, the Railroad Labor Act (known as the Watson-Parker Act) abolished the **Railroad Labor Board** and replaced it with a National Board of Mediation. The Board of Mediation was to hear all disputes not settled by bipartisan boards of adjustment created by **railroads** to represent management and labor. Where settlements were not reached the Board could refer disputes to courts of arbitration. The intention of the act was to allow collective bargaining and voluntary agreements to settle disputes in the railroad industry. However, the railroads failed to establish boards of adjustment and continued to maintain company unions, and the board had no power to impose penalties on the employers. Nonetheless, the act marked a step toward union recognition in the railroads. In providing a mechanism for mediating public disputes and introduced a cooling-off period in which no changes could be made to existing conditions, it also brought some peace to the troubled industry.

See also TRADE UNIONS.

RAILROAD LABOR BOARD. Created under the **Railroad Transportation Act** of 1920, the Railroad Labor Board was a nine-man tribunal with three members each representing public, labor, and management respectively and empowered to settle labor disputes and make awards relating to hours and wages. However, the Board proved unable to enforce its decisions and was abolished in 1926 by the **Railroad Labor Act**.

See also RAILROADS.

RAILROADS. The railroad industry, which began in the early nineteenth century and grew with increasing rapidity from the 1830s on, was central to American economic growth. By 1860 there were over thirty thousand miles of rail track in the United States, two-thirds of it in northern states. The greatest wave of railroad construction came after the Civil War in conjunction with westward expansion and settlement and massive industrialization in the east. The first transcontinental railroad was completed in 1869, and by the start of the twentieth century over two hundred thousand miles of track had been laid.

The railroad industry also witnessed the development of huge corporations headed by entrepreneurs often described as "robber barons." Despite the beginning of regulation with the creation of the Interstate Commerce Commission in 1886, the ruthless profiteering and shady business practices of such men led to calls for reform and were a key element in both the Populist and **Progressive** movements. Legislation aimed at curbing railroad monopolies and the control of the rates charged by companies was passed under both **Theodore Roosevelt** and **Woodrow Wilson**. During **World War I** the government took over the running of the railroads and although there were calls for this to continue, they were returned to private ownership under the **Railroad Transportation Act** of 1920. Postwar readjustments led to labor conflict in the industry and a major **railroad strike** in 1922. The development of the **automobile** and of air transportation, and the earlier overexpansion of uneconomic lines, placed the industry in an increasingly unfavorable position from the 1920s on. Railroad mileage, which had peaked at 254,000 miles in 1916, had fallen to 249,619 by 1930.

See also ECONOMY.

RAILROAD STRIKE, 1922. When the **Railroad Labor Board** withdrew wage increases granted in 1920 and at the same time failed to enforce agreements to abandon company unions, the **railroad** shop and nonoperative unions went on strike. The employers also demanded an end to union seniority rights in the industry and employed strikebreakers to keep the lines running.

In 1923 attorney general **Harry Daugherty** obtained a sweeping injunction prohibiting picketing and even communication between the strikers and their supporters, and the strikers were forced to return to work.

See also TRADE UNIONS.

RAILROAD TRANSPORTATION ACT, 1920. Known as the Esch-Cummins Act, the Railroad Transportation Act was passed to ease the transition from wartime government control back to private ownership after the war. It increased the size of the Interstate Commerce Commission from seven to eleven members and gave the commission power to fix rates to yield a return of 6 percent of the estimated value of **railroads**. An appropriation of $200 million was made to help railroads reestablish their prewar status, and a $300 million "revolving fund" was created to provide loans to financially weak companies. The commission was also authorized to draw up plans for the consolidation of the railroads into between twenty and thirty-five systems. The act also prohibited multiple directorships after December 1921.

RANDOLPH, ASA PHILIP (1889–1979). A. Philip Randolph was born in Florida and attended the Cookman Institute. In 1911 he moved to New York City and took courses at City College. Together with **Chandler Owen**, Randolph opened an employment office in Harlem to try to unionize fellow **African American** migrants and enlist black recruits for the **Socialist Party**. In 1917 Randolph and Owen began to produce *The Messenger*, a left-wing journal aimed at black audiences. Their opposition to African American participation in the war effort during **World War I** led to them being charged under the **Sedition Act**, but the charge was dismissed because the judge believed they were the dupes of white radicals. During the **Red Scare** *The Messenger* was described as the "most able and most dangerous" of all black publications.

After World War I Randolph voiced opposition to **Marcus Garvey**'s call for racial separatism and from 1925 on was involved in trying to organize the Pullman Car porters into a union. He established the Brotherhood of Sleeping Car Porters (BSCP) with *The Messenger* as its official publication. The BSCP was finally given a charter by the **American Federation of Labor** in 1935 and recognized by the Pullman Company in 1937. Randolph was the BSCP president until his retirement in 1968. Randolph was appointed to the New York City Commission on Race in 1935 and also became president of the National Negro Congress concerned with the economic situation of African Americans. Faced with continued discrimination in the developing defense industries, in 1940 Randolph called for a March on Washington to protest in July 1941. Threatened by a potentially embarrassing demonstration, president **Franklin D. Roosevelt** issued an executive order outlawing discrimination and establishing a Fair Employment Practices Committee to investigate complaints, and the march was called off. Randolph unsuccessfully campaigned for the establishment of a permanent fair employment practices act. With the reintroduction of Selective Service after World War II, Randolph mobilized black opinion to protest against segregation in the armed forces, and in 1948 president Harry S. Truman issued an executive order initiating the integration of the military.

During the 1950s Randolph organized a Prayer Pilgrimage in Washington, D.C., in 1957 and supported Youth Marches for Integrated Schools in 1958 and 1959. In 1955 Randolph was appointed one of the vice presidents of the newly merged AFL-CIO. It was Randolph who in 1963 suggested a March on Washington for Jobs and Freedom for African Americans. The March was one of the highpoints of the civil rights demonstrations of the 1960s. However, Randolph subsequently agreed to a moratorium on demonstrations in order to support Lyndon Johnson in the presidential election. The same year Randolph established the Randolph Institute to encourage links between labor organizations and the civil rights movement. Although such actions separated him from the increasingly militant and separatist Black Power groups, Randolph remained an influential figure in civil rights until his death.

See also TRADE UNIONS.

RANKIN, JEANETTE (1880–1973). Jeanette Rankin was a graduate of the University of Montana (1902) and the New York School of Philanthropy (1909). She was a **social worker** in Seattle in 1909 and then became involved in the **women's suffrage** campaign. Following Montana's acceptance of female suffrage in 1914, Rankin was the first woman to serve in the U.S. Congress when she was elected on a progressive **Republican** platform in 1916. She voted against America's entry into **World War I**. Having failed to be elected to the Senate in 1918 Rankin returned to social work and became active in a number of **women**'s causes and was particularly active in peace organizations. She was returned to the House of Representatives in 1940 and once again voted against war in 1941. Rankin did not seek reelection in 1942 but turned instead to lecturing and work for the **National Consumers' League** and Women's International League for Peace and Freedom. She later campaigned against the war in Vietnam.

RANSOM, JOHN CROWE (1888–1974). The southern poet John Ransom graduated from Vanderbilt University, Nashville, in 1909, studied at Oxford as a Rhodes Scholar from 1910 to 1913, and then took a teaching position at Vanderbilt, where he remained until 1937. Ransom served in the artillery in France during **World War I** and shortly after his first book, *Poems about God*, was published. His second volume, *Chills and Fever*, appeared in 1924, and the third, *Two Gentlemen in Bonds*, in 1927. Ransom wrote little new poetry after this, but was still highly regarded. His book *Selected Poems* (1963) was awarded the National Book Award in 1964.

Ransom was one of a group of sixteen poets—including **Donald Davidson**, **Allen Tate**, and Robert Penn Warren—known as the Fugitives. They met in Nashville from 1915 to 1928 to read and criticize one another's work and to produce a magazine, *The Fugitive* (1922–1925), in which they explored the southern heritage but offered an alternative to the old clichés of the South. They responded to the criticism of southern ways in coverage of the **Scopes Monkey Trial**, and in *I'll Take My Stand* (1930) Ransom and others defended agrarian culture. Ransom offered a defense of religion in his *God Without Thunder: An Unorthodox Defense of Orthodoxy* (1930).

Ransom moved to Kenyon College, Ohio, in 1937. There he edited the *Kenyon Review* from 1939 to 1959, and together with the publication of *The New Criticism* (1941) with its emphasis on close, systematic textual analysis, this made him one of America's most respected literary figures.

See also LITERATURE AND THEATER.

RECONSTRUCTION FINANCE CORPORATION (RFC). The Reconstruction Finance Corporation was established by Congress on the recommendation of **Herbert Hoover** in 1932 "to provide emergency financing facilities for financial institutions" and "to aid in financing **agriculture**, commerce, and industry" in order to counter the effects of the **Great Depression**. Its primary concern was to halt the run on **banks** and to restore faith in the financial system in order to encourage a revival of industry. It was headed initially by **Charles Dawes** and was described by some as a "rich man's dole." Before the end of the Hoover Administration the RFC had lent $1.5 billion to banks, mortgage loan companies, **railroads**, insurance companies, and agricultural credit organizations. Although it was not particularly successful, the RFC's life was extended, and it was grouped with other agencies as the Federal Loan Agency in 1939. It survived in various forms and was involved in financing a number of war-related activities. Its capital stock, originally $500 million, was reduced in 1948 to $100 million. Revelations of various financial irregularities and misuse of funds in the 1950s led to its abolition in 1954.

See also ECONOMY.

RED SCARE, 1919. Following the end of World War I the United States was gripped by a wave of antiradical hysteria that was directed against real or imagined Bolsheviks (supporters of the 1917 Russian communist revolution). Strikes such as those in **Seattle** and the **Boston police strike** were characterized as the work of "reds," and fears of impending revolution were fanned by a wave of bombing outrages in April and June. Radical groups and **trade unionists** celebrating May Day were attacked. Attorney general **A. Mitchell Palmer** and a Justice Department official, **J. Edgar Hoover**, announced that a revolution was planned and launched the **Palmer raids** in December 1919. When no revolution materialized, many observers began to protest against the attack on civil liberties, and gradually the violence declined. However, xenophobia continued to be evident in the legislation to limit **immigration**, in the rise of the **Ku Klux Klan**, and in the trial and execution of **Sacco and Vanzetti**.

The Red Scare can be seen in part as a reaction to the dislocations of war and uncertainty about the postwar settlement. It was also a continuation of the anti-German hysteria and "100 percent Americanism" of the war years and of the anti-immigrant sentiment evident in the prewar years.

RED SUMMER, 1919. As well as a wave of antiradicalism in the **Red Scare**, 1919 witnessed an upsurge of violence directed against **African Americans**. Lynching, which had been increasing during World War I, reached an even higher level when over eighty African Americans were brutally murdered by mobs in 1919. In addition twenty-five race riots varying in scale and intensity broke out across the country in towns and cities as far apart as Charleston, South Carolina; **Longview**, Texas; Omaha, Nebraska; **Elaine**, Arkansas; and in Washington, D.C., itself. The worst incidents took place in **Chicago**, where at least twenty-three African Americans and fifteen white Americans died. However, out of the mood of disillusionment emerged a "**New Negro**," more assertive and less prepared to turn the other cheek.

See also CRIME AND POLICING.

REED, JOHN SILAS (1887–1920). The writer and revolutionary John Reed went to Harvard University from 1906 to 1910. Shortly after his graduation Reed joined the **Greenwich Village** bohemian community and began writing for the *American Magazine*, *Collier's*, and other publications. In 1912 he became an editor of *The Masses*, a radical journal dedicated to free expression. In 1913 Reed went to Paterson, New Jersey, to report on the strike of silk workers. He and his friends then staged a pageant in Madison Square Garden in support of the strike. He subsequently went to **Mexico** to cover the revolution for the *New York World*, and his reports helped to popularize **Pancho Villa** in the United States. When war in Europe broke out in 1914, Reed attempted to get to the western front but failed. Instead he went to Russia and published *The War in Eastern Europe* in 1916. After a brief sojourn in the United States, where he and his partner, Louise Bryant, established the Provincetown Players with **Eugene O'Neill**, Reed returned to

Russia to cover the outbreak of the revolution. When he arrived back in the United States in 1918, Reed was put on trial under the **Espionage Act** for his antiwar writing in *The Masses*. He was acquitted, arrested, and tried a second time, and once more acquitted with his fellow editors. In 1919 he published *Ten Days That Shook the World*, his account of the Russian Revolution. Reed helped to found the Communist Labor Party in America and began editing its journal in 1919. He returned to Russia in 1919, was detained in Finland trying to return to the United States, and was forced to return to Russia. Suffering from typhus, Reed died in Moscow and was buried in the Kremlin. In the 1920s and 1930s groups who shared his left-wing sympathies established several John Reed clubs in the United States.

See also LITERATURE AND THEATER.

REPUBLICAN PARTY. For much of the latter half of the nineteenth and early years of the twentieth centuries, the party of Abraham Lincoln dominated politics, controlling both the White House and Congress. However, from the turn of the century on the conservative element in the party was increasingly challenged by **progressive** insurgents demanding reform. For a while both factions united uneasily behind **Theodore Roosevelt**, but the divisions reappeared during the presidency of **William Howard Taft** and culminated in the defection of many reformers to Roosevelt and the **Progressive Party** in 1912. As a result of this split, **Woodrow Wilson** won the presidential election, and the **Democrats** gained control of both the House and the Senate. The demise of the reform impulse and the reaction to the **Versailles peace settlement** and **League of Nations** at the end of World War I restored some unity to the Republican Party. In control of the White House under presidents **Warren Harding**, **Calvin Coolidge**, and **Herbert Hoover**, Republicans had majorities in the House and Senate from 1919 until the **Great Depression** brought a Democratic landslide in the election of 1932. However, the continued presence of a reformist element, united with the midwestern Farm Bloc, ensured that none of the presidents in the interwar years could completely rely on partisan support for their policies.

See also POLITICAL PARTIES.

RICE, ELMER (1892–1967). Born Elmer Leopold Reizenstein in New York City, Rice graduated from New York Law School in 1912 but abandoned the legal profession two years later to concentrate on his writing. His first successful play, *On Trial* (1914), the first to use flashbacks in a stage production, was subsequently adapted for cinema in 1917, 1928, and 1939. After a number of other plays—*The Iron Cross* (1917), *The Home of the Free* (1918), *It Is the Law* (1922)—Rice had a major success with *The Adding Machine* (1923), a play depicting the regimentation of the machine age. His realistic study of life in the slums, *Street Scene* (1929), won the Pulitzer Prize and was adapted as a musical by Kurt Weill in 1947. Other plays looked at expatriate life and the legal profession—*The Left Bank* (1931), *We, the People* (1933)—while *Judgment Day* (1934) and *Between Two Worlds* (1934) looked at the impact of Nazism and ideological issues. Rice was briefly the first director of the New York office of the Works Progress Administration's Federal Theater Project (1935–1936). His political views led him to be labeled a communist, his most successful later play was *Dream Girl* (1945), and his last play was *Cue for Passion* (1958). Rice wrote a critical study of American drama, *The Living Theater* (1960); his autobiography, *Minority Report*, was published in 1963.

See also LITERATURE AND THEATER.

RICKENBACKER, EDWARD VERNON (1890–1973). Edward Rickenbacker worked in automobile manufacturing and sales before **World War I**. In 1909 he took up motorcar racing and became a full-time driver in 1912. With the outbreak of war in 1917 Rickenbacker joined the army and became a driver but then learned to fly and was commissioned in the Army Air Service. By the time the war ended, Rickenbacker had become America's top air ace, having fought in 134 aerial contests and downed 26 German airplanes and balloons. He was awarded the French Croix de Guerre, the American Distinguished Service Cross with oak leaf clusters, and the Congressional Medal of Honor.

After the war Rickenbacker created an automobile manufacturing company but took to speedway management when his business failed. In 1934 he became manager of Eastern Airlines, and then became president and general manager in 1938. Although originally opposed to American involvement in World War II, once the country had entered the conflict Rickenbacker toured the United States, the Pacific, China, and the Soviet Union on morale boosting and diplomatic missions. He survived three weeks at sea on a raft after his airplane crashed in the Pacific in 1942. In 1953 Rickenbacker became chairman of the Eastern Airlines board of directors.

See also AVIATION.

ROARING TWENTIES. The decade of the 1920s was described variously as "the **Jazz** Age," "the age of prosperity," and the "roaring twenties." The latter suggested a rapid period of change—the adjective had been applied first to the 1840s as "the roaring forties." A **movie** titled *The Roaring 20s* about bootlegging and starring James Cagney appeared in 1939.

ROBERTS, OWEN JOSEPHUS (1875–1955). The **Supreme Court** justice Owen Roberts was educated at the University of Pennsylvania and the University of Pennsylvania Law School, where he graduated in 1898. He practiced law in Philadelphia and for twenty-two years also taught at the University of Pennsylvania Law School. In 1918 Roberts became a special deputy U.S. attorney and was involved in prosecutions under the **Espionage Act**. In 1924 president **Calvin Coolidge** appointed Roberts, together with **Atlee Pomerene**, to prosecute those involved in the **Teapot Dome** scandal.

In 1930 president **Herbert Hoover** nominated Roberts to fill the seat on the Supreme Court vacated following the death of Edward Sanford. With the new chief justice **Charles Evans Hughes**, Roberts held the balance between the conservatives and liberals in the court. Increasingly the court became more liberal on issues of freedom of speech and, in the case of the **Scottsboro boys**, on the right of defendants to have counsel appointed for their defense. However, Roberts tended to side with the conservatives in cases concerning the extension of government authority under the **New Deal**. But following **Franklin D. Roosevelt**'s attempt to alter the composition of the court Roberts made "a switch in time that saved nine" and sided with the liberal group to uphold minimum wage laws, the National Labor Relations Act (1935), and the Social Security Act (1935). Roberts tended to be more conservative on civil rights and civil liberties and supported white primaries in 1935, and compulsory flag salutes and the pledge of allegiance in public schools in 1940. However, he dissented against the decision to uphold the evacuation of Japanese Americans during World War II.

Following his retirement in 1945, Roberts was dean of the University of Pennsylvania Law School from 1948 to 1951. He was also chair of the security board of the Atomic Energy commission (AEC). His Holmes lectures at Harvard Law School in 1951 were published as *The Court and the Constitution*.

ROBERTSON, ALICE MARY (1854–1931). Largely self-educated, Alice Robertson became a clerk in the Indian Office in Washington, D.C., in 1873. In 1879 she returned to Oklahoma Indian Territory to teach. Robertson was appointed government supervisor of Creek Indian Schools from 1900 to 1905 and was postmaster of Muskogee, Oklahoma, 1905 to 1913. In 1920 she was elected as a Republican to the U.S. Congress but failed to win reelection in 1922. President **Warren Harding** appointed her as a welfare worker at the Veterans' Hospital in Muskogee in 1923.

See also NATIVE AMERICANS; WOMEN.

ROBESON, PAUL LEROY BUSTILL (1898–1976). The great American singer, actor, athlete, and civil rights activist Paul Robeson attended Rutgers University (then a college). An outstanding scholar and athlete, he became the first **African American** All-American in football. Following his graduation 1919, Robeson went to Columbia Law School, where he obtained his degree in 1923 and began work in a New York City law firm. Following a racial slight, Robeson gave up law and joined **Eugene O'Neill**'s Provincetown Players and starred in *All God's Chillun Got Wings* and *The Emperor Jones* in 1924. Robeson began his solo singing career with a performance of gospel songs at Carnegie Hall in 1925 and became celebrated for singing and acting in various musicals, most famously for his rendition of "Ol' Man River" in *Show Boat* (1928). In 1930 he achieved critical acclaim for his portrayal of *Othello* in London. Robeson went on to appear in eleven **movies** including *Song of Freedom* (1936), *King Solomon's Mines* (1937), and *Proud Valley* (1940), in addition to film versions of his stage successes and was the best-known black entertainer of his day.

Embittered by race prejudice in the United States, Robeson increasingly spent time performing in Europe after 1928. In the 1930s he visited the Soviet Union and became an advocate of communism. He returned to the United States with the outbreak of World War II and achieved a great success when he became the first African American to play the lead in *Othello* in America. After the war Robeson's communist sympathies led to his investigation by congressional committees and his blacklisting as an entertainer. His passport was revoked from 1950 to 1958, effectively destroying his career. Robeson left the United States in 1958 and did not return until 1963. He lived out his remaining years in virtual seclusion but was remembered in several awards for his contributions to the arts and to civil rights.

See also LITERATURE AND THEATER; MUSIC AND DANCE.

ROBINS, MARGARET DREIER (1868–1945). Margaret Robins (née Dreier, sister of **Mary Dreier**) committed herself to voluntary work while still a teenager. In 1902 she joined the New York Charities Aid Association and the **Women**'s Municipal League, and in 1904 she joined the Women's **Trade Union** League (WTUL). Robins was to devote most of her career and her personal wealth to the WTUL. Originally treasurer, in 1907 Dreier became president of the WTUL, a position she held until 1922. She also edited the WTUL journal, *Life and Labor*, for several years. Dreier campaigned for municipal reform and for **women's suffrage**, worked on behalf of the **Progressive Party** in 1912, and supported **Republican Charles Evans Hughes** in 1916.

During **World War I** Robins was involved in the Illinois Women's Council of National Defense. After the war she convened the first International Congress of Working Women and organized the International Federation of Working Women in 1922. During the 1920s Robins was active in the national Republican Party but later supported the **New Deal**.

ROBINSON, EDWIN ARLINGTON (1869–1935). Regarded as the first major American poet of the twentieth century, Edwin Robinson studied at Harvard University from 1891 to 1893 but was forced to leave due to family difficulties. His first poetry was published as *The Torrent and the Night Before* in 1896 and *The Children of the Night* in 1897. With the support of president **Theodore Roosevelt** he found a job at the New York Customs House from 1905 to 1909 that enabled him to continue writing. He published *The Town down the River* in 1909. A series of Arthurian poems, *Merlin*, *Lancelot*, and *Tristram*, were published in 1917, 1920, and 1927, respectively. Robinson's volume of Collected *Poems* was awarded the first Pulitzer Prize for poetry in 1921; he won a second Pulitzer for *The Man Who Died Twice* (1924) and a third for *Tristram*. His other writings included *Avon's Harvest* (1921), *Roman Bartholow* (1925), *The Glory of the Nightingales* (1930), and *Nicodemus* (1932). Robinson was awarded honorary degrees from Yale and Bowdoin.
   See also LITERATURE AND THEATER.

ROBINSON, JAMES HARVEY (1863–1936). The historian James Robinson completed his undergraduate and master's degrees at Harvard University in 1888 and traveled to Europe, where he studied for his PhD. A year after his graduation in 1890 Robinson began teaching European history at the University of Pennsylvania. His emphasis on the use of primary sources led to the publication of five volumes of *Translations and Reprints* in 1894. In 1895 Robinson was appointed professor in European history at Columbia University, where he remained until 1919. At Columbia Robinson became one of America's leading historians, inspiring a generation of scholars, including **Charles A. Beard**, Carl Becker, and Arthur Schlesinger Sr., who would later become famous in their own right. In his many publications Robinson stressed the "new history," incorporating social, economic, and cultural aspects rather than merely concentrating on the political and military. He also argued that history was relevant to contemporary issues. His books included *An Introduction to the History of Western Europe* (1902, 1903), *Readings in European History* (1904, 1906), *The Development of Modern Europe* (1907–1908) [with Charles A. Beard], and *Outlines of Euro-*

pean History (1912) [also with Beard]. In *The New History* (1912) Robinson argued that history must draw upon the social sciences to better understand the past.

Robinson became increasingly disillusioned during **World War I**, and after Columbia dismissed two professors for their opposition to American entry into the war, he resigned to establish the New School for Social Research in 1919. The new institution had no entry requirements and offered no degrees. Robinson left in 1921 to concentrate on his own writing. He produced *The Mind in the Making* (1921), *The Humanizing of Knowledge* (1922), and *The Ordeal of Civilization* (1926). Robinson was elected president of the American Historical Association in 1929.

See also EDUCATION.

ROCKEFELLER, ABBY ALDRICH (1874–1948). Abby Greene Aldrich, the daughter of Nelson Aldrich, senator for Rhode Island, grew up in Providence, Rhode Island, and was educated by private tutor and in a girl's school. She traveled in the United States and Europe. In 1901 she married **John D. Rockefeller Jr.**, one of the world's richest men. Rockefeller had six children between 1903 and 1915. In addition to raising a family, Abby Rockefeller was involved on her own and with her husband in many philanthropic activities. The Rockefellers supported the restoration of colonial Williamsburg, and Abby donated to the Rockefeller Folk Art collection there. Abby was also instrumental in the creation of the New York Museum of Modern Art in 1929 and was an active supporter throughout her life. She served on the board of trustees and donated several works by Henri Matisse, Pablo Picasso, Diego Rivera, and others, and with her son Nelson, she established a purchase fund for the museum.

See also WOMEN.

ROCKEFELLER, JOHN DAVISON, JR. (1874–1960). John D. Rockefeller was the only son of the head of Standard Oil, millionaire industrialist John D. Rockefeller Sr. Rockefeller Jr. graduated from Brown University in 1897 and began work as an associate in Standard Oil. Ill health led to his retirement from the business, and he began instead to manage the various Rockefeller philanthropic organizations. In 1913 he became president of the newly created Rockefeller Foundation.

Rockefeller supported a wide range of concerns including religious groups such as the Interchurch World Movement; conservation projects included the establishment of the Grand Teton National Park in Wyoming and Acadia National Park in Maine, and the development of colonial Williamsburg in Virginia. The foundation also financed an International **Education** Board to support academic research activities abroad and "International Houses" to provide residences for foreign students at U.S. universities. From 1918 to 1929 Rockefeller was president of the Laura Spelman Rockefeller Memorial that provided philanthropic support for concerns related to **women** and children. Rockefeller also supported preservation and building projects in New York City including work on the Cloisters Museum and Palisades Park. In 1928 building began on Rockefeller Center in New York City, originally as a home for the Metropolitan Opera. When the Opera withdrew RCA became the tenant of "**Radio** City."

ROCKNE, KNUTE (1888–1931). Born Knute Kenneth Rokne in Voss, Norway, Rockne arrived in the United States with his family in 1893 and settled in Chicago. After working at a variety of jobs Rockne entered Notre Dame University in 1910 and took part successfully in a number of **sports**. He shone particularly at football as captain of the team. After graduating in chemistry and pharmacology in 1914, Rockne took a coaching post at a high school, but later that year he was appointed as a chemistry instructor and assistant football coach at Notre Dame, where he became head coach in 1918. The team dominated the game from 1919 to 1924, and Rockne became a national celebrity. His team was famous for its backfield, known as the "Four Horsemen of Notre Dame," Harry Stuhldreher, Donald Miller, James Crowley, and Elmer Layden. In 1928 Rockne's Notre Dame team achieved near-mythical status when his halftime appeal to the memory of former half-back George Gipp resulted in an emotional 12-6 upset victory over the Army team. The team won the national championships again in 1929 and 1930. In 1931 Rockne died in an airplane crash en route to help make a film, *The Spirit of Notre Dame*. A film of his life, *Knute Rockne, All-American*, was made in 1940.

ROGERS, WILL (WILLIAM PENN ADAIR) (1879–1935). A Cherokee born in the Indian Territory of Oklahoma, Will Rogers began his career as a cowboy in Texas in 1898. In 1902 he traveled to Argentina as a cowhand, and then on to South Africa. It was in South Africa that Rogers found work in a Wild West Show riding and roping. He toured New Zealand and Australia before returning to the United States. During performances with the *Ziegfeld Follies* in 1916 Rogers developed his style of humorous social commentary. In 1920 he began to write columns for the press and particularly for the *Saturday Evening Post*. In 1918 Rogers also began appearing in motion pictures, and he made 48 silent comedies before turning to sound film in 1929. A series of **movies** in which he played different western persona appeared in the 1930s—*State Fair* (1933), *David Harum* (1934), and *Steamboat 'Round the Bend* (1935). Rogers became a well-known radio personality during the 1930s, and his folksy wit and humorous observations on political and other matters seemed to capture a popular mood for nostalgia. When he died in an airplane crash in Alaska in 1935, Rogers was much mourned.

ROOSEVELT, (ANNA) ELEANOR (1884–1962). Eleanor Roosevelt was born in New York City into America's social elite. Her uncle was president **Theodore Roosevelt**, and Eleanor benefited from the best education available, despite the death of her parents at an early age. When she returned from her schooling in London Eleanor joined the **National Consumers League** and worked with immigrant children. In 1905 she married **Franklin Delano Roosevelt**, a sixth cousin once removed. She bore him six children between 1906 and 1916, one of whom died as an infant. She was for a long time dominated by her husband's mother, but during **World War I** Eleanor began to develop an independent public role when she worked for the Red Cross and Navy League. She came to an accommodation with Franklin after discovering his affair with her own social secretary, Lucy Mercer, and became more involved in activities with **women's suffrage** groups and **trade unions**, particularly the **League of Women Voters**, the Women's Trade Union League, and Women's division of the Democratic Committee. Her independence developed further in 1921 following Franklin's affliction with poliomyelitis, a crippling viral infection that left him permanently disabled. Eleanor helped him to overcome the disability and to continue his political career.

By 1928 Eleanor headed the women's division of the **Democratic Party**, and when Franklin became governor of New York she often carried out inspections of state facilities on his behalf. Once Franklin Roosevelt became president Eleanor took on the role as an active first lady, transforming the position much as her husband did the presidency. She was often attacked for her actions on behalf of women and **African Americans**, and for her views expressed in speeches, radio broadcasts, and her daily newspaper column, "My Day," which began in 1935. In 1939 Eleanor Roosevelt publicly announced her resignation from the Daughters of the American Revolution (DAR) after the organization had refused to allow the black opera singer Marian Anderson to perform in Constitution Hall. Roosevelt helped to arrange an alternative performance at the Lincoln Memorial. She continued to campaign on behalf of African Americans during World War II.

During the war Mrs. Roosevelt was briefly assistant director of the Office of Civil Defense, but this ended following congressional criticism. She worked energetically throughout the war on morale-raising activities, visiting many parts of the United States, the Caribbean, the Pacific, and Great Britain. Following Franklin Roosevelt's death in 1945, Eleanor was appointed U.S. representative to the United Nations (UN), a position she held until 1953. She chaired the Human Rights Commission from 1946 to 1951 and was instrumental in the adoption of the Universal Declaration of Human

Rights in 1948. Eleanor twice visited the USSR in the 1950s. She also campaigned on behalf of birth control and continued to have some influence in the Democratic Party. John F. Kennedy appointed her as representative to the UN once more in 1961 and as chair of the National Commission on the Status of **Women**.

ROOSEVELT, FRANKLIN DELANO (1882–1945). Thirty-second president of the United States. Born in Hyde Park, New York, into a wealthy family, Franklin Roosevelt was educated at Groton, Harvard, and Columbia Law School. He briefly practiced law in New York City before entering the state senate as a **Democrat** in 1910. In 1913 he was appointed assistant secretary of the navy, a post previous held by his uncle, **Theodore Roosevelt**. His role in the Navy Department enhanced his reputation, and after the war he was nominated as the Democratic Party's vice presidential candidate to run with **James M. Cox** in the unsuccessful campaign of 1920. In 1921 he developed polio, which left him severely paralyzed and threatened to destroy his political career. However, aided by his wife, **Eleanor Roosevelt**, he fought to overcome the handicap and in 1928 succeeded **Al Smith** as governor of New York. As the effects of the **Depression** began to tell, Roosevelt introduced measures to develop public electric power, reduce utility rates, and provide relief for the unemployed. He defeated Smith and **John Nance Garner** to win the Democratic presidential nomination in 1932 and he broke with tradition and flew to Chicago to accept the nomination. In his speech on 2 July he promised "a new deal for the American people," and this quickly became the label applied to his program. His election campaign was impressively vague in specifics, but he projected a positive air and promised an "enlightened administration." He was critical of **Herbert Hoover** for failing to balance the budget and for increasing government bureaucracy.

Roosevelt won a convincing victory with 57 percent of the popular vote to Hoover's 40 percent, and 472 Electoral College votes to 59. He did little between his victory and his inauguration but did survive **Guiseppe Zangara**'s assassination attempt in February 1933. However, declaring there was "nothing to fear but fear itself," in his inaugural address in March he promised a wide-ranging program of measures to combat the deepening depression. He followed this with a remarkable wave of action in what became known as the "First Hundred Days," establishing the **New Deal** as a reforming administration of unprecedented proportions. The New Deal was to form the basis of the modern welfare state and the framework of American politics for the next half century. Roosevelt served an unprecedented four terms having been reelected in 1936, 1940, and 1944. He successfully led the nation through World War II and in the process assumed the leading role in international diplomacy through his meetings with prime minister Winston Churchill of Great Britain and premier Josef Stalin of the USSR.

ROOSEVELT, THEODORE (1858–1919). Twenty-sixth president of the United States. Theodore Roosevelt was born in New York City into a wealthy family. Sickly as a child, he improved his health and physique through exercise and subsequently remained a lifelong advocate of the strenuous life. He was educated privately and then at Harvard University and Columbia Law School. His first book, *The Naval War of 1812*, was published in 1882. Roosevelt visited the West in 1883, acquired a ranch, became a cowboy, and developed a lasting affinity with that region. He wrote an account of *Hunting Trips of a Ranchman* (1885) and a four-volume history, *Winning the West* (1889–1896).

In 1881 Roosevelt was elected to the New York State Assembly and served from 1882 to 1884. He was a member of the U.S. Civil Service Commission, 1889–1895, and president of New York City Board of Police Commissioners, 1895–1897. He was appointed assistant secretary of the navy by president William McKinley in 1897 but resigned in 1898 to organize a volunteer cavalry unit, the "Rough Riders," to serve in the Spanish-American War. Roosevelt rose to national prominence when he led the "Rough Riders" in the battle at San Juan Hill, Cuba, in 1898. He enhanced his reputation as a reformer while governor of New York, 1899–1900, and was chosen by the **Republican Party** as William McKinley's vice presidential running mate largely in order to keep him in control. However, Roosevelt became president after an anarchist assassinated McKinley in 1901. He was elected in his own right in 1904.

Flamboyant and assertive, Roosevelt reinvigorated the presidency. Beginning with the antitrust proceedings against J. P. Morgan's Northern Securities Company, Roosevelt made a reputation as "trustbuster" in restricting industrial monopolies in forty-three separate actions under the Sherman Antitrust Law (1890). In 1903 Roosevelt created the Department of Commerce and Labor and supported the regulation of the **railroads**. He initiated policies of land conservation, and approved the Pure Food and Drug and Meat Inspection Acts in 1906. Roosevelt backed an aggressive **foreign policy** in the Caribbean, using the phrase "speak softly and carry a big stick" and asserting "dollar diplomacy" to further U.S. interests, particularly in Panama. Under Roosevelt, U.S. troops occupied Santo Domingo (1904) and Cuba (1907). He supported the expansion of U.S. naval strength and was active in bringing about a number of international arbitration treaties. His role as mediator in the Russo-Japanese War (1905) won him the Nobel Peace Prize.

Having promised in 1904 not to seek reelection, Roosevelt was responsible for the nomination of **William Howard Taft** as his successor in 1908. When Taft failed to continue his policies, particularly on conservation, Roosevelt attempted to regain the Republican Party nomination in 1912. When he was unsuccessful he assumed the leadership of the National **Progressive Party** but was defeated by the **Democratic** candidate, **Woodrow**

Wilson. He was critical of many of Wilson's policies and after the outbreak of war in Europe in 1914 called for the strengthening of the U.S. military. Once America entered **World War I** he proposed raising another volunteer regiment and unsuccessfully sought a military appointment. Roosevelt called for total loyalty and spoke out against "hyphenated Americans." He gave only qualified support for the **League of Nations** and was insistent that America remained an independent military power.

ROOT, ELIHU (1845–1937). Elihu Root graduated from New York University Law School in 1867 and started his own law firm in 1869. From 1883 to 1885 Root served as U.S. attorney in the southern district of New York, and it was there he developed his relationship with **Theodore Roosevelt**. In 1899 President McKinley appointed Root secretary of war. He was largely responsible for developing policies with regard to the territories acquired from Spain in 1898 (Puerto Rico and the Philippines) and for establishing the basis for Cuban independence. He resigned from the post in 1904 but returned to office as secretary of state in 1905. Root began the process of professionalizing the Foreign Service, and he established better relations with Latin America and cosponsored the Central American Peace Conference in 1907. Root also resolved disagreements with Canada over North Atlantic coastal fishing rights. Through the Root-Takahira agreement with Japan in 1908 Root secured Japanese agreement to maintain the status quo in the Pacific and accept the independence and integrity of China. In 1912 he was awarded the Nobel Peace Prize for his work.

Root resigned as secretary of state in 1909. He was elected senator for New York in 1908 and served until 1915. He supported **William Howard Taft** in 1912. In April 1917 **Woodrow Wilson** appointed Root to head a mission to Russia following the overthrow of the tsar. The appointment was not a success, and as a result Root was not included in the **Versailles Peace Conference**. Root favored ratification of the **League of Nations** with reservations, a proposal rejected by the "**Irreconcilables**" to U.S. membership. Root was a delegate to the **Washington Naval Conference** and was a member of the commission of international law experts appointed by the League of Nations to draft the constitution of the **Permanent Court of International Justice**. He declined an invitation to become one of the court's judges but remained an advocate of American membership. Root was also president of the Carnegie Endowment for International Peace.

ROSENWALD, JULIUS (1862–1932). The business executive and philanthropist Julius Rosenwald entered the clothing business in 1879. He established his own clothing manufacturing company in Chicago in the 1880s. In 1896 Rosenwald joined the Sears, Roebuck mail order company. He was vice president of the company from 1895 to 1910, president from 1910 to 1925, and chairman of the board, 1923 to 1932. In addition to expanding the business and establishing retail outlets, Rosenwald established health-care provision and profit sharing schemes for employees. Rosenwald's investments in the company made him a multimillionaire. By 1925 he was worth an estimated $125 million. Rosenwald aimed to use one-third of his wealth for charity and became a leading philanthropist. The Julius Rosenwald Fund was established in 1917 through which over $4 million was given toward the construction of 5,357 public schools, shops, and teachers' homes in **African American** communities in the South. He also made donations to the University of Chicago, Chicago's Museum of Science and Industry, the Young Men's Christian Association (YMCA) and Young Women's Christian Association (YWCA), and a number of Jewish causes.

ROSEWOOD MASSACRE, 1923. Following unconfirmed reports that an **African American** male had assaulted a white **woman** near the black township of Rosewood, Florida, on 1 January 1923, a white mob gathered, set fire to the buildings in Rosewood, and murdered eight people. The rest of the 120 black inhabitants fled the town and did not return. No one was ever indicted for the incident.

See also CRIME AND POLICING.

ROSS, EDWARD ALSWORTH (1866–1951). Edward Ross was educated at Coe College, Iowa, then studied in Berlin, France, and England before taking his PhD at Johns Hopkins in 1891. Following his graduation Ross held a succession of teaching posts in Indiana, Cornell, and Stanford Universities. His contract at Stanford was terminated because of his outspoken progressive views, and the furor that followed led to the campaign to secure tenured protection for academics. Ross was employed as professor of sociology at the University of Nebraska from 1901 to 1906, when he was appointed professor in sociology at the University of Wisconsin, a position he held until 1937. In 1914 and 1915 Ross was elected president of the American Sociological Society. Ross wrote many academic works, chiefly *Social Control* (1901), *Foundations of Sociology* (1905), *Sin and Society* (1907), and *Social Psychology* (1908). Widely traveled, he also wrote *The Changing Chinese* (1911), *Russia in Upheaval* (1918), *The Social Revolution in Mexico* (1923), and *The Russian Soviet Republic* (1923). From 1940 to 1950 Ross was chair of the **American Civil Liberties Union**.

See also EDUCATION.

ROSS, NELLIE TAYLOE (1876–1977). In 1924 Nellie Tayloe Ross became the first female state governor when she completed the term of office of her deceased husband, William Bradford Ross, in Wyoming. She served out the two remaining years in office and saw a number of measures such as a new **banking** code and a **child labor** law passed. Although selected to run again by the Wyoming **Democrats**, Ross failed to win reelection in 1926 in her solidly **Republican** state. She continued to be active within the Democratic Party and was vice chair of the party's national convention in 1928. She moved to Washington, D.C., that year and was active in mobilizing Democratic **women**. Her support for **Franklin D. Roosevelt** was rewarded with her appointment as head of the U.S. Mint in 1933, a position she held for twenty years.

ROTHSTEIN, ARNOLD (1883–1928). A professional gambler from an early age, Arnold Rothstein ran gambling houses in New York City, Saratoga Springs, and Long Beach, operated a racing stable, a real estate business, and a bail bond firm. Rothstein was alleged to have been behind the fixing of the 1919 **World Series** when the Chicago White Sox lost to the Cincinnati Reds. Rothstein was shot dead in a New York hotel while playing cards.
    See also CRIME AND POLICING; SPORTS.

RURAL CREDITS ACT, 1916. Passed as part of the "preparedness" campaign prior to U.S. entry into **World War I**, the Rural Credits Act established twelve Federal Farm Banks similar to those in the **Federal Reserve**. The Farm Banks were to provide long-term mortgages to farmers at low interest rates to reduce farm debt and encourage greater production.
    See also FARMING.

RUSSIAN CIVIL WAR, INTERVENTION IN, 1918–1920. While the Bolshevik (Communist) revolution of October 1917 was greeted with some misgivings by **Woodrow Wilson**'s administration, it was not until the new Soviet government had signed the treaty of Brest Litovsk with Germany and withdrawn from **World War I** in March 1918 that the U.S. government became openly antagonistic. In August 1918 three regiments of U.S. troops were sent as part of an allied force to Murmansk, Archangel, and Vladivostok, ostensibly to protect U.S. personnel and property but in practice aiding the anti-Bolshevik forces. Some eight thousand troops were in Russia until their eventual withdrawal in April 1920, and 275 died in various confrontations with the Soviet forces.
    See also FOREIGN POLICY.

RUTH, GEORGE HERMAN "BABE" (1895–1948). The great baseball player Babe Ruth was committed to an industrial school for boys in Baltimore as a delinquent child in 1902. It was there that Ruth developed his early prowess as a baseball player. In 1914 he was signed by the Baltimore Orioles, where he acquired his nickname, "Babe." Later that year Ruth was sold to the American League side, the Boston Red Sox. Initially an outstanding pitcher, he switched to the outfield in 1919 and rapidly made his mark as a batter, establishing a league record by hitting twenty-nine home runs. In 1920 Ruth was sold to the New York Yankees for a then record $125,000.

In New York Ruth became a national figure and the best-known sportsman of his day as the "Sultan of Swat." His presence helped bring about the Yankees' domination of major league baseball, and in 1923 they moved to a newly built Yankee Stadium, popularly known as "the House that Ruth Built." Ruth was a legend not just for his baseball but also for his legendary appetite for food, beer, and women. By 1925 he was overweight, playing badly, and often in conflict with Yankees' manager Miller Huggins. However, he regained his home-run title in 1926 and kept it for six seasons. In 1927 he hit sixty home runs, a record not beaten until 1961. Ruth played his last game for the Yankees in 1934, joined the Boston Braves as assistant manager but retired after only twenty-eight games in 1935. Ruth's big-hitting style of play helped to transform baseball, and his presence on and off the field made him the most widely acclaimed sportsman and best-known figure of his day. His total of 714 home runs survived until the 1970s. He was among the first five players admitted to the National Baseball Hall of Fame when it opened in Cooperstown, New York, in 1939. When he died of cancer in 1948, two hundred thousand fans passed his body as it lay in state at Yankee Stadium, and one hundred thousand watched the funeral procession. For many observers Ruth remains the greatest baseball player ever.

See also SPORTS.

S

SACCO, NICOLA (1891–1927). The Italian **immigrant** famously convicted with **Bartolomeo Vanzetti** in the **Sacco and Vanzetti** case was born in Torremaggiore, Italy. He immigrated to the United States in 1908 and found work in shoe factories in Massachusetts. Between 1912 and 1917 Sacco and Vanzetti were active as fund-raisers and in strike activities for the anarchist movement. In 1917 both men fled to Mexico to avoid the draft. They returned to the United States and resumed their association with the anarchist movement and were arrested in May 1920 with other Italians in connection with those activities. However, Sacco and Vanzetti were subsequently charged with robbing two shoe factories and killing a guard and paymaster at the factory in South Braintree, Massachusetts. Found guilty in 1921, they were electrocuted at Charlestown State Prison on 23 August 1927.

SACCO AND VANZETTI CASE. The arrest, trial, conviction, and ultimate execution of the two Italian anarchists **Nicola Sacco** and **Bartolomeo Vanzetti** became an international cause célèbre between 1921 and 1927. Arrested initially for their political activities, the two men were subsequently charged with the robbery of two shoe factories in 1920 involving the killing in one at South Braintree, Massachusetts, of a guard and the paymaster. The trial in Dedham, Massachusetts, took place against a background of hysteria during the **Red Scare** and the **Palmer Raids**, and the trial was conducted in a prejudicial manner in focusing on their **immigrant** backgrounds, avoidance of the draft, and anarchist involvement. Their conviction on 14 July 1921, despite obvious weaknesses in the prosecution case and evidence of bias on the part of the judge, led to national and international protests. After eight motions for retrial were denied and the Massachusetts Supreme Court upheld their convictions, Sacco and Vanzetti were sentenced to death in April 1927. A commission appointed by the state governor also found that "on the whole" the trial and appeals process had been fair. The two men were electrocuted on 23 August 1927. Arguments about their guilt or innocence are still the subject of much historical debate.

See also CRIME AND POLICING.

SANDBURG, CARL (1878–1967). After a time as an itinerant worker and serving in the Spanish-American War, the poet and writer Carl Sandburg became a reporter in Milwaukee and then for the Chicago *Daily News*. His poetry celebrating the city and working people, *Chicago Poems* (1915), *Cornhuskers* (1918), and *Smoke and Steel* (1920), won him prizes and national and international recognition as a "poet of the people." He was awarded a Pulitzer Prize in 1940 for his four-volume biography of Abraham Lincoln, *The War Years* (1939), and for his *Complete Poems* in 1951. He was awarded the gold medal of the American Academy of Arts and Letters in 1952 for his work in history and biography. He published *Harvest Poems* in 1960 and *Honey and Salt* in 1963.

See also LITERATURE AND THEATER.

SANFORD, EDWARD TERRY (1865–1923). The **Supreme Court** justice Edward Sanford studied at the University of Tennessee, Harvard University, and Harvard Law School, where he obtained his LLB in 1889. He practiced law in Knoxville, Tennessee, until 1907, when he became assistant attorney general. Sanford also taught law at the University of Tennessee between 1897 and 1916. From 1908 until 1923 he sat as a federal trial judge in Tennessee, earning a reputation for patience and impartiality. In 1923 president **Warren G. Harding** appointed Sanford to the Supreme Court on the recommendation of **William Howard Taft**. Sanford was often among the more liberal minority in court decisions about federal and economic regulation and voted to invalidate all-white primaries in *Nixon v. Herndon* (1927). However, he wrote the decision upholding racially restrictive covenants. His most important contribution was in cases relating to the First Amendment in which he argued that speeches advocating the violent overthrow of government had a "bad tendency" that placed them outside of the protection of free speech. In the course of his argument Sanford extended the Bill of Rights to apply to the states through the Fourteenth Amendment's "due process" clause, a position that was to have considerable significance in the 1950s. Coincidentally, Sanford died on the same day as Taft.

SANGER, MARGARET HIGGINS (1883–1966). Margaret Sanger trained as a nurse and studied under Havelock Ellis, the sexual psychologist, and Dr. Marie Stopes, the pioneer birth control advocate. In 1914 she became editor of *Woman Rebel*, which encouraged the use of contraception. When the publication was declared indecent Sanger was arrested but fled to England. In 1916 she opened the first birth control clinic in the United States and was charged with maintaining a public nuisance and jailed for thirty days. In 1921 she founded the American Birth Control League, which she headed until

1929, when she established the National Committee on Federal Legislation for Birth Control. The Planned Parenthood Federation of America emerged from this in 1942.

SCHENCK V. UNITED STATES, 1919. One of several cases brought to the **Supreme Court** to test the validity of the **World War I Espionage** and **Sedition Acts**. Justice **Oliver Wendell Holmes** used not just the consequences of the actions in question, but the circumstances of "clear and present danger" to uphold the conviction of the socialist Charles T. Schenck for distributing literature encouraging resistance to the draft. The decision of the court was unanimous.

SCHULTZ, DUTCH (1902–1935). Born Arthur Flegenheimer in the Bronx, New York City, Schultz adopted his new name in the early 1920s when he became the owner of illegal saloons and a **bootlegger**. He was known as one of the most powerful gangsters in New York and often compared to **Al Capone**. Using his political connections, Schultz was able to gain an influence in food servicing unions and also in the gambling rackets in **Harlem**. Attempts to convict Schultz of tax evasion failed in 1935. However, fearing that he planned to assassinate the district attorney for New York, Thomas Dewey, Schultz's gangland associates had him murdered in October 1935.
    See also CRIME AND POLICING.

SCHURMAN, JACOB GOULD (1854–1942). Born in Canada, Jacob Schurman attended university in London and Edinburgh followed by a further period of study in Europe. He began teaching in Canada in 1880 and published *Kantian Ethics and the Ethics of Evolution* in 1881. In 1886 he was appointed professor of philosophy at Cornell, where he remained for twenty-eight years, becoming president of the university in 1892. Schurman published several works including *The Ethical Import of Darwinism* (1888) and was the founding editor of the *Philosophical Review* from 1892 to 1905.
    Schurman became a naturalized U.S. citizen in 1892 and was involved in political affairs. He opposed the annexation of the Philippines in 1898 but in 1899 was appointed president of the first U.S. commission to the islands. From 1912 to 1913 Schurman was the U.S. minister to Greece and Montenegro and published a study of *The Balkan Wars, 1912–13* (1914). Following his retirement from Cornell in 1920, Schurman was appointed U.S. minister to China and ambassador to Germany in 1925. He held that position until 1930.
    See also EDUCATION.

SCHWAB, CHARLES MICHAEL (1862–1939). Charles Schwab began his career in the steel industry aged seventeen and in 1889 became superintendent of the Carnegie Homestead Works in Pennsylvania. In 1897 Andrew Carnegie made Schwab president of the Carnegie Steel Company. When the company was sold to John Pierpoint Morgan in 1901 Schwab became president of the newly created U.S. Steel Company. In 1903 he resigned and assumed control of the Bethlehem Steel Corporation, which he built up to become the largest independent steel company. During **World War I** Woodrow **Wilson** appointed Schwab head of the Emergency Fleet Corporation. After the war he lived in semiretirement but from 1927 to 1932 was president of the Iron and Steel Institute.

SCHWIMMER, ROSIKA (1877–1948). Born in Budapest, Hungary, Rosika Schwimmer organized the National Association of Women Office Workers in 1897 and the Hungarian Association of Working **Women** in 1903. Inspired by the American suffragist **Carrie Chapman Catt**, Schwimmer organized the Hungarian Feminist Association in 1904. In 1914 she drew up a proposal for a conference of neutral nations to end **World War I**, and she traveled to the United States to appeal to **Woodrow Wilson** and **William Jennings Bryan** for support. In 1915 she joined with **Jane Addams** to create the **Woman's Peace Party**. Schwimmer was the international secretary. In 1915 Schwimmer persuaded **Henry Ford** to sponsor a peace conference in Sweden, and she sailed on the peace ship *Oscar II* to convene the conference in February 1916. The conference ended in failure, and Schwimmer remained in Europe. In 1918 the Hungarian government appointed her minister to Switzerland.

Following a counterrevolution in Hungary, Schwimmer fled first to Austria and then in 1921 to the United States. In America she was labeled a radical and pacifist, and in 1928 her application for citizenship was denied. Her case was argued before the **Supreme Court** in *Schwimmer v. United States* but was denied on the grounds that she was "an uncompromising pacifist with no sense of national loyalty." Justices **Oliver Wendell Holmes** and **Louis D. Brandeis** dissented from the majority decision. Schwimmer remained in the United States as a resident alien and continued to work for world government. She was nominated for the Nobel Peace Prize by several international representatives in 1948 but died before an award was made.

SCOPES, JOHN T. (1900–1970). John Scopes was a high school biology teacher in Dayton, Tennessee, charged with breaking the Butler Act, a state law passed in 1925 that prohibited the teaching of the theory of evolution. His trial, known as the **Scopes Monkey Trial**, became famous nationally and internationally.

SCOPES MONKEY TRIAL. The trial in Dayton, Tennessee, of **John Scopes**, the biology teacher accused of breaking the Tennessee law prohibiting the teaching of the theory of evolution. The trial lasted from 10 July to 25 July 1925 and was known as the "Monkey Trial" because it was argued that evolutionists believed men were descended from apes. The defense, funded by the **American Civil Liberties Union** and argued by the famous labor lawyer **Clarence Darrow**, challenged the constitutionality of the law, given the scientific validity of evolution. The prosecution was led by **William Jennings Bryan**, who supported the literal interpretation of the Bible. The climax of the trial came when Darrow put Bryan on the stand to defend his fundamentalist views and exposed him to public ridicule. Although Scopes was found guilty of breaking the law, he was given the minimum penalty of a $100 fine. The Butler Act remained on the statutes until 1967.

SCOTT, EMMETT JAY (1873–1957). The **African American** educator and publicist Emmett Scott attended Wiley College in Texas briefly before leaving to become a journalist in 1890. After becoming a reporter at the Houston *Post*, Scott became an editor of the black **newspaper** the *Texas Freeman* in 1894. In 1897 he was hired as private secretary to the African American spokesman and principal of Tuskegee Institute, Booker T. Washington. Scott helped Washington to influence and control elements of the black press and other black leaders. He was involved in the creation of the Negro Business League and was its secretary from 1900 to 1922. In 1909 president **William Howard Taft** appointed Scott as one of the members of the American Commission to Liberia in Africa.

During **World War I** Scott was appointed assistant to the secretary of war, **Newton D. Baker**, to advise on race relations, and he was to write *Scott's Official History of the American Negro in the World War* (1919) and *Negro Migration during the War* (1920). From 1919 to 1932 Scott was secretary-treasurer and business manager at Howard University in Washington, D.C. A supporter of the **Republican Party**, he was a special adviser on race to the Republican National Convention in 1924 and assistant publicity director for the National Republican Committee from 1939 to 1942. During World War II Scott established an African American shipyard at the Sun Shipbuilding Company in Chester, Pennsylvania. He retired when the war ended.

SCOTT, EVELYN NÉE DUNN (1893–1963). The writer Evelyn Scott was born in Clarksville, Tennessee, but her family moved to Kentucky, Indiana, then Missouri, before finally settling in New Orleans. She joined the **Woman** Suffrage Association at the age of seventeen and published her first short story using the pseudonym of Hiram Hagan Beck (she was also to publish under the names of Ernest Souza and Elsie Dunn). At the age of twenty Dunn ran away with a married man and assumed the name of Scott. She and her partner lived in Brazil until 1919, when they returned to the United States; they separated in 1922. Scott published two trilogies of novels in quick succession: *The Narrow House* (1921), *Narcissus* (1922), and *The Golden Door* (1925); and *Migrations* (1927), *The Wave* (1929), and *A Calendar of Sin* (1931). In between she wrote an autobiography, *Escapade* (1923), and a further novel, *Ideals* (1927). Although not an enormous best seller, Scott's writing was well received critically and represented the modernist literature emerging in the 1920s.

Scott was also very critical of the position of women in traditional southern society and wrote very favorably of the work of **William Faulkner**. In addition to her novels, she published poetry, *Precipitations* (1920), *The Winter Alone* (1930), and a further autobiography, *Background in Tennessee* (1937). Two further novels, *Breathe upon These Slain* (1934) and *Bread and a Sword* (1937), were the last significant pieces of work she produced. Scott lived most of the time in New York City until her marriage to an English writer in the 1930s, when she subsequently moved to Canada and then England. She returned to the United States in 1952 but remained largely unrecognized until some considerable time after her death.

See also LITERATURE AND THEATER.

SCOTTSBORO BOYS. In March 1931 nine **African American** teenagers riding a freight train from Chattanooga to Memphis, Tennessee, were seized in Alabama and accused of raping two young white women riding the same train. Tried in Scottsboro, the case of the boys became an international cause célèbre because of the doubts about the evidence and the racial nature of the trials. Eight of the boys were convicted by an all-white jury and sentenced to death. One conviction was reversed on the grounds that the accused was a juvenile when the **crime** was committed. (The nine boys were Roy and Andy Wright, Eugene Williams, Heywood Patterson, Ozie Powell, Clarence Norris, Olen Montgomery, Charlie Weems, and Willie Roberson. Roy Wright's trial was declared a mistrial.)

Clarence Darrow was originally involved in the boys' defense following their first conviction. However, he withdrew because of the role of the **Communist Party** in the defense committee. In November 1932 the **Supreme Court** reversed the convictions on the other eight boys because Alabama had failed to provide adequate assistance of counsel. In subsequent retrials, despite doubts about the evidence of the two supposed victims, the boys were once against found guilty and sentenced to death, but in 1935 the Supreme Court overturned the convictions because African Americans were excluded from juries in Alabama. The boys were subsequently retried once more and four were convicted, two of whom were sentenced to death. Charges were dropped against the remaining four. The death sentences were commuted, and by 1950 all of the Scottsboro boys were free by parole, appeal, or escape.

SEABURY, SAMUEL (1873–1958). Samuel Seabury qualified and practiced law in New York City. From 1907 to 1914 he served as a justice on the Supreme Court of New York, and from 1914 to 1916 was associate judge to the New York Court of Appeals. Seabury rose to national prominence as chairman of the committee investigating **crime** in New York City politics, 1930–1931. The results of the investigation led to the resignation of Mayor **James J. Walker** in 1932 and subsequent election of **Fiorello La Guardia** on a reform Fusion ticket. Seabury was the author of *The New Federalist* (1950).

SEATTLE GENERAL STRIKE, 1919. On 21 January 1919 shipyard workers in Seattle went on strike over a wage claim. Support from other unions turned this into a general strike on 6 February as sixty thousand workers withdrew their labor. The strike was characterized by mayor **Ole Hanson** as the work of Bolsheviks and the first step toward revolution in the United States. Hanson mobilized the police and military against the strikers, and faced with growing public disapproval, the strikers ended their action on 10 February. The strike was one of several major labor disputes that year contributing to a mood of unrest that provoked the **Red Scare**.
   See also TRADE UNIONS.

SECOND CHILD LABOR LAW, 1919. Passed after the **Supreme Court** had invalidated the **Keating-Owen Act**, 1916, the second Child Labor Law imposed a tax of 10 percent on the profits of any factory employing children younger than fourteen or mines and quarries employing children under the age of sixteen. The law was declared unconstitutional by the Supreme Court in *Bailey v. Drexel Furniture Company*, 1922.

SEDITION ACT, 1918. In May 1918 the **Espionage Act** was amended to prohibit any incitement of disloyalty or refusal of duty, or "the uttering, printing, writing, or publishing" of "any disloyal, profane, scurrilous, or abusive language about the form of government of the United States, or the Constitution of the United States, or the military or naval forces . . . or the flag . . . or the uniform." Convictions were punishable by a fine of up to $20,000 and up to twenty years' imprisonment. Under this and the previous legislation some 450 conscientious objectors were sentenced to military prison, and a total of 2,168 cases of sedition were brought, of which by 1921 1,055 had been convicted. Among those convicted were the Socialists **Victor**

Berger and **Eugene Debs**, and the **Industrial Workers of the World** leader, "Big Bill" **(William) Haywood**. The Espionage and Sedition legislation was upheld by the **Supreme Court** in *Schenck v. United States*. The Sedition Act was repealed in 1921.

See also WORLD WAR I, 1914–1918.

SEEGER, ALAN (1888–1916). The poet Alan Seeger was born in New York City and spent his early childhood on Staten Island and then in Mexico City. He entered Harvard University in 1906, a contemporary of **John Reed**. He graduated in 1910 and joined the bohemian community of artists and writers in **Greenwich Village**. In 1912 he moved to Paris and in 1914 joined the French Foreign Legion in order to participate in **World War I**. Some of his poems were published in *Atlantic Monthly*, and he also wrote from the front for the *New York Sun* and *New Republic*. "I Have a Rendezvous with Death," his most famous poem, written while he was ill in the hospital, was published posthumously in *New Republic* shortly after he was killed during the battle of the Somme. *Poems by Alan Seeger* and his *Letters and Diaries* were published in 1916 and 1917 respectively. Lines from his "Ode in Memory of the American Volunteers Fallen for France" were included on a memorial dedicated to the American dead in Paris in 1923. In 1916 Seeger was awarded the Croix de Guerre, the highest French military award, and in 1924 he was recognized with the Medaille Militaire. His poetry is generally seen as representative of the romantic notions of war that were destroyed on the Western Front.

See also HEMINGWAY, ERNEST MILLER (1899–1961); LITERATURE AND THEATER; "LOST GENERATION".

SELECTIVE SERVICE ACT, 1917. Passed in May 1917, the Selective Service Act was effectively the first full military draft law passed in U.S. history and was passed despite some opposition both inside and outside Congress. The act required all men between the ages of twenty-one and thirty to register for military service on 5 June. Draft boards were established in 4,648 districts, and they administered the four calls for service issued during **World War I**. A total of 26 million men out of a male population of 54 million were registered, and 4 million were drafted.

SELZNICK, DAVID O. (1902–1965). David Selznick took over his father's filmmaking business in 1923 and after some success moved to Metro-Goldwyn-Mayer (MGM) and became a producer. He moved to Paramount in 1928 and produced a number of successful **movies**. He established his own production unit in 1931 and then worked for RKO, for whom he made *King Kong* in 1933. Selznick returned to MGM in 1933 and produced some famous films, particularly versions of literary works such as *David Copperfield* (1935) and *Anna Karenina* (1935). His later productions included *Little Lord Fauntleroy* (1936), *The Prisoner of Zenda* (1937), and *Gone with the Wind* (1939). Selznick later made a number of major movies with the director Alfred Hitchcock, including *Rebecca* (1940) and *Spellbound* (1945). Following the success of *Gone with the Wind* Selznick was awarded the Irving G. Thalberg Memorial Award by the Academy of Arts for his outstanding contribution to the movie industry. He continued to produce films into the 1950s, despite declining success and failing health.

SENNETT, MACK (1880–1960). The future pioneer of silent **movie** comedies Mack Sennett was born Michael Sinnott in Canada. His family moved to the United States in 1897, and he found work in burlesque theater before getting a job with the Biograph Film Company in 1908. Sennett successfully developed a number of slapstick comic films while at Biograph. In 1912 he became production head of the Keystone Film Company, where he made several successful films, particularly those featuring the crazy antics of the Keystone Kops. Sennett's success faded in the later 1920s, and by 1929 he worked for a minor company, Educational Pictures. He was declared bankrupt during the 1930s. In 1937 Sennett received a special Academy Award for his contribution to screen comedy.

SETTLEMENT HOUSES. The Settlement House movement that sprang up in the late nineteenth and early twentieth century across the United States was a major part of the **progressive movement**. Inspired by the example of Toynbee Hall in London, the settlement house was a residential community center established in poor, working-class, or **immigrant** urban areas to provide social welfare, educational, and leisure facilities. Stanton Coit and Charles B. Stover established the first settlement in the United States at the University Settlement in New York City in 1886. It was followed in 1889 by the Hull Street Settlement in Chicago, established by **Jane Addams**, and the Henry Street Settlement in New York City in 1893, led by **Lillian Wald**. By 1916 there were some four hundred settlements in different towns and cities. Some 70 percent of the workers in them were **women**, and the settlement houses were closely linked with the **women's suffrage** campaign as well as the calls for wider social and political reform.

See also SOCIAL WORK.

SEVENTEENTH AMENDMENT, 1913. The Seventeenth Amendment, passed by Congress in May 1912 and ratified 31 May 1913, established the direct popular election of U.S. senators rather than by state legislatures. (See appendix 2.)

SHARKEY, JACK (1902–1994). Born Josef Paul Zukauskas, Jack Sharkey changed his name shortly before he left the navy and became a professional boxer in 1924. After a rapid rise through the ranks of heavyweight boxers, Sharkey fought **Jack Dempsey** in 1927 but was knocked out in the seventh round. After beating a number of other contenders Sharkey fought Max Schmeling of Germany for the heavyweight championship in 1930, but he lost by disqualification for a low blow. In 1932 Sharkey won the rematch and became the world heavyweight champion. He lost the title in 1933 to the Italian Primo Carnera. After a comeback in 1935 Sharkey fought the **African American** Joe Louis in 1935, but he was knocked out in the third round and retired from boxing.

See also SPORTS.

SHEELER, CHARLES RETTEW (1883–1965). Charles Sheeler studied **art** in Philadelphia at the Pennsylvania Academy of Fine Arts. He traveled widely in Europe and was influenced by the Impressionist painters in his paintings of still life and architecture. In 1910 he began work as a commercial photographer while also continuing to paint. Several of his paintings were included in the **Armory Exhibition** in 1913 and the 1916 Forum exhibition of leading modern American artists. In 1919 Sheeler moved to New York City and established a reputation for his photographs and paintings of the city. He also produced photographs for *Vogue*, *Vanity Fair*, and advertising agencies. In 1927 he completed a widely published series of photographic studies of **Henry Ford**'s River Rouge factory in Michigan. In addition to photographs, Sheeler also painted many industrial landscapes, and his career, which continued through to the 1950s, included commissions from Kodak, U.S. Steel, and **General Motors**. In 1962 Sheeler was awarded the American Academy of Arts and Letters' Merit Medal, and he was elected to the National Institute of Arts and Letters in 1963.

SHEPPARD, MORRIS (1875–1941). Morris Sheppard graduated in law from the University of Texas in 1897 and obtained a master of law degree from Yale in 1898. After practicing law in Texas he was elected to Congress as a progressive **Democrat** in 1902 and served until 1913, when he was elected to the U.S. Senate on a prohibition platform. Sheppard introduced a constitutional amendment providing for **Prohibition** in 1913; it was passed in 1917 and ratified as the **Eighteenth Amendment** in 1919. Sheppard coauthored the **Sheppard-Towner Act** and was also one of the founders of the congressional "Farm Bloc," formed in 1921 to lobby on behalf of agricultural interests. He supported **Franklin D. Roosevelt** and the **New Deal** but was chair of the Senate Investigating Committee on Campaign Expenditures, which criticized the political role played by members of the Works Progress

Administration. As chair of the Military Affairs Committee, Sheppard supported the administration's preparations for war including the introduction of Selective Service in 1940.

SHEPPARD-TOWNER ACT. Passed in 1921, the Sheppard-Towner Act, or Maternity and Infancy Care Act, provided federal-state funding for child and maternal health centers, some three thousand of which were established between 1921 and 1929, when its funding was ended by Congress.
See also SHEPPARD, MORRIS (1875–1941).

SIMMONS, WILLIAM JOSEPH (1880–1945). The founder of the second **Ku Klux Klan**, William Simmons went into the church ministry at an early age. After service in the Spanish-American War (1898), Simmons was licensed to preach for the Methodist Church, and he preached in Florida and Alabama until 1912. After breaking with the church Simmons worked with fraternal organizations and became district manager of the Woodmen of the World in Atlanta. Inspired by **D. W. Griffith**'s film *The Birth of a Nation*, Simmons launched the Ku Klux Klan in 1915.

In 1920 Simmons hired Edward Y. Clarke and Elizabeth Tyler of the Southern Publicity Association to expand Klan membership. Capitalizing on the conservative postwar mood, Clarke and Tyler increased membership from a few thousand to 2 million, and the Klan spread beyond the South into Indiana and Illinois and into urban areas. Clarke and then Hiram W. Evans replaced Simmons as "imperial wizard" in 1922. Simmons attempted to regain control in 1923 and eventually agreed to sell his interests back to the Klan for $90,000 in 1924. Simmons established another organization, the Knights of the Flaming Sword, but like the Klan it faded away, and with it so did Simmons.

SINCLAIR, HARRY FORD (1876–1956). Harry Sinclair first qualified as a pharmacist and ran his father's drugstore in Wheeling, West Virginia. Having lost the business in 1901, he began work in the oil industry buying and selling oil leases. He was successful enough to buy his own well in 1905, and, following a series of successful investments, Sinclair established the Sinclair Oil and Refining Corporation in 1916. He served as a member of the oil subcommittee of an advisory committee to the **Council of National Defense**. After the war he continued to build up his business empire, and in 1923 it was revealed in a Senate investigation that he had leased naval oil reserves in **Teapot Dome**, Wyoming, from the Department of the Interior without competitive bidding. Sinclair refused to testify before the Senate committee and was held in contempt. In 1927 he was tried with secretary of the interior **Albert Fall** on a charge of criminal conspiracy, but the case ended in a mistrial. He was tried again in 1928 after Fall had been convicted separately on other charges. Sinclair refused to testify and was found in contempt for shadowing jurors. He was jailed for nine months in 1929 on the two contempt charges, but was never convicted for other charges relating to Teapot Dome.

Sinclair's oil business continued to grow even through the **Great Depression**. During World War II he served on the Petroleum Industry War Council. By 1950 the Sinclair Oil Company was the seventh largest integrated petroleum company in the United States.

SINCLAIR, UPTON BEALL (1878–1968). Educated at the City College of New York and Columbia University, the author Upton Sinclair began publishing with his *Springtime Harvest* in 1901. This was followed by several other books, but his first major success came with *The Jungle* in 1906, an exposé of the life and working experience of **immigrants** in Chicago. Sinclair's writing reflected his socialism, and among his other more successful books was *Cry for Justice*, an anthology of social protest published in 1915, and the novels *King Coal* (1917) and *Oil* (1927). His *Boston* (1928) dealt with the **Sacco and Vanzetti case**.

Sinclair moved to California after World War I and stood, unsuccessfully, as the **Socialist** candidate for the U.S. House of Representatives in 1920 and for governor of California in 1926 and 1930. In 1934 he ran for governor on the **Democratic** ticket and a platform to End Poverty in California (EPIC). He was unsuccessful. Sinclair later wrote a number of political novels dealing with Hitler and the rise of Fascism and his "Lanny Budd" novels, *World's End* (1940), *Between Two Worlds* (1941), and *Wide Is the Gate* (1943), for which he was awarded the Pulitzer Prize. Altogether Sinclair wrote more than ninety books.

See also LITERATURE AND THEATER.

SISSLE, NOBLE (1889–1975). The **African American** songwriter and bandleader Noble Sissle began singing professionally in 1908, formed his first orchestra in 1915, and also performed as a singer. During **World War I** Sissle was a drum major in the 369th U.S. Infantry band under James Reese Europe. After the war Sissle toured with his partner in songwriting, pianist Eubie Blake. Together they wrote the **music** for *Shuffle Along*, which opened on Broadway in May 1921. *Shuffle Along* included famous songs such as "Love Will Find a Way" and "I'm Just Wild about Harry," helped popularize jazz **dancing**, and is regarded by some critics as the opening of the **Harlem Renaissance**. Other musicals followed—*Elsie* (1923), *Chocolate Dandies* (1924), and *Keep Shufflin'* (1928). In 1926 Sissle and Blake toured in Europe, and Sissle continued to perform in Paris and London, with visits back to the United States, through to 1930. Through the 1930s Sissle and Blake were reunited, and their band included at various times such performers as Sidney Bechet, **Duke Ellington**, and Lena Horne. Sissle performed in various tours for troops during World War II and continued playing through to the 1960s. He was one of the founders of the Negro Actors' Guild and was its first president.

SIXTEENTH AMENDMENT, 1913. Passed by Congress in 1909, the Sixteenth Amendment was ratified on 30 March 1913. It provided Congress with the power to tax incomes. (See appendix 2.)

SLEMP, CAMPBELL BASCOM (1870–1943). A graduate of Virginia Military Institute and the University of Virginia Law School, Campbell Slemp practiced law in Virginia until 1907, when he was elected as a **Republican** to fill his dead father's seat in the U.S. House of Representatives. Slemp was a staunch support of **William Howard Taft** and then of **Warren Harding**, and he helped secure the Republican victories in southern states in 1920. In 1923 he became secretary to president **Calvin Coolidge** and in 1924 was Coolidge's campaign manager. Slemp resigned his position as secretary in 1925 and resumed his law practice in Washington, D.C. Slemp published a positive account of Coolidge's presidency in *The Mind of the President* in 1926. He continued to be active in the Republican National Committee and supported **Herbert Hoover** in 1928. He was appointed American commissioner general at the French Colonial Exposition in 1931.

SMITH, ALFRED EMANUEL (1873–1944). "Al" Smith, as he came to be known, was born and brought up in New York City, where he worked in a variety of jobs including the fish market. He was involved in local politics at an early age and was elected to the New York State legislature in 1903, and served until to 1915, becoming **Democratic Party** leader in 1911 and speaker in 1913. Smith took part in the state factory commission established after the Triangle shirtwaist factory fire that killed 146 people in 1911, and he sponsored a number of bills to protect the health and safety of workers, particularly **women** and children. Smith was sheriff of New York County from 1915 to 1917 and president of the New York Board of Aldermen in 1917. In 1918 he was elected governor of New York and he served for four terms: 1919–1920, 1923–1928. Following his failure to win reelection in 1920, Smith served on the National Board of Indian Commissioners and Port Authority of New York. He also acted as chairman of the U.S. Trucking Corporation.

Smith's period as governor was associated with the continuation of a reform program: limiting the working hours of women and children, improving **railroad** safety, expanding public **education**, and reforming state government. Smith also supported measures to repeal **Prohibition**. In 1924 Smith failed to win the Democratic Party's presidential nomination. He won the nomination in 1928, but lost the election in part because of his Irish Catholic background and his opposition to Prohibition. However, given the apparent prosperity at the time, **Herbert Hoover**'s election victory for the **Republicans** was probably fairly inevitable. Hoover gained more than 58 percent of the popular vote and won 444 electoral college votes to Smith's 87. Following his defeat Smith became manager of the company that managed the Empire State Building in New York City. He supported **Franklin D. Roosevelt**'s nomination in 1932 but increasingly became critical of the **New Deal** for creating what he saw as class conflict. In 1936 he campaigned against Roosevelt and in favor of the Republican Alfred M. Landon. In 1940 Smith supported Wendell Willkie.

SMITH, BESSIE (1894–1937). The great blues singer Bessie Smith began performing on the streets of Chattanooga, Tennessee, at the age of nine. She joined other **African American** performers in a touring show in 1912 and spent several years in minstrel and vaudeville shows. By 1920 Smith was established as a star among the black community and in 1921 she produced her first record, but she was not signed by Columbia Records until 1923. Her first single sold 780,000 copies in six months, and the "Empress of the Blues," as Smith was billed, became probably the most successful African American performer of the 1920s. She made over 180 recordings, performed in a number of revues, and appeared in one film, *St. Louis Blues*, made in 1929. Smith's career began to wane in the 1930s, but she continued to tour theaters in the South and to perform occasionally in **Harlem**, New York. In 1937 she was seriously injured in a car crash in Mississippi, but denied treatment at the nearest white hospitals, she died, having been taken two hundred miles to an African American hospital.
See also JAZZ; MUSIC AND DANCE; WOMEN.

SMITH-HUGHES ACT, 1917. The Smith-Hughes Act established a Federal Board for Vocational **Education** to encourage training in **agriculture**, home economics, vocational subjects, commerce, trade, and industry by providing federal funds to states on a matching basis.

SMITH-LEVER ACT, 1914. The Smith-Lever Act provided an appropriation of $500,000, with additional appropriations of the same amount annually until 1923 to be distributed equally to the states to support adult **education** in **agriculture**.

SMOOT, REED (1862–1941). A graduate of Brigham Young University, Reed Smoot was a banker and official in the Mormon Church prior to becoming the first Mormon elected to the U.S. Senate by the state legislature in 1902. He held his seat until 1933. Smoot was a conservative **Republican**, and he opposed the **League of Nations**. In 1930 he cosponsored the **Hawley-Smoot Tariff Act**. He was defeated in the election of 1932 and returned to Salt Lake City.
    See also TARIFFS.

SNYDER, RUTH (1895–1928). Ruth Snyder became the center of public attention in 1927 after she and her lover, Judd Gray, were arrested for the murder of her husband, the editor of *Motor Boating*, Albert Snyder. The trial was the subject of a great deal of lurid news coverage in which Ruth Snyder was painted as the "femme fatale." Found guilty on 9 May 1927, Snyder became only the second **woman** to be electrocuted when she was executed in Sing Sing prison, New York, on 12 January 1928. Thomas Howard photographed the moment of her death using a concealed camera, and the shocking picture appeared on the front page of the *New York Daily News*. Judd was executed shortly after Snyder. The murder formed the basis of James M. Cain's book *Double Indemnity* (1943), made into a film in 1944.
    See also CRIME AND POLICING; NEWSPAPERS AND MAGAZINES.

SOCIALIST LABOR PARTY (SLP). The Socialist Labor Party began as the Workingmen's Party in 1876 but was renamed in 1877. It fielded its first presidential candidate in 1892. Committed to the idea of socialist industrial unions, the SLP tried unsuccessfully to forge links with the **American Federation of Labor (AFL)** but was later to have some support within the **Industrial Workers of the World (IWW)**. In the 1890s the party was led by Daniel De Leon, but ideological divisions within the party led to the formation of the **Socialist Party of America (SPA)** in 1901. Nonetheless, the smaller SLP survived until 2008 and fielded presidential candidates in every election up to and including 1976. In the 1920s the SLP never got more than 31,084 votes; in 1932 it received 34,038, and its highest ever number of votes was 53,814 in 1972.
    See also POLITICAL PARTIES.

SOCIALIST PARTY OF AMERICA (SPA). In 1897 **Eugene V. Debs** established a Social Democratic Party, and in 1901 this joined with reformist elements of the Socialist Labor Party led by **Morris Hillquit** to establish the Socialist Party of America. The Socialist Party was committed to state ownership of the means of production and the equitable distribution of wealth among the working classes. It sought to achieve these ends through evolutionary rather than revolutionary means, and supported social and economic reform through the political process. Support for the Socialist Party was particularly strong in working-class **immigrant** communities, but it began to attract middle-class intellectuals like **Upton Sinclair**, **Walter Lippmann**, and **John Reed** in the years before 1914. However, when the party opposed America's entry into **World War I**, many people deserted it, and the majority of its leaders were jailed under the **Espionage** and **Sedition Acts**. Debs ran as the party's presidential candidate in every election except 1916 (when A. L. Benson stood) up to and including that of 1920, when he received almost 1 million votes despite being in prison. In 1912 he secured 6 percent of the popular vote with over nine hundred thousand votes. At the end of the war the party divided between those who wished to follow a revolutionary path along Russian lines and those who continued to espouse a reformist path. The "**Red Scare**" further discredited and weakened them, and its membership fell from 24,661 in 1921 to a mere 8,477 by 1926. In 1924 the SPA endorsed the **Progressive Party** candidate **Robert M. La Follette**. In the 1930s and 1940s the leader of the party was **Norman Thomas**, but even at the height of the **Depression** he could attract only less than nine hundred thousand votes, about 2 percent of the vote (the total number of voters having increased considerably since 1912 with the enfranchisement of **women**). The SPA continued to field presidential candidates through to 1956.

See also BERGER, VICTOR LOUIS (1860–1929); POLITICAL PARTIES; SOCIALIST LABOR PARTY (SLP); TRADE UNIONS.

SOCIAL WORK. The social work profession emerged in the period between the late nineteenth century and the late 1930s out of the philanthropic, charitable, and community welfare programs. As industrialization, **immigration**, and urbanization developed from the 1870s on, mounting concern about urban poverty, crime, and ill health brought a variety of responses. The Charity Organization Societies (COS) sought to better organize the traditional voluntary charitable responses to poverty, unemployment, and hardship through investigators who would assess need and allocate resources. Other educated middle-class workers, many of them **women** like **Jane Addams**, turned to **settlement houses** to provide assistance, education, and a meeting point for the immigrant working classes and American middle classes. Many of the people concerned about social problems joined the **progressive movement** to call for political reform to improve conditions at work and in the cities and to make politics more responsive to social need.

The study of social problems and provision of different forms of social welfare led to the emergence of professional social workers. The National Conference of Charities and Corrections (NCCC), formed in 1874, became the National Conference of Social Work in 1917. People like **Edith Abbott** and **Sophonisba Breckinridge** established new educational programs and schools, and an American Association of Social Workers (AASW) was created in 1921. Increasingly in the 1920s the focus was less on the social aspect and more on case studies and the individual and psychological causes of social problems. With the coming of the **Great Depression**, however, social welfare once more became a national issue. Under the reform programs of the **New Deal** social work moved from the private into the public sector and completed the professionalization of social work in a modern, often federally funded, welfare system.

SPEAKEASY. Speakeasies were illegal, unlicensed drinking establishments. Although they had existed before the passage of the **National Prohibition Act** in 1919, speakeasies reached a height of popularity during the mid-1920s. Speakeasies varied from restaurants, clubs, or basic bars to which admittance was gained by payment of a fee or private membership.

See also BOOTLEGGING; CRIME AND POLICING; PROHIBITION.

SPINGARN, JOEL ELIAS (1875–1939). After obtaining a PhD from Columbia in 1899, Joel Spingarn took up a teaching position in **literature** at the university. He became a professor in 1909 but was dismissed in 1911 for his criticism of university policy. Although he published several collections of poetry, Spingarn established a reputation as a literary critic, publishing several works including *The New Criticism* (1911). In 1919 he became one of the founders of the Harcourt, Brace and Company publishers and edited its European library series.

Spingarn was active in progressive politics and attended the **Progressive Party** conventions in 1912 and 1916. In 1910 he became a member of the executive of the **National Association for the Advancement of Colored People** (NAACP) and succeeded **Oswald Garrison Villard** as chairman in 1914. In 1913 he established the Spingarn Medal, an annual award to **African Americans** of achievement. In 1917 Spingarn, who served as an Army intelligence officer, used his influence to win the establishment of a segregated officer-training school for black soldiers. Spingarn was president of the NAACP from 1930 to 1939.

SPORTS. The years prior to **World War I** had already witnessed an increase in professional sports, but it was the 1920s, often described as a "Golden Age," that witnessed the real rise of sports as a national, professional commercial enterprise. While college sports became ever more popular, even among those who had never been to college, professional sports emerged as equally important. New stadiums such as Comiskey Park in Chicago, Ebbets Field in Brooklyn, Fenway Park in Boston, and Wrigley Field in Chicago were built for baseball and football before the war. The original Yankee Stadium in the Bronx, New York City, opened in 1923. Major league baseball had already emerged as the national sport by the end of the nineteenth century and was organized under the American and National Leagues, who staged the World Series from 1903 on. The game lost some of its following due to low-scoring games and because of the scandal in 1919 when several members of the Chicago White Sox were found to have "fixed" the **World Series**. Interest in the game resumed due to the impact of live **radio** broadcasts, which began in 1920, and the appearance of some of the sport's greatest players, particularly **"Babe" George Herman Ruth**, who played first for the Boston Red Sox and then for the New York Yankees. The record-breaking hitting of Ruth and **Lou Gehrig** attracted huge crowds to the game.

Baseball had become racially segregated in the late nineteenth century, and **African American** players had to establish their own National Negro League (NNL) in 1920. It existed until 1931, when it collapsed due to the effects of the **Great Depression**. The Eastern Colored League (ECL) was created in 1923, and the Negro World Series was staged between the ECL and NNL until 1928, when the Eastern League disintegrated and was later replaced by the American Negro League. A Negro Southern League also existed for a while.

The American Football Association was founded by eleven teams in September 1920 and in 1922 became the National Football League (NFL). While **Knute Rockne**'s Notre Dame football team dominated the game for much of the decade, support for noncollege teams grew, and **Red Grange** successfully made the switch from college football to professional in 1925. He was watched by a crowd of over sixty-five thousand when his Chicago Bears beat the New York Giants at the Polo Grounds in New York City. Basketball was a minor sport in comparison with football and baseball, but the formation of the American Basketball League (ABL) in 1925 helped to provide a more secure base on which to build. Ice hockey was predominantly a Canadian game, and the first significant American team did not appear until the Boston Bruins were formed in 1924.

Individual sports also became big spectator sports, none more so than professional boxing. Prizefighting was still illegal in several states before **World War I**, but with its acceptance as an Olympic sport at the 1904 St.

Louis games, the establishment of boxing commissions, and the use of boxing in military training during the war, it became more professional, more organized, more commercial, and more popular after 1918. The National Boxing Association was formed in 1921. Like other sports, boxing was segregated, although an African American, Jack Johnson, had held the world heavyweight championship from 1910 until his eventual defeat by the "Great White Hope," Jess Willard. In 1919 Willard lost the title to **Jack Dempsey** in a brutal fight. Dempsey was defeated by **Gene Tunney** in 1926 and again, controversially, in a rematch billed as "the fight of the century" in 1927. Both fights took place before huge crowds and were also broadcast on the **radio** to audiences estimated to be close to 50 million.

Golf developed as a popular sport as several cities established municipal golf courses, and players such as **Bobby Jones** and **Walter Hagen** dominated the amateur and professional game. **Women** were also becoming accepted in golf, and players like Edith Cummings (the inspiration for a character in **F. Scott Fitzgerald**'s novel *The Great Gatsby*) and Glenna Collett Vare dominated the game. Women's increased acceptance in sports was aided by the contributions of **Helen Wills** in tennis and the swimmer **Gertrude Ederle**, who won three medals in the Paris Olympics in 1924. **Bill Tilden** dominated the men's tennis game until his retirement in 1930.

See also COBB, TYRUS RAYMOND (1886–1961); DAVIS, DWIGHT FILLEY (1879–1945); WEISSMULLER, JOHNNY (1904–1984).

STARR, ELLEN GATES (1859–1940). Ellen Starr, who with **Jane Addams** founded **Hull House**, studied briefly at Rockford Female Seminary before taking up teaching in 1878. She and Addams traveled to Europe in 1888 and opened Hull House in Chicago the following year. Starr was particularly interested in **art** and **education**, and in 1894 she formed the Chicago Public School Art Society to place art in school classrooms. In 1897 Starr went to London, England, to study bookbinding and returned in 1898 to open a bookbindery at Hull House. Starr was actively involved in a number of industrial disputes between 1895 and 1915, and she campaigned against low wages, long hours, and the exploitation of **women** workers. She helped to found the Chicago branch of the Women's Trade Union League in 1904. Starr joined the **Socialist Party** and stood unsuccessfully as a candidate in local elections. She converted to Catholicism in 1920 and, suffering from ill health, she entered a convent in 1930.

See also SETTLEMENT HOUSES; TRADE UNIONS.

STEEL STRIKE, 1919. Encouraged by gains in membership and strength during **World War I**, the **American Federation of Labor** hoped to organize the steel industry in the aftermath of the conflict. Organized labor had failed to make inroads in the steel industry since major defeats in the 1890s and in 1902. The labor force often worked a twelve-hour day, seven days a week. A National Committee for Organizing Iron and Steel Workers was established under the leadership of **William Z. Foster**, and the strike began on 22 September 1919, when 250,000 workers came out. The employers, led by **Elbert Gary** of U.S. Steel, characterized the strikers and Foster as "Bolsheviks" and refused to take part in any collective bargaining. They used strikebreakers, police, and federal troops to overcome the strike, which was effectively over by December and officially called off on 8 January 1920. The twelve-hour day remained in force until the mid-1920s.

See also TRADE UNIONS.

STEICHEN, EDWARD JEAN (1879–1973). The famous photographer was born Édouard Jean Steichen in Luxembourg. His family came to the United States in 1881, and he grew up in Chicago. He studied for four years at the American Fine **Art** Company in Milwaukee and also the Milwaukee Art Students League. Like many of his contemporaries he spent time in Europe from 1900 to 1902 and held his first one-man exhibition in Paris in 1902. Steichen met and began a lasting professional relationship with **Alfred Stieglitz** in 1900 and was involved in the production of the influential *Camera Work* in 1903. Steichen was a frequent contributor to the journal, which ran until 1917. In 1911 his photographs of gowns in *Art et Décorum* probably began modern fashion photography. During **World War I** Steichen commanded a photographic division with the **American Expeditionary Force (AEF)**. After the war he photographed many of the leading **movie** actors of the day including **Charlie Chaplin** and perhaps most famously, in 1928, **Greta Garbo**. Many of his photographs were published between 1923 and 1938 in the magazines *Vogue* and *Vanity Fair*. During World War II Steichen worked with the U.S. Navy and directed a documentary film, *The Fighting Lady* (1945), which won an Academy Award for the best documentary. After the war Steichen became director in the Department of Photography of the New York Museum of Modern Art. He was awarded the President's Medal of Freedom by Lyndon Baines Johnson in 1963.

See also NEWSPAPERS AND MAGAZINES.

STEIMER, MOLLIE (1897–1980). Born in Russia, Mollie Steimer immigrated to the United States with her family in 1913. Steimer found work in the garment industry in New York City and became active in the **trade union** movement. She became an anarchist and was part of a group that opposed U.S. entry into **World War I**. Steimer and five others were arrested under the **Espionage Act** in 1918. Steimer was sentenced to fifteen years in jail and a $500 fine. Her conviction was upheld despite protests from people such as

Roger Baldwin and **Margaret Sanger**. While in prison it was decided that Steimer should be deported with other radicals, including **Emma Goldman**, held in the **Palmer Raids**, and she was sent to Russia. In 1922 she was arrested for political activities and sent to Siberia. In 1923 Steimer was deported to Germany and settled in Berlin. She fled Germany following Adolf Hitler's rise to power and eventually settled in Mexico, where she died still true to her anarchist beliefs.

See also WOMEN.

STEIN, GERTRUDE (1874–1951). A graduate of Radcliffe College, Gertrude Stein lived in Paris from 1902, where the salon she established was the center of the group of American literary exiles, including **Sherwood Anderson, F. Scott Fitzgerald**, and **Ernest Hemingway**, during the interwar period. It was Stein who characterized Hemingway and others as a **"lost generation."** She was the author of several books, collections of poems, and essays, many marked by an avant-garde, stream-of-consciousness style. Among the best known are *Three Lives* (1909), *Making of Americans* (1925), *The Autobiography of Alice B. Toklas* (1933), *Four Saints in Three Acts* (1934), and *Picasso* (1938).

See also LITERATURE AND THEATER; WOMEN.

STIEGLITZ, ALFRED (1864–1946). Educated first in New York, Alfred Stieglitz moved with his family to Europe and continued his education in Berlin, Germany, in the 1880s. It was while in Germany that Stieglitz began to study photography and he began to exhibit and publish his photographs. He returned to New York in 1890 and set up the Photochrome Engraving Company. Stieglitz was not committed to business, and in 1893 he became the editor of *American Amateur Photographer*. In 1896 he was involved in the foundation of the Camera Club of New York, and he established the official publication, *Camera Notes*, the following year. By the turn of the century he had established himself through publications and exhibitions as the best-known photographer in the United States. He had an enormous influence and helped to establish the Photo-Secession group with **Edward Steichen**, and edited *Camera Work* from 1903 to 1917. The studio he and Steichen established, known simply as 291, was famous for showing the work of young American artists and leading European artists such as Pablo Picasso, Henri Matisse, and Auguste Rodin. Stieglitz later established other galleries in New York City, where he continued to show the work of new photographers and artists such as **Paul Strand**, Ansell Adams, and Walker Evans. He married **Georgia O'Keefe** in 1924 and encouraged her artistic development in the 1920s. From 1923 Stieglitz put on regular one-man shows of his work, or jointly with O'Keefe; he gave his last one-man exhibition in 1934, a year after donating much of his work to the Metropolitan Museum of Art.

See also ART.

STIMSON, HENRY LEWIS (1867–1950). One of America's longest serving statesmen, Henry Stimson graduated from Yale University in 1888, attended Harvard Law School, qualified in law, and practiced in New York City. Stimson was U.S. attorney for southern New York State and in 1910 ran unsuccessfully as the **Republican** candidate for governor. In 1911 president **William Howard Taft** appointed him secretary of war. During **World War I** Stimson served as a colonel with the artillery in France. In 1927 president **Calvin Coolidge** appointed Stimson to mediate between warring factions in Nicaragua. From 1927 to 1929 he served as governor general of the Philippines and resisted early moves toward independence.

In 1928 president **Herbert Hoover** appointed Stimson as secretary of state, and in that capacity he chaired the U.S. delegation to the **London Naval Conference**, 1930–1931. In 1931 Stimson issued a statement that became known as the "Stimson Doctrine" expressing U.S. opposition to the Japanese conquest of Manchuria and refusing to accept any change in territorial possession as a consequence of the invasion. Stimson tried to mobilize European opposition to Japanese aggression and would have preferred to take stronger action but bowed to Hoover's wishes to maintain a purely limited diplomatic response. In 1940 Stimson was one of two Republicans appointed to the cabinet when president **Franklin D. Roosevelt** made him secretary of war. Stimson was also the president's senior adviser on atomic weapons. During World War II he recommended offering the Japanese terms for surrender that would allow them to keep the emperor. He also supported the dropping of the atomic bombs in 1945 and was responsible for the choice of targets.

See also FOREIGN POLICY.

ST. MIHIEL SALIENT. German position held in the **Argonne** for four years during **World War I**. The salient was attacked by the American 1st Army on 12 September 1918 and taken by 16 September. The victory may have inflated the self-esteem of the U.S. forces, leading them to underestimate the task which faced them in the subsequent Argonne offensive, but it did provide an important boost to **Allied** morale and vindicated general **John Pershing**'s policy of maintaining the U.S. army as an independent force.

STOCK MARKET CRASH. *See* WALL STREET CRASH, 1929.

STODDARD, (THEODORE) LOTHROP (1883–1950). Born in Brookline, Massachusetts, Stoddard graduated from Harvard College, Boston, in 1905 and studied law at Boston University. He was admitted to the bar in 1908. Following an extensive tour of Europe, Stoddard studied political science at Harvard University, obtaining his master of arts degree in 1910 and a PhD in history in 1914. His PhD thesis was on the slave revolt in Haiti and was published as *The French Revolution in San Domingo* in 1914. He was, however, best known for his writing on race—his *The Rising Tide of Color Against White World-Supremacy* (1920) was a popular success. Sharing some of the views of **Madison Grant**, Stoddard warned of the threat of a population explosion among the nonwhite population of the world. His *Revolt Against Civilization* (1922) advocated **immigration** control and birth control legislation, and Stoddard served on the board of directors of the American Birth Control League. Stoddard also wrote on *The New World of Islam* (1921). He shared some of the views of the Nazis in Germany and he spent time as a journalist there between 1939 and 1940 and wrote a study, *Into the Darkness* (1940), that although sympathetic to Nazi theories on race and eugenics, was nonetheless critical of the restrictions on democracy under Adolf Hitler. From 1940 to 1945 he was a **foreign policy** adviser with the Washington *Evening Star*. However, his views on race were discredited during World War II, and subsequently much of his writing was dismissed or ignored.

STOKES, ROSE PASTOR (1879–1933). Stokes was born Rose Wieslander in Poland but moved first to London, England, and then to Cleveland, Ohio, as a child. In 1900 she became a journalist for the Cleveland *Yidisher Tageblatt*, then moved to New York City, where she met and, in 1905, married James Graham Phelps Stokes, a leader in the **settlement house** movement. Stokes became an active campaigner for reform and socialist causes. She supported U.S. entry into **World War I** and initially broke with the **Socialist Party of America**. However, she returned to the party following the Bolshevik Revolution in Russia and in 1918 was charged under the **Espionage Act** for criticizing the involvement in the war. Her conviction was overturned on appeal. She joined the **Communist Party USA** after the war and was one of the few **women** elected to the executive committee.

STONE, HARLAN FISKE (1872–1946). Harlan Fiske Stone graduated from Amherst College in 1894 and Columbia Law School in 1898. He practiced law in New York City and in 1902 became a professor and then, in 1910, dean in the Columbia Law School. Stone held that post until he was appointed attorney general by president **Calvin Coolidge** to succeed **Harry S. Daugherty** in 1924. In 1925 Coolidge appointed Stone to the **Supreme**

Court, where, with **Oliver Wendell Holmes** and **Louis Brandeis**, he became one of the liberal dissenting voices. He defended legislation to protect the rights of **women**, children, and workers, and in 1940 became chief justice.

STONE, WILLIAM JOEL (1848–1918). A graduate of the University of Missouri and a qualified lawyer, William Stone was elected **Democratic** congressman to the U.S. House of Representatives for three terms from 1884 to 1890, and then governor of Missouri from 1893 to 1897. As governor he supported the employers' liability law but was defeated by opposition from the **railroad** companies. Stone was also conspicuous for his support of "free silver," the use of silver coinage to expand currency supply in the mid-1890s. In 1903 he was elected to the U.S. Senate and served until his death. As a senator Stone supported **Woodrow Wilson** and helped to secure the passage of the **Underwood-Simmons tariff** in 1913.

As chair of the Senate Foreign Relations Committee from 1914 Stone increasingly disagreed with Wilson's policies with regard to Germany and in 1917 was one of the "little group of willful men" who opposed giving the president the power to arm merchant ships. Once America had entered **World War I** Stone offered his full support, and although coming from a state with a large German-American population, said there could be "no divided patriotism." Stone supported the notion of a "peace without victory" but died before the war had ended.

STORRS, JOHN HENRY BRADLEY (1885–1956). Often described as "one of the most important **modernist** sculptors" of the early twentieth century, John Storrs was born in Chicago. He attended the Chicago Manual Training School, where he graduated in 1905. After traveling in Europe, Storrs studied at the **Art** Institute of Chicago, the School of the Museum of Fine Arts in Boston, and the Pennsylvania Academy of Fine Arts before going to Paris in 1911, where he worked for a time with Auguste Rodin. He was to spend most of his life in France but returned to America periodically to work and exhibit. He married the French writer Marguerite De Ville Chabrol in 1914.

Storrs held his first one-man show in 1920 in Chicago, and his abstract sculptures such as the aptly named *Abstraction* showed the influence of Native American art as well as Cubism. However, the son of an architect, and influenced by the work of Marcel Duchamps, **Man Ray**, and the buildings of Frank Lloyd Wright, Storrs's work increasingly resembled the skyscrapers of Manhattan, and his tall, sleek, geometrical designs in metals such as brass and copper were appropriately named "Studies in Architectural Form" (1923–1927). His piece titled *Auto Tower* (1922) combined the shape of a tower block when vertical with that of an automobile when horizontal. His thirty-one-foot-high figure of *Ceres* was commissioned by the Chicago Board of Trade in 1928 and stood on top of its building, combining sculpture with architecture.

As materials became more expensive or in short supply, Storrs turned to paintings in the 1930s. However, he was imprisoned twice by the Germans during World War II, and his output declined. He was made a Chevalier of the French Legion of Honor in 1938.

STRAND, PAUL (1890–1976). The photographer Paul Strand was born in New York City, the son of immigrants from what was Bohemia, now part of the Czech Republic. From 1904 to 1909 he attended the New York City Ethical Culture School, where he was taught by the famous photographer Lewis Hine. From 1911 to 1913 Strand worked in insurance but was also a self-employed photographer. He was much influenced by a visit to **Alfred Stieglitz**'s 291 gallery in 1907, and he subsequently joined the Camera Club that included Stieglitz and **Edward Steichen**; in 1916 some of his work appeared in *Camera Work*, the magazine established by Stieglitz. His photograph of *Wall Street* (1915) was inspirational in the new studies of the city and buildings. Strand had already established himself as a leading pictorial photographer known for his portraits of New York City street dwellers and ordinary people when he enlisted in the Army Medical Corps toward the end of **World War I**. After the war Strand made a short film with **Charles Sheeler** portraying New York City, *Manhattan* (1920). During the 1920s Strand increasingly concentrated on close-up images of natural objects, rocks, pieces of wood, and landscapes, similar to the work of **Georgia O'Keefe**. In the 1930s Strand was invited to head the film and photography department at the Museum of Fine Arts in Mexico and he made a film, *Redes* (1936), released in the United States as *The Wave*. He also worked with Pare Lorentz on the film *The Plow That Broke the Plains* (1936), *People of the Cumberlands* (1937), and *Native Land* (1942). During World War II Strand was involved in making government propaganda films. After the war Strand was subject to congressional investigation because of his left-wing leanings, and following the trial of Alger Hiss he left the United States to live in France for the remainder of his life.

See also ART.

STRATTON-PORTER, GENE (1863–1924). Gene Stratton-Porter's career initially began as a photographer and naturalist. Her photographs of birds and moths were published in the magazines *Recreation* and *Outing*, and she acted as photographic consultant for *National Geographic*. She combined her interest in nature with romance in works of fiction, and her first novel, *Song of the Cardinal*, was published in 1903. The following year Stratton-Porter achieved popular success with *Freckles*, a novel that idealized the values of hard work and bravery and a love of nature. Similar themes featured in *A Girl of the Limberlost* (1909), *The Harvester* (1911), and *Laddie* (1913). Her other work included *Michael O'Halloran* (1915), *A Daughter of the Land* (1918), *Her Father's Daughter* (1921), and the posthumous *The Magic Garden* (1927). In addition Stratton-Porter wrote editorials in *McCall's* advancing **women**'s equality, and in 1922 she established her own film company. At the time of her death in an automobile accident, Stratton-Porter was one of the country's most popular writers.

See also LITERATURE AND THEATER.

STRONG, BENJAMIN (1872–1928). After a successful career in **banking**, Benjamin Strong became governor of the newly established **Federal Reserve** Bank of New York in 1914. Strong provided effective leadership during **World War I** when the "Fed" operated as the fiscal agent for the Treasury. After the war Strong worked to ensure the Fed's independence. He was also active in trying to bring stability to the currencies of Germany, Belgium, Italy, and Poland during the 1920s.

SULLIVAN, MARK (1874–1952). Mark Sullivan began his career in journalism while he was still at high school writing for a small-town paper that he also co-owned. He attended Harvard University and Harvard Law School, and graduated in 1903. Sullivan found work first with *McClure's* in 1905, and then with *Collier's* in 1906. He edited *Collier's* from 1914 to 1917. Sullivan supported **Theodore Roosevelt** and the **Progressives**. After **World War I** he reported on the **Versailles peace settlement** for *Collier's* and then wrote first for the *New York Evening Post*, and then the *New York Tribune* (later the *Herald-Tribune*), and he became one of the United States' best-known journalists.

Sullivan was a friend and supporter of **Herbert Hoover**. He opposed **Franklin D. Roosevelt**'s election in 1932 but initially seemed open-minded about the **New Deal**. Gradually he became more critical of the Roosevelt Administration. In addition to his success as a journalist, Sullivan also published an informative six-volume history, *Our Times: The United States 1900–1925*, between 1926 and 1935. He retired from journalism in 1945.

See also NEWSPAPERS AND MAGAZINES.

SUNDAY, BILLY (1862–1935). Born William Ashley Sunday, Billy Sunday achieved early success as a baseball player in Nevada, Iowa, and then Marshalltown. In 1883 he joined the Chicago White Stockings and then the Pittsburgh Alleghenies in 1888, before moving on to the Philadelphia Phillies in 1890. In 1891 at the height of his success Sunday quit sports to become an evangelist with the Chicago Young Men's Christian Association (YMCA). After a few years Sunday became a traveling evangelist and achieved a national reputation that survived into the 1920s. In 1920 he unsuccessfully sought the **Republican** presidential nomination and then agreed to run on a Prohibitionist party ticket, but the party failed to organize. Nonetheless, Sunday was credited with aiding the passage of the **Eighteenth Amendment**. Although his following gradually declined as the 1920s progressed, thousands of mourners gathered to view his coffin after he died in Chicago.

SUPREME COURT. The highest federal court in the land consisting of nine justices, each appointed by the president for life, had in the late nineteenth century increasingly upheld the principles of laissez-faire and notions of freedom of contract to empower business corporations, often to the detriment of **trade unions**. There was a slight shift in the court's attitudes during the **progressive** period, particularly with appointment of **Oliver Wendell Holmes**, **John H. Clarke**, and **Louis Brandeis**, who recognized the law should respond to social change. Prior to **World War I** the court upheld limitations on working hours where the health and safety of workers, men and **women**, were affected, but not where it violated workers' rights to accept whatever working conditions they chose. Regulation of trusts was upheld but increasingly narrowed to apply only to "unreasonable" restraint of trade. Shortly after the war the court upheld the limitations imposed on civil liberties in the **Espionage** and **Sedition acts** in *Schenck v. United States* and *Abrams v. United States*, although Holmes and Brandeis dissented.

In the 1920s the court once more tended to protect business and private property. **Warren Harding**'s appointment of **William Howard Taft** as chief justice, with three other conservative justices (**Pierce Butler**, **Edward Sanford**, and **George Sanford**), resulted in decisions against **child labor laws** (*Bailey v. Drexel Furniture*) and a minimum wage law for women (*Adkins v. Children's Hospital*) but upholding restrictions on trade unions. Faced with a predominantly conservative body that threatened to undermine the **New Deal** in the 1930s, president **Franklin D. Roosevelt** attempted to alter the court's composition. Although his "court packing" failed, the court increasingly adopted a more liberal position and approved the later reform measures.

See also CARDOZO, BENJAMIN NATHAN (1870–1938); FRANK-FURTER, FELIX (1882–1965); MCREYNOLDS, JAMES CLARK (1862–1946); ROBERTS, OWEN JOSEPHUS (1875–1955); SUTHERLAND, (ALEXANDER) GEORGE (1862–1942); VAN DEVANTER, WILLIS (1859–1941).

SUSSEX. The *Sussex* was a French liner torpedoed by a German submarine on 24 March 1916. Not only was this an apparent breach of the pledge made after the sinking of the *Arabic*, but also among those injured were four Americans. On 19 April president **Woodrow Wilson** announced that if such attacks were not suspended, his administration would sever diplomatic links with the German government. On 4 May the German government pledged that all vessels would be visited for inspection prior to any future submarine attack.

See also *LUSITANIA*; WORLD WAR I, 1914–1918.

SUTHERLAND, (ALEXANDER) GEORGE (1862–1942). Born in England, George Sutherland moved to Utah with his family in 1864. Sutherland graduated from the Brigham Young Academy in 1881 and later enrolled in the University of Michigan law school. Having qualified in law Sutherland established a practice in Salt Lake City. He was elected state senator in Utah's first state legislature in 1896 as a **Republican** and in 1900 became Utah's congressman in the U.S. House of Representatives. In 1905 the legislature elected him to the U.S. Senate. In 1915 Sutherland introduced a constitutional amendment to grant **women** the vote. Like the amendment, Sutherland was defeated in his bid for reelection in 1916 and established a law practice in Washington, D.C.

Sutherland supported the election of **Warren Harding** in 1920 and in 1922 was appointed to the **Supreme Court**. Generally a conservative in outlook, Sutherland wrote the majority opinion in *Adkins v. Children's Hospital* (1923) against the law allowing the federal government to fix minimum wages for women in Washington, D.C. However, in *Powell v. Alabama* in 1932, he wrote the opinion setting aside the conviction of one of the **Scottsboro boys** because he had been denied adequate counsel. Sutherland retired in 1938 after **Franklin D. Roosevelt**'s attempt to alter the composition of the Supreme Court had failed but also after *Adkins* had been overturned in *West Coast Hotel v. Parrish*.

SWANSON, GLORIA (1899–1983). The **movie** actress Gloria Swanson was born Gloria May Josephine Svensson. She began her acting career as an extra in Chicago and moved to California in 1915, where she adopted her stage name. Swanson worked for **Mack Sennett** at the Keystone Film Company. She later moved to the Triangle Picture Company but became a star after joining Paramount in 1919 and working with **Cecil B. De Mille**. Swanson starred in *For Better, for Worse* (1919), *Male and Female* (1919), *Why Change Your Wife?* (1920), *The Great Moment* (1921), *Her Gilded Cage*

(1922), *Prodigal Daughters* (1923), *Bluebeard's Eighth Wife* (1923), *Zaza* (1923), *The Humming Bird*, *A Society Scandal*, *Manhandled*, *Her Love Story*, and *Wages of Virtue* (all in 1924).

By the mid-1920s Swanson was the best-known silent screen actress, famous for her looks and her often-extravagant costumes. In 1926 she left Paramount to form her own company, which released films through United Artists. She made *The Love of Sunya* in 1927 and *Sadie Thompson*, a movie version of Somerset Maugham's novel *Rain*, in 1928, and *The Trespasser* in 1929. Her various films in the 1930s were generally less than successful, and she went into retirement. Swanson's comeback after World War II was not successful either, but she did gain an Academy Award for her role in *Sunset Boulevard* in 1950. Her last appearance in the movies was as herself in *Airport* (1975).

See also WOMEN.

SWOPE, GERARD (1872–1957). Swope was an engineer with the Western Electric Company in Chicago who served as an assistant to **George W. Goethals** during **World War I**. In 1919 he joined General Electric as president of its international operations and became chairman of General Electric itself in 1922. With **Owen Young** as chairman, Swope took control of day-to-day running of the company and with great attention to detail helped to increase sales and production through increased efficiency and a reduced workforce. Swope, who had lived and worked at **Hull House settlement** in the 1890s, was instrumental in the introduction of policies of "**welfare capitalism**" but was unsuccessful in gaining employee approval for an unemployment insurance plan.

In response to the **Wall Street Crash** Swope proposed the "Swope Plan" in 1931, which called upon companies to organize by industry and agree to codes of fair competition with agreed working hours and conditions. Elements of the plan were discernible in the **New Deal**'s National Recovery Administration (NRA). Swope chaired the **Department of Commerce**'s Business Advisory and Planning Council formed to advise the NRA in 1933. He later worked toward the implementation of Social Security and labor relations legislation, and was a member of the National Labor Relations Board. He accepted union recognition within General Electric between 1936 and 1939 and after his retirement in 1939 he served as chair of the New York City Housing Authority. He briefly returned to General Electric during World War II. After the war he chaired the Institute of Pacific Relations looking at U.S. **foreign policy** in the Far East.

T

TAFT, WILLIAM HOWARD (1957–1930). Twenty-seventh president of the United States. Born in Cincinnati, Ohio, William Howard Taft graduated from Yale University in 1878 and Cincinnati Law School in 1880. He was admitted to the bar and practiced law in Cincinnati. Taft served as a judge in the Ohio Superior Court, 1887–1890; U.S. solicitor general, 1890–1892; U.S. Circuit Court judge, 1892–1900; and first governor of the Philippines, 1901–1904. He was appointed secretary of war by **Theodore Roosevelt** in 1904, and in 1908, largely at Roosevelt's suggestion, was nominated as the **Republican Party**'s presidential candidate. He defeated the **Democratic** candidate **William Jennings Bryan** by 7.6 million votes to 6.4 million and by 321 Electoral College votes to 162. As president Taft created a separate **Department of Labor** in 1913 and established the **Children's Bureau**. He also supported the Mann-Elkins Act (1910) regulating **railroads** and supported U.S. business investments overseas as part of "dollar diplomacy."

Taft vigorously continued Roosevelt's anti-trust policies, but lost his mentor's support over tariff issues and the dismissal of the chief forester, **Gifford Pinchot**. He lost the presidency to **Woodrow Wilson** in 1912, when many Republicans supported Roosevelt and the **Progressive Party**. Taft became professor of constitutional law at Yale from 1913 to 1921 and during the war he cochaired the War Labor Conference Board with **William Wilson** and served on the **War Labor Board**. He was appointed chief justice of the **Supreme Court** by **Warren Harding** in 1921 and served until 1930. He generally took a conservative position, writing the majority opinion in *Bailey v. Drexel Furniture Co.* (1922), but he dissented from the decision that invalidated minimum wages for **women** in the capital in *Adkins v. Children's Hospital* (1923). Taft was the only person in history to hold the office of president and chief justice.

TARBELL, IDA MINERVA (1857–1944). Ida Tarbell was educated at Allegheny College and then at the Sorbonne, in Paris, from 1891–1894. She became the most famous female journalist of her day through her work with *McClure's*, particularly the series of exposés of the practices of the Standard

Oil Company she wrote between 1902 and 1904 and published as the *History of the Standard Oil Company* in two volumes in 1904. From 1906 to 1915 Tarbell contributed to the *American Magazine*. Tarbell also authored *The Business of Being a Woman* (1912) and *The Ways of a Woman* (1915), both of which revealed something of her conservatism with regard to female equality. She was not a supporter of **women's suffrage** and expressed fairly traditional views on **women**'s "true nature." After **World War I** Tarbell served on president **Woodrow Wilson**'s **Industrial Conference** in 1919 and on president **Warren Harding**'s **Unemployment Conference** in 1921. Tarbell also authored a number of books on history and economics, including *Life of Abraham Lincoln* (1900).

See also NEWSPAPERS AND MAGAZINES.

TARIFFS. The system of duties or taxes levied on imports to raise revenue and to protect U.S. manufacturers began with the policies of Alexander Hamilton and the tariff of 1789 and continued through various forms and amendments thereafter. Attempts to reform the tariff system in order to lower prices became a part of the **Democratic Party**'s platform in the late nineteenth century, particularly after the McKinley tariff of 1890 had raised duties to new levels. Tariff reform was a central part of **Woodrow Wilson**'s **New Freedom** program to bring about fairer competition. He succeeded with the passage of the **Underwood-Simmons Act** of 1913.

President Wilson vetoed an Emergency Agricultural Tariff bill in 1920, but **Warren Harding** passed it in 1921. The attempt to protect U.S. farm prices and the expansion of industry into the South and West helped to erode tariff opposition and enabled the passage of the **Fordney-McCumber Act** in 1922 raising tariffs to a new high. The **Hawley-Smoot Act** (1930) raised tariffs yet further in an attempt to stave off the deepening economic **depression** after the **Wall Street Crash**. It turned out to be counterproductive as other nations were unable to earn dollars to purchase U.S. commodities, and they also responded with their own protective measures.

See also ECONOMY.

TARKINGTON, BOOTH (1869–1946). The novelist and playwright Booth Tarkington first achieved literary success with the publication of *The Gentleman from Indiana* in 1899. He wrote a series of best sellers examining life in Indiana, including *The Two Vanrevels* (1902), *The Conquest of Canaan* (1905), *The Flirt* (1913), *The Turmoil* (1915), and a play that was a box-office success, *The Man from Home* (1908). His collections of boys' stories, beginning with *Penrod* in 1914, were also very popular with all ages. His best-known work, later a famous film, was *The Magnificent Ambersons* (1918), which won Tarkington a Pulitzer Prize. *Alice Adams* (1921) won him

a second Pulitzer. During the early 1920s Tarkington wrote several successful plays. In addition to his studies of Indiana and Indianapolis, Tarkington wrote novels about Maine, and more children's stories through to the 1940s.
See also LITERATURE AND THEATER.

TATE, (JOHN ORLEY) ALLEN (1899–1979). The critic and poet Allen Tate studied at Vanderbilt University, Nashville, between 1918 and 1923. While there he joined a group of poets and writers known as the Fugitives, including **John Crowe Ransom, Donald Davidson**, and Robert Penn Warren, who were part of the southern literary renascence. In 1924 Tate moved to New York City, where he contributed reviews and articles to journals such as the *New Republic* and the *Nation*. In 1928 Tate published a collection of poems, *Mr. Pope and Other Poems* (which included "Ode to the Confederate Dead"), and a biography, *Stonewall Jackson*, followed in 1929 by *Jefferson Davis*. In 1930 Tate, with other Fugitives, was a contributor to the defense of southern agrarianism in *I'll Take My Stand*. In addition to further collections of poetry, Tate published a Civil War novel, *The Fathers*, in 1938. He then became poet in residence at Princeton University until 1942. In 1943 he was appointed consultant in poetry at the Library of Congress, and in 1944 he began to edit the *Sewanee Review*. In 1948 two further collections of poetry and essays were published, and Tate accepted a three-year appointment at New York University. In 1951 he went to the University of Minnesota, where he remained until 1968. Tate continued to publish essays and poetry through the 1950s, and in 1956 he was awarded the Bollingen Prize.
See also LITERATURE AND THEATER.

TAYLOR, (JOSEPH) DEEMS (1885–1966). After graduating from New York University in 1906, Deems Taylor worked for a number of encyclopedias including *Encyclopedia Britannica*. However, Taylor's career lay in **music** and he began writing musical works while still a student. He composed *The Siren Song* in 1912, *Through the Looking Glass* (1918), and *Jurgen* (1925). He achieved some popular success with his operas, *The King's Henchman* (1927) based on a libretto by **Edna St. Vincent Millay**, and again with *Peter Ibbetson* in 1931. Taylor supported himself by journalism and was music critic for the *New York World* from 1921 to 1925, editor of *Musical America* 1927–1929, and music critic for the *New York American*. In the 1930s and 1940s he worked as a radio commentator on music programs. From 1933 until 1966 Taylor was a director of the American Society of Composers, Authors, and Publishers (ASCAP) and its president from 1942 to 1948.

TEAPOT DOME. Near Salt Creek, Wyoming, Teapot Dome was the location of U.S. Navy oil reserves that, together with those in Elk Hills, California, were transferred to the authority of the Department of the Interior in 1921. In 1922 the secretary of the interior, **Albert B. Fall**, leased the reserves to oil companies owned by **Harry F. Sinclair** and **Edward L. Doheny** without any competitive bidding in return for bribes totaling $400,000. This arrangement became public in 1924 following the Senate investigations initiated by **Robert F. LaFollette** and led by **Thomas J. Walsh**. Civil and criminal suits eventually resulted in Fall's conviction for corruption and Sinclair's for criminal contempt. Teapot Dome subsequently became synonymous with the corruption surrounding the administration of **Warren G. Harding**.

See also CRIME AND POLICING.

THALBERG, IRVING GRANT (1899–1936). Irving Thalberg went into business straight from high school and in 1918 entered the **movie** industry when he was employed as a private secretary by the head of Universal Studios, Carl Laemmle. By 1920 Thalberg was general manager in charge of production at Universal City in California. He successfully managed the production of two box-office hits, *Foolish Wives* (1921) and *The Hunchback of Notre Dame* (1923). That same year Thalberg joined **Louis B. Mayer** and was involved in the formation of Metro-Goldwyn-Mayer. The studio soon became the richest and most important in Hollywood.

Thalberg developed a reputation for detailed planning and organization of movie production. He also opposed **trade unions** and fought to keep them out of the industry. In his long career Thalberg was associated with the production of such classics as *The Big Parade* (1925), *The Barretts of Wimpole Street* (1934), *Mutiny on the Bounty* (1935), and *Romeo and Juliet* (1936).

See also GOLDWYN, SAMUEL (1882–1974).

THOMAS, NORMAN MATTOON (1884–1968). **Socialist** leader Norman Thomas studied politics under **Woodrow Wilson** at Princeton University and then turned to theology. He was a Presbyterian pastor and worked in the New York **settlement houses** until 1918. A pacifist, Thomas opposed entry into **World War I**, and was one of the founders of the Fellowship of Reconciliation, a group of pacifist clergymen. He was also one of the founders of the **American Civil Liberties Union**. He was an associate editor of *The Nation* (1921–1922) and codirector of the League of Industrial Democracy from 1922 to 1937. Thomas ran unsuccessfully as the **Socialist** candidate in the New York gubernatorial campaign in 1924 and as the party's presidential candidate in 1928, 1932, and 1936, offering a moderate, non-Marxist brand of socialism critical of Soviet-style communism. He supported U.S. entry into World War II but opposed certain government policies, such as the internment of Japanese Americans. He became the Socialist presidential candidate again in 1940, 1944, and 1948 but later suggested that the party should abandon such campaigns and support progressive **Democrats**. Thomas resigned his official positions in the party in 1955 but continued as its leading spokesman. In his later years he spoke out against U.S. military involvement in Vietnam.

THOMPSON, WILLIAM BOYCE (1869–1930). The mining entrepreneur and financier William Thompson attended Phillips Exeter Academy, New Hampshire, and Columbia University School of Mines. In 1897 Thompson established a mining investment company in Butte, Montana, and in 1899 created the Colorado Mining Company, which successfully developed profitable mines in Arizona and in Nevada. His mining interests quickly spread to other states, and by 1914 he also had investments in mines in Peru and Brazil. Thompson joined with **Bernard Baruch** to develop other mines in Asia and he also worked with J. P. Morgan. During **World War I** Thompson helped to raise funds for **Herbert Hoover**'s Belgian Relief Fund, for the **Liberty Loans**, and for the Red Cross. He also visited Russia and tried to aid the Kerensky regime following the first Russian Revolution. After the war Thompson called for the recognition of the Soviet Union. In 1918 and 1919 Thompson provided financial support for the **Republican Party** and supported **Theodore Roosevelt**'s bid for the presidential nomination. When Roosevelt died, Thompson led the call for a national memorial. During the 1920s Thompson was involved in oil investments and was linked with **Henry Sinclair**.

THOMPSON, WILLIAM HALE (1867–1944). After working for a number of years as a cowboy William Thompson assumed the management of his family's real estate business in Chicago in 1891. He became known nationally as an outstanding football player for the Chicago Athletic Club. In 1900 Thompson entered politics as a **Republican** alderman on Chicago city council. He then served as Cook County commissioner from 1902 to 1904. After a period out of political office Thompson was elected mayor of Chicago with a huge majority in 1915. Opposed to American entry into **World War I**, Thompson ran for the U.S. Senate in 1918 on an **isolationist** platform. He was unsuccessful but in 1919 regained the mayor's position by a narrow margin. Thompson's victory was due in large measure to the support of **African American** voters, and during the **1919 race riots** he delayed in calling in the National Guard for three days.

Thompson's second term as mayor was notable for a major program of public works, but it was also marked by a wave of gangsterism and crime in part due to Thompson's failure to enforce **Prohibition**. Thompson did not seek reelection in 1923. He regained the position in 1927 and promised to recognize individual civil liberties, that is, not uphold Prohibition. He received financial aid from **Al Capone**. Thompson also made a national reputation for his outspoken anti-British views, and he suspended the Chicago superintendent for allowing the use of pro-British history texts in school. Despite his undoubted success in appealing to black, German, and Irish voters, Thompson was defeated in the election of 1931. He was defeated in the gubernatorial election in 1936 and failed to gain the Republican nomination for governor in 1939. He ran as an independent but was defeated.

TILDEN, WILLIAM ("BILL") TATUM 1893–1953). Bill Tilden dominated tennis in America throughout the 1920s. He began playing tennis as a child. In 1913 and 1914 he won the U.S. mixed doubles title with Mary Kendall Browne. Tilden enlisted in the army during **World War I** and played exhibition games around the country. In 1918, while still in the service, he won the national clay court championship and the U.S. doubles championship with Vinnie Richards. After winning the Wimbledon championship in London in 1920 Tilden went on to win his first U.S. singles title the same year. He held on to the first ranking in the United States for six years, winning six U.S. singles titles, a second Wimbledon title, the World Hard Court title in 1921, and fifteen Davis Cup singles contests. In addition Tilden held various clay court doubles and mixed doubles titles. He won the U.S. title again in 1929 and his last Wimbledon championship in 1930, the year he retired from the amateur game.

In 1930 Tilden became a tennis professional, playing exhibition matches and coaching. He won the professional championship singles titles in 1931 and 1935, and doubles titles in 1931 and 1932 with Frank Hunter and Bruce Barnes, respectively. Tilden continued to play exhibition fund-raisers during World War II. In 1945 Tilden was one of the organizers of the Professional Tennis Players Association. His reputation was, however, shattered in 1946 following his arrest and conviction for committing a homosexual act with a minor. He served a one-year prison sentence but was convicted of a similar offense in 1949. Despite this he was regarded for a long time as the greatest tennis player during the first fifty years of the twentieth century. In addition to playing tennis, Tilden wrote several books about the game and authored a number of stage plays.

See also SPORTS.

TOKLAS, ALICE BABETTE (1877–1967). Born in San Francisco, Alice B. Toklas moved to Paris, France, in 1907. There she became **Gertrude Stein**'s partner in the famous salon that became a center for members of the "**lost generation**" of American writers, such as **Ernest Hemingway**, who became voluntary exiles in Europe during the 1920s. Toklas published Stein's work and after her friend's death wrote two cookbooks and her own memoirs, *What Is Remembered* (1963).

See also LITERATURE AND THEATER.

TOOMER, (NATHAN) JEAN (1894–1967). Born of mixed race, and educated first in all-black schools, then all-white, Jean Toomer attended a number of colleges and universities without graduating before finding employment in 1921 in a small college in Sparta, Georgia. While there Toomer began writing short stories that were published in various journals. In 1923 his book *Cane* was published to critical acclaim and was seen as part of the **Harlem Renaissance**. Toomer subsequently became a disciple of the Russian mystic Georgi Gurdjieff, and he dedicated his life to teaching Gurdjieff's lessons, first in Harlem, then Chicago, and later Taos, New Mexico. He published little other than a few short stories after *Cane*.

See also AFRICAN AMERICANS; LITERATURE AND THEATER.

TOWNER, HORACE MANN (1855–1937). A **Republican** congressman from Iowa, Horace Towner was educated at the University of Chicago and Union College of Law and admitted to the bar in 1877. He served as county superintendent of schools in Adams County, Iowa, from 1880 to 1884 and was elected judge of the third judicial district in 1890 and served until 1911. Towner also lectured on constitutional law at the University of Iowa. He was elected to the U.S. House of Representatives in 1910 and served until 1923, when he was appointed governor of **Puerto Rico**. Towner held that position until 1929, when he returned to his private law practice. As a legislator Towner was best known for cosponsoring the **Sheppard-Towner Act** (1921).

TOWNLEY, CHARLES ARTHUR (1880–1959). After failing as a farmer in North Dakota in 1912, Charles Townley became involved with the **Socialist Party**. In 1915 Townley formed an organization to focus simply on the needs of farmers known as the **Nonpartisan League** (NPL). Under Townley's effective leadership the NPL endorsed a number of successful candidates in 1916, including Governor Lynn J. Frazier. However, Townley opposed U.S. entry into **World War I**, and he was twice tried under the **Espi-**

onage and **Sedition Acts** and served a brief jail sentence. Unsuccessful in his attempt to win election to Congress from North Dakota in 1920, Townley's influence declined, and he resigned from the position of leader in 1922.

During the 1930s Townley was involved in organizing the Farm Holiday Association, and he edited a farmers' newspaper. During the 1950s he supported Joseph McCarthy and accused some of his former colleagues of being communist sympathizers. Townley died in a car accident.

TRADE UNIONS. The organization of working people in a particular craft or industry began in the early nineteenth century in response to industrialization and the rise of the factory system. The growing power of industrial corporations after the Civil War (1861–1865) and the decline of the independent craftsman led to different attempts to organize. Following the failure of the reformist all-inclusive Knights of Labor in the 1880s, the **American Federation of Labor** (AFL) headed by **Samuel Gompers** emerged as an organization of skilled workers using collective bargaining to achieve better wages and conditions in the workplace. While the AFL concentrated on skilled workers, the unskilled **immigrant** and **African American** workers were largely ignored.

The failure of unions to organize the steel industry in 1892 and the **railroad** workers in 1894 saw the rise of more radical bodies. The **Socialist Party**, led by **Eugene Debs**, sought political solutions, and the **Industrial Workers of the World** (IWW) attempted to mobilize all workers, particularly the unskilled, in one big union, in order ultimately to bring about a revolutionary change in society. These radical challenges did much to prompt **progressive** reformers into action but in the long run had only a limited appeal to American workers.

During **World War I** unions gained in strength and recognition as a consequence of labor shortages and their participation in the mobilization of manpower. While the AFL hoped to capitalize upon these gains at the end of the war, employers were equally determined to return to the prewar position. This conflict led to a series of strikes in 1919, one of the most significant being the **steel strike**. Most of these disputes ended in failure for the unions, and the 1920s witnessed a decline in membership from a high of 5 million to less than 3 million as prosperity and the employers' use of **welfare capitalism** to some extent undermined their appeal. The conservative attitude of the **Republican** administrations and the antipathy of the **Supreme Court** also contributed to this weakened position.

Faced with even greater losses during the **Great Depression**, some union leaders, particularly **John L. Lewis**, called for a revitalized effort to organize workers on an industrial basis and including the unskilled. This caused a rift with the AFL and was to lead to the emergence of the Congress of Industrial Organizations (CIO) in 1935. Granted recognition under the Labor Relations

Act of the **New Deal**, unions were to go through one of their greatest periods of growth during the 1930s. These gains were consolidated during World War II as trade unions finally became an established part of American life. The AFL and CIO merged in the 1950s.

See also DUBINSKY, DAVID (1892–1982); GREEN, WILLIAM (1870–1952); HAYWOOD, WILLIAM DUDLEY (1869–1928); HILLMAN, SIDNEY (1887–1946).

TRADING WITH THE ENEMY ACT, 1917. Passed in October 1917, the Trading with the Enemy Act prohibited trade with the **Central Powers** and established a blacklist of all companies suspected of having commercial links with enemy countries. The act also established the office of the **Alien Property Custodian**.

See also WORLD WAR I, 1914–1918.

TRANSPORTATION. *See* AUTOMOBILE; AVIATION; FEDERAL HIGHWAY ACTS, 1916, 1921, 1925; RAILROADS; RAILROAD STRIKE, 1922; RAILROAD TRANSPORTATION ACT, 1920; U.S. RAILROAD ADMINISTRATION (USRA).

TROTTER, WILLIAM MONROE (1872–1934). The **African American** leader William Monroe Trotter grew up in Boston and was educated at Harvard University, where he earned both a BA and a master's degree. In 1901 Trotter established a crusading weekly **newspaper**, *The Boston Guardian*, which he edited until his death. Trotter was among the first African Americans to criticize Booker T. Washington's "accommodationist" leadership and in 1903 was involved in disrupting a public meeting in Boston addressed by Washington. Trotter was briefly jailed for his part in the so-called "Boston riot." In 1905 Totter joined with **W. E. B. Du Bois** to establish the Niagara Movement, a civil rights organization that helped pave the way for the **National Association for the Advancement of Colored People** (NAACP). Trotter wanted the latter organization to be exclusively black and disagreed with Du Bois on this and other issues.

In 1914 Trotter was among a delegation of African Americans who met **Woodrow Wilson** at the White House. When Trotter insistently chided the president for his failure to combat lynching, Wilson terminated the meeting. Trotter also encouraged African Americans to protest against **D. W. Griffith**'s film *The Birth of a Nation* for its glorification of the **Ku Klux Klan**. In 1919 Trotter managed to attend the **Versailles Peace Conference** despite being denied a passport by the U.S. government, and in doing so helped to publicize race issues. His stormy temperament, however, ensured that Trotter was always a rather marginal figure. He lost his newspaper in 1934 in the **Depression** and committed suicide shortly after.

TULSA RACE RIOT, 1921. Tulsa, Oklahoma, was the scene of a three-day race riot in which at least fifty white and two hundred black people were killed in the confrontation that began on 31 May 1921. The riot began after members of the **African American** community, who had gathered to ensure the safety of a black man in police custody, exchanged shots with gathering white men. Most of Greenwood, the area inhabited by Tulsa's eight thousand African Americans—sometimes known as the "Black Wall Street"—was destroyed by the white mob. Governor J. B. A. Robertson declared martial law and mobilized units of the National Guard to restore order. A commission established in 1997 held the police largely responsible for not preventing the conflict.

TUMULTY, JOSEPH PATRICK (1879–1954). Qualified as a lawyer in New Jersey, Joseph Tumulty established a practice in Jersey City in 1902 and became involved in **Democratic Party** politics. He served on the New Jersey Assembly from 1907 to 1910, when he became governor **Woodrow Wilson**'s personal secretary. He continued in that position when Wilson entered the White House in 1912. Tumulty was an influential figure until after Wilson's second marriage in 1916. His relationship with the president finally ended in 1922, and he returned to the private practice of law.

TUNNEY, (JAMES JOSEPH) GENE (1897–1978). Gene Tunney began his career as a professional boxer in 1916. In 1918 he enlisted in the Marine Corps and was sent to France, where he became the camp boxing champion and lightweight champion of the **American Expeditionary Force**. Back in civilian life Tunney won the U.S. light heavyweight title in 1922. From then until 1925 Tunney won all but one contest as a light heavyweight, losing and regaining his title to Harry Greb (1922, 1923), and famously defeating Georges Carpentier in 1924.

In 1926 Tunney defeated the heavy weight champion **Jack Dempsey** in front of a record audience of 120,000. Another 100,000 watched the rematch in 1927. The fight became one of the most famous in boxing history. Having led for six rounds, Tunney was knocked down in the seventh but benefited from a famous "long count" because Dempsey did not retire to a neutral corner. Tunney recovered and won the fight. In 1928 Tunney retired as undefeated heavyweight champion. He went on to write articles on health and fitness and two autobiographies (*A Man Must Fight* [1933], *Arms for a Living* [1941]) and after 1928 became a business executive. During World War II Tunney directed the U.S. Navy's physical fitness program.

See also SPORTS.

TWENTIETH AMENDMENT. Passed on 3 March 1932 and ratified on 23 January 1933, the Twentieth Amendment reduced the gap between the election of a new president and Congress in November to January rather than March. It also ended "lame duck" Congresses that had met from December to March and had included congressmen defeated in the November elections. (See appendix 2.)

TWENTY-FIRST AMENDMENT. Passed in February 1933 and ratified on 5 December 1933, the Twenty-first Amendment repealed the **Eighteenth** and so ended **Prohibition** in the United States. The amendment was ratified directly by state conventions, the first time such a device had been used since the approval of the Constitution itself. The vote for delegates in favor of repeal was approximately 73 percent of votes cast. Control of alcohol after 1933 became a state rather than a federal issue. (See appendix 2.)

UNDERWOOD, OSCAR WILDER (1862–1929). After studying at the University of Virginia, Oscar Underwood established a successful law practice in Birmingham, Alabama, in 1884. In 1895 he was elected as a **Democrat** to the U.S. House of Representatives, lost the seat in 1896 but was returned in 1897. He remained in the House until 1915, when he was elected to the Senate on an anti-**Prohibition** platform. As a congressman Underwood became chair of the House Ways and Means committee and, following the election of **Woodrow Wilson**, led the Democrats to secure passage of the president's **New Freedom** program including **tariff** reform. The latter was achieved with the **Underwood-Simmons Tariff Act**. Underwood supported Wilson's war program and also the **Treaty of Versailles**. In 1920 Underwood became Senate minority leader. He was a delegate to the **Washington Naval Conference** in 1921 and helped to secure ratification of the treaties. Underwood resigned as minority leader in 1923 and planned a campaign to secure the Democratic presidential nomination in 1924. His opposition to the **Ku Klux Klan** cost him the support of the South, and his bid was unsuccessful. He did not seek reelection in 1926.

UNDERWOOD-SIMMONS TARIFF. Passed in 1913, the Underwood-Simmons Act was a key measure in **Woodrow Wilson**'s **New Freedom** program. It was the first significant reform of the **tariff** since the Civil War, and it reduced tariffs on 958 goods or items. However, rates were left unchanged on over three hundred items, maintaining the protectionist element.
   See also UNDERWOOD, OSCAR WILDER (1862–1929).

UNEMPLOYMENT CONFERENCE, 1921. *See* PRESIDENT'S UNEMPLOYMENT CONFERENCE, 1921.

U.S. EMERGENCY FLEET CORPORATION (USEFC). The Emergency Fleet Corporation, headed by **Charles Schwab**, replaced the **U.S. Shipping Board** in following America's entry into **World War I** in April 1917. It embarked on a huge shipbuilding program, spending more than $1 billion. During the war the number of shipyards increased from 61 to 341, with an increase in the workforce from 45,000 to 380,000. By 1921 the tonnage of U.S. vessels involved in foreign trade had risen from about 3 million to 11 million. After the war, government-built ships were sold to private operators.

U.S. FOOD ADMINISTRATION. Established under the **Lever Food and Fuel Act** in 1917 the Food Administration was responsible for ensuring the adequate production and for controlling the price and supply of food and feeds during the war. As head of the administration, **Herbert Hoover** set the prices of certain commodities such as wheat, sugar, and hogs but refused to introduce rationing. The Food Administration relied on voluntary cooperation mobilized by a massive program of exhortation and propaganda urging the population to conserve food supplies and observe "wheatless, meatless, and porkless" days.

U.S. FUEL ADMINISTRATION. The Fuel Administration was established with the U.S. **Food Administration** in 1917 under the **Lever Food and Fuel Act** in order to ensure the adequate provision of fuel for the war effort. **Harry Garfield**, president of Williams College and son of former president James Garfield, headed the administration. He took action to stabilize coal prices but, faced with continuing shortages and a transportation deadlock, he ordered all factories east of the Mississippi to close for a week in January 1918. While this helped to resolve the situation, it led to considerable criticism of **Woodrow Wilson**'s administration.

U.S. HOUSING CORPORATION (USHC). Faced with considerable housing shortages in many war industry centers, in 1918 president **Woodrow Wilson** approved the creation of the U.S. Housing Corporation to build homes for war workers. Although short-lived the Corporation built some 6,000 homes in 80 cities across the country. After the war completed projects were sold off, but the USHC established an important precedent for later federal housing programs.

U.S. RAILROAD ADMINISTRATION (USRA). Following America's entry into **World War I** in 1917 the various **railroad** companies attempted to coordinate their services voluntarily through a Railroads War Board. However, this proved inadequate, and by December of that year the system had virtually come to a standstill. Using his wartime executive authority president **Woodrow Wilson** established the U.S. Railroad Administration to take over the temporary running of the system. Headed by secretary of the treasury **William Gibbs McAdoo**, the new agency successfully coordinated timetables, pooled rolling stock, unified the use of terminals, and built additional rail cars. The railroad companies were guaranteed annual compensation, and the federal government paid all railroad costs for the duration of the war.

U.S. SHIPPING BOARD (USSB). The five-man U.S. Shipping Board was created under the Merchant Marine Act on 7 September 1916 to build, purchase, lease, and operate merchant ships during **World War I** and for a five-year period after. In April 1917 it became the **U.S. Emergency Fleet Corporation**. The Shipping Board assumed a largely regulatory role under the **Merchant Marine Act** of 1920.

V

VALENTINO, RUDOLPH (1895–1923). Born Rodolfo Alfonzo Raffaele Pierre Philibert Guglielmi in Italy, Rudolph Valentino entered the United States in 1913, where he became one of the greatest silent **movie** idols in the role as the Latin lover. He began work as an extra in the movies after working variously as a gardener, waiter, and café dancer. His big breakthrough came with *The Four Horsemen of the Apocalypse* (1921). Valentino then starred in a series of movies as male seducer who was tamed by his would-be victim, beginning with *The Sheik* (1921). His other films in a similar role included *Blood and Sand* (1922), *Monsieur Beaucaire* (1924), and *The Son of the Sheik* (1926). Valentino's funeral after his sudden death of peritonitis in New York attracted huge crowds of hysterical women, and he remained the personification of the male screen heartthrob for generations.

VAN DEVANTER, WILLIS (1859–1941). Willis Van Devanter graduated from Cincinnati Law School in 1881 and practiced law in Indiana for three years before establishing a practice in Wyoming. Van Devanter was actively involved in Wyoming politics as a **Republican**, and was Cheyenne City attorney from 1887 to 1888 and then representative to the state legislature. In 1889 Van Devanter was appointed chief justice of the territorial supreme court and then became first chief justice of Wyoming's Supreme Court after it achieved statehood in 1890. He abandoned the position for private practice.

In 1897 Van Devanter was appointed assistant U.S. attorney general in the Department of the Interior, and in 1903 became judge of the Eighth Circuit Court of Appeals. In 1910 president **William Howard Taft** appointed him to the U.S. **Supreme Court**. Van Devanter was a staunch conservative. He was a strong supporter of property rights and business interests, and opposed demands for labor reform. Van Devanter was one of the authors of the Judiciary Act of 1925, which gave the Supreme Court power to regulate and control its own business and so determine which cases it would examine. He wrote the opinion upholding the **Eighteenth Amendment** and **Prohibition**, and was steadfast in his opposition to the **New Deal** in the 1930s. Van Devanter was the first justice to retire with full pay under the terms of the Supreme Court Retirement Act (1937).

VAN DOREN, CARL (CLINTON) (1885–1950). Carl Van Doren studied at Illinois University and Columbia University, where he gained his PhD in 1911. He was an assistant professor in the English Department at Columbia from 1911 to 1934, during which time he edited the *Cambridge History of American Literature* (1917–1921), was literary editor of *The Nation* (1919–1922) and *Century Magazine* (1922–1925), and was editor for the Literary Guild (1926–1934). Van Doren was particularly important in encouraging black writers in the **Harlem Renaissance**.

See also LITERATURE AND THEATER.

VAN RENSSELAER, MARTHA (1864–1932). Martha Van Rensselaer was for a while a schoolteacher before she became school commissioner for Cattaraugus County, New York, from 1893 to 1899. In 1911 she joined Cornell University to organize an extension program of home economic courses for **agricultural** communities, and in 1911 Van Rensselaer became professor of home economics. She was a leading writer on home economics and contributed regularly to the *Ladies' Home Journal*. From 1914 to 1916 Van Rensselaer was president of the Home Economic Association. During **World War I** she was a member of the **U.S. Food Administration**. In 1923 she was voted one of the most outstanding **women** in the United States.

VAN VECHTEN, CARL (1880–1964). Following his graduation from the University of Chicago in 1899 Carl Van Vechten began work as a society reporter and photographer for the *Chicago American*. In 1906 Van Vechten moved to New York City, where he became the assistant **music** critic of the *New York Times*. He was the paper's Paris correspondent from 1908 to 1909, and then continued as **art** and music critic until 1913. Van Vechten was a close acquaintance of **Mabel Dodge Luhan**, **Gertrude Stein**, and the literary and artistic inhabitants of **Greenwich Village**. Van Vechten wrote several novels dealing with this social milieu—*Peter Whiffle* (1922), *The Blind Bow Boy* (1923), *The Tattooed Countess* (1924)—and also several works of music criticism—*Music after the Great War* (1915), *The Music of Spain* (1918), and *Red: Papers on Musical Subjects* (1925).

Perhaps Van Vechten's greatest significance, however, was in his role as a popularizer of **African American** arts and entertainment and as a supporter of the **Harlem Renaissance**. Van Vechten captured something of the excitement of New York's black community in his novel *Nigger Heaven* (1926) although some African Americans disliked the book's title and subject matter. During the 1930s Van Vechten became a keen portrait photographer and captured many of the images of famous black and white personalities for posterity.

See also LITERATURE AND THEATER.

VANZETTI, BARTOLOMEO (1888–1927). Born in Villafalletto, Italy, Bartolomeo Vanzetti immigrated to the United States in 1908. He worked in a number of menial jobs and became a fish peddler. With **Nicola Sacco** he was involved in anarchist activities, which led to his arrest in 1920. He and Sacco were, however, subsequently charged with robbery and murder. Following their trial, conviction, and death sentence, the **Sacco and Vanzetti case** became an international cause célèbre. Despite protests from around the world, both men were electrocuted at Charlestown State Prison on 23 August 1927.

VARDAMAN, JAMES KIMBLE (1861–1930). After studying law at Carrollton University, Mississippi, James Vardaman was admitted to the bar in 1881 and began a law practice in Winona, where he also became editor of the Winona *Advance*. He continued to practice law and publish newspapers after his move to Greenwood, Mississippi. A **Democrat**, Vardaman served in the state house of representatives, 1890–1896, and was speaker in 1894. He was an unsuccessful candidate for governor of Mississippi in 1895 and 1899, and served in Cuba during the Spanish-American War. In 1904 Vardaman was elected governor following his virulent criticism of **African Americans**. He served one term before winning election to the U.S. Senate on his third attempt in 1912. Vardaman was one of the six senators who opposed American entry into **World War I** in 1917, and because of this he failed to be reelected in 1918 and again in 1922. His other notable contribution as a senator was to oppose **Selective Service** and particularly the recruiting of African Americans into the services. Vardaman retired to Birmingham, Alabama, in 1922.

VERA CRUZ. In 1913 Victoriano Huerta seized power in **Mexico**. The American president, **Woodrow Wilson**, refused to recognize the new regime. Following an incident in which U.S. seamen were arrested in Tampico, Mexico, in 1914, admiral Henry Mayo demanded a salute for the U.S. flag in addition to the release of the servicemen, which had already occurred. When this was refused Wilson approved the bombardment and seizure of Vera Cruz. On 21 April his instructions were carried out with the loss of two hundred Mexican and nineteen American lives. The U.S. forces were withdrawn in June after a mediated settlement negotiated by Argentina, Brazil, and Chile, but relations with Mexico continued to be fragile for several years.

See also ABC MEDIATION, 1914; FOREIGN POLICY.

VERSAILLES PEACE CONFERENCE. Following the **Armistice** in November 1918, the victorious **Allies** met from 18 January to 28 June 1919 in Versailles to agree to the terms of the peace settlement. Although attended by representatives from thirty-two countries initially working through various committees, the conference was dominated by the "Big Five," president **Woodrow Wilson**, Georges Clemenceau of France, Prime Minister David Lloyd George of Great Britain, Vittorio Orlando of Italy, and Marquis Saionji Kinmochi of Japan. Ignoring the principle of "open covenants openly arrived at" as proposed in Wilson's **Fourteen Points**, the meetings were held behind closed doors.

See also VERSAILLES, TREATY OF, 1919; WORLD WAR I, 1914–1918.

VERSAILLES, TREATY OF, 1919. The treaty that emerged from the **Versailles Peace Conference** ending **World War I** was signed by thirty-two nations in June 1919 and presented to the German representatives for signature. It consisted of 440 articles, many of a punitive character. These included: a war guilt clause; acceptance of the demilitarization of the Rhineland; the cession of Alsace and Lorraine and the Saar to France, Sudentenland to the newly created Czechoslovakia, and other territory to Belgium and to Poland, and the loss of all colonies; the scrapping of the German navy and air force; and the imposition of reparations, which were to be agreed on at a future date. The last clause provided for the establishment of a **League of Nations**. President **Woodrow Wilson** accepted the treaty as politically expedient on the expectation that it could be modified subsequently by the League of Nations. However many **progressives**, both in and outside of the **Democratic Party**, were dismayed by the harsh terms of the treaty. Conservatives in both major parties were not prepared to accept the commitments involved in the League of Nations, and as a consequence the treaty failed to get the two-thirds support needed for ratification in the U.S. Senate. The United States ended formal hostilities with Germany by a two-nation agreement in 1921.

See also FOREIGN POLICY.

VIDOR, KING WALLIS (1894–1982). The motion picture producer and director began work in the film industry in Texas producing films of real events such as the Galveston hurricane and the Houston sugar refining industry. In 1915 Vidor moved to California and began work with the Vitagraph studio. After working for a number of companies, Vidor established his own in 1920 and produced several **movies** starring his wife, Florence Vidor. From

1924 until 1933 he worked as a director for Metro-Goldwyn-Mayer. He produced the sound musical *The Big Parade* in 1925. Vidor's first big success came with *La Bohème* starring **Lillian Gish** in 1926. His film *The Crowd* won an Academy Award nomination the same year. Several more successful films followed. Vidor worked as an independent producer-director for several years after 1933 but returned to MGM in 1938. *The Citadel*, his first film that year, won four Academy Award nominations; *Northwest Passage* (1940) was a huge box-office success.

During World War II Vidor served in the photographic unit of the armed forces, and after the war he worked on several films with producer **David O. Selznick**. Vidor's last film was *Solomon and Sheba* (1959). Vidor received many awards in recognition of his contribution to filmmaking, and in 1979 the Academy gave him its Lifetime Achievement Award.

VILLA, FRANCISCO ("PANCHO") (1877–1923). Born Doroteo Arango, Pancho Villa was a Mexican revolutionary and bandit who fought against the government first of Victoriano Huerta (1911–1915) and then of Venustiano Carranza (1914–1915). Initially supported by the U.S. government and admired in the press, which dubbed him "the Robin Hood of Mexico," **Woodrow Wilson**'s administration ceased supplying Villa arms once Carranza assumed power. In January 1916 Villa seized a train and killed eighteen American passengers in an attempt to discredit Carranza and provoke U.S. intervention. When that failed Villa crossed the border into Texas and New Mexico, where he burned the town of **Columbus** and killed seventeen inhabitants on 9 March 1916. Villa was then pursued unsuccessfully by a **punitive expedition** led by General **John Pershing** deep into **Mexico**. In 1919 Villa agreed to retire to his ranch, but he was assassinated in 1923.

VILLARD, OSWALD GARRISON (1872–1949). Born in Germany, Villard was the grandson of the abolitionist and pacifist William Lloyd Garrison. After graduating from Harvard University, he began work as an editorial writer on his father's **newspaper**, the New York *Evening Post*. When his father died in 1900, Villard became owner/editor of the *Post* and its weekly edition, the *Nation*. He turned the latter into a leading liberal journal and was an advocate of **women's suffrage**, recognition of **trade unions**, and civil rights. He was one of the founders of the **National Association for the Advancement of Colored People** (NAACP) in 1909. As a pacifist Villard opposed U.S. entry into **World War I**, and as a result was forced to sell the *Post* in 1918. He bought the *Nautical Gazette* the same year and owned it until 1935. In 1918 Villard wrote critical accounts of the **Versailles Peace Conference** and **Versailles Treaty** for *The Nation*, and during the 1920s he campaigned on behalf of imprisoned conscientious objectors, in support of antilynching legislation, and against **Prohibition**. During the 1920s and 1930s he published material on newspapers and journalism, several studies of German history and development, a critique of the U.S. defense establishment, and his own autobiography, *Fighting Years: Memoirs of a Liberal Editor*, in 1939.

VINSON, FREDERICK MOORE (1890–1953). Frederick Vinson graduated from Kentucky Normal College in 1908 and gained his law degree from Center College, Danville, in 1911. He established a law practice in Louisa, Kentucky, and served as city attorney from 1913 to 1914. Vinson was elected commonwealth attorney for the 32nd judicial district of Kentucky in 1921, a position he held until his election as a **Democrat** to the U.S. House of Representatives in 1924. He was defeated in 1928 and resumed his law practice in Ashland, Kentucky. Vinson returned to the House of Representatives in 1931 and held his seat until 1938.

A supporter of the **New Deal**, Vinson was appointed associate justice to the U.S. Circuit Court of Appeals in the District of Columbia and he served in that position from 1938 until 1943. From 1943 until 1945 he was director of the Office of Economic Stabilization, a wartime agency. In 1945 he was appointed first as Federal Loan Administrator and then director of War Mobilization and Reconstruction. President Harry S. Truman appointed Vinson as secretary of the treasury in 1945, and he was involved in drawing up the Bretton Woods Agreement in 1944 and in establishing the International Monetary Fund. Following the death of Chief Justice **Harlan F. Stone** in 1946, Truman appointed Vinson as replacement, and he served until his death. Not especially outstanding, Vinson approved the decision in 1951 to uphold the conviction of eleven members of the **Communist Party** charged under the Smith Act (1940).

VOLSTEAD ACT. The Volstead Act was the popular name for the **National Prohibition Act** that was introduced in Congress by Congressman Andrew Volstead of Minnesota in 1919 to enforce the **Eighteenth Amendment**. Initially vetoed by **Woodrow Wilson**, Congress overrode the president, and the act went into force on 1 January 1920.

VOLSTEAD, ANDREW JOHN (1860–1947). Andrew Volstead was admitted to the Minnesota bar in 1884 and in 1886 was elected **Republican** prosecuting attorney for Yellow Medicine County. He was elected to the U.S. House of Representatives in 1902 and served until 1923. He consistently opposed **Woodrow Wilson**'s **New Freedom** legislation. As chair of the Judiciary Committee Volstead gave his name to the legislation to enforce

Prohibition. Volstead was defeated in the election of 1922 and became legal adviser to Minnesota's Northwest Prohibition Enforcement District until 1931, when he returned to his law practice.

See also NATIONAL PROHIBITION ACT, 1919.

WAGNER, ROBERT FERDINAND (1877–1953). Robert Wagner was born in Germany and immigrated to the United States with his family in 1885. They settled in New York City, where Wagner went on to qualify and practice in law. He was elected as **Democrat** to the New York State assembly in 1905 and then to the state senate. He was chairman of the State Factory Investigating Committee from 1911 to 1915, and justice of the supreme court of New York, 1919 to 1926. Together with **Al Smith**, Wagner promoted several pieces of reform legislation to improve labor conditions in New York. He was elected to the U.S. Senate in 1926, where he served until his resignation due to ill health in 1949.

Wagner chaired several committees and sponsored several pieces of social reform legislation such as the National Industrial Recovery Act and the Social Security Act. He was best known as the author of the National Labor Relations Act (Wagner Act) of 1935, which established the National Labor Relations Board and recognized workers' rights of free collective bargaining. He was a delegate to the United Nations Monetary and Financial Conference at Bretton Woods in 1944.

WALD, LILLIAN (1867–1940). Lillian Wald was a nurse, **social worker**, and public health official active in the progressive reform movement as a social worker and **women**'s activist. Wald trained as a nurse in the New York Hospital training school and graduated in 1891. Having become aware of the plight of **immigrant** workers on the Lower East Side, Wald abandoned her training to become a doctor and with Mary Brewster established the Henry Street Settlement in New York City in 1893. Wald pioneered public health nursing when she developed the Visiting Nurse society to provide health care among the immigrant population. She also persuaded Columbia University to establish a department of nursing and health. In 1912 Wald became the first president of the National Organization for Public Health Nursing.

Wald was influential in securing the establishment of the **Federal Children's Bureau** and the Red Cross rural nursing service, both in 1912. Wald was also a supporter of **women's suffrage** and of the peace movement.

When American entered **World War I** she chaired the Committee on Community Nursing of the American Red Cross and led the campaign to combat the outbreak of **influenza** in 1918. In 1919 she represented the United States at the international Red Cross conference in France. She attended the International Conference on Women for Peace in Zurich that led to the foundation of the Women's International League for Peace and Freedom. Wald was a supporter of the **League of Nations**. Wald's prewar **pacifism** and her friendship with people like **Emma Goldman** led her to be listed as a radical during the **Red Scare**. Nonetheless, in 1922 the *New York Times* named Wald one of the twelve greatest living American women. Paradoxically, Wald lobbied in support of **Prohibition** and also supported **Al Smith**'s candidacy for president in 1928. Wald wrote two autobiographical accounts—*The House on Henry Street* (1915) and *Windows on Henry Street* (1934). She retired from Henry Street in 1933 due to ill health.

WALKER, JAMES JOHN (1881–1946). Although he completed a law degree in 1904, "Jimmy" Walker first worked as a songwriter. However, in 1909 Walker began his political career when he was elected to the state assembly, and in 1914 he entered the New York state senate. He served until 1925, supporting a series of progressive social welfare measures. In 1925 Walker successfully campaigned to become mayor of New York City, and he was reelected in 1929, defeating Republican **Fiorello La Guardia**.

Although his administrations witnessed the expansion of the transit system, improved public hospitals, and a new sanitation department, Walker left the details of government to others, particularly the machine politicians of Tammany Hall. Walker enjoyed the good life and a colorful private life. His extravagant lifestyle and casual approach to the business of government lost its appeal with the onset of the **Depression**, and investigations headed by **Samuel Seabury** in 1931 revealed widespread corruption in the Walker administration. Walker resigned in September 1932. Despite all this, Walker remained popular in New York. In 1937 he was appointed assistant counsel of the New York State Transit Commission, and in 1940 La Guardia appointed him as "impartial chairman" of the Women's Cloak Industry.

WALLACE, HENRY CANTWELL (1866–1924). Henry Cantwell Wallace studied briefly at Iowa State Agricultural College before taking over one of his father's farms in 1887. In 1892 he was appointed professor of dairying at Iowa State College. In 1895 he joined his father in taking over what became *Wallaces' Farmer*, and he helped turn it into an influential agricultural journal. He was active in the wartime mobilization of **farming** during **World War I** but opposed **Herbert Hoover**'s policies as food administrator. In 1921 **Warren Harding** appointed Wallace secretary of agriculture. Wallace expanded the role of the Department of Agriculture, and he supported the proposed **McNary-Haugen Plan** to maintain farm prices. However the plan had little support from the Harding administration and was opposed by president **Calvin Coolidge** under whom Wallace served briefly before he succumbed to illness. Wallace's son, Henry Agard Wallace, also became secretary of agriculture and later secretary of commerce in **Franklin D. Roosevelt**'s administration.

WALL STREET BOMBING, 1920. Just after midday on 16 September 1920 a bomb exploded on the corner of Wall Street and Broad Street, the heart of the financial district in New York City. Thirty-eight people were killed and more than 140 were injured. Despite a prolonged investigation by New York police department and the new Bureau of Investigation headed by **J. Edgar Hoover**, no arrests were made. The attack was linked to the wave of bombings the previous year, and it was believed that supporters of the deported Italian anarchist Luigi Galleani might have been responsible. Such thinking probably influenced the trial of **Nicola Sacco** and **Bartolomeo Vanzetti**.

See also RED SCARE, 1919.

WALL STREET CRASH, 1929. The greatest financial crash in the history of the United States occurred in October 1929. Following several months in which security prices fell, on "Black Thursday," 24 October, over 13 million shares were traded on the stock exchange. On 29 October, "Black Tuesday," "the most devastating day in the history of the New York stock market," more than 16 million shares were sold and share prices fell by $40 billion. By July 1933 the decline in value was $74 billion, and the great boom in stocks, the "bull market" of the 1920s, was over.

The speculation boom of the 1920s was fueled by the expansion of manufacturing and the growth of consumerism based on new products such as the **automobile**, **radio**, and other electrical appliances. The mood of optimism was reflected in rising share prices, and shares themselves then became seen as a way of making money quickly, rather than as investments in the country's industrial future. The market, however, was largely unregulated and suffered serious flaws. Investors could buy shares on "margin," that is, paying a fraction (sometimes as little as 10 percent) of the value of the shares and borrowing the rest from brokers. As prices rose shares could be sold, the balance paid off and a profit was made; when prices fell panic set in as investors realized the yield would not meet outstanding balance. Holding companies and investment trusts sprang up offering shares that often bore little relation to industrial assets or profits, and sometimes were simply exercises in speculation. Brokers' loans rose from $3.5 million in June 1927 to $8 million in September 1929 and about 4 million Americans owned stock, 1.5 million of them using brokers. When share prices began to fall, panic quickly set in, especially among those who had bought on margin.

The Crash wiped out the savings of individuals and the investments of **banks** and insurance companies. The loss of confidence in financial institutions due to failure and tales of fraud and embezzlement added to this downward spiral. The rush of savers to withdraw money from banks compounded the crisis that led to a general collapse in financial institutions. By 1932 almost four thousand banks had failed. This in turn contributed to the onset of the **Great Depression** as investment in industry fell and loans to companies, farms, homeowners, and international banks were called in.

See also ECONOMY.

WALSH, THOMAS JAMES (1859–1933). The lawyer and **Democratic Party** politician Thomas Walsh gained a degree in law at the University of Wisconsin, settled briefly in the Dakota Territory, and in 1890 established a law practice in Montana. He was unsuccessful in his bid to win election to the U.S. House of Representatives in 1906 but was elected to the Senate in 1912 and held the position until his death. Walsh managed **Woodrow Wilson**'s western campaign in 1916 and supported the Wilson program in peace and war. It was Walsh whose investigations while chair of the Public Land Committee after the war opened up the **Teapot Dome** scandal and won him a reputation for probity. In 1932 Walsh supported the nomination of **Franklin D. Roosevelt**, and he was offered the appointment of attorney general in the new administration. He died while en route to the inaugural ceremonies.

WAR FINANCE CORPORATION (WFC). The War Finance Corporation was created in 1918 to provide credit facilities for war industries by making loans to banks. After **World War I** it provided loans to **railroad** companies. The powers of the WFC were augmented in 1919 to aid exporters. In 1921 the WFC provided funds to help agricultural exporters and by 1924, when it was abolished, had lent $700 million.

See also ECONOMY.

WAR INDUSTRIES BOARD (WIB). The War Industries Board was established in 1917 to coordinate U.S. industrial mobilization, fix prices, allocate raw material, and determine production levels during **World War I**. In 1918 the WIB's powers were further increased, and **Bernard Baruch** was appointed chairman. Although the WIB relied on voluntary methods and used an enormous number of committees staffed primarily with "dollar-a-year men" from business who could afford to work for a nominal salary, it did have enforcement powers. Such was its power that some commentators viewed the Board as a form of "war socialism." The WIB was abolished in January 1919.

See also ECONOMY.

WAR LABOR BOARD (WLB). The War Labor Board was established in April 1918 to mediate in labor-management disputes in defense industries and lessen the potential disruption of the war effort by strikes. The WLB recognized the right to collective bargaining and the need for a minimum living wage and a basic eight-hour day. It adjudicated in over twelve hundred cases during the war.

See also ECONOMY.

WASHINGTON NAVAL CONFERENCE, 1921–1922. A conference held in Washington, D.C., to consider the limiting of naval armaments involving the United States, Great Britain, France, Italy, the Netherlands, Belgium, Portugal, Japan, and China. The conference resulted in several treaties—the **Washington Naval Treaty**, **Four-Power Treaty**, Nine-Power Treaty, and a "naval holiday." Significantly it left Japan as the strongest naval power in the Far East.

WASHINGTON NAVAL TREATY. The Washington Naval Treaty, or Five-Power Treaty, signed by the United States, Great Britain, Japan, France, and Italy at the **Washington Naval Conference**. It provided for the scrapping of a number of battleships and a "naval holiday" to establish a ratio in terms of ships' tonnage to 5:5:3 for the United States, Britain, and Japan, and 1.75 each for France and Italy.

WATERS, ETHEL (1896–1977). The **African American** blues, gospel, and **jazz** singer and actress Ethel Waters began performing in vaudeville in 1917. She began recording for Black Swan Records in 1921 and performed in a number of musical plays and reviews, including *African* (1927), *Blackbirds of 1930* (1930), *As Thousands Cheer* (1933), in **DuBose Heyward**'s *Mamba's Daughters* (1938), and in *Cabin in the Sky* (1940). Waters also appeared in films, most notably the **movie** version of *Cabin in the Sky* with **Louis Armstrong** and other leading African American performers in 1943. She was nominated for the best supporting actress Academy Award for her role in *Pinky* in 1949. Waters also appeared on radio shows and later as "Beuhla" on television.

See also LITERATURE AND THEATER; MUSIC AND DANCE.

WEBB-POMERENE ACT. Passed in April 1918, the Webb-Pomerene Act, or Webb Export Act, exempted export trade associations from the provisions of antitrust legislation provided that they did not attempt to restrain competition or prices within the domestic market. The act was intended to stimulate foreign trade.

See also ECONOMY.

WEEKS, JOHN WINGATE (1860–1926). John Weeks graduated from the U.S. Naval Academy in 1881 and served in the navy for two years. After working as a surveyor in Florida he moved to Boston, where he successfully established a banking and brokerage company. Weeks served briefly in local politics before being elected to Congress as a **Republican** representative for Massachusetts in 1904. He served until 1913. He played a part in drawing up the Currency Act in 1908 and the Postal Savings Bank in 1910. He was elected to the U.S. Senate by the Massachusetts legislature in 1913 and played an important part in securing the passage of the **Federal Reserve Act** in 1913. Weeks lost his seat to his Democratic opponent in 1918. However, he continued to be active in Republican Party politics. As a member of the National Committee in 1920 Weeks supported **Warren G. Harding**'s nomination. He was rewarded with the appointment as secretary of war in 1921. Untainted by the scandals in the Harding administration, he kept his position under **Calvin Coolidge** until ill health forced him to retire in 1925.

WEISSMULLER, JOHNNY (1904–1984). Born Janos Weissmuller in Rumania, the future swimming champion was brought to the United States as an infant. He changed his name in 1924. Weissmuller began entering swimming competitions in 1921 and, using the new crawl stroke, he had set sixty-seven world records at different distances by 1922. Weissmuller won three gold medals at the 1924 Paris Olympics and five in the 1928 games at Amsterdam. Having turned professional in 1929, Weissmuller became an international **movie** star in the 1930s as Tarzan, the hero of the novels by **Edgar Rice Burroughs**. Weissmuller established the formulaic characteristics of the primitive hero—his limited speech, his famous jungle yodel, and his athleticism—in a series of movies from *Tarzan the Ape Man* (1932) through to *Tarzan and the Mermaids* (1948), and in similar movies through to the 1950s. Weissmuller retired in the late 1950s. He was elected a charter member to the U.S. Olympic Hall of Fame in 1983.

See also SPORTS.

WELFARE CAPITALISM. A term applied to programs introduced by large corporations during the 1920s to improve labor relations, stabilize the workforce, and limit the appeal of **trade unions**. They included offering profit sharing and stock subscription schemes to workers, pension and insurance plans, paid vacations, social and welfare clubs and activities, and improved facilities on the shop floor. These plans were more paternalistic forms of the **American Plan**, which had emerged in defense of the open shop and in response to union gains during **World War I**. Company unions were often allowed, but without bargaining rights or the right to strike, and benefits were generally determined by the length of service. By 1926 50 percent of the top fifteen hundred companies had comprehensive plans in operation, and more than four hundred companies had pension plans available to their 4 million workers. Such schemes rarely reached the smaller businesses, nor did they do much to avert the impact of the **Great Depression**.

WESTON, EDWARD HENRY (1886–1958). Born in Chicago, the photographer Edward Weston took courses in photography at the Illinois College of Photography and began work as a commercial photographer in 1911. His first photograph was published in 1906. The Photographers' Association of America recognized Weston as a leading pictorialist photographer in 1916, and he was a frequent prizewinner. Weston's work was, however, becoming increasingly more artistic, and he gradually abandoned his commercial career. He moved to Mexico in 1923 and began to produce photographs of ordinary objects shot from unusual perspectives. In 1928 he opened a studio in San Francisco before settling the following year in Carmel. Studies of landscapes, rock formations, and sand dunes now followed his photographs of stones, shells, and other objects. Weston continued to produce prints of his work until his death. With **Alfred Stieglitz** Weston helped to establish modern American photography.

See also ART.

WHARTON, EDITH NEWBOLD (1862–1937). The writer Edith Wharton was born of wealthy parents in New York City. She began writing early in life and had already published several poems by the age of sixteen. After her marriage in 1885 she traveled frequently to Europe and wrote a number of books on European architecture. Several of her short stories were published in collections as *The Greater Inclination* (1899), *Crucial Instances* (1901), and *The Descent of Man* (1904). Wharton's first novel, *The Valley of Decision*, was published in 1902, but her critical and popular success as an author began with her critique of New York high society in *The House of Mirth* in 1905. *Ethan Frome* (1911), reflecting her own personal experience, was concerned with a love triangle.

Wharton's support of France during **World War I** and her activities on behalf of Belgian refugees won her the award of the Legion of Honor and Order of Leopold. In 1920 her novel *The Age of Innocence*, mourning the loss of tradition in the war, won the Pulitzer Prize. Her subsequent writing, written in France, was less successful.

See also LITERATURE AND THEATER; WOMEN.

WHEELER, BURTON KENDALL (1882–1975). After gaining a law degree from the University of Michigan in 1905, Burton Wheeler established a law practice in Butte, Montana. He served a term as a **Democrat** in the Montana House of Representatives from 1910 to 1912 and then became U.S. district attorney for Montana from 1913 to 1918. He was unsuccessful in his attempt to become governor of Montana in 1918 but was elected senator in 1920 and served until he lost the Democratic primary in 1946. As a western progressive Wheeler fought against the power of the Anaconda Copper Mining Company in Montana and the popular hysteria during **World War I**.

Wheeler led the hearings in 1924 into Attorney General **Harry Daugherty**'s failure to investigate the **Teapot Dome** scandal, and was the vice presidential running mate with **Robert M. La Follette** and the **Progressive Party** the same year. In 1930 Wheeler was one of the first Democrats to support the nomination of **Franklin D. Roosevelt** for the presidency, and he supported most of Roosevelt's **New Deal** measures. However, Wheeler opposed Roosevelt's attempt to alter the composition of the **Supreme Court** in 1937. He also was a supporter of neutrality and opposed Roosevelt's increasing support for Great Britain and France and spoke at America First rallies across the country in 1941. He supported the war effort after Pearl Harbor, and voted for American membership in the United Nations in 1945. After leaving the Senate he practiced law in Washington, D.C.

WHITE, EDWARD DOUGLASS (1845–1921). Edward White left Georgetown College (now a university) in 1861 to fight for the Confederacy in the Civil War. After the war White studied law and was admitted to the Louisiana bar in 1868. In 1874 he was elected to the Louisiana Senate and in 1879 was appointed to the Louisiana Supreme Court. Because of a new age requirement he gave up his seat in 1880 and practiced law. In 1888 White was elected to the U.S. Senate as a **Democrat**.

In 1894 president Grover Cleveland appointed White to the U.S. **Supreme Court** and in 1910 president **William Howard Taft** raised him to chief justice, the first time a sitting justice had assumed the position. White held the position until his death and provided stability in the court during a period of rapid change in personnel. His position was generally conservative, supportive of business rather than labor interests or social reform measures, and upholding racial segregation. White argued for a narrow reading of the Sherman Antitrust Act and opposed a number of decisions against monopolies. In 1908 he wrote the opinion in the *Employers' Liability Cases* against federal laws making **railroads** liable for injuries to their workers and was in the majority in *Adair v. United States*, upholding "yellow-dog contracts" prohibiting union membership. White was also in the majority decision against the prohibition of **child labor** in *Hammer v. Dagenhart* (1918). He did, however, dissent when the Court ruled against a law limiting working hours in *Lochner v. New York* (1905), and he joined the unanimous decision in *Muller v. Oregon* (1908), which upheld the law limiting the hours women could work. In both cases White believed the states had policing powers in the workplace.

White supported the federal government's broad taxation rights in a series of cases and also the federal power to suppress civil liberties. He voted to uphold all of the federal prosecutions during **World War I** under the **Espionage** and **Sedition Acts**. White also voted to uphold racial segregation in decisions from *Plessy v. Ferguson* on. However, he did agree with decisions against "grandfather clauses" that undermined the right to vote. White's major contribution to constitutional law was in developing the "insular doctrine," which stated that constitutional rights and guarantees did not "follow the flag" without express congressional approval, but otherwise his role in the Supreme Court was largely unmemorable.

WHITE, WALTER FRANCIS (1893–1955). The **African American** civil rights leader graduated from Atlanta University in 1916 and worked for two years in insurance. In 1918 he was appointed assistant executive secretary to the **National Association for the Advancement of Colored People** (NAACP). He held the position until 1929 and then became executive secretary of the organization. White took advantage of his light color to investigate and report on lynching in the South during the 1920s, and his reports were used in support of the **Dyer antilynching bills** in 1922, 1937, and 1940. His book on the subject, *Rope and Faggott: A Biography of Judge Lynch*, was published in 1929. White also wrote two novels, *The Fire in the Flint* (1924) and *Flight* (1926), and actively supported other members of the **Harlem Renaissance**. He later wrote of the situation of black soldiers during World War II in *A Rising Wind* (1945) and his autobiography, *A Man Called White* (1948).

White and the NAACP successfully opposed the nomination of John J. Parker to the **Supreme Court** in 1930 because of racist comments he had made during his career. White was also instrumental in initiating the NAACP's legal challenges to discrimination, and through his friendship with **Eleanor Roosevelt** gained some influence in the White House. His marriage to a white woman in 1949 alienated some white and African American supporters of the NAACP, and White increasingly had differences with fellow activists in the organization before his death.

WHITE, WILLIAM ALLEN (1868–1944). William Allen White was a leading **progressive newspaper** editor, journalist, and writer. He was educated at Emporia College and the University of Kansas. In 1891 he began work with the *Kansas City Journal* but soon moved to the *Kansas City Star*. White established his own paper, the *Emporia Gazette*, in 1895 and turned it into a commercial success. White wrote for magazines and published several collections of short stories and novels. After meeting and becoming friendly with **Theodore Roosevelt**, White became a leading voice among progressive **Republicans**. He joined a number of like-minded writers at *The American Magazine* and published a series of his articles there as *The Old Order Changeth* (1910). White supported the **Progressive Party** in 1912 but returned to the **Republicans** in 1916. White supported **Woodrow Wilson**'s wartime domestic programs and the **League of Nations**. In 1923 White's editorial in defense of free speech won him a Pulitzer Prize. He stood unsuccessfully as an independent candidate for governor of Kansas in 1924 in order to challenge the influence of the **Ku Klux Klan** but was outspoken in his attacks on **Al Smith** in 1928. In 1930 he became a member of the committee appointed by president **Herbert Hoover** to study conditions in **Haiti**. White was lukewarm in his support for **Franklin D. Roosevelt** and the **New Deal** due to the increased power of the federal government. In 1940 he led the Committee to Defend America by Aiding the Allies and helped secure support for the Lend-Lease Act in 1941. White's *Autobiography* was published posthumously in 1946 and awarded the Pulitzer Prize.

WHITEMAN, PAUL SAMUEL (1890–1967). Paul Whiteman grew up in a musical family and played viola with the Denver Symphony Orchestra at the age of sixteen. He moved to San Francisco in 1912 and worked with the San Francisco Symphony Orchestra until 1916, when he turned to **jazz**. In 1917 Whiteman joined the U.S. Navy and served as a bandleader. After **World War I**, Whiteman formed his own band and in 1920 moved to New York to perform on Broadway and make recordings. He had major hits in 1920 with "Whispering" and "Japanese Sandman," and even greater success with "Three O'Clock in the Morning" in 1926. In 1924 the Whiteman orchestra performed the first jazz symphony in New York with **George Gershwin** playing *Rhapsody in Blue*. Whiteman was one of the leading musical influences in the 1920s. His band toured Great Britain several times and did much to make jazz widely known. Whiteman also wrote popular books on jazz. His first film in 1930 was *The King of Jazz*, and he appeared in several more films subsequently. After a break through illness, Whiteman returned to **radio** in 1942 and later made television appearances. He was vice president of the ABC network from 1947 to 1955. Whiteman, although white, was often known as the "King of Jazz" because he gave many white jazz performers, such as Bix Beiderbecke, Tommy Dorsey, Hoagy Carmichael, and singer Bing Crosby, their start in show business.

See also MUSIC AND DANCE.

WICKERSHAM, GEORGE WOODWARD (1858–1936). George Wickersham qualified as a lawyer at the University of Pennsylvania and practiced law in New York City from 1883 until his death. In 1909 **William Howard Taft** appointed him attorney general. Wickersham brought more than eighty prosecutions under the Sherman Antitrust Act against companies, including Standard Oil and American Tobacco. He returned to his law practice after 1912 but remained active in **Republican Party** politics. Wickersham was a strong internationalist and supported U.S. involvement in the **League of Nations**. He served on the League's committee to codify international law and was president of the International Arbitral Tribunal from 1932 to 1936. In 1929 president **Herbert Hoover** appointed Wickersham to chair the National Commission on Law Observance and Enforcement that reported on **Prohibition** in 1931. The commission concluded that the enforcement of Prohibition was a failure that had undermined law enforcement generally and led to widespread corruption. However, the report did not categorically reject the principle of prohibition itself.

See also CRIME AND POLICING.

WILDER, THORNTON NIVEN (1897–1975). Thornton Wilder was educated at Oberlin College and Yale University, and was awarded an MA in French literature from Princeton in 1926. Wilder served in the coast guard during **World War I**. He taught French and English at Lawrenceville School and at the University of Chicago from 1930 to 1937. As a writer Wilder used myth and allegory to explore the meaning of life and the themes of love and tolerance. His best-known book, *The Bridge of San Luis Rey* (1927), won a Pulitzer Prize, as did *Heaven's My Destination* (1935) and the plays *Our Town* (1938) and *The Skin of Our Teeth* (1942). Wilder enlisted during World War II, served in the air force, and was awarded the Legion of Merit and the Bronze Star. In the 1950s he held a chair in poetry at Harvard University and was awarded the National Medal for Literature in 1962. His comedy *The Matchmaker* (1954) was successfully turned into the film musical *Hello, Dolly!* in 1969. Wilder continued to write until his death. His last book, *Theophilus North*, was published in 1973.

See also LITERATURE AND THEATER.

WILLIAMS, WILLIAM CARLOS (1883–1963). The poet, writer, and physician William Carlos Williams was born in Rutherford, New Jersey. After his early schooling in Rutherford he was sent to Geneva and Paris in 1897. In 1902 he was admitted to the University of Pennsylvania Medical School, where he graduated in 1906. He established his private medical practice in Rutherford in 1910 and continued to work as a doctor and as a poet. It was as a student that he established his close friendship with fellow poet **Ezra Pound** and the artist **Charles Demuth**. He was also friends with **Man Ray** and the French modernist artist Marcel Duchamp and shared the imagist approach to poetry with the emphasis on clarity and precision in language evident in his first collection, *Poems*, in 1909 and *The Tempers* (1913) and *Al Que Quiere* (1917). However, his innovative and experimental style became most evident in *Kora in Hell: Improvisations* (1920), which even Pound described as "incoherent." His collection of poetry and prose, *Spring and All* (1923), included one of his best-known poems, "The Red Wheelbarrow."

Very much affected by **T. S. Eliot**'s *The Waste Land*, Williams struggled to produce his own epic work. However, he persisted in use of ordinary idiom and American themes. His collection of essays, *In the American Grain* (1925), provided sketches of historical figures and themes ranging from Puritans, George Washington, through to Abraham Lincoln. He finally published the first part of his epic work in 1946 with *Paterson*, a free-verse collection centered on the industrial city; subsequent volumes appeared in later years, the last in 1958. His concern to show ordinary people and their lives can be seen in his poetry and some his short stories such as *The Farmers' Daughters* (1963). He published his autobiography in 1951. Williams met with a mixed reception in his own time but had a considerable influence on later poets, including members of the Beat Generation, and he is now recognized as one of the major modernist writers.

See also LITERATURE AND THEATER.

WILLS, HELEN NEWINGTON (MOODY) (1905–1998). Born in Centreville, California, and a graduate in Fine Arts from the University of California at Berkeley, Helen Wills was regarded as the first American **woman** to achieve international recognition as a **sports** person. She dominated tennis during the 1920s, winning thirty-one Grand Slam titles including seven U.S. Lawn Tennis singles titles, eight Wimbledon singles titles, and four French singles championships. She won her first national title in 1923 and in 1924 won gold medals in the women's singles and mixed doubles at the Paris Olympics. Noted for her apparent lack of emotion while playing, Mills was known as "Little Miss Poker Face," and her determination enabled her to come back from ill health on more than one occasion. Like a number of other

women players, Mills championed wearing knee-length skirts rather than the restrictive full-length skirts worn previously. In 1933 she beat the eighth-ranked male player, Phil Neer, in an exhibition game. She retired in 1938.

Wills was also an artist who exhibited her painting and drawing, and she wrote and illustrated a coaching manual, *Tennis* (1928), and her autobiography, *Fifteen-Thirty: The Story of a Tennis Player* (1937). She married Frederick Moody in 1929, was divorced in 1937, and married Aidan Roark in 1939. In 1998, Wills funded the building of a neuroscience institute at the University of California, Berkeley, which became the Helen Wills Neuroscience Institute.

WILSON, EDITH BOLLING GALT (1872–1961). The second wife of **Woodrow Wilson**, Edith Wilson was previously married to Norman Galt, a jeweler. When Galt died in 1908, Edith took over the operation of the jewelry store for a number of years before selling the business. In 1915 she met and married President Wilson. Mrs. Wilson accompanied the president whenever he traveled and advised him on many political matters. She accompanied him to the **Versailles Peace Conference** in 1919 and on his tour of the United States to support the **Versailles Treaty** and U.S. entry into the **League of Nations**. When the president suffered a stroke, Mrs. Wilson played a key, even controversial, role in vetting his visitors and the business he handled. Edith Wilson cared for her husband until his death in 1924 and after helped in the publication of his authorized biography. Her own book, *My Memoir* (1938), was critical of many politicians for failing her husband. She continued to attend political functions until her death.

See also WOMEN.

WILSON, EDMUND (1895–1972). The author and critic Edmund Wilson was born in Red Bank, New Jersey, and educated at Hill School, Pottstown, Pennsylvania. He graduated from Princeton University in 1916 and worked for a time as a reporter for the *New York Evening Sun*. During **World War I** Wilson served in a medical unit and then the intelligence service. He returned to the United States in 1919 and established himself as a literary critic and essayist with *Vanity Fair* (1920–1921, 1923) and then as an editor with the *New Republic* (1926–1931), and later the *New Yorker* (1944–1948). His first publication was an anthology of short stories and poetry based on his war experience, *The Undertaker's Garland* (1922). His novel *I Thought of Daisy* (1929) and collection of short stories *Memoirs of Hecate County* (1946) were based on the bohemian literary circle in New York City. Following the **Wall Street Crash** he toured the country and produced a series of reports published as *The American Jitters: A Year of the Slump* (1932). Wilson is, however, best known for his critical literary and social studies: *Axel's Castle*

(1931) on symbolist **literature**, including pieces on **T. S. Eliot** and **Gertrude Stein**; *To the Finland Station* (1940) on socialist and revolutionary theory; *The Wound and the Bow: Seven Studies in Literature* (1941); and *Patriotic Gore: Studies in the Literature of the American Civil War* (1962). His other many works included plays, memoirs, and essays. Despite his opposition to the Cold War and to the war in Vietnam, Wilson was awarded the Medal of Freedom by president Lyndon Johnson in 1963. Various essays of his were published after his death, including on *The Twenties* (1975).

WILSON, ELLEN AXSON (1860–1914). The first wife of president **Woodrow Wilson**, Ellen Wilson was a graduate of Rome Female College in Georgia. She married Wilson in 1885 and bore him three daughters. While supporting her husband in his professional and political career, Ellen Wilson developed her own work in art from the 1890s on. Some of her work won prizes and she held several exhibitions. As first lady Mrs. Wilson organized the running of the White House and participated in official functions. Although not a prominent public figure, she also supported a number of social issues relating to conditions for federal employees and housing conditions in the capital.

See also WOMEN.

WILSON, WILLIAM BAUCHOP (1862–1934). Wilson was the first secretary of labor in the United States following the creation of the **Department of Labor** in 1912. A former miner and a member of the Mineworkers union, he served in congress as a **Democratic** representative from Pennsylvania 1907–1913. During **World War I** he cochaired the War Labor Conference Board with **William Howard Taft** and served on the **War Labor Board**. After the war Wilson was president of the International Labour Conference in 1919 and he chaired the **Federal Board for Vocational Training** from 1920 to 1921 and also the second **Industrial Conference**. In 1926 Wilson made an unsuccessful attempt to win the Democratic Party nomination to become senator for Pennsylvania.

WILSON, (THOMAS) WOODROW (1856–1924). Twenty-eighth president of the United States. Born in Staunton, Virginia, and educated at Princeton and the University of Virginia, Woodrow Wilson was admitted to the bar in 1882 and practiced law in Atlanta, Georgia. In 1886 he obtained his PhD in history from Johns Hopkins University. His thesis was published as *Congressional Government* in 1885. He was to write a number of other studies in politics and history, including a five-volume *History of the American People* (1902). Wilson taught political science and history at Bryn Mawr, Wesleyan, and Princeton, where he became president from 1902 to 1910. He introduced a number of reforms to the university system, including challenging the exclusive eating clubs. Faced with opposition to these measures, he resigned in 1910.

In 1910 Wilson became **Democratic** governor of New Jersey and served from 1911 to 1913. He disassociated himself from the old state party machine and supported a corrupt practices act, workmen's compensation legislation, the direct primary, and regulation of public utilities. He was nominated as the Democratic Party's presidential candidate in 1912 with the support of **William Jennings Bryan**. Wilson won the 1912 presidential election in a three-cornered contest against the **Progressive** candidate, **Theodore Roosevelt**, and **Republican William Howard Taft**. Wilson gained 6,296,547 votes, Roosevelt 4,118,571, and Taft 3,486,720 but won 435 Electoral College votes to Roosevelt's 88 and Taft's 8. Wilson was the first southerner to become president since the Civil War.

Wilson's "**New Freedom**" program was essentially a classical liberal program of using government power to restore free-market competition. Like Theodore Roosevelt, Wilson saw the presidency as central to an activist federal government. He met with Democratic Party leaders to formulate policy and broke with tradition in going directly to address Congress in person. He continued the antitrust policies of his Republican predecessors and established the **Federal Trade Commission**, supported the **Clayton Antitrust act**, federal workmen's compensation, and a federal **child labor law**. He reduced **tariffs** in 1913, introduced income tax to recoup the lost revenues, and provided for **bank** regulation with the passage of the **Federal Reserve** act. On other issues such as race relations and votes for **women**, Wilson was a conservative. Racial segregation in the federal government increased under his administration, and it was only after 1915 that he began to support **women's suffrage**. Wilson was reelected again in 1916, narrowly defeating **Charles Evans Hughes** by 9,127, 695 votes to 8,533,507 and 277 Electoral College votes to 254.

When the war in Europe broke out in 1914, Wilson called on Americans to remain impartial "in thought as well as action," and he initiated a policy of neutrality. However, Americans were not forbidden from traveling on ships of belligerent nations, nor from traveling to Europe. Nor were they were forbidden from trading with European powers. Instead the Wilson Administration insisted that American citizens had the right to free passage on the high seas. Such policies brought the government into conflict with both Great Britain and Germany, but particularly the latter when they announced a policy of unrestricted submarine warfare in 1915. Although the president protested following the sinking of the *Lusitania*, he also said that there was such a thing as being "too proud to fight." Support for his policy was indicated when, in the course of Wilson's nomination at the Democratic Party convention, the slogan "he kept us out of war" emerged as a campaign slogan.

President Wilson also attempted to bring an end to the conflict through mediation in 1915 and again in 1916. In 1917 he called for "peace without victory," but this was rejected when the German government announced the resumption of unrestricted submarine warfare. The subsequent sinking of several American vessels made war inevitable. The decision was made easier by the publication of the **Zimmerman telegram** indicating that Germany might form an alliance with **Mexico** in the event of war with the United States. In his address to Congress on 2 April 1917, Wilson said the war was to make the world "safe for democracy." America entered the war on April 6.

During **World War I** the Wilson administration took steps to mobilize the population through the **Committee of Public Information** and to suppress opposition via **Espionage** and **Sedition** legislation. Control over food and fuel was achieved through the **Food** and **Fuel** administrations, and industrial mobilization was led by the **Committee for National Defense** and the **War Industries Board**. A National **War Labor Board** was created to mediate in labor disputes in the defense industry. In total during the war government powers were extended to unprecedented levels.

President Wilson spelled out his program for the postwar settlement and a liberal new order in his **Fourteen Points** speech to Congress on 8 January 1918 promising a liberal world order based on national self-determination. It was on this basis that Germany sued for peace in October 1918, and the **armistice** was agreed in November. Wilson went to Paris to take part personally in the peace conference at **Versailles**. Although forced to compromise with the British leader Lloyd George and the French premier, Georges Clemenceau, on a number of issues, he won acceptance for the **League of Nations** central to his promise of a world without war. The Germans were forced to accept the treaty, including a war guilt clause and demand for reparations, in June 1919.

On his return to the United States, President Wilson met considerable opposition from **Republicans** and some Democrats to the commitments implied in the League of Nations. Wilson, however, refused any compromise and would accept no amendments. Faced with congressional opposition led by **Henry Cabot Lodge**, Wilson went to the country to appeal to the people directly. On 2 October 1919 he suffered a massive stroke and as a result was severely incapacitated. The treaty was rejected in November 1919. With the defeat of the Democrats in the 1920 election Wilson retired to his home in Washington, D.C.

WOLFE, THOMAS (1900–1938). The author Thomas Wolfe was a graduate of the University of North Carolina at Chapel Hill, and Harvard University. From 1924 until 1930 he worked in the English department of Washington Square College in New York City. In 1929 his study of small-town southern life, based on his own family, was published to critical acclaim as the novel *Look Homeward, Angel*. The sequel, *Of Time and the River*, was published in 1935. A collection of short stories was also published in 1935 as *From Death to Morning*. A memoir, *The Story of a Novel*, appeared in 1936, and *The Web and the Rock* (1939) and *You Can't Go Home Again* (1940) were both produced from manuscripts after his death.

See also LITERATURE AND THEATER.

WOMAN'S PEACE PARTY (WPP). Founded following a meeting of peace campaigners led by **Jane Addams** in 1915, by 1917 the WPP had a membership of between twenty-five thousand and forty thousand. The party was somewhat discredited when it was linked with **Henry Ford**'s failed peace campaign in 1916 and declined in support after the United States entered **World War I** in 1917. It was renamed the Women's International League for Peace and Freedom in 1921.

See also PEACE MOVEMENTS.

WOMEN. The situation of women in the United States went through considerable change from the late nineteenth century up to the 1930s. Following the Civil War (1861–1865) there was a considerable increase in opportunities for women in higher education, and the number of women more than doubled between 1880 and 1900. At the same time there was also an increase in female employment. In 1870 less than 15 percent of women (4 million) were in paid work; by 1910 this was 24 percent (8 million). The great majority of these (85 percent) were single and under the age of twenty-five, and the biggest single area of employment was domestic service. Most working women were **immigrants** or **African Americans**. However, new job opportunities other than the traditional ones of teaching and nursing were growing for native-born American women with the development of the typewriter, telephone, and cash register, and also in teaching with the growth of **education**. Many college-educated women, like **Jane Addams** and **Edith** and **Grace Abbott**, also found a vocation in the **settlement house** movement, 70 percent of whose workers were female.

The changing status of women was reflected in the **progressive** movement's calls for regulation of women's work and in the demand for the vote. The **women's suffrage** movement, spearheaded by the **National American Woman Suffrage Association (NAWSA)**, grew in support in the late nineteenth and early twentieth centuries and was reinvigorated under the new leadership of people like **Carrie Chapman Catt** and **Alice Paul**, and also by the inspiration of the suffragettes in Great Britain. **World War I** brought further gains through the increased use of women in war work and in the stress placed on the "war for democracy." While the importance of women's work was now recognized in the creation of a **Women's Bureau**, the passage of the **Nineteenth Amendment** in June 1919 finally brought women into politics, and they were able to vote nationally for the first time in 1920.

Women's suffrage was just one campaign in which they were engaged in the public arena. Many were active in the peace movement through the **Woman's Peace Party (WPP)**, the temperance movement in the **Women's Christian Temperance Union (WCTU)**, and in **trade unions** particularly in the Women's Trade Union League (WTUL). **African American** women also were active in the **National Association for the Advancement of Colored People (NAACP)**, and women of both races were involved in their separate club organizations. Some women, such as **Emma Goldman**, **Kate O'Hare**, and **Rose Pastor Stokes**, were involved in more radical activities and played a part in the **Socialist Party of America**. Although not holding any official office, the wives of presidents sometimes played a role in particular organizations and so exercised some influence. President **Woodrow Wilson**'s second wife, **Edith Wilson**, did play an important role after her husband had suffered a stroke in 1919.

For many observers, such as **Frederick Lewis Allen**, the acquisition of the vote signaled the birth of a "new woman" in the 1920s. The number of women in paid employment rose from 8.6 million to 10.7 million during the decade, and the proportion of women in clerical and sales occupations continued to rise. The proportion of female workers who were married doubled between 1900 and 1930. However, the percentage of women in paid work remained constant at around 25 percent, and equally the percentage of the labor force that was female remained at about the same figure; 60 percent of all employed women were black or foreign.

Nonetheless, the "**flapper**" symbolized both the greater economic opportunities enjoyed by many women, and a greater social and sexual liberation reflected and shaped by advertising and the **movies**. Leading stars of the day included **Clara Bow**, **Louise Brooks**, and **Lillian Gish**. A number of women also became well known for their achievements in **sports**, ranging from **Gertrude Ederle** in swimming to **Helen Wills** in tennis. **Amelia Earhart** was almost equally as famous as **Charles Lindbergh** for her achievements in **aviation**. Women were also some of leading figures in **art** and **literature**: **Georgia O'Keefe** stood out in photography and painting, while **Edith Wharton** continued to be one of the best-selling authors.

A key area of employment and influence for women outside of the home was in education. The expansion in the number of schools at all levels during this period brought an increased demand for teachers, met at the primary and secondary levels especially by women. Women such as **Bertha Landes** and **Julia Lathrop** also played a leading role in **social work** or government agencies dealing with women's work or the care of children. The **Women's Bureau** and **Children's Bureau** were largely staffed and headed by women such as Mary Anderson and Grace Abbott.

However, for those women still tied to the home, chores may have become lighter with the greater use of electric refrigerators, cleaners, and irons, but their roles as mothers and wives were essentially the same. These differences may account in part for the divisions within the women's movement after 1920. Although some were satisfied with the vote, there were those who campaigned for an **Equal Rights Amendment**, while others argued for legislation to protect women at work. The limits to the progress toward gender equality became apparent in the 1930s when, faced with impact of the **Great Depression**, many Americans felt men should be given priority over women in the workplace, and a number of states tried to legislate against the employment of married women.

See also BALCH, EMILY GREENE (1867–1961); BARA, THEDA (NÉE THEODOSIA BURR GOODMAN) (1885–1955); BEARD, MARY RITTER (1876–1958); BLATCH, HARRIOT STANTON (1856–1940); CARAWAY, HATTIE OPHELIA WYATT (1878–1950); CATHER, WILLA SILBERT (1876–1947); COOLIDGE, GRACE ANNA GOODHUE (1879–1957); CROSBY, CARESSE (NÉE MARY "POLLY" JACOB) (1892–1970); DEWSON, MOLLY (MARY WILLIAMS) (1874–1962); DORR, RHETA CHILDE (1866–1948); DREIER, MARY ELIZABETH (1875–1963); EARHART, AMELIA (1898–1937); EASTMAN, CRYSTAL (1881–1928); FAUSET, JESSIE REDMON (1882–1961); FERGUSON, MIRIAM AMANDA WALLACE ("MA") (1875–1961); FITZGERALD, ZELDA SAYRE (1900–1948); FLYNN, ELIZABETH GURLEY (1890–1964); GARBO, GRETA (1905–1990); GILMAN, CHARLOTTE PERKINS (1860–1935); GISH, DOROTHY (1898–1968); GLASGOW, ELLEN ANDERSON GHOLSON (1873–1945); HARDING, FLORENCE MABEL KLING DEWOLFE (1860–1924); HURSTON, ZORA NEALE (1891–1960); HOOVER, LOU HENRY (1874–1944); KELLER, HELEN (1880–1968); KELLEY, FLORENCE (1859–1932); KELLOR, FRANCES ALICE (1873–1952); LARSEN, NELLA (1891–1964); LOMBARD, CAROLE (1908–1942); LOOS, (CORINNE) ANITA (1893–1981); LUHAN, MABEL DODGE (1879–1962); LYND, HELEN MERRELL (1896–1982); MCPHERSON, AIMEE SEMPLE (1890–1944); MILLAY, EDNA ST. VINCENT (1892–1950); MILLS, FLORENCE (1896–1927); MOSKOWITZ, BELLE LINDNER ISRAELS (1877–1933); NATIONAL WOMAN'S PARTY (NWP); NEGRI, POLA (1899–1987); OVINGTON, MARY WHITE (1865–1951); OWEN, RUTH BRYAN (1885–1954); PARKER, DOROTHY (1893–1967); PAUL, ALICE (1885–1977); PERKINS, FRANCES (1882–1965); PICKFORD, MARY (1892–1979); RANKIN, JEANETTE (1880–1973); ROBINS, MARGARET DREIER (1868–1945); ROCKE-

FELLER, ABBY ALDRICH (1874–1948); ROOSEVELT, (ANNA) EL-EANOR (1884–1962); ROSS, NELLIE TAYLOE (1876–1977); SANGER, MARGARET HIGGINS (1883–1966); SCHWIMMER, ROSIKA (1877–1948); SCOTT, EVELYN NÉE DUNN (1893–1963); SMITH, BES-SIE (1894–1937); SNYDER, RUTH (1895–1928); STARR, ELLEN GATES (1859–1940); STEIMER, MOLLIE (1897–1980); STEIN, GERTRUDE (1874–1951); STRATTON-PORTER, GENE (1863–1924); SWANSON, GLORIA (1899–1983); TARBELL, IDA MINERVA (1857–1944); TOK-LAS, ALICE BABETTE (1877–1967); VAN RENSSELAER, MARTHA (1864–1932); WALD, LILLIAN (1867–1940); WATERS, ETHEL (1896–1977); WILSON, ELLEN AXSON (1860–1914); YEZIERSKA, AN-ZIA (1880–1970).

WOMEN'S BUREAU. Developed from the Women in Industry Service established during **World War I** in response to the increased employment of **women**, the Women's Bureau was created as an office in the **Department of Labor** in 1920 to investigate and report on issues relating to female employment. It provided guidelines to employers on women's employment through the 1920s and 1930s and reported on conditions of female employment in specific industries.

WOMEN'S CHRISTIAN TEMPERANCE UNION (WCTU). The WCTU was created in 1874 to campaign in favor of the legal prohibition of alcohol. It quickly grew into the largest single organization of **women** in the United States and was often linked to the **women's suffrage** movement. The WCTU campaign encouraged a number of states to enact **Prohibition** prior to the introduction of the **Eighteenth Amendment** in 1920.

WOMEN'S SUFFRAGE MOVEMENT. The campaign for **women**'s suffrage had its origins in the 1830s and was particularly associated with the Abolitionist movement. The Seneca Falls declaration (1848) was a call for equal rights. However, the movement was swallowed up in the conflict over slavery and divided after the Civil War when the Fourteenth Amendment specifically acknowledged the rights of men. In 1869 a New York–based group led by Elizabeth Cady Stanton and Susan B. Anthony, the National Woman Suffrage Association (NWSA), was formed to promote an amendment to enfranchise women. An alternative and less radical group, the American Woman Suffrage Association (AWSA), led by Lucy Stone, concentrated on local activities and state-by-state campaigns for the franchise. In 1890 the two organizations came together to form the **National American**

Woman Suffrage Association (NAWSA), and this was led by Anthony from 1892 until 1900. Three western states, Wyoming, Colorado, and Utah, granted women the vote in the 1890s.

There was powerful opposition to women's suffrage from the South (fearful of changes that would affect the racial status quo), the brewing industry (aware of women's support for **Prohibition**), industrialists (alarmed at the thought of regulation of female and **child labor**), and machine politicians (worried about the possibility of reform). However, under the new leadership of **Carrie Chapman Catt** (1900–1904), NAWSA began to grow by appealing to middle-class society and club women, and the newly college educated. They also adopted the tactics used by the British suffragists. Many women in the **settlement house** and **progressive movements** became supporters of suffrage. Catt's return to the leadership and **Alice Paul**'s advocacy of militant tactics gave the movement a new vigor. Between 1910 and 1914 another ten states granted women the vote. The final impetus to reform came during **World War I** as women harnessed their campaign to the "war for democracy" and as war work broke down some of the barriers in the workplace. The **Nineteenth Amendment** was approved by Congress in 1919 and finally ratified on 26 August 1920. Women voted for the first time nationally that November.

WOOD, GRANT (1892–1942). Grant Wood, regarded as "one of the most American of America's artists," learned his trade at the Minneapolis School of Design and in night classes at the University of Iowa and **Art** Institute of Chicago. He taught in Cedar Rapids, Iowa, but after military service during **World War I** was one of the many artists and writers who spent time in Paris, France. In 1927 he received a commission for a stained glass window commemorating war veterans in Cedar City. His design, using German glass, caused some controversy, a fact that influenced his satirical painting *Daughters of Revolution* (1932). A number of Wood's paintings shared this ironic view, most famously his austere depiction of a farmer and his wife in *American Gothic* (1930). Other work showing the influence of American folk art and the sense of irony included the *Midnight Ride of Paul Revere* (1931) and *Parson Weems' Fable* (1939).

In the 1930s Wood became a leading figure in the Regionalist school of artists celebrating the richness of the land and offering a vision of hope during the **Great Depression** in work ranging from *Fall Plowing* and *Birthplace of **Herbert Hoover*** (both 1931), through to *Iowa Cornfield* (1941). During the 1930s Wood was head of the Iowa Works Progress Administration (WPA) Art Project and taught at the University of Iowa. In 1935 he was elected to the National Academy of Design, and much of his work in the mid-1930s was printmaking and illustration.

WOOD, LEONARD (1860–1927). Leonard Wood qualified as a doctor at Harvard Medical School in 1884. Having been dismissed from Boston City Hospital for infringing rules with regard to surgery, Wood entered the U.S. Army as a surgeon in 1885. In 1898, together with **Theodore Roosevelt**, he formed and then led the "Rough Riders," a volunteer military unit in the Spanish-American War. He subsequently became military governor of Cuba (1899–1902) and then commander of the U.S. forces in the Philippines (1903–1908). In this latter position he was responsible for the bloody suppression of the Moro people. Wood was appointed army chief of staff from 1910 to 1914 and became an advocate of the policy of "preparedness." He was a candidate for the Republican presidential nomination in 1916 and 1920, losing to **William Howard Taft** and **Warren Harding**, respectively. As governor-general of the Philippines from 1921 until 1927, he resisted demands for self-government in the island, a policy for which he was subsequently criticized.

WOODS, ROBERT ARCHEY (1865–1925). Robert Woods was educated at Amherst College and Andover Theological Seminary. In 1892 he took over control of Andover House, the first **settlement house** in Boston. In 1895 Woods renamed it South End House, and he was to develop it into one of the leading settlement houses in the country. Woods particularly stressed the need for empirical evidence in social reform and popularized the use of the social survey. His own study, *The City Wilderness: A Study of the South End*, was published in 1898, and he conducted further studies of Boston published as *Americans in Progress* in 1902.

In 1911 Woods organized the National Federation of Settlements (later the National Association of Social Workers), and he acted as president and secretary until his death. He published many articles and monographs on the nature and ethos of the settlement house movement.

WORK, HUBERT (1860–1942). Hubert Work studied at the University of Michigan and then the University of Pennsylvania, where he obtained his medical qualification in 1885. Work established a practice in Colorado and founded the Woodcroft Hospital for mental illness at Pueblo in 1896. He was director until 1917. Work was a leading activist in the Colorado medical profession and was president of the State Board of Health. In 1917 he joined the Army Medical Reserve.

Work was a leading **Republican** and a member of the National Committee from 1913 to 1919. He supported **Warren Harding** and was appointed assistant postmaster general in 1921 and postmaster general in 1922. When **Albert Fall** resigned as secretary of the interior in 1923, Harding named Work as his successor, and he endeavored to overcome the taint of corruption left by his predecessor. Work called for the preservation of grazing lands, and he also helped to establish the Federal Oil Conservation Board in 1924 following the **Teapot Dome** scandal. Work commissioned a study of the role of the Indian Bureau that called for widespread changes in policy when it was published in 1928. Work had, however, resigned to campaign on behalf of **Herbert Hoover**. After the victory, he retired to practice medicine in Denver, Colorado.

WORLD DISARMANENT CONFERENCE, 1932–1934. In February 1932 the **League of Nations** convened a conference of fifty-seven nations at Geneva, Switzerland, to discuss general disarmament. The United States was one of the nonleague members to be represented. Attempts to produce disarmament agreements foundered on disagreements over exact terms and the withdrawal of Germany in October 1933.

WORLD SERIES, 1919. In 1919 eight players from the Chicago White Sox were accused of throwing the World Series against the Cincinnati Reds. Few people could accept the possibility that the national sport could be corrupt, despite evidence to the contrary. Although acquitted in the trial that lasted from 1920 to 1921, the players were banned from professional baseball for life. They toured as the Chicago Black Sox. A baseball commission under **Kenesaw Mountain Landis** was subsequently established to clean up the game.
See also SPORTS.

WORLD WAR I, 1914–1918. The first of two world wars in the twentieth century, often known as the "Great War," World War I was caused by an explosion of a complex series of big power rivalries over colonies, naval strengths, and territorial disputes, particularly in the Balkans. The outbreak began following the assassination of Archduke Franz Ferdinand of Austria in Sarajevo, Serbia, on 28 June 1914. Two opposing alliance systems, the **Allies** and **Central Powers**, built up since the 1890s, were then drawn into the conflict as Austria, backed by Germany, issued an ultimatum to Serbia, in turn backed by Russia. When Austria mobilized and declared war on Serbia, Russia ordered general mobilization on 30 July. Fearful that Russia's ally, France, might enter any ensuing conflict, and following preestablished military plans, the German government declared war on France and on 4 August invaded Belgium, which had refused passage of German troops. The German invasion prompted a British declaration of war in honor of treaty obligations with Belgium. The war spread as Turkey was drawn in against Russia and Italy against Austria, and the Japanese against Germany.

The reaction of Americans to the outbreak of war in Europe was shock and horror. Many **Progressives** were associated with **peace movements** and regarded the war as a descent into barbarity; others believed that it confirmed the validity of the policy of **isolation**. With a large **immigrant** population, particularly of German-American and Irish-American origin, and traditional links with Great Britain and France, sympathies were divided. British propaganda made much of the German invasion of Belgium and "war atrocities." It was not surprising, then, that president **Woodrow Wilson** called on the American people to be "impartial in thought as well as in action."

Despite this intention no restriction was imposed on trade with belligerents, nor on travel across the Atlantic. American industry was quick to supply munitions and as a consequence of British control of the seas, trade quickly began to favor the Allies. By 1916 the value of trade with Great Britain and France was $3.5 billion compared with only $1 million to the Central Powers. Germany responded by using submarines (U-boats) to attack merchant and passenger ships. President Wilson described the sinking of the *Lusitania* in 1915 as "illegal and inhuman" but later declared that there was such a thing "as a nation too proud to fight." Increasingly, however, the United States could not sit idly on the sidelines, and the Wilson administration made several unsuccessful attempts to arrive at a mediated settlement in 1915 and 1916. This culminated in his call for "peace without victory" in January 1917. Having committed so much and suffered such huge losses, neither side was prepared to accept this position.

When Germany, faced with stalemate and desperate to break the blockade, resumed the campaign of unrestricted submarine warfare in 1917, war was inevitable. Diplomatic relations with Germany were severed in February, and the publication of the **Zimmerman telegram** increased the growing anti-German mood. The Russian Revolution in March ended tsarist autocracy and enabled Wilson to argue that the Allies were fighting for the cause of democracy. After several American vessels had been torpedoed, on 2 April the president went before Congress to ask for a declaration of war in order to "make the world safe for democracy." The declaration was approved in the Senate by eighty-two votes to six on 4 April and by the House of Representative, 373 votes to 50, on 6 April.

Although only directly involved for eighteen months, the war had a considerable impact on American society. The mobilization of manpower for the armed forces with the introduction of **Selective Service**, and the expansion of industry and **farming** to feed, cloth, and arm the United States and continue to supply her allies, affected different social groups and government itself. Faced with continued opposition to the war from **Socialists**, peace groups, and some Midwestern farmers, the Wilson administration immediately established a **Committee on Public Information** (CPI) under **George Creel** to rally public opinion. The **Espionage Act**, passed in 1917, introduced to stifle dissent and deal with enemy sympathizers, was further strengthened by the **Sedition Act** in 1918. Both were used against Socialists and the leaders of the **Industrial Workers of the World** (IWW), but also fostered a mood of "100 percent Americanism" that brought hysterical attacks on individuals of German origin and, in some cases, foreigners from whatever country.

The economic mobilization was first led by the **Council of National Defense** (CND) and its **Advisory Commission** and then by the **War Industries Board** (WIB). The **Lever Food and Fuel Act** established federal agencies to maximize food production and control prices and to facilitate the best use of fuel. **Railroads** came under the control of the **U.S. Railroad Administration** (USRA). A **War Labor Board** (WLB) was created to settle disputes in war industries. One consequence of this was increased recognition of **trade unions** and certain minimum standards in pay and conditions. As a million additional **women** workers joined the labor force, they too gained recognition in the Women in Industry Service in the **Department of Labor**. The majority of women peace activists abandoned their prewar position. The **women's suffrage** campaign, however, continued, and the participation of women in defense industries strengthened their case and contributed to the final passage of the **Nineteenth Amendment**. **African Americans** were less fortunate. Segregated and discriminated against in the military, their armed service was belittled. Employment opportunities in northern industries encouraged a **Great Migration** from the South that resulted in better jobs and greater freedom but was met by race violence in **East St. Louis** in 1917 and in several towns and cities in the North and South during the "**Red Summer**" of 1919.

By the time the United States entered the war, the conflict had long reached a stalemate in the trench warfare on the western front. Resisting Allied calls to incorporate American forces in their own armies, the U.S. commander, general **John J. Pershing**, insisted on the independence of an **American Expeditionary Force** (AEF). Nonetheless, in the face of a renewed German offensive in March 1918, the first U.S. troops fought under French and British command and played a crucial role in the second battle of the **Marne** at **Chateau-Thierry** and **Belleau Wood**. The presence of the American troops was enormously important psychologically. In September half a million members of the AEF fought at in the battle at **St. Mihiel** and then more took part in the **Meuse-Argonne** offensive, which eventually saw success in November. By the time the war ended, 4 million men had joined the armed forces, and the AEF had suffered 255,970 casualties, including 50,280 dead.

After four years of trench warfare in the west, a second revolution in Russia, and a total of almost 10 million war dead, the war had ended with an Allied victory. Four empires, the German, Austro-Hungarian, Russian, and Turkish, collapsed. The **Treaty of Versailles** drawn up in 1919 also established a **League of Nations** that was hoped would prevent further wars. The U.S. Senate's failure to approve the treaty and/or American involvement in the League, despite president Woodrow Wilson's wishes, did much to undermine the settlement. The legacies of the war and the failures of the peace settlement in many ways paved the way for the rise of Adolf Hitler in 1933 and the outbreak of World War II in 1939.

See also ARMED FORCES; AMERICAN AMBULANCE FIELD SERVICE (AAFS); AMERICAN UNION AGAINST MILITARISM (AUAM); ARMISTICE; BARUCH, BERNARD MANNES (1870–1965); CONSCIENTIOUS OBJECTORS; CROWDER, ENOCH HERBERT (1859–1932); DEMOBILIZATION; FOSDICK, RAYMOND BLAINE; GERARD, JAMES WATSON (1867–1952); GOETHALS, GEORGE WASHINGTON (1858–1928); LEGGE, ALEXANDER (1866–1933); LEHMAN, HERBERT HENRY (1878–1963); LEVER FOOD AND FUEL ACT, 1917; MARCH, PEYTON CONWAY (1864–1955); MCADOO, WILLIAM GIBBS (1863–1941); MARNE, BATTLE OF; MITCHELL, WILLIAM LENDRUM (1879–1936); RICKENBACKER, EDWARD VERNON (1890–1973); YORK, ALVIN CULLUM (1887–1964).

WRIGHT, HAROLD BELL (1872–1944). The novelist Harold Bell Wright trained for the ministry at Hiram College, Ohio, 1892–1894, and although he did not complete the course, he served as a minister in a number of states between 1897 and 1908. His first book, *That Printer of Udell's*, based on his readings to his congregation, was published in 1903 and sold almost five hundred thousand copies. His second, *The Shepherd of the Hills* (1907), was also an enormous success, and Wright became a full-time writer. In 1909 he produced another best seller, *The Calling of Dan Matthews*, and yet another, *The Winning of Barbara Worth*, in 1911. These successes were followed by *The Eyes of the World* (1914) and *When a Man's a Man* (1916). Set mainly in California and Arizona, Wright's books stressed manly virtues, hard work, patriotism, and self-reliance, the benefits of outdoor life, and the power of Christian faith.

Although he continued to write through the 1920s and 1930s, Wright's later novels did not match his earlier works' commercial success. However, his novel *The Re-creation of Brian Kent* (1919) sold many more copies in its first two years of publication than **F. Scott Fitzgerald**'s *This Side of Paradise* (1920), and film versions of *The Winning of Barbara Worth*, starring Gary Cooper in 1926, and *The Shepherd of the Hills*, starring John Wayne in 1941, were successful. Wright published his autobiography, *To My Sons*, in 1934.

See also LITERATURE AND THEATER.

YEZIERSKA, ANZIA (1880–1970). Anzia Yezierska, who also wrote under the name Hattie Mayer, was born on the Russian-Polish border. Her family immigrated to New York in about 1890. Yezierska won a scholarship to Columbia University and graduated as a domestic science teacher in 1904. She taught from 1908 to 1915 but turned increasingly to writing. Her collection of short stories, *Hungry Hearts*, was published in 1920. It was followed by her novels *Salome of the Tenements* (1923), *Bread Givers* (1925), *Arogant Beggar* (1927), and *All I Could Never Be* (1932). The main theme of Yezierka's writing was the struggle of **immigrant women** to escape poverty and achieve the "American Dream." Yezierska worked for the WPA during the 1930s and also wrote about the Puerto Rican community.

See also LITERATURE AND THEATER.

YORK, ALVIN CULLUM (1887–1964). York was a soldier who had originally claimed conscientious objector status on religious grounds when America entered **World War I** but was persuaded that he would be fighting for God in a righteous conflict. Having joined the Army, on 8 October 1918 York became a national hero when during the **Argonne offensive** he single-handedly killed or captured nearly 150 Germans in a single day armed only with a rifle and Colt .45. He was awarded the Medal of Honor and returned home to a hero's welcome. *Sergeant York*, a film of his life starring Gary Cooper, was made in 1941.

YOUNG, CHARLES (1864–1922). Born a slave in Kentucky, Charles Young grew up and went to school in Ripley, Ohio. In 1884 he became only the third **African American** to enter West Point Military Academy (after Henry O. Flipper and John H. Alexander). He graduated in 1889 and served initially with the all-black 9th Cavalry and then the 10th U.S. Cavalry before moving to Wilberforce College, Ohio, in 1894 to teach military science. He subsequently was posted to the Philippines and then in 1903 became the first African American to be appointed a park superintendent when he assumed the role in the Sequoia and General Grant national parks. In 1912 Young became the first black military attaché when he was posted to Liberia. He returned in 1898 and served as a major in the 10th Cavalry during the **punitive expedition** to Mexico in 1916. He was promoted to lieutenant colonel but placed on the inactive list because of supposed health issues. In order to challenge the decision and to stake his claim for promotion to general, Young rode on horseback from Wilberforce to Washington, D.C., in 1918. He was reinstated to full colonel just after **World War I** came to an end and in 1919 Young was posted back to Liberia. He died of tropical fever in Nigeria while still on active service.

See also ARMED FORCES.

YOUNG, OWEN D. (1874–1962). A graduate of Boston Law School and a corporation lawyer, Owen Young joined General Electric (GE) as general counsel and vice president in 1913. He settled strikes in several GE plants during **World War I**, and in 1919 he served on the **Second Industrial Conference**. In 1921 he chaired the subcommittee on Business Cycles and Unemployment of president **Warren Harding**'s **Unemployment Conference**. He also led the American delegation to the International Chamber of Commerce's Court of Arbitration. From 1925 to 1928 Young chaired the International Chamber of Commerce itself.

In 1919 **Woodrow Wilson** asked Young to join GE with Westinghouse, AT&T, and Western Electric to form a company to prevent the British Marconi company from monopolizing long-distance radio communication. The result was the Radio Corporation of America (RCA), which, with Young as chairman until 1929, pooled American radio technology and equipment. Young entered into agreements with foreign companies dividing the world into radio zones in order to facilitate communication. Under his leadership RCA became the largest radio company in the world. In 1926 Young also helped to establish the National Broadcasting Company (NBC) and in 1928 the movie chain Radio-Keith-Orpheum (RKO).

In 1922 Young became chair of the board of GE with **Gerard Swope** as president. The two men were associated with the introduction of programs of "**welfare capitalism**," which did much to influence labor relations during the 1920s.

Young was a representative to the Reparations Conference in 1924 and was instrumental in securing the acceptance of the **Dawes Plan**. In 1929 he chaired the meetings that agreed on the **Young Plan**. President **Herbert Hoover** appointed Young to the **President's Committee on Recent Economic Changes** in 1929 and as chair of the Committee on Mobilization of Relief Resources of the **President's Unemployment Relief Commission** in 1931. He chaired the American Youth Commission, 1936–1942, and was a member of the New York regional committee of the War Manpower Commission in 1942. Having retired from GE in 1939, Young returned as acting chair to supervise the manufacture of war orders in 1942. He finally retired in 1944, but after the war served on president Harry S. Truman's Advisory Committee on Foreign Aid (1947) and chaired the New York Commission on the Need for a State University (1946).

See also ECONOMY.

YOUNG PLAN, 1929. The Young Plan was drawn up by a committee headed by **Owen D. Young** and replaced the **Dawes Plan** in setting a revised schedule of annual payments of war reparations by Germany. The Young Plan reduced the total amount of reparations to $27 billion spread over fifty-nine years to be paid through a Bank for International Settlement in Basle, Switzerland. As Germany was unable to make any payments in 1931–1932 due to the onset of the Depression and Hitler refused to make payments after 1933, the Young Plan was ineffective.

Z

ZANGARA, GUISEPPE (1900–1933). Born in Italy, Giuseppe Zangara immigrated to the United States in 1923. He worked for a while in New Jersey and California before settling in Miami, Florida. Depressed due to lack of employment, he blamed first president **Herbert Hoover** and then president-elect **Franklin Roosevelt**. When Roosevelt visited Florida in February 1933, Zangara fired several shots at him in an attempted assassination. He missed Roosevelt but wounded several bystanders and the mayor of Chicago, **Anton Cermak**, who was meeting Roosevelt. Sentenced initially to eighty-four years in prison, when Cermak died from his wounds Zangara was sentenced to death. He was executed on 20 March 1933.

ZANUCK, DARRYL FRANCIS (1902–1979). The Hollywood **movie** tycoon Darryl Zanuck served in the U.S. Army from 1916 to 1918 before moving to California to establish a career as a writer. He became a screenwriter with Warner Brothers studio in 1923 and in 1925 became head of production. Following a dispute with Jack Warner, Zanuck left the company in 1933 and began work with Twentieth Century films, later Twentieth-Century Fox. In 1935 Zanuck became vice president, and he held the position until 1956. Zanuck was responsible for the production of many significant films including *The Grapes of Wrath* (1940), *Gentlemen's Agreement* (1947), and *The Robe* (1953). During World War II he served with the Signal Corps and made films about the war effort. After breaking with Twentieth-Century Fox in 1956, Zanuck returned to take over the company in 1962. The success of his *The Longest Day* (1962) helped get the studio back on its feet, and this was followed with *The Sound of Music* (1965) and *Planet of the Apes* (1968). Internal disputes forced Zanuck to resign in 1971.

ZIMMERMAN TELEGRAM. A telegram from the German foreign secretary Arthur Zimmerman to the German minister in **Mexico** was intercepted by the British government in January 1917. On 24 February the note was given to the U.S. ambassador in London. It indicated that Germany would resume unrestricted submarine warfare and proposed a Mexican-German alliance in the event of U.S. entry into **World War I**. If victorious, Mexico would recover Texas, New Mexico, and Arizona. When the telegram was published on 1 March it caused considerable public anger and added support to **Woodrow Wilson**'s call for a declaration of war on 2 April 1917.

ZUKOR, ADOLPH (1873–1976). Born in Ricse, Hungary, Adolph Zukor immigrated to the United States in 1889 and established a fur company in Chicago in 1893. In 1903 Zukor opened a penny arcade with kinetoscopes—peep-show viewers—which he eventually turned into a "nickelodeon" **movie** theater. Zukor studied filmmaking and, using the technique of employing stars from the theater, established the Famous Players Film Company in 1912. By 1918 he employed a number of the big names in the new industry, including **Mary Pickford** and **Douglas Fairbanks**. By 1916 he had added distribution to showing and producing films, and had taken over the Paramount company. In 1919 Zukor began to build a chain of larger "picture places" to show first-run movies, a practice **Samuel Goldwyn** and **William Fox** were also to follow. Paramount was forced into bankruptcy in 1933 as a consequence of the **Great Depression**, but Zukor remained as chairman and later president of the reorganized company. In creating a vertically integrated company that controlled filmmaking from production to exhibition, Zukor had helped to establish the studio system that dominated the industry until 1948, when the **Supreme Court** ruled that the studio constituted a monopoly in breach of antitrust laws. His "contribution to the industry" was recognized with a special Academy Award in 1949.

Appendix 1

Presidents and Their Administrations, 1913–1933

WOODROW WILSON (1913–1921)

Election results:

	Popular Votes	Electoral Votes
1912		
Woodrow Wilson	4,118,571	88
William Howard Taft	3,486,720	8
1916		
Woodrow Wilson	9,127,695	277
Charles Evans Hughes	8,533,507	254

Vice President: Thomas R. Marshall (1913–1921)

Cabinet

Secretaries of State

    William J. Bryan (1913–1915)
    Robert Lansing (1915–1920)
    Bainbridge Colby (1920–1921)

Secretaries of the Treasury

    William G. McAdoo (1913–1918)
    Carter Glass (1918–1920)
    David F. Houston (1920–1921)

Secretaries of War

    Lindley M. Garrison (1913–1916)
    Newton D. Baker (1916–1921)

Attornies General

James C. McReynolds (1913–1914)
Thomas W. Gregory (1914–1919)
Alexander M. Palmer (1919–1921)

Postmaster General: Albert S. Burleson (1913–1921)

Secretary of the Navy: Josephus Daniels (1913–1921)

Secretaries of the Interior

Franklin K. Lane (1913–1920)
John B. Payne (1920–1921)

Secretaries of Agriculture

David F. Houston (1913–1920)
Edwin T. Meredith (1920–1921)

Secretaries of Commerce

William C. Redfield (1913–1919)
Joshua W. Alexander (1919–1921)

Secretary of Labor: William B. Wilson (1913–1921)

WARREN HARDING 1921–1923

Election results:

	Popular Votes	Electoral Votes
1920		
Warren G. Harding	16,143,407	404
James M. Cox	9,130,328	127

Vice President: Calvin Coolidge (1921–1923)

Cabinet

Secretary of State: Charles Evans Hughes (1921–1923)
Secretary of the Treasury: Andrew W. Mellon (1921–1923)
Secretary of War: John W. Weeks (1921–1923)
Attorney General: Harry M. Daugherty (1921–1923)

Postmasters General

William H. Hays (1921–1922)
Hubert Work (1922–1923)
Harry S. New (1923)

Secretary of the Navy: Edwin Denby (1921–1923)
Secretaries of the Interior

Albert B. Fall (1921–1923)
Hubert Work (1923)

Secretary of Agriculture: Henry C. Wallace (1921–1923)
Secretary of Commerce: Herbert Hoover (1921–1923)
Secretary of Labor: James J. Davis (1921–1923)

CALVIN COOLIDGE (1923–1929)

Election results:

	Popular Votes	Electoral Votes
1924		
Calvin Coolidge	15,718,211	382
John W. Davis	8,385,283	136
Robert M. LaFollette	4,831,289	13

Vice President: Charles G. Dawes (1925–1929)

Cabinet

Secretaries of State

Charles Evans Hughes (1923–1925)
Frank B. Kellogg (1925–1929)

Secretary of the Treasury: Andrew W. Mellon (1923–1929)
Secretaries of War

John W. Weeks (1923–1925)
Dwight F. Davis (1925–1929)

Attornies General

Harry M. Daugherty (1923–1924)
Harlan F. Stone (1924–1925)
John G. Sargent (1925–1929)

Postmaster General: Harry S. New (1923–1929)
Secretaries of the Navy

Edwin Denby (1923–1924)
Curtis D. Wilbur (1924–1929)

Secretaries of the Interior

Hubert Work (1923–1928)
Roy O. West (1929)

Secretaries of Agriculture

Henry C. Wallace (1923–1924)
Howard M. Gore (1924–1925)
William M. Jardine (1925–1929)

Secretaries of Commerce

Herbert Hoover (1923–1928)
William F. Whiting (1928–1929)

Secretary of Labor: James J. Davis (1923–1929)

HERBERT HOOVER (1929–1933)

Election results:

	Popular Votes	Electoral Votes
1928		
Herbert C. Hoover	21,391,993	444
Alfred E. Smith	15,016,169	87
1932		
Franklin D. Roosevelt	22,809,638	472
Herbert C. Hoover	15,758,901	59

Vice President: Charles Curtis (1929–1933)

Cabinet

Secretary of State: Henry L. Stimson (1929–1933)
Secretaries of the Treasury

Andrew W. Mellon (1929–1932)
Ogden L. Mills (1932–1933)

Secretaries of War

James W. Good (1929)
Patrick J. Hurley (1929–1933)

Attorney General: William DeWitt Mitchell (1929–1933)
Postmaster General: Walter F. Brown (1929–1933)
Secretary of the Navy: Charles F. Adams (1929–1933)
Secretary of the Interior: Ray L. Wilbur (1929–1933)
Secretary of Agriculture: Arthur M. Hyde (1929–1933)
Secretaries of Commerce

Robert P. Lamont (1929–1932)
Roy D. Chapin (1932–1933)

Secretaries of Labor

James J. Davis (1929–1930)
William N. Doak (1930–1933)

Appendix 2

Constitutional Amendments

SEVENTEENTH AMENDMENT

Passed by Congress 16 May 1912. Ratified 31 May 1913.

The Senate of the United States shall be composed of two Senators from each state, elected by the people thereof, for six years; and each Senator shall have one vote. The electors in each state shall have the qualifications requisite for electors of the most numerous branch of the state legislatures.

When vacancies happen in the representation of any state in the Senate, the executive authority of such state shall issue writs of election to fill such vacancies: Provided, that the legislature of any state may empower the executive thereof to make temporary appointments until the people fill the vacancies by election as the legislature may direct.

This amendment shall not be so construed as to affect the election or term of any Senator chosen before it becomes valid as part of the Constitution.

EIGHTEENTH AMENDMENT

Passed by Congress 17 December 1917. Ratified 29 January 1919.

Section 1. After one year from the ratification of this article the manufacture, sale, or transportation of intoxicating liquors within, the importation thereof into, or the exportation thereof from the United States and all territory subject to the jurisdiction thereof for beverage purposes is hereby prohibited.

Section 2. The Congress and the several states shall have concurrent power to enforce this article by appropriate legislation.

Section 3. This article shall be inoperative unless it shall have been ratified as an amendment to the Constitution by the legislatures of the several states, as provided in the Constitution, within seven years from the date of the submission hereof to the states by the Congress.

NINETEENTH AMENDMENT

Passed by Congress 5 June 1919. Ratified 26 August 1920.

The right of citizens of the United States to vote shall not be denied or abridged by the United States or by any state on account of sex.

Congress shall have power to enforce this article by appropriate legislation.

TWENTIETH AMENDMENT

Passed by Congress 3 March 1932. Ratified 23 January 1933.

Section 1. The terms of the President and Vice President shall end at noon on the 20th day of January, and the terms of Senators and Representatives at noon on the 3d day of January, of the years in which such terms would have ended if this article had not been ratified; and the terms of their successors shall then begin.

Section 2. The Congress shall assemble at least once in every year, and such meeting shall begin at noon on the 3d day of January, unless they shall by law appoint a different day.

Section 3. If, at the time fixed for the beginning of the term of the President, the President elect shall have died, the Vice President elect shall become President. If a President shall not have been chosen before the time fixed for the beginning of his term, or if the President elect shall have failed to qualify, then the Vice President elect shall act as President until a President shall have qualified; and the Congress may by law provide for the case wherein neither a President elect nor a Vice President elect shall have qualified, declaring who shall then act as President, or the manner in which one who is to act shall be selected, and such person shall act accordingly until a President or Vice President shall have qualified.

Section 4. The Congress may by law provide for the case of the death of any of the persons from whom the House of Representatives may choose a President whenever the right of choice shall have devolved upon them, and for the case of the death of any of the persons from whom the Senate may choose a Vice President whenever the right of choice shall have devolved upon them.

Section 5. Sections 1 and 2 shall take effect on the 15th day of October following the ratification of this article.

Section 6. This article shall be inoperative unless it shall have been ratified as an amendment to the Constitution by the legislatures of three-fourths of the several states within seven years from the date of its submission.

TWENTY-FIRST AMENDMENT

Passed by Congress 20 February 1933. Ratified 5 December 1933.

Section 1. The eighteenth article of amendment to the Constitution of the United States is hereby repealed.

Section 2. The transportation or importation into any state, territory, or possession of the United States for delivery or use therein of intoxicating liquors, in violation of the laws thereof, is hereby prohibited.

Section 3. This article shall be inoperative unless it shall have been ratified as an amendment to the Constitution by conventions in the several states, as provided in the Constitution, within seven years from the date of the submission hereof to the states by the Congress.

Bibliography

CONTENTS

INTRODUCTION

There is a huge amount of literature covering the period 1913 to 1933. Normally the progressive era, World War I, and the 1920s would be dealt with separately, and each area would merit its own extensive bibliography. A few general works do take a broader view—some older works such as Preston William Slosson's *The Great Crusade and After 1914–1928*, and Mark Sullivan's multivolume *Our Times 1900–1925*, for example, often provide useful detail and insight. More recent works are stronger on analytic content. One of the best of these in terms of detailed basic coverage is still Arthur S. Link with William B. Catton, *American Epoch: A History of the United States since the 1890s* (2 vols. covering 1897–1920, 1921–1941). Longer surveys such as Walter La Feber, *The American Century: A History of the United States since the 1890s*, and James T. Patterson, *America in the Twentieth Century: A History*, are particularly good. Also useful is Page Smith, *America Enters the World: A People's History of the Progressive Era and World War*.

The prewar reform movement known as Progressivism is the subject of much historical debate. Initially seen by people like George E. Mowry in *The California Progressives* and Arthur S. Link, *Woodrow Wilson and the Progressive Era*, as a liberal response to the problems of industrial society and the beginnings of the welfare state, later writers questioned the motives of the reformers and suggested varying degrees of self-interest. Richard Hofstadter in *The Age of Reform* was the key authority, and he was joined by Robert H. Wiebe with *The Search for Order* and Henry F. May in *the End of American Innocence*. The debate has been brought up to date by Michael McGerr in *A Fierce Discontent: Rise and Fall of the Progressive Movement in America, 1870–1920* and in Steven J. Diner's biographical focus in *A Very Different Age: Americans of the Progressive Era*. A useful short summary can be found in Brett Flehinger, *The 1912 Election and the Power of Progressivism: A Brief History*.

The authority on Woodrow Wilson is Arthur S. Link. Link's edited *Papers of Woodrow Wilson*, Princeton University Press, was published in sixty-nine volumes between 1965 and 1994 and is an essential source. His definitive biography *Wilson* was also published in several volumes, all by Princeton University Press: *The Road to the White House* (1947); *The New Freedom* (1956); *The Struggle for Neutrality, 1914–1915* (1960); *Confusions and Crises, 1915–1916*; and *Campaigns for Progressivism and Peace, 1916–1917* (1965). Link's short survey *Woodrow Wilson and the Progressive Era, 1910–1917* is also extremely good on the major political developments but has little to say on social and economic matters. A stimulating comparison that reveals a great deal about the progressive period is John M. Cooper's *The Warrior and the Priest: Woodrow Wilson and Theodore Roosevelt*, and Cooper's biography of *Woodrow Wilson* is also of value. Kendrick A. Clements provides a very good overview in *The Presidency of Woodrow Wilson*.

An established authority on the entry of the United States into the war is Ernest R. May, *The World War and American Isolation, 1914–1917*. More up to date is John Milton Cooper, *The Vanity of Power: American Isolationism and the First World War* and Thomas J. Knock's prize-winning study *To End All Wars: Woodrow Wilson and the Quest for a New World Order*. More recently, Ross Kennedy's *The Will to Believe: Woodrow Wilson, World War*

I, and America's Strategy for Peace and Security offers a fresh critical examination of the topic. Cooper's *Breaking the Heart of the World: Woodrow Wilson and the Fight for the League of Nations* is an excellent account of the failed peace settlement. Older surveys such as Frederic L. Paxson's three-volume *American Democracy and the World War* are still useful although very political in emphasis.

Two good single accounts of the American military experience during World War I are Laurence Stallings's *The Doughboys: The Story of the AEF, 1917–1918* and Gary Mead's similarly titled *The Doughboys: America and the First World War*. Jennifer Keene has written widely on the subject, and her *The American Soldier Experience* is a good general basic introduction to the subject. Two contrasting views are presented by participants in General John Pershing's *My Experience in the Great War* and Peyton C. March's *The Nation at War*. David Trask's *The AEF and Coalition Warmaking, 1917–1918* is a critical study of Pershing's leadership, while individual campaigns are thoroughly examined in Paul F. Braim's *The Test of Battle*, Robert H. Ferrell's *Collapse at Meuse-Argonne*, and James Hallas's *Squandered Victory*.

Historical works dealing with the United States home front during World War I fall essentially into two groups: the semiofficial studies written shortly after the war, often by participants; and the newer more critical studies in the later twentieth century. In addition to Paxson's *American Democracy and the World War*, Grosvenor B. Clarkson's *Industrial America in the World War*, Benedict Crowell and Robert F. Wilson's six-volume *How America Went to War*, W. D. Hines, *The War History of American Railroads*, and Gordon S. Watkins, *Labor Problems and Labor Administration in the United States during World War I*, all provide detailed factual accounts. Some later work was more critical in tone: John Maurice Clark, *The Costs of the World War to the American People*, and James R. Mock and Cedric Larson, *Words That Won the War: The Story of the Committee of Public Information 1917–1919*, are two excellent examples. A more balanced view is available in the later analytical studies. Groundbreaking in offering a new analysis that combines the military experience with the domestic is David M. Kennedy's *Over Here: The First World War and American Society*.

Domestic issues are dealt with in more detail by Neil A. Wynn, *From Progressivism to Prosperity: World War I and American Society*, while a comprehensive synthesis is provided by Robert H. Zeiger, *America's Great War: World War I and the American Experience*, and Robert Schaffer, *America in the Great War*. John Milton Cooper Jr., in *Pivotal Decades: The United States, 1900–1920*, looks at the progressive era and war together while Ellis Hawley's illuminating study, *The Great War and the Search for Modern Order: A History of the American People and Their Institutions, 1917–1933*, locates the war in the context of later developments. The wartime state is the subject of a number of works: Christopher Capozzola's *Uncle Sam Wants You: World War I and the Making of the Modern American Citizen* provides a more up-to-date study of the impact of wartime mobilization on different groups, while Steven Vaughn established the links between progressivism and the propaganda activities of the Committee on Public Information in his *Holding Fast the Inner Lines: Democracy, Nationalism, and the Committee on Public Information*; Valerie Jean Conner links prewar and postwar labor relations with the war in her excellent study, *The National War Labor Board: Stability, Social Justice, and the Voluntary State in World War I*.

The impact of the war on underprivileged groups has also been increasingly a subject of study. Barbara J. Steinson's *American Women's Activism in World War I* is a useful corrective. Maurine Weiner Greenwald's examination of the economic effects, *Women, War, and Work*, is the most detailed study of this important area and helps to fill many gaps. While Arthur E. Barbeau and Florette Henri's slim study of *The Unknown Soldiers: Black American Troops in World War I* remains the best work on the military experience of African Americans, Mark Ellis's *Race, War, and Surveillance: African Americans and the United States Government during World War I* offers the most detailed study of black attitudes and the government's response to them.

Excellent surveys of all of these subjects and a useful bibliography can be found in the Organization of American Historians' *Magazine of History* 17:1 (October 2002).

The transition to peacetime and the conflicts that erupted in the "Red Scare" have not been subject to much study beyond Burl Noggle's *Into the Twenties: The United States from Armistice to Normalcy* and Robert K. Murray's *Red Scare: A Study in National Hysteria 1919–1920*. A recent useful study is Todd J. Pfannestiel's *Rethinking the Red Scare: The Lusk Committee and New York's Crusade Against Radicalism, 1919–1923*.

Views of the "Jazz Age" were for a long time colored by Frederick Lewis Allen's journalistic study *Only Yesterday* and the short stories and novels of F. Scott Fitzgerald, both of which tended to emphasize the "revolution in manners and morals" and apparently carefree spirit of the decade. More critical appraisals appeared after World War II with George Soule's economic reassessment in *Prosperity Decade* and William E. Leuchtenburg's broader *The Perils of Prosperity*. Although more balanced, these studies still had elements of the traditional views evident in their discussion of broad cultural developments and politics judged against the coming of the Great Depression. Leuchtenburg's sympathetic analysis of the New Deal, shared by other writers like Arthur M. Schlesinger Jr., also colored their perspective of the 1920s. Later writers focused more on social and cultural diversity and the survival particularly of ethnic and racial divisions. Lynn Dumenil's *The*

Modern Temper, Ann Douglas's *Terrible Honesty: Mongrel Manhattan in the 1920s*, and David J. Goldberg's shorter *Discontented America* are among the best of more recent work on the 1920s. However, they tend to present social history without the politics, and they should be read in conjunction with political studies such as Niall Palmer's *The Twenties in America: Politics and History* or Ronald Allen Goldberg's excellent, if brief, general survey, *America in the Twenties*. David E. Kyvig's more recent excellent and wide-ranging social study, *Daily Life in the United States, 1920–1940*, provides a great deal of interesting detail of basic social conditions. Robert and Helen Merrell Lynd's famous study of Muncie, Indiana, *Middletown: A Study in Modern American Culture*, provides fascinating contemporary insights on small-town life and values, and the report by The President's Research Committee on Recent Social Trends, *Recent Social Trends in the United States*, contains much detailed information.

Just as views of the 1920s as a whole have changed, so the appreciation of presidents Harding, Coolidge, and Hoover has undergone some revision. Warren G. Harding's presidency was for a long time regarded as one of the worst in American history, associated with political scandal and failure to adapt to the changing economic and cultural forces of modern society. Revelations of corruption that emerged after his death in the investigations of Teapot Dome and other affairs involving his administration, coupled with accusations of marital infidelity and the suggestion he had fathered an illegitimate child, ensured that Harding would be dealt with harshly by historians. From the 1920s on with works such as William Allen White's *Masks in a Pageant* through to Mark Sullivan's volume of *Our Times: The Twenties*, Harding became more of a caricature than a real figure. Revision of these portrayals began with the opening of the Harding papers in 1964, but the most substantial reconsideration did not appear until Robert K. Murray's study of *The Harding Era: Warren G. Harding and His Administration* in 1969. Robert K. Ferrell's *The Strange Deaths of President Harding* provides a stimulating survey of some of the debates surrounding the Harding administration, and president Richard Nixon's former White House counsel John W. Dean provides a favorable overview in *Warren G. Harding* but adds little new.

President Calvin Coolidge has been placed only marginally higher than Harding in the historical rankings. While his honesty and sobriety was always emphasized, his inactivity and willingness to allow business a free hand were judged harshly by post-Depression critics. The Coolidge administration was given little consideration in Frederick Lewis Allen's *Only Yesterday*, and, as the title suggests, William Allen White's biography, *A Puritan in Babylon*, only confirmed what had become the established view of the 1920s. Even almost thirty years later Donald R. McCoy's study *Calvin Coolidge: The Quiet President* did little to alter the image of "Silent Cal," which survived until Robert Sobel's aptly titled *Coolidge, An American Enigma* another twenty-five years later. A recent brief survey is offered by David Greenberg in *Calvin Coolidge* and Amity Shlaes's sympathetic *Coolidge*, but the best reassessment of the Coolidge administration can be found in John Earl Haynes's edited collection, *Calvin Coolidge and the Coolidge Era: Essays on the History of the 1920s*. The bibliographic essays by John Braeman and Lynn Dumenil are especially useful and cover the decade as a whole.

Much of the rewriting of the political history of the 1920s focused on governmental structures and the rise of the "managerial" or "associational" state. Work by Ellis W. Hawley in a number of journal articles and in *The Great War and the Search for Modern Order* demonstrated that the Republican administrations were far from the *laissez faire* governments they were once portrayed as. Central to this new perspective was Herbert Hoover, both as secretary of commerce and as president. Hoover's reputation was left in tatters as a consequence of the Wall Street Crash and the catastrophic depression that followed. Even his defenders represented him as a conservative, upholding traditional values in contrast to the later "radical" departures of the New Deal. However, as historians after World War II began to revise their views of both Progressivism and the New Deal, so Hoover's role was subject to reexamination, and that process sped up with the opening of the Hoover Library in 1966. George H. Nash's magisterial three-volume biography, *The Life of Herbert Hoover*, is the essential starting point. Later studies by Kendrick Clements and Glen Jeansonne follow on from Nash's work. The biographies by Joan Hoff Wilson and David Burner, *Herbert Hoover: Forgotten Progressive* and *Herbert Hoover: A Public Life*, established continuities between the reform ethos, war years, and 1920s. Increasingly too, the Hoover administration was seen as paving the way for the New Deal rather than standing in contrast to it. These views were expressed in different ways by Harris G. Warren in *Herbert Hoover and the Great Depression*, Albert U. Romasco in *The Poverty of Abundance: Hoover, the Nation, the Depression*, and Ellis W. Hawley et al., *Herbert Hoover and the Crisis of American Capitalism*. This changing historiography is outlined fully in the edited collections by Martin L. Fausold and George T. Mazuzan, *The Hoover Presidency: A Reappraisal*, and Mark M. Dodge, *Herbert Hoover and the Historians*. A good short summary can be found in William E. Leuchtenburg's *Herbert Hoover*. Useful coverage of all presidential elections can be found in Arthur M. Schlesinger Jr.'s multivolume *History of American Presidential Elections*.

The various social, cultural, and economic trends of the 1920s are clearly outlined in the books by Dumenil, Goldberg, and Leuchtenburg cited above. Paula Fass's *The Damned and the Beautiful: American Youth in the 1920s* is also very useful in examining key aspects of the decade. African American life during this period is the subject of a growing scholarship, much of it concentrating on the Great Migration and settlement in particular northern centers. Several chapters in Joe William Tuttle Jr.'s *The African American Experience* provide a good general survey and detailed bibliography. Similarly William H. Chafe's *The American Woman: Her Changing Economic and Political Roles, 1920–1970* offers a good introduction and overview to another area of expanding literature, and some of the key debates on women's issues are examined in Amy E. Butler's study of the *Two Paths to Equality: Alice Paul and Ethel M. Smith in the Era Debate*. The prewar period in labor history is well dealt with in Melvyn Dubofsky's *Industrialism and the American Worker*, while the classic study of labor in the 1920s remains Irving Bernstein's *The Lean Years*. A useful study of literature, the arts, and entertainment is *American Culture in the 1920s* by Susan Currell.

The Wall Street Crash and causes and consequences of the Great Depression are well handled in Robert McElvaine's *The Great Depression* and also in David M. Kennedy's Pulitzer Prize–winning *Freedom from Fear*. Kennedy also provides a good synopsis of the material relating to Franklin D. Roosevelt and the New Deal, and Anthony J. Badger's *The New Deal* is one of the best more recent studies of the subject.

Several archive collections are particularly useful for this period. The Library of Congress has the private papers of many of the leading figures during this period. Presidential papers, some of which are more useful than others, can be found in the Library of Congress and presidential libraries. The Wilson papers in the Library of Congress and at Princeton University, New Jersey, and the Hoover papers at the Hoover Library in West Branch, Iowa, are exceptionally full collections. The records of federal agencies held in the National Archives in Washington, D.C., also provide rich sources. Some of this material can be accessed via websites. Information on presidents and their administrations can be found via www.whitehouse.gov/history/presidents and www.pl.org/div/potus. Material on Coolidge and the decade as a whole is included in the Calvin Coolidge Memorial foundation's site, www.calvin-coolidge.org. The Library of Congress provides a great deal of material online, and particularly useful is the American Memory site, "Prosperity and Thrift: The Coolidge Era and the Consumer Economy," at http://memory.loc.gov/ammem/coolhtml/coolhome.html. Among other very useful websites are http://historymatters.gmu.edu and www.galeuk.com.

BIBLIOGRAPHIES AND ENCYCLOPEDIAS

Bruccoli, Mary. *Concise Dictionary of American Literary Biography: The Twenties, 1917–1929*. Farmington Hills, MI: Cengage Gale, 1989.

Buenker, John D., and Edward R. Kantowicz, eds. *Historical Dictionary of the Progressive Era, 1890–1920.* Westport, CT: Greenwood, 1988.

Carnes, Mark C., ed. *American History.* New York: Simon & Schuster/Macmillan, 1996.

Cayton, Mary Kupiec, and Peter W. Williams, eds. *Encyclopedia of American Cultural and Intellectual History.* Vol. 1. New York and London: Charles Scribner, 2001.

Ciment, James, ed. *Encyclopedia of the Great Depression and New Deal.* Armonk, NY: M. E. Sharpe, 2000.

———. ed. *Encyclopedia of the Jazz Age: From the End of World War I to the Great Crash.* New York: M. E. Sharpe, 2007.

Garraty, John A., and Mark Carnes, eds. *The American Dictionary of National Biography.* 24 vols. New York: American Council of Learned Societies and Oxford University Press, 1999. Also available at www.anb.org.

Hogg, Ian V. *Historical Dictionary of World War I.* Lanham, MD: Scarecrow Press, 1998.

Howlett, Charles F. *The American Peace Movement: References and Resources.* Boston: G. K. Hall, 1997.

Kellner, Bruce. *The Harlem Renaissance: A Historical Dictionary for the Era.* New York: Methuen, 1987.

Martin, Michael, and Leonard Gelber, eds. *Dictionary of American History.* Totowa, NJ: Littlefield, Adams, 1965.

O'Brien, Patrick G., comp. *Herbert Hoover: A Bibliography.* Westport, CT: Greenwood Press, 1993.

Olson, James S. *Historical Dictionary of the 1920s: From World War I to the New Deal, 1919–1933.* Westport, CT: Greenwood Press, 1988.

Renshaw, Patrick. *America in the Era of the Two World Wars, 1910–1945.* New York: Addison Wesley Longman, 1996.

Rollyson, Carl, ed. *The Twenties in America.* 3 vols. Ipswich, MA: Salem Press, 2012.

Schaffer, Ronald, ed. *The United States in World War I: A Selected Bibliography.* Santa Barbara, CA: ABC-Clio, 1978.

Tucker, Spencer C., and Priscilla Mary Roberts, eds. *The Encyclopedia of World War I: A Political, Social, and Military History.* 5 vols. Santa Barbara: ABC-Clio, 2005.

U.S. Bureau of the Census. *Historical Statistics of the United States, Colonial Times to 1970.* Washington, D.C.: Government Printing Office, 1976.

Venson, Anne Cipriano, ed. *The United States in the First World War: An Encyclopedia.* Hamden, CT: Garland, 1996.

Wintz, Carl D., and Paul Finkleman. *Encyclopedia of the Harlem Renaissance.* New York: Routledge, 2004.

Woodward, David R., and Robert Franklin Maddox, eds. *America and World War I: A Selected Annotated Bibliography of English Language Sources.* New York: Garland, 1985.

GENERAL SURVEYS

Cashman, Sean Dennis. *America in the Twenties and Thirties: The Olympian Age of Franklin Delano Roosevelt.* New York: New York University Press, 1989.

Graham, Otis L. *The Great Campaigns: Reform and War in America, 1900–1928.* Englewood Cliffs, NJ: Prentice Hall, 1971.

Karl, Barry D. *The Uneasy State: The United States from 1915 to 1945.* Chicago: University of Chicago Press, 1983.

La Feber, Walter. *The American Century: A History of the United States since the 1890s,* 5th ed. New York: McGraw-Hill, 1998.

Link, Arthur S., with William B. Catton. *American Epoch: A History of the United States since the 1890s* (2 vols., 1897–1920, 1921–1941). New York: Alfred Knopf, 1963.

Patterson, James T. *America in the Twentieth Century: A History,* 5th ed. Fort Worth: Harcourt, 2000.

Ridings, William J., Jr., and Stuart B. McIver. *Rating the Presidents.* New York: Citadel Press, 2000.

Schlesinger, Arthur M., Jr. *History of American Presidential Elections.* New York: McGraw Hill, 1971.

Slosson, Preston William. *The Great Crusade and After 1914–1928.* New York: Macmillan, 1930.

Smith, Page. *America Enters the World: A People's History of the Progressive Era and World War II.* New York: McGraw-Hill, 1985.

Sullivan, Mark. *Our Times 1900–1925.* New York: Charles Scribner's Sons, 1925–1935.

PREWAR PROGRESSIVISM, 1913–1917

Addams, Jane. *Twenty Years at Hull House.* New York: Macmillan, 1910.

Ashby, Le Roy. *William Jennings Bryan: Champion of Democracy.* New York: Macmillan, 1987.

Berson, Robin Kadison. *Jane Addams: A Biography.* Westport, CT: Greenwood Press, 2004.

Brown, Victoria Bissell. *The Education of Jane Addams: Politics and Culture in Modern America.* Philadelphia: University of Pennsylvania, 2004.

Chambers, Clarke A. *Seedtime of Reform: American Social Service and Social Action, 1918–1933*. Ann Arbor: University of Michigan, 1967.

———. *Paul U. Kellogg and the "Survey": Voices for Social Reform and Social Justice*. Minneapolis: University of Minnesota Press, 1971.

Chambers, John W., III. *The Tyranny of Change: Americans in the Progressive Era, 1890–1920*. New York: St. Martin's Press, 1992.

Chatfield, Charles. *For Peace and Justice: Pacifism in America, 1914–1941*. Knoxville: University of Tennessee Press, 1971.

Cooper, John Milton, Jr. *Pivotal Decades: The United States, 1900–1920*. New York: W. W. Norton, 1990.

———. *The Warrior and the Priest: Woodrow Wilson and Theodore Roosevelt*. Cambridge, MA: Harvard University Press, 1983.

Davis, Allen F. *Spearheads for Reform*. New York: Oxford University Press, 1967.

———. *American Heroine: The Life and Legend of Jane Addams*. New York: Oxford University Press, 1973.

DeBenedetti, Charles. *The Peace Reform in American History*. Bloomington: Indiana University Press, 1984.

Diner, Steven J. *A Very Different Age: Americans of the Progressive Era*. New York: Hill & Wang, 1998.

Dubofsky, Melvyn. *We Shall Be All: A History of the Industrial Workers of the World*. Chicago: Quadrangle, 1969.

Duffy, Bernard K., and Carl R. Burgchard. *Robert M. La Follette Sr.: The Voice of Conscience*. Westport, CT: Greenwood Press, 1992.

Flanagan, Maureen. *America Reformed: Progressives and Progressivisms, 1890s–1920s*. New York: Oxford University Press, 2007.

Flehinger, Brett. *The 1912 Election and the Power of Progressivism*. Boston: Bedford/St. Martins, 2003.

Forcey, Charles. *The Crossroads of Liberalism: Croly, Weyl, Lippmann and the Progressive Era, 1900–1925*. New York: Oxford University Press, 1961.

Gilmore, Glenda Elizabeth. *Who Were the Progressives?* Boston: Bedford/St. Martin's, 2002.

Goldman, Eric. *Rendezvous with Destiny: A History of Modern American Reform*. New York: Vintage, 1956.

Higgens-Evenson, R. Rudy. *The Price of Progress: Public Services, Taxation, and the American Corporate State, 1877 to 1929*. Baltimore: Johns Hopkins University Press, 2003.

Higham, John. *Strangers in the Land: Patterns of American Nativism, 1860–1925*. New York: Atheneum, 1963.

Hofstadter, Richard. *The Age of Reform*. New York: Knopf, 1955.

Hoxie, Frederick E. *A Final Promise: The Campaign to Assimilate the Indians, 1880–1920*. Lincoln: University of Nebraska Press, 2001.

Jeansonne, Glen. *Transformation and Reaction: America 1921–1945*. New York: HarperCollins, 1994.

Kazin, Michael. *A Godly Hero: The Life of William Jennings Bryan*. New York: Knopf, 2006.

LaFollette, Belle Case, and Fola La Follette. *Robert M. La Follette*. 2 vols. New York: Macmillan, 1953.

Lears, T. J. Jackson. *No Place of Grace: Antimodernism and the Transformation of American Culture, 1880–1920*. New York: Pantheon, 1981.

Leiby, J. *A History of Social Welfare and Social Work in the United States*. New York: Columbia University Press, 1979.

Link, Arthur. *Woodrow Wilson and the Progressive Era, 1910–1917*. New York: Harper & Row, 1954.

Link, Arthur, and Richard L. McCormick. *Progressivism*. Arlington Heights, IL: Harlan Davidson, 1983.

Lubove, R. *The Professional Altruist: The Emergence of Social Work as a Career 1880–1930*. Boston: Harvard University Press, 1965.

Marchand, C. Roland. *The American Peace Movement and Social Reform*. Princeton, NJ: Princeton University Press, 1973.

May, Henry F. *The End of American Innocence: A Study of the First Years of Our Own Time, 1912–1917*. Chicago: Quadrangle, 1964.

McGerr, Michael. *A Fierce Discontent: The Rise and Fall of the Progressive Movement in America, 1870–1920*. New York: Free Press, 2003.

Mowry, George F. *The California Progressives*. Berkeley: University of California Press, 1951.

Parrish, Michael E. *Felix Frankfurter and His Time*. New York: Free Press, 1982.

Piott, Steven. *American Reformers 1870–1920*. Lanham: Rowman & Littlefield Publishers, 2006.

Schutz, Aaron. *Social Class, Social Action, and Education: The Failure of Progressive Democracy*. Basingstoke: Palgrave Macmillan, 2010.

Stansell, Christine. *American Moderns: Bohemian New York and the Creation of a New Century*. New York: Metropolitan, 2000.

Steel, Ronald. *Walter Lippmann and the American Century*. Boston: Little, Brown and Company, 1980.

Stromquist, Shelton. *Reinventing "The People": The Progressive Movement, the Class Problem, and the Origins of Modern Liberalism*. Urbana: University of Illinois Press, 2006.

Urofsky, Melvin I. *Big Steel and the Wilson Administration: A Study in Business-Government Relations*. Columbus, OH: Ohio State University Press, 1969.

Weinstein, James. *The Corporate Ideal in the Liberal State: 1900–1918*. Boston: Beacon Press, 1968.

———. *The Decline of Socialism in America, 1912–1925*. New York: Vintage, 1969.

Wiebe, Robert. *The Search of Order, 1877–1920*. New York: Hill & Wang, 1967.

Zunz, Olivier. *The Changing Face of Inequality: Urbanization, Industrial Development, and Immigrants in Detroit, 1880–1920*. Chicago: University of Chicago Press, 1982.

WOODROW WILSON

Auchinloss, Louis. *Woodrow Wilson*. New York: Viking, Penguin, 2000.

Baker, Ray Stannard. *Woodrow Wilson: Life and Letters.* 8 vols. New York: Doubleday, 1927–1939.

Brands, H. W. *Woodrow Wilson.* New York: Times Books, 2003.

Clements, Kendrick A. *The Presidency of Woodrow Wilson*. Lawrence: University Press of Kansas, 1992.

———. "Woodrow Wilson and World War I." *Presidential Studies Quarterly* 34:1 (2004).

Cooper, John Milton, Jr. *Woodrow Wilson: A Biography*. New York: Knopf, 2009.

Heckscher, August. *Woodrow Wilson*. New York: Macmillan/Collier, 1991.

Levin, Phyllis Lee. *Edith and Woodrow: The Wilson White House*. New York: Scribner's, 2001.

Link, Arthur S. *The Road to the White House*. Princeton, NJ: Princeton University Press, 1947.

———. *Woodrow Wilson and the Progressive Era, 1910–1917*. New York: Harper & Row, 1954.

———. *The New Freedom*. Princeton, NJ: Princeton University Press, 1956.

———. *The Struggle for Neutrality, 1914–1915*. Princeton, NJ: Princeton University Press, 1960.

———. *Confusions and Crises, 1915–1916*. Princeton, NJ: Princeton University Press, 1964.

———. *Campaigns for Progressivism and Peace*. Princeton, NJ: Princeton University Press, 1965.

Miller, Kristie. *Ellen and Edith: Woodrow Wilson's First Ladies*. Lawrence: University Press of Kansas, 2010.

Mulder, John M., et al., eds. *Woodrow Wilson: A Bibliography*. Westport, CT: Greenwood Press, 1997.

Pestrillo, Ronald J. *Woodrow Wilson and the Roots of Modern Liberalism*. Lanham, MD: Rowman & Littlefield, 2004.

Startt, James D. *Woodrow Wilson and the Press: Prelude to the Presidency.* New York: Palgrave Macmillan, 2004.

Thompson, J. A. *Woodrow Wilson.* London: Longman, 2002.

Thorsen, Niels Aaga. *The Political Thought of Woodrow Wilson, 1875–1910.* Princeton, NJ: Princeton University Press, 1988.

Walworth, Arthur C. *Woodrow Wilson.* 2 vols. New York: W. W. Norton, 1958.

Weinstein, Edwin A. *Woodrow Wilson: A Medical and Psychological Biography.* Princeton, NJ: Princeton University Press, 1981.

FOREIGN RELATIONS

Ambrosius, Lloyd E. *Wilsonianism: Woodrow Wilson and His Legacy in American Foreign Policy.* New York: St. Martin's Press, 2002.

Bacino, Leo J. *Reconstructing Russia: U.S. Policy in Revolutionary Russia, 1917–1922.* Kent, OH: Kent State University Press, 1999.

Boghardt, Thomas. *The Zimmermann Telegram: Intelligence, Diplomacy and America's Entry into World War I.* Annapolis, MD: Naval Institute Press, 2012.

Calhoun, Frederick S. *Power and Principle: Armed Intervention in Wilsonian Foreign Policy.* Kent, OH: Kent State University Press, 1986.

———. *Uses of Force and Wilsonian Foreign Policy.* Kent, OH: Kent State University Press, 1993.

Clements, Kendrick A. *Woodrow Wilson: World Statesman.* Boston: Twayne, 1987.

Davis, Donald E., and Eugene P. Trani. *First Cold War: The Legacy of Woodrow Wilson in U.S.-Soviet Relations.* Columbia and London: University of Missouri Press, 2002.

Fogelsong, David S. *America's Secret War against Bolshevism: U.S. Intervention in the Russian Civil War, 1917–1920.* Chapel Hill: University of North Carolina Press, 1995.

Katz, F. *The Secret War in Mexico: Europe, the United States and the Mexican Revolution.* Chicago: University of Chicago Press, 1981.

Kindall, S. G. *American Soldiers in Siberia.* New York: R. Smith, 1945.

Levin, N. Gordon. *Woodrow Wilson and World Politics: America's Response to War and Revolution.* New York: Oxford University Press, 1968.

Link, Arthur S. *The Higher Realism of Woodrow Wilson.* Nashville, TN.: Vanderbilt University Press, 1971.

———, ed. *Woodrow Wilson and a Revolutionary World, 1913–1920.* Chapel Hill: University of North Carolina Press, 1982.

McFadden, D. W. *Alternative Paths: Soviets and Americans, 1917–1920.* New York: Oxford University Press, 1993.

Melton, Carol Kingsland Willcox. *Between War and Peace: Woodrow Wilson and the American Expeditionary Force in Siberia, 1918–1921.* Macon, GA: Mercer University Press, 2001.

Ninkovich, Frank. *The Wilsonian Century: U.S. Foreign Policy since 1900.* Chicago: University of Chicago Press, 1999.

Quirk, R. E. *Affair of Honor: Woodrow Wilson and the Occupation of Veracruz.* New York: W. W. Norton, 1967.

Rhodes, B. D. *The Anglo-American Winter War with Russia, 1918–1919.* Westport, CT: Greenwood Press, 1988.

Saul, Norman E. *War and Revolution: The United States and Russia, 1914–1921.* Lawrence: University Press of Kansas, 2001.

Silverlight, John. *The Victor's Dilemma: Allied Intervention in the Russian Civil War.* London: Barrie & Jenkins, 1970.

Tucker, Robert W. Woodrow Wilson and the Great War: Reconsidering America's Neutrality, 1914–1917. Charlottesville: University Press of Virginia, 2007.

Tulchin, Joseph S. *The Aftermath of War: World War I and U.S. Policy Toward Latin America.* New York: New York University Press, 1971.

THE WILSON ADMINISTRATION, WORLD WAR I, AND THE VERSAILLES TREATY

Alef, Daniel. *Bernard Baruch: Lone Wolf of Wall Street.* Santa Barbara, CA: Titans of Fortune Publishing, 2007.

Ambrosius, Lloyd E. *Wilsonian Statecraft.* Wilmington, DE: Scholarly Resource Books, 1991.

Andelman, David A. *A Shattered Peace: Versailles 1919 and the Price We Pay Today.* New York: Wiley, 2007.

Bailey, Thomas A. *Woodrow Wilson and Lost Peace.* London: Macmillan, 1944.

Boemeke, Manfred F., et al., eds. *The Treaty of Versailles: A Reassessment after 75 Years.* Washington, D.C.: German Historical Institute, 1998.

Cooper, John Milton, Jr. *The Vanity of Power: American Isolationism and the First World War.* Westport, CT: Greenwood Press, 1969.

———. *Breaking the Heart of the World: Woodrow Wilson and the Fight for the League of Nations.* Cambridge and New York: Cambridge University Press, 2001.

Craig, Douglas B. *Progressives At War: William G. McAdoo and Newton D. Baker, 1863–1941.* Baltimore: Johns Hopkins University Press, 2013.

Dawley, Alan. *Changing the World: American Progressives in War and Revolution*. Princeton and Oxford: Princeton University Press, 2003.

Devlin, Patrick. *Too Proud to Fight: Woodrow Wilson's Neutrality*. New York: Oxford University Press, 1975.

Ferrell, Robert H. *Woodrow Wilson and World War I, 1917–1921*. New York: Harper & Row, 1985.

Finnegan, John Patrick. *Against the Specter of a Dragon: The Campaign for American Military Preparedness, 1914–1917*. Westport, CT: Greenwood Press, 1974.

Fleming, Thomas. *The Illusion of Victory: America in World War I*. New York: Basic Books, 2003.

Grant, James. *Bernard Baruch: The Adventures of a Wall Street Legend*. Mount Jackson, VA: Axios Press, 2012.

Hodgson, Godfrey. *Woodrow Wilson's Right Hand: The Life of Colonel Edward M. House*. New Haven, CT: Yale University Press, 2006.

Keene, Jennifer D. *The United States and the First World War*. Harlow, England: Pearson Education, 2000.

Kendrick, A. Clements. *The Presidency of Woodrow Wilson*. Lawrence: University of Kansas, 1992.

Kennedy, Ross. *The Will to Believe: Woodrow Wilson, World War I, and America's Strategy for Peace and Security*. Kent, OH: Kent State University Press, 2004.

Knock, Thomas J. *To End All Wars: Woodrow Wilson and the Quest for a New World Order*. New York: Oxford University Press, 1992.

Levin, N. Gordon. *Woodrow Wilson and World Politics: America's Response to War and Revolution*. London: Oxford University Press, 1968.

Macmillan, Margaret. *Paris 1919: Six Months That Changed the World*. New York: Random House, 2001.

May, Ernest R. *The World War and American Isolation, 1914–1917*. Cambridge, MA: Harvard University Press, 1959.

Mayer, Arno J. *The Political Origins of the New Diplomacy, 1917–1918*. New Haven, CT: Yale University Press, 1959.

———. *The Politics and Diplomacy of Peacemaking*. London: Weidenfeld & Nicholson, 1968.

Mee, Charles L. *The End of Order: Versailles, 1919*. New York: Dutton, 1980.

Nelson, Keith L. *Victors Divided: America and the Allies in Germany, 1918–1923*. Berkeley: University of California Press, 1975.

Paxson, Frederic L. *American Democracy and the World War*. 3 vols. Boston: Houghton Mifflin, 1936–1948.

Peterson, H. C. *Propaganda for War: The Campaign Against American Neutrality, 1914–1917*. Port Washington, NY: Kennikat Press, 1968.

Seymour, C. *American Diplomacy during the War*. Baltimore, MD: Johns Hopkins, 1934.

Sharp, Alan. *The Versailles Settlement: Peacemaking in Paris, 1919*. New York: St. Martin's, 1991.

Slotkin, Richard. *Lost Battalions: The Great War and the Crisis of American Nationality*. New York: Henry Holt, 2005.

Smith, Daniel M. *The Great Departure: The United States and World War I*. New York: John Wiley, 1965.

Tucker, Robert W. *Robert Lansing and American Neutrality, 1914–1917*. Berkeley: University of California Press, 1958.

———. *Woodrow Wilson and the Great War: Reconsidering America's Neutrality, 1914–1917*. Charlottesville: University of Virginia Press, 2007.

Walworth, Arthur S. *America's Moment: 1918: American Diplomacy at the End of the War*. New York: Norton, 1977.

———. *Wilson and His Peacemakers: American Diplomacy at the Paris Peace Conference, 1919*. New York: Norton, 1986.

THE AMERICAN EXPEDITIONARY FORCE

Ayres, L. P. *The War with Germany: A Statistical Summary*. Washington, D.C.: U.S. War Department, 1919.

Beaver, Daniel R. *Newton D. Baker and the American War Effort, 1917–1919*. Lincoln: University of Nebraska, 1966.

Braim, Paul F. *The Test of Battle: The American Expeditionary Forces in the Meuse-Argonne Campaign*. Newark: University of Delaware Press, 1987.

Britten, Thomas A. *American Indians in World War I: At Home and Abroad*. Albuquerque, NM: University of New Mexico, 1997.

Bruce, Robert B. *Fraternity of Arms: America and France in the Great War*. Lawrence, KS: University of Kansas Press, 2003.

Chambers, John Whitelly, III. *To Raise an Army: The Draft Comes to Modern America*. New York: Free Press, 1987.

Clark, George B. *The American Expeditionary Force in World War I: A Statistical History, 1917–1919*. Jefferson, NC, and London: McFarland, 2013.

Coffman, Edward M. *The Hilt of the Sword: The Career of Peyton C. March*. Madison: University of Wisconsin Press, 1966.

———. *The War to End All Wars: The American Military Experience in World War*. Oxford: Oxford University Press, 1968.

Cornebise, Alfred E. *The Stars and Stripes: Doughboy Journalism in World War I*. Westport, CT: Greenwood Press, 1984.

Eisenhower, John. *Yanks: The Epic Story of the American Army in World War I*. New York: Free Press, 2001.

Evans, Martin Marix, ed. *American Voices of World War I: Primary Source Documents, 1917–1920*. Chicago: Fitzroy Dearborn Publishers, 2001.

Farwell, Byron. *Over There: The United States in the Great War, 1917–1918*. New York: W. W. Norton, 1999.

Ferrell, Robert H. *Collapse at Meuse-Argonne: The Failure of the Missouri-Kansas Division*. Columbia: University of Missouri Press, 2004.

———. *Meuse-Argonne Diary: A Division Commander in World War I*. Columbia: University of Missouri Press, 2004.

Ford, Nancy Gentile. *Americans All! Foreign-born Soldiers in World War I*. College Station, TX: Texas A&M University Press, 2001.

Freidel, Frank. *Over There: The Story of America's First Great Overseas Crusade*. New York: McGraw-Hill, 1990.

Gilbert, James L. *World War I and the Origins of U.S. Military Intelligence*. Lanham, MD: Scarecrow Press, 2012.

Grotelneschen, Mark Ethan. *The AEF Way of War: The American Army and Combat in World War I*. New York: Cambridge University Press, 2007.

Hallas, James H. *Squandered Victory: The American First Army at St. Mihiel*. Westport, CT: Praeger, 1995.

———, ed. *Doughboy War: The American Expeditionary Force in World War I*. Boulder, CO: Lynne Rienner Publishing, 2000.

Hamburger, Kenneth E. *Learning Lessons in the American Expeditionary Forces*. Washington, D.C.: U.S. Army Center of Military History, 1997.

Harbord, James G. *The American Army in France, 1917–1919*. Boston, MA: Houghton Mifflin, 1936.

Harris, Stephen L. *Harlem's Hell Fighters: The African American 369th Infantry in World War I*. Washington, D.C.: Brassey's, 2003.

Hart, Peter. *The Great War: A Combat History of the First World War*. New York: Oxford University Press, 2013.

Hoff, Thomas A. *U.S. Doughboy, 1916–1919*. Oxford: Osprey Publishing, 2005.

James, D. Clayton, and Anne Sharp Wells. *America and the Great War, 1914–1920*. Wheeling, IL: Harlan Davidson, 1998.

Johnson, Herbert A. *Wingless Eagle: U.S. Army Aviation through World War I*. Chapel Hill: University of North Carolina Press, 2001.

Keene, Jennifer. *The United States and the First World War*. New York: Longman, 2000.

———. *Doughboys: The Great War and the Remaking of America*. Baltimore, MD: Johns Hopkins University Press, 2001.

———. *World War I: The American Soldier Experience*. Lincoln and London: University of Nebraska Press, 2011.

Knudson, Michael J., and Ann G. Knudson. *Warriors in Khaki: Native American Doughboys from North Dakota*. Los Gatos, CA: Robertson Publishing, 2012.

Krause, Susan Applegate. *North American Indians in the Great War*. Lincoln: University of Nebraska Press, 2009.

Lee, David D. *Sergeant York: An American Hero*. Lexington: University Press of Kentucky, 1985.

Liggett, Hunter. *Commanding an American Army: Recollections of the Great War*. Boston, MA: Houghton Mifflin, 1925.

March, Peyton C. *The Nation at War*. New York: Doubleday, 1932.

Marshall, R. Jackson, III. *Memories of World War I: North Carolina Doughboys on the Western Front*. Raleigh, NC: Division of Archives and History, North Carolina Department of Cultural Resources, 1998.

McCartin, Joseph A. *Labor's Great War: The Struggle for Industrial Democracy and the Origins of Modern American Labor Relations*. Chapel Hill, NC: University of North Carolina Press, 1997.

Mead, Gary. *The Doughboys: America and the First World War*. New York: Penguin, 2000.

Meigs, Mark. *Optimism at Armageddon: Voices of American Participants in the First World War*. New York: New York University Press, 1997.

Mitchell, William. *Memoirs of World War I*. New York: Random House, 1960.

Palmer, F. *Our Greatest Battle: The Meuse Argonne*. New York: Dodd, 1919.

Pencak, William. *For God and Country: The American Legion, 1919–1941*. Boston: Northeastern University Press, 1989.

Pershing, John J. *My Experience in the Great War*. New York: Frederick Stokes, 1931.

Roberts, Frank E. *The American Foreign Legion: Black Soldiers of the 93rd in World War I*. Annapolis, MD: Naval Institute Press, 2004.

Rossano, Geoffrey. *Hero of the Angry Sky: The World War I Diary and Letters of David S. Ingalls, America's First Naval Ace*. Athens, OH: Ohio University Press, 2013.

Rubin, Richard. *The Last of the Doughboys: The Forgotten Generation and Their Forgotten World War*. New York: Houghton Mifflin Harcourt, 2013.

Smythe, Donald. *Pershing, General of the Armies*. Bloomington: Indiana University Press, 1986.

Snell, Mark A., ed. *Unknown Soldiers: The American Expeditionary Forces in Memory & Remembrance*. Kent, OH: Kent State University Press, 2008.

Stallings, Laurence. *The Doughboys: The Story of the AEF, 1917–1918*. New York: Harper, 1963.

Sterba, Christopher M. *Good Americans: Italian and Jewish Immigrants during the First World War*. New York: Oxford University Press, 2003.

Trask, David F. *The United States in the Supreme War Council*. Middletown, CT: Wesleyan University Press, 1961.

———. *The AEF and Coalition Warmaking, 1917–1918*. Lawrence: University Press of Kansas, 1993.

U.S. War Department. *United States Army in the World War, 1917–1919*. 17 vols. Washington, D.C.: U.S. Government Printing Office.

Vandiver, Frank E. *Black Jack: The Life and Times of John J. Pershing*. College Station, TX: Texas A&M University, 1977.

Zeiger, Susan. *In Uncle Sam's Service: Women Workers with the American Expeditionary Force, 1917–1919*. Ithaca, NY: Cornell University Press, 1999.

WORLD WAR I AT HOME

Baruch, Bernard. *American Industry in the War*. New York: Prentice-Hall, 1941.

Beaver, Daniel R. *Newton D. Baker and the American War Effort, 1917–1919*. Lincoln: University of Nebraska Press, 1966.

Blakey, George T. *Historians on the Homefront: American Propagandists for the Great War*. Lexington: University Press of Kentucky, 1970.

Breen, William J. *Uncle Sam at Home: Civilian Mobilization, Wartime Federalism, and the Council of National Defense, 1917–1919*. Westport, CT: Greenwood Press, 1984.

———. *Labor Market Politics and the Great War: The Department of Labor, the States, and the First U.S. Employment Service, 1907–1933*. Kent, OH: Kent State University Press, 1997.

Bristow, Nancy K. *Making Men Moral: Social Engineering during the Great War*. New York: New York University Press, 1996.

Britten, Thomas, A. *American Indians in World War I: At Home and at War*. Albuquerque: University of New Mexico Press, 1997.

Capozzola, Christopher. *Uncle Sam Wants You: World War I and the Making of the Modern American Citizen*. New York: Oxford University Press, 2008.

Chafee, Zechariah, Jr. *Free Speech in the United States*. Cambridge, MA: Harvard University Press, 1941.

Clark, John Maurice. *The Costs of the World War to the American People*. New Haven, CT: Yale University Press, 1931.

Clarkson, Grosvenor B. *Industrial America in the World War: The Strategy Behind the Lines*. Boston, MA: Houghton Mifflin, 1923.

Clayton, James D., and Anne Sharp Wells. *America and the Great War, 1914–1920*. Wheeling, IL: Harlan Davidson, 1998.

Conner, Valerie Jean. *The National War Labor Board: Stability, Social Justice, and the Voluntary State in World War I.* Chapel Hill: University of North Carolina Press, 1983.

Cornebise, Alfred E. *War as Advertised: The Four Minute Men and America's Crusade, 1918–1918.* Philadelphia: American Philosophical Society, 1984.

Creel, George. *How We Advertised America.* New York: Harper & Brothers, 1920.

Crowell, Benedict. *America's Munitions 1917–1918.* Washington, DC: U.S. Government Printing Office, 1919.

———. *Demobilization: Our Industrial and Military Demobilization after the Armistice, 1918–1920.* New Haven, CT: Yale University Press, 1921.

Crowell, Benedict, and Robert F. Wilson, *How America Went to War.* 6 vols. New Haven, CT: Yale University Press, 1921.

Cuff, Robert D. *The War Industries Board: Business-Government Relations during World War II.* Baltimore: Johns Hopkins University Press, 1973.

Davis, Allen F. "Welfare, Reform, and World War I." *American Quarterly* 19 (Fall 1967): 516–33.

DeBauches, Leslie Midkiff. *Reel Patriotism: The Movies and World War I.* Madison: University of Wisconsin Press, 1997.

Donohue, William A. *The Politics of the American Civil Liberties Union.* New Brunswick, NJ: Transaction Publishers, 1985.

Ellis, Edward Robb. *Echoes of Distant Thunder: Life in the United States, 1914–1918.* New York: Coward, McCann & Geoghegan, 1975.

Ford, Nancy Gentile. *The Great War and America: Civil Military Relations during World War I.* Westport, CT: Praeger Security International, 2008.

Freeberg, Ernest. *Democracy's Prisoner: Eugene V. Debs, the Great War, and the Right to Dissent.* Boston: Harvard University Press, 2009.

Gabrielan, Randall. *Explosion at Morgan: The World War I Middlesex Munitions Disaster.* Charleston, SC: The History Press, 2012.

Gilbert, Charles. *American Financing of World War I.* Westport, CT: Greenwood, 1970.

Grubbs, Frank L. *The Struggle for Labor Loyalty: Gompers, the A. F. of L. and the Pacifists, 1917–1920.* Durham, NC: Duke University Press, 1968.

———. *Samuel Gompers and the Great War: Protecting Labor's Standards.* Wake Forest, NC: Meridional Publications, 1982.

Gruber, Carol S. *Mars and Minerva: World War I and the Uses of the Higher Learning in America.* Baton Rouge: Louisiana State University Press, 1975.

Harries, Meirion, and Susan Harries. *The Last Days of Innocence: America at War, 1917–1918.* New York: Random House, 1997.

Haydu, Jeffrey *Making American Industry Safe for Democracy: Comparative Perspectives on the State and Employee Representation in the Era of World War I.* Urbana: University of Illinois Press, 1997.

Hines, Walter D. *The War History of American Railroads.* New Haven, CT: Yale University Press, 1928.

Irwin, Julia F. *Making the World Safe: The American Red Cross and a Nation's Humanitarian Awakening.* New York: Oxford University Press, 2013.

Jantzen, Steven. *Hurrah for Peace, Hooray for War: The United States during World War I.* New York: Knopf, 1972.

Jensen, Joan. *The Price of Vigilance.* Chicago: Rand McNally, 1968.

Johnson, Donald. *The Challenge to American Freedoms: World War I and the Rise of the American Civil Liberties Union.* Lexington: University of Kentucky Press, 1963.

Jordan, William G. *Black Newspapers and America's War for Democracy, 1914–1920.* Chapel Hill: University of North Carolina Press, 2001.

Kennedy, David M. *Over Here: The First World War and American Society.* New York: Oxford University Press, 1980.

Kerr, K. Austin. *American Railroad Politics, 1914–1920: Rates, Wages, and Efficiency.* Pittsburgh: University of Pittsburgh Press, 1969.

Kohn, Stephen M. *American Political Prisoners: Prosecutions under the Espionage and Sedition Acts.* Westport, CT: Praeger, 1994.

Koistinen, Paul A. C. *Mobilizing for Modern War: The Political Economy of American Warfare, 1865–1919.* Lawrence: University of Kansas Press, 1997.

Link, Arthur S., ed. *The Impact of World War I.* New York: Harper & Row, 1969.

Livermore, Seward W. *Woodrow Wilson and the War Congress, 1916–1918.* Seattle: University of Washington Press, 1966.

Luebke, Frederick C. *Bonds of Loyalty: German-Americans and World War I.* DeKalb, IL: Northern Illinois University Press, 1974.

McCartin, Joseph A. *Labor's Great War: The Struggle for Industrial Democracy and the Origins of Modern Labor Relations, 1912–1921.* Chapel Hill: University of North Carolina Press, 1997.

Mock, James R., and Cedric Larson. *Words that Won the War: The Story of the Committee on Public Information, 1917–1919.* Princeton, NJ: Princeton University Press, 1939.

Mullendore, William Clinton. *History of the United States Food Administration, 1917–1919.* Stanford, CA: Stanford University Press, 1941.

Murphy, Paul L. *World War I and the Origin of Civil Liberties in the United States.* New York: Norton, 1979.

Offer, Avner. *The First World War: An Agrarian Interpretation.* Oxford: Clarendon Press, 1989.

Paxson, Frederic L. *American Democracy and the World War*. 3 vols. Boston: Houghton Mifflin, 1936–1948.

Petersen, H. C., and Gilbert C. Fite. *Opponents of War, 1917–1918*. Seattle: University of Washington Press, 1968.

Polenberg, Richard. *Fighting Faiths: The Abrams Case, the Supreme Court, and Free Speech*. New York: Viking, 1987.

Preston, William, Jr. *Aliens and Dissenters: Federal Suppression of Radicals, 1903–1933*. New York: Harper & Row, 1966.

Rochester, Stuart I. *American Liberal Disillusionment in the Wake of World War I*. University Park: Pennsylvania State University Press, 1977.

Schaffer, Ronald. *America in the Great War: The Rise of the War Welfare State*. New York: Oxford University Press, 1991.

Scheiber, Harry N. *The Wilson Administration and Civil Liberties, 1917–1921*. Ithaca, NY: Cornell University Press, 1960.

Sterba, Christopher M. *Good Americans: Italian and Jewish Immigrants during the First World War*. New York: Oxford University Press, 2003.

Thomas, William H., Jr. *Unsafe for Democracy: World War I and the U.S. Justice Department's Covert Campaign to Suppress Dissent*. Madison: University of Wisconsin Press, 2008.

Thompson, John A. *Reformers and War: American Progressive Publicists and the First World War*. Cambridge, England: Cambridge University Press, 1987.

Trask, David F., ed. *World War I at Home: Readings on American Life, 1914–1920*. New York: Wiley, 1970.

Vaughn, Stephen. *Holding Fast the Inner Lines: Democracy, Nationalism, and the Committee on Public Information*. Chapel Hill: University of North Carolina Press, 1980.

Ward, Larry Wayne. *The Motion Picture Goes to War: The U.S. Government Film Effort during World War I*. Ann Arbor: University of Michigan Research Press, 1985.

Watkins, Gordon S. *Labor Problems and Labor Administration in the United States during World War I*. Urbana: University of Illinois, 1919.

Wittke, Carl. *German-Americans and the World War*. Columbus: Ohio State Archaeological and Historical Society, 1936.

Wynn, Neil A. *From Progressivism to Prosperity: World War I and American Society*. New York: Holmes and Meier, 1986.

Zeiger, Robert H. *America's Great War: World War I and the American Experience*. Lanham, MD: Rowman & Littlefield, 2000.

POSTWAR

Ackerman, Kenneth D., *Young J. Edgar: Hoover, the Red Scare, and the Assault on Civil Liberties*. New York: Carroll & Graf, 2007.

Bagby, Wesley M. *The Road to Normalcy*. Baltimore: Johns Hopkins University Press, 1962.

Barry, John M. *The Great Influenza: The Epic Story of the Deadliest Plague in History*. New York: Penguin, 2004.

Byerly, Carol R. *Fever of War: The Influenza Epidemic in the U.S. Army during World War I*. New York: New York University Press, 2005.

Coben, Stanley. *A. Mitchell Palmer: Politician*. New York: Columbia University Press, 1963.

———. "A Study in Nativism: The American Red Scare of 1919–1920." *Political Science Quarterly* 79 (March 1964): 52–75.

Copeland, Tom. *The Centralia Tragedy of 1919: Elmer Smith and the Wobblies*. Seattle, WA: University of Washington Press, 1993.

Crosby, Alfred W. *America's Forgotten Pandemic: The Influenza of 1918*. Westport, CT: Greenwood, 1976.

Ellis, Mark. "J. Edgar Hoover and the 'Red Summer' of 1919." *Journal of American Studies* 28:1 (April 1994): 39–50.

Foner, Philip S. *History of the Labor Movement in the United States: Postwar Struggles 1918–1920*. New York: International Publishers Co., 1987.

Gage, Beverly. *The Day Wall Street Exploded: A Story of America in the First Age of Terror*. New York: Oxford University Press, 2009.

Gengarelly, W. Anthony. *Distinguished Dissenters and Opposition to the 1919–1920 Red Scare*. Lewiston, NY: Edwin Mellen Press, 1996.

Gentry, Curt. *J. Edgar Hoover: The Man and the Secrets*. New York: Norton, 2001.

Hagedorn, Ann. *Savage Peace: Hope and Fear in America, 1919*. New York: Simon & Schuster, 2007.

Jaffe, Julian F. *Crusade against Radicalism: New York during the Red Scare, 1914–1924*. Port Washington, NY: Kennikat Press, 1972.

Klingaman, William K. *1919: The Year Our World Began*. New York: St. Martin's, 1987.

Kornweibel, Theodore. *"Seeing Red": Federal Campaigns against Black Militancy, 1919–1925*. Bloomington: Indiana University Press, 1998.

Littlewood, Thomas B. *Soldiers Back Home: The American Legion in Illinois, 1919–1939*. Carbondale: Southern Illinois University Press, 2004.

McWhirter, Cameron. *Red Summer: The Summer of 1919 and the Awakening of Black America*. New York: Henry Holt, 2011.

Miller, William D. *Pretty Bubbles in the Air: America in 1919*. Chicago: University of Illinois Press, 1991.

Murray, Robert K. *The Red Scare: A Study in National Hysteria.* Minneapolis: University of Minnesota Press, 1955.

Nielson, Kim E. *Un-American Womanhood: Anti-Radicalism, Anti-Feminism, and the First Red Scare.* Columbus: Ohio State University Press, 2001.

Noggle, Burl. *Into the 1920s: America from Armistice to Normalcy.* Urbana: University of Illinois Press, 1974.

Pencak, William. *For God and Country: The American Legion, 1919–1941.* Boston: Northeastern University Press, 1989.

Pfannestiel, Todd J. *Rethinking the Red Scare: The Lusk Committee and New York's Crusade Against Radicalism, 1919–1923.* New York and London: Routledge, 2003.

Rochester, Stuart I. *American Liberal Disillusionment in the Wake of World War I.* University Park: Pennsylvania State University Press, 1977.

Rumer, Thomas A. *The American Legion: An Official History, 1919–1989.* New York: M. Evans, 1990.

Russell, Francis. *A City in Terror, 1919: The Boston Police Strike.* New York: Viking, 1975.

Schmidt, Regin. *Red Scare: FBI and the Origins of Anticommunism in the United States, 1919–1943.* Copenhagen: Museum Tusculanum Press, 2000.

Theoharis, Athan G. *The FBI and American Democracy: A Brief Critical History.* Kansas: University Press, 2004.

Voogd, Jan. *Race Riots and Resistance: The Red Summer of 1919.* New York: Peter Lang, 2008.

THE 1920S—GENERAL

Alchon, Guy. *The Invisible Hand of Planning: Capitalism, Social Science, and the State in the 1920s.* Princeton, NJ: Princeton University Press, 1985.

Allen, Frederick Lewis. *Only Yesterday: An Informal History of the 1920s.* New York: Harper & Brothers, 1931.

———. *Since Yesterday: The Nineteen Thirties in America, September 3, 1929–September, 3 1939.* New York: Harper & Row, 1940.

Ashby, Leroy. *The Spearless Leader: Senator Borah and the Progressive Movement in the 1920s.* Urbana: University of Illinois Press, 1972.

Baatz, Simon. *For the Thrill of It: Leopold, Loeb, and the Murder That Shocked Chicago.* New York: HarperCollins, 2008.

Bak, Richard. *Henry and Edsel: The Creation of the Ford Empire.* Hoboken, NJ: Wiley, 2003.

Barry, John M. *Rising Tide: The Great Mississippi Flood of 1927 and How It Changed America.* New York: Simon & Schuster, 1997.

Berg, A. Scott. *Lindbergh.* New York: G. P. Putnam's Sons, 1998.

Berger, Michael. *The Devil Wagon in God's Country: The Automobile and Social Change in Rural America, 1892–1929.* Hamden, CT: Archon Books, 1979.

Best, Gary Dean. *The Dollar Decade: Mammon and the Machine in 1920s America.* Westport, CT: Praeger, 2003.

Braeman, John, Robert Bremner, and David Brophy, eds. *Change and Continuity in Twentieth Century America: The 1920s.* Columbus: Ohio State University Press, 1968.

Brink, Randall. *Lost Star: The Search for Amelia Earhart.* New York: W. W. Norton & Company, 1994.

Brodsky, Alyn. *The Great Mayor: Fiorello La Guardia.* New York: Truman Talley Books, 2003.

Burner, David. *The Politics of Provincialism: The Democratic Party in Transition, 1919–1932.* New York: Alfred Knopf, 1968.

Butler, Susan. *East to the Dawn: The Life of Amelia Earhart.* Reading, MA: Addison-Wesley, 1997.

Campbell, Mike. *Amelia Earhart: The Truth At Last.* Camp Hill, PA: Sunbury Press, 2012.

Carter, Paul A. *Another Part of the Twenties.* New York: Columbia University Press, 1977.

———. *The Twenties in America.* New York: Columbia University Press, 1977.

Chernow, Ron. *Titan: The Life of John D. Rockefeller Sr.* New York: Vintage Books, 2004.

Cohen, Lizabeth. *Making a New Deal.* New York: Cambridge University Press, 1990.

Collier, Peter, and David Horowitz. *The Fords, An American Epic.* New York: Summit Books, 1987.

Craig, Douglas B. *After Wilson: The Struggle for Control of the Democratic Party, 1920–1934.* Chapel Hill, NC, and London: University of North Carolina Press, 1992.

Critchley, David. *The Origins of Organized Crime in America: The New York City Mafia, 1891–1931.* New York and London: Routledge, 2008.

Devine, Thomas E. *Eye Witness: The Amelia Earhart Incident.* Frederick, CO: Renaissance House, 1987.

Dinnerstein, Leonard. *The Leo Frank Case.* Athens and London: University of Georgia Press, 2008.

Douglas, Ann. *Terrible Honesty: Mongrel Manhattan in the 1920s.* New York: Farrar, Straus and Giroux, 1995.

Drowne, Kathleen Morgan, and Patrick Huber, eds. *The 1920s*. Westport, CT: Greenwood Press, 2004.

Dumenil, Lynn. *The Modern Temper: American Culture and Society in the 1920s*. New York: Hill & Wang, 1995.

Eldot, Paula. *Governor Alfred E. Smith: The Politician as Reformer*. New York: Garland, 1983.

Elliott, Lawrence. *Little Flower: The Life and Times of Fiorello La Guardia*. New York: William Morrow, 1983.

Farrell, John A. *Clarence Darrow: Attorney for the Damned*. New York: Random House, 2011.

Fass, Paula, *The Damned and the Beautiful: American Youth in the 1920s*. New York: Oxford University Press, 1977.

Finan, Christopher M. *Alfred E. Smith: The Happy Warrior*. New York: Hill & Wang, 2002.

Fitzgerald, F. Scott. "May Day." In *the Diamond as Big as the Ritz and Other Stories*. Harmondsworth, England: Penguin, 1962.

———. "Echoes of the Jazz Age." In *The Crack-Up with Other Pieces and Stories*. Harmondsworth, England: Penguin, 1965.

———. *The Great Gatsby*. New York: Collier, 1992 [1926].

Flink, James J. *The Automobile Age*. Cambridge, MA: MIT Press, 1988.

Goldberg, David J. *Discontented America: The United States in the 1920s*. Baltimore, MD: Johns Hopkins University Press, 1999.

Goldberg, Ronald Allen. *America in the Twenties*. Syracuse: Syracuse University Press, 2003.

Gordon, Colin, ed. *Major Problems in American History 1920–1945*. Boston: Houghton Mifflin, 1999.

Green, Harvey. *The Uncertainty of Everyday Life*. New York: HarperCollins, 1992.

Hakim, Joy. *War, Peace, and All That Jazz*. New York: Oxford University Press, 1995.

Hawley, Ellis W. *The Great War and the Search for a Modern Order: A History of the American People and Their Institutions, 1917–1933*. New York: St. Martin's Press, 1992.

Hicks, John D. *Republican Ascendancy, 1921–1933*. New York: Harper & Row, 1960.

Hoffman, Frederick J. *The Twenties: American Writing in the Postwar Decade*. New York: Free Press, 1965.

Jardim, Anne. *The First Henry Ford: A Study in Personality and Business Leadership*. Cambridge, MA: MIT Press, 1970.

Jeffers, Paul H. *The Napoleon of New York: Mayor Fiorello La Guardia*. New York: Wiley, 2002.

Kaplan, Edward S. *American Trade Policy 1923–1995*. London: Greenwood Press, 1996.

Kazin, Michael. *A Godly Hero: The Life of William Jennings Bryan*. New York: Knopf, 2006.

Kessner, Thomas. *Fiorello H. La Guardia and the Making of Modern New York*. New York: McGraw-Hill, 1989.

———. *The Flight of the Century: Charles Lindbergh and the Rise of American Aviation*. New York: Oxford University Press, 2010.

Kyvig, David. *Daily Life in the United States, 1920–1939: Decades of Promise and Pain*. Westport, CT: Greenwood Press, 2002.

Lacey, Robert. *Ford: The Men and the Machine*. London: Heinemann, 1986.

Leach, William. *Land of Desire: Merchants, Power, and the Rise of a New American Culture*. New York: Pantheon Books, 1993.

Leighton, Isabel, ed. *The Aspirin Age 1919–1941*. New York: Simon & Schuster, 1949.

Leinwand, Gerald. *William Jennings Bryan: An Uncertain Trumpet*. Lanham, MD: Rowman & Littlefield, 2006.

Leuchtenburg, William E. *The Perils of Prosperity, 1914–1932*. Chicago: University of Chicago Press, 1958.

Levine, Lawrence. *Defender of the Faith: William Jennings Bryan: The Last Decade, 1915–1925*. Boston: Harvard University Press, 1987.

Link, Arthur S. "What Happened to the Progressive Movement in the 1920s?" *American Historical Review* 64 (1959): 833–51.

Long, Elgen M., and Marie K. Long *Amelia Earhart: The Mystery Solved*. New York: Simon & Schuster, 1999.

Lunedin, Rolf. *Business and Religion in the American 1920s*. Westport, CT: Greenwood Press, 1988.

Lurie, Jonathan. *William Howard Taft: Progressive Conservative*. Cambridge: Cambridge University Press, 2011.

Lynd, Robert S., and Helen M. Lynd. *Middletown: A Study in Modern American Culture*. New York: Harcourt Brace, 1929.

Marchand, Roland. *Advertising the American Dream: Making Way for Modernity, 1920–1940*. Berkeley: University of California Press, 1985.

Mason, Alpheus. *William Howard Taft, Chief Justice*. New York: Simon & Schuster, 1964.

May, Henry F. "Shifting Perspectives on the 1920s." *Mississippi Valley Historical Review* 43:3 (December 1956): 405–27.

May, Lary. *Screening Out the Past: The Birth of Mass Culture and the Motion Picture Industry*. Oxford: Oxford University Press, 1980.

McRae, Donald. *The Old Devil: Clarence Darrow*. London: Pocket Books, 2009.

Miller, Nathan. *New World Coming: The 1920s and the Making of Modern America*. New York: Scribner, 2003.

Moore, Lucy. *Anything Goes: A Biography of the Roaring Twenties*. London: Atlantic Books, 2008.

Mowry, George Edwin. *The Twenties: Fords, Flappers, & Fanatics*. Englewood Cliffs, NJ: Prentice-Hall, 1963.

Nash, Roderick. *The Nervous Generation: American Thought, 1917–1930*. Chicago: Rand McNally, 1970.

Neal, Donn C. *The World Beyond the Hudson: Alfred E. Smith and National Politics*. New York: Garland, 1983.

Nevins, Allan, and Frank E. Hill. *Ford: Expansion and Challenge, 1915–1933*. New York: Scribner, 1957.

Palmer, Niall. *The Twenties in America: Politics and History*. Edinburgh: Edinburgh University Press, 2006.

Parrish, Michael E. *Anxious Decades: America in Prosperity and Depression, 1920–1941*. New York: W. W. Norton, 1992.

———. *The Hughes Court: Justices, Rulings and Legacy*. Santa Barbara, CA: ABC-CLIO, Inc., 2002.

Paschen, Stephen H., and Leonard Schlip, eds. *The United States in the 1920s as Observed in Contemporary Documents: The Ballyhoo Years*. Lewiston, NY: Edwin Mellen Press, 2007.

Pietrusza, David. *Rothstein: The Life, Times and Murder of the Criminal Genius Who Fixed the 1919 World Series*. New York: Carroll & Graf, 2003.

———. *1920: The Year of the Six Presidents*. New York: Basic Books, 2008.

Plesur, Milton, ed. *The 1920s: Problems and Paradoxes*. Boston: Allyn and Bacon, 1969.

President's Committee on Recent Economic Changes. *Recent Economic Changes in the United States; Report of the Committee on Recent Economic Changes, of the President's Conference on Unemployment; Herbert Hoover, Chairman; Including the Reports of a Special Staff of the National Bureau of Economic Research*. 2 vols. New York: McGraw-Hill, 1929.

President's Research Committee on Social Trends. *Recent Social Trends in the United States; Report of the President's Research Committee on Social Trends; with a Foreword by Herbert Hoover*. 2 vols. New York: McGraw-Hill, 1933.

Prothro, James W. *The Dollar Decade: Business Ideas in the 1920s*. Baton Rouge, LA: Louisiana State University Press, 1954.

Purcell, Edward. *Brandeis and the Progressive Constitution*. New Haven: Yale University Press, 2000.

Rhodes, Chip. *Structures of the Jazz Age: Mass Culture, Progressive Education, and Racial Disclosures in American Modernism*. London: Verso, 1998.

Rose, Cynthia, ed. *American Decades: Primary Sources, 1920–1929*. Detroit: Gale Publishing, 2004.

Rosenthal, Michael. *Nicholas Miraculous: The Amazing Career of the Redoubtable Nicholas Murray Butler*. New York: Farrar, Straus and Giroux, 2006.

Saloutos, Theodore, and John F. Hicks. *Agricultural Discontent in the Middle West, 1900–1939*. Madison: University of Wisconsin Press, 1951.

Schlesinger, Arthur M., Jr. *The Age of Roosevelt: The Crisis of the Old Order, 1919–1933*. Boston: Houghton Mifflin, 1957.

Schriftgiesser, Karl. *This Was Normalcy: An Account of Party Politics during Twelve Republican Years, 1920–1932*. New York: Oriole Editions, 1973.

Sellers, Alvin V. *The Trial of Leo Frank*. Farmington Mills, MI: Gale, 2012.

Shannon, David. *Between the Wars: America, 1919–1941*. Boston: Houghton Mifflin, 1979.

Sitton, Tom, and William Deverell. *Metropolis in the Making: Los Angeles in the 1920s*. Berkeley: University of California Press, 2001.

Sklar, Robert, ed. *The Plastic Age, 1917–1930.* New York: George Braziller, 1970.

Slayton, Robert A. *Empire Statesman: The Rise and Redemption of Alfred Smith*. New York: Free Press, 2001.

Snowman, Daniel. *America Since 1920*. London: Heinemann Educational, 1978.

Soule, George. *Prosperity Decade: From War to Depression, 1917–1929*. New York: Rinehart, 1947.

Starr, Kevin, ed. *Material Dreams: Southern California through the 1920s*. New York: Oxford University Press, 1990.

Stevenson, Elizabeth. *Babbitts and Bohemians: From the Great War to the Great Depression*. New Brunswick, NJ: Transaction Publishers, 1998.

Temkin, Moshik. *The Sacco-Vanzetti Affair: America on Trial*. New Haven: Yale University Press, 2009.

Tindall, George B. *The Emergence of the New South, 1913–1945*. Baton Rouge: Louisiana State University Press, 1967.

Tobin, Eugene M. *Organize or Perish: America's Independent Progressives, 1913–1933*. Westport, CT: Greenwood Press, 1986.

Topp, Michael M. *The Sacco and Vanzetti Case: A Brief History with Documents*. Boston: Bedford/St. Martin's, 2005.

Vine, Phyllis. *One Man's Castle: Clarence Darrow in Defense of the American Dream.* New York: Amistad, 2005.

Watson, Bruce. *Sacco and Vanzetti: The Men, the Murders, and the Judgment of Mankind*. New York: Viking Press, 2007.

Young, William, and David E. Kaiser. *Postmortem: New Evidence in the Case of Sacco and Vanzetti*. Amherst, MA: University of Massachusetts Press, 1985.

WARREN HARDING AND HIS ADMINISTRATION

Anthony, Carl S. *Florence Harding: The First Lady, the Jazz Age and the Death of America's Most Scandalous President*. New York: William Morrow, 1998.

Britton, Nan. *The President's Daughter*. New York: Elizabeth Ann Guild, 1927.

Burton, David H. *Taft, Holmes, and the 1920s Court: An Appraisal*. Madison, NJ: Fairleigh Dickinson University Press, 1998.

———. *William Howard Taft, Confident Peacemaker*. New York: Fordham University Press, 2004.

Cannadine, David. *Mellon: An American Life*. New York: Knopf, 2006.

Dean, John W. *Warren G. Harding*. New York: Times Books, 2004.

Downes, Randolph C. *The Rise of Warren Gamaliel Harding, 1865–1920*. Columbus: Ohio State University Press, 1970.

Ferrell, Robert K. *The Strange Deaths of President Harding*. Columbia: University of Missouri Press, 1996.

Frederick, Richard G., ed. *Warren G. Harding: A Bibliography*. Westport, CT: Greenwood Press, 1992.

Giglio, James N., *H. M. Daugherty and the Politics of Expediency*. Kent, OH: Kent State University Press, 1978.

Gleason, Mildred Diane, and H. Micheal Tarver. *Warren G. Harding: Harbinger of Normalcy*. Hauppauge, NY: Nova Science Publishers, Inc., 2013.

Hubbard, Preston J. *Origins of the TVA: The Muscle Shoals Controversy, 1920–1932*. Nashville: Vanderbilt University Press, 1961.

Mee, Charles L. *The Ohio Gang: The World of Warren G. Harding*. New York: Evans, 1981.

Moran, P., ed. *Warren G. Harding, 1865–1923: Chronology, Documents, Bibliographic Aids*. New York: Oceana Publications, 1970.

Morello, John A. *Selling the President, 1920: Albert D. Lasker, Advertising and the Election of Warren G. Harding*. Wesport, CT: Praeger, 2001.

Murray, Robert K. *The Harding Era: Warren G. Harding and His Administration*. Minneapolis: University of Minneapolis Press, 1969.

———. *The Politics of Normalcy: Governmental Theory and Practice in the Harding-Coolidge Era*. New York: Norton, 1973.

Noggle, Burl. *Teapot Dome: Oil and Politics in the 1920s*. Baton Rouge: Louisiana State University Press, 1962.

Payne, Phillip G. *Dead Last: The Public Memory of Warren G. Harding's Scandalous Legacy*. Athens: Ohio University Press, 2009.

Russell, Francis. *The Shadow of Blooming Grove: Warren G. Harding in His Times*. New York: McGraw-Hill, 1968.

Sherman, Richard B. "The Harding Administration and the Negro: An Opportunity Lost." *Journal of Negro History* 49 (July 1964): 151–68.

Sibley, Katherine A. S. *First Lady Florence Harding: Behind the Tragedy and Controversy.* Lawrence: University Press of Kansas, 2009.

Sinclair, Andrew. *The Available Man: The Life Behind the Masks of Warren Gamaliel Harding.* New York: Macmillan, 1965.

Stratton, David H. *Tempest over Teapot Dome: The Story of Albert B. Fall.* Norman: University of Oklahoma Press, 1998.

Trani, Eugen P., and David L. Wilson. *The Presidency of Warren G. Harding.* Lawrence: Regents Press of Kansas, 1977.

White, William Allen. *Masks in a Pageant.* New York: Macmillan, 1928.

Wilson, David L. *The Presidency of Warren G. Harding.* Lawrence: Regents Press of Kansas, 1977.

CALVIN COOLIDGE AND HIS ADMINISTRATION

Bittinger, Cynthia D. *Grace Coolidge: Sudden Star.* Hauppauge, NY: Nova Publishers, 2005.

Booraem, Hendrik V. *The Provincial: Calvin Coolidge and His World, 1885–1895.* Lewisburg, PA: Bucknell University Press, 1994.

———. *The Price of Freedom: Speeches and Addresses.* New York: Scribner's Sons, 1924.

Coolidge, Calvin. *Foundations of the Republic: Speeches and Addresses.* New York: Scribner's Sons, 1926.

———. *The Autobiography of Calvin Coolidge.* New York: Cosmopolitan Book Corporation, 1929.

Coolidge, Grace. *Grace Coolidge: An Autobiography.* Edited by Lawrence F. Wikander and Robert H. Ferrell. Worland, WY: High Plains Publishing, 1992.

Ferrell, Robert H. *The Presidency of Calvin Coolidge.* Lawrence: University Press of Kansas, 1998.

———. *Grace Coolidge: The People's Lady in Silent Cal's White House.* Lawrence: University of Kansas Press, 2008.

Fleser, Arthur L. *A Rhetorical Study of the Speaking of Calvin Coolidge.* Lewiston, NY: Edwin Mellen Press, 1990.

Fuess, Claude Moore. *Calvin Coolidge, The Man from Vermont.* Boston: Little, Brown and Company, 1940.

Gilbert, Robert E. *The Tormented President: Calvin Coolidge, Death, and Clinical Depression.* Westport, CT: Praeger, 2003.

Greenberg, David. *Calvin Coolidge.* New York: Times Books, 2006.

Hannaford, Peter. *The Quotable Calvin Coolidge: Sensible Words for a New Century*. Bennington, VT: Images from the Past, 2001.

Haynes, John Earl, ed. *Calvin Coolidge and the Coolidge Era: Essays on the History of the 1920s*. Washington, DC: Library of Congress, 1998.

Johnson, Charles C. *Why Coolidge Matters: Leadership Lessons from America's Most Underrated President*. New York: Encounter Books, 2013.

Krug, Larry L. *The 1924 Coolidge-Dawes Lincoln Tour*. Atglen, PA: Schiffer Publishing, 2007.

MacKay, Kenneth. *The Progressive Movement of 1924*. New York: Columbia University Press, 1947.

Maddox, Robert James. "Keeping Cool with Coolidge." *Journal of American History* 53:4 (March 1967): 772–80.

McCoy, Donald R. *Calvin Coolidge: The Quiet President*. Lawrence: University Press of Kansas, 1988.

Murray, Robert K. *The Politics of Normalcy: Governmental Theory and Practice in the Harding-Coolidge Era*. New York: Norton, 1973.

Pietrusza, David, ed. *Calvin Coolidge: A Documentary Biography*. Church & Reid Books, 2013.

Quint, Howard H., and Robert H. Ferrell, eds. *The Talkative President: The Off-the-Record Press Conferences of Calvin Coolidge*. Amherst: University of Massachusetts Press, 1964.

Ross, Ishbel. *Grace Coolidge and Her Era: The Story of a President's Wife*. New York: Dodd Mead, 1962.

Shlaes, Amity. *Coolidge*. New York: Harper Collins, 2013.

Silver, Thomas B. *Coolidge and the Historians*. Durham, NC: Academic Press for the Claremont Institute, 1982.

Slemp, C. Bascom. *The Mind of the President*. Garden City, NY: Doubleday, Page, 1926.

Sobel, Robert. *Coolidge, An American Enigma*. Washington, DC: Regnery Publishing Inc., 2000.

Tucker, Garland S., III. *The High Tide of Conservatism: Davis, Coolidge, and the 1924 election*. Austin: Emerald Books Co., 2010.

Wallace, Jerry L. *Calvin Coolidge: Our First Radio President*. Plymouth Notch, VT: Calvin Coolidge Memorial Foundation, 2008.

White, William Allen. *A Puritan in Babylon: The Story of Calvin Coolidge*. New York: Macmillan, 1938.

Wikander, Lawrence E., and Robert H. Ferrell, eds. *Grace Coolidge: An Autobiography*. Worland, WY: High Plains Publishing Co., 1992.

HERBERT HOOVER AND HIS ADMINISTRATION

Allen, Anne Beiser. *An Independent Woman: The Life of Lou Henry Hoover.* Westport, CT: Greenwood Press, 2000.

Barber, William J. *From New Era to New Deal: Herbert Hoover, the Economists, and American Economic Policy, 1921–1933.* Cambridge: Cambridge University Press, 1985.

Best, Gary Dean. *The Politics of American Individualism: Herbert Hoover in Transition, 1918–1929.* Westport, CT: Greenwood, 1975.

———. *Herbert Hoover: The Post-presidential Years, 1933–1964.* Stanford, CA: Hoover Institution Press, 1983.

Brandes, Joseph. *Herbert Hoover and Economic Diplomacy: Department of Commerce Policy, 1921–1928.* Pittsburgh, PA: University of Pittsburgh Press, 1962.

Buhite, Russell D. *Patrick J. Hurley and American Foreign Policy.* Ithaca: Cornell University Press, 1973.

Burner, David. *Herbert Hoover: The Public Life.* New York: Alfred A. Knopf, 1978.

Burns, Richard Dean. *Herbert Hoover: A Bibliography of His Times and Presidency.* Wilmington, DE: Scholarly Resources, 1991.

Calder, James D. *The Origins and Development of Federal Crime Control Policy: Herbert Hoover's Initiatives.* Westport, CT: Praeger, 1993.

Clements, Kendrick A. *Hoover, Conservation, and Consumerism: Engineering the Good Life.* Lawrence: University Press of Kansas, 2000.

———. *The Life of Herbert Hoover: Imperfect Visionary, 1918–1928.* New York: Palgrave Macmillan, 2010.

Dodge, Mark M., ed. *Herbert Hoover and the Historians.* West Branch, IA: Herbert Hoover Presidential Library Association, 1989.

Eble, Kenneth. *Herbert Hoover.* Boston: G. H. Hall, 1980.

Fausold, Martin L. *The Presidency of Herbert C. Hoover.* Lawrence: University Press of Kansas, 1985.

Fausold, Martin L., and George Mazuzan, eds. *The Hoover Presidency: A Reappraisal.* Albany: State University of New York Press, 1974.

Gaddis, Vincent H. *Herbert Hoover, Unemployment, and the Public Sphere: A Conceptual History, 1919–1933.* Lanham, MD: University Press of America, 2005.

Gelfand, Lawrence E., ed. *Herbert Hoover: The Great War and Its Aftermath, 1914–1923.* Iowa City: University of Iowa Press, 1979.

Hamilton, David E. *From New Day to New Deal: American Farm Policy from Hoover to Roosevelt, 1928–1933.* Chapel Hill: University of North Carolina Press, 1991.

Hawley, Ellis W. "Herbert Hoover, the Commerce Secretariat and the Vision of an 'Associative State,' 1921–1928." *Journal of American History* 61:1 (June 1974): 116–40.

———, ed. *Herbert Hoover as Secretary of Commerce: Studies in New Era Thought and Practice.* Iowa City: University of Iowa Press, 1981.

Hawley, Ellis W., et al. *Herbert Hoover and the Crisis of American Capitalism.* Cambridge, MA: Schenkman, 1973.

———, et al. *Herbert Hoover and the Historians.* West Branch, Iowa: Herbert Hoover Presidential Association, 1989.

Hoover, Herbert C. *The Memoirs of Herbert Hoover.* 3 vols. New York: Macmillan, 1951–1952.

Jeansonne, Glen. *The Life of Herbert Hoover: Fighting Quaker, 1928–1933.* New York: Palgrave Macmillan, 2012.

Kaufman, Andrew L. *Cardozo.* Cambridge: Harvard University Press, 1998.

Krog, Carl E., and William R. Tanner, eds. *Herbert Hoover and the Republican Era: A Reconsideration.* Lanham: University Press of America, 1984.

Leonard, Charles A. *A Search for a Judicial Philosophy: Mr. Justice Roberts and the Constitutional Revolution of 1937.* Port Washington, NY: Kennikat Press, 1971.

Leuchtenburg, William E. *Herbert Hoover.* New York: Times Books, 2013.

Lichtman, Allan J. *Prejudice and the Old Politics: The Presidential Election of 1928.* Chapel Hill: University of North Carolina Press, 1979.

Liebovich, Louis W. *Bylines in Despair: Herbert Hoover, the Great Depression, and the U.S. News Media.* Westport, CT: Praeger, 1991.

Lisio, Donald J. *The President and Protest: Hoover, MacArthur, and the Bonus Riot.* Columbia: University of Missouri Press, 1974.

———. *Hoover, Blacks, and Lily-Whites: A Study of Southern Strategies.* Chapel Hill: University of North Carolina Press, 1985.

Lloyd, Craig. *Aggressive Introvert: A Study of Herbert Hoover and Public Relations Management, 1912–1932.* Columbus: Ohio State University Press, 1973.

Morison, Elting E. *Turmoil and Tradition: A Study of the Life and Times of Henry L. Stimson.* Boston: Houghton Mifflin, 1960.

Nash, George H. *Herbert Hoover and Stanford University.* Stanford, CA: Hoover Institution Press, 1988.

———. *The Life of Herbert Hoover: The Engineer 1874–1914* (vol. 1); *The Humanitarian* (vol. 2); *Master of Emergencies, 1917–1918* (vol. 3). New York: W. W. Norton, 1983, 1988, 1996.

Nash, Lee, ed. *Understanding Herbert Hoover: Ten Perspectives.* Stanford, CA: Hoover Institution Press, 1987.

Norton, Richard. *An Uncommon Man: The Triumph of Herbert Hoover.* New York: Simon & Schuster, 1989.

O'Brien, Patrick G. *Herbert Hoover: A Bibliography*. Westport, CT: Greenwood, 1993.

Olson, James S. *Herbert Hoover and the Reconstruction Finance Corporation, 1931–1933*. Ames: Iowa State University Press, 1977.

———. *Saving Capitalism: The Reconstruction Finance Corporation and the New Deal, 1933–1940*. Princeton, NJ: Princeton University Press, 1988.

Parrish, Michael E. *The Hughes Court: Justices, Rulings and Legacy*. Santa Barbara, CA: ABC-CLIO, Inc., 2002.

Polenberg, Richard. *The World of Benjamin Cardozo: Personal Values and the Judicial Process*. Cambridge: Harvard University Press, 1997.

Romasco, Albert U. *The Poverty of Abundance: Hoover, the Nation, the Depression*. New York: Oxford University Press, 1965.

Rosen, Elliott A. *Hoover, Roosevelt, and the Brains Trust: From Depression to New Deal*. New York: Columbia University Press, 1977.

Schmitz, David F. *Henry L. Stimson: The First Wise Man*. Wilmington, DE: SR Books, 2001.

Schwarz, Jordan A. *The Interregnum of Despair: Hoover, the Nation, and the Depression*. Urbana: University of Illinois Press, 1970.

Smith, Gene. *The Shattered Dream: Herbert Hoover and the Great Depression*. New York: William Morrow, 1970.

Smith, Richard Norton. *An Uncommon Man: The Triumph of Herbert Hoover*. New York: Simon & Schuster, 1984.

Sobel, Robert. *Herbert Hoover at the Onset of the Great Depression, 1929–1930.* Philadelphia: J. B. Lippincott, 1975.

Walch, Timothy, ed. *Uncommon Americans: The Lives and Legacies of Herbert and Lou Hoover*. Westport, CT: Praeger, 2003.

Walch, Timothy, and Dwight M. Miller. *Herbert Hoover and Franklin D. Roosevelt: A Documentary History*. Westport, CO: Greenwood Press, 1998.

Weed, Clyde P. *The Nemesis of Reform: The Republican Party during the New Deal*. New York: Columbia University Press, 1994.

Wert, Hal Elliott. *Hoover, the Fishing President: Portrait of the Private Man and His Life Outdoors*. Mechanicsburg, PA: Stackpole Books, 2005.

Wilson, Joan Hoff. *Herbert Hoover: Forgotten Progressive*. Boston: Little Brown, 1975.

Young, Nancy Beck. *Lou Henry Hoover: Activist First Lady*. Lawrence: University Press of Kansas, 2004.

FOREIGN AFFAIRS

Adler, Selig. *The Uncertain Giant, 1921–1941: American Foreign Policy Between the Wars.* New York: Macmillan, 1965.

Aldcroft, Derek. *From Versailles to Wall Street, 1919–1929.* Berkeley: University of California Press, 1977.

Buckley, Thomas H. *The United States and the Washington Conference, 1921–1922.* Knoxville: University of Tennessee Press, 1970.

Cohen, Warren I. *Empire without Tears: America's Foreign Relations, 1921–1933.* Philadelphia: Temple University Press, 1987.

Costigliano, Frank. *Awkward Dominion: American Political, Economic and Cultural Relations with Europe, 1919–1933.* Ithaca, NY: Cornell University Press, 1984.

Curry, Earl R. *Hoover's Dominican Diplomacy and the Origins of the Good Neighbor Policy.* New York: Garland, 1979.

DeBenedetti, Charles. *Origins of the Modern American Peace Movement, 1915–1929.* New York: Kraus International, 1978.

DeConde, Alexander. *Herbert Hoover's Latin American Policy.* Stanford, CA: Stanford University Press, 1951.

Dunne, Michael. *The United States and the World Court, 1920–35.* New York: St. Martin's Press, 1988.

Ellis, L. Ethan. *Republican Foreign Policy, 1921–1933.* New Brunswick, NJ: Rutgers University Press, 1968.

Feis, Herbert. *The Diplomacy of the Dollar, 1919–1932.* New York: Norton, 1966.

Ferrell, Robert H. *Peace in Their Time: The Origins of the Kellogg-Briand Pact.* New Haven, CT: Yale University Press, 1952.

———. *American Diplomacy in the Great Depression: Hoover-Stimson Foreign Policy, 1929–1933.* New Haven, CT: Yale University Press, 1957.

Filene, Peter G. *Americans and the Soviet Experiment, 1917–1933.* Cambridge: Harvard University Press, 1967.

Glad, Betty. *Charles Evans Hughes and the Illusions of Innocence.* Urbana: University of Illinois Press, 1966.

Grieb, Kenneth J. *The Latin American Policy of Warren G. Harding.* Fort Worth: Texas Christian University Press, 1976.

Kamman, William. *A Search for Stability: United States Diplomacy toward Nicaragua, 1925–1933.* Notre Dame, IN: University of Notre Dame Press, 1968.

Kuehl, Warren, and Lynne Dunn. *Keeping the Covenant: American Internationalists and the League of Nations, 1920–1939.* Kent, OH: Kent State University Press, 1997.

Leffler, Melvyn P. *The Elusive Quest: America's Pursuit of European Stability and French Security, 1919–1933.* Chapel Hill: University of North Carolina Press, 1979.

Louria, Margot. *Triumph and Downfall: America's Pursuit of Peace and Prosperity, 1921–1933.* Westport, CT: Greenwood Press, 2001.

Marks, Sally. *The Illusion of Peace: International Relations, 1918–1933.* New York: Palgrave Macmillan, 2003.

Munro, Dana C. *The United States and the Caribbean Republics, 1921–1933.* Princeton: Princeton University Press, 1974.

Myers, William Starr. *The Foreign Policies of Herbert Hoover, 1929–1933.* New York: Scribners, 1940.

O'Connor, Raymond G. *Perilous Equilibrium: The United States and the London Disarmament Conference of 1930.* Lawrence: University of Kansas Press, 1962.

Ostrower, Gary B. *Collective Insecurity: The United States and the League of Nations during the Early Thirties.* Lewisburg: Bucknell University Press, 1979.

Powaski, Ronald E. *Toward an Entangling Alliance: American Isolationism, Internationalism, and Europe, 1901–1950.* New York: Greenwood Press, 1991.

Randall, Stephen J. *United States Foreign Oil Policy, 1919–1948.* Kingston, Ontario: McGill-Queens University Press, 1986.

Schmitz, David F. *The United States and Fascist Italy, 1922–1940.* Chapel Hill: University of North Carolina Press, 1988.

Tulchin, Joseph S. *The Aftermath of War: World War I and U.S. Foreign Policy toward Latin America.* New York: New York University Press, 1971.

Wheeler, Gerald E. *Prelude to Pearl Harbor: The United States Navy and the Far East, 1921–1931.* Columbia: University of Missouri Press, 1963.

Wilson, Joan Hoff. *American Business and Foreign Policy, 1920–1933.* Lexington: University of Kentucky Press, 1971.

———. *Ideology and Economics: U.S. Relations with the Soviet Union, 1918–1933.* Columbia: University of Missouri Press, 1974.

Wood, Bryce. *The Making of the Good Neighbor Policy.* New York: Columbia University Press, 1961.

ENTERTAINMENT, SPORTS, AND THE MEDIA

Abel, Richard, ed. *Silent Film.* New Brunswick, NJ: Rutgers University Press, 1996.

Barfield, Ray. *Listening to Radio, 1920–1950*. Westport, Conn: Praeger Publishers, 1996.

Barnouw, Eric. *A Tower in Babel: A History of Broadcasting in the United States to 1933*. New York: Oxford University Press, 1995.

Burk, Robert F. *Never Just a Game: Players, Owners, and American Baseball to 1920*. Chapel Hill: University of North Carolina Press, 1994.

———. *Much More than a Game: Players, Owners, and American Baseball since 1921*. Chapel Hill: University of North Carolina Press, 2001.

Carney, Gene. *Burying the Black Sox: How Baseball's Cover-Up of the 1919 World Series Fix Almost Succeeded*. Dulles, VA: Potomac Books, 2007.

Coben, Stanley. *Rebellion against Victorianism: The Impetus for Cultural Change in 1920s America*. New York: Oxford University Press, 1991.

Covert, Catherine L., and John D. Stevens. *Mass Media between the Wars: Perceptions of Cultural Tension, 1918–1941*. Syracuse: Syracuse University Press, 1984.

Crafton, Donald. *The Talkies: American Cinema's Transition to Sound, 1926–1931*. New York: Simon & Schuster, 1997.

Currell, Susan. *American Culture in the 1920s*. Edinburgh: Edinburgh University Press, 2009.

Douglas, George H. *The Early Days of Radio Broadcasting*. Jefferson, NC: McFarland, 1987.

Douglas, Susan J. *Listening In: Radio and the American Imagination*. Minneapolis: University of Minnesota Press, 2004.

Erenburg, Lewis A. *Steppin' Out: New York Nightlife and the Transformation of American Culture*. Westport, CT: Greenwood Press, 1981.

Gomery, Douglas. *Shared Pleasures: A History of Movie Presentations in the United States*. Madison: University of Wisconsin Press, 1992.

———. *The Coming of Sound: A History*. New York: Routledge, 2004.

Gorn, Elliott, and Warren Goldstein. *A Brief History of American Sports*. New York: Hill & Wang, 1993.

Jacobs, Lea. *The Decline of Sentiment: American Film in the 1920s*. Berkeley, CA: University of California Press, 2008.

Kemp, Philip ed. *Cinema: The Whole Story*. London: Thames & Hudson, 2011.

Leider, Emily. *Dark Lover: The Life and Death of Rudolph Valentino*. New York: Farrar, Straus and Giroux, 2003.

May, Lary. *Screening Out the Past: The Birth of Mass Culture and the Motion Picture Industry*. New York: Oxford University Press, 1980.

Montville, Leigh. *The Big Bam: The Life and Times of Babe Ruth*. New York: Broadway Books, 2006.

Nasaw, David. *Going Out: The Rise and Fall of Public Amusements*. New York: Basic Books, 1993.

Neft, David S., Richard M. Cohen, and Rick Korch. *The Complete History of Professional Football from 1892 to the Present.* New York: St. Martin's Press, 1994.

Reisler, Jim. *Babe Ruth: Launching the Legend.* New York: McGraw-Hill, 2004.

Riess, Steven A. *City Games: The Evolution of American Urban Society and the Rise of Sports.* Urbana: University of Illinois Press, 1989.

Rosen, Philip T. *The Modern Stentors: Radio Broadcasters and the Federal Government, 1920–1934.* Westport, CT: Greenwood Press, 1980.

Sarris, Andrew. *You Ain't Heard Nothin' Yet: The American Talking Film— History and Memory, 1927–1949.* New York: Oxford University Press, 1998.

Schatz, Thomas. *The Genius of the System: Hollywood Filmmaking in the Studio Era.* Minneapolis: University of Minnesota Press, 2010.

Sklar, Robert. *Movie-made America: A Social History of American Movies,* New York: Random House, 1975.

Smulyan, Susan. *Selling Radio: The Commercialization of American Broadcasting, 1920–1934.* Washington, DC: Smithsonian Institution Press, 1994.

Sullivan, Dean A., ed. *Middle Innings: A Documentary History of Baseball, 1900–1948.* New York: Bison Books, 2001.

Weintraub, Robert. *The House That Ruth Built: A New Stadium, the First Yankees Championship, and the Redemption of 1923.* New York: Little Brown and Company, 2011.

LITERATURE, MUSIC, AND THE ARTS

Baigell, Matthew. *Artist and Identity in Twentieth-Century America.* New York: Cambridge University Press, 2001.

Barr, Alfred Hamilton. *American Art of the 20's and 30's.* New York: Arno Press, 1969.

Baur, John. *Revolution and Tradition in Modern American Art.* Cambridge, MA: Harvard University Press, 1951.

Berman, Ronald. *Fitzgerald, Hemingway, and the Twenties.* Tuscaloosa, AL: University of Alabama Press, 2002.

Bilton, Alan, and Philip Melling, eds. *America in the 1920s: Literary Sources and Documents.* 3 vols. Robertsbridge, England: Helm Information, 2004.

Bordman, Gerald, and Thomas Hischak. *The Oxford Companion to American Theater.* New York: Oxford University Press, 2004.

Bradbury, Malcolm, and David Palmer, eds. *The American Novel and the 1920s*. London: Hodder & Stoughton, 1971.

Brown, Milton W. *American Painting from the Armory Show to the Depression*. Princeton, NJ: Princeton University Press.

Carroll, Anne Elizabeth. *Word, Image, and the New Negro: Representation and Identity in the Harlem Renaissance*. Bloomington, IN: Indiana University Press, 2005.

Cassidy, Donna M. *Painting the Musical City: Jazz and Cultural Identity in American Art 1910–1940*. Washington DC: Smithsonian Institute, 1997.

Cooperman, Stanley. *World War I and the American Novel*. Baltimore, MD: Johns Hopkins University, 1967.

Corn, Wanda. *The Great American Thing: Modern Art and National Identity 1915–1933*. Berkeley, CA: University of California Press, 2000.

Cowley, Malcolm. *Exile's Return: A Literary Odyssey of the 1920s*. New York: Penguin, 1995.

Craven, Wayne. *American Art: History and Culture*. Boston: McGraw-Hill, 1994.

Curnutt, Kirk. *A Historical Guide to F. Scott Fitzgerald*. New York: Oxford University Press, 2004.

Daniel, Malcolm. *Stieglitz, Steichen, Strand: Masterworks from the Metropolitan Museum of Art*. New York: Metropolitan Museum of Art, 2011.

Davidson, Abraham A. *Early American Modernist Painting, 1910–1935*. New York: Harper & Row, 1981.

Doss, Erika. *Twentieth Century American Art*. New York: Oxford University Press, 2002.

Evans, Nicholas. *Writing Jazz: Race, Class, Nationalism and Modern Culture in the 1920s*. New York and London: Garland Publishing, Inc., 2000.

Foulkes, Julia L. *Modern Bodies: Dance and American Modernism from Martha Graham to Alvin Ailey*. Chapel Hill, NC: University of North Carolina Press, 2002.

Gerwitz, Arthur, and James J. Kolb, eds. *Art, Glitter and Glitz: Mainstream Playwrights and Popular Theater in the 1920s*. Westport, CT: Praeger Publishers, 2004.

Gioia, Ted. *The History of Jazz*. New York: Oxford University Press, 1999.

Hadlock, Richard. *Jazz Masters of the 20s*. New York: Da Capo Press, 1988.

Haskell, Barbara. *The American Century: Art and Culture, 1900–1950*. New York: Whitney Museum of American Art, 1999.

Hatock, Jennifer. *At Home: Domesticity and World War I in American Literature*. Columbus, OH: Ohio State University Press, 2003.

Hoffman, Frederick. *The Twenties: American Writing in the Postwar Decade*. New York: Free Press, 1965.

James, Pearl. *The New Death: American Modernism and World War I*. Charlottesville and London: University of Virginia Press, 2013.

Jasen, David A. *Tin Pan Alley: An Encyclopedia of the Golden Age of American Song*. New York: Routledge, 2003.

Johnson, Stewart J. *American Modern, 1925–1940: Design for a New Age*. New York: Harry Abrams, 2000.

Kingsbury, Celia Malone. *The Peculiar Sanctity of War: Hysteria in the Literature of World War I*. Lubbock: Texas Tech University Press, 2002.

Krutch, Joseph Wood. *The American Drama since 1918: An Informal History*. New York: George Braziller, 1957.

Levy, Sophie, ed. *Transatlantic Avant-Garde: American Artists in Paris, 1918–1939*. Berkeley, CA: University of California Press, 2003.

MacDonald, Gail. *American Literature and Culture, 1900–1960: An Introduction*. Malden, MA: Blackwell Publishing, 2008.

Marchand, Roland. *Advertising the American Dream: Making Way for Modernity, 1920–1940*. Berkeley: University of California Press, 1985.

Martin, Carol. *Dance Marathons: Performing American Culture of the 1920s and 1930s*. Jackson, MS: University Press of Mississippi, 1994.

Miller, Jordan, and Winifred Frazer. *American Drama between the Wars: A Critical History*. Boston: Twayne Publishers, 1991.

Ogren, Kathy J. *The Jazz Revolution: Twenties America and the Meaning of Jazz*. New York: Oxford University Press, 1989.

Oja, Carol J. *Making Music Modern: New York in the 1920s*. New York: Oxford University Press, 2000.

Phelan, James. *Reading the American Novel, 1920–2010*. Chichester, UK: Wiley-Blackwell, 2013.

Pohl, Frances K. *Framing America: A Social History of American Art*. New York: Thames & Hudson, 2002.

Prigozy, Ruth. *The Cambridge Companion to F. Scott Fitzgerald*. Cambridge, UK: Cambridge University Press, 2001.

Raub, Patricia. *Yesterday's Stories: Popular Women's Novels of the Twenties and Thirties*. Westport, CT: Greenwood Press, 1994.

Rawls, Walton. *Wake Up, America! World War I and the American Poster*. New York: Abbeville Publishers, 1988.

Shaw, Arnold. *The Jazz Age: Popular Music in the 1920s*. New York: Oxford University Press, 1990.

Skipwith, Joanna, ed. *Rhapsodies in Black: Art of the Harlem Renaissance*. Berekey, CA: University of California Press, 1997.

Stearns, Marshall W. *The Story of Jazz*. New York: Oxford University Press, 1956.

Suskin, Steven. *Show Tunes: The Songs, Shows, and Careers of Broadway's Major Composers*. New York: Oxford University Press, 2000.

Trout, Steven. *Memorial Fictions: Willa Cather and the First World War*. Lincoln, NE: University of Nebraska, 2002.

————. *American Prose Writers of World War I: A Documentary Volume.* Detroit: Thomson/Gale, 2005.

Wilson, Richard Guy, Dianne Pilgrim, and Dickran Tashjian. *The Machine Age in America, 1918–1941.* New York: The Brooklyn Museum, 1986.

Zabel, Barbara. *Assembling Art: The Machine and the American Avant-Garde.* Jackson, MS: University Press of Mississippi, 2004.

PROHIBITION

Ashbury, Herbert. *The Great Illusion: An Informal History of Prohibition.* Garden City, NY: Doubleday, 1950.

Behr, Edward. *Prohibition: Thirteen Years That Changed America.* New York: Arcade Publishing, 1996.

Burns, Eric. *The Spirits of America: A Social History of Alcohol.* Philadelphia: Temple University Press, 2004.

Clark, Norman H. *Deliver Us from Evil: An Interpretation of American Prohibition,* New York: W. W. Norton, 1976.

————. *The Dry Years: Prohibition and Social Change in Washington.* Seattle: University of Washington Press, 1988.

Coffey, Thomas M. *The Long Thirst: Prohibition in America 1920–1933.* New York: W. W. Norton, 1975.

Drowne, Kathleen. *Spirits of Defiance: National Prohibition and Jazz Age Literature, 1920–1933.* Columbus: Ohio State University Press, 2005.

Heimel, Paul W. *Eliot Ness: The Real Story.* Nashville: Cumberland House, 2000.

Kerr, K. A. *Organized for Prohibition: A New History of the Anti-Saloon League.* New Haven, CT: Yale University Press, 1985.

Kobler, John. *Ardent Spirits: The Rise and Fall of Prohibition.* New York: G. P. Putnam, 1973.

Kyvig, David E. *Repealing National Prohibition.* Chicago: University of Chicago Press, 1979.

————, ed. *Law, Alcohol, and Order: Perspectives on National Prohibition.* Westport, Conn: Greenwood Press, 1985.

Lender, Mark E., and James K. Martin. *Drinking in American History.* New York: The Free Press, 1982.

Lerner, Michael. *Dry Manhattan.* Cambridge, MA: Harvard University Press, 2007.

Mappen, Marc. *Prohibition Gangsters: The Rise and Fall of a Bad Generation.* New Brunswick, NJ: Rutgers University Press, 2013.

Mason, Philip P. *Rumrunning and the Roaring Twenties.* Detroit: Wayne State University Press, 1995.

Murdock, Catherine Gilbert. *Domesticating Drink: Women, Men, and Alcohol in America, 1870–1940*. Baltimore: Johns Hopkins University Press, 1998.

Okrent, Daniel. *Last Call: The Rise and Fall of Prohibition*. New York: Scribner, 2011.

Sinclair, Andrew. *Prohibition: The Era of Excess*, Boston: Little, Brown, 1962.

Timberlake, J. H. *Prohibition and the Progressive Movement, 1900–1920*. Cambridge, MA: Harvard University Press, 1963.

SOCIAL CONFLICTS AND IMMIGRATION

Abrams, Douglas Carl. *Selling the Old-Time Religion: American Fundamentalism and Mass Culture, 1920–1940*. Athens: University of Georgia Press, 2001.

Alexander, Michael. *Jazz Age Jews*. Princeton: Princeton University Press, 2003.

Baatz, Simon. *For the Thrill of It: Leopold, Loeb, and the Murder That Shocked Chicago*. New York: HarperCollins, 2008.

Baker, Kelly J. *Gospel According to the Klan: The KKK's Appeal to Protestant America*. Lawrence: University Press of Kansas, 2011.

Baldwin, Neil. *Henry Ford and the Jews: The Mass Production of Hate*. New York: Public Affairs, 2001.

Blee, Kathleen M. *Women of the Klan: Racism and Gender in the 1920s*. Berkeley: University of California Press, 1991.

Bodnar, John, et al. *Lives of their Own: Blacks, Italians, and Poles in Pittsburgh, 1900–1960*. Urbana: University of Illinois Press, 1982.

Bornet, Vaughn D. *Labor Politics in a Democratic Republic*. Washington, DC: Spartan, 1964.

Bruns, Roger. *Preacher: Billy Sunday and Big-Time American Evangelism.* New York: W. W. Norton, 1992.

Chalmers, David M. *Hooded Americanism: The History of the Ku Klux Klan*. Garden City, NY: Doubleday, 1965.

Divine, Robert. *American Immigration Policy 1924–1952*. New Haven, CT: Yale University Press, 1957.

Eldot, Paula. *Governor Alfred E. Smith: The Politician as Reformer*. New York: Garland, 1983.

Farrell, John Aloysius, *Clarence Darrow: Attorney for the Damned*. New York: Doubleday, 2011.

Feldman, Glenn. *Politics, Society, and the Klan in Alabama, 1915–1949*. Tuscaloosa: University of Alabama Press, 1999.

Fox, Craig. *Everyday Klansfolk: White Protestant Life and the KKK in 1920s Michigan.* East Lansing, MI: Michigan State University Press, 2011.

Furniss, Norman F. *The Fundamentalist Controversy, 1918–1931.* New Haven, CT: Yale University Press, 1954.

Ginger, Ray. *Six Days or Forever? Tennessee v. John Thomas Scopes.* Boston: Beacon Press, 1958.

Gonzales, Manuel G. *Mexicanos: A History of Mexicans in the United States.* Bloomington: Indiana University Press, 2000.

Gonzales, Manuel G., and Cynthia M. Gonzales. *En Aquel Entonces [In Years Gone By]: Readings in Mexican-American History.* Bloomington: Indiana University Press, 2000.

Guterl, Matthew Pratt. *The Color of Race in America, 1900–1940.* Harvard: Harvard University Press, 2004.

Higham, John. *Strangers in the Land: The Patterns of American Nativism, 1860–1925.* New York: Atheneum, 1981.

Huthmacher, Joseph J. *Massachusetts People and Politics, 1919–1933.* Cambridge, MA: Belknap Press, 1959.

Jackson, Kenneth T. *The Ku Klux Klan in the City, 1915–1930.* New York: Oxford University Press, 1967.

Josephson, Matthew, and Hanna Josephson. *Al Smith: Hero of the Cities.* Boston: Houghton Mifflin, 1969.

Kaiser, David E. *Postmortem: New Evidence in the Case of Sacco and Vanzetti.* Boston: University of Massachusetts, 1985.

Kazin, Michael. *A Godly Hero: The Life of William Jennings Bryan.* New York: Knopf, 2006.

Larson, Edward J. *Summer for the Gods: The Scopes Trial and America's Continuing Debate over Science and Religion.* New York: Basic Books, 1997.

Leinwald, Gerlad. *1927: High Tide of the 1920s.* New York: Four Walls Eight Windows, 2001.

Lichtman, Allen J. *Prejudice and Old Politics: The Presidential Election of 1928.* Chapel Hill: University of North Carolina Press, 1979.

MacLean, Nancy. *Behind the Mask of Chivalry: The Making of the Second Ku Klux Klan.* New York: Oxford University Press, 1994.

Martin, Robert F. *Hero of the Heartland: Billy Sunday and the Transformation of American Society, 1862–1935.* Bloomington: Indiana University Press, 2002.

McVeigh, Rory. *The Rise of the Ku Klux Klan: Right-Wing Movements and National Politics.* Minneapolis, MN: University of Minnesota Press, 2009.

Melnick, Jeffrey Paul. *Black-Jewish Relations on Trial: Leo Frank and Jim Conley in the New South.* Jackson: University Press of Mississippi, 2000.

Moore, Leonard J. *Citizen Klansmen: The Ku Klux Klan in Indiana, 1921–1928.* Chapel Hill: University of North Carolina Press, 1991.

Moore, R. Laurence. *Selling God: American Religion in the Marketplace of Culture*. New York: Oxford University Press, 1995.

Morone, Jame A. *Hellfire Nation: The Politics of Sin in American History*. New Haven, CT: Yale University Press, 2003.

O'Connor, Richard. *The First Hurrah: A Biography of Alfred E. Smith*. New York: Putnam, 1970.

Oney, Steve. *And the Dead Shall Rise: The Murder of Mary Phagan and the Lynching of Leo Frank*. New York: Pantheon, 2003.

Pegram, Thomas R. *One Hundred Percent American: The Rebirth and Decline of the Ku Klux Klan in the 1920s*. Lanham: Rowman & Littlefield, 2011.

Pietrusza, David. *Rothstein: The Life, Times and Murder of the Criminal Genius Who Fixed the 1919 World Series*. New York: Carroll & Graf, 2003.

Russell, Francis. *Tragedy at Dedham: The Story of the Sacco-Vanzetti Case*. New York: McGraw-Hill, 1962.

Silva, Ruth C. *Rum, Religion, and Votes: 1928 Reexamined*. University Park: Pennsylvania State University Press, 1962.

Slayton, Robert A. *Empire Statesman: The Rise and Redemption of Al Smith*. New York: Free Press, 2001.

Spiro, Jonathan P. *Defending the Master Race: Conservation, Eugenics, and the Legacy of Madison Grant*. Burlington, VT: University of Vermont Press, 2009.

Takaki, Ronald T. *Strangers from a Different Shore: A History of Asian Americans*. Boston: Back Bay Books, 1998.

Temkin, Moshik. *The Sacco-Vanzetti Affair: America on Trial*. New Haven and London: Yale University Press, 2009.

AFRICAN AMERICANS

Anderson, Jervis. *This Was Harlem: A Cultural Portrait, 1900–1950*. New York: Farrar, Straus and Giroux, 1981.

———. *A. Philip Randolph: A Biographical Portrait*. Berkeley: University of California Press, 1986.

Barbeau, Arthur E., and Florette Henri. *The Unknown Soldiers: Black American Troops in World War I*. Philadelphia: Temple University Press, 1974.

Blackmon, Douglas A. *Slavery by Another Name: The Re-Enslavement of Black Americans from the Civil War to World War II*. New York: Anchor Books, 2009.

Boyle, Kevin. *Arc of Justice: A Saga of Race, Civil Rights and Murder in the Jazz Age*. New York: Henry Holt & Company, 2004.

Brophy, Alfred L. *Reconstructing the Dreamland: The Tulsa Race Riot of 1921, Race Reparations, and Reconciliation*. New York: Oxford University Press, 2002.

Carter, Dan T. *Scottsboro: A Tragedy of the American South*. New York: Oxford University Press, 1971.

Cronon, David. *Black Moses: The Story of Marcus Garvey and the Universal Negro Improvement Association*. Madison: University of Wisconsin Press, 1955.

Drake, St. Clair, and Horace R. Cayton. *Black Metropolis: A Study of Negro Life in a Northern City*. 2 vols. New York: Harcourt, Brace and World, 1945.

Ellis, Mark. *Race, War, and Surveillance: African Americans and the United States Government during World War I*. Bloomington: Indiana University Press, 2001.

Ellsworth, Scott. *Death in a Promised Land: The Tulsa Race Riot of 1921*. Baton Rouge: Louisiana State University Press, 1982.

Fairclough, Adam. *Better Day Coming: Blacks and Equality, 1890–2000*. New York: Viking, 2001.

Franklin, John Hope, and Alfred A. Moss. *From Slavery to Freedom*. New York: McGraw-Hill, 1994.

Franklin, John Hope, Alfred A. Moss, and August Meier, eds. *Black Leaders of the Twentieth Century*. Urbana: University of Illinois Press, 1982.

Goodman, James. *Stories of Scottsboro: The Rape Case That Shocked 1930s America and Revived the Struggle for Equality*. New York: Pantheon Books, 1994.

Gottlieb, Peter. *Making Their Own Way: Southern Blacks' Migration to Pittsburgh, 1916–30*. Urbana: University of Illinois Press, 1987.

Greenberg, Cheryl Lynn. *Or Does It Explode?: Black Harlem in the Great Depression*. New York: Oxford University Press, 1991.

Griffin, Farah Jasmine. *"Who Set You Flowin'?": The African-American Migration Narrative*. New York: Oxford University Press, 1995.

Grossman, James R. *Land of Hope: Chicago, Black Southerners, and the Great Migration*. Chicago: University of Chicago Press, 1989.

Harris, William H. *Keeping the Faith: A. Philip Randolph, Milton P. Webster, and the Brotherhood of Sleeping Car Porters, 1925–1937*. Urbana: University of Illinois Press, 1977.

Harrison, Alferdteen, ed. *Black Exodus: The Great Migration from the American South*. Jackson: University Press of Mississippi, 1991.

Haynes, Robert V. *Night of Violence: The Houston Riot of 1917*. Baton Rouge: Louisiana State University Press, 1976.

Helbing, Mark. *The Harlem Renaissance: The One and the Many.* Westport CT: Greenwood Press, 1999.

Hill, Laban Carrick. *Harlem Stomp: A Cultural History of the Harlem Renaissance.* New York: Little, Brown, 2003.

Hill, Robert A., ed. *The Marcus Garvey and Universal Negro Improvement Association Papers.* Berkeley: University of California Press, 1983–1986.

Hirsch, James S. *Riot and Remembrance: The Tulsa Race War and Its Legacy.* Boston, MA: Houghton Mifflin, 2002.

Huggins, Nathan. *Harlem Renaissance.* New York: Oxford University Press, 1971.

Hunton, Addie W., and Kathryn M. Johnson. *Two Colored Women with the American Expeditionary Forces.* New York: G. K. Hall, 1997.

Jones, Sharon L. *Rereading the Harlem Renaissance: Race, Class, and Gender in the Fiction of Jessie Fauset, Zora Neale Hurston, and Dorothy West.* Westport, CT: Greenwood Press, 2002.

Kellogg, Charles Flint. *NAACP: A History of the National Association for the Advancement of Colored People, Volume 1: 1909–1920.* Baltimore: Johns Hopkins University Press, 1967.

Kornweibel, Theodore, Jr. *"No Crystal Stair": Black Life and the Messenger, 1917–1928.* Westport, CT: Greenwood Press, 1975.

———. *"Seeing Red": Federal Campaigns against Black Militancy, 1919–1925.* Bloomington: Indiana University Press, 1998.

Kramer, Victor A., and Robert A. Russ, eds. *Harlem Renaissance Re-Examined.* Troy, NY: Whitston Publishing Co., 1997.

Lamon, Lester C. *Black Tennesseans, 1900–1930.* Knoxville: University of Tennessee Press, 1977.

Lentz-Smith, Adriane. *Freedom Struggles: African Americans and World War I.* Boston: Harvard University Press, 2011.

Levine, David Alan. *Internal Combustion: The Races in Detroit, 1915–1926.* Westport, CT: Greenwood Press, 1976.

Lewis, David Levering. *When Harlem Was in Vogue.* New York: Oxford University Press, 1981.

———. *W. E. B. Du Bois: Biography of a Race, 1868–1919.* New York: Henry Holt, 1993.

Lisio, Donald J. *Hoover, Blacks, & Lily-Whites: A Study of Southern Strategies.* Chapel Hill: University of North Carolina Press, 1985.

Little, A. W. *From Harlem to the Rhine: The Story of New York's Colored Volunteers.* New York: Covici, 1936.

Locke, Alain, ed. *The New Negro.* New York: Atheneum, 1968.

Madigan, Tim. *The Burning: Massacre, Destruction, and the Tulsa Race Riot of 1921.* New York: Thomas Dunne Books, 2001.

Martin, Tony. *Race First: The Ideological and Organizational Struggles of Marcus Garvey and the Universal Negro Improvement Association*. Westport, CT: Greenwood Press, 1976.

McMillen, Neil R. *Dark Journey: Black Mississippians in the Age of Jim Crow*. Urbana: University of Illinois Press, 1990.

McWhirter, Cameron. *Red Summer: The Summer of 1919 and the Awakening of Black America*. New York: Henry Holt, 2011.

Mjagkij, Nina. *Loyalty in Time of Trial: The African American Experience during World War I*. Lanham, MD: Rowman & Littlefield, 2011.

Nielson, David G. *Black Ethos: Northern Urban Life and Thought, 1890–1930*. Westport, CT: Greenwood Press, 1977.

Osofsky, Gilbert. *Harlem: The Making of a Ghetto, 1890–1930*. New York: Harper & Row, 1966.

Patter, Nicholas. *Jim Crow and the Wilson Administration: Protesting Federal Segregation in the Early Twentieth Century*. Boulder: University Press of Colorado, 2004.

Perry, Jeffrey B. *Hubert Harrison: The Voice of Harlem Radicalism, 1883–1918*. New York: Columbia University Press, 2009.

Phillips, Kimberley L. *Alabama North: African-American Migrants, Community and Working-Class Activism in Cleveland, 1915–1945*. Urbana: Illinois State University Press, 1999.

Reed, Christopher Robert. *The Rise of Chicago's Black Metropolis, 1920–1929*. Urbana: University of Illinois Press, 2011.

Rudwick, Elliott M. *Race Riot at East St. Louis, July 2, 1917*. New York: Atheneum, 1972.

Scott, Emmett J. *The American Negro in the World War*. Chicago: Homewood Press, 1919.

———. *Negro Migration during the Great War*. New York: Oxford University Press, 1920.

Sherman, Richard B. *The Republican Party and Black America: From McKinley to Hoover, 1896–1933*. Charlottesville: University of Virginia Press, 1973.

Spear, Allen H. *Black Chicago: The Making of a Negro Ghetto, 1890–1920*. Chicago: University of Chicago Press, 1967.

Stein, Judith. *The World of Marcus Garvey: Race and Class in Modern Society*. Baton Rouge: Louisiana State University Press, 1986.

Stockley, Grif. *Blood in Their Eyes: The Elaine Race Massacre of 1919*. Fayetteville: University of Arkansas Press, 2001.

Thomas, Richard W. *Life for Us Is What We Make It: Building Black Community in Detroit, 1915–1945*. Bloomington: Indiana University Press, 1992.

Trotter, Joe William, Jr. *Black Milwaukee: The Making of an Industrial Proletariat, 1915–1945*. Urbana: University of Illinois Press, 1985.

————. *Coal, Class, and Color: Blacks in Southern West Virginia, 1915–32.* Urbana: University of Illinois Press, 1990.

————, ed. *The Great Migration in Historical Perspective: New Dimensions of Race, Class, and Gender.* Bloomington: Indiana University Press, 1991.

Tuttle, William M. *Race Riot: Chicago in the Red Summer of 1919.* New York: Atheneum, 1970.

Voogd, Jan. *Race Riots and Resistance: The Red Summer of 1919.* New York: Peter Lang, 2008.

Weiss, Nancy J. *The National Urban League, 1910–1940.* New York: Oxford University Press, 1974.

Whitaker, Robert. *On the Laps of Gods: The Red Summer of 1919 and the Struggle for Justice That Remade a Nation.* New York: Random House, 2008.

Williams, Chad L. *Torchbearers of Democracy: African American Soldiers in the World War I Era.* Chapel Hill: University of North Carolina Press, 2010.

Williams, Lee E., and Lee E. Williams II. *Anatomy of Four Race Riots: Racial Conflict in Knoxville, Elaine, Tulsa, and Chicago, 1919–1921.* Jackson: University and College Press of Mississippi, 1972.

Williams, Lillian Serece. *The Development of a Black Community: Buffalo, New York, 1900–1940.* Bloomington: Indiana University Press, 1999.

WOMEN

Adams, Katherine H., and Michael L. Keene. *Alice Paul and the American Suffrage Campaign.* Urbana and Chicago: University of Illinois, 2008.

Alonso, Harriet Hyman. *Peace as a Women's Issue: A History of the U.S. Movement for World Peace and Women's Rights.* Syracuse, NY: Syracuse University Press, 1993.

Baker, Jean H. *Votes for Women: The Struggle for Suffrage Revisited.* New York: Oxford University Press, 2002.

————. *Sisters: The Lives of America's Suffragists.* New York: Hill & Wang, 2005.

Becker, Susan. *The Origins of the Equal Rights Amendment: American Feminism Between the Wars.* Westport, CO,: Garland Publishing, 1985.

Brown, Dorothy M. *Setting a Course: American Women in the 1920s.* Boston: Twayne, 1987.

Buechler, Steven M. *The Transformation of the Woman Suffrage Movement.* New Brunswick, NJ: Rutgers University Press, 1986.

————. *Women's Movements in the United States: Woman Suffrage, Equal Rights and Beyond.* New Brunswick, NJ: Rutgers University Press, 1990.

Butler, Amy E. *Two Paths to Equality: Alice Paul and Ethel M. Smith in the Era Debate, 1921–1929.* Albany: State University of New York Press, 2002.

Chafe, William H. *The American Woman: Her Changing Economic and Political Roles, 1920–1970.* New York: Oxford University Press, 1972.

Coates, Patricia Walsh. *Margaret Sanger and the Origin of the Birth Control Movement, 1910–1930: The Concept of Women's Sexual Autonomy.* New York: Edwin Mellen Press, 2008.

Conor, Liz. *The Spectacular Modern Woman: Feminine Visibility in the 1920s.* Bloomington, IN: Indiana University Press, 2004.

Cook, Blanche Wiesen. *Eleanor Roosevelt: A Life.* New York: Viking, 1992.

Cooney, Robert P. J. *Winning the Vote: The Triumph of the American Woman Suffrage Movement.* Santa Cruz, CA: American Graphic Press, 2005.

Davis, Allen F. *American Heroine: The Life and Legend of Jane Addams.* New York: Oxford University Press, 1973.

Davis, Simone Weil. *Living Up to the Ads: Gender Fictions of the 1920s.* Durham, NC: Duke University Press, 2000.

Degler, Carl. *At Odds: Women and the Family in America from the Revolution to the Present.* New York: Oxford University Press, 1980.

Elshtain, Jean Bethke. *Jane Addams and the Dream of American Democracy.* New York: Basic Books, 2001.

Engelman, Peter C. *A History of the Birth Control Movement in America.* Santa Barbara, CA: ABC-CLIO, 2011.

Finnegan, Margaret. *Selling Suffrage: Consumer Culture and Votes for Women.* New York: Columbia University Press, 1999.

Flexner, Eleanor. *A Century of Struggle: The Women's Rights Movement in the United States.* Cambridge, MA: Harvard University Press, 1959.

Foster, Carrie. *The Women and the Warriors: The United States Section of the Women's International League for Peace and Freedom, 1915–1946.* Syracuse, NY: Syracuse University Press, 1995.

Freeman, Jo. *A Room at a Time: How Women Entered Party Politics.* Lanham: Rowman & Littlefield, 2002.

Gavin, Lettie. *American Women in World War I: They Also Served.* Boulder: University Press of Colorado, 1999.

Greenwald, Maurine. *Women, War, and Work: The Impact of World War I on Women Workers in the United States.* Westport, CT: Greenwood, 1980.

Hajo, Cathy Moran. *Birth Control on Main Street: Organizing Clinics in the United States, 1916–1939.* Urbana and Chicago: University of Illinois Press, 2010.

Harvey, Anna L. *Votes without Leverage: Women in American Electoral Politics, 1920–1970.* Cambridge: Cambridge University Press, 1998.

Higgonnet, Margaret R., ed. *Nurses at the Front: Writing the Wounds of the First World War.* Boston: Northeastern University Press, 2001.

Hunton, Addie W., and Kathryn M. Johnson. *Two Colored Women with the American Expeditionary Forces*. New York: G. K. Hall, 1997.

Kennedy, Kathleen. *Disloyal Mothers and Scurrilous Citizens: Women and Subversion during World War I*. Bloomington: Indiana University Press, 1999.

Kessler-Harris, Alice. *Out to Work: A History of Wage-earning women in the United States*. New York: Oxford University Press, 1990.

Kraditor, Aileen. *The Ideas of the Woman Suffrage Movement, 1890–1920*. New York: Columbia University Press, 1965.

Lemons, J. Stanley. *The Woman Citizen: Social Feminism in the 1920s*. Urbana: University of Illinois Press, 1975.

Lunardini, Christine A. *From Equal Suffrage to Equal Rights: Alice Paul and the National Woman's Party, 1910–1928*. New York: iUniverse, 1986.

Mackrell, Judith. *Flappers: Six Women of a Dangerous Generation*. London: Macmillan, 2013.

May, Elaine Tyler. *Great Expectations: Marriage and Divorce in Post-Victorian America*. Chicago: University of Chicago Press, 1983.

O'Neill, William L. *Everyone Was Brave: A History of Feminism in America*. Chicago: Quadrangle, 1971.

Paulson, Ross Evans. *Women's Suffrage and Prohibition: A Comparative Study of Equality and Social Control*. Glenview, IL: Scott Foresman/Addison Wesley, 1973.

Rose, Kenneth. *American Women and the Repeal of Prohibition*. New York: New York University Press, 1996.

Rosenberg, Rosalind. *Divided Lives: American Women in the Twentieth Century*. New York: HarperCollins, 2008.

Scharf, Lois. *Eleanor Roosevelt: First Lady of American Liberalism*. Boston: Twayne, 1988.

Scharf, Lois, and Joan Jensen, eds. *Decades of Discontent: The Women's Movement, 1920–1940*. Westport, CT: Greenwood Press, 1983.

Schneider, Dorothy, and Carl J. Schneider. *Into the Breach: American Women Overseas in World War I*. New York: Viking, 1991.

Steinson, Barabara. *American Women's Activism in World War I*. New York: Garland, 1982.

Strom, Sharon Hartman. *Beyond the Typewriter: Gender, Class, and the Origins of Modern Office Work*. Urbana: University of Illinois Press, 1992.

Walker, Nancy A. *Shaping Our Mothers' World: American Women's Magazines*. Jackson: University Press of Mississippi, 2000.

Walton, Mary. *A Woman's Crusade: Alice Paul and the Battle for the Ballot*. New York: Palgrave Macmillan, 2010.

Wheeler, Marjorie Sprull, ed. *One Woman, One Vote: Rediscovering the Woman Suffrage Movement*. New York: NewSage Press, 1995.

Zeiger, Susan. *In Uncle Sam's Service: Women Workers with the American Expeditionary Force, 1917–1919*. Ithaca, NY: Cornell University Press 1999.

Zeitz, Joshua. *Flapper: A Madcap Story of Sex, Style, Celebrity and the Women Who Made America Modern*. New York: Crown, 2006.

LABOR MOVEMENTS

Barrett, James R. *William Z. Foster and the Tragedy of American Radicalism*. Urbana: University of Illinois Press, 1999.

Bernstein, Irving. *The Lean Years: A History of the American Worker, 1920–1933*. Boston: Houghton Mifflin, 1960.

Brandes, Stuart D. *American Welfare Capitalism, 1880–1940*. Chicago: University of Chicago Press, 1976.

Brody, David. *Labor in Crisis: The Steel Strike of 1919*. Philadelphia: Lippincott, 1965.

———. *Workers in Industrial America: Essays on the Twentieth Century Struggle*. New York: Oxford University Press, 1980.

Bucki, Cecelia. *Bridgeport's Socialist New Deal, 1915–36*. Urbana: University of Illinois Press, 2001.

Carlson, Peter. *Roughneck: The Life and Times of Big Bill Haywood*. New York: W. W. Norton, 1983.

Cole, Peter. *Wobblies on the Waterfront: Interracial Unionism in Progressive-Era Philadelphia*. Urbana: University of Illinois Press, 2007.

Dubofsky, Melvyn. *We Shall Be All: A History of the Industrial Workers of the World*. New York: Quadrangle, 1969.

———. *'Big Bill' Haywood*. Manchester, England: Manchester University Press, 1987.

———. *Industrialism and the American Worker, 1865–1920*. Wheeling, IL: Harlan Davidson, 1996.

Dubofsky, Melvyn, and Warren R. Van Tine. *John L. Lewis: A Biography*. Urbana: University of Illinois Press, 1986.

Esposito, Anthony V. *The Ideology of the Socialist Party of America, 1901–1917*. New York: Garland Publishing, 1997.

Foner, Philip S. *History of the Labor Movement in the United States*. Vol. 6: *On the Eve of America's Entrance into World War I, 1915–16*. New York: International Publishers, 1982.

———. *History of the Labor Movement in the United States: Postwar Struggles 1918–1920*. New York: International Publishers, 1987.

———. *History of the Labor Movement in the United States*. Vol. 7: *Labor and World War I*. New York: International Publishers, 1987.

Gerstle, Gary. *Working-Class Americanism: The Politics of Labor in a Textile City, 1914–1960*. Princeton, NJ: Princeton University Press, 2002.

Green, James R. *The World of the Worker: Labor in Twentieth Century America*. Urbana: University of Illinois Press, 1998.

Greene, Julie. *Pure and Simple Politics: The American Federation of Labor and Political Activism, 1881–1917*. Cambridge: Cambridge University Press, 1998.

Hall, Greg. *Harvest Wobblies: The Industrial Workers of the World and Agricultural Laborers in the American West, 1905–1930*. Eugene: University of Oregon Press, 2001.

Higbie, Frank Tobias. *Indispensable Outcasts: Hobo Workers and Community in the American Midwest, 1880–1930*. Urbana: University of Illinois Press, 2003.

Kaufman, Stuart B., et al., eds. *The Samuel Gompers Papers*. 4 vols. Urbana: University of Illinois Press, 1986–1992.

Kipnis, Ira. *The American Socialist Movement 1897–1912*. Chicago: Haymarket Books, 2005.

Lipset, Seymour Martin, and Gary Marks. *It Didn't Happen Here: Why Socialism Failed in the United States*. New York: Norton, 2000.

Livesay, Harold. *Samuel Gompers and Organized Labor in America*. Boston: Little, Brown, 1978.

McCartin, Joseph A. *Labor's Great War: The Struggle for Industrial Democracy and the Origins of Modern American Labor Relations, 1919–1921*. Chapel Hill: University of North Carolina Press, 1997.

McCormick, John S., and John R. Sillito. *A History of Utah Radicalism: Startling, Socialistic, and Decidedly Revolutionary*. Logan: Utah State University Press, 2011.

Montgomery, David. *Workers' Control in America: Studies in the History of Work, Technology, and Labor Struggles*. New York: Cambridge University Press, 1979.

———. *The Fall of the House of Labor: The Workplace, the State, and American Labor Activism, 1865–1925*. Cambridge: Cambridge University Press, 1987.

Renshaw, Patrick. *The Wobblies: The Story of the IWW and Syndicalism in the United States*. New York: Doubleday, 1967.

Schatz, Ronald W. *The Electrical Workers: A History of Labor at General Electric and Westinghouse, 1923–1960*. Urbana: University of Illinois Press, 1987.

Sellars, Nigel A. *Oil, Wheat, and Wobblies: The Industrial Workers of the World in Oklahoma, 1905–1930*. Norman: University of Oklahoma Press, 1998.

Shannon, David A. *The Socialist Party of America: A History*. New York: Macmillan, 1955.

Shogan, Robert. *The Battle of Blair Mountain: The Story of America's Largest Labor Uprising*. Boulder, CO: Westview Press, 2004.

Weinstein, James. *The Decline of Socialism in America, 1912–1925*. Brunswick, NJ: Rutgers University Press, 1984.

Zieger, Robert. *Republicans and Labor, 1919–1929*. Lexington: University of Kentucky Press, 1969.

———. *American Workers, American Unions*. Baltimore, MD: Johns Hopkins University Press, 1994.

THE CRASH AND THE GREAT DEPRESSION

Bernanke, Ben S. *Essays on the Great Depression*. Princeton: Princeton University Press, 2000.

Bernstein, Michael A. *The Great Depression: Delayed Recovery and Economic Change in America, 1929–1939*. Cambridge: Cambridge University Press, 1987.

Bird, Caroline. *The Invisible Scar*. New York: McKay, 1966.

Bordo, Michael D., Claudia Goldin, and Eugene N. White, eds. *The Defining Moment: The Great Depression and the American Economy in the Twentieth Century*. Chicago: University of Chicago Press, 1998.

Chandler, Lester V. *America's Greatest Depression, 1919–1941*. New York: Harper, 1970.

Daniels, Roger. *The Bonus March: An Episode of the Great Depression*. Westport, CT: Greenwood Press, 1941.

Fearon, Peter. *War, Prosperity and Depression, 1919–1941*. Deddington, Oxfordshire: Philip Allan, 1987.

Friedman, Milton, and Anna Jacobson Schwartz. *The Great Contraction, 1929–1933*. Princeton, NJ: Princeton University Press, 1965.

Galbraith, John Kenneth. *The Great Crash: 1929*. Boston: Houghton Mifflin, 1955.

Garraty, John A. *The Great Depression: An Inquiry into the Causes, Course, and Consequences of the Worldwide Depression of the Nineteen Thirties*. New York: Harcourt Brace Jovanovich, 1986.

Irwin, Douglas. *Peddling Protectionism: Smoot-Hawley and the Great Depression*. Princeton, NJ: Princeton University Press, 2011.

Klingaman, William K. *1929: The Year of the Great Crash*. New York: Harper & Row, 1989.

Lisio, Donald J. *The President and Protest: Hoover, Conspiracy, and the Bonus Riot*. Columbia: University of Missouri Press, 1974.

Lowitt, Richard, and Maurine Beasley, eds. *One Third of a Nation: Lorena Hickock Reports on the Great Depression*. Urbana: University of Illinois Press, 1981.

McElvaine, Robert S. *The Great Depression: America 1929–1941*. New York: Times Books, 1984.

Olson, James Stuart. *Herbert Hoover and the Reconstruction Finance Corporation, 1931–1933*. Ames: Iowa State University Press, 1977.

Rosen, Elliott. *Hoover, Roosevelt, and the Brains Trust: From Depression to New Deal*. New York: Columbia University Press, 1977.

Rothbard, Murray N. *America's Greatest Depression*. Princeton, NJ: D. Van Nostrand, 1963.

Schlaes, Amity. *The Forgotten Man: A New History of the Great Depression*. New York: HarperCollins, 2007.

Schlesinger, Arthur M., Jr. *The Age of Roosevelt: The Politics of Upheaval*. Boston: Houghton Mifflin, 1960.

Singleton, Jeff. *The American Dole: Unemployment Relief and the Welfare State in the Great Depression*. Westport, CT: Greenwood Press, 2000.

Smiley, Gene. *Rethinking the Great Depression*. Chicago: Ivan R. Dee, 2002.

Terkel, Studs. *Hard Times: An Oral History of the Great Depression*. New York: Pantheon, 1970.

Thomas, Gordon, and Morgan-Witts, M. *The Day the Bubble Burst: A Social History of the Wall Street Crash of 1929*. New York: Doubleday and Company, 1979.

Watkins, T. H. *The Great Depression: America in the 1930s*. Boston: Little, Brown, 1993.

FRANKLIN D. ROOSEVELT, THE ELECTION OF 1932, AND THE NEW DEAL

Alter, Jonathan. *The Defining Moment: FDR's Hundred Days and the Triumph of Hope*. New York: Simon & Schuster, 2006.

Badger, Anthony J. *The New Deal: The Depression Years, 1933–40*. New York: Hill & Wang, 1989.

———. *FDR: The First Hundred Days*. New York: Hill & Wang, 2008.

Bellush, Bernard. *Franklin D. Roosevelt as Governor of New York*. New York: Columbia University Press, 1955.

Burns, James MacGregor. *Roosevelt: The Lion and the Fox*. New York: Harcourt Brace, 1956.

———. *Roosevelt: The Soldier of Freedom*. New York: Harcourt Brace Jovanovich, 1970.

Cook, Blanch Wiesen. *Eleanor Roosevelt: Vol. 1, 1884–1933*. New York: Penguin, 1992.

Davis, Kenneth S. *FDR*. 4 vols. New York: Random House, 1985–1993.

De Kay, James Tertius. *Roosevelt's Navy: The Education of a Warrior Preside, 1882–1920*. New York: Pegasus, 2012.

Friedel, Frank *Franklin D. Roosevelt: The Triumph*. Boston: Little, Brown, 1956.

Houck, David, and Amos Kiewe. *FDR's Body Politics: The Rhetoric of Disability*. College Station, TX: Texas A&M University Press, 2003.

Kennedy, David M. *Freedom from Fear: The American People in Depression and War, 1929–1945*. New York: Oxford University Press, 1999.

Lash, Joseph. *Eleanor and Franklin*. New York: W. W. Norton, 1971.

Leuchtenburg, William E. *Franklin D. Roosevelt and the New Deal, 1932–1940*. New York: Harper & Row, 1963.

Ritchie, Donald A. *Electing FDR: The New Deal Campaign of 1932*. Lawrence: University Press of Kansas, 2007.

Rowley, Hazel. *Franklin and Eleanor: An Extraordinary Marriage*. New York: Farrar, Straus and Giroux, 2010.

Schlesinger, Arthur M., Jr. *The Coming of the New Deal*. Boston: Houghton Mifflin, 1958.

Smith, Jean Edward. *FDR*. New York: Random House, 2007.

Winkler, Allan M. *Franklin D. Roosevelt and the Making of Modern America*. New York: Longman Publishing, 2006.

About the Author

Neil Alan Wynn was born in 1947 to British parents in The Hague, Holland. Dr. Wynn completed his school education in Edinburgh, Scotland, where he also attended university from 1965 to 1969. Following his graduation with an MA in history, he went to the Open University in England to undertake research for his PhD. After four years, including a year as a graduate assistant at State University of New York at Buffalo, Wynn was awarded the first PhD in history at the Open University in 1973 for his thesis on "The Afro-American and the Second World War."

In 1973 Dr. Wynn took up an appointment as lecturer in history at what was then Glamorgan Polytechnic (later the Polytechnic of Wales and from 1989 the University of Glamorgan) to develop and teach courses in American history and American studies. He was subsequently promoted to senior lecturer, principal lecturer, and in 1994 became reader in history and American studies. In 1979 Dr. Wynn was awarded a fellowship by the American Council of Learned Societies and spent a year engaged in research in Washington, D.C. He has taught on international programs at Central Missouri State University and at the Maastricht Center for Transatlantic Studies in the Netherlands, of which he was a director. In 2003 he was appointed professor of twentieth-century American history at the University of Gloucestershire in Cheltenham, England.

Dr. Wynn is the author of *Historical Dictionary of the Roosevelt-Truman Era* (2008), *The African American Experience during World War* II (2010), *The Afro American and the Second World War* (1976, 1993), and *From Progressivism to Prosperity: World War I and American Society* (1986). He has authored chapters in several collections and various journal articles on African American and American history and culture. He edited *Cross the Water Blues: African American Music in Europe* (2007) and coedited *Transatlantic Roots Music: Folk, Blues and National Identities* (2012) and *America's Century: Perspectives on U.S. History since 1900* (1993). From 1990 to 2003, he reported on events in the United States for the *Annual Register*, and he has often broadcast on national and local BBC radio on American history and current affairs.